ADOBE® COLDFUSION® 8
Application Development

web application construction kit
VOLUME 2

Ben Forta and Raymond Camden

with Charlie Arehart, John C. Bland II, Leon Chalnick, Ken Fricklas,
Paul Hastings, Mike Nimer, Sarge Sargent, and Robi Sen

Adobe ColdFusion 8 Web Application Construction Kit, Volume 2: Application Development

Ben Forta and Raymond Camden
with Charlie Arehart, John C. Bland II, Leon Chalnick, Ken Fricklas, Paul Hastings, Mike Nimer, Sarge Sargent, and Robi Sen

This Adobe Press book is published by Peachpit.

Peachpit Press
1249 Eighth Street
Berkeley, CA 94710
510/524-2178
510/524-2221 (fax)

Find us on the Web at: www.peachpit.com
To report errors, please send a note to errata@peachpit.com

Peachpit is a division of Pearson Education

Editor: Judy Ziajka
Technical Reviewer: Jim Gibson
Production Editor: Lupe Edgar
Compositor: Maureen Forys, Happenstance Typo-O-Rama
Proofreader: Liz Welch
Indexer: Ron Strauss
Cover design: Charlene Charles-Will

ISBN 13: 978-0-321-51546-9

ISBN 10: 0-321-51546-3

9 8 7 6 5 4 3 2 1

Printed and bound in the United States of America

Biographies

Ben Forta

Ben Forta is Director of Platform Evangelism at Adobe Systems, Inc., and has more than two decades of experience in the computer software industry, in product development, support, training, and marketing. Ben is the author of the best-selling ColdFusion book of all time, *Macromedia ColdFusion MX 7 Web Application Construction Kit*, as well as books on SQL, JavaServer Pages, Windows development, Regular Expressions, and more. Over half a million Ben Forta books have been printed in more than a dozen languages worldwide. Ben helped create the official Adobe ColdFusion training materials, as well as the certification tests and study guides for those tests. He writes regular columns on ColdFusion and Internet development and spends a considerable amount of time lecturing and speaking on application development worldwide. Ben welcomes your e-mail at ben@forta.com and invites you to visit his Web site at http://forta.com/ and his blog at http://forta.com/blog.

Charlie Arehart

A veteran ColdFusion developer since 1997, Charlie Arehart is a longtime contributor to the community and a recognized Adobe Community Expert. He's a Certified Advanced ColdFusion Developer and an instructor for ColdFusion 4, 5, 6, and 7 and served as technical editor for the *ColdFusion Developers Journal* until 2003. Now an independent contractor (carehart.org) living in Alpharetta, Georgia, Charlie provides high-level troubleshooting and tuning assistance and training and mentoring for ColdFusion teams. He also helps run the Online ColdFusion Meetup (coldfusionmeetup.com, an online ColdFusion user group) and is frequently invited to speak at developer conferences and user groups worldwide.

John C. Bland II

John C. Bland II, co-founder and CEO of Katapult Media, Inc., began his journey as a Web developer in 1996. In 2001 he started his first company, jDev, Inc., with a main focus on computer and technical training and eventually Web development. Later, wanting to focus the company vision, John and his wife, Tia, decided to close jDev and start a new company named Katapult Media, Inc., focusing on Web development using technologies such as ColdFusion, the Adobe Flash platform, PHP, and the .NET platform. John has written for the *ColdFusion Developers Journal* and the Adobe Developer Center. As the manager of the Arizona Flash Platform User Group (www.gotoandstop.org), John continues to give back to the community that helped mold him into the developer he is today. Through Katapult, he continues to work diligently on countless Web sites and desktop applications, most of which can be viewed at www.katapultmedia.com. John blogs regularly at www.johncblandii.com on numerous topics, concepts, and (mainly) code.

Ken Fricklas

Ken Fricklas is co-author of several ColdFusion books, has spoken at many conferences, and teaches ColdFusion nationally. He even has a copy of ColdFusion 1.5 sitting on a shelf somewhere. In his spare time, he enjoys music, performs improvisational comedy, and is a programmer-consultant. More information can be found at `http://kensblog.fricklas.com`.

Leon Chalnick

Leon Chalnick, one of the contributing authors of the original edition of this book, is the president of Advanta Solutions, LLC (`www.AdvantaSolutions.com`), a consulting firm specializing in system analysis and Web application development in the Los Angeles area. When not busy on client work (or this book!), Leon is busy playing his guitar, working on old tube amps and cabs, or cycling the hills in the south Bay Area.

Mike Nimer

Mike Nimer is a founding partner, with Jeff Tapper, of Tapper, Nimer and Associates, whose focus is training, mentoring, and development of rich Internet applications. Mike is a formerly a member of the Adobe ColdFusion engineering team, responsible in part for the Flex integration with ColdFusion and a number of other features in the ColdFusion Server. Before joining the Adobe/Macromedia engineering team, he spent three years working as a senior consultant with the Macromedia consulting group, where he provided onsite assistance to customers around the world with their architecture planning, code reviews, performance tuning, and general code issues.

Paul Hastings

Paul Hastings, who after over 20 years of IT work is now a perfectly fossilized geologist, is CTO at Sustainable GIS, a consulting firm specializing in Geographic Information Systems (GIS) technology, ColdFusion Internet and intranet applications for the environment and natural resource markets, and, of course, ColdFusion globalization. Paul is based in Bangkok, Thailand, but says that it's not nearly as exciting as it sounds. He can be reached at `paul@sustainableGIS.com`.

Ray Camden

Raymond Camden is the owner of Camden Media, Inc., a Web development and training company. A longtime ColdFusion user, Raymond has worked on numerous ColdFusion books, including the *Macromedia ColdFusion MX 7 Web Application Construction Kit*, and has contributed to the *Fusion Authority Quarterly Update* and the *ColdFusion Developers Journal*. He also gives presentations at numerous conferences and contributes to online Webzines. He has founded many community Web sites, including `CFLib.org`, `ColdFusionPortal.org`, and `ColdFusionCookbook.org`, and is the author of open source applications, including the popular BlogCFC (`www.blogcfc.com`) blogging application. Raymond can be reached at his blog (`www.coldfusionjedi.com`) or via email at `ray@camdenfamily.com`. He is the happily married proud father of three kids and is somewhat of a *Star Wars* nut.

Robi Sen

Robi Sen is a managing partner with Twin Technologies, a premiere Web 2.0 software development house specializing in delivering mission-critical Web applications for Fortune 500 companies as well as the defense, intelligence, and healthcare sectors. Robi has also been in executive leadership positions with Department 13 and Vobis Communications in the course of a distinguished 20-year career in the software industry.

Sarge Sargent

Sarge Sargent is a former senior product support engineer for ColdFusion and JRun with Adobe's North American Customer Care organization. During his tenure with Allaire, Macromedia, and now Adobe, he has also supported Breeze/Connect, Contribute Publishing Services, and Flex. He is well-known in the ColdFusion community as an expert in configuration, optimization, scalability, security, and LDAP integration. A Certified ColdFusion Developer and MCSE, he has served as contributor and technical editor or reviewer for several ColdFusion books, written several Developer Connection and Knowledgebase articles for the Adobe Web site, and spoken at several conferences and user groups. Sarge is currently Adobe's technical account manager for Flash and Flash Media Server. Although his focus is now on serving the Adobe Flash platform community, ColdFusion will forever remain in his blood. Sarge continues to share his onion on his blog at www.sargeway.com.

Dedications

Charlie Arehart

I'd like to dedicate this book to my wife of seven years and the love of my life, Kim. I couldn't do all I do without your patience, support, and encouragement. Thank you, my love. God truly blessed me when He brought you into my life.

John C. Bland II

I would like to dedicate this book to Tia, Alex, and Lil' John for the continuous support of my career and the time involved helping me become the man, business mind, and developer I am today. I owe and love you guys big time!

Ken Fricklas

To my family, long may you roam.

Paul Hastings

I would like to dedicate this book to my family: my wife Mao and our three children, Meow, Ning, and Joe, as well as my in-laws Edwin and Pu and their still whirling-dervish daughter Nadia.

Ray Camden

To my wife, Jeanne—you are my best supporter, my best friend, and the absolute best thing in my life. Thank you.

Sarge Sargent

As always, I dedicate my work to my fam.

Acknowledgments

Ben Forta

Thanks to my co-authors, Ray Camden, Charlie Arehart, John. C. Bland, Ken Fricklas, Leon Chalnick, Mike Nimer, Paul Hastings, Robi Sen, and Sarge Sargent, for their outstanding contributions. Although these book are affectionately known to thousands as "the Ben Forta books," they are, in truth, as much theirs as mine. An extra thank you to Ray Camden for once again bravely accepting the role of lead co-author. Thanks to Nancy Ruenzel and the crew at Peachpit for allowing me the creative freedom to build these books as I see fit. Thanks to Wendy Sharp for stepping in as acquisitions editor on this revision, and to Judy Ziajka for so ably shepherding this book through the publication process. Thanks to Jim Gibson for his careful and methodical tech edit. Thanks to Damon Cooper, Tom Jordahl, Dean Harmon, and the rest of the ColdFusion team for creating yet another phenomenal edition of an already phenomenal product. Thanks to the thousands of you who write to me with comments, suggestions, and criticism (thankfully not too much of the latter)—I do read each and every message (and even attempt to reply to them all, eventually), and all are appreciated. And last, but by no means least, a loving thank you to my wife, Marcy, and our children for putting up with (and allowing) my often hectic work schedule. Their love and support make all I do possible.

Charlie Arehart

First, I want to thank Ben for having me as a contributor to this series. With so many excellent authors among the current and past contributors, I really feel privileged. I also want to thank him for all his contributions to the community. Again, as with my fellow authors, I follow in the footsteps of giants. In that regard, I want to acknowledge the awesome ColdFusion community. I've so enjoyed being a part of it, as both beneficiary and contributor, since 1997. This book's for you.

John C. Bland II

Sarge, as you always say, Ayo! Dude, you continue to help me in any way you can, and for that Tia and I are grateful. You are a true friend. Ben, I appreciate your support and understanding during the writing process. It was great working with you on such an amazing product. Michael Hagel, I know this book put a strain on a few projects, but you always understood—thanks! Cody Beckner, you are the epitome of a friend and an amazing sounding board. Momma, Pac, Joe, and Bubba, you guys are amazing. Keep doing what you do and thank you for encouraging me to better myself professionally. Oh, and I'm going to quiz you on the book, too, so you better read it! :-)

Leon Chalnick

I would like to thank Matt Howard for his time and support of the use of his Mach-II Contact Manager application.

Ken Fricklas

Thanks to Ben and the Adobe team, Carolyn and Bryce for putting up with me, Mike (and family), Susan (and family), and my parents for all your support.

Mike Nimer

I'd like to thank my amazing and lovely wife, Angela, for her support and editing skills, Baby Nimer, and Lucy the dog (for the Frisbee breaks).

Paul Hastings

Once again, I'd like to thank the "usual suspects" at Adobe, Damon Cooper and Tom Jordahl, for such a fine product and to offer this as a way of showing my appreciation for all the hard work that went into making ColdFusion 8. I'd also like to thank Ben Forta for the opportunity to again work on this book. Thanks everybody.

Ray Camden

I want to thank my wife and kids for their understanding while I worked night after night. I want to thank Ben for once again asking me to help out with this monster of a book. Thank you to Adobe for answering my unending stream of questions and also putting up with my suggestions. (They were all good ideas, really!)

Sarge Sargent

Thanks to Ben for having me on the project again. Special thanks to my family for being a rock and a refuge for me. Xtra-special thanks to my wife, Nicole, for granting me permission to work on this project and for being my "Ambassador of Quon." Bob!

CONTENTS AT A GLANCE

CONTENTS

Introduction

Who Should Use This Book?

Adobe ColdFusion was the first Web application server (created actually before the term existed) and remains the world's leading cross-platform Web development tool. Although ColdFusion remains an easy (and even fun) product to learn, some of its more advanced features and technologies require substantial know-how and experience.

This book was written for ColdFusion programmers. If you have yet to write ColdFusion code, this is not the book you need—at least not yet. Instead, grab a copy of the first book in this series, *Adobe ColdFusion 8 Web Application Construction Kit, Volume 1: Getting Started* (ISBN 0-321-51548-X). That book teaches you everything you need to know to get up and running (including extensive information about prerequisite technologies such as Internet fundamentals, the basics of application and database design, and the SQL language). It also teaches you everything you need to know to write real-world Web-based applications.

ColdFusion 8, the latest version of ColdFusion, introduces and extends many new high-end technologies designed to let you create highly secure, scalable, and extensible applications. This book teaches you how these technologies work, how they are used, and how to incorporate them into your own applications.

And when you are done with this book, you'll be ready for the final installment of the trilogy, *Adobe ColdFusion 8 Web Application Construction Kit, Volume 3: Advanced Application Development* (ISBN 0-321-51547-1).

How to Use This Book

This is the eighth edition of *Adobe ColdFusion Web Application Construction Kit*, and what started off as a single volume a decade ago has had to grow to three volumes to adequately cover ColdFusion 8. The books are organized as follows:

- **Volume 1:** *Adobe ColdFusion 8 Web Application Construction Kit, Volume 1: Getting Started* includes Chapters 1–23 and is targeted at beginning ColdFusion developers.

- **Volume 2:** *Adobe ColdFusion 8 Web Application Construction Kit, Volume 2: Application Development* includes Chapters 24–40 and covers the ColdFusion features and language elements that are used by most ColdFusion developers most of the time.

- **Volume 3:** *Adobe ColdFusion 8 Web Application Construction Kit, Volume 3: Advanced Application Development* includes Chapters 41–81 and covers the more advanced ColdFusion functionality, including extensibility features, as well as security and management features that will be of primary interest to those responsible for larger and more critical applications.

These book are designed to serve two different, but complementary, purposes.

First, as the books used by most ColdFusion developers, they are a complete tutorial covering everything you need to know to harness ColdFusion's power. As such, the books are divided into sections, and each section introduces new topics building on what has been discussed in prior sections. Ideally, you will work through these sections in order, starting with ColdFusion basics and then moving on to advanced topics. This is especially true of the first two books.

Second, the books are an invaluable desktop reference tool. The accompanying Web site contains reference chapters that will be of use to you while developing ColdFusion applications. Those reference chapters are cross-referenced to the appropriate tutorial sections, so that step-by-step information is always readily available to you.

The following paragraphs describe the contents of *Adobe ColdFusion 8 Web Application Construction Kit, Volume 2: Application Development*.

Part V: Creating Functions, Tags, and Components

Chapter 24, "Building User-Defined Functions, " introduces the `<cffunction>` tag and explains how it can (and should) be used to extend the CFML language.

Chapter 25, "Creating Custom Tags," teaches you how to write your own tags to extend the CFML language—tags written in CFML itself.

ColdFusion Components are the most important application building block in ColdFusion, and Chapter 26, "Building Reusable Components," teaches the basics of ColdFusion Component development.

Chapter 27, "Creating Advanced ColdFusion Components," continues exploring ColdFusion Components by introducing advanced topics, including persistence, encapsulation, and inheritance.

Part VI: ColdFusion Configuration and Performance

Chapter 28, "ColdFusion Server Configuration," revisits the ColdFusion Administrator, this time explaining every option and feature, while providing tips, tricks, and hints you can use to tweak your ColdFusion server.

Chapter 29, "Improving the User Experience," helps you create applications that really get used. You learn important user interface concepts, how to build sophisticated browser screens, and much more.

Chapter 30, "Managing Threads," explains asynchronous development and how to use multi-threaded processing to improve application performance.

Developers are always looking for ways to tweak their code, squeezing a bit more performance wherever possible. Chapter 31, "Improving Performance," provides tips, tricks, and techniques you can use to create applications that will always be snappy and responsive.

Part VII: Integrating with ColdFusion

Adobe PDF files are the standard for high-fidelity document distribution and online forms processing, and ColdFusion features extensive PDF integration as explained in Chapter 32, "Working with PDF Files."

Chapter 33, "ColdFusion Image Processing," teaches you how to read, write, and manipulate image files using ColdFusion tags and functions.

Chapter 34, "Advanced ColdFusion-Powered Ajax," continues to explore Ajax user interface controls and concepts.

Chapter 35, "Understanding ColdFusion-Powered Flex," introduces the basics of ColdFusion-powered Flex applications.

Chapter 36, "Building ColdFusion-Powered Flex Applications," continues the discussion of Cold-Fusion and Flex, exploring Flash Remoting, LiveCycle Data Services, and more.

Chapter 37, "Creating Presentations," teaches you how to use ColdFusion to build dynamic Acro-bat Connect presentations.

ColdFusion is primarily used to generate Web content, but that is not all it can do. In Chapter 38, "Generating Non-HTML Content," you learn how to use `<cfcontent>` to generate content for popular applications (such as Microsoft Word and Microsoft Excel), along with other output options.

Chapter 39, "Full-Text Searching," introduces the Verity search engine. Verity provides a mechanism that performs full-text searches of all types of data. The Verity engine is bundled with the ColdFusion Application Server, and the `<cfindex>` and `<cfsearch>` tags provide full access to Verity indexes from within your applications.

Chapter 40, "Event Scheduling," teaches you how to create tasks that execute automatically and at timed intervals. You also learn how to dynamically generate static HTML pages using ColdFusion's scheduling technology.

The Web Site

The accompanying Web site contains everything you need to start writing ColdFusion applications, including:

- Links to obtain ColdFusion 8
- Links to obtain Adobe Dreamweaver
- An explanation of how to obtain Eclipse and the ColdFusion Eclipse plug-ins
- Source code and databases for all the examples in this book
- Electronic versions of some chapters
- An errata sheet, should one be required
- An online discussion forum

The book Web page is at `http://www.forta.com/books/0321515463`.

And with that, turn the page and start reading. In no time, you'll be taking advantage of the power of ColdFusion 8.

PART V

Creating Functions, Tags, and Components

CHAPTER 24

Building User-Defined Functions

This chapter introduces you the brave new world of user-defined functions (UDFs), a feature that received a complete overhaul in ColdFusion MX. You can now create your own functions to do just about anything you can think of. User-defined functions are easy to write and even easier to use. You use them just like ColdFusion's built-in functions.

Thinking About Extending CFML

Throughout this book, you have been learning how to use CFML's built-in tags and functions to produce dynamic Web pages. You have used tags like `<cfquery>` and `<cfoutput>` to display information stored in databases, and you have used functions like `uCase()` and `dateFormat()` to further tweak your work.

For the next few chapters, you will be exploring how to *extend* the CFML language by creating your own tags, functions, and components. Once you see how easy it is to do so, you will find that you can make your application code much more elegant and maintainable. It's a very exciting topic. It's even fun.

There are four basic ways in which you can extend ColdFusion:

- **User-Defined Functions.** As the name implies, UDFs are functions that you create yourself. If you feel that some function is missing from ColdFusion's list of built-in ones, or that a particular function would be especially handy for an application you're building, you can just make the function yourself. UDFs are what this chapter is all about.

- **Custom Tags.** UDFs let you make your own functions, but Custom Tags allow you to create your own CFML tags. Of all the extensibility methods listed here, Custom Tags remain the most flexible and powerful. For more information, see Chapter 25, "Creating Custom Tags."

- **ColdFusion Components (CFCs).** CFCs are conceptually similar to Custom Tags, but imply a more structured, object-oriented manner of programming. CFCs are also at the heart of ColdFusion 8's Flash and Web Services integration. See Chapter 26, "Building Reusable Components," for details.

- **CFX Tags.** It is also possible to write your own CFX tags. You can write the code to make the tag do its work in either Java or C++. For more information about writing CFX tags, see the ColdFusion 8 documentation or see *Adobe ColdFusion 8 Web Application Construction Kit, Volume 3: Advanced Application Development.*

NOTE

If you wish, you can also extend ColdFusion 8 by writing JSP tag libraries, COM/ActiveX controls, Java classes or JavaBeans, and more. The list above simply summarizes the extensibility methods specific to ColdFusion.

In this chapter, I will concentrate on the first option, user-defined functions. I recommend that you also read Chapters 25 and 26 so that you know the extensibility options available to you. In many cases, you can get a particular task done by creating a tag or a function, so it helps to have an understanding of both.

Functions Turn Input into Output

Think about the CFML functions you already know. Almost all of them accept at least one piece of information, do something with the information internally, and then return some kind of result. For instance, ColdFusion's uCase() function accepts one piece of information (a string), performs an action (converts it to uppercase), then returns a result.

So you can think of most functions as being like little engines, or mechanisms on an assembly line. Some functions accept more than one piece of information (more than one argument), but the point is still the same: almost all functions are about accepting input and creating some kind of corresponding output. A function's *arguments* provide the input, and its output is passed back as the function's *return value*.

As the designer of your own functions, you get to specify the input by declaring one or more arguments. You also get to pass back whatever return value you wish.

Building Your First UDF

As a ColdFusion developer for Orange Whip Studios, you often need to display movie titles. It's easy enough to write a <cfquery> tag that retrieves the title for a particular movie based on its ID, but that can get repetitive if you need to do it on many different pages. Also, you must keep the database's design in mind at all times, instead of just concentrating on the task at hand.

You find yourself wishing you had a function called getFilmTitle() that would return the title of whatever FilmID you passed to it. So, for example, if you wanted to display the title of film number 8, you could just use this:

```
<cfoutput>#getFilmTitle(8)#</cfoutput>
```

Well, it turns out that ColdFusion 8 makes it remarkably easy to create this function. And you get to create it using the good old <cfquery> tag you already know and love. All you need to do is to surround the <cfquery> with a few extra tags!

Let's take a look at what it will take to put this new function into place.

Basic Steps

To create a user-defined function, you follow four basic steps:

1. Start with a pair of <cffunction> tags. You will insert all the code needed to make the function do its work between the opening and closing <cffunction> tags.

2. Add a <cfargument> tag for each argument your function will be using as input. If you wish, you can specify some arguments as required and others as optional.

3. After the <cfargument> tags, add whatever CFML code is needed to make your function do its work. Feel free to use whatever tags and functions you want in this section.

4. The last step is to use the <cfreturn> tag to return the result of whatever computations or processing your function does. In other words, you use <cfreturn> to specify what your function's output should be.

NOTE

The <cffunction> and related tags discussed in this chapter were introduced in ColdFusion MX. In previous versions of Cold-Fusion, the only way to create UDFs was with the less powerful <cfscript> tag, which isn't discussed specifically in this book. If you come across a UDF that was created using <cfscript>, you can use it in your code just like the ones discussed in this chapter. For creating new UDFs, we strongly recommend using <cffunction> rather than the older, script-based method.

I could now introduce the syntax and attributes for each of these new tags, but in this case it's easier if we just jump right in so you can see how the tags work together.

Here is the code needed to create the getFilmTitle() user-defined function:

```
<cffunction name="getFilmTitle">
 <cfargument name="filmID" type="numeric" required="Yes">

<!--- Get the film's title --->
 <cfquery name="getFilm" datasource="#datasource#"
 cachedwithin="#createTimespan(0,1,0,0)#">
 SELECT MovieTitle FROM Films
 WHERE FilmID = #ARGUMENTS.filmID#
 </cfquery>

<!--- Return the film's title --->
 <cfreturn getFilm.MovieTitle>
</cffunction>
```

As you can see, all three UDF-related tags are used here. First, a pair of <cffunction> tags surrounds the code for the whole function. Next, a <cfargument> tag at the top of the function defines what its input should be. Finally, a <cfreturn> tag at the end returns the function's output. Nearly all UDFs are constructed using this basic pattern.

Everything else between the `<cffunction>` tags is the actual CFML code that will be executed each time the function is invoked. In this simple example, the only processing that needs to occur to generate the function's output is a simple database query.

As you can see, a special ARGUMENTS scope will contain the value of each argument when the function is actually used. So, if the number 8 is passed to the function's `filmID` argument, then the value of the `ARGUMENTS.filmID` variable will be 8. In this case, `ARGUMENTS.filmID` dynamically creates the SQL that will retrieve the appropriate film title from the database. All that's left to do is to return the title as the function's output, using the `<cfreturn>` tag. It's that easy.

Using the Function

Once you've written a UDF, you can use it just like any other function. For instance, after the `<cffunction>` code shown above, you can use the function to display the title for a film, like this:

```
<cfoutput>#getFilmTitle(8)#</cfoutput>
```

When ColdFusion encounters the function, it will run the code between the corresponding `<cffunction>` tags. For the `getFilmTitle()` function, this means running the `<cfquery>` tag and returning the film title that gets retrieved from the database.

Of course, you can provide input to the function's arguments dynamically, as with any other function. For instance, if you have a form field named `showFilmID`, you could use code like the following to display the title corresponding to the ID number that the user provides on the form:

```
<cfoutput>#getFilmTitle(FORM.showFilmID)#</cfoutput>
```

You can also use UDFs in `<cfset>` tags or any other place where you would use a CFML expression. For instance, the following `<cfset>` tag would create a variable called `myFilmInUpperCase`, which is the uppercase version of the selected film's title:

```
<cfset myFilmInUpperCase = uCase(getFilmTitle(FORM.showFilmID))>
```

UDF Tag Syntax

Now that you've seen a simple example of how the code for a user-defined function is structured, let's take a closer look at the attributes supported by each of the tags involved: `<cffunction>`, `<cfargument>`, and `<cfreturn>`. Tables 24.1, 24.2, and 24.3 show the syntax supported by these three important tags.

Table 24.1 `<cffunction>` Tag Syntax

ATTRIBUTE	PURPOSE
name	The name of the new function. To actually use the function, you will call it using the name you provide here. The name needs to be a valid CFML identifier, which means it can contain only letters, numbers, and underscores, and its first character must be a letter.
returnType	Optional. You can use this attribute to indicate the type of information that the function will return, such as string, numeric, date, and so on. This attribute is optional, but it helps ensure your UDF runs correctly and should be used.

Table 24.1 (CONTINUED)

ATTRIBUTE	PURPOSE
output	Optional. While most UDFs will simply return a value, a UDF can actually output data as well. This shouldn't be used very often, so in general you should set this value to False. Setting it to False also reduces the white space generated by a call to the UDF.

NOTE

The `<cffunction>` tag actually supports several more attributes, which are relevant only when the tag is used within the context of a ColdFusion Component. You will learn about the other `<cffunction>` attributes in Chapter 26.

Table 24.2 `<cfargument>` Tag Syntax

ATTRIBUTE	PURPOSE
name	The name of the argument. Within the function, a variable will be created in the ARGUMENTS scope that contains the value passed to the argument when the function is actually used.
type	Optional. The data type that should be supplied to the argument when the function is actually used. If you supply a TYPE, ColdFusion will display an error message if someone tries to use the function with the wrong kind of input.
required	Optional. Whether the argument is required for the function to be able to do its work. The default is No (i.e., not required).
default	Optional. For optional arguments (that is, when required="No"), this determines what the value of the argument should be if a value isn't passed to the function when it is actually used.

One of the neatest things about the UDF framework is how easy it is to create functions that have required arguments, optional arguments, or both:

- If a `<cfargument>` tag uses required="Yes", the argument must be provided when the function is actually used. If the argument isn't provided at run time, ColdFusion will display an error message.

- If required="No" and a default attribute have been specified, the function can be called with or without the argument at run time. Go ahead and use the ARGUMENTS scope to refer to the value of the argument. If a value is provided when the function is actually used, that value will be what is present in the ARGUMENTS scope. If not, the default value will be what is in the ARGUMENTS scope.

- If required="No" and the default attribute has *not* been specified, the argument is still considered optional. If the function is called without the argument, there will be no corresponding value in the ARGUMENTS scope. You can use the isDefined() function to determine whether the argument was provided at run time. For instance, you would use isDefined("ARGUMENTS.filmID") within a function's code to determine if an optional filmID argument was provided.

You will see optional arguments at work in Listing 24.4 later in this chapter.

NOTE

By "run time," I just mean "at the time when the function is actually used." Programmers often use this term to refer to the actual moment of execution for a piece of code.

Table 24.3 `<cfreturn>` Tag Syntax

RETURN VALUE	PURPOSE
(any expression)	The `<cfreturn>` tag doesn't have any attributes per se. Instead, you place whatever string, number, date, variable, or other expression you want directly within the `<cfreturn>` tag.

For instance, if you wanted your function to always return the letter *A*, you would use:

```
<cfreturn "A">
```

If you wanted your function to return the current time, you would use:

```
<cfreturn timeFormat(now())>
```

You can use complex expressions as well, like this:

```
<cfreturn "The current time is: " & timeFormat(now())>
```

Using Local Variables

To get its work done, a UDF often needs to use `<cfset>` or other tags that create variables. Most of the time, you don't want these variables to be visible to pages that use the function.

Why Local Variables Are Important

Consider the `getFilmTitle()` function, which you have already seen. The code for this function runs a query named `getFilm` within the body of the function (that is, between the `<cffunction>` tags). That query returns only one column, `MovieTitle`. You probably don't want that query object to continue existing after the function is called. After all, what if someone already has a `<cfquery>` called `getFilm` that selects *all* columns from the Films table, then calls the UDF? That's right—after the UDF runs, the function's version of the `getFilm` query (which has only one column) will overwrite the one that the page created before calling the function, and any subsequent code that refers to `getFilms` probably won't work as expected.

NOTE

Developers often refer to this type of situation as a "variable collision" or a "namespace collision." Whatever the name, it's bad news, because it can lead to unpredictable or surprising results, especially if you are using a UDF that someone else wrote.

What you need is some way to tell ColdFusion that a particular variable should be visible only within the context of the `<cffunction>` block. Such a variable is called a *local variable*.

How to Declare a Local Variable

It's easy to create local variables in a UDF. All you need to do is *declare* the variable as a local variable, using the `<cfset>` tag and the var keyword, like this:

```
<cfset var myLocalVariable = "Hello">
```

The var keyword tells ColdFusion that the variable should cease to exist when the `<cffunction>` block ends, and that it shouldn't interfere with any other variables elsewhere that have the same name. You almost always want to declare all variables you create within a `<cffunction>` block as local with the var keyword.

NOTE

You usually don't want a function to have any "side effects" other than producing the correct return value. That way, you know it is always safe to call a function without having to worry about its overwriting any variables you might already have defined.

Here are some rules about local variables:

- You can declare as many local variables as you want. Just use a separate `<cfset>` for each one, using the var keyword each time.

- The `<cfset>` tags needed to declare local variables must be at the very top of the `<cffunction>` block, right after any `<cfargument>` tags. If ColdFusion encounters the var keyword after any line of code that does anything else, it will display an error message.

- It isn't possible to declare a local variable without giving it a value. That is, `<cfset var myLocalVariable>` alone isn't valid. There has to be an equals sign (=) in there, with an initial value for the variable. You can always change the value later in the function's code, so just set the variable to an empty string if you're not ready to give it its real value yet.

To make the `getFilmTitle()` function work correctly so that the `getFilm` query object is discarded after the function does its work, you need to add a `<cfset>` tag at the top of the function body, declaring the `getFilm` variable as a local variable, like so:

```
<cffunction name="getFilmTitle">
 <cfargument name="filmID" type="numeric" required="Yes">

 <!--- This variable is for this function's use only --->
 <cfset var getFilm = "">

 <!--- Get the film's title --->
 <cfquery name="getFilm" datasource="#datasource#"
 cachedwithin="#createTimespan(0,1,0,0)#">
 SELECT MovieTitle FROM Films
 WHERE FilmID = #ARGUMENTS.filmID#
 </cfquery>

 <!--- Return the film's title --->
 <cfreturn getFilm.MovieTitle>
</cffunction>
```

Because the `<cfset>` uses the `var` keyword, ColdFusion now understands that it should discard the `getFilm` variable after the function executes, and that it shouldn't interfere with any variables elsewhere that have the same name.

NOTE

This `<cfset>` sets the `GetFilm` variable to an empty string. It doesn't matter what this initial value is, since the variable will be set to the results of `<cfquery>` on the next line. In other languages, you might use an initial value of `null`, but CFML doesn't support the notion of a null value. Every variable always has some kind of value.

Where to Save Your UDFs

Now that you have seen what a completed `<cffunction>` block looks like, you may be wondering where exactly you are supposed to place it. The answer is simple: you can place your `<cffunction>` blocks anywhere you want, in any ColdFusion template. Your code can make use of the function anywhere after it encounters the `<cffunction>` block.

Creating and Using a UDF in the Same File

For instance, Listing 24.1 is a template that uses the `<cffunction>` block shown earlier to create the `getFilmTitle()` function, then uses the function to display a list of films (Figure 24.1).

Figure 24.1

The `getFilmTitle()` function makes it easy to display film titles.

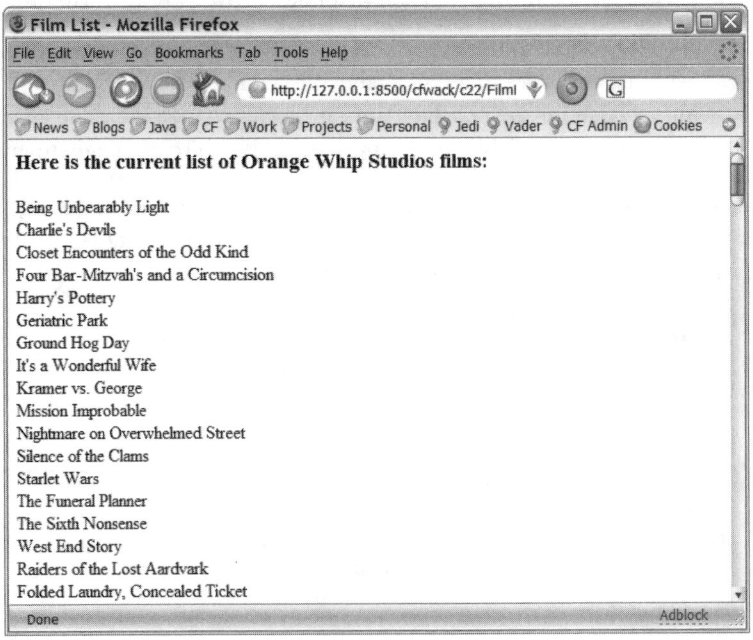

Listing 24.1 FilmList.cfm—Creating and Using a UDF

```
<!---
 Filename: FilmList.cfm
 Created by: Nate Weiss (NMW)
 Please Note Displays a list of films
 --->

<!--- ****** BEGIN FUNCTION DEFINITIONS ****** --->
<!--- Function: getFilmTitle() --->
<!--- Returns the title of a film, based on FilmID --->
<cffunction name="getFilmTitle">
 <!--- One argument: FilmID --->
 <cfargument name="filmID" type="numeric" required="Yes">

 <!--- This variable is for this function's use only --->
 <cfset var getFilm = "">

 <!--- Get the film's title --->
 <cfquery name="getFilm" datasource="ows"
 cachedwithin="#createTimespan(0,1,0,0)#">
 SELECT MovieTitle FROM Films
 WHERE FilmID = #Arguments.filmID#
 </cfquery>

 <!--- Return the film's title --->
 <cfreturn getFilm.MovieTitle>
</cffunction>
<!--- ****** END FUNCTION DEFINITIONS ****** --->

<!--- Get a list of all FilmIDs --->
<cfquery name="getFilms" datasource="ows">
 SELECT FilmID
 FROM Films
</cfquery>

<html>
<head><title>Film List</title></head>
<body>
 <h3>Here is the current list of Orange Whip Studios films:</h3>

 <!--- Now it is extremely easy to display a list of film links --->
 <cfoutput query="getFilms">
 #getFilmTitle(FilmID)#<br>
 </cfoutput>

</body>
</html>
```

Saving UDFs in Separate Files for Easy Reuse

In Listing 24.1, you saw how to create and use a user-defined function, all in the same ColdFusion template. While the function works just fine, it doesn't really make anything any easier. You wouldn't want to have to retype that function every time you wanted to display a movie's title.

Most of the time, you'll want to keep your UDFs in separate files to make them easy to reuse in your various ColdFusion pages. For instance, it would probably be a good idea to create a file named FilmFunctions.cfm that contains the getFilmTitle() function.

Later, as you create other film-related functions, you could put them in the same file. Once you have this file in place, you can simply include the file with a <cfinclude> tag to use the function it contains.

Listing 24.2 shows how to create such a file. As you can see, this is the same <cffunction> block shown in Listing 24.1; here it's simply dropped into its own template.

Listing 24.2 FilmFunctions1.cfm—Placing a UDF in a Separate File

```
<!---
Filename: FilmFunctions1.cfm
Created by: Nate Weiss (NMW)
Purpose: Creates a library of user-defined functions
related to films
--->

<!--- Function: GetFilmTitle() --->
<!--- Returns the title of a film, based on FilmID --->
<cffunction name="getFilmTitle">
 <!--- One argument: FilmID --->
 <cfargument name="filmID" type="numeric" required="Yes">

 <!--- This variable is for this function's use only --->
 <cfset var getFilm = "">

 <!--- Get the film's title --->
 <cfquery name="getFilm" datasource="ows"
 cachedwithin="#createTimespan(0,1,0,0)#">
 SELECT MovieTitle FROM Films
 WHERE FilmID = #ARGUMENTS.filmID#
 </cfquery>

 <!--- Return the film's title --->
 <cfreturn getFilm.MovieTitle>
</cffunction>
```

Once you have a file like this in place, you just need to include the file via a simple <cfinclude> tag to be able to use the function(s) it contains. For instance, Listing 24.3 is a revised version of the Film List template from Listing 24.1. The results in the browser are exactly the same (Figure 24.2), but the code is much cleaner.

Figure 24.2

UDFs can encapsulate scripting, HTML, or other lower-level code.

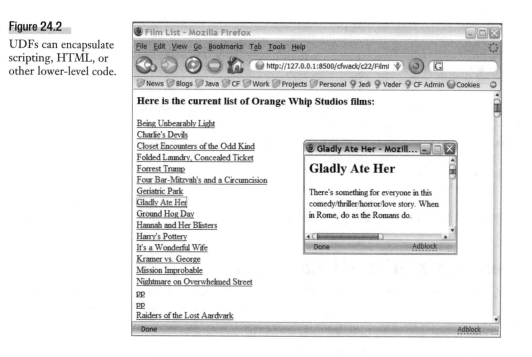

Listing 24.3 `FilmList2.cfm`—Using UDFs Stored in a Separate File

```
<!---
 Filename: FilmList2.cfm
 Created by: Nate Weiss (NMW)
 Purpose: Displays a list of films
--->

<!--- Include the set of film-related user-defined functions --->
<cfinclude template="FilmFunctions1.cfm">

<!--- Get a list of all FilmIDs --->
<cfquery name="getFilms" datasource="ows">
 SELECT FilmID
 FROM Films
 ORDER BY MovieTitle
</cfquery>

<html>
<head><title>Film List</title></head>
<body>
 <h3>Here is the current list of Orange Whip Studios films:</h3>

 <!--- Now it is extremely easy to display a list of film links --->
 <cfoutput query="getFilms">
 #getFilmTitle(FilmID)#<br>
 </cfoutput>

</body>
</html>
```

Reusing Code Saves Time and Effort

The `<cfinclude>` tag at the top of Listing 24.3 allows you to use the `getFilmTitle()` function later in the same template. You could use this same `<cfinclude>` tag in any other templates that need to use the function.

In other words, once you have created a user-defined function, it is incredibly easy to reuse it wherever you need. This makes your work easier and more efficient. And if you ever have to make a correction in the `getFilmTitle()` function, you only need to do so in one place. This makes your project much easier to maintain over time.

TIP

If you want to be able to use the functions in a particular file throughout your entire application, just move the `<cfinclude>` tag to your `Application.cfc` file. You're then free to use the functions wherever you wish.

Creating Libraries of Related UDFs

ColdFusion developers often refer to a file of conceptually related UDFs as a *UDF library*. Actually, there are no specific rules about what kinds of UDFs you can collect into a library, but it makes sense to group your UDFs into files according to some kind of common concept.

In fact, you have already seen a small UDF library: the `FilmFunctions1.cfm` file shown in Listing 24.2. It contains only one function, but you can still think of it as a library that you could expand to include other film-related functions in the future.

Designing the UDF Library

Let's say your team needs some more film-related functions added to the `FilmFunctions` library. Sounds like fun! You decide to create a new version of the library file, called `FilmFunctions2.cfm`. You sit down with the other members of your team, and come up with the list of functions shown in Table 24.4.

Table 24.4 Functions in the `FilmFunctions` UDF Library

FUNCTION	PURPOSE
`getFilmsQuery()`	This function returns a query object that contains information about films in the database. It supports one argument called `filmID`, which is optional. If the function is called without `filmID`, the function simply executes a `<cfquery>` that gets information about all films from the database and returns the query object. If a `filmID` is provided, however, the query object will only contain one row, corresponding to the specified film.
`getFilmTitle()`	This behaves in the same way as the `getFilmTitle()` function created in the first version of the library file. It takes one argument, `filmID`, which is the ID of the film to get the title for. Internally, this function can make use of the `getFilmsQuery()` function.

Table 24.4 (CONTINUED)

FUNCTION	PURPOSE
getFilmURL()	This function is similar to getFilmTitle(). It takes one argument, filmID. Instead of returning the film's title, however, it returns a standardized URL to a page called ShowFilm.cfm containing details about the film. The function includes the film's ID number in the URL so the ShowFilm.cfm template can display information about the correct film.
makeFilmPopupLink()	This function also accepts a filmID argument. It returns the HTML code needed to display a link for the selected film. When the link is clicked, a pop-up window appears with some basic information about the selected film. Internally, this function calls a general-purpose UDF function called JavaScriptPopupLink(), discussed later in this section.

Listing 24.4 shows the code for the new FilmFunctions2.cfm UDF library.

Listing 24.4 FilmFunctions2.cfm—A UDF Function Library

```
<!---
Filename: FilmFunctions2.cfm
Created by: Nate Weiss (NMW)
Purpose: Creates a library of user-defined functions
related to films
--->

<!--- Function: getFilmsQuery() --->
<!--- Returns a query object from the Films table in the database --->
<cffunction name="getFilmsQuery" returntype="query" output="false">
 <!--- Optional argument: FilmID --->
 <cfargument name="filmID" type="numeric" required="No">

 <!--- This variable is for this function's use only --->
 <cfset var filmsQuery = "">

 <!--- Query the database for information about all films --->
 <!--- The query is cached to improve performance --->
 <cfquery name="filmsQuery" datasource="ows"
  cachedwithin="#createTimespan(0,1,0,0)#">
 SELECT * FROM Films
  <!--- If a FilmID argument was provided, select that film only --->
 <cfif isDefined("ARGUMENTS.filmID")>
 WHERE FilmID = #ARGUMENTS.filmID#
 <!--- Otherwise, get information for all films, in alphabetical order --->
 <cfelse>
 ORDER BY MovieTitle
 </cfif>
 </cfquery>

 <!--- Return the query --->
 <cfreturn filmsQuery>
</cffunction>

<!--- Function: getFilmTitle() --->
<!--- Returns the title of a film, based on FilmID --->
```

Listing 24.4 (CONTINUED)

```
<cffunction name="getFilmTitle" returnType="string" output="false">
  <!--- One argument: FilmID --->
  <cfargument name="filmID" type="numeric" required="Yes">

  <!--- This variable is for this function's use only --->
  <cfset var getFilm = "">

  <!--- Get a query object of all films in the database --->
  <cfset getFilm = getFilmsQuery(ARGUMENTS.filmID)>

  <!--- Return the film's title --->
  <cfreturn getFilm.MovieTitle>
</cffunction>

<!--- Function: getFilmURL() --->
<!--- Returns the URL to a film's detail page, based on FilmID --->
<cffunction name="getFilmURL" returnType="string" output="false">
  <!--- One argument: FilmID --->
  <cfargument name="filmID" type="numeric" required="Yes">

  <!--- Return the appropriate URL --->
  <cfreturn "ShowFilm.cfm?FilmID=#ARGUMENTS.filmID#">
</cffunction>

<!--- Include another UDF function library --->
<!--- This one creates the JavaScriptPopupLink() function --->
<cfinclude template="SimpleJavaScriptFunctions.cfm">


<!--- Function: MakeFilmPopupLink() --->
<!--- Returns an HTML link for a film, based on FilmID --->
<cffunction name="MakeFilmPopupLink" returnType="string" output="false">
  <!--- One argument: FilmID --->
  <cfargument name="filmID" type="numeric" required="Yes">

  <!--- Return a link for the film --->
  <cfreturn javaScriptPopupLink(getFilmURL(ARGUMENTS.filmID),
  getFilmTitle(ARGUMENTS.FilmID))>
</cffunction>
```

Each of the <cffunction> blocks in Listing 24.4 is fairly simple. It's interesting to note here that UDFs can call other UDFs in the same file. They can even call functions in other files, as long as the <cfinclude> tag has been used to include the other files.

Let's take a closer look at each one of these new UDFs individually:

- For the getFilmsQuery(), note that the <cfargument> tag includes a required="No" attribute, which means the argument is optional. The first thing this function does is execute a <cfquery> tag to obtain film information from the database. Within the query, a simple isDefined("ARGUMENTS.filmID") test is used to find out whether the optional filmID argument has been provided when the function is actually used. If so, a WHERE clause is dynamically included in the SQL statement (so the query retrieves just the information about the specified film).

- The getFilmTitle() function has been reworked a bit, mainly to demonstrate that UDFs can call any other UDFs in the same file. Now, instead of using a <cfquery> tag within the body of the function, the new, convenient getFilmsQuery() function is used instead. Note that the filmID argument provided to getFilmTitle() is in turn passed to getFilmsQuery() internally, which means that the returned query contains data about the specified film only. It is then a simple matter to return the film's title using the <cfreturn> tag.

- The getFilmURL() function is the simplest of all the UDFs in this library. It just returns a URL that points to a template called ShowFilm.cfm, passing along the specified filmID as a URL parameter. The nice thing about this function is that it abstracts the idea of a film's Detail Page. If the URL that people should go to for more information about a film changes in the future, you can just edit the function in one place, rather than in multiple places throughout the application.

- The makeFilmPopupLink() function is interesting because it calls three functions internally. It uses both getFilmURL() and getFilmTitle() to get the URL and title of the specified film, respectively. It then passes the returned values to the javaScriptPopupLink() function, created in a separate UDF library file called SimpleJavaScriptFunctions.cfm. You will see the code for this function in a moment. For now, just take it on faith that the function returns the HTML and JavaScript code needed to create a link that opens a pop-up window.

Putting the UDF Library to Use

Listing 24.5 shows a new version of the Film List page (see Listings 24.1 and 24.3 for the previous versions). This version gets its work done with just a few lines of code, and it's more functional, too! Now, when the user clicks a film's title, a small pop-up window displays more information about that film (Figure 24.2).

Listing 24.5 FilmList3.cfm—Using Several UDFs Together

```
<!---
 Filename: FilmList3.cfm
 Created by: Nate Weiss (NMW)
 Purpose: Displays a list of films
--->

<!--- Include the set of film-related user-defined functions --->
<cfinclude template="FilmFunctions2.cfm">

<!--- Get a query object about films in database --->
<cfset getFilms = getFilmsQuery()>

<html>
<head><title>Film List</title></head>
<body>
 <h3>Here is the current list of Orange Whip Studios films:</h3>

 <!--- Now it is extremely easy to display a list of film links --->
```

Listing 24.5 (CONTINUED)

```
    <cfoutput query="getFilms">
    #makeFilmPopupLink(getFilms.FilmID)#<br>
    </cfoutput>
    </body>
    </html>
```

First, a `<cfinclude>` tag is used to include the new library of film-related UDFs. That makes it possible to call the `getFilmsQuery()` function to get a query object full of information about the films in the company's database. The value returned by the function is assigned to the local `getFilms` variable. From that point on, the `getFilms` query object can be used just as if there was an actual `<cfquery name="getFilms">` tag on the page.

Now it just takes a simple call to `makeFilmPopupLink()` to create a pop-up–enabled link for each film in the `getFilms` query. Through the magic of the UDF framework, that one line of code looks up the movie's title, obtains the correct URL to display details about the film, and generates the JavaScript code needed to pop up the detail page in a small window. And it's all eminently reusable.

Don't user-defined functions rock?

Creating General-Purpose UDFs

The functions in the `FilmFunctions` UDF library (refer to Table 24.4) are all related to the film concept, which is in turn somewhat related to the Films table in the ows database. As such, the library is really of interest only to the developers working on the Orange Whip Studios site. It's not going to be of much use to other ColdFusion developers.

It is, however, possible to create user-defined functions that have no ties to a particular application. You can think of such functions as *general-purpose functions*. They are useful for many different types of applications.

For instance, consider the `javaScriptPopupLink()` function used internally by the `FilmFunctions` library in Listing 24.4. That function isn't expecting any input that is specific to Orange Whip Studios or any other type of application. And its purpose—to create pop-up windows easily—might come in handy in any Web-based application.

Things to Consider

You don't need to do anything special to create a general-purpose function. Go ahead and use the same `<cffunction>`, `<cfargument>`, and `<cfreturn>` syntax you have already learned about. Just bear these things in mind as you go along:

Keep the list of arguments as short as possible. ColdFusion will let you create UDFs with many, many arguments, but such functions quickly become unwieldy. If you feel you need to have lots of arguments, consider creating a CFML Custom Tag instead, as discussed in the next chapter.

Keep code reuse in mind. If the problem at hand has both an application-specific aspect and a general-purpose aspect, try to isolate the two parts of the problems in two different functions. For instance, the problem of displaying a pop-up window about a film has an application-specific aspect (the film) and a general-purpose aspect (the pop-up window). By creating two different functions, you can reuse the pop-up aspect in situations that don't have anything to do with films.

In Chapter 25, you will learn how to create your own Custom Tags and Components (CFCs) as well as functions. Custom Tags are significantly more powerful and flexible than custom functions. Try to use UDFs for simple matters, especially quick retrieval and formatting. Use Custom Tags and Components for more involved processes, especially those you can think of as discrete actions rather than simple "massaging."

Writing the `SimpleJavaScriptFunctions` Library

As an example of a general-purpose UDF library, let's consider the `SimpleJavaScriptFunctions.cfm` library we used earlier, in Listing 24.4. Presently, this library contains only one function, `javaScriptPopupLink()`, which is responsible for creating a link that opens a pop-up window when clicked. This function supports four arguments, as listed in Table 24.5.

Table 24.5 `javaScriptPopupLink()` Function Syntax

ARGUMENT	DESCRIPTION
`linkURL`	Required. The URL for the page that should appear in the pop-up window when the user clicks the link.
`linkText`	Required. The text of the link—that is, the text the user will click to open the pop-up window. This text will also appear in the browser's status bar when the pointer hovers over the link.
`popupWidth`	Optional. The width of the pop-up window, in pixels. If this argument isn't provided, a default width of `300` is used.
`popupHeight`	Optional. The height of the pop-up window, in pixels. If this argument isn't provided, a default width of `200` is used.
`popupTop`	Optional. The vertical position of the pop-up window. If this argument isn't provided, a default value of `200` is used.
`popupLeft`	Optional. The horizontal position of the pop-up window. If this argument isn't provided, a default value of `300` is used.

NOTE

The `popupWidth`, `popupHeight`, `popupTop`, and `popupLeft` arguments correspond to the `width`, `height`, `top`, and `left` values supported by the JavaScript `window.open()` method. Consult a JavaScript reference for details

The function uses all these pieces of information to assemble the HTML code for an anchor element (that is, an `<a href>` tag) containing the appropriate JavaScript code to get the desired effect. The code is returned as the function's result (as a string).

Listing 24.6 is the ColdFusion code required to create `javaScriptPopupLink()`.

NOTE

The goal here isn't to teach you about JavaScript (that would take a whole book in itself), but rather to show you how you can distill something like JavaScript code and package it into a UDF for your ColdFusion pages. The nice thing about this kind of abstraction is that people can use the UDF without needing to understand the JavaScript code it generates.

Listing 24.6 SimpleJavaScriptFunctions.cfm—Creating a General-Purpose UDF

```
<!---
Filename: SimpleJavaScriptFunctions.cfm
Created by: Nate Weiss (NMW)
Purpose: Creates a library of ColdFusion functions that
encapsulate JavaScript ideas
--->


<!--- Function: JavaScriptPopupLink() --->
<!--- Returns an HTML link that opens a pop-up window via JavaScript --->
<cffunction name="javaScriptPopupLink" returnType="string" output="false">
 <!--- One argument: FilmID --->
 <cfargument name="linkURL" type="string" required="Yes">
 <cfargument name="linkText" type="string" required="Yes">
 <cfargument name="popupWidth" type="numeric" default="300">
 <cfargument name="popupHeight" type="numeric" default="200">
 <cfargument name="popupTop" type="numeric" default="200">
 <cfargument name="popupLeft" type="numeric" default="300">

 <!--- These variables are for this function's use only --->
 <cfset var features = "">
 <cfset var linkCode = "">

 <!--- Window features get passed to JavaScript's window.open() command --->
 <cfset features = "width=#ARGUMENTS.PopupWidth#,"
 & "height=#ARGUMENTS.PopupHeight#,top=#ARGUMENTS.PopupTop#,"
 & "left=#ARGUMENTS.PopupLeft#,scrollbars=yes">

 <!--- Create variable called LinkCode, which contains HTML / JavaScript --->
 <!--- needed to display a link that creates a pop-up window when clicked --->
 <cfsavecontent variable="linkCode">
 <cfoutput>
<a href="#ARGUMENTS.linkURL#" onclick="popupWin =
window.open('#ARGUMENTS.linkURL#','myPopup','#features#'); popupWin.focus(); return
false;" >#ARGUMENTS.LinkText#</a> </cfoutput>
 </cfsavecontent>

 <!--- Return the completed link code --->
 <cfreturn linkCode>
</cffunction>
```

NOTE

This listing includes some JavaScript code, such as `window.open()`, `focus()`, `window.status`, and `return true`. These are very basic JavaScript concepts. If you aren't familiar with them, consult any reference or online guide.

As with the earlier UDF examples in this chapter, the first thing this code does is define the function's arguments with the <cfargument> tag. This is actually the first UDF example that accepts more than one argument. As you can see, you can add as many arguments as you like. Just don't get totally carried away, since functions with dozens of arguments will probably be somewhat harder to use.

Next, a variable called `features` is created; this is the list of "window features" that will be supplied to the JavaScript `window.open()` method. You can find out more about how to specify window features in a JavaScript reference guide, but the basic idea is that this describes the physical pop-up window, including its position and size. When the function executes, the value of `features` will be something like this (depending on the actual arguments used):

```
width=300,height=200,top=200,left=300,scrollbars=yes
```

The next block of code uses the `<cfsavecontent>` tag to create a variable named `linkCode`. Cold-Fusion will process and evaluate all the code between the opening and closing `<cfsavecontent>` tags, then assign the final result to the `linkCode` variable. This makes it easier to create a variable that contains multiple lines, a variety of quotation marks, and so on. In this kind of situation, it's a lot easier than using the `<cfset>` tag. You can even use tags like `<cfloop>` within this type of block. That said, a `<cfset>` (or several `<cfset>` tags) would work equally well. The code might just be a bit harder to follow.

Within the `<cfsavecontent>` block, the basic idea is to generate a normal HTML `<a>` tag, with a normal `href` attribute. In addition to the `href` attribute, the `<a>` tag is also given `onclick`, `onmouseover`, and `onmouseout` attributes. These attributes contain JavaScript code that will execute when the user clicks the link, hovers over the link, and hovers away from the link, respectively.

NOTE

It is also necessary to use a pair of `<cfoutput>` tags here to force ColdFusion to evaluate the variables and expressions within this block. The final result (after all number signs (#), tags, and functions have been evaluated) is "captured" by `<cfsavecontent>` and placed into the `linkText` variable.

The result is the behavior shown earlier in Figure 24.2: when the user clicks the link, a pop-up window appears. If the user's browser doesn't support JavaScript, or if scripting has been disabled, the Film Details page simply appears in the main window (as a normal link would). You can use your browser's View Source option to examine the final HTML and JavaScript code that gets sent to the browser.

Sharing UDF Libraries with Others

Of course, you can download and use UDF function libraries that other people have written. Just save the `.cfm` file that contains the functions to an appropriate place on your server's drive, then include the file with `<cfinclude>`, just like the other examples in this chapter. You can also share your own general-purpose UDF libraries with others for fun or profit.

One place to exchange UDF function libraries is the Adobe Developer Exchange, at `http://www.adobe.com/cfusion/exchange/index.cfm`.

Another great place to find or share user-defined functions is the Common Function Library Project, at `http://www.cflib.org`. CFLib, as the library is commonly known, currently has over 800 UDFs released (Figure 24.3).

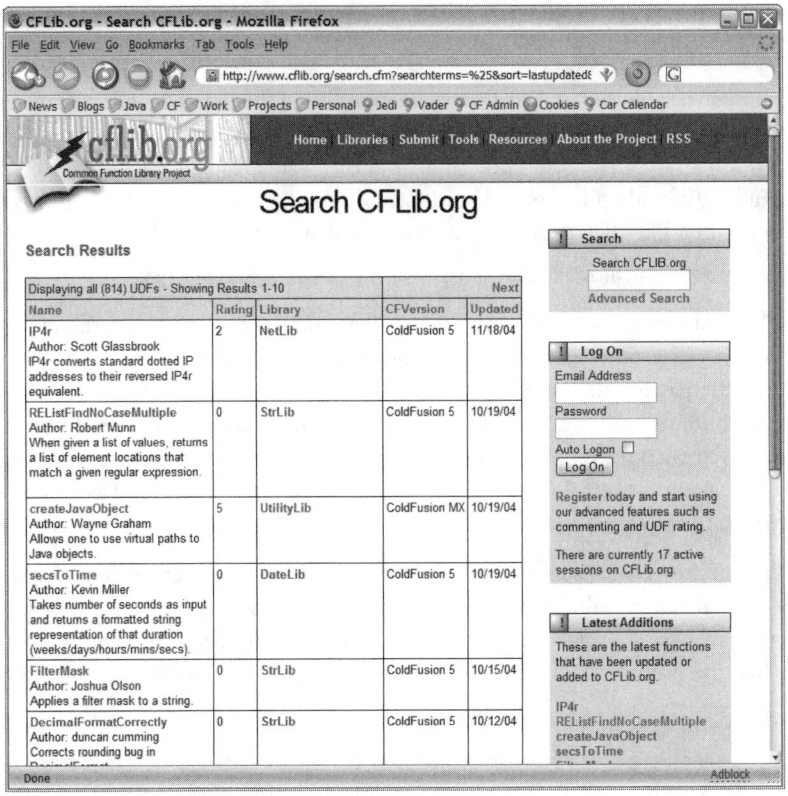

Figure 24.3

The Common
Function Library
Project's Web site
is another great place
to find user-defined
functions.

CHAPTER 25

Creating Custom Tags

Easy, Powerful Extensibility

In Chapter 24, "Building User-Defined Functions," you learned how to create your own user-defined functions (UDFs). These are exciting because they allow you to add to the CFML language to better suit your needs. Once you have written a UDF, you can use it just like one of ColdFusion's own built-in functions. Extending ColdFusion's language lets you reuse your code in many different places. That makes your job easier and more productive—plus, it's fun!

Let's recap the four basic ways of extending ColdFusion:

- **User-Defined Functions.** If there is some function that you feel is missing from ColdFusion's list of built-in functions, or that would be handy for an application you're building, you can just make the function yourself.

- **Custom Tags.** While UDFs allow you to make your own functions, custom tags let you create your own CFML tags. Of all the extensibility methods listed here, custom tags are the most flexible and powerful.

- **ColdFusion Components (CFCs).** Conceptually, CFCs are similar to custom tags, but imply a more structured, object-oriented manner of programming. CFCs are also at the heart of ColdFusion's Flash and Web Services integration.

- **CFX Tags.** It is also possible to write your own CFX tags in either Java or C++. For more information about writing CFX tags, see the ColdFusion documentation or consult *Adobe ColdFusion 8 Web Application Construction Kit, Volume 3: Advanced Application Development.*

Introducing CFML Custom Tags

The UDF framework introduced in Chapter 24 is probably the easiest and most straightforward way to extend the language. That said, the most *flexible* way to extend ColdFusion is by creating your own tags. Like UDFs, custom tags let you add your own tags to the CFML language, for whatever purpose you want. Unlike UDFs, the custom tag framework has been around since ColdFusion 3.0, and has become a rich and mature part of the product. As of this writing, there are many more custom tags than UDFs. Custom tags excel at encapsulating concepts and processes and are the bedrock of many existing ColdFusion applications.

You can solve many problems using either framework. And you can write extensions in ColdFusion's native language, CFML, regardless of which framework you choose for a particular task. This means you already know most of what you need, and can get started right away.

The Basic Custom Tag Idea

The idea behind custom tags is simple: to enable ColdFusion developers like you to package chunks of ordinary CFML code into reusable modules. From that point on, you can refer to the modules by name, using ColdFusion's familiar tag-based syntax. You get to define attributes for your tags, just as for regular CFML tags. Your tags can run queries, generate HTML, and perform calculations. They have almost no special requirements or limitations.

Generally, custom tags are self-contained and goal-oriented. They take care of whatever processing is necessary to perform a particular task or set of related tasks. In short, custom tags can be many different things, depending on your needs.

Why Modularity Is a Good Thing

As you will soon see, custom tags are easy to write, but you need to think about exactly how you want them to work. A process that might take half an hour to code as a normal ColdFusion template might require an extra 10 or 15 minutes to implement as a custom tag, because you will need to put some extra thought into how to modularize your code.

If it takes extra time, why bother with all this modularity business? Because breaking your code into independent, manageable chunks has a number of significant advantages.

Modularity Means Being Self-Contained

Because custom tags are modular, they usually end up being entirely self-contained. For instance, you might create a custom tag called <cf_PlaceOrder> that takes care of all aspects of placing an order, whatever that means in practice for your application. Because this custom tag is self-contained, other developers can place the tag in their templates wherever they need to, without worrying about what your custom tag actually does internally.

Modules Are Easy to Maintain

When you're using a custom tag, you can make any changes in just one place. Again, consider the hypothetical custom tag called <cf_PlaceOrder>. If you need to add some new step to the actual processing of each order, you can update the custom tag without having to touch each template that uses the tag. Additionally, because custom tags generally represent self-contained, well-defined chunks of code that do just one thing and do it well, they are usually easier for various members of a team to maintain. Their single-mindedness and sense of purpose make them more self-documenting and easier to understand than ordinary templates.

Modularity Encourages Code Reuse

Why reinvent the wheel? If someone else already has written code that gets a particular task done, it's almost always easier and more efficient to simply reuse that code, and get on to the next item in your schedule. Conversely, if you write some code that solves a problem, why not package it in such a way that you can easily use it again later?

How to Use Custom Tags

It's sometimes said that lazy people make the best programmers because they tend to solve problems by taking advantage of proven, working solutions that are already in place. Lazy or not, it's often a great idea to reuse work others have done. Before you get started on a project or tackle a piece of code, see whether someone has already written a custom tag that does what you need. If so, you can just use it. It's almost like getting the entire ColdFusion developer community to help you write the code for your application.

Finding Tags on the Developer Exchange

You can look for custom tags online in a number of places. By far the largest and most popular is the Developer Exchange portion of Adobe's own Web site, which offers thousands of custom tags for the taking. In many situations, a simple search will reveal that someone else has already solved your problem for you.

The Developer Exchange is located at `http://www.adobe.com/cfusion/exchange/index.cfm`. You can run keyword searches to find tags or browse through tags by category, popularity, or date of posting.

NOTE

Other items are available besides custom tags at the Developer Exchange, so when you run a search, be sure to specify that you want custom tags only.

How to "Install" a Custom Tag

A single ColdFusion template (`.cfm`) file represents each custom tag. Generally, the `.cfm` file and some type of documentation are placed together in a `.zip` file for easy downloading.

There isn't really any special installation step. All you have to do is place the custom tag template into the special `CustomTags` folder on your ColdFusion server's drive.

To install a custom tag, follow these steps:

1. Find the custom tag you want and download the `.zip` file that contains the tag. If you have been given the `.cfm` file directly rather than compressed in a `.zip` file, go to step 3.

2. Open the `.zip` file, using a utility such as WinZip from `http://www.winzip.com`, and find the custom tag template (`.cfm`) file itself. The template's file name will be the name of the custom tag, without the `cf_` prefix. So if you have downloaded a custom tag called `<cf_PlaceOrder>`, you should look for a file called `PlaceOrder.cfm`.

3. Place the custom tag template file into the `CustomTags` folder, located within the `ColdFusion8` folder on your ColdFusion server's drive. In a default Windows installation, this is the `c:\ColdFusion8\ CustomTags` folder.

That's it. The custom tag is now installed, and you can start using it in your code.

TIP

If you want to organize the custom tag templates you download (or write) into subfolders within the `CustomTags` folder, go ahead. As long as they are somewhere within the `CustomTags` folder, ColdFusion will find and use them in your applications.

NOTE

If you don't have access to the special `CustomTags` folder, or if you plan to use the custom tag in just one or two of your own templates, place the custom tag template into the folder where you plan to use it. See "Placing Custom Tags in the Current Directory," later in this chapter.

You can move the location of the special `CustomTags` folder, or create additional special custom tag folders. See "Changing the Custom Tag Search Path," later in this chapter.

Some custom tags might require other tags or files to be present as well. The documentation that comes with the tag should point out what you need to know.

Using Custom Tags

After you install a custom tag by placing its template in the special `CustomTags` folder, it's ready for use in your code. To help you get your feet wet, this book's Web site includes a custom tag in the listings for this chapter. The custom tag, `<cf_coolImage>`, allows you to easily create JavaScript-based rollovers. For example, you may want an image to switch to a "glowing" version when the mouse moves over it.

Using `<cf_CoolImage>`

Users and graphic designers love rollover images, in which an image changes when you move your pointer over it, usually to suggest that the image is live and can—should! must!—be clicked. Normally, you must write or borrow some JavaScript to get this done.

Listing 25.1 shows how you can use the `<cf_CoolImage>` custom tag to easily place a rollover image on one of your pages. If you visit this listing in your Web browser, you will see that the image does indeed roll over when you move the pointer over it. (Be sure you have copied over the images from the book Web site.)

Listing 25.1 `UsingCoolImage.cfm`—Using `<cf_CoolImage>` to Create a Rollover Effect

```
<!---
 Filename: UsingCoolImage.cfm
 Author: Nate Weiss (NMW)
 Purpose: Demonstrates how to use a custom tag
--->

<html>
<head><title>Using a Custom Tag</title></head>
<body>

<h2>Using a Custom Tag</h2>
<p>Hover your mouse over the logo, baby, yeah!</p>

<!--- Display a "Mouse Rollover" Image via groovy --->
<!--- <CF_CoolImage> Custom Tag by Jeremy Allaire --->
<!--- The tag will include all needed code for us --->
<cf_CoolImage
imgName="MyImage"
src="Logo.gif"
overSrc="LogoOver.gif"
width="300"
height="139"
border="0"
href="http://www.adobe.com/"
alt="Click for Adobe Home Page">
</body>
</html>
```

The attributes for `<cf_CoolImage>` are fairly self-explanatory and are not detailed here (you can look them up on the Developer Exchange if you want). The purpose of this listing is to show you how to use a custom tag in your code and give you a sense of what you can do with custom tags.

Thinking About Custom Tags as Abstractions

If you visit `UsingCoolImage.cfm` and then view its HTML code using your browser's View Source option, you will see that all the appropriate JavaScript and HTML code has been generated for you, based on the attributes you provided to the tag in Listing 25.1. I don't have the space here to go into a line-by-line explanation of the generated code, but the custom tag takes care of writing it correctly for you, so you don't really need to understand it.

In fact, that's the great thing about the tag. It lets you focus on the task at hand—inserting a rollover image—without worrying about the actual code you would normally need to write. You can think about the rollover at a higher, or more abstract, level. Developers often refer to this type of phenomenon as *abstraction*.

The more concepts or coding steps a tag wraps into one task-based or goal-oriented chunk, the more fully that tag becomes a helpful abstraction of the underlying concepts. You are free to make your custom tags do whatever you want them to and have them represent whatever level of abstraction you feel is appropriate.

NOTE

If you want to know more about the JavaScript code generated by `<cf_CoolImage>`, you can easily decipher it with the help of a JavaScript reference text or online tutorial. You can also refer to the JavaScript reference built into Dreamweaver.

Changing the Custom Tag Search Path

As you have already learned, when you use a custom tag in one of your ColdFusion templates, the ColdFusion Application Server looks in the special `CustomTags` folder for the corresponding custom tag template. So when you use the `<cf_CoolImage>` custom tag in your own code, ColdFusion looks for the `CoolImage.cfm` file in the `c:\ColdFusion8\CustomTags` folder (assuming you are running ColdFusion on a Windows machine and that you accepted the default installation options).

If you want, you can change the location of the special `CustomTags` folder, or specify additional folders for ColdFusion to look in. Say you want to place the custom tags for the Orange Whip Studios project in a folder called `C:\OrangeWhipCustomTags`, instead of `C:\ColdFusion8\CustomTags`. All you need to do is add the new folder to the custom tag search path. The custom tag search path is a list of folders ColdFusion looks through whenever you call a custom tag in one of your application templates. When you first install ColdFusion, only one folder is in the search path (the `CustomTags` folder within `ColdFusion8`).

After you add a new folder to the search path, you are free to place some custom tags in the new folder and others in the original `CustomTags` folder. Now, when you first refer to a custom tag in your own templates, the ColdFusion server first looks in the special `CustomTags` folder (and its subfolders) and then in your newly specified folder (and any of its subfolders).

NOTE

If all this path searching sounds like a lot of overhead for ColdFusion to incur, don't worry. Once ColdFusion successfully finds a custom tag template in the search paths you have configured, it remembers the template's location for all subsequent requests (until the server is restarted or until the server's template cache is exhausted). In other words, the custom tag search path is searched only once per custom tag per server restart, so there isn't much of a penalty for adding folders to the search path. Remember that if you test a custom tag and then move it, you will need to restart ColdFusion to have it "find" the custom tag again.

To add a folder to the custom tag search path, follow these steps:

1. Navigate to the Custom Tag Paths page of the ColdFusion Administrator (Extensions > Custom Tag Paths).

2. Specify the path and name of the folder you want to add to the custom tag search path. You can use the Browse Server button to avoid having to type the folder's path manually.

3. Click the Add Path button. The new folder appears in the list of custom tag paths.

4. Now you can place your custom tag templates in the folder you just added or in the original.

You can also remove folders from the custom tag search path using the Delete button. After you remove a folder from the search path, ColdFusion will no longer find custom tag templates in that folder.

Placing Custom Tags in the Current Directory

Sometimes placing custom tag templates in the special `CustomTags` folder isn't possible or convenient (see the section "How to 'Install' a Custom Tag," earlier in this chapter). For instance, if an Internet Service Provider is hosting your ColdFusion application, you might not have access to the ColdFusion Administrator or the `CustomTags` folder.

In such a situation, you can place the custom tag template (`CoolImage.cfm`, for example) in the same folder as the template you want to use it in. When ColdFusion encounters the custom tag in your code, it first looks for the appropriate file in the current folder. (It doesn't automatically look in the parent folder or subfolders of the current folder.) If ColdFusion can't find the `.cfm` file for the custom tag in the current folder, it then looks in the special `CustomTags` folder (and its subfolders).

Placing the custom tag template in the current folder is a good idea when:

- You don't have access to the special `CustomTags` folder.

- You are still developing and testing the custom tag. Just don't forget to restart ColdFusion so it can "find" it again if you subsequently move it to the `CustomTags` folder.

- You know you won't use the custom tag extensively, so you don't mind its being available only to code templates in the current folder.

- You want to simplify the distribution of your application and would rather not require that the custom tag template be dealt with separately.

These situations aside, it's smart to use the special `CustomTags` folder described earlier in this chapter. You will find all your custom tags in one place, and you won't have to maintain multiple copies of the same custom tag template (one for each folder in which you want to use the tag).

Controlling Template Locations with `<cfmodule>`

ColdFusion provides an alternative way to use custom tags in your templates that is helpful in a number of situations. Instead of calling your custom tags using the usual `<cf_` prefix, you use the `<cfmodule>` tag. You don't need to change anything in the custom tag template itself. You can use any custom tag with either method.

Introducing the `<cfmodule>` Tag

The `<cfmodule>` tag executes a ColdFusion template as a *module*, which is just another name for a CFML custom tag. Basically, you specify which custom tag you want to use with the `name` or `template` attribute. Then you add whatever additional attributes you need to pass to the tag, just as you would if you were calling the module using the normal `<cf_`-style custom tag syntax.

Table 25.1 explains the attributes you can supply to the `<cfmodule>` tag.

TIP

You provide either the `name` attribute or the `template` attribute when using `<cfmodule>`, but not both.

Table 25.1   `<cfmodule>` Tag Syntax

ATTRIBUTE	PURPOSE
name	The name of the custom tag you want to use, not including the `<cf_` prefix. ColdFusion will look for the tag in the current folder and then the special `CustomTags` folder, just as it would if you were calling the custom tag normally. So instead of using `<cf_PlaceOrder>` in your code, you would use `<cfmodule>` with `name="placeOrder"`.
template	The relative file name of the custom tag template, including the `.cfm` extension. You can provide a relative path to the template, just like the `template` attribute of the `<cfinclude>` tag. ColdFusion won't automatically look for the tag in the special `CustomTags` folder, because you are specifying the location explicitly. So instead of using `<cf_PlaceOrder>` in your code, you might use `<cfmodule>` with `template="PlaceOrder.cfm"`. You can also use a pathname expanded from a ColdFusion mapping.
attributeCollection	Optional. A structure that contains name-value pairs to consider as attributes. See "Passing Attributes with `attributeCollection`," later in this chapter.

Calling Modules by Name

As mentioned previously, you can use `<cfmodule>` to call modules either by name with the `name` attribute or by template location with the `template` attribute. In this section, you learn about calling modules by name.

Understanding the `name` Attribute

At its simplest, you can use `<cfmodule>` to call custom tags by simply providing the name of the tag, without the customary `<cf_` prefix. ColdFusion will use the same logic it does normally to find the corresponding template file (first looking in the current directory and then looking in the special `CustomTags` folder). Provide `<cfmodule>` with whatever additional attributes you would normally supply to the custom tag.

For instance, you might have a custom tag called `<cf_PlaceOrder>` that's normally called with two attributes called `orderID` and `sendConfirmation`, like this:

```
<!--- Place order --->
<cf_PlaceOrder
 orderID="#myOrderID#"
 sendConfirmation="Yes">
```

To call the tag with <cfmodule>, you would use the following:

```
<!--- Place Order --->
<cfmodule
 name="PlaceOrder"
 orderID="#myOrderID#"
 sendConfirmation="Yes">
```

No huge advantage exists to using <cfmodule> in this way versus the traditional <cf_ method. It's simply an alternative syntax you can use if you prefer.

NOTE

One advantage that can be helpful in certain situations is that this syntax can determine the NAME attribute dynamically. For example, you could create a string variable called `CallThisModule`, which would hold the name of the module you wanted to call, based on whatever logic you needed. You could then call <cfmodule> with `template="#CallThisModule#"` to execute the module. There would be no way to accomplish this using the traditional <cf_ syntax.

Using Dot Notation to Avoid Conflicts

As you saw earlier, you can place custom tag templates anywhere within the special CustomTags folder. You can place them in the CustomTags folder itself, or you can create any number of folders and subfolders within it (see the section "Using Custom Tags," earlier in this chapter).

This is a great feature, but it can cause problems if more than one custom tag with the same file name exists. For instance, what if two of your Web applications are running on the same Cold-Fusion server, and both use <cf_PlaceOrder> custom tags that do different things internally? You could place one in a subfolder of CustomTags called OrangeWhip and the other in a subfolder called PetStore, but you would have no way to tell ColdFusion which one of these to use at any given time. ColdFusion would simply use the first one it found for all requests, regardless of which folder the calling template was in.

To address this type of situation, ColdFusion allows you to use dot notation in <cfmodule>'s name attribute, where the dots indicate subfolders within the special CustomTags folder.

For instance, to specify that you want to use the version of the PlaceOrder module located within the OrangeWhip subfolder of the CustomTags folder, you would use the following:

```
<!--- Place order via custom tag --->
<cfmodule
 name="OrangeWhip.PlaceOrder">
```

To specify that you want to use the custom tag template PlaceOrder.cfm located in a folder called Commerce within a folder called OrangeWhip in the special CustomTags folder, you would use the following:

```
<!--- Place Order --->
<cfmodule
 name="OrangeWhip.Commerce.PlaceOrder"
 action="Delete"
 filmID="5">
```

As you can see, this special dot notation lets you set up hierarchies of custom tag modules, simply by establishing subfolders nested within the `CustomTags` folder. This can be important if you'll be installing your application on a server along with other ColdFusion applications.

NOTE

If you prefer the `<cf_` syntax to `<cfmodule>` but are still worried about naming conflicts, you can add a consistent prefix to each of your custom tag file names. Instead of naming a custom tag file `PlaceOrder.cfm`, for instance, you might call it `owsPlaceOrder.cfm`. The chance of there being two tags with the same file name on the same server is very unlikely. Then you could use the tag with `<cf_owsPlaceOrder>` syntax. It's a less formal solution, but it will generally work.

Calling Modules by Template Location

You can also use `<cfmodule>` with its `template` attribute instead of the `name` attribute to explicitly specify the location of your custom tag template. Use this method in situations where you don't want ColdFusion to attempt to find your tag's template automatically (in the current folder, the `CustomTags` folder, or anywhere else).

NOTE

The `template` attribute effectively takes away the magic effect created by your custom tags, as they appear to become part of ColdFusion. So using the word module instead of custom tag starts to make more sense.

The `template` attribute works just like the `template` attribute of the `<cfinclude>` tag. You can provide a relative path to the template, using slashes to indicate subdirectories. You can also use the usual URL-style `../` notation to indicate the parent folder.

For instance, just as all images for the Orange Whip Studios project are stored in the `images` subfolder within the `ows` folder, you could keep all your modules in a subfolder called `modules`. Then, assuming you want to call a template from a different subfolder of ows (such as a subfolder called 25 for this chapter of this book), you could refer to the custom tag template using a relative path that starts with `../modules/`, as shown in the following code.

So, instead of this:

```
<!--- Place order --->
<cf_PlaceOrder
  orderID="#MyOrderID#"
  sendConfirmation="Yes">
```

or this:

```
<!--- Place order --->
<cfmodule
  name="PlaceOrder"
  orderID="#MyOrderID#"
  sendConfirmation="Yes">
```

you might use something such as this:

```
<!--- Place order --->
<cfmodule
  template="../modules/PlaceOrder.cfm"
  orderID="#MyOrderID#"
  sendConfirmation="Yes">
```

You can also use ColdFusion mappings with the template attribute of the `cfmodule` tag. So if you created a mapping called ows, you can create a folder under it called `customtags` and call `PlaceOrder` like this:

```
<!--- Place order --->
<cfmodule template="/ows/customtags/PlaceOrder.cfm"
  ordered="#myOrderID#"
  sendConfirmation="yes">
```

NOTE

You can't provide an absolute file system-style path to the **TEMPLATE** attribute, so drive letters or UNC paths are not allowed.

Writing Custom Tags That Display Information

Now that you understand how to use existing custom tags, it's time to write your own. This section introduces you to the basic concepts involved in creating a custom tag. As you will soon see, it's an easy and productive way to write your code.

Writing Your First Custom Tag

It's traditional to illustrate a new language or technique with a "Hello, World" example. Listing 25.2 shows a custom tag that outputs a `"Hello, World"` message in the current Web page, formatted with ordinary HTML table syntax.

Save this listing as `HelloWorld.cfm` in either the special `CustomTags` folder or the folder you've been using as you follow along in this chapter.

Listing 25.2 `HelloWorld.cfm`—A Simple Custom Tag Template

```
<!---
 Filename: HelloWorld.cfm
 Author: Nate Weiss (NMW)
 Purpose: Creates the <CF_HelloWorld> custom tag example
--->

<table border="5" cellPadding="5">
 <tr><th bgcolor="yellow">
 <b>Hello, World, from Orange Whip Studios.</b><br>
 </th></tr>
 <tr><td bgcolor="orange">
 Orange whip... two orange whips... three orange whips!<br>
 </td></tr>
</table>
```

Now you can use the custom tag just by adding a `cf_` prefix to the tag's file name (without the `.cfm` part). This means you have just created a custom tag called `<cf_HelloWorld>`, which you can use in code as shown in Listing 25.3.

Listing 25.3 `UsingHelloWorld.cfm`—Testing the `<CF_HelloWorld>` Custom Tag

```
<!---
Filename: UsingHelloWorld.cfm
Author: Nate Weiss (NMW)
Purpose: Shows how <CF_HelloWorld> can be used in a ColdFusion page
--->

<!--- Display Hello World Message, via Custom Tag --->
<cf_HelloWorld>
```

It's a start, but this custom tag isn't terribly exciting, since it will always output exactly the same thing. In fact, at this point, you could just replace the reference to the custom tag in Listing 25.3 with an ordinary `<cfinclude>` tag and the results would be the same:

```
<!--- Display Hello World Message, via Custom Tag --->
<cfinclude template="HelloWorld.cfm">
```

Things get a lot more interesting after you start making custom tags that accept attributes, just like ColdFusion's built-in tags.

Introducing the `attributes` Scope

To make your own custom tags really useful, you want them to accept tag attributes, just as normal CFML and HTML tags do. ColdFusion makes this very easy by defining a special `attributes` scope for use within your custom tag templates.

The `attributes` scope is a ColdFusion structure that is automatically populated with any attributes provided to the custom tag when it is actually used in code. For instance, if an attribute called `message` is provided to a tag, as in `<cf_HelloWorld message="Country and Western">`, then the special `attributes` scope will contain a `message` value, set to `Country and Western`. You could output this value to the page by referring to `#ATTRIBUTES.message#` between `<cfoutput>` tags within the custom tag template.

Outputting Attribute Values

Listing 25.4 shows another custom tag called `<cf_HelloWorldMessage>`, which is almost the same as `<cf_HelloWorld>` from Listing 25.2. The difference is the fact that this tag accepts an attribute called `message`, which gets displayed as part of the `"Hello, World"` message.

Listing 25.4 `HelloWorldMessage.cfm`—Defining Attributes for Your Custom Tags

```
<!---
Filename: HelloWorldMessage.cfm
Author: Nate Weiss (NMW)
Purpose: Creates a custom tag that accepts attributes
--->

<!--- Tag Attributes --->
<cfparam name="ATTRIBUTES.message" type="string">

<!--- Output message in HTML table format --->
```

Listing 25.4 (CONTINUED)

```
<cfoutput>
<table border="5" cellPadding="5">
<tr><th bgcolor="yellow">
<b>Hello, World, from Orange Whip Studios.</b><br>
</th></tr>
<tr><td bgcolor="orange">
#ATTRIBUTES.message#<br>
</td></tr>
</table>
</cfoutput>
```

The `<cfparam>` tag at the top of Listing 25.4 makes it clear that a `message` parameter is expected to be provided to the tag and that it is expected to be a string value. The `<cfoutput>` block near the end outputs the value of the `message` parameter provided to the tag. Listing 25.5 shows how to supply the `message` parameter that the tag now expects.

NOTE

To make this listing work, you must save the previous listing (Listing 25.4) as `HelloWorldMessage.cfm`, either in the same folder as Listing 25.5 or in the special `CustomTags` folder.

Listing 25.5 `UsingHelloWorldMessage.cfm`—Supplying Attributes to Your Custom Tags

```
<!---
Filename: UsingHelloWorldMessage.cfm
Author: Nate Weiss (NMW)
Purpose: Shows how to use the <CF_HelloWorldMessage> custom tag
--->

<!--- Display Hello World Message, via Custom Tag --->
<cf_HelloWorldMessage
message="We're getting the band back together!">
```

NOTE

Attribute names are not case sensitive. There is no way to determine whether a parameter was passed to a tag with code such as `Message="Hello"` or `MESSAGE="Hello"`. Of course, the case of each attribute's value is preserved, so there is a difference between `message="Hello"` and `message="HELLO"`.

Using `<cfparam>` to Declare Attributes

You don't have to include the `<cfparam>` tag in Listing 25.4. As long as the `message` attribute is actually provided when the tag is used, and as long as the parameter is a string value, the `<cfparam>` tag doesn't do anything. It only has an effect if the attribute is omitted (or provided with a value that can't be converted to a string), in which case it displays an error message.

However, I strongly suggest that you declare each of a custom tag's attributes with a `<cfparam>` tag at the top of the tag's template, for the following reasons:

- Always having your custom tag's attributes formally listed as `<cfparam>` tags at the top of your templates makes your custom tag code clearer and more self-documenting.

- Specifying the expected data type with `<cfparam>`'s `type` attribute acts as a convenient sanity check in case someone tries to use your tag in an unexpected way.

- If you declare all your tag's attributes using `<cfparam>` tags at the top of a tag's template, you know that the rest of the template will never run if the attributes aren't provided properly when the tag is actually used. This prevents problems or data inconsistencies that could arise from partially executed code.

- As discussed in the next section, you can easily make any of your tag's attributes optional by simply adding a `default` attribute for the corresponding `<cfparam>` tag.

➔ See Chapter 8, "The Basics of CFML," in *Adobe ColdFusion 8 Web Application Construction Kit, Volume 1: Getting Started,* for more information about the `<cfparam>` tag.

NOTE

You can use the `<cftry>` and `<cfcatch>` tags to provide friendly error messages when the attributes passed to a custom tag do not comply with the rules imposed by the custom tag's `<cfparam>` tags. See the version of the `<cf_PlaceOrder>` custom tag presented in Chapter 51, "Error Handling," online, for an example.

Making Attributes Optional or Required

When you start working on a new custom tag, one of the most important things to consider is which attributes your new tag will take. You want to ensure that the attribute names are as clear, intuitive, and self-describing as possible.

Often, you will want to make certain attributes optional, so they can be omitted when the tag is actually used. That way, you can provide lots of attributes for your tags (and thus flexibility and customizability), without overburdening users of your tags with a lot of unnecessary typing if they just want a tag's normal behavior.

Using `<cfparam>` to Establish Default Values

The most straightforward way to declare an optional attribute for a custom tag is to provide a `default` attribute to the corresponding `<cfparam>` tag at the top of the tag's template.

Look at the version of the `<cf_HelloWorldMessage>` tag shown in Listing 25.6. This version is the same as the previous one (shown in Listing 25.4), except that it defines five new attributes: `topMessage`, `topColor`, `bottomColor`, `tableBorder`, and `tablePadding`. The values are given sensible default values using the `default` attribute.

Listing 25.6   `HelloWorldMessage2.cfm`—Making Certain Attributes Optional

```
<!---
  Filename: HelloWorldMessage2.cfm
  Author: Nate Weiss (NMW)
  Purpose: Creates a custom tag that accepts attributes
--->

<!--- Tag Attributes --->
<cfparam name="ATTRIBUTES.message" type="string">
```

Listing 25.6 (CONTINUED)

```
<cfparam name="ATTRIBUTES.topMessage" type="string"
 default="Hello, World, from Orange Whip Studios.">
<cfparam name="ATTRIBUTES.topColor" type="string" default="yellow">
<cfparam name="ATTRIBUTES.bottomColor" type="string" default="orange">
<cfparam name="ATTRIBUTES.tableBorder" type="numeric" default="5">
<cfparam name="ATTRIBUTES.tablePadding" type="numeric" default="5">

<!--- Output message in HTML table format --->
<cfoutput>
 <table border="#ATTRIBUTES.tableBorder#" cellPadding="#ATTRIBUTES.tablePadding#">
 <tr><th bgcolor="#ATTRIBUTES.topColor#">
 <b>#ATTRIBUTES.topMessage#</b><br>
 </th></tr>
 <tr><td bgcolor="#ATTRIBUTES.bottomColor#">
 #ATTRIBUTES.message#<br>
 </td></tr>
 </table>
</cfoutput>
```

If the tag is explicitly provided with a `topColor` value when it is used, that value will be available as `ATTRIBUTES.topColor`. If not, the `default` attribute of the `<cfparam>` tag kicks in and provides the default value of `Yellow`. The same goes for the other new attributes: if values are supplied at run time, the supplied values are used; if not, the default values kick in.

NOTE

There's generally no harm in defining more attributes than you think people will need, as long as you supply default values for them. As a rule of thumb, try to provide attributes for just about every string or number your tag uses, rather than hard-coding them. This is what Listing 25.6 does.

Assuming you save Listing 25.6 as a custom tag template called `HelloWorldMessage.cfm`, you can now use any of the following in your application templates:

```
<cf_HelloWorldMessage
message="We're getting the band back together!">

<cf_HelloWorldMessage
topMessage="Message of the Day"
message="We're getting the band back together!">

<cf_HelloWorldMessage
message="We're getting the band back together!"
topColor="Beige"
bottomColor="##FFFFFF"
tableBorder="0">
```

Using Functions to Test for Attributes

Instead of using the `<cfparam>` tag, you can use the `isDefined()` function to test for the existence of tag attributes. This is largely a matter of personal preference. For instance, instead of this:

```
<cfparam name="ATTRIBUTES.message" type="string">
```

you could use this:

```
<cfif not isDefined("ATTRIBUTES.message") >
 <cfabort showError="You must provide a Message attribute">
</cfif>
```

Or instead of this:

```
<cfparam name="ATTRIBUTES.topColor" type="string" default="Yellow">
```

you could use this:

```
<cfif not isDefined("ATTRIBUTES.topColor")>
 <cfset ATTRIBUTES.topColor="Yellow">
</cfif>
```

NOTE

Since the **ATTRIBUTES** scope is implemented as a ColdFusion structure, you can also use CFML's various structure functions to test for the existence of tag attributes. For instance, instead of `isDefined("ATTRIBUTES.topColor")`–shown in the previous code snippet–you could use `structKeyExists(ATTRIBUTES, "topColor")` to get the same effect.

NOTE

Because the special **ATTRIBUTES** scope exists only when a template is being called as a custom tag, you can use `isDefined("ATTRIBUTES")` if you want to be able to detect whether the template is being visited on its own or included via a regular `<cfinclude>` tag.

Who Are You Developing For?

Before you get started on a new custom tag, think about who its audience will be. Keep that audience in mind as you think about the tag's functionality and what its attributes and default behavior should be. Custom tags generally fall into one of these two groups:

- **Application-Specific Tags**. These display something or perform an action that makes sense only within your application (or within your company). These tags generally either relate to your application's specific database schema or are in charge of maintaining or participating in business rules or processes specific to your company. This type of tag extends the CFML language to the exclusive benefit of your application, creating a kind of tool set for your code's internal use.

- **General-Purpose Tags.** These don't have anything specific to do with your application; instead, they provide some functionality you might need in a variety of scenarios. Rather than being of interest mainly to you or your programming team, these tags are of interest to the ColdFusion developer community at large. This type of tag extends the CFML language for all ColdFusion programmers who download or buy it.

The type of code you use to write the two types of tags isn't categorically different, but it is still helpful to keep the tag's audience in mind as you work—whether that audience is just you, or ColdFusion developers all over the world. If you are creating an application-specific tag, think about the people who might need to look at the code in the future. If you're creating a general-purpose tag, imagine fellow developers using your tag in various contexts.

Then ask yourself these questions:

- **How can I name the tag so that its purpose is self-explanatory?** In general, the longer the tag name, the better. Also, the tag name should hint not only at what the tag does, but also at what it acts on. Something such as `<cf_DisplayMovie>` or `<cf_ShowMovieCallout>` is better than just `<cf_Movie>` or `<cf_Display>`, even if the shorter names are easier to type or seem obvious to you.

- **How can I name the attributes so that they are also self-explanatory?** Again, there's little harm in using long attribute names. Long names make the tags—and the code that uses them—more self-documenting.

- **Which attributes will the audience need, and which should be optional versus required?** A good rule of thumb is that the tag's optional attributes should have sensible enough default values so that the tag works in a useful way with only the required attributes. The optional attributes should be gravy.

NOTE

Try to make your tag's name and attribute names come together in such a way that the tag's use in code reads almost like a sentence. It's really great when you can understand a tag's purpose just by looking at its usage in actual code templates.

Querying and Displaying Output

Now that you know how to create a custom tag that accepts a few attributes to control its behavior, let's make a tag that really does something useful. This section demonstrates how easy it is to create tags that look up and display information. You can then reuse them throughout your application.

Running Queries in Custom Tags

You can use any tag in the CFML language within a custom tag template, including `<cfquery>`, `<cfoutput>`, and `<cfset>`. Listing 25.7 turns the movie-display code from the `FeaturedMovie.cfm` template in Chapter 19, "Introducing the Web Application Framework," in Vol. 1, *Getting Started*, into a custom tag called `<cf_ShowMovieCallout>`.

The first half of the `FeaturedMovie.cfm` example randomly determines which of the available movies to show. The second half queries the database for the selected movie and displays its title, description, and other information. This custom tag does the work of the second half of that example (that is, it only shows a movie's information, without the randomizing aspect). It takes just one required attribute, a numeric attribute called `filmID`. Within the custom tag, you can use the `ATTRIBUTES.filmID` value in the criteria for a `<cfquery>` to retrieve the appropriate film information.

At its simplest, this tag can be used as follows—a neat, tidy, helpful abstraction of the CFML, HTML, and CSS code that the tag generates:

```
<!--- Show movie number five, formatted nicely --->
<cf_ShowMovieCallout
  filmID=5">
```

Listing 25.7 `ShowMovieCallout.cfm`—Query/Display a Particular Film Record

```
<!---
<CF_ShowMovieCallout> Custom Tag
Retrieves and displays the given film

Example of Use:
<cf_ShowMovieCallout
FilmID="5">
--->

<!--- Tag Attributes --->
<!--- FilmID Attribute is Required --->
<cfparam name="ATTRIBUTES.filmID" type="numeric">
<!--- Whether to reveal cost/release dates (optional) --->
<cfparam name="ATTRIBUTES.showCost" type="boolean" default="yes">
<cfparam name="ATTRIBUTES.showReleaseDate" type="boolean" default="Yes">
<!--- Optional formatting and placement options --->
<cfparam name="ATTRIBUTES.tableAlign" type="string" default="right">
<cfparam name="ATTRIBUTES.tableWidth" type="string" default="150">
<cfparam name="ATTRIBUTES.caption" type="string" default="Featured Film">
<!--- Use "ows" datasource by default --->
<cfparam name="ATTRIBUTES.DataSource" type="string" default="ows">

<!--- Get important info about film from database --->
<cfquery name="getFilm" datasource="#ATTRIBUTES.dataSource#">
SELECT
MovieTitle, Summary,
AmountBudgeted, DateInTheaters
FROM Films
WHERE FilmID = #ATTRIBUTES.filmID#
</cfquery>

<!--- Display error message if record not fetched --->
<cfif getFilm.recordCount neq 1>
 <cfthrow message="Invalid FilmID Attribute"
 detail="Film #ATTRIBUTES.filmID# doesn't exist!">
</cfif>

<!--- Format a few queried values in local variables --->
<cfset productCost = ceiling(val(getFilm.AmountBudgeted) / 1000000)>
<cfset releaseDate = dateFormat(getFilm.DateInTheaters, "mmmm d")>

<!--- Now Display The Specified Movie --->
<cfoutput>
 <!--- Define formatting for film display --->
 <style type="text/css">
 th.fm { background:RoyalBlue;color:white;text-align:left;
 font-family:sans-serif;font-size:10px}
 td.fm { background:LightSteelBlue;
 font-family:sans-serif;font-size:12px}
 </style>

 <!--- Show info about featured movie in HTML Table --->
 <table width="#ATTRIBUTES.tableWidth#" align="#ATTRIBUTES.tableAlign#"
 border="0"
 cellSpacing="0">
```

Listing 25.7 (CONTINUED)

```
<tr><th class="fm">#ATTRIBUTES.caption#</th></tr>

<!--- Movie Title, Summary, Rating --->
<tr><td class="fm">
<b>#getFilm.MovieTitle#</b><br>
#getFilm.Summary#<br>
</td></tr>

<!--- Cost (rounded to millions), release date --->
<cfif ATTRIBUTES.showCost or ATTRIBUTES.showReleaseDate>
<tr><th class="fm">
<!--- Show Cost, if called for --->
<cfif ATTRIBUTES.showCost>
Production Cost $#ProductCost# Million<br>
</cfif>
<!--- Show release date, if called for --->
<cfif ATTRIBUTES.showReleaseDate>
In Theaters #ReleaseDate#<br>
</cfif>
</th></tr>
</cfif>
</table>
<br clear="all">
</cfoutput>
```

TIP

It's often helpful to put an Example of Use comment at the top of your custom tag as shown here, even if you provide better documentation elsewhere. If nothing else, the hint will serve as a quick reminder to you if you need to revise the tag later.

At the top of this listing, a number of `<cfparam>` tags make clear what the tag's required and optional parameters will be. Only the `filmID` attribute is required; because its `<cfparam>` tag doesn't have a `default` attribute, ColdFusion will throw an error message if a `filmID` isn't provided at run time. The `showCost` and `showReleaseDate` attributes are Boolean values, meaning that either `Yes` or `No` (or an expression that evaluates to `True` or `False`) can be supplied when the tag is actually used; the `default` for each is defined to be `Yes`. The `tableAlign`, `tableWidth`, `caption`, and `dataSource` attributes are also given sensible default values so they can be omitted when the tag is used.

Next, the `<cfquery>` named `getFilm` retrieves information about the appropriate film, using the value of `ATTRIBUTES.filmID` in the `WHERE` clause. Then two local variables called `productCost` and `releaseDate` are set to formatted versions of the `AmountBudgeted` and `DateInTheaters` columns returned by the query.

NOTE

These two variables are referred to as local because they exist only in the context of the custom tag template itself, not in the calling template where the tag is used. The `getFilm` query is also a local variable. See the section "Local Variables in Custom Tags," later in this chapter, for more information.

Custom tags should be able to deal gracefully with unexpected situations. For that reason, a `<cfif>` block is used right after the `<cfquery>` to ensure that the query retrieved one record as expected. If not, a <cfthrow> tag halts all processing with a customized, diagnostic error message. For more information about <cfthrow>, see Chapter 51.

NOTE

The error message generated by the <cfthrow> tag will be displayed using the appropriate look-and-feel template if the <cferror> tag or onError() method is used in Application.cfc, as discussed in Chapter 19.

The rest of the template is essentially unchanged from the FeaturedMovie.cfm template as it originally appeared in Chapter 19. The film's title, summary, and other information are shown in an attractive table format. The <cfif> logic at the end of the template enables the display of the Production Cost and Release Date to be turned off by setting the showCost or showReleaseDate attributes of the tag to No.

After you've saved Listing 25.7 as a custom tag template called ShowMovieCallout.cfm (in the special CustomTags folder or in the same folder as the templates in which you want to use the tag), it is ready for use. Listing 25.8 shows how easily you can use the tag in your application's templates.

Listing 25.8   UsingShowMovieCallout.cfm—Using the <cf_ShowMovieCallout> Custom Tag

```
<!---
  Filename: UsingShowMovieCallout.cfm
  Author: Nate Weiss (NMW)
  Purpose: Demonstrates how to use the <CF_ShowMovieCallout> custom tag
--->

<!--- Page Title and Text Message --->
<h2>Movie Display Demonstration</h2>

<!--- Display Film info as "callout", via Custom Tag --->
<cf_ShowMovieCallout filmID="20">
```

Local Variables in Custom Tags

The previous section pointed out that the getFilm, productCost, and releaseDate variables are local variables, meaning they exist only within the scope of the custom tag template itself.

This is an important aspect of ColdFusion's custom tag functionality. Whenever a custom tag is executed, it gets a private area in the server's memory to store its own variables. Unless you use a scope prefix (such as ATTRIBUTES, APPLICATION, or SESSION), all references to variables in the custom tag template refer only to this private area. The result is what some other programming languages call a namespace—an interim memory space for the tag to do its work, without regard to how it will affect the template in which it is used.

For instance, if you attempt to display the value of the productCost variable in Listing 25.8, after the <cf_ShowMovieCallout> tag, you would get an error message saying that the variable doesn't exist—because the variable exists only within the custom tag's template itself. After the tag finishes its work, all its variables are discarded and are no longer available.

This is what enables custom tags to be so modular and independent. Because they don't affect the variables in the templates in which they run, they are free to create variables and run queries in any way they need to. All kinds of problems would arise if this weren't the case.

For instance, what if Listing 25.8 needs to run its own query named `getFilms` before it uses the `<cf_ShowMovieCallout>` tag? If custom tags didn't have their own local variables, the `<cfquery>` inside the custom tag template would overwrite any variable called `getFilms` that was set before the tag was called. This could lead to all sorts of strange behavior, especially if you were using a custom tag that you didn't write, because you would need to know all the variable names the custom tag uses internally and to avoid using them in your templates.

Remember these important points:

- Variables in custom tags are always local, unless you specify a special scope name (discussed shortly).

- Variables set before the tag is used aren't available within the custom tag itself.

- Similarly, variables set in the custom tag's template aren't available as normal variables in code that uses the tag.

- The ATTRIBUTES scope enables you to pass specific values into the tag.

- The special CALLER scope, which you will learn about shortly, lets you access or set specific variables in the calling template.

Custom Tags Versus `<cfinclude>`

Previously you learned about the `<cfinclude>` tag, which lets you put ordinary CFML code in a separate template and include it anywhere else you need to use it. You might be thinking that including a template with the `<cfinclude>` tag is pretty similar to calling a custom tag. That's true, but custom tags are more sophisticated because they have their own variable name spaces, as explained above.

Although you can often get the same results using `<cfinclude>` instead of creating a custom tag, your code will usually be harder to maintain and debug because variables set in the calling template might interfere with the way the included template behaves, and vice versa.

Custom Tags That Process Data

So far, we have concentrated on creating custom tags that display information, such as the `<cf_ShowMovieCallout>` custom tag. Many of the custom tags you will write are likely to be similar to it in that they will be in charge of wrapping up several display-related concepts (querying the database, including formatting, outputting the information, and so on).

However, you can also create custom tags that have different purposes in life: to process or gather information. This type of custom tag generally doesn't generate any HTML to be displayed on the current page. Instead, these tags perform some type of processing, often returning a calculated result to the calling template.

You might call these tags nonvisual, or perhaps number crunchers, to set them apart from tags that generate something visual, such as the `<cf_ ShowMovieCallout>` and `<cf_HelloWorldMessage>` examples you have already seen.

Introducing the `CALLER` Scope

ColdFusion defines two special variable scopes that come into play only when you're creating custom tags:

- The `ATTRIBUTES` Scope—You have already learned about this scope, which passes specific information to a custom tag each time it is used.

- The `CALLER` Scope—Gives a custom tag a way to set and use variables in the template in which you're using the tag (the calling template).

The special `CALLER` scope is easy to understand and use. Within a custom tag template, you prefix any variable name with `CALLER` (using dot notation) to access the corresponding variable in the calling template. Through the `CALLER` scope, you have full read-write access to all variables known to the calling template, meaning that you can set variables as well as access their current values. For instance, you can set variables in the calling template using an ordinary `<cfset>` tag.

Returning Variables to the Calling Template

Let's say you're writing a custom tag called `<cf_PickFeaturedMovie>`, which will choose a movie from the list of available films. In the calling template, you plan on using the tag like so:

```
<cf_PickFeaturedMovie>
```

Inside the custom tag template (`PickFeaturedMovie.cfm`), you could set a variable using a special `CALLER` prefix, such as this:

```
<cfset CALLER.featuredFilmID = 5>
```

This prefix would make `featuredFilmID` available in the calling template as a normal variable. For instance, this code snippet would call the custom tag and then output the value of the variable it returns:

```
<cf_PickFeaturedMovie>
<cfoutput>
 The featured Film ID is:
 #featuredFilmID#
</cfoutput>
```

Of course, using these snippets, the value of `featuredFilmID` would always be 5, so the custom tag wouldn't be all that useful. Listing 25.9 shows how to expand the previous snippets into a useful version of the `<cf_PickFeaturedMovie>` custom tag. The purpose of the code is to select a single film's ID number in such a way that all films are rotated evenly on a per-session basis.

Listing 25.9 `PickFeaturedMovie.cfm`—Setting a Variable in the Calling Template

```
<!---
 Filename: PickFeaturedMovie.cfm
 Author: Nate Weiss (NMW)
 Purpose: Creates the <CF_PickFeaturedMovie> custom tag
--->

<!--- Tag Attributes --->
<!--- Use "ows" datasource by default --->
<cfparam name="ATTRIBUTES.dataSource" type="string" default="ows">

<cflock scope="session" type="exclusive" timeout="30">

  <!--- List of movies to show (list starts out empty) --->
  <cfparam name="SESSION.movieList" type="string" default="">

  <!--- If this is the first time we're running this, --->
  <!--- Or we have run out of movies to rotate through --->
  <cfif SESSION.movieList eq "">
    <!--- Get all current FilmIDs from the database --->
    <cfquery name="getFilmIDs" datasource="#ATTRIBUTES.dataSource#">
    SELECT FilmID FROM Films
    ORDER BY MovieTitle
    </cfquery>

    <!--- Turn FilmIDs into a simple comma-separated list --->
    <cfset SESSION.movieList = valueList(getFilmIDs.FilmID)>
  </cfif>

  <!--- Pick the first movie in the list to show right now --->
  <cfset thisMovieID = listFirst(SESSION.movieList)>

  <!--- Re-save the list, as all movies *except* the first --->
  <cfset SESSION.movieList = listRest(SESSION.movieList)>
</cflock>

<!--- Return chosen movie to calling template --->
<cfset CALLER.featuredFilmID = thisMovieID>
```

The `<cfparam>` tag at the top of this custom tag template establishes a single optional attribute for the tag called `dataSource`, which will default to ows if not provided explicitly. We begin by using a `<cflock>` tag to ensure that the code here is thread-safe. Since we are reading and writing to a shared scope, it's important that we control how the code is accessed. We use `<cfparam>` to default the list of movies to an empty string. If the SESSION variable already exists, this line will do nothing. If the `movieList` variable equals an empty string, it means we either just created the variable, or the list of movies has already been used. If this is the case, we run a query to grab all the film IDs. We then use the `valueList()` function to copy out the list of IDs from the query. The `listFirst()` function is used to get the first film ID from the list, and `listRest()` is used to remove the ID and resave the list to the `SESSION.movieList` variable. Because the final `<cfset>` uses the special CALLER scope, the featured movie that the tag has chosen is available for the calling template to use normally.

Listing 25.10 shows how you can put this version of the `<cf_PickFeaturedMovie>` custom tag to use in actual code.

Listing 25.10 `UsingPickFeaturedMovie1.cfm`—Using a Variable Set by a Custom Tag

```
<!---
 Filename: UsingPickFeaturedMovie1.cfm
 Author: Nate Weiss (NMW)
 Purpose: Shows how <cf_PickFeaturedMovie> can be used in a ColdFusion page
--->

<!--- Page Title and Text Message --->
<h2>Movie Display Demonstration</h2>

<!--- Pick rotating Featured Movie to show, via Custom Tag --->
<cf_PickFeaturedMovie>

<!--- Display Film info as "callout", via Custom Tag --->
<cf_ShowMovieCallout
 filmID="#featuredFilmID#">
```

NOTE

The CALLER scope is for use only within custom tag templates. Don't use it in your ordinary ColdFusion templates. Doing so won't generate an error message, but it could produce unexpected results.

If you are calling a custom tag from within another custom tag, the CALLER scope of the innermost tag will refer to the local variables in the first custom tag template, not the variables in the top-level page template. To access the variables of the top-level template from the innermost tag, you must use CALLER.CALLER.VariableName instead of CALLER.VariableName. In some cases, this can be a pain; the REQUEST scope provides an effective solution, as explained in the section "The REQUEST Scope," later in this chapter.

First, the `<cf_PickFeaturedMovie>` custom tag from Listing 25.9 is called. As the custom tag executes, it selects the film ID it feels is appropriate and saves the value in the `featuredFilmID` variable in the calling template (which, in this case, is Listing 25.10). Next, the featured movie is actually displayed to the user, using the `<cf_ShowMovieCallout>` custom tag presented earlier in this chapter.

NOTE

These two custom tags (`<cf_PickFeaturedMovie>` and `<cf_ShowMovieCallout>`) each do something useful on their own and can be used together, as shown here. As you design custom tags for your applications, this type of synergy between tags is a nice goal to shoot for.

Of course, to make Listing 25.10 work, you need to enable session management by using an `Application.cfc` file. See Chapter 19 for details. You will find a simple `Application.cfc` file for this chapter at the book's Web site.

NOTE

The more a custom tag relies on variables in the calling template, the less modular it becomes. So, although the CALLER scope gives you read-write access to variables in the calling template, you should use it mainly for setting new variables, rather than accessing the values of existing ones. If you find that you are accessing the values of many existing variables in the calling template, maybe you should just be writing a normal `<cfinclude>` style template rather than a custom tag, or maybe the values should be passed into the tag explicitly as attributes.

Variable Names as Tag Attributes

In the version of the <cf_PickFeaturedMovie> custom tag shown in Listing 25.9, the selected film ID is always returned to the calling template as a variable named featuredFilmID. Designing a custom tag to accept an additional returnVariable attribute allows a calling template to control the name of the variable modified by the custom tag template.

For instance, for the <cf_PickFeaturedMovie> custom tag, you might add an attribute called returnVariable, which allows the calling template to specify the variable in which to place the featured film's ID number.

To use the tag, change this line from Listing 25.9:

```
<!--- Pick rotating featured movie to show via custom tag --->
<cf_PickFeaturedMovie>
```

to this:

```
<!--- Pick rotating featured movie to show via custom tag --->
<cf_PickFeaturedMovie
returnVariable="FeaturedFilmID">
```

This makes the custom tag less intrusive because it doesn't demand that any particular variable names be set aside for its use. If for whatever reason the developer coding the calling template wants the selected film to be known as myFeaturedFilmID or showThisMovieID, he or she can simply specify that name for the returnVariable attribute. The calling template is always in control.

NOTE

Also, code that uses the <cf_PickFeaturedMovie> tag will be a bit more self-documenting and easier to understand because it is now evident from where exactly the FeaturedFilmID variable is coming.

NOTE

If you think about it, a number of ColdFusion's own CFML tags use the same technique. The most obvious example is the <cfquery> tag's name attribute, which tells the tag which variable to store its results in. The name attributes of the <cfdirectory> and <cfsearch> tags are similar, as are the OUTPUT attribute for <cfwddx> and the VARIABLE attributes for <cffile> and <cfsaveoutput>.

Using <cfparam> with type="variableName"

You have already seen the <cfparam> tag used throughout this chapter to make it clear which attributes a custom tag expects and to ensure that the data type of each attribute is correct. When you want the calling template to accept a variable name as one of its attributes, you can set the type of the <cfparam> tag to variableName.

Therefore, the next version of the <cf_PickFeaturedMovie> custom tag will include the following lines:

```
<!--- Variable name to return selected FilmID as --->
<cfparam name="ATTRIBUTES.returnVariable" type="variableName">
```

When the <cfparam> tag is encountered, ColdFusion ensures that the actual value of the attribute is a legal variable name. If it's not, ColdFusion displays an error message stating that the variable name is illegal. This makes for a very simple sanity check. It ensures that the tag isn't being provided with something such as returnValue="My Name", which likely would result in a much uglier error message later on because spaces aren't allowed in ColdFusion variable names.

NOTE

In ColdFusion, variable names must start with a letter, and the other characters can only be letters, numbers, and underscores. Any string that doesn't conform to these rules won't get past a <cfparam> of type="variableName". What's nice is that if the rules for valid variable names changes in a future version of ColdFusion, you won't have to update your code.

Setting a Variable Dynamically

After you've added the <cfparam> tag shown previously to the <cf_PickFeaturedMovie> custom tag template, the template can refer to ATTRIBUTES.returnVariable to get the desired variable name. Now the final <cfset> variable in Listing 25.9 just needs to be changed so that it uses the dynamic variable name instead of the hard-coded variable name of featuredFilmID. Developers sometimes get confused about how exactly to do this.

Here's the line as it stands now, from Listing 25.9:

```
<!--- Return chosen movie to calling template --->
<cfset CALLER.featuredFilmID = thisMovieID>
```

People often try to use syntax similar to the following to somehow indicate that the value of ATTRIBUTES.returnVariable should be used to determine the name of the variable in the CALLER scope:

```
<!--- Return chosen movie to calling template --->
<cfset CALLER.#ATTRIBUTES.returnVariable# = thisMovieID>
```

Or they might use this:

```
<!--- Return chosen movie to calling template --->
<cfset #CALLER.##ATTRIBUTES.returnVariable### = thisMovieID>
```

These are not legal because ColdFusion doesn't understand that you want the value of ATTRIBUTES.returnVariable evaluated before <cfset> is actually performed. ColdFusion will just get exasperated, and display an error message.

Using Quoted <cfset> Syntax

ColdFusion provides a somewhat odd-looking solution to this problem. You simply surround the left side of the <cfset> expression, the part before the equals (=) sign, with quotation marks. This forces ColdFusion to first evaluate the variable name as a string before attempting to actually perform the variable setting. The resulting code looks a bit strange, but it works very well and is relatively easy to read.

So, this line from Listing 25.9:

```
<!--- Return chosen movie to calling template --->
<cfset CALLER.featuredFilmID = thisMovieID>
```

can be replaced with this:

```
<!--- Return chosen movie to calling template --->
<cfset "CALLER.#ATTRIBUTES.returnVariable#" = thisMovieID>
```

Listing 25.11 shows the completed version of the <cf_PickFeaturedMovie> custom tag. This listing is identical to Listing 25.9, except for the first and last lines, which are the <cfparam> line and the updated <cfset> line shown previously.

Listing 25.11 PickFeaturedMovie2.cfm—Revised Version of <cf_PickFeaturedMovie>

```
<!---
 Filename: PickFeaturedMovie2.cfm
 Author: Nate Weiss (NMW)
 Purpose: Creates the <CF_PickFeaturedMovie> custom tag
--->

<!--- Tag Attributes --->

<!--- Variable name to return selected FilmID as --->
<cfparam name="ATTRIBUTES.returnVariable" type="variableName">

<!--- Use "ows" datasource by default --->
<cfparam name="ATTRIBUTES.dataSource" type="string" default="ows">

<cflock scope="session" type="exclusive" timeout="30">

  <!--- List of movies to show (list starts out empty) --->
  <cfparam name="SESSION.movieList" type="string" default="">

  <!--- If this is the first time we're running this, --->
  <!--- Or we have run out of movies to rotate through --->
  <cfif SESSION.movieList eq "">
    <!--- Get all current FilmIDs from the database --->
    <cfquery name="getFilmIDs" datasource="#ATTRIBUTES.dataSource#">
    SELECT FilmID FROM Films
    ORDER BY MovieTitle
    </cfquery>

    <!--- Turn FilmIDs into a simple comma-separated list --->
    <cfset SESSION.movieList = valueList(getFilmIDs.FilmID)>
  </cfif>

  <!--- Pick the first movie in the list to show right now --->
  <cfset thisMovieID = listFirst(SESSION.movieList)>

  <!--- Re-save the list, as all movies *except* the first --->
  <cfset SESSION.movieList = listRest(SESSION.movieList)>
</cflock>

<!--- Return chosen movie to calling template --->
<cfset "CALLER.#ATTRIBUTES.returnVariable#" = thisMovieID>
```

Listing 25.12 shows how to use this new version of the custom tag. This listing is nearly identical to Listing 25.10, except for the addition of the returnVariable attribute. Note how much clearer the cause and effect now are. In Listing 25.10, the featuredFilmID variable seemed to appear out of nowhere. Here, it's very clear where the showThisMovieID variable is coming from.

Listing 25.12 UsingPickFeaturedMovie2.cfm—Using the returnVariable Attribute

```
<!---
 Filename: UsingPickFeaturedMovie2.cfm
 Author: Nate Weiss (NMW)
 Purpose: Shows how <cf_PickFeaturedMovie2> can be used in a ColdFusion page
--->

<!--- Page Title and Text Message --->
<h2>Movie Display Demonstration</h2>

<!--- Pick rotating Featured Movie to show, via Custom Tag --->
<cf_PickFeaturedMovie2 returnVariable="showThisMovieID">

<!--- Display Film info as "callout", via Custom Tag --->
<cf_showMovieCallout filmID="#showThisMovieID#">
```

Using the setVariable() Function

Another way to solve this type of problem is with the setVariable() function. This function accepts two parameters. The first is a string specifying the name of a variable; the second is the value you want to store in the specified variable. (The function also returns the new value as its result, which isn't generally helpful in this situation.)

So, this line from Listing 25.11:

```
<!--- Return chosen movie to calling template --->
<cfset "CALLER.#ATTRIBUTES.returnVariable#" = thisMovieID>
```

could be replaced with this:

```
<!--- Return chosen movie to calling template --->
<cfset temp = setVariable("CALLER.#ATTRIBUTES.returnVariable#", thisMovieID)>
```

Because the result of the function is unnecessary here, this line can be simplified to:

```
<!--- Return chosen movie to calling template --->
<cfset setVariable("CALLER.#ATTRIBUTES.returnVariable#", thisMovieID)>
```

Using struct Notation

One more way a custom tag can return information to the calling document is to simply treat the CALLER scope as a structure.

So, this line from Listing 25.11:

```
<!--- Return chosen movie to calling template --->
<cfset "CALLER.#ATTRIBUTES.returnVariable#" = thisMovieID>
```

could be replaced with this:

```
<!--- Return chosen movie to calling template --->
<cfset CALLER[ATTRIBUTES.returnVariable] = thisMovieID>
```

Either method—the quoted <cfset> syntax mentioned previously, the SetVariable() method shown, or struct notation—produces the same results. Use whichever method you prefer.

Custom Tags That Encapsulate Business Rules

It's often helpful to create custom tags to represent the business rules or logic your application needs to enforce or adhere to. After these custom tags are written correctly, you can rest assured that your application won't violate the corresponding business rules.

For instance, looking at the tables in the ows example database, it's easy to see that several tables will be involved when someone wants to place an order from Orange Whip Studios' online store. For each order, a record will be added to the MerchandiseOrders table, and several records can be added to the MerchandiseOrdersItems table (one record for each item the user has in the shopping cart). In addition, you will need to verify the user's credit-card number and perhaps send a confirmation email as an acknowledgment of the user's order. In a real-world application, you might also need to decrease the current number of items on hand after the order has been placed, and so on.

You could place all those steps in a single custom tag. It could be called something such as <cf_PlaceMerchandiseOrder> and take a few simple and easily understood parameters that represent everything necessary to complete an order successfully. The tag might look like this when used in code:

```
<!--- Place order for selected items and get new Order ID --->
<cf_PlaceMerchandiseOrder
 contactID="4"
 merchIDList="2,6,9"
 shipToCurrentAddress="Yes"
 sendReceiptViaEmail="Yes"
 returnVariable="NewOrderID">
```

In fact, a version of the <cf_PlaceMerchandiseOrder> tag is developed in Chapter 22, "Online Commerce," online.

Custom Tags for General-Purpose Use

So far in this chapter, you have learned how to make custom tags that are mainly for internal use within your application or company. The <cf_ShowMovieCallout> custom tag might be enormously useful in building projects for Orange Whip Studios, but probably not all that helpful to the average ColdFusion programmer.

In contrast, you will sometimes find yourself writing a custom tag you know will be helpful not only to yourself but to other developers as well. If so, you can package it and make it available to others via the Developer Exchange on the Adobe Web site, either free or for a fee.

Perhaps you need to convert sentences to title case, meaning that the first letter of each word should be capitalized. You could write a custom tag, perhaps called <cf_TextToTitleCase>, to get the job done. After the tag is complete, you could share it with other developers you know or even post it for free download by the entire ColdFusion developer community.

Listing 25.13 shows code that creates the <CF_TextToTitleCase> custom tag. The tag has two required attributes—input and output. The tag looks at the text passed to it via the input attribute, capitalizes the first letter of each word, and returns the capitalized version of the string back to the calling template by storing it in the variable specified by the output attribute.

A third, optional attribute, `dontCapitalizeList`, can be supplied with a comma-separated list of words that should *not* be capitalized. If this attribute isn't provided, it uses a default list of words: a, an, the, to, for, and of. If a word from the input is in this list, it is appended to the output string verbatim, its case preserved.

NOTE

The output attribute here works just like the `ReturnVariable` attribute in some of this chapter's other examples. Depending on the situation, simplified attribute names, such as `input` and `output`, can be easier for other developers to use. In other cases, more verbose attribute names, such as `textToConvert` and `returnVariable`, might make more sense. Geeky as it might sound, coming up with the names is part of the fun.

Listing 25.13 `TextToTitleCase.cfm`—Source Code for `<cf_TextToTitleCase>`

```
<!---
 Filename: TextToTitleCase.cfm
 Author: Nate Weiss (NMW)
 Purpose: Creates the <cf_TextToTitleCase> custom tag
--->

<!--- Tag Parameters --->
<cfparam name="ATTRIBUTES.input" type="string">
<cfparam name="ATTRIBUTES.output" type="variableName">
<cfparam name="ATTRIBUTES.dontCapitalizeList" type="string"
 default="a,an,the,to,for,of">
<!--- Local Variables --->
<cfset result = "">

<!--- For each word in the input --->
<cfloop list="#ATTRIBUTES.input#" index="thisWord" delimiters=" ">

 <!--- Assuming this is a word that should be capitalized --->
 <cfif listFindNoCase(ATTRIBUTES.dontCapitalizeList, thisWord) eq 0>

   <!--- Grab the first letter, and convert it to uppercase --->
   <cfset firstLetter = uCase( mid(thisWord, 1, 1) )>
   <!--- Grab remaining letters, convert them to lowercase --->
   <cfset restOfWord = lCase( mid(thisWord, 2, len(thisWord)-1) )>

   <!--- Append the completed, capitalized word to result --->
   <cfset result = listAppend(result, firstLetter & restOfWord, " ")>

 <!--- If this is a word that should *not* be capitalized --->
 <cfelse>

   <cfset result = listAppend(result, thisWord, " ")>

 </cfif>

</cfloop>

<!--- Return result to calling template --->
<cfset "CALLER.#ATTRIBUTES.output#" = result>
```

Listing 25.13 relies on the idea that you can think of a set of words (similar to a sentence) as a list, just like an ordinary, comma-separated list of values. The only difference is that the list is delimited by spaces instead of commas. Therefore, by supplying a space as the delimiter to ColdFusion's list functions, such as listAppend(), you can treat each word individually or loop through the list of words in a sentence.

NOTE

For more information about lists, see the various list functions (such as listFind(), listGetAt(), and listDeleteAt()). See also the discussion of CFML data types in Chapter 8.

First, three <cfparam> tags declare the tag's input and output attributes as well as the optional attribute, dontCapitalizeList. A variable called result is set to an empty string. Then, a <cfloop> tag loops over the words supplied by the input attribute. If the word is found in dontCapitalizeList then the word is appended to the output list by the <cfelse> clause. Otherwise, for each word, the first letter is capitalized and stored in the firstLetter variable. The remaining letters, if any, are stored in the restOfWord variable. So, when the firstLetter and restOfWord variables are concatenated using the & operator, they form the capitalized form of the current word. The listAppend() function then appends the word to the list of capitalized words in result, again using the space character as the delimiter. When the <cfloop> is finished, all the words in input have been capitalized and the tag's work is done. It then passes the completed result back to the calling template using the usual quoted <cfset> syntax.

NOTE

Because of the way ColdFusion's list functionality behaves, consecutive space characters from the original string are not preserved in the tag's output. ColdFusion treats multiple delimiters as a single delimiter. So if the Input contained three words with five spaces between each word, the resulting output would still contain three words (in title case), but with only one space between each word. This is the defined, documented behavior and isn't a bug. Depending on the situation, the multiple-delimiter behavior can work for you or against you. Just keep it in mind.

Listing 25.14 shows how you and other developers can use this custom tag in actual code.

Listing 25.14 UsingTextToTitleCase.cfm—Using <cf_TextToTitleCase>

```
<!---
 Filename: UsingTextToTitleCase.cfm
 Author: Nate Weiss (NMW)
 Purpose: Demonstrates how to use the <cf_TextToTitleCase> custom tag
--->

<h2>Using &lt;cf_TextToTitleCase&gt;</h2>

<!--- Text to convert to "Title Case" --->
<cfset originalText = "The rest of the band's around back.">

<!--- Convert Text to Title Case, via Custom Tag --->
<cf_textToTitleCase input="#originalText#" output="fixedCase">

<!--- Output the text, now in Title Case --->
<cfoutput>
<p><b>Original Text:</b><br>
```

Listing 25.14 (CONTINUED)

```
#originalText#<br>

<p><b>Processed Text:</b><br>
#FixedCase#<br>
</cfoutput>
```

Sharing Your Custom Tags

As explained in the section "Finding Tags on the Developer Exchange," earlier in this chapter, the Developer Exchange on the Adobe Web site is the first place most ColdFusion developers go when they are looking for custom tags to purchase or download. If you want to share one of your custom tags with others, consider posting it to the Developer Exchange.

Additional Custom Tag Topics

So far, we have dealt with simple tags, and the rules we have learned work well enough for most uses, but ColdFusion also provides advanced features that can really enhance custom tags.

Passing Attributes with `attributeCollection`

In addition to the special `name` and `template` attribute names (discussed in the section "Controlling Template Locations with `<cfmodule>`," earlier in this chapter), a third attribute name exists: `attributeCollection`. ColdFusion reserves the `attributeCollection` attribute name for a special use: if a structure variable is passed to a custom tag as an attribute called `attributeCollection`, the values in the structure become part of the ATTRIBUTES scope inside the custom tag template.

That is, instead of doing this:

```
<!--- Display Hello World Message, via Custom Tag --->
<cf_HelloWorldMessage
 message="We're getting the band back together!"
 topColor="yellow"
 bottomColor="orange">
```

or this:

```
<!--- Display Hello World Message, via Custom Tag --->
<cfmodule
 name="HelloWorldMessage"
 message="We're getting the band back together!"
 topColor="yellow"
 bottomColor="orange">
```

you could do this:

```
<!--- Set up attribute structure --->
<cfset attribs = structNew()>
<cfset attribs.message = "We're getting the band back together!"">
<cfset attribs.topColor = "yellow">
<cfset attribs.bottomColor = "orange">
```

```
<!--- Display Hello World Message, via Custom Tag --->
<cfmodule
 name="HelloWorldMessage"
 attributeCollection="#attribs#">
```

This is most useful in certain specialized situations, such as when you are calling a custom tag recursively (using the custom tag within the custom tag's own template, so that the tag calls itself repeatedly when used). You would be able to call a tag a second time within itself, passing the second tag the same attributes that were passed to the first, by specifying `attributeCollection= "#ATTRIBUTES#"`.

The REQUEST Scope

In addition to the CALLER and ATTRIBUTES scopes, ColdFusion defines a third special variable scope called REQUEST, which is relevant to a discussion of custom tags. Although it isn't specifically part of ColdFusion's custom tag framework, it comes into play only in situations in which you have custom tags that might in turn use other custom tags.

Making Variables Available to All Custom Tags

Consider a situation where you might want to create a custom tag that uses the `<cf_ShowMovieCallout>` tag from Listing 25.7 internally. The new custom tag defines an optional `dataSource` attribute, which defaults to ows. That value is then passed to the `<cf_ShowMovieCallout>` tag from Listing 25.7. Wouldn't it be more convenient to use the `dataSource` variable defined in the `Application.cfc` file, in a process similar to that of earlier templates? That way, if your application needed to use a different data source name, you could just make the change in one place, in `Application.cfc`.

But how could you refer to that `dataSource` variable? Normally, you would refer to it directly in the `dataSource` attribute for each `<cfquery>` tag, as in the `datasource="#dataSource#"` attribute that has appeared in previous chapters. Of course, in a custom tag template, that variable wouldn't exist because the tag has its own local variable scope. You could access the value using the CALLER scope, as in `dataSource="#CALLER.dataSource#"`, but there's a problem with that, too. When the new tag calls `<cf_ShowMovieCallout>`, the code template for `<cf_ShowMovieCallout>` won't be capable of referring to CALLER.dataSource because there is no local variable named DataSource in the calling template. In this situation, `<cf_ShowMovieCallout>` could refer to CALLER.CALLER.dataSource. That would work, but your code will get messier and messier if you start nesting tags several levels deep.

The answer is the REQUEST scope, a special scope shared among all ColdFusion templates participating in the page request—whether they are included via `<cfinclude>`, called as a custom tag, or called via `<cfmodule>`.

This means you can change these lines in the `Application.cfc` file:

```
<!--- Any variables set here can be used by all our pages --->
<cfset dataSource = "ows">
<cfset companyName = "Orange Whip Studios">
```

to this:

```
<!--- Any variables set here can be used by all our pages --->
<cfset REQUEST.dataSource = "ows">
<cfset REQUEST.companyName = "Orange Whip Studios">
```

Then you will be able to provide the `REQUEST.dataSource` variable to the `dataSource` attribute of every `<cfquery>` tag in your application, regardless of whether the query is in a custom tag.

So you may ask: Why not use the `APPLICATION` scope? You certainly *could* use the `APPLICATION` scope. In general, developers tend to use either `REQUEST` or `APPLICATION`—not both. `REQUEST` scope variables were more useful in earlier versions of ColdFusion, where accessing the `APPLICATION` scope required extensive locking. Now that locking isn't needed as much, most of the time you will use `APPLICATION` variables for values that don't change.

Maintaining Per-Request Flags and Counters

You can also use the `REQUEST` scope to create custom tags that are aware of how many times they have been included on a page. For instance, if you look at the code for the `<cf_ShowMovieCallout>` tag in Listing 25.7, you will see that it includes a `<style>` block defining how the callout box will appear. If you include this custom tag several times on the same page, that `<style>` block will be included several times in the page's source, which will cause the final page to have a longer download time than it should.

You could use the `REQUEST` scope to ensure that the `<style>` block gets included in the page's source code only once, by surrounding the block with a `<cfif>` test that checks to see whether a variable called `REQUEST.calloutStyleIncluded` has been set. If not, the `<style>` block should be included in the page. If it has been set, the tag knows that the block has already been included on the page, presumably because the tag has already been used earlier on the same page.

The `<style>` block in `ShowMovieCallout.cfm` would be adjusted to look like this:

```
<!--- If the <style> isn't included in this page yet --->
<cfif not isDefined("REQUEST.calloutStyleIncluded") >
 <!--- Define formatting for film display --->
 <style type="text/css">
 th.fm { background:RoyalBlue;color:white;text-align:left;
 font-family:sans-serif;font-size:10px}
 td.fm { background:LightSteelBlue;
 font-family:sans-serif;font-size:12px}
 </style>

 <!--- Remember that the <STYLE> has been included --->
 <cfset REQUEST.calloutStyleIncluded = "Yes">
</cfif>
```

Listing 25.15 provides the complete code for the revised `ShowMovieCallout.cfm` template.

Listing 25.15 `ShowMovieCallout2.cfm`—Tracking Variables Between Tag Invocations

```
<!---
<cf_ShowMovieCallout2> Custom Tag
Retrieves and displays the given film
```

Listing 25.15 (CONTINUED)

```
  Example of Use:
  <cf_ShowMovieCallout
  FilmID="5">
--->

<!--- Tag Attributes --->

<!--- FilmID Attribute is Required --->
<cfparam name="ATTRIBUTES.filmID" type="numeric">

<!--- Whether to reveal cost/release dates (optional) --->
<cfparam name="ATTRIBUTES.showCost" type="boolean" default="yes">
<cfparam name="ATTRIBUTES.showReleaseDate" type="boolean" default="yes">

<!--- Optional formatting and placement options --->
<cfparam name="ATTRIBUTES.tableAlign" type="string" default="right">
<cfparam name="ATTRIBUTES.tableWidth" type="string" default="150">
<cfparam name="ATTRIBUTES.caption" type="string" default="Featured Film">

<!--- Use "ows" datasource by default --->
<cfparam name="ATTRIBUTES.dataSource" type="string" default="ows">

<!--- Get important info about film from database --->
<cfquery name="getFilm" datasource="#ATTRIBUTES.dataSource#">
 SELECT
 MovieTitle, Summary,
 AmountBudgeted, DateInTheaters
 FROM Films
 WHERE FilmID = #ATTRIBUTES.filmID#
</cfquery>

<!--- Display error message if record not fetched --->
<cfif getFilm.recordCount neq 1>
 <cfthrow
 message="Invalid FilmID Attribute"
 detail="Film #ATTRIBUTES.filmID# doesn't exist!">
</cfif>

<!--- Format a few queried values in local variables --->
<cfset productCost = ceiling(val(getFilm.AmountBudgeted) / 1000000)>
<cfset releaseDate = dateFormat(getFilm.DateInTheaters, "mmmm d")>

<!--- Now Display The Specified Movie --->
<cfoutput>
 <!--- If the <STYLE> not included in this page yet --->
 <cfif not isDefined("REQUEST.calloutStyleIncluded")>
   <!--- Define formatting for film display --->
   <style type="text/css">
   th.fm { background:RoyalBlue;color:white;text-align:left;
   font-family:sans-serif;font-size:10px}
   td.fm { background:LightSteelBlue;
   font-family:sans-serif;font-size:12px}
   </style>

   <!--- Remember that the <STYLE> has been included --->
```

Listing 25.15 (CONTINUED)

```
    <cfset REQUEST.calloutStyleIncluded = "Yes">
</cfif>

<!--- Show info about featured movie in HTML Table --->
<table width="#ATTRIBUTES.tableWidth#" align="#ATTRIBUTES.tableAlign#"
border="0" cellSpacing="0">

<tr><th class="fm">
#ATTRIBUTES.caption#
</th></tr>

<!--- Movie Title, Summary, Rating --->
<tr><td class="fm">
<b>#getFilm.MovieTitle#</b><br>
#getFilm.Summary#<br>
</td></tr>

<!--- Cost (rounded to millions), release date --->
<cfif ATTRIBUTES.showCost or ATTRIBUTES.showReleaseDate>
<tr><th class="fm">
<!--- Show Cost, if called for --->
<cfif ATTRIBUTES.showCost>
Production Cost $#productCost# Million<br>
</cfif>
<!--- Show release date, if called for --->
<cfif ATTRIBUTES.showReleaseDate>
In Theaters #ReleaseDate#<br>
</cfif>
</th></tr>
</cfif>
</table>
<br clear="all">
</cfoutput>
```

NOTE

Because the **REQUEST** scope isn't shared between page requests, you don't need to use the `<cflock>` tag when setting or accessing **REQUEST** variables.

Working with `<cfimport>`

The introduction of ColdFusion MX brought the capability to import a directory of CFML custom tags, by using the `<cfimport>` tag. If you are familiar with JavaServer Pages (JSP), you'll recognize that this method is similar to the method you use to import a JSP tag library (`taglib`). In fact, the `<cfimport>` tag does double duty: It also allows you to import JSP tag libraries for use in your Cold-Fusion page (JSP `taglib` importing is available in the Enterprise version only). Table 25.2 summarizes the `<cfimport>` tag and its attributes.

Table 25.2   **Attributes of** `<cfimport>`

ATTRIBUTE	REQUIRED	DEFAULT	DESCRIPTION
`taglib`	Yes	None	Directory containing CFML custom tags; can also point to a JSP tag library descriptor or JAR file.
`prefix`	Yes	None	Prefix for addressing imported CFML or JSP tags. To import without a prefix, pass an empty string (`""`).

As you can see from Table 25.2, you simply point the `taglib` attribute to a directory containing CFML custom tags and assign that directory to a tag prefix. Let's start with a directory named `mylib` under the `ows/25` directory. You set the `<cfimport>` tag's `taglib` attribute to `mylib`, and the `prefix` attribute to `lib`. You can call all the tags in the specified directory like this: `<lib:ThisTagName>`.

You would use this JSP (or XML) style of syntax only when accessing tags whose directory has been imported through `<cfimport>`. You call custom tags in other directories with the standard `<cf_ThisTagName>` syntax. If the `<cfimport>` tag's `prefix` attribute is passed an empty string, it results in HTML-style syntax with no `CF_` or JSP-style prefix (as in `<ThisTagName>`). The next code snippet shows this syntax.

NOTE

When using the `<cfimport>` tag, you must first ensure that the custom tag directory that you want to import–in this case, `mylib`–is located under one of the custom tag locations mentioned at the beginning of this section.

The `ows/25/mylib` directory contains a sample tag library that includes the `IntelligentForm.cfm` and `IntelligentInput.cfm` custom tags (covered in depth later in this chapter). You can call them using `<cfimport>`, like this:

```
<cfimport taglib="mylib" prefix="lib">

<lib:IntelligentForm formName="MyForm">
  <lib:IntelligentInput fieldName="SSN" size="12" maxLength="11"/>
  <lib:IntelligentInput fieldName="FirstName" size="22" maxLength="20"/>
  <lib:IntelligentInput fieldName="LastName" size="22" maxLength="20"/>
</lib:IntelligentForm>
```

You can also call these custom tags without using a tag prefix, like this:

```
<cfimport taglib="mylib" prefix="">

<IntelligentForm formName="MyForm">
  <IntelligentInput fieldName="SSN" size="12" maxLength="11"/>
  <IntelligentInput fieldName="FirstName" size="22" maxLength="20"/>
  <IntelligentInput fieldName="LastName" size="22" maxLength="20"/>
</IntelligentForm>
```

The use of `<cfimport>` gives you an advantage in large applications that use many custom tags from various sources. That's because you can isolate custom tags with identical names yet different logic into separate directories, import each directory using a different tag prefix, and call identically named tags without one tag occluding the other since you're effectively isolating each custom tag library in its own namespace. Although we do not have a listing that demonstrates `<cfimport>`, you can certainly build one that uses any of the custom tags discussed so far.

But before you go changing all your custom tag calls using `<cfimport>` syntax, be aware of these disadvantages:

- Because `<cfimport>` is a compile-time directive, you must place a call to `<cfimport>` on every page on which you intend to use `<cfimport>` syntax to call a custom tag.

- Because `<cfimport>` is processed at compile time, you cannot use any ColdFusion expressions as the values of attributes, which means that you must hard-code the value of `taglib` every time you call `<cfimport>`. This sometimes makes it difficult to migrate from development to staging and then to deployment—especially in shared hosting environments where a mapping name has already been assigned to another application.

Now that you've been through this review of custom tag fundamentals, you're probably thinking, "So what's the big deal about custom tags, anyway? They seem like glorified `cfinclude` tags to me." And up to this point, you're right: simple custom tags are little more than separate templates of stand-alone code that can modify their behavior by changing the values of the attributes with which they are called.

Advanced custom tags, however, are to this day among the most powerful development tools in all of ColdFusion. You can build complete application subsystems of highly reusable code that adapt to the environments in which they are deployed. Well-written advanced custom tags can be instantly reused from application to application with little or no modification at all.

In the remainder of this chapter you'll learn how to leverage the hidden workings of advanced custom tags, and you'll put that knowledge to use by building step by step a family of related custom tags that can easily be adapted to handle multiple tasks in an application. The chapter also includes a number of diagrams and dumps of complex objects to help you visualize the process flow and data flow between related custom tags.

Paired Custom Tags

All of the custom tags you've seen here so far are called *empty* custom tags because they do not span a region of content or code. *Paired* custom tags *do* span, or wrap, a region of content or code and act upon that region in some way. You deal with this concept every day; for example:

```
<b>The force is strong in this one.</b>
```

The HTML `Bold` element is a typical paired tag that acts on the span of content between its opening and closing tags. This may seem like baby steps to you, but the exact same process is applied to ColdFusion paired custom tags.

Essentially, a paired tag of any kind always executes *twice*—once for the opening tag (Start mode) and once for the closing tag (End mode)—and performs a distinct operation in both Start mode and End mode. The HTML `Bold` tag, for example, in the opening tag establishes the beginning of the content to be modified; the closing tag establishes the end of that content and also instructs the browser to make the content bold. As you continue reading, keep in mind this concept of a paired tag executing twice and doing something different in each execution.

The Execution Cycle

A paired custom tag goes through three modes of execution, in order, when it is called:

- Start mode, which executes immediately after the opening tag and triggers the first execution of the paired custom tag.

- Inactive mode, which is the idle period between the opening and closing tags.

- End mode, which executes immediately after the closing tag and triggers the second execution of the paired custom tag.

In a ColdFusion paired custom tag, the opening tag triggers the first execution, during which `ThisTag.ExecutionMode` is `"Start"`. `ThisTag` is a special scope that exists within custom tags and refers to specific properties of the custom tag, such as its current execution mode, whether the custom tag has an end tag (as a paired tag would), and more, as you'll see later in this chapter.

After the first execution of the paired custom tag, the tag goes into Inactive mode, during which time the contents in the body of the tag are accumulated into `ThisTag.GeneratedContent`. The closing tag then triggers the second execution of the paired custom tag, during which `ThisTag.ExecutionMode` is `"End"`.

You separate Start mode logic from End mode logic using a simple `If` construct:

```
<cfif ThisTag.ExecutionMode EQ "Start">

<cfelse>

</cfif>
```

We test only for `ThisTag.ExecutionMode EQ "Start"` and assume that the `<cfelse>` clause refers to the End mode, even though there are two other execution modes besides Start. This is because Inactive mode isn't actually executed; it's an idle mode, during which the content is accumulated into `ThisTag.GeneratedContent`.

Like any other type of custom tag, a paired custom tag may take attributes that can be passed to the logic in the custom tag to modify its behavior. These attributes become part of the `Attributes` scope just as they do in other types of custom tags. Because attributes are always passed in an opening tag, those attributes are "seen" by and can therefore be used by logic in the Start mode of the paired custom tag. Once an execution mode gains access to something, any other execution modes that follow will also have access; therefore, because the Start mode can access the attributes passed into the tag, so can the Inactive and End modes.

NOTE

The Inactive mode doesn't do any processing of its own, but you'll learn later that it passes process flow to any child tags nested in the body (between the opening and closing tags) of the paired tag. Those child tags can then gain access to the objects seen by their parent tag's Start mode.

The Start mode may execute logic or output content, but it can neither see nor modify any content or code in the body of the paired tag. The Inactive mode is the first point at which the content in the body of the paired tag can be seen, but the only thing the Inactive mode can do with this content is accumulate it into a special variable. The End mode, which can see, access, and modify everything that happened in the execution modes before it, is therefore the most powerful execution mode, and as such it's often where the majority of paired custom tag logic is executed.

Confusion often exists about ColdFusion paired custom tags because of their added ability to programmatically modify the content in the span between the opening and closing tags, but you'll soon see how to visualize the process in a very simple way that eliminates confusion.

Let's look at a practical example of a paired custom tag that wraps a relatively large passage of content and outputs only a specified portion of that content formatted in a div container. We'll call the custom tag TruncateQuote, and it's called like this:

```
<cf_TruncateQuote numberOfCharacters="125">
Four score and seven years ago our fathers brought forth on this continent a new
nation, conceived in liberty and dedicated to the proposition that all men are
created equal. Now we are engaged in a great civil war, testing whether that nation
or any nation so conceived and so dedicated can long endure. We are met on a great
battlefield of that war. We have come to dedicate a portion of that field as a final
resting-place for those who here gave their lives that that nation might live. It is
altogether fitting and proper that we should do this.
</cf_TruncateQuote>
```

If you'd like to try this, type the preceding call to <cf_TruncateQuote> in a file named Test.cfm.

Listing 25.16 shows cf_TruncateQuote's code. As long as you save this custom tag file within the same directory as the page that calls it (Test.cfm), you can run the calling page and see the results.

Listing 25.16 TruncateQuote.cfm—Implementing a Paired Tag

```
<!--- Author: Adam Phillip Churvis -- ProductivityEnhancement.com --->
<!--- Truncates and formats a body of text --->

<cfparam name="Attributes.numberOfCharacters" type="numeric" default="300">

<cfif ThisTag.ExecutionMode EQ "Start">
  <div style="border: 1px solid Black; width:300px;">
<cfelse>
  ...
  </div>

  <cfset ThisTag.GeneratedContent = Left(ThisTag.GeneratedContent,
    Attributes.numberOfCharacters)>
</cfif>
```

The most confusing thing for most developers is why that ellipsis appears at the *end* of the truncated quote and not before, since it appears in order in the code. The answer lies in the way that content is accumulated during the Inactive mode and modified in the End mode.

The Concept of `GeneratedContent`

As mentioned earlier, during Inactive mode a paired custom tag accumulates the content that spans the range between the opening and closing tags in a special variable named `ThisTag.Generated-Content`. Since a paired custom tag has only two opportunities to run (once in Start mode and once in End mode), and since you can't yet see or modify `ThisTag.GeneratedContent` in the Start mode, the only place you can modify `ThisTag.GeneratedContent` is in the End mode. In the same way that the closing HTML `Bold` tag modifies the contents between it and the opening tag, so does Cold-Fusion by manipulating `ThisTag.GeneratedContent` in the End mode.

But why does the ellipsis appear at the end? It's because of the way ColdFusion prepares and outputs the results of running a paired custom tag—sort of like preparing a sandwich in reverse (from the top down) and then serving it.

ColdFusion gathers into a buffer any content that is output during Start mode. Then, in Inactive mode, the content accumulated in `ThisTag.GeneratedContent` is added to the buffer. Then, in End mode, any content that is output directly during the End mode is added to the buffer. Any manipulation of `ThisTag.GeneratedContent` by the End mode is performed after this "sandwich" has been assembled in order. The completed package is then output from the buffer as a single chunk of content.

So even though the ellipsis appeared before the manipulation of `ThisTag.GeneratedContent`, the ellipsis was directly output by the End mode, so it was placed after `ThisTag.GeneratedContent`.

Custom Tags That May Be Called as Paired or Empty

You may sometimes need similar functionality that applies to an entire ColdFusion page, or to only a section of a page, but that behaves a little differently in each case. For example, you may want to create a custom tag that makes checking for authentication and authorization easy. So if you want to ensure that users attempting to access a ColdFusion page are both authenticated and authorized with the ADMIN role, you can call the custom tag as an empty (unpaired) tag at the top of the page, like this:

```
<cf_Auth roles="ADMIN">

<p>You won't see this page unless you're logged in and have been assigned the ADMIN
role.</p>
```

And if you want to prevent only a portion of a page from being displayed unless the user is both authenticated and authorized with the ADMIN role, you can call the custom tag as a paired tag, like this:

```
<cf_Auth roles="ADMIN">
  <p>You won't see this section unless you're logged in and have been assigned the
ADMIN role.</p>
</cf_Auth>

<p>You'll see this section no matter who you are, and you don't have to be logged
in, either.</p>
```

But you want the tag to react differently in each case. If it's called as an empty tag and the user isn't authorized, you want to redirect to a page that tells the user that he or she has insufficient privileges; on the other hand, if the tag is called as a paired tag under the same conditions, then you want anything in the body of the tag disregarded: both content and code. To determine whether a custom tag is called as an empty tag or a paired tag, you check the value of `ThisTag.HasEndTag`.

Using `ThisTag.HasEndTag`

As mentioned earlier, the `ThisTag` scope contains a variable named `ThisTag.HasEndTag` that describes whether or not a custom tag has a corresponding closing tag (that is, whether or not it is a paired tag). Here's how you would use `HasEndTag` in our scenario:

```
<!--- Check to see if the user is logged in --->
<cflogin>
  <cfif ThisTag.HasEndTag>
    <!--- If this tag is called as a paired tag and the user is not logged in,
    exit the tag now to prevent execution of any code between the start and
    end tags. --->
    <cfexit method="ExitTag">
  <cfelse>
    <!--- If this tag is not called as a paired tag and the user is not logged
    in, redirect to the login form. --->
    <cflocation url="#Application.urlRoot#/login/LoginForm.cfm" addtoken="No">
  </cfif>
</cflogin>
```

Although this code tests only the authentication portion of the security check, it gives you a clear idea of how you can create a custom tag that can adapt its behavior based on how it is called: either as an empty tag or as a paired tag.

Using `cfexit` to Control Custom Tag Processing Flow

Paired custom tags aren't relegated to only modifying content; they can also prevent code in the body of the paired tag from being executed, or they can control the flow of logic in such code. Let's see how this works.

Notice the `<cfexit method="ExitTag">` in the preceding code. It tells the flow of logic to ignore the remainder of the custom tag and continue immediately after the end tag. So if the user hasn't logged in yet, the `<cflogin>` section executes, and if the custom tag was called as a paired tag, it ignores the rest of the custom tag, its execution cycles, its output—everything. Any content wrapped with this custom tag will not be displayed, and any wrapped code will not be executed.

Keep this principle in mind as you review Listing 25.17, which is the completed `<cf_Auth>` custom tag.

Listing 25.17 `Auth.cfm`—Using `cfexit` to Control Custom Tag Processing Flow

```
<!--- Author: Adam Phillip Churvis -- ProductivityEnhancement.com --->
<!--- Ensures that user is authenticated and authorized --->

<cfparam name="Attributes.roles" type="string" default="">
```

Listing 25.17 (CONTINUED)

```
<cfif ThisTag.ExecutionMode EQ "Start">

  <!--- Check to see if the user is logged in --->
  <cflogin>
    <cfif ThisTag.HasEndTag>
      <!--- If this tag is called as a paired tag and the user is not logged in,
      exit the tag now to prevent execution of any code between the start and
      end tags. --->
      <cfexit method="ExitTag">
    <cfelse>
      <!--- If this tag is not called as a paired tag and the user is not logged
      in, redirect to the login form. --->
      <cflocation url="#Application.urlRoot#/login/LoginForm.cfm" addtoken="No">
    </cfif>
  </cflogin>

  <!--- Check to see if the user must be a member of one or more roles --->
  <cfif Len(Trim(Attributes.roles)) GT 0>
    <!--- We must now see if at least one of the user's roles match those in
    Attributes.roles --->

    <!--- Loop over the list of required roles --->
    <cfset inRole = FALSE>
    <cfif isUserInAnyRole(attributes.roles)>
    <cfset inRole = true>
    </cfif>

    <!--- Check to see if the user may access content. --->
    <cfif NOT inRole>
      <cfif ThisTag.HasEndTag>
        <!--- If this tag is called as a paired tag and the user cannot access
        content, exit the tag now to prevent execution of any code between the
        start and end tags. --->
        <cfexit method="ExitTag">
      <cfelse>
        <!--- If this tag is not called as a paired tag and the user cannot
        access content, redirect to the login form. --->
        <cflocation url="#Application.urlRoot#/login/InsufficientPrivileges.cfm"
          addtoken="No">
      </cfif>
    </cfif>
  </cfif>

</cfif>
```

As shown in Table 25.3, `<cfexit>` has three possible methods: ExitTag, which exits the entire custom tag; ExitTemplate, which exits the current execution mode of the custom tag and continues with the next; and Loop, which exits the End mode and starts over again in the Inactive mode (most often used to repetitively execute nested child tags). As you'll see later in this chapter, if the body of the paired tag contains nested child tags, Inactive mode passes processing to the first such child tag.

Table 25.3   `<cfexit>` **Method's Effect on Flow Control**

METHOD	LOCATION	BEHAVIOR
`ExitTag`	Calling page	Terminate processing
	Start mode	Continue after end tag
	End mode	Continue after end tag
`ExitTemplate`	Calling page	Terminate processing
	Start mode	Jump down to Inactive mode
	End mode	Continue after end tag
`Loop`	Calling page	(Error)
	Start mode	(Error)
	End mode	Jump back into Inactive mode

We'll go deeper into `<cfexit>` later in this chapter when we start using the more advanced aspects of custom tag design.

Nested Custom Tags

A *nested tag* is a paired tag that "nests" related tags in its body. *Related* means related in purpose, as with an HTML `<form>` tag and its related `<input>` tags.

A paired tag that surrounds one or more related tags is called a *parent tag*, and the related tags it surrounds are called *child tags*. A parent tag doesn't change its paired tag stripes just because it surrounds child tags; everything about its execution cycle remains exactly the same, `ThisTag.GeneratedContent` is still created and output in the proper order, and so on. The most significant difference between a paired tag that surrounds content and a paired tag that surrounds other tags is that during Inactive mode flow, control passes to the first child tag in the body of the parent. Once all the child tags have finished processing their own execution cycles, flow control passes back to the parent tag's End mode.

You already work with nested tags every day (in forms and inputs, `cfquery` and `cfqueryparam`, and so forth), and you understand how they are called—so I won't bore you with the basics of *calling* nested custom tags. Let's instead learn how to avoid a common but serious problem that often occurs with nested custom tags when they are called using `cfmodule` syntax rather than `cf_` syntax.

The `cfmodule` Caveat

You'll often develop your code using `cf_` syntax but have to deploy it using `cfmodule` syntax, to prevent your custom tag calls from being occluded with custom tags of the same name (but different logic) used by other applications on the same shared server. You might think the worst problem you'll have is converting all those easy-to-read `cf_` calls over to `cfmodule`, but when most of your custom tags stop working altogether, you'll find out this is the least of your problems.

Here's why. Calling the form using cf_ syntax appears to work correctly, but it masks a potentially serious problem:

```
<cf_IntelligentForm formName="MyForm">
  <cf_IntelligentInput fieldName="SSN" size="12" maxLength="11">
  <cf_IntelligentInput fieldName="FirstName" size="22" maxLength="20">
  <cf_IntelligentInput fieldName="LastName" size="22" maxLength="20">
</cf_IntelligentForm>
```

Everything looks okay on the surface, but problems lurk underneath.

So you convert the calls to <cfmodule> syntax:

```
<cfmodule template="IntelligentForm.cfm" formName="MyForm">
  <cfmodule template="IntelligentInput.cfm" fieldName="SSN" size="12"
    maxLength="11">
  <cfmodule template="IntelligentInput.cfm" fieldName="FirstName" size="22"
    maxLength="20">
  <cfmodule template="IntelligentInput.cfm" fieldName="LastName" size="22"
    maxLength="20">
</cfmodule>
```

But now the closing <cfmodule> tag at the end of the listing doesn't know which tag to close. The result is that it closes the first unclosed tag above it, which in this case is the LastName field.

So now the DisplayField (this file can be found at the book's Web site) custom tag for the LastName field is being called as a closed tag, which means the LastName field is also being called as a paired tag because any tag with a closing tag is also a paired tag. This in turn means that the DisplayField custom tag for the LastName field is *run twice*.

So we'll solve the problem of cfmodule not knowing which tag to close by explicitly closing all custom tag calls on the page:

```
<cfmodule template="IntelligentForm.cfm" formName="MyForm">
  <cfmodule template="IntelligentInput.cfm" fieldName="SSN" size="12"
    maxLength="11"/>
  <cfmodule template="IntelligentInput.cfm" fieldName="FirstName" size="22"
    maxLength="20"/>
  <cfmodule template="IntelligentInput.cfm" fieldName="LastName" size="22"
    maxLength="20"/>
</cfmodule>
```

But now we have another problem: *All* the form fields are output twice. The reason lies in how the child tag was coded:

```
<cfparam name="Attributes.fieldName" type="string">
<cfparam name="Attributes.size" type="numeric">
<cfparam name="Attributes.maxLength" type="numeric">
<cfparam name="Attributes.label" type="string" default="#Attributes.fieldName#">

<cfoutput>
<tr>
  <td>#Attributes.label#  </td>
  <td>
    <input
      type="text"
```

```
          name="#Attributes.fieldName#"
          size="#Attributes.size#"
          maxlength="#Attributes.maxlength#" >
    </td>
  </tr>
</cfoutput>
```

Remember that closed tags are also considered to be paired tags, and paired tags are always called twice—once in Start mode and once in End mode. Since we're not sure how the child tag will be called, we have to make sure it will work using either cf_ syntax or cfmodule syntax, and that means outputting the child tag's contents only in Start mode. If we output only in End mode, then calling the child tag using cf_ syntax would fail because it's not called as a paired tag and therefore doesn't have an End mode.

So let's fix this in Listing 25.18.

Listing 25.18   NoComm/IntelligentInput.cfm—Fixing the cfmodule Problem

```
<cfparam name="Attributes.fieldName" type="string">
<cfparam name="Attributes.size" type="numeric">
<cfparam name="Attributes.maxLength" type="numeric">
<cfparam name="Attributes.label" type="string" default="#Attributes.fieldName#">

<cfif ThisTag.ExecutionMode EQ "Start">
  <cfoutput>
  <tr>
    <td>#Attributes.label#  </td>
    <td>
      <input
        type="text"
        name="#Attributes.fieldName#"
        size="#Attributes.size#"
        maxlength="#Attributes.maxlength#" >
    </td>
  </tr>
  </cfoutput>
</cfif>
```

Now the custom tag is working the way it really should.

So remember to always structure your custom tags from the very beginning with tests for ThisTag.ExecutionMode EQ "Start", and separate Start mode logic from End mode logic. And if your custom tag is really meant to be called only as an empty tag, make sure to execute all logic in the Start mode of the tag.

Now let's move on to the real meat of this chapter, which is the communication mechanism between parent and child tags that makes them related to one another.

Communicating Between Parent and Child Custom Tags

There are four possible models of communication between parent and child custom tags:

- Neither tag communicates with the other.

- The child tag communicates with the parent tag.

- The parent tag communicates with the child tag.

- Both tags communicate with each other.

We're going to carefully explore each of these four methods using a familiar topic: Web forms.

Nested Custom Tags That Don't Communicate

Just because parent and child custom tags are related in their functionality doesn't necessarily mean that they need to communicate with one another. In fact, the only reason for custom tags to communicate is so they can know about and use each other's data for their own purposes.

The IntelligentForm and IntelligentInput tags shown earlier are good examples of parent and nested child custom tags that are related but don't need to know anything about each other—each tag is entirely self-contained and handles its job without needing anything from the other tag.

Process flow passes from the parent tag's Inactive mode to the nested child tag's Start mode as it normally does, but the child tag doesn't tell the parent tag anything about itself, and it doesn't ask the parent about the parent's data. But sharing data can lead to better functionality with less overall effort, so let's tell the parent tag about the child tag's data and see what we can do with that information.

Child to Parent

A nested child tag can send its attributes to its parent tag using the <cfassociate> tag. The parent tag receives those attributes in its ThisTag scope into an array named AssocAttribs.

Listing 25.19 creates a form using the same calls to IntelligentForm and IntelligentInput that you saw earlier, but the IntelligentForm tag in Listing 25.20 adds a new twist by focusing the cursor in the first form field when the field is displayed—all based on its use of the child tag's data.

Listing 25.19 `Child2Parent/CallingPage.cfm`—Creating the Form

```
<!--- Author: Adam Phillip Churvis -- ProductivityEnhancement.com --->

<cf_IntelligentForm formName="MyForm">
  <cf_IntelligentInput fieldName="SSN" size="12" maxLength="11">
  <cf_IntelligentInput fieldName="FirstName" size="22" maxLength="20">
  <cf_IntelligentInput fieldName="LastName" size="22" maxLength="20">
</cf_IntelligentForm>
```

Listing 25.20 `Child2Parent/IntelligentForm.cfm`—An Intelligent Form Custom Tag

```
<!--- Author: Adam Phillip Churvis -- ProductivityEnhancement.com --->

<cfparam name="Attributes.formName" type="string" default="formName">

<cfoutput>
<cfif ThisTag.ExecutionMode EQ "Start">
  <table cellspacing="0" cellpadding="0" border="0">
```

Listing 25.20 (CONTINUED)

```
          <form name="#Attributes.formName#" method="Post">
    <cfelse>
      <tr>
        <td> </td>
        <td><input type="submit" value="Submit Form"></td>
      </tr>
      </form>
      </table>

      <cfdump var="#ThisTag#" label="ThisTag as seen by the end mode of the form">

      <script type="text/javascript">
        #Attributes.formName#.#ThisTag.AssocAttribs[1].FieldName#.focus();
      </script>
    </cfif>
    </cfoutput>
```

I've placed a `cfdump` call in Listing 25.20 to show the contents of the `ThisTag` scope so that you can visualize what's happening. We'll look at that a little later, but for now let's see how the child tag sends its data to its parent in Listing 25.21.

Listing 25.21 `Child2Parent/IntelligentInput.cfm`—Intelligent Form Field That Informs Its Parent

```
    <!--- Author: Adam Phillip Churvis -- ProductivityEnhancement.com --->

    <cfparam name="Attributes.fieldName" type="string">
    <cfparam name="Attributes.size" type="numeric">
    <cfparam name="Attributes.maxLength" type="numeric">
    <cfparam name="Attributes.label" type="string" default="#Attributes.fieldName#">

    <cfif ThisTag.ExecutionMode EQ "Start">

      <cfassociate basetag="CF_INTELLIGENTFORM">

      <cfoutput>
      <tr>
        <td>#Attributes.label#  </td>
        <td>
          <input
            type="text"
            name="#Attributes.fieldName#"
            size="#Attributes.size#"
            maxlength="#Attributes.maxlength#" >
        </td>
      </tr>
      </cfoutput>
    </cfif>
```

That call to `<cfassociate>` is what does the trick.

When a child tag is called, the Start mode sends its `Attributes` scope (which, like all scopes, is a structure) to the parent tag, and the parent adds the `Attributes` scope structure as the value of an element in its `ThisTag.AssocAttribs` array.

So we can now tell on which field to focus, because it's stored in the first element of the AssocAttribs array:

```
<script type="text/javascript">
  #Attributes.formName#.#ThisTag.AssocAttribs[1].FieldName#.focus();
</script>
```

This is a very simple example of what a parent can do with its child tags' data, but as long as you understand the basic mechanisms involved, you can figure out some rather involved ways to use such child tag data in your own parent tags.

Now let's work from the other direction: sharing a parent tag's data with its child tags.

Parent to Child

A child tag can request its parent tag's data using the GetBaseTagData() function, which returns the parent tag's data. The data returned to the child includes the parent tag's Attributes scope, its Caller scope, and its ThisTag scope as keys in a structure.

Listing 25.22 looks familiar, but we've added a new inputStyle attribute that we're going to propagate down to the child tags.

Listing 25.22 Parent2Child/CallingPage.cfm—Creating the Form

```
<!--- Author: Adam Phillip Churvis -- ProductivityEnhancement.com --->

<cf_IntelligentForm formName="MyForm" inputStyle="color:##FF3399;">
  <cf_IntelligentInput fieldName="SSN" size="12" maxLength="11">
  <cf_IntelligentInput fieldName="FirstName" size="22" maxLength="20">
  <cf_IntelligentInput fieldName="LastName" size="22" maxLength="20">
</cf_IntelligentForm>
```

Listing 25.23 can't do anything with the child tags' data because the child tags didn't send their data to the IntelligentForm parent tag. Listing 25.24, however, makes use of its parent tag's inputStyle attribute, which is now available through the child tag's parentData structure.

Listing 25.23 Parent2Child/IntelligentForm.cfm—Intelligent Form Custom Tag

```
<!--- Author: Adam Phillip Churvis -- ProductivityEnhancement.com --->

<cfparam name="Attributes.formName" type="string" default="formName">
<cfparam name="Attributes.inputStyle" type="string" default="">

<cfoutput>
<cfif ThisTag.ExecutionMode EQ "Start">
  <table cellspacing="0" cellpadding="0" border="0">
  <form name="#Attributes.formName#" method="Post">
<cfelse>
  <tr>
    <td> </td>
    <td><input type="submit" value="Submit Form"></td>
  </tr>
  </form>
  </table>
</cfif>
</cfoutput>
```

Listing 25.24 `Parent2Child/IntelligentInput.cfm`—Intelligent Form Field Requests Data

```
<!--- Author: Adam Phillip Churvis -- ProductivityEnhancement.com --->

<cfparam name="Attributes.fieldName" type="string">
<cfparam name="Attributes.size" type="numeric">
<cfparam name="Attributes.maxLength" type="numeric">
<cfparam name="Attributes.label" type="string" default="#Attributes.fieldName#">

<cfif ThisTag.ExecutionMode EQ "Start">

  <cfset parentData = GetBaseTagData("CF_INTELLIGENTFORM")>

  <cfdump var="#parentData#" label="parentData as seen by #Attributes.fieldName#">

  <cfoutput>
  <tr>
    <td>#Attributes.label#  </td>
    <td>
      <input
        type="text"
        name="#Attributes.fieldName#"
        size="#Attributes.size#"
        maxlength="#Attributes.maxlength#"
        style="#parentData.Attributes.inputStyle#">
    </td>
  </tr>
  </cfoutput>
</cfif>
```

I've included a `cfdump` of the `parentData` structure that is the result of the `GetBaseTagData()` function, which is called in each child tag.

The `parentData` structure's contents are identical in each child tag because each gets the same collection of parent tag data.

Now comment out the call to `cfdump`, rerun the page, and enter some data in each of the fields. Each of the fields generated by the child tags is formatted the same, according to the `inputStyle` attribute passed to the parent tag.

Now let's combine and leverage the power of both techniques by using bidirectional communication between both tags.

Bidirectional

All communications among related custom tags are handled by the child tag: child-to-parent communication is handled via the `<cfassociate>` tag, and parent-to-child communication is handled via the `GetBaseTagData()` function. Bidirectional communication is simply the combination of both methods.

Listings 25.25, 25.26, and 25.27 combine the techniques shown thus far to implement bidirectional communication between parent and nested child custom tags.

Listing 25.25 Bidirectional/CallingPage.cfm—Creating the Form

```
<!--- Author: Adam Phillip Churvis -- ProductivityEnhancement.com --->

<cf_IntelligentForm formName="MyForm"
  inputStyle="color:##003399;font-weight:bold;">
  <cf_IntelligentInput fieldName="SSN" size="12" maxLength="11">
  <cf_IntelligentInput fieldName="FirstName" size="22" maxLength="20">
  <cf_IntelligentInput fieldName="LastName" size="22" maxLength="20">
</cf_IntelligentForm>
```

Listing 25.26 Bidirectional/IntelligentForm.cfm—Intelligent Form Custom Tag

```
<!--- Author: Adam Phillip Churvis -- ProductivityEnhancement.com --->

<cfparam name="Attributes.formName" type="string" default="formName">
<cfparam name="Attributes.inputStyle" type="string" default="">

<cfoutput>
<cfif ThisTag.ExecutionMode EQ "Start">
  <table cellspacing="0" cellpadding="0" border="0">
  <form name="#Attributes.formName#" method="Post">
<cfelse>
  <tr>
    <td> </td>
    <td><input type="submit" value="Submit Form"></td>
  </tr>
  </form>
  </table>

  <cfdump var="#ThisTag#" label="ThisTag as seen by the end mode of the form">

  <script type="text/javascript">
     #Attributes.formName#.#ThisTag.AssocAttribs[1].fieldName#.focus();
  </script>
</cfif>
</cfoutput>
```

Listing 25.27 Bidirectional/IntelligentInput.cfm—Form Field That Gives and Receives Data

```
<!--- Author: Adam Phillip Churvis -- ProductivityEnhancement.com --->

<cfparam name="Attributes.fieldName" type="string">
<cfparam name="Attributes.size" type="numeric">
<cfparam name="Attributes.maxLength" type="numeric">
<cfparam name="Attributes.label" type="string" default="#Attributes.fieldName#">

<cfif ThisTag.ExecutionMode EQ "Start">

  <cfassociate basetag="CF_INTELLIGENTFORM">

  <cfset parentData = GetBaseTagData("CF_INTELLIGENTFORM")>

  <cfdump var="#parentData#"
    label="parentData as seen by #Attributes.fieldName#">

  <cfoutput>
```

Listing 25.27 (CONTINUED)

```
    <tr>
      <td>#Attributes.label#  </td>
      <td>
        <input
          type="text"
          name="#Attributes.fieldName#"
          size="#Attributes.size#"
          maxlength="#Attributes.maxlength#"
          style="#parentData.Attributes.inputStyle#">
      </td>
    </tr>
    </cfoutput>
</cfif>
```

It's interesting to see how each call to `<cfassociate>` adds another `AssocAttribs` entry to the parent tag's `ThisTag` scope, which is then returned to the child tag via its call to `GetBaseTagData()`.

You've seen how the basic mechanisms of nested custom tags work, and I've given you some simple yet practical examples of how to leverage their communication mechanisms.

NOTE

The child tags can all format themselves based on the formatting attributes passed to the parent tag and shared with the child tags, and the parent tag can determine the first field in which to focus the cursor based on the child tags' data passed to it.

Where to Go From Here

If you've been thinking of ways to leverage advanced custom tags in your own applications now that you know how to design them, don't hesitate. Start experimenting!

Try incorporating some of the following functionality into what you've already created in this chapter:

- Add formatting functionality like that used in the `IntelligentForm.cfm` and `IntelligentInput.cfm` examples in this chapter.

- Change the focus-first-field script to use the `AssocAttribs` technique we used in `IntelligentForm.cfm` and `IntelligentInput.cfm`.

- Add client-side validation to `DisplayField.cfm`.

- Add server-side validation to `DisplayField.cfm`.

- Create additional form-control custom tags, such as select menus and radio button groups.

After you've made some or all of these enhancements to your custom tags, add more of the Company table's columns to your forms by just duplicating one of the calls to `<cf_DisplayField>` and changing its attributes. Now do you see the power of creating advanced custom tags? How long would it take you to adapt all of an application's forms to a modified database schema using custom tags like these? A few minutes at most? This should prove that it's definitely worth the time and effort to learn about and build a library of custom tags to serve your application development needs.

And finally, if you come up with a killer set of custom tags, make sure to share them with the Cold-Fusion community through your local ColdFusion user group, discussion lists, blogs, and anywhere else frequented by ColdFusion developers. Everyone will be glad you did.

Building Reusable Components

Introducing ColdFusion Components

An important part of ColdFusion is its ColdFusion Components framework. Think of the CFC framework as a special way to combine key concepts from custom tags and user-defined functions into *objects*. These objects might represent concepts (such as individual films or actors), or they might represent processes (such as searching, creating special files, or validating credit card numbers).

About ColdFusion Components

You can think of CFCs as a structured, formalized variation on custom tags. Whereas custom tags are very free in form and don't necessarily imply any kind of "correct" way to go about your work as a developer, the CFC framework gently forces developers to work in a more systematic way. If you choose to use the CFC framework for parts of your application, you will find yourself thinking about those aspects in a slightly more theoretical, abstract manner. And this has lots of benefits.

Because CFCs are more structured, the code is generally very easy to follow and troubleshoot. Think of the CFC framework as a way to write smart code, guiding you as a developer to adopt sensible practices.

But the most dramatic benefit is that the structured nature of CFCs makes it possible for ColdFusion to look into your CFC code and find the important elements, such as what functions you have included in the CFC and what each function's arguments are. This knowledge allows ColdFusion to act as a kind of interpreter between your CFC and other types of applications, such as Dreamweaver, Flash, and Web Services. If you want them to, these components become part of a larger world of interconnected clients and servers, rather than only being a part of your ColdFusion code.

CFCs Can Be Called in Many Different Ways

This chapter and the last have been all about making it easier to reuse the code that you and other developers write. CFCs take the notion of code reuse to a whole new level, by making it ridiculously easy to reuse your code not only within ColdFusion, but in other types of applications as well.

All of the following can share and use CFCs:

- **ColdFusion Pages**. Once you have written the code for a CFC, you can call its methods from your normal ColdFusion pages, much as you can call the user-defined functions and custom tags you write. In this sense, you can think of CFCs as a third way of extending the CFML language.

- **Flash**. Client-side applications written with Flash can easily access ColdFusion Components. The Flash 6 player contains scriptable support for communicating with a ColdFusion server and interacting with your CFCs. In other words, CFCs become the logical gateway between your ColdFusion code and the Flash player. The integration between CFCs and Flash is tight. It is almost as easy to use CFCs within Flash code as it is within another ColdFusion page

- **Web Browsers**. If you wish, you can allow Web browsers to visit and interact with your CFCs directly, without your even needing to create a separate ColdFusion page that uses the CFC. Of course, you can control whether this is allowed, whether the user first needs to log in, and so on.

- **Other Applications That Support Web Services**. You can turn any ColdFusion Component into a Web Service by adding just one or two additional attributes to your CFC code. It will then be available as a resource that can be used over the Internet by any other application that supports Web Services, like other Web application servers, the various pieces of the .NET and J2EE platforms, and other languages such as Perl.

In other words, if you like the idea of reusing code, you'll love the CFC framework even more than the UDF and custom tag frameworks.

CFCs Are Object-Oriented Tools

Depending on your background, you may be familiar with object-oriented programming (OOP). Whether you know OOP or not, CFCs give you the most important real-world benefits of object-oriented programming without getting too complicated—exactly what you would expect from ColdFusion.

NOTE

> Don't let the OOP term scare you—this isn't your father's object orientation. The introduction of CFCs hasn't turned ColdFusion or CFML into a complex, full-blown object-oriented language. CFCs aren't obsessive-compulsive. Whether your father may be is a different story.

Without getting too deeply into the specifics, you can think of object-oriented programming as a general programming philosophy. The philosophy basically says that most of the concepts in an application represent objects in the real world, and should be treated as such. Some objects, like films or merchandise for sale, might be physical. Others, like expense records or individual merchandise orders, might be more conceptual but still easy to imagine as objects—or objectified, like many of Orange Whip Studios' better-looking actors.

ColdFusion's CFC framework is based on these object-oriented ideas:

- **Classes.** In traditional object-oriented programming, the notion of a class is extremely important. For our purposes, just think of an object class as a type of object. For instance, Orange Whip Studios has made many films during its proud history. If you think of each individual film as an object, then it follows that you can consider the general notion of a film (as opposed to a particular film) as a class. Hence, each individual film object belongs to the same class, perhaps called Film. In ColdFusion you don't actually ever create a class; CFCs are your classes.

- **Methods.** In the object-oriented world, each type of object (that is, each class) will have a few *methods*. Methods are functions that have been conceptually attached to a class. A method represents something you can do to an object. For instance, think about a car as an object. You can start it, put it into gear, stop it, and so on. So, for a corresponding object class called car, it might have methods named `Car.startEngine()`, `Car.changeGear()`, `Car.avoidPedestrian()`, and so on.

- **Instances.** If there is a class of object called Film, then you also need a word to refer to each individual film the studio makes. In the OOP world, this is described as an *instance*. Each individual film is an instance of the class called Film. Each instance of an object usually has some information associated with it, called its *instance data*. For example, Film A has its own title and stars. Film B and Film C have different titles and different stars.

- **Properties.** Most real-world objects have properties that make them unique, or at least distinguish them from other objects of the same type. For instance, a real-world car has properties such as its color, make, model, engine size, number of doors, license plate and vehicle identification number, and so on. At any given moment, it might have other properties such as whether it is currently running, who is currently driving it, and how much gas is in the tank. If you're talking about films, the properties might be the film's title, the director, how many screens it is currently shown on, or whether it is going to be released straight to video. Properties are generally stored as instance data.

CFCs and Method Inheritance

In addition to the OOP concepts just listed, ColdFusion's CFC framework also supports the notion of *inheritance*, where different object classes can be derived from a parent object class. There might be other types of objects that are related to the Film class, but have additional, more specific characteristics (perhaps ComedyFilm, which would track additional information about how funny it is, and ActionFilm, which would track how many explosions occur per minute).

NOTE

Once you start talking about this concept, you usually need to start using other object-oriented vocabulary words, such as subclassing, overriding, overloading, descendants, polymorphism, and so on. If none of those words means anything to you, don't worry. The CFC framework implements the concept in a straightforward way that sidesteps many of the thornier points of traditional OOP implementations.

➡ You can learn all about CFC inheritance in *Adobe ColdFusion 8 Web Application Construction Kit, Volume 3: Advanced Application Development.*

The Two Types of Components

Most CFCs fall into two broad categories: *static* components and *instance-based* components.

Static Components

I'll use the term *static* to refer to any component where it doesn't make sense to create individual instances of the component. Often you can think of such components as *services* that are constantly listening for and answering requests. For instance, if you were creating a film-searching component that made it easy to search the current list of films, you probably wouldn't need to create multiple copies of the film-searching component.

Static components are kind of like Santa Claus, the Wizard of Oz, or your father—only one of each exists. You just go to that one and make your request.

Instance-Based Components

Other components represent ideas where it is very important to create individual instances of a component. For instance, consider a CFC called ShoppingCart, which represents a user's shopping cart on your site. Many different shopping carts exist in the world at any given time (one for each user). Therefore, you need to create a fresh instance of the ShoppingCart CFC for each new Web visitor, or perhaps each new Web session. You would expect most of the CFC's methods to return different results for each instance, depending on the contents of each user's cart.

Your First CFC

The best news about CFCs is that there is really very little to learn about them. For the most part, you just write functions in much the same way that you learned in Chapter 24, "Building User-Defined Functions." You then save them in a special file and surround them with a `<cfcomponent>` tag. That's really about it.

Let's take a closer look.

The Structure of a CFC File

Each ColdFusion component is saved in its own file, with a `.cfc` extension. Except for one new tag, `<cfcomponent>`, everything in the file is ordinary CFML code. With the `.cfc` extension instead of `.cfm`, the ColdFusion server can easily detect which files represent CFC components.

Table 26.1 describes the various parts of a component definition file.

Table 26.1 The Parts of a Component

PART	DESCRIPTION
`<cfcomponent>` block	Surrounds everything else in the CFC file. Place an opening `<cfcomponent>` tag at the top of your `.cfc` file, and a closing tag at the bottom.

Table 26.1 (CONTINUED)

PART	DESCRIPTION
`<cffunction>` blocks	Within the `<cfcomponent>` tag, use `<cffunction>` blocks to create each of the component's methods. There are a few additional attributes in the `<cffunction>` tag for CFCs, but for the most part, you write these functions the same way you learned in Chapter 24. Within each `<cffunction>` tag, you will use `<cfargument>` to define the method's arguments, `<cfreturn>` to return whatever result you want the method to return, and so on.
Initialization code	Any CFML code that is inside the `<cfcomponent>` block but not within any of the `<cffunction>` tags will execute the first time an instance of the component is used. I call this initialization code because the main reason you would want code to run when the CFC is first created would be to set values in the THIS (or VARIABLES) scope to their initial values.

Introducing the `<cfcomponent>` Tag

The `<cfcomponent>` tag doesn't have any required attributes, so in its simplest use, you can just wrap opening and closing `<cfcomponent>` tags around everything else your CFC file contains (mainly `<cffunction>` blocks). That said, you can use two optional attributes, `hint` and `displayName`, to make your CFC file more self-describing (see Table 26.2).

If you provide these optional attributes, ColdFusion and Dreamweaver can automatically show `hint` and `displayName` in various places, to make life easier for you and the other developers who might be using the component. See the "Exploring CFCs in Dreamweaver" section, later in this chapter, for more on where you will see this information displayed.

Table 26.2 `<cfcomponent>` Tag Syntax

ATTRIBUTE	DESCRIPTION
`hint`	What your component does, in plain English (or whatever language you choose, of course). I recommend that you provide this attribute.
`displayName`	An alternative, friendlier phrasing of the component's name. Make the component's actual name (that is, the file name) as self-describing as possible, rather than relying on the `displayName` to make its purpose clear.

NOTE

As you will soon see, the `<cffunction>` and `<cfargument>` tags also have `hint` and `displayName` attributes. Each aspect of a CFC that someone would need to know about to actually use it can be described more completely within the component code itself.

Using `<cffunction>` to Create Methods

The biggest part of a CFC is the ColdFusion code you write for each of the CFC's methods. (Remember, I use the word *method* to refer to a function attached to a CFC.) To create a component's methods, you use the `<cffunction>` tag in much the same way you learned in Chapter 24. If the method has any required or optional arguments, you use the `<cfargument>` tag, again as shown in Chapter 24.

The `<cffunction>` and `<cfargument>` tags each take a few additional attributes that Chapter 24 didn't discuss because they are only relevant for CFCs. The most important new attributes are `hint` and `displayName`, which all the CFC-related tags have in common. A summary of all `<cffunction>` and `<cfargument>` attributes is provided in Tables 26.3 and 26.4.

Table 26.3   `<cffunction>` Syntax for CFC Methods

ATTRIBUTE	DESCRIPTION
name	Required. The name of the function (method), as discussed in Chapter 24.
hint	Optional. A description of the method. Like the `hint` attribute for `<cfcomponent>`, this description will be visible in Dreamweaver to make life easier for you and other developers. It is also included in the automatic documentation that ColdFusion produces for your components.
displayName	Optional. Like the `displayName` attribute for `<cfcomponent>` (see Table 26.4).
returnType	Optional. The type of data that the function returns (for instance, a `date` or a `string`). You aren't required to specify the `returnType`, but I recommend it. If you do, the return type will be conveniently displayed in Dreamweaver and by ColdFusion itself, making it a lot easier to keep track of which methods do what. Also, the `returnType` is required if you want the method you're creating to be available as a Web Service.
returnFormat	Optional. The format in which the data should be returned when accessed remotely. By default, all data is returned in WDDX format, unless `returnType` is XML. You can specify WDDX, JSON (for JSON format), or plain (for no formatting).
access	Optional. This attribute defines how your method can be used. If `access="remote"`, the method can be accessed over the Internet as a Web Service, by Web browsers, or by the Flash Player. If `access="public"`, the method can be used internally by any of your ColdFusion pages (similar to a UDF or custom tag), but not by Flash, browsers, or Web Services. If `access="private"`, the method can only be used internally by other methods in the same component. If `access="package"`, the method can only be used internally by other methods in the same component, or other components in the same directory.
roles	Optional. A list of security roles or user groups that should be able to use the method. This attribute only has meaning if you are using the `<cflogin>` security framework discussed in Chapter 23, "Securing Your Applications," online. If a `roles` attribute is provided, and the current user has not logged in as a member of one of the allowed roles, that user won't be able to access the method. The effect is similar to using the `isUserInRole()` function to deny access within normal ColdFusion pages, as discussed in Chapter 23. Note that the `roles` attribute for a CFC method lists a set of roles. If users are in one of those roles, they can call the method. The `isUserInRole()` function, however, uses a list of roles the user must exist in. In other words, the user can be in any role when using the `roles` attribute, but must be in all the roles when using `isUserInRole()`.

NOTE

The valid data types you can provide for returnType are any, array, binary, component, Boolean, date, guid, numeric, query, string, struct, uuid, variableName, and xml. If the method isn't going to return a value at all, use returnType="void". If the method is going to return an instance of another component, you can provide that component's name (the file name without the .cfc) as the returnType value.

Table 26.4   <cfargument> Syntax for CFC Method Arguments

ATTRIBUTE	SYNTAX
name	Required. The name of the argument, as discussed in Chapter 24.
hint	An explanation of the argument's purpose. Like the HINT attribute for <cfcomponent> and <cffunction>, this description will be visible in Dreamweaver to make life easier for you and other developers. It is also included in the automatic documentation that ColdFusion produces for your components.
displayName	Optional. Like the displayName attribute for <cfcomponent> (see Table 26.2).
type	Optional. The data type of the argument, as discussed in Chapter 24. You can use any of the values mentioned in the note under Table 26.3 except for void.
required	Optional. Whether the argument is required. See Chapter 24 for details.
default	Optional. A default value for the argument, if required="No". See Chapter 24.

NOTE

There is actually another CFC-related tag, called <cfproperty>. In this version of ColdFusion the <cfproperty> tag doesn't affect how a CFC works; it only helps the CFC be more self-documenting, mainly for the benefit of Web Services. See the "Documenting Properties with <cfproperty>" section, near the end of this chapter.

A Simple Example

Let's look at a simple example of a CFC. Say you want to create a CFC called FilmSearchCFC, which provides a simplified way to search for films. You like the idea of being able to reuse this component within your ColdFusion pages, instead of having to write queries over and over again. You'd also like to be able to flip a switch and have the component available to the Flash Player or Web Services.

Listing 26.1 is a simple version of the FilmSearchCFC.

Listing 26.1   FilmSearchCFC.cfc—A Simple CFC

```
<!---
 Filename: FilmSearchCFC.cfc
 Author: Nate Weiss (NMW)
 Purpose: Creates FilmSearchCFC, a simple ColdFusion Component
--->

<!--- The <CFCOMPONENT> block defines the CFC --->
<!--- The filename of this file determines the CFC's name --->
<cfcomponent output="false">
```

Listing 26.1 (CONTINUED)

```
<!--- ListFilms() method --->
<cffunction name="listFilms" returnType="query" output="false">
  <!--- Optional SearchString argument --->
  <cfargument name="searchString" required="no" default="">

  <!--- var scoped variables --->
  <cfset var getFilms = "">
  <!--- Run the query --->
  <cfquery name="getFilms" datasource="ows">
  SELECT FilmID, MovieTitle FROM Films
  <!--- If a search string has been specified --->
  <cfif ARGUMENTS.searchString neq "">
  WHERE (MovieTitle LIKE '%#ARGUMENTS.searchString#%'
  OR Summary LIKE '%#ARGUMENTS.searchString#%')
  </cfif>
  ORDER BY MovieTitle
  </cfquery>

  <!--- Return the query results --->
  <cfreturn getFilms>

</cffunction>

</cfcomponent>
```

NOTE

Earlier, I explained that there are two types of components: static components, which just provide functionality, and instance-based components, which provide functionality but also hold information. This CFC is an example of a static component. You will see how to create instance-based components shortly.

This version of the CFC only has one method, called `listFilms()`, which queries the database for a listing of current films. The query object is returned as the method's return value (this is why `returnType="query"` is used in the method's `<cffunction>` tag).

The `listFilms()` method takes one optional argument called `searchString`. If the `searchString` argument is provided, a WHERE clause is added to the database query so that only films with titles or summaries containing the argument string are selected. If the `searchString` isn't provided, all films are retrieved from the database and returned by the new method.

As you can see, building a simple component isn't much different from creating a user-defined function. Now that you've created the component, let's take a look at how to use it in your Cold-Fusion code.

TIP

You can use the Create Component dialog in Dreamweaver to create the basic skeleton of `<cfcomponent>`, `<cffunction>`, `<cfargument>`, and `<cfreturn>` tags. Then all you need to do is add the appropriate logic to the `<cffunction>` blocks. See the "Using the Create Component Dialog" section, later in this chapter.

Using the CFC in ColdFusion Pages

Once you have completed your CFC file, there are two basic ways to use the new component's methods in your ColdFusion code:

- With the <cfinvoke> tag, as discussed next.

- With <cfscript> syntax, in the form component.methodName(). To use this syntax, you must first create an instance of the CFC with the <cfobject> tag or the createObject() function.

In general, you will probably use the <cfinvoke> syntax for static components (like the FilmSearchCFC), and the <cfscript> syntax when interacting with a specific instance of a component. See "The Two Types of Components," earlier in this chapter.

Calling Methods with <cfinvoke>

The most straightforward way to call a CFC method is with the <cfinvoke> tag. <cfinvoke> makes your CFC look a lot like a custom tag. To provide values to the method's arguments, as in the optional searchString argument in Listing 26.1, you can either add additional attributes to <cfinvoke> or you can nest a <cfinvokeargument> tag within the <cfinvoke> tag. Tables 26.5 and 26.6 show the attributes supported by <cfinvoke> and <cfinvokeargument>.

Table 26.5 <cfinvoke> Tag Syntax

ATTRIBUTE	DESCRIPTION
component	The name of the component, as a string (the name of the file in which you saved the component, without the .cfc extension) or a component instance.
method	The name of the method you want to use.
returnVariable	A variable name in which to store whatever value the method decides to return.
(method arguments)	In addition to the component, method, and returnVariable attributes, you can also provide values to the method's arguments by providing them as attributes. For instance, the listFilms() method from Listing 26.1 has an optional argument called SearchString. To provide a value to this argument, you could use searchString="Saints" or SearchString="#FORM.keywords#". You can also provide arguments using the separate <cfinvokeargument> tag (see Table 26.6).
argumentCollection	Optional, and for special cases only. This attribute lets you provide values for the method's arguments together in a single structure. It works the same way as the attributeCollection attribute of the <cfmodule> tag.

NOTE

For the `component` attribute, you can use the component name alone (that is, the file without the `.cfc` extension) if the .cfc file is in the same folder as the file that is using the `<cfinvoke>` tag. You can also specify a `.cfc` in another folder, using dot notation to specify the location of the folder relative to the Web server root, where the dots represent folder names. For instance, you could use the `FilmSearchCFC` component by specifying `component="ows.26.FilmSearchCFC"`. For more information, see the ColdFusion 8 documentation.

NOTE

You can also save `.cfc` files in the special `CustomTags` folder or its subfolders. For the **COMPONENT** attribute of `<cfinvoke>`, specify the location relative to the `CustomTags` folder, again using dots to separate the folder names. This is the same way that you can specify folder locations for the `name` attribute of the `<cfmodule>` tag. You can also start the `component` attribute with a logical path defined in the Mappings page of the ColdFusion Administrator.

Table 26.6 `<cfinvokeargument>` Tag Syntax

ATTRIBUTE	DESCRIPTION
name	The name of the argument. So, to provide a value to an argument called searchString, you could use a `<cfinvokeargument>` tag with name="searchString".
value	The value of the argument. To provide the value of a form field to the searchString argument, you could use value="#FORM.searchString#".

Listing 26.2 shows how to use `<cfinvoke>` to call the `listFilms()` method of the `FilmSearchCFC` component created in Listing 26.1.

Listing 26.2 `UsingFilmSearchCFC1.cfm`—Invoking a Component Method

```
<!---
 Filename: UsingFilmSearchCFC1.cfm
 Author: Nate Weiss (NMW)
 Purpose: Uses the FilmSearchCFC component to display a list of films
--->

<html>
<head><title>Film Search Example</title></head>
<body>

<!--- Invoke the ListFilms() method of the FilmSearchComponent --->
<cfinvoke component="FilmSearchCFC" method="listFilms"
 returnVariable="FilmsQuery">

<!--- Now output the list of films --->
<cfoutput query="filmsQuery">
 #FilmsQuery.MovieTitle#<br>
</cfoutput>

</body>
</html>
```

First, the `<cfinvoke>` tag invokes the `listFilms()` method provided by the `FilmSearchCFC1` component. Note that the correct value to provide to `component` is the name of the component file name, but without the `.cfc` extension. When this page is visited with a browser, ColdFusion will see the `<cfinvoke>` tag and look for the corresponding CFC file (`FilmSearchCFC.cfc`). It will then execute the code in the `<cffunction>` block with `name="listFilms"`.

The `returnVariable` attribute has been set to `FilmsQuery`, which means that `FilmsQuery` will hold whatever value the method returns. The method in question, `listFilms()`, returns a query object as its return value. Therefore, after the `<cfinvoke>` tag executes, the rest of the example can refer to `filmsQuery` as if it were the results of a normal `<cfquery>` tag. Here, a simple `<cfoutput>` block outputs the title of each film.

The result is a simple list of film titles, as shown in Figure 26.1.

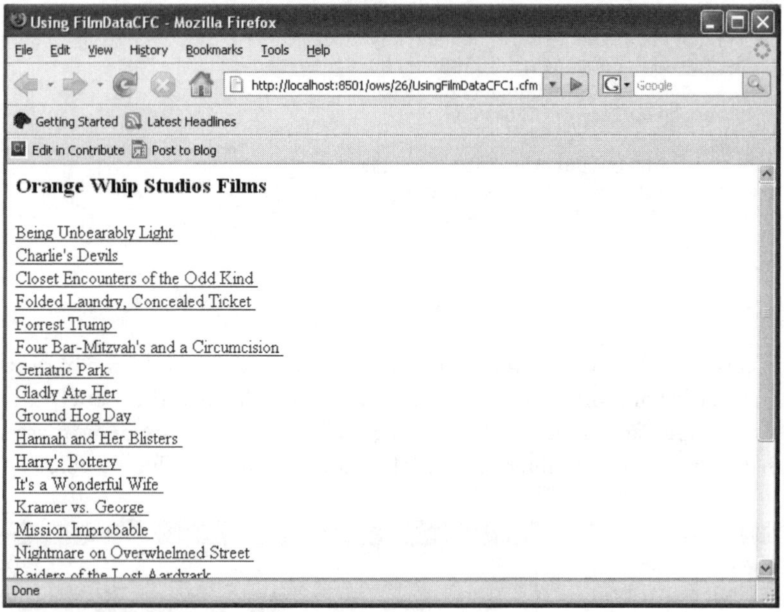

Figure 26.1

It's easy to execute a component's methods and use the results.

Supplying Arguments

The `listFilms()` method from Listing 26.1 takes an optional argument called `searchString`. This argument was not provided to the method in Listing 26.2, so the method will always return all films. Listing 26.3 shows how to supply values to method arguments by adding an attribute to the `<cfinvoke>` tag.

Listing 26.3 `UsingFilmSearchCFC2.cfm`—Supplying Arguments with `<cfinvoke>`

```
<!---
 Filename: UsingFilmSearchCFC2.cfm
 Author: Nate Weiss (NMW)
 Purpose: Uses the FilmSearchCFC component to display a list of films
--->
```

Listing 26.3 (CONTINUED)

```html
<html>
<head><title>Film Search Example</title></head>
<body>

<!--- FORM parameter called Keywords, empty by default --->
<cfparam name="FORM.keywords" default="">

<!--- Simple form to allow user to filter films --->
<cfform>
 <cfinput name="keywords" value="#FORM.keywords#">
 <input type="submit" value="Filter">
</cfform>

<!--- Invoke the ListFilms() method of the FilmSearchComponent --->
<!--- Pass the user's search keywords to the SearchString argument --->
<cfinvoke component="FilmSearchCFC" method="listFilms"
 searchString="#FORM.keywords#"
 returnVariable="filmsQuery">

<!--- Now output the list of films --->
<cfoutput query="filmsQuery">
 #filmsQuery.MovieTitle#<br>
</cfoutput>

</body>
</html>
```

In this example, a very simple search form has been added at the top of the page, where the user can filter the list of films by typing in a keyword. The value that the user types is passed to the search-String argument of the listFilms() method. The method responds by returning only those films that contain the user's filter string in their title or summary (Figure 26.2).

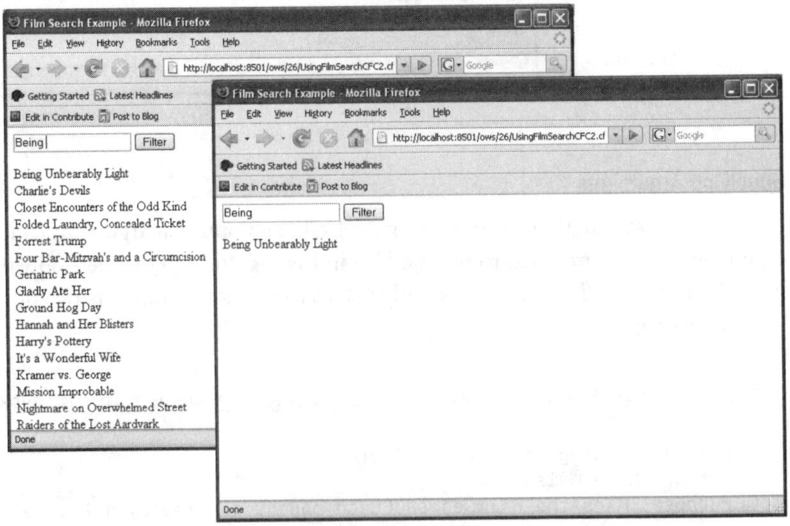

Figure 26.2

The <CFINVOKE> tag makes it easy to pass values to methods.

NOTE

You can use the `<cfinvokeargument>` tag to supply the `SearchString` argument (or any other argument), instead of providing the argument as an attribute of `<cfinvoke>`. You can see this in action in the next example (Listing 26.4).

Calling an Instance's Methods

In the last listing, you saw how to use the `<cfinvoke>` tag to call a CFC method. Calling methods this way isn't much different from calling a custom tag with `<cfmodule>`, or calling a UDF. It's also possible to create an instance of a CFC, and then call the instance's methods. If the CFC doesn't track instance data (a shopping cart, say, or information about a particular film), there isn't much of a functional difference. But it's worth taking a look at now, because it underscores the notion of a CFC as an object that provides functionality (in the form of methods).

To work with methods in this way, two steps are involved:

1. Create an instance of the CFC with the `<cfobject>` tag or `createObject()` function.

2. Invoke whatever methods you want, using the `<cfinvoke>` tag as you learned in the last section. But instead of specifying the component by name, you pass the component instance directly to the `component` attribute. You can repeat this part as many times as you like, using the same component instance.

Table 26.7 shows the attributes you supply to the `<cfobject>` tag to create an instance of a CFC.

Table 26.7   `<cfobject>` Tag Syntax for CFC Instantiation

ATTRIBUTE	DESCRIPTION
component	Required. The name of the component (that is, the CFC file name without the `.cfc` extension).
name	Required. A variable name in which to store the CFC instance. After the `<cfobject>` tag executes, your code can refer to the variable named here to interact with the instance.

NOTE

You can use the `<cfobject>` tag to create instances of other types of objects, not just CFCs. For instance, it can create instances of JavaBeans and Windows COM controls. Only the attributes relevant for CFCs are included in Table 26.7. For information on the other uses of `<cfobject>`, see Vol. 3, *Advanced Application Development*.

Listing 26.4 is a simple example of CFC instantiation and method calling. This listing does the same thing as the previous one, except that it calls the `listFilms()` method using an *instance* of the `FilmSearchCFC1` component, rather than the component itself.

Listing 26.4   `UsingFilmSearchCFC3.cfm`—Creating a Component Instance

```
<!---
 Filename: UsingFilmSearchCFC3.cfm
 Author: Nate Weiss (NMW)
```

Listing 26.4 (CONTINUED)

```
   Purpose: Uses the FilmSearchCFC component to display a list of films
   --->

<html>
<head><title>Film Search Example</title></head>
<body>

<!--- FORM parameter called Keywords, empty by default --->
<cfparam name="FORM.keywords" default="">

<!--- Simple form to allow user to filter films --->
<cfform>
 <cfinput name="keywords" value="#FORM.keywords#">
 <input type="submit" value="Filter">
</cfform>

<!--- Create an instance of the CFC --->
<cfobject component="FilmSearchCFC" name="myFilmSearcher">

<!--- Invoke the ListFilms() method of the CFC instance --->
<cfinvoke component="#myFilmSearcher#" method="listFilms"
 returnVariable="filmsQuery">
 <!--- Pass the user's search keywords to the SearchString argument --->
 <cfinvokeargument name="searchString" value="#FORM.keywords#">
</cfinvoke>

<!--- Now output the list of films --->
<cfoutput query="filmsQuery">
 #filmsQuery.MovieTitle#<br>
</cfoutput>

</body>
</html>
```

Calling Methods with `<cfscript>` Syntax

You've seen how you can call a component's methods using `<cfinvoke>`. You can also call methods using a `<cfscript>` syntax, where you call a CFC's methods in a way that makes them look more obviously like functions.

To call methods using the `<cfscript>` syntax, you just use the method like a function (either a built-in CFML function or a UDF), as in a `<cfset>` tag. The only difference is that you precede the function name with a component instance, separated with a dot. So, if you have an object instance called myFilmSearcher, you could use this line to call its listFilms() method:

```
<cfset filmsQuery = myFilmSearcher.listFilms()>
```

Functionally, this way of calling a method isn't any different than using `<cfinvoke>`, but it's more concise, so you may prefer it. Listing 26.5 is the same as the previous listing, but with the `<cfinvoke>` tag replaced with the script-style syntax.

Listing 26.5 `UsingFilmSearchCFC4.cfm`—Calling Methods Using `<cfscript>` Syntax

```
<!---
 Filename: UsingFilmSearchCFC4.cfm
 Author: Nate Weiss (NMW)
 Purpose: Uses the FilmSearchCFC component to display a list of films
--->

<html>
<head><title>Film Search Example</title></head>
<body>

<!--- FORM parameter called Keywords, empty by default --->
<cfparam name="FORM.keywords" default="">

<!--- Simple form to allow user to filter films --->
<cfform>
 <cfinput name="keywords" value="#FORM.keywords#">
 <input type="submit" value="Filter">
</cfform>

<!--- Create an instance of the CFC --->
<cfobject component="FilmSearchCFC" name="myFilmSearcher">

<!--- Invoke the CFC's ListFilms() method --->
<cfset filmsQuery = myFilmSearcher.listFilms(FORM.keywords)>

<!--- Now output the list of films --->
<cfoutput query="filmsQuery">
 #filmsQuery.MovieTitle#<br>
</cfoutput>

</body>
</html>
```

Instantiating Components with `createObject()`

The last two examples used the `<cfobject>` tag to create an instance of a CFC. As an alternative, you can use the `createObject()` function to do the same thing. Provide the word `component` as the function's first argument, and the name of the desired CFC as the second argument. The function will return the component instance, which you can then use to call methods.

In other words, you could replace the `<cfobject>` tag in Listing 26.4 with this line:

```
<cfset myFilmSearcher = createObject("component","FilmSearchCFC")>
```

Neither `<cfobject>` nor `createObject()` is better. Just use whichever one you prefer.

A More Complete CFC

Listing 26.6 shows a slightly more complex variation on the `FilmSearchCFC` component created in Listing 26.1. The idea behind this CFC is to provide not only a search facility, but also a way to get and display detailed information about films. To reflect this expanded role, I'll call this version `FilmDataCFC1` instead of `FilmSearchCFC`.

CFCs as Collections of Functions

In addition to the listFilms() method, Listing 26.6 also includes a new method, getFilmData(), which takes a film's ID number as input and returns a structure containing the film's title, summary, and actors. You can think of this CFC as a collection of conceptually related functions, since both methods are about data retrieval pertaining to records in the Films database table. In a big-picture way, this is what many CFCs are all about: collecting related functionality into a single bundle.

Also, this listing uses the hint attribute in the <cfcomponent> tag and each of the <cffunction> and <cfargument> tags to allow the component to be self-documenting.

NOTE

In fact, once you create a CFC, you can view automatically generated documentation for it by visiting the .cfc file with your browser. For details, see Figure 26.5 later in this chapter.

Listing 26.6 FilmDataCFC1.cfc—Providing Descriptive Information About Methods

```
<!---
Filename: FilmDataCFC1.cfc
Author: Nate Weiss (NMW)
Purpose: Creates the FilmDataCFC1 ColdFusion Component, which provides
search and data retrieval services for films in the ows database.
--->

<!--- The <CFCOMPONENT> block defines the CFC --->
<!--- The filename of this file determines the CFC's name --->
<cfcomponent
hint="Provides a simple interface for searching for and getting detailed
information about films in the Orange Whip Studios database."
output="false">

  <!--- ListFilms() method --->
  <cffunction name="listFilms" returnType="query"
hint="Returns a query object containing film information." output="false">

    <!--- Optional SearchString argument --->
    <cfargument name="searchString" type="string" required="No"
hint="Optional search criteria; if not given, all films are returned.">

    <!--- Optional SearchString argument --->
    <cfargument name="actorID" type="numeric" required="No"
hint="Allows searching for films by actor.">

    <!--- var scope variables --->
    <cfset var getFilms = "">

    <!--- Run the query --->
    <cfquery name="getFilms" datasource="ows">
    SELECT FilmID, MovieTitle FROM Films
    WHERE 0=0
    <!--- If a search string has been specified --->
    <cfif isDefined("ARGUMENTS.searchString")>
    AND (MovieTitle LIKE '%#ARGUMENTS.searchString#%'
    OR Summary LIKE '%#ARGUMENTS.searchString#%')
    </cfif>
```

Listing 26.6 (CONTINUED)

```
        <!--- If an actor's name has been specified --->
        <cfif isDefined("ARGUMENTS.actorID")>
        AND FilmID IN
        (SELECT FilmID FROM FilmsActors
        WHERE ActorID = #ARGUMENTS.actorID#)
        </cfif>
        ORDER BY MovieTitle
      </cfquery>

      <!--- Return the query results --->
      <cfreturn getFilms>
    </cffunction>


    <!--- GetFilmData() method --->
    <cffunction name="getFilmData" returnType="struct" output="false"
    hint="Returns structured information about the specified film.">

      <!--- FilmID argument --->
      <cfargument name="filmID" type="numeric" required="Yes"
      hint="The film that you want information about.">

      <!--- This is what this method originally returns --->
      <!--- The var keyword makes it local to the method --->
      <cfset var filmData = structNew()>
      <cfset var getFilm = "">
      <cfset var getActors = "">

      <cfset filmData.filmID = ARGUMENTS.filmID>

      <!--- Select data about the film from the database --->
      <cfquery name="getFilm" datasource="ows">
      SELECT MovieTitle, Summary FROM Films
      WHERE FilmID = #ARGUMENTS.filmID#
      </cfquery>

      <!--- Populate the FilmData structure with film info --->
      <cfset filmData.movieTitle = getFilm.MovieTitle>
      <cfset filmData.summary = getFilm.Summary>

      <!--- Run second query to get actor information --->
      <cfquery name="getActors" datasource="ows">
      SELECT ActorID, NameFirst, NameLast
      FROM Actors
      WHERE ActorID IN
      (SELECT ActorID FROM FilmsActors
      WHERE FilmID = #ARGUMENTS.filmID#)
      </cfquery>

      <!--- Make the GetActors query results part of the returned structure --->
      <cfset filmData.actorsQuery = getActors>

      <!--- Return the final structure --->
      <cfreturn FilmData>
    </cffunction>

</cfcomponent>
```

TIP

> As the number of methods provided by each CFC increases, you will want to have some way of keeping track of them. Dreamweaver addresses this need by allowing you to explore the methods and arguments for each CFC in the Components tree. See the "Exploring CFCs in Dreamweaver" section, later in this chapter.
>
> You can use the Create Component dialog in Dreamweaver to create the basic skeleton of `<cfcomponent>` and related tags. See the "Using the Create Component Dialog" section, later in this chapter.

The `listFilms()` method was in the last version, but I've adapted it slightly here. It now accepts two optional arguments, `searchCriteria` and `actorName`, which can filter the returned query object based on keywords or the name of an actor.

Using the `FilmData` CFC

The code in Listing 26.6 creates two methods: the `listFilms()` method can be used to display a list of films, and the `getFilmData()` method can be used to display detailed information about a particular film. The next two listings show how you can use these methods together to create a simple film-browsing interface.

Listing 26.7 uses the `listFilms()` method to display a list of films. This isn't much different from the first listing that used the `FilmSearchCFC` component (Listing 26.2), as shown in Figure 26.3. The only real difference is each film is now presented as a link to a detail page, where the details about the selected film will be shown.

Listing 26.7   `UsingFilmDataCFC1.cfm`—Using a CFC in a Master-Detail Data Interface

```
<!---
 Filename: UsingFilmDataCFC1.cfm
 Author: Nate Weiss (NMW)
 Purpose: Uses the FilmDataCFC component to display a list of films
--->

<html>
<head><title>Using FilmDataCFC</title></head>
<body>

<h3>Orange Whip Studios Films</h3>

<!--- Invoke the ListFilms() method of the FilmSearchComponent --->
<cfinvoke component="FilmDataCFC1" method="listFilms"
 returnVariable="filmsQuery">
  <cfif isDefined("url.actorID") and isNumeric(url.actorID)>
    <cfinvokeargument name="actorID" value="#url.actorID#">
  </cfif>
</cfinvoke>

<!--- Now output the list of films --->
<cfoutput query="filmsQuery">
 <a href="UsingFilmDataCFC1_Detail.cfm?FilmID=#FilmID#">#MovieTitle#</a><br>
</cfoutput>

</body>
</html>
```

Figure 26.3

The GetFilmData() method can be used to produce a page such as this.

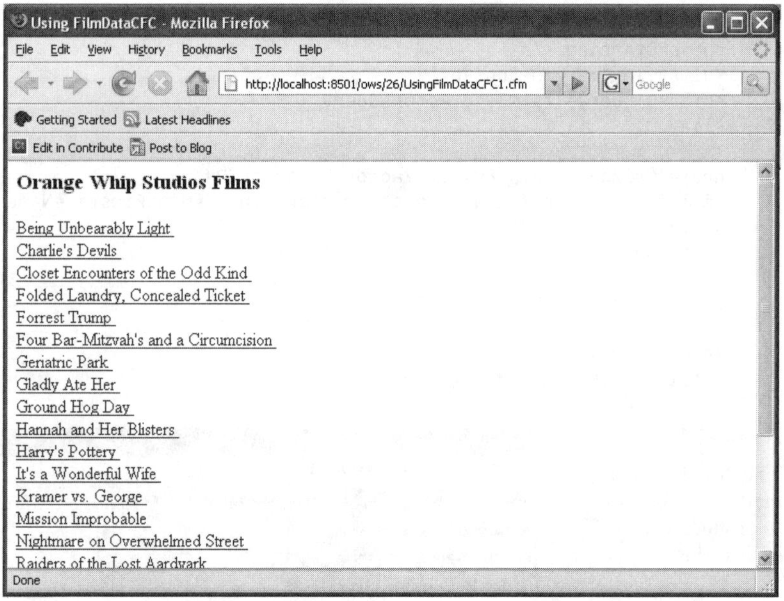

Listing 26.8 is the detail page a user gets if they click one of the links created by Listing 26.7. It simply calls the getFilmData() method exposed by the FilmDataCFC1 component, then displays the information using an ordinary <cfoutput> block (Figure 26.4).

Listing 26.8 UsingFilmDataCFC1_Detail.cfm—Creating the Film Details Page

```
<!---
 Filename: UsingFilmDataCFC1_Detail.cfm
 Author: Nate Weiss (NMW)
 Purpose: Uses the FilmDataCFC component to display one film
--->

<html>
<head><title>Using FilmDataCFC</title></head>
<body>

<!--- We need to have a FilmID parameter in the URL --->
<cfparam name="URL.filmID" type="numeric">

<!--- Call the GetFilmData() method of the FilmDataCFC1 component --->
<cfinvoke component="FilmDataCFC1" method="getFilmData"
 filmID="#URL.filmID#"
 returnVariable="filmData">

<!--- Produce the simple film display --->
<cfoutput>
 <h3>#filmData.MovieTitle#</h3>
 <p>#filmData.Summary#</p>

 <!--- Include a list of actors --->
```

Listing 26.8 (CONTINUED)

```
<p><b>Starring:</b>
<ul style="margin-top:2px">
<cfloop query="filmData.ActorsQuery">
<li>
<a
href="UsingFilmDataCFC1.cfm?actorID=#actorID#"
title="Click for films this actor stars in.">#NameFirst# #NameLast#</a>
</li>
</cfloop>
</ul>
</cfoutput>

</body>
</html>
```

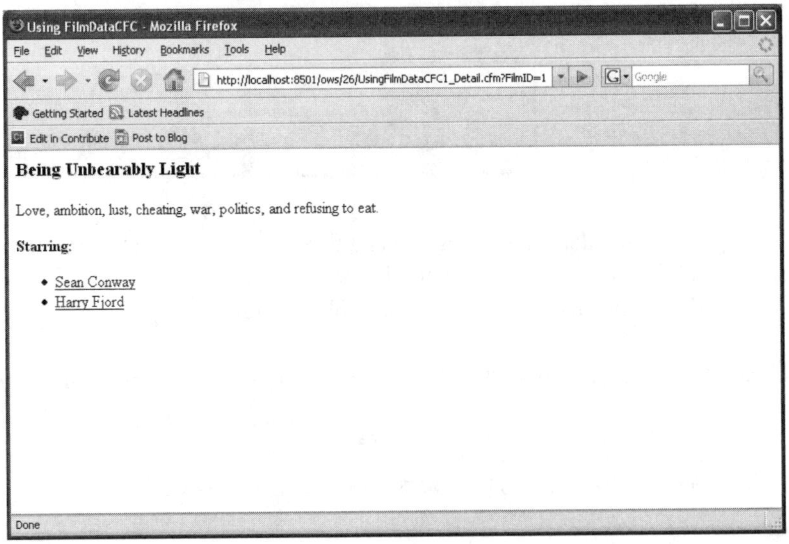

Figure 26.4

The GetFilmData()
method can be used
to produce a page
such as this.

Note that the <cfloop> tag in this listing uses filmData.ActorsQuery as its query attribute. The
filmData variable is a structure returned by the getFilmData() method created in Listing 26.6. If
you look back at that listing, you will find that getFilmData() returns a structure. The structure
contains simple string properties such as movieTitle and summary, but it also contains a property
called actorsQuery, which is a query result set object returned by a <cfquery> tag. Because the
actorsQuery properties contains a query object, it can be used as the query attribute of a <cfloop>
(or, for that matter, of <cfmail>, <cfchartseries>, or any other tag that accepts a query object).

NOTE

The getFilmData() method demonstrates that although component methods can only return a single return value, you can easily have that return value be a structure that contains as much information as you need.

The result is a set of pages that lets the user browse through films, using the actors' names as a way
to get from film to film. When a user first visits Listing 26.7, a simple list of films appears. When

users click a film's title, they are brought to Listing 26.8, which displays details about the selected film, including a list of actors. Users can click the actors' names, which sends them back to Listing 26.7. This time, though, the selected actor's ID number is passed to the `listFilms()` method, which means that only that actor's films are shown. Users can click any of those films to see the other actors in the selected film, and so on.

Separating Logic from Presentation

As you saw in the last three listings, it's relatively easy to create a CFC and use its methods to display data, perhaps to create some sort of master-detail interface. The process is basically to first create the CFC, then create a normal ColdFusion page to interact with each of the methods.

When used in this fashion, the CFC is a container for *logic* (such as extraction of information from a database), leaving the normal ColdFusion pages to deal only with *presentation* of information. Many developers find it's smart to keep a clean separation of logic and presentation while coding.

This is especially true in a team environment, where different people are working on the logic and the presentation. By keeping your interactions within databases and other logic packaged in CFCs, you can shield the people working on the presentation from the guts of your application. They can focus on making the presentation as attractive and functional as possible, without needing to know any CFML other than `<cfinvoke>` and `<cfoutput>`. And they can easily bring up the automatically generated documentation pages for each component to stay up to date on the methods each component provides.

Accessing a CFC via a URL

You have seen how to use CFC methods in your `.cfm` pages using the `<cfinvoke>` and `<cfobject>` tags. It's also possible to access methods directly with a Web browser. That is, if you place a `.cfc` file in a location that is accessible via a URL, people can use the component's methods by visiting that URL directly.

NOTE

I recommend that you use CFCs by invoking their methods within a `.cfm` page (using `<cfinvoke>` or the `<cfscript>` method syntax), as you have seen already, rather than having browsers visit the CFC's methods directly. This keeps the separation of functionality and presentation clean. If you do decide to have your CFCs accessed directly via a URL, keep the parts of the code that output HTML in separate methods, as the example in this section does.

Visiting the Correct URL

Assuming you installed ColdFusion on your local machine and are saving this chapter's listings in the `ows/26` folder within your Web server's document root, the URL to access a component called `FilmDataCFC2` would be:

```
http://localhost:8500/ows/26/FilmDataCFC2.cfc
```

If you visit this URL with your browser, you will get the automatically generated documentation page for the component. (You will be asked for a password before the documentation page will appear; use your ColdFusion Administrator or RDS password.)

To use one of the component's methods, just add a URL parameter named `method`, where the value of the parameter is the name of the method you want to call. For instance, to use the method called `ProduceFilmListHTML`, you would visit this URL with your browser:

```
http://localhost:8500/ows/26/FilmDataCFC2.cfc?method=ProduceFilmListHTML
```

NOTE

It is only possible to access a method via a URL if the `<cffunction>` block that creates the method contains an `access="remote"` attribute. If you try to use the URL to access a method that has a different `access` level (including the default value "public"), ColdFusion will display an error message.

When calling a method via the URL, you can supply values for the method's arguments by including the arguments as name-value pairs in the URL. So, to call the `produceFilmHTML` method, supplying a value of 3 to the method's `filmID` argument, you would use this URL:

```
http://localhost:8500/ows/26/FilmDataCFC2.cfc?method=produceFilmHTML&filmID=3
```

To provide values for multiple arguments, just provide the appropriate number of name-value pairs, always using the name of the argument on the left side of the equals (=) sign and the value of the argument on the right side of the equals sign.

NOTE

If the value of the argument might contain special characters such as spaces or slashes, you need to escape the value with Cold-Fusion's `URLEncodedFormat()` function. This is the case for any URL parameter, not just for CFCs. In fact, it's the case for any Web application environment, not just ColdFusion.

This is a bit of an advanced topic, but If you need to provide non-simple arguments such as arrays or structures, you can do so by creating a structure that contains all of your arguments (similar to creating a structure to pass to the `attributeCollection` attribute of the `<cfmodule>` tag), using the `<cfwddx>` tag to convert the structure to a WDDX packet, then passing the packet as a single URL parameter called `argumentCollection`. Or, if you are accessing the CFC via a form, you can provide such a packet as a form field named `argumentCollection`.

Creating Methods That Generate HTML

Just because it's possible to access a method with your browser doesn't mean the browser will understand what to do with the result. For instance, if you look at the `FilmDataCFC1` component from Listing 26.6, one of the methods returns a query and the other returns a structure. These are ColdFusion concepts; no browser is going to understand what to do with them.

For a CFC to be able to do anything meaningful if accessed via a URL, you must make sure that any methods accessed in this way return HTML that the browser can understand. The most straightforward way to do this is to add additional methods to your CFC that produce the appropriate HTML. Internally, these methods can call the CFC's other methods to retrieve data or perform other processing. To make sure that only the HTML-generating methods are accessible via a URL, only those methods should have an `access="remote"` attribute.

Listing 26.9 contains the code that we have already been exploring in the previous topic: `FilmDataCFC2.cfc`. It is a revised version of the `FilmDataCFC1` component from Listing 26.6. This version adds two new methods called `produceFilmListHTML()` and `produceFilmHTML()`. These methods basically contain the same code and produce the same result as Listing 26.7 and Listing 26.8, respectively. In other words, the component now takes care of both logic and presentation.

Listing 26.9 `FilmDataCFC2.cfc`—Adding Methods That Generate HTML

```
<!---
 Filename: FilmDataCFC2.cfc
 Author: Nate Weiss (NMW)
 Purpose: Creates the FilmDataCFC2 ColdFusion Component, which provides
 search and data retrieval services for films in the ows database.
--->

<!--- The <CFCOMPONENT> block defines the CFC --->
<!--- The filename of this file determines the CFC's name --->
<cfcomponent
 hint="Provides a simple interface for searching for and getting detailed
 information about films in the Orange Whip Studios database."
 output="false">

  <!--- ListFilms() method --->
  <cffunction name="listFilms" returnType="query"
 hint="Returns a query object containing film information." output="false">

    <!--- Optional SearchString argument --->
    <cfargument name="searchString" type="string" required="No"
    hint="Optional search criteria; if not given, all films are returned.">

    <!--- Optional SearchString argument --->
    <cfargument name="actorID" type="numeric" required="No"
    hint="Allows searching for films by actor.">

    <!--- var scope variables --->
    <cfset var getFilms = "">

    <!--- Run the query --->
    <cfquery name="getFilms" datasource="ows">
     SELECT FilmID, MovieTitle FROM Films
     WHERE 0=0
     <!--- If a search string has been specified --->
     <cfif isDefined("ARGUMENTS.searchString")>
     AND (MovieTitle LIKE '%#ARGUMENTS.searchString#%'
     OR Summary LIKE '%#ARGUMENTS.searchString#%')
     </cfif>

     <!--- If an actor's name has been specified --->
     <cfif isDefined("ARGUMENTS.actorID")>
     AND FilmID IN
     (SELECT FilmID FROM FilmsActors
     WHERE ActorID = #ARGUMENTS.actorID#)
     </cfif>
     ORDER BY MovieTitle
    </cfquery>

    <!--- Return the query results --->
    <cfreturn getFilms>
  </cffunction>
```

Listing 26.9 (CONTINUED)

```coldfusion
<!--- GetFilmData() method --->
<cffunction name="getFilmData" returnType="struct" output="false"
hint="Returns structured information about the specified film.">

  <!--- FilmID argument --->
  <cfargument name="filmID" type="numeric" required="Yes"
  hint="The film that you want information about.">

  <!--- This is what this method originally returns --->
  <!--- The var keyword makes it local to the method --->
  <cfset var filmData = structNew()>
  <cfset var getFilm = "">
  <cfset var getActors = "">

  <cfset filmData.filmID = ARGUMENTS.filmID>

  <!--- Select data about the film from the database --->
  <cfquery name="getFilm" datasource="ows">
  SELECT MovieTitle, Summary FROM Films
  WHERE FilmID = #ARGUMENTS.filmID#
  </cfquery>

  <!--- Populate the FilmData structure with film info --->
  <cfset filmData.movieTitle = getFilm.MovieTitle>
  <cfset filmData.summary = getFilm.Summary>

  <!--- Run second query to get actor information --->
  <cfquery name="getActors" datasource="ows">
  SELECT ActorID, NameFirst, NameLast
  FROM Actors
  WHERE ActorID IN
  (SELECT ActorID FROM FilmsActors
  WHERE FilmID = #ARGUMENTS.filmID#)
  </cfquery>

  <!--- Make the GetActors query results part of the returned structure --->
  <cfset filmData.actorsQuery = getActors>

  <!--- Return the final structure --->
  <cfreturn FilmData>
</cffunction>

  <!--- ProduceFilmListHTML() method --->
  <cffunction name="produceFilmListHTML" access="remote" output="true"
  returntype="void" hint="Produces a simple HTML display">

  <!--- This variable is local to only to this function --->
  <cfset var filmsQuery = "">
  <cfset var actorData = "">

  <!--- Call the ListFilms() method to get data about all films--->
  <!--- Pass along any arguments that were passed to this method --->
  <cfinvoke method="listFilms" returnVariable="filmsQuery"
  argumentCollection="#ARGUMENTS#">
```

Listing 26.9 (CONTINUED)

```
      <!--- Begin displaying output --->
      <cfoutput>
      <!--- If an ActorID was provided as an argument, then we are --->
      <!--- only displaying films that star the specified actor --->
      <cfif isDefined("ARGUMENTS.actorID")>
        <cfset actorData = getFilmData(filmsQuery.FilmID).actorsQuery>
        <h3>Films Starring #actorData.NameFirst# #actorData.NameLast#</h3>
        <p><a href="FilmDataCFC2.cfc?method=produceFilmListHTML">
        [List Of All Films]</a></p>
      <!--- Otherwise, all Orange Whip films are being displayed --->
      <cfelse>
        <h3>Orange Whip Studios Films</h3>
      </cfif>

      <!--- For each film, display the title as a link --->
      <!--- to this component's ProduceFilmHTML() method --->
      <cfloop query="filmsQuery">
      <a href="FilmDataCFC2.cfc?method=produceFilmHTML&FilmID=#FilmID#">
      #MovieTitle#</a><br>
      </cfloop>
      </cfoutput>

  </cffunction>
  <!--- ProduceFilmHTML() method --->
  <cffunction name="produceFilmHTML" access="remote" output="true"
  returntype="void" hint="Produces a simple HTML display">

      <!--- FilmID argument --->
      <cfargument name="filmID" type="numeric" required="Yes"
      hint="The ID number of the film to display information about">

      <!--- Call the GetFilmData() method to get basic film information --->
      <cfset var filmData = getFilmData(ARGUMENTS.filmID)>

      <!--- Produce the simple film display --->
      <cfoutput>
      <h3>#filmData.MovieTitle#</h3>
      <p>#filmData.Summary#</p>

      <!--- Include a list of actors --->
      <p><b>Starring:</b>
      <ul style="margin-top:2px">
      <cfloop query="FilmData.ActorsQuery">
      <li>
      <a href="FilmDataCFC2.cfc?method=produceFilmListHTML&ActorID=#ActorID#">
      #NameFirst# #NameLast#</a>
      </li>
      </cfloop>
      </ul>
      </cfoutput>

  </cffunction>

</cfcomponent>
```

Within the produceFilmListHTML() method, the component's own listFilms() method retrieves a list of films. Then a <cfoutput> block generates the HTML that should be returned to the browser. This <cfoutput> code is fairly similar to the code after the <cfinvoke> in Listing 26.7. The main difference is that the href attributes of the links that this code generates point to the produceFilmHTML() method of this same component instead of to a normal ColdFusion page. That is, the HTML generated by this method contains links that will execute other methods of the same component.

NOTE

Look at the argumentCollection="#ARGUMENTS#" attribute used in the <cfinvoke> tag in this listing. Any arguments passed to the produceFilmListHTML() method will be passed along to the listFilms() method as it is invoked. You can use this syntax whenever you want to call a method within another method and want the nested method to receive the same arguments as the outer method.

Another interesting thing about this <cfinvoke> tag: it doesn't include a component attribute. Normally, component is a required attribute, but you can leave it out if you are using <cfinvoke> within another method. ColdFusion assumes that you are referring to another method within the same component.

The code for the second new method, produceFilmHTML(), works similarly. Again, this new method calls one of the non-remote methods, getFilmData(), to obtain the information it needs to display. For variety's sake, getFilmData() is called via the <cfscript> syntax, rather than the <cfinvoke> tag.

NOTE

In general, methods that generate HTML or other output with <cfoutput> should not also produce a return value. In other words, you generally shouldn't use <cfoutput> and <cfreturn> within the same method.

Now that you've completed this component, you can visit it using the following URL:

```
http://localhost:8500/ows/26/FilmDataCFC2.cfc?method=ProduceFilmListHTML
```

The result for the user is the same master-detail film-browsing interface created with Listings 26.6 and 26.7. The only difference is that the CFC is doing all the work on its own, rather than needing separate .cfm files to invoke it. As far as the user is concerned, the only difference is the .cfc extension in the URL.

NOTE

All of the methods, including the non-Remote ones (listFilms() and getFilmData()), are still available for use within normal ColdFusion pages via <cfinvoke> or <cfobject>.

Other Ways of Separating CFC Logic from Presentation

Listing 26.9 contains two logic methods and two presentation methods. Although only the presentation methods can be accessed directly with a Web browser (because of the access="remote" attribute), they are all included in the same CFC file.

If you wanted, you could create a separate CFC for the presentation methods. You would just use the <cfinvoke> tag within the presentation CFC to call the logic methods.

Another option is to store the presentation methods in their own .cfc file, adding an extends attribute that specifies the name of the logic CFC. This would cause the presentation CFC to *inherit* the methods from the logic CFC so it could use them internally, as shown in Listing 26.9. Component inheritance and a complete discussion of the extends attribute are beyond the scope of this chapter. For details, consult the ColdFusion documentation or Vol. 3, *Advanced Application Development*.

Accessing a CFC via a Form

It is also possible to access a method directly from a browser using a form. Conceptually, this is very similar to accessing a method via a URL, as discussed in the previous section, "Accessing a CFC via a URL." Just use the URL for the .cfc file as the form's action, along with the desired method name. Then add form fields for each argument that you want to pass to the method when the form is submitted. For example, the following snippet would create a simple search form, which, when submitted, would cause a list of matching films to appear.

```
<cfform action="FilmDataCFC2.cfc?method=ProduceFilmListHTML">
 <input name="searchString">
 <input type="Submit" value="Search">
</cfform>
```

NOTE

Again, the method must use access="remote" in its <cffunction> tag. Otherwise, it can't be accessed directly over the Internet via a Form or a URL.

Exploring CFCs in Dreamweaver

Once you've written your CFCs, they become a part of Adobe Dreamweaver. You can explore each CFC's hints and methods, display automatic documentation for each CFC, and drag and drop methods into your ColdFusion pages. These features make it even easier for you and your team to reuse code with CFCs.

The heart of the Dreamweaver-CFC integration is the Components tab in the Application panel, which is displayed by default if you chose the HomeSite/Coder interface while you were installing Dreamweaver. If you don't see the Application panel, select Window > Components from the main menu.

TIP

As a shortcut, you can use Ctrl-F7 (or equivalent) to show the Application panel.

If the tabs in the Application panel are dimmed (disabled), open a file that is associated with a site that uses ColdFusion as the Application Server type. You've probably already done this for the **ows** folder in your Web server's document root, so just open any of the .cfm files within **ows**. That should enable the Application panel.

Viewing All Your CFCs

With the Application panel expanded, click the Components tab. You will notice a drop-down list at the top of the tab, with choices for CF Components or Web Services. Make sure CF Components is selected.

You should now see a tree with items for each folder on your Web server that contains a `.cfc` file. For instance, you should see an item for `ows.26` (the `26` folder within the `ows` folder); this will contain the CFCs created in this chapter.

NOTE

I am assuming that you have copied all the example files for this chapter from the Web site into your Web server's document root. If not, do so now–or keep in mind that only the `.cfc` files that are actually present on your server will be shown in the tree in Dreamweaver.

Go ahead and expand the `ows.26` item in the tree. The CFCs for this chapter, including the `Film-SearchCFC`, `FilmDataCFC`, and `FilmRotationCFC` components, will display as nested items in the tree. You can expand each CFC to reveal its methods, and you can expand each method to reveal its input arguments (Figure 26.5).

Figure 26.5

Dreamweaver makes it easy to keep track of your CFCs and their methods.

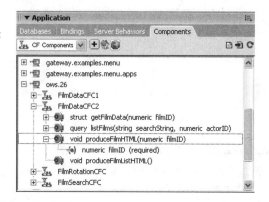

NOTE

If you add to or change a CFC, click the Refresh button at the top-right corner of the Components tab to make the tree reflect your changes.

ColdFusion and Dreamweaver refer to the ability to display this kind of information about components as component introspection. The fact that the server can look into the component file to learn about its methods, return values, and arguments is a key feature of the new CFC framework. Component introspection makes many things possible, including the tight Dreamweaver integration you are seeing here, the Flash integration you will learn about in Chapter 26, and ColdFusion's ability to automatically expose your CFCs as Web Services.

Jumping to CFC Code from the Tree

Once you have the Components tree showing in the Application tab (see the previous section, "Viewing All Your CFCs"), you can double-click the items in the tree to open the corresponding `.cfc` file.

If you double-click

- a component (like the `FilmDataCFC` item), Dreamweaver will open up the `.cfc` file, ready for your edits.

- a method within a component (like `getFilmData` or `listFilms`), Dreamweaver will open the file, then scroll down and highlight the corresponding `<cffunction>` block.

- an argument within a method (like `searchString` or `filmID`), Dreamweaver will open the file and scroll down to the corresponding `<cfargument>` tag.

Inserting `<cfinvoke>` Tags via Drag and Drop

If you're working on a ColdFusion page and want to call one of your CFC's methods, Dreamweaver can automatically write the appropriate `<cfinvoke>` code for you. Just click the method in the Components tree (see Figure 26.5), then drag it to the appropriate spot in your code. When you release the mouse, a `<cfinvoke>` tag will be added to your code with the `component`, `method`, and other attributes already filled in for you. In addition, a `<cfinvokeargument>` tag will be added for each of the method's required arguments. This can be a real time-saver.

TIP

You can insert the same code by right-clicking (Windows) or Control-clicking (Mac) the method and choosing Insert Code from the context menu.

Viewing CFC Details

To get more information about an item in the Components tree, right-click (Windows) or Control-click (Mac) the item, then select Get Details from the context menu. A message box will appear, displaying detailed information about the component, method, or argument.

Viewing CFC Documentation

One of the coolest CFC features in ColdFusion is the ability to generate a documentation page automatically for each of your components. You can use the page as a live reference guide to the CFC. (If you are familiar with Java, this is analogous to a JavaDoc page.)

To view the automatic reference page for a component, right-click (Windows) or Control-click (Mac) the component (or any of its methods or arguments) in the Components tree and select Get Description from the context menu. Dreamweaver will launch your browser with the documentation page showing. For instance, the generated documentation page for the `FilmDataCFC1` component is shown in Figure 26.6.

Viewing CFC Documentation Without Dreamweaver

You don't have to use Dreamweaver to generate the documentation page for a CFC. You can view the documentation page at any time by just navigating your browser to the URL for the `.cfc` file. For instance, assuming you have installed ColdFusion on your local machine, you can get to the documentation page at `http://localhost:8500/ows/26/FilmDataCFC2.cfc`.

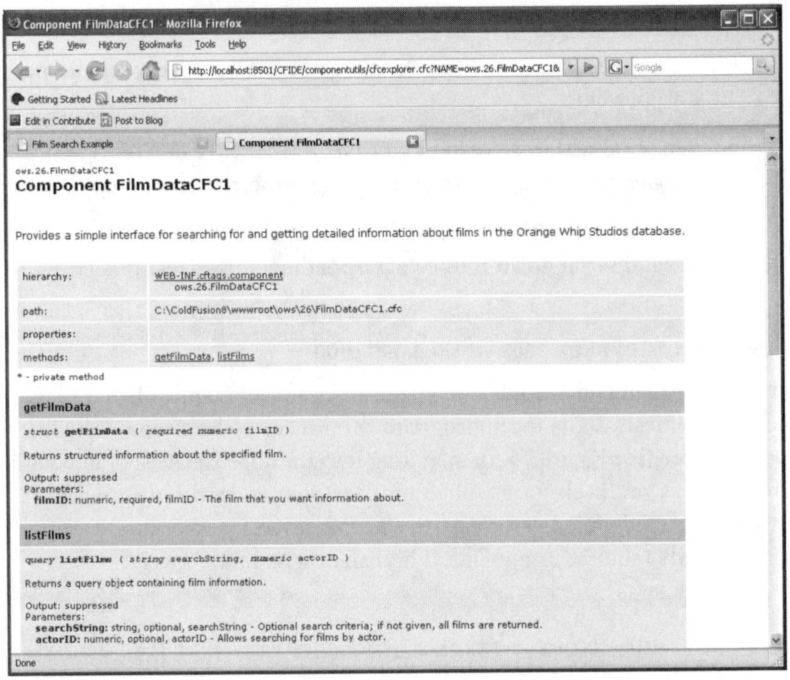

Figure 26.6

ColdFusion will generate an automatic reference page for any CFC.

TIP

Of course, once you have the generated documentation page open in your browser, you can always use your browser's File > Save As command to save the HTML file to some permanent location on your local hard drive. That way, you can view or print the documentation even when you can't connect to the ColdFusion server.

Using the Create Component Dialog

Wizards aren't for everyone, but if you like them, Dreamweaver provides a very nice Create Component dialog that you can use to create new .cfc files. This wizard-style interface makes it easy to design a new CFC. You just fill in the blanks about your new component's name, hints, methods (functions), arguments, and so on.

To launch the Create Component dialog, click the button marked with a plus sign (+) at the top of the Components tab in the Application panel. Or you can right-click (Windows) or Control-click (Mac) anywhere in the Components tab and select Create New CFC from the context menu. The Create Component dialog will appear (Figure 26.7). Just fill in the desired blanks on each of the various pages. Except for the component's name and directory, you can leave any of the other items blank.

When you click OK, Dreamweaver will generate the appropriate skeleton of <cfcomponent>, <cffunction>, <cfargument>, and <cfreturn> tags for you. All that remains is to add the appropriate method code to each of the <cffunction> blocks.

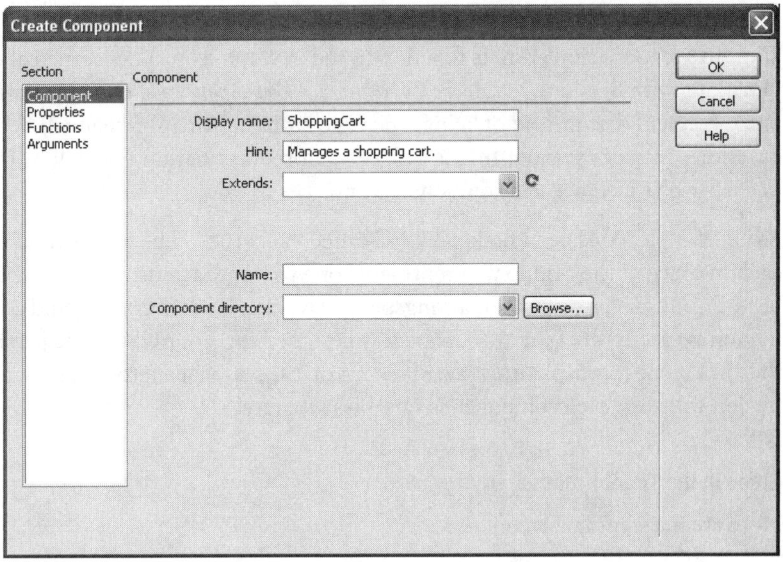

Figure 26.7

The Create Component dialog can make it easier to design a new CFC.

Components That Hold Instance Data

The ColdFusion components discussed so far in this chapter (the `FilmSearchCFC` and `FilmDataCFC` examples) have both been *static* components, meaning they don't hold any instance data. That is, although you can create an instance of a component with `<cfobject>` before using it, there really isn't any need to do so. One instance of a component isn't going to behave any differently from any other instance, so it's fine to simply call the CFC's methods directly.

If you create components that hold instance data, though, each instance of the component lives on its own and has its own memory in which to store information. If your component is about films, each instance might be an individual film and the instance data might be the film's title, budget, gross receipts, or even critics' reviews. If your component is about shopping carts, each instance of the component would represent a separate user's shopping cart, and the instance data would be the cart's contents.

This section will explain how to create this type of component.

Introducing the `THIS` Scope

The CFC framework sets aside a special variable scope called `THIS`, which stands for *this instance* of a component. You can think of the word `THIS` as meaning "this film" or "this shopping cart" or "this object," depending on what you intend your component to represent.

The THIS Scope Represents an Instance

The THIS scope is similar in its function to the SESSION scope you learned about in Chapter 20, "Working with Sessions," in *Adobe ColdFusion 8 Web Application Construction Kit, Volume 1: Getting Started*, except that instead of being a place to store information that will be remembered for the duration of a user's session, THIS is a place to store information that will be remembered for as long as a particular instance of a component continues to exist.

As an example, consider a fictional CFC called ParrotCFC. The idea behind the component is that each instance of the component represents one parrot. Each instance of the component needs to have a name, an age, a gender, a wingspan, a favorite word or cracker, and so on. This kind of information is exactly what the THIS scope was designed for. Your CFC code just needs to set variables in the THIS scope (perhaps THIS.favoriteWord or THIS.wingSpan) to remember these values. Cold-Fusion will keep each component's variables separate.

Steps in the THIS Process

Here are the steps involved:

1. Create the CFC file. Within the file, use the THIS scope as the component's personal memory space, keeping in mind that each instance of the component (that is, each parrot) will get its own copy of the THIS scope for its own use.

2. In your ColdFusion pages, create an instance of the CFC with <cfobject> before you use any of the component's methods. If you want the instance to live longer than the current page request, you can place the instance in the SESSION or APPLICATION scope.

3. Now go ahead and use the instance's methods with the <cfinvoke> tag as you learned in previous examples. Make sure that you specify the instance (that is, the individual parrot) as the component attribute of the <cfinvoke> tag, rather than as the name of the CFC.

In this scenario, each individual instance of the ParrotCFC has a life of its own. The <cfobject> tag is what makes a particular parrot come to life. The THIS scope automatically maintains the parrot's characteristics.

Extending the metaphor, if the parrot is the pet of one of your Web users, you can make the parrot follow the user around by having it live in the user's SESSION scope. Or if the parrot doesn't belong to a particular person but instead belongs to your application as a whole (perhaps the parrot is your site's mascot), you could have it live in the APPLICATION scope. Or you might have a bunch of parrots that are looking for owners. You could keep these parrots (each one an instance of the ParrotCFC component) in an array in the APPLICATION scope. When a user wants to take one of the parrots home as a pet, you could move the parrot out of the array and into the SESSION scope.

OK, that's enough about parrots. The idea here is to think of a CFC as an independent thing or object with its own properties. You store individual instances of the object in the APPLICATION or SESSION scope if you want it to remain in memory for a period of time, or just leave it in the normal scope if you only need the instance to live for the current page request.

NOTE

By definition, a component that doesn't refer to the THIS scope at all in its methods doesn't need to be instantiated with <cfobject> before calling its methods, and can therefore be considered a static component. Any component that does use the THIS scope internally probably needs to be instantiated to function properly.

An Instance Data CFC Example

Let's look at a simple example of a CFC that holds instance data. The component is called FilmRotationCFC, and its purpose is to keep track of a featured film.

Designing FilmRotationCFC

To demonstrate the use of multiple methods within an instantiated component, the FilmRotation-CFC component will contain five methods, as listed in Table 26.8.

Table 26.8   Methods Provided by FilmRotationCFC

METHOD	DESCRIPTION
currentFilmID()	Returns the ID number of the currently featured film. Because this method uses access="Private", it can only be used internally within the FilmRotationCFC.
isFilmNeedingRotation()	Returns TRUE if the current film has been featured for more than the amount of time specified as the rotation interval (5 seconds by default). Returns FALSE if the current film should be left as is for now. This is a private method that can only be used internally.
rotateFilm()	Rotates the currently featured film if it has been featured for more than the amount of time specified as the rotation interval (5 seconds by default). Internally, this method calls isFilmNeedingRotation() to find out if the current film has expired. If so, it sets the current film to be the next film in the rotation.
getCurrentFilmID()	Rotates the current movie (if appropriate), then returns the currently featured film. Internally, this function calls rotateFilm() and then returns the value of currentFilmID(). This is a public method.
getCurrentFilmData()	Returns the title, summary, and other information about the currently featured film. Internally, this function calls getCurrentFilmID() and then returns the information provided by the GetFilmData() method of the FilmDataCFC2 component. This method is included mainly to show how to call one component's methods from another component.
randomizedFilmList()	Returns a list of all FilmID numbers in the ows database, in random order. Internally, this uses the listRandomize() method to perform the randomization.
listRandomize(list)	Accepts any comma-separated list and returns a new list with the same items in it, but in a random order. Because this method uses access="Private", it can only be used internally within the FilmRotationCFC. This method really doesn't have anything to do with this CFC in particular; you could reuse it in any situation where you wanted to randomize a list of items.

TIP

In this CFC, I am adopting a convention of starting all public method names with the word `Get`. You might want to consider using naming conventions such as this when creating your own component methods.

It is conventional in many programming languages to start the name of any function that returns a Boolean value with the word `Is`. You might want to consider doing the same in your own CFCs.

Building `FilmRotationCFC`

Listing 26.10 shows the code for the `FilmRotationCFC` component. Because this component includes a number of methods, this code listing is a bit long. Don't worry. The code for each of the individual methods is quite short.

Listing 26.10 `FilmRotationCFC.cfc`—Building a CFC That Maintains Instance Data

```
<!---
 Filename: FilmRotationCFC.cfc
 Author: Nate Weiss (NMW)
 Purpose: Creates FilmRotationCFC, a ColdFusion Component
--->

<cfcomponent output="false">

  <!--- *** begin initialization code *** --->
  <cfset THIS.filmList = randomizedFilmList()>
  <cfset THIS.currentListPos = 1>
  <cfset THIS.rotationInterval = 5>
  <cfset THIS.currentUntil = dateAdd("s", THIS.rotationInterval, now())>


  <!--- *** end initialization code *** --->
  <!--- Private function: RandomizedFilmList() --->
  <cffunction name="randomizedFilmList" returnType="string" access="private"
  output="false"
  hint="For internal use. Returns a list of all Film IDs, in random order.">

    <!--- This variable is for this function's use only --->
    <cfset var getFilmIDs = "">

    <!--- Retrieve list of current films from database --->
    <cfquery name="getFilmIDs" datasource="ows"
    cachedwithin="#CreateTimeSpan(0,1,0,0)#">
    SELECT FilmID FROM Films
    ORDER BY MovieTitle
    </cfquery>

    <!--- Return the list of films, in random order --->
    <cfreturn listRandomize(valueList(getFilmIDs.FilmID))>
  </cffunction>

  <!--- Private utility function: ListRandomize() --->
  <cffunction name="listRandomize" returnType="string"
  output="false"
  hint="Randomizes the order of the items in any comma-separated list.">
```

Listing 26.10 (CONTINUED)

```
      <!--- List argument --->
      <cfargument name="list" type="string" required="Yes"
      hint="The string that you want to randomize.">

      <!--- These variables are for this function's use only --->
      <cfset var result = "">
      <cfset var randPos = "">

      <!--- While there are items left in the original list... --->
      <cfloop condition="listLen(ARGUMENTS.list) gt 0">
        <!--- Select a list position at random --->
        <cfset randPos = randRange(1, listLen(ARGUMENTS.list))>
        <!--- Add the item at the selected position to the Result list --->
        <cfset result = listAppend(result, listGetAt(ARGUMENTS.list, randPos))>
        <!--- Remove the item from selected position of the original list --->
        <cfset ARGUMENTS.list = listDeleteAt(ARGUMENTS.list, randPos)>
      </cfloop>

      <!--- Return the reordered list --->
      <cfreturn result>
  </cffunction>

  <!--- Private method: IsFilmNeedingRotation() --->
  <cffunction name="isFilmNeedingRotation" access="private" returnType="boolean"
  output="false"
  hint="For internal use. Returns TRUE if the film should be rotated now.">

      <!--- Compare the current time to the THIS.CurrentUntil time --->
      <!--- If the film is still current, DateCompare() will return 1 --->
      <cfset var dateComparison = dateCompare(THIS.currentUntil, now())>

      <!--- Return TRUE if the film is still current, FALSE otherwise --->
      <cfreturn dateComparison neq 1>
  </cffunction>

  <!--- RotateFilm() method --->
  <cffunction name="rotateFilm" access="private" returnType="void" output="false"
  hint="For internal use. Advances the current movie.">

      <!--- If the film needs to be rotated at this time... --->
      <cfif isFilmNeedingRotation()>
        <!--- Advance the instance-level THIS.CurrentListPos value by one --->
        <cfset THIS.currentListPos = THIS.currentListPos + 1>

        <!--- If THIS.CurrentListPos is now more than the number of films, --->
        <!--- Start over again at the beginning (the first film) --->
        <cfif THIS.currentListPos gt listLen(THIS.FilmList)>
          <cfset THIS.currentListPos = 1>
        </cfif>

        <!--- Set the time that the next rotation will be due --->
        <cfset THIS.currentUntil = dateAdd("s", THIS.rotationInterval, now())>
      </cfif>
  </cffunction>
```

Listing 26.10 (CONTINUED)

```
    <!--- Private method: CurrentFilmID() --->
    <cffunction name="currentFilmID" access="private" returnType="numeric"
    output="false"
    hint="For internal use. Returns the ID of the current film in rotation.">

      <!--- Return the FilmID from the current row of the GetFilmIDs query --->
      <cfreturn listGetAt(THIS.filmList, THIS.currentListPos)>
    </cffunction>

    <!--- Public method: GetCurrentFilmID() --->
    <cffunction name="getCurrentFilmID" access="public" returnType="numeric"
    output="false"
    hint="Returns the ID number of the currently 'featured' film.">
      <!--- First, rotate the current film --->
      <cfset rotateFilm()>

      <!--- Return the ID of the current film --->
      <cfreturn currentFilmID()>
    </cffunction>

    <!--- Public method: GetCurrentFilmData() --->
    <cffunction name="getCurrentFilmData" access="remote" returnType="struct"
    output="false"
    hint="Returns structured data about the currently 'featured' film.">

      <!--- This variable is local just to this function --->
      <cfset var currentFilmData = "">

      <!--- Invoke the GetCurrentFilmID() method (in separate component) --->
      <!--- Returns a structure with film's title, summary, actors, etc. --->
      <cfinvoke component="FilmDataCFC2" method="getFilmData"
      filmID="#getCurrentFilmID()#" returnVariable="currentFilmData">

      <!--- Return the structure --->
      <cfreturn currentFilmData>
    </cffunction>

  </cfcomponent>
```

The most important thing to note and understand about this CFC is the purpose of the first few <cfset> tags at the top of Listing 26.10. Because these lines sit directly within the body of the <cfcomponent> tag, outside any <cffunction> blocks, they are considered *initialization code* that will be executed whenever a new instance of the component is created. Notice that each of these <cfset> tags creates variables in the special THIS scope, which means they are assigned to each instance of the component separately. Typically, all that happens in a CFC's initialization code is that it sets instance data in the THIS scope.

NOTE

It's important to understand that these lines don't execute each time one of the instance's methods is called. They execute only when a new instance of the component is brought to life with the <cfobject> tag.

The <cfset> tags at the top of the listing create these instance variables:

- THIS.filmList is a list of all current films, in the order in which the component should show them. The component's randomizedFilmList() method creates the sequence. This order will be different for each instance of the CFC.

- THIS.currentListPos is the current position in the randomized list of films. The initial value is 1, which means that the first film in the randomized list will be considered the featured film.

- THIS.rotationInterval is the number of seconds that a film should be considered featured before the component features the next film. Right now, the interval is 5 seconds.

- THIS.currentUntil is the time at which the current film should be considered expired. At that point, the CFC will select the next film in the randomized list of films. When the component is first instantiated, this variable is set to 5 seconds in the future.

Let's take a quick look at the <cffunction> blocks in Listing 26.10.

The randomizedFilmList() method will always be the first one to be called, since it is used in the initialization code block. This method simply retrieves a record set of film IDs from the database. Then it turns the film IDs into a comma-separated list with ColdFusion's valueList() function and passes the list to the CFC's listRandomize() method. The resulting list (which is a list of films in random order) is returned as the method's return value.

The listRandomize() method uses a combination of ColdFusion's list functions to randomize the list supplied to the list argument. The basic idea is to pluck items at random from the original list, adding them to the end of a new list called result. When there are no more items in the original list, the result variable is returned as the method's return value.

The currentFilmID() method simply returns the FilmID in the current position of the CFC's randomized list of films. As long as THIS.currentListPos is set to 1, this method returns the first film's ID.

The isFilmNeedingRotation() method uses dateCompare() to compare THIS.currentUntil to the current time. If the time has passed, this method returns TRUE to indicate that the current film is ready for rotation.

The rotateFilm() method is interesting because it actually makes changes to the variables in the THIS scope first created in the initialization code block. First, it uses isFilmNeedingRotation() to see whether the current film has been featured for more than 5 seconds already. If so, it advances the This.currentListPos value by 1. If the new currentListPos value is greater than the length of the list of films, that means all films in the sequence have been featured, so the position is set back to 1. Lastly, the method uses ColdFusion's dateAdd() function to set the THIS.currentUntil variable to 5 seconds in the future.

The getCurrentFilmID() method ties all the concepts together. Whenever this method is used, the rotateFilm() method is called (which will advance the current film to the next item in the sequence if the current one has expired). It then calls currentFilmID() to return the current film's ID.

Storing CFCs in the APPLICATION Scope

Now that the FilmRotationCFC component is in place, it's quite simple to put it to use. Listing 26.11 shows one way of using the component.

Listing 26.11 UsingFilmRotationCFCa.cfm—Instantiating a CFC at the Application Level

```
<!---
 Filename: UsingFilmRotationCFCa.cfm
 Author: Nate Weiss (NMW)
 Purpose: Demonstrates storage of CFC instances in shared memory scopes
--->

<html>
<head>
 <title>Using FilmRotationCFC</title>
</head>

<body>

<!--- If an instance of the FilmRotatorCFC component hasn't been created --->
<!--- yet, create a fresh instance and store it in the APPLICATION scope --->
<cfif not isDefined("APPLICATION.filmRotator")>
 <cfobject component="FilmRotationCFC" name="APPLICATION.FilmRotator">
</cfif>

<!--- Invoke the GetCurrentFilmID() method of the FilmRotator CFC object --->
<cfinvoke component="#APPLICATION.filmRotator#" method="getCurrentFilmID"
 returnVariable="featuredFilmID">

<p>The callout at the right side of this page shows the currently featured film.
The featured film changes every five seconds.
Just reload the page to see the next film in the sequence.
The sequence will not change until the ColdFusion server is restarted.</p>

<!--- Show the current film in a callout, via custom tag --->
<cf_ShowMovieCallout
 filmID="#featuredFilmID#">

</body>
</html>
```

The idea here is to keep an instance of FilmRotationCFC in the APPLICATION.filmRotator variable. Keeping it in the APPLICATION scope means that the same instance will be kept in the server's memory until the ColdFusion server is restarted. All sessions that visit the page will share the instance.

First, a simple isDefined() test sees if the CFC instance called APPLICATION.filmRotator already exists. If not, the instance is created with the <cfobject> tag. So, after this <cfif> block, the instance is guaranteed to exist. Keep in mind that the CFC's initialization code block is executed when the instance is first created (refer to Listing 26.10).

NOTE

If you wanted the CFC instance to be available to all pages in the application, you could move the <cfif> block in Listing 26.11 to your Application.cfc file.

Displaying the currently featured film is simply a matter of calling the `getCurrentFilmID()` method with the `<cfinvoke>` tag and passing it to the `<cf_ShowMovieCallout>` custom tag (created in Chapter 25, "Creating Custom Tags"). When a browser visits this listing, the currently featured movie is displayed. If you reload the page repeatedly, you will see that the featured movie changes every 5 seconds. If you wait long enough, you will see the sequence of films repeat itself. The sequence will continue to repeat until the ColdFusion server is restarted, at which point a new sequence of films will be selected at random.

Storing CFCs in the SESSION Scope

One of the neat things about CFCs is their independence. You will note that the code for the `RotateFilmCFC` component doesn't contain a single reference to the APPLICATION scope. In fact, it doesn't refer to any of ColdFusion's built-in scopes at all, except for the THIS scope.

This means it's possible to create some instances of the CFC that are kept in the APPLICATION scope, and others that are kept in the SESSION scope. All the instances will work properly, and will maintain their own versions of the variables in the THIS scope.

To see this in action, go back to either Listing 26.10 or Listing 25.11 and change the code so that the CFC instance is kept in the SESSION scope instead of the APPLICATION scope. Now each Web session will be given its own `FilmRotator` object, stored as a session variable. You can see how this looks in Listing 26.12 (in the upcoming section "Modifying Properties from a ColdFusion Page").

To see the difference in behavior, open up the revised listing in two different browsers (say, Firefox and Internet Explorer 7), and experiment with reloading the page. You will find that the films are featured on independent cycles, and that each session sees the films in a different order. If you view the page on different computers, you will see that each machine also has its own private, randomized sequence of featured films.

Instance Data as Properties

As I've explained, the code for the `FilmRotationCFC` component uses the THIS scope to store certain variables for its own use. You can think of these variables as *properties* of each component instance, because they are the items that make a particular instance special, that give it its individuality, its life.

Sometimes you will want to display or change the value of one of these properties from a normal ColdFusion page. ColdFusion makes it very easy to access an instance's properties. Basically, you can access any variable in a CFC's THIS scope as a property of the instance itself.

Modifying Properties from a ColdFusion Page

If you have a CFC instance called `SESSION.myFilmRotator` and you want to display the current value of the `currentUntil` property (that is, the value of the variable that is called `THIS.currentUntil` within the CFC code), you can do so with the following in a normal `.cfm` page:

```
<cfoutput>
 #timeFormat(SESSION.myFilmRotator.currentUntil)#
</cfoutput>
```

To change the value of the `rotationInterval` property (referred to as `THIS.rotationInterval` in the `FilmRotationCFC.cfc` file) to 10 seconds instead of the usual 5 seconds, you could use this line:

```
<cfset SESSION.myFilmRotator.rotationInterval = 10>
```

After you changed the `rotationInterval` for the `SESSION.FilmRotator` instance, then that session's films would rotate every 10 seconds instead of every 5 seconds. Listing 26.12 shows how all this would look in a ColdFusion page.

Listing 26.12 `UsingFilmRotationCFCc.cfm`—Interacting with a CFC's Properties

```
<!---
 Filename: UsingFilmRotationCFCc.cfm
 Author: Nate Weiss (NMW)
 Purpose: Demonstrates storage of CFC instances in shared memory scopes
--->

<html>
<head>
 <title>Using FilmRotationCFC</title>
</head>

<body>

<!--- If an instance of the FilmRotatorCFC component hasn't been created --->
<!--- yet, create a fresh instance and store it in the SESSION scope --->
<cfif not isDefined("SESSION.myFilmRotator")>
 <cfobject component="FilmRotationCFC" name="SESSION.myFilmRotator">

 <!--- Rotate films every ten seconds --->
 <cfset SESSION.myFilmRotator.rotationInterval = 10>
</cfif>

<!--- Display message --->
<cfoutput>
 <p>
 The callout at the right side of this page shows the currently featured film.
 Featured films rotate every #SESSION.myFilmRotator.rotationInterval# seconds.
 Just reload the page to see the next film in the sequence.
 The sequence will not change until the web session ends.</p>
 The next film rotation will occur at:
 #timeFormat(SESSION.myFilmRotator.currentUntil, "h:mm:ss tt")#
</cfoutput>

<!--- Show the current film in a callout, via custom tag --->
<cf_ShowMovieCallout filmID="#SESSION.myFilmRotator.getCurrentFilmID()#">

</body>
</html>
```

NOTE

You can experiment with changing the `RotationInterval` property to different values. Keep in mind that the code in the `<cfif>` block will only execute once per session, so you may need to restart ColdFusion to see a change. If you are using J2EE Session Variables, you can just close and reopen your browser. Or you could move the `<cfset>` line outside the `<cfif>` block.

What all this means is that the CFC's methods can access an instantiated CFC's properties internally via the THIS scope, and your ColdFusion pages can access them via the instance object variable itself. As you learned in the introduction to this topic, CFCs can be thought of as containers for data and functionality, like many objects in the real world. You know how to access the data (properties) as well as the functionality (methods).

CFCs and the VARIABLES Scope

The THIS scope isn't the only way to persist data within a CFC. Each CFC also has a VARIABLES scope. This scope acts just like the VARIABLES scope within a simple CFM page. Like the THIS scope, each method in the CFC can read and write to the scope. However, unlike the THIS scope, you can't display or modify the value outside of the CFC.

Some people consider this a good thing. Look at the code in Listing 26.12. One line uses the timeFormat() function to display the CFC's currentUntil variable. Now imagine that many other CFM pages on your site do the same thing. What happens if the writer of the CFC changes the name of that variable? All of sudden you have a bunch of errors on your site, since these documents were using the internal currentUntil variable of the CFC. The whole point of encapsulation is to prevent problems like this. How can we prevent this?

I would suggest doing two things. Whenever you need to access a value from within a CFC, build a method. So for example, instead of directly accessing the currentUntil value of the CFC, the CFC itself could define a getCurrentUntil() method. Any CFM that needs this value would simply use the method. If the CFC changed the internal value, it wouldn't break anything, since the other documents would be using the method instead of directly accessing the value.

Along with using methods to return instance data, consider using the VARIABLES scope instead of the THIS scope. This will actually prevent CFMs from reading the data, forcing you to use methods to access the data itself.

Documenting Properties with <cfproperty>

As you learned earlier, you can easily view a CFC's methods in the Component tree in the Dreamweaver's Application panel. You can also view them in the automatically generated reference page that ColdFusion produces if you visit a CFC's URL with your browser. Since a CFC's properties are also important, it would be nice if there was an easy way to view them too.

ColdFusion provides a tag called <cfproperty> that lets you provide information about each variable in the this scope that you want to document as an official property of a component. The <cfproperty> tags must be placed at the top of the CFC file, just within the <cfcomponent> tag, before any initialization code.

The syntax for the <cfproperty> tag is shown in Table 26.9.

NOTE

The <cfproperty> tag doesn't actively create a property in this version of ColdFusion. Adding the tag to a .cfc file doesn't cause your component to behave differently. It simply causes the information you provide in the <cfproperty> tag to be included in the automatic documentation and in the Dreamweaver interface.

If you're using the CFC framework to create Web Services, the <cfproperty> tag becomes important, because the property will become part of the published description of the service. Creating Web Services isn't much harder than creating ordinary CFCs, but it's beyond the scope of this book. For details, see Vol. 3, *Advanced Application Development*.

Table 26.9   <cfproperty> Tag Syntax

ATTRIBUTE	DESCRIPTION
name	The name of the property. This should match the name of the variable in the THIS scope that is used within the component's methods.
type	The data type of the property, such as numeric, string, or query.
required	Whether the property is required.
default	The initial value of the property.
hint	An explanation of what the property does or represents.
displayName	An alternate name for the property.

To document the rotationInterval property officially, you could add the following <cfproperty> tag to Listing 26.10, between the opening <cfcomponent> tag and the series of <cfset> tags:

```
<!--- Property: Rotation Interval --->
<cfproperty
name="RotationInterval"
type="numeric"
required="No"
default="5"
hint="The number of seconds between film rotations.">
```

NOTE

Remember that the <cfproperty> idoesn't actively create a property in this version of ColdFusion. Just because you add the <cfproperty> tag to document the THIS.rotationInterval property, it doesn't mean that you can remove the <cfset> tag that actually creates the variable and gives it its initial value.

CFCs, Shared Scopes, and Locking

In Chapter 19, "Introducing the Web Application Framework," in Vol. 1, *Getting Started*, you learned that it's important to beware of *race conditions*. A race condition is any type of situation where strange, inconsistent behavior might arise if multiple page requests try to change the values of the same variables at the same time. Race conditions aren't specific to ColdFusion development; all Web developers should bear them in mind. See Chapter 19 for more information about this important topic.

Since these last few examples have encouraged you to consider storing instances of your CFCs in the APPLICATION or SESSION scope, you may be wondering whether there is the possibility of logical race conditions occurring in your code, and whether you should use the <cflock> tag or some other means to protect against them if necessary.

The basic answer is that packaging your code in a CFC doesn't make it more or less susceptible to race conditions. If the nature of the information you are accessing within a CFC's methods is such that it shouldn't be altered or accessed by two different page requests at the same time, you most likely should use the <cflock> tag to make sure one page request waits for the other before continuing.

Direct Access to Shared Scopes from CFC Methods

If your CFC code is creating or accessing variables in the APPLICATION or SESSION scope directly (that is, if the words APPLICATION or SESSION appear in the body of your CFC's <cffunction> blocks), place <cflock> tags around those portions of the code. The <cflock> tags should appear inside the <cffunction> blocks, not around them. Additionally, you should probably place <cflock> tags around any initialization code (that is, within <cfcomponent> but outside any <cffunction> blocks) that refers to APPLICATION or SESSION. In either case, you would probably use scope= "SESSION" or scope="APPLICATION" as appropriate; alternatively, you could use <cflock>'s NAME attribute as explained in Chapter 19 if you wanted finer-grained control over your locks.

Also, ask yourself why you're even using the APPLICATION or SESSION scope in your CFC code. Is it really necessary? If the idea is to persist information, why not simply store the CFC itself in one of the persistent scopes? This will be helpful if you decide that the information needs to be specific to the SESSION and not to the APPLICATION. If you never directly referenced any scope in your CFC code, but instead simply stored the CFC in one of the scopes, "moving" the CFC then becomes a simple matter.

Locking Access to the THIS Scope

The FilmRotationCFC example in this chapter (Listing 26.10) doesn't manipulate variables in the APPLICATION or SESSION scopes; instead, the CFC is designed so that entire instances of the CFC can be stored in the APPLICATION or SESSION scope (or the SERVER scope, for that matter) as the application's needs change over time. This is accomplished by only using variables in the THIS scope, rather than referring directly to SESSION or APPLICATION, within the CFC's methods.

You may wonder how to approach locking in such a situation. I recommend that you create a unique lock name for each component when each instance is first instantiated. You can easily accomplish this with ColdFusion's CreateUUID() function. For instance, you could use a line like this in the component's initialization code, within the body of the <cfcomponent> tag:

```
<cfset THIS.lockName = CreateUUID()>
```

The THIS.lockName variable (or property, if you prefer) is now guaranteed to be unique for each instance of the CFC, regardless of whether the component is stored in the APPLICATION or the

SERVER scope. You can use this value as the `name` of a `<cflock>` tag within any of the CFC's methods. For instance, if you were working with a CFC called `ShoppingCartCFC` and creating a new method called `addItemToCart()`, you could structure it according to this basic outline:

```
<cffunction name="addItemToCart">
 <cflock name="#THIS.lockName#" type="Exclusive" timeout="10">
 <!--- Changes to sensitive data in THIS scope goes here --->
 </cflock>
</cffunction>
```

In Chapter 22, a shopping-cart component is created that locks accesses to the THIS scope using this technique. Refer to the `ShoppingCart.cfc` example in that chapter for a complete example. For more information on the `<cflock>` tag, especially when to use `type="Exclusive"` or `type="ReadOnly"`, see the "Using Locks to Protect Against Race Conditions" section in Chapter 19.

Learning More About CFCs

In Chapter 22, there is a CFC called `ShoppingCart`, which is another example of a component that is designed to be stored in the SESSION scope. Look at this example to see another way in which a helpful and independent CFC can be created that encapsulates a real-world concept or metaphorical object (in this case, a shopping cart).

Learning About Advanced CFC Concepts

This chapter has introduced you to the most important concepts about the new ColdFusion Components functionality in ColdFusion. That said, there is more to the CFC framework than I have been able to present here.

→ In Vol. 3, *Advanced Application Development,* you will find chapters on advanced CFC concepts such as: component inheritance and method overriding using the `extends` attribute of the `<cfcomponent>` tag; securing access to individual CFC methods with the `roles` attribute of the `<cffunction>` tag; use of the `getMetaData()` function to determine a CFC's characteristics programmatically at runtime; accessing component methods with JSP tag library style syntax, using the `<cfimport>` tag; and exposure of CFC methods as Web Services so that other systems, including participants in Microsoft's .NET Framework or systems that work under Sun's Java umbrella, can use the methods over the Internet.

CHAPTER 27

Creating Advanced ColdFusion Components

The previous chapter covered the basics of ColdFusion Components: how to create them, use them, store data in them, and make them persist. But you can do a lot more with ColdFusion Components. This chapter presents many of the more advanced features of ColdFusion Components, including inheritance, security, type checking, and serialization. This chapter also covers a few features of components new to ColdFusion 8.

Specifying Data Types and Type Checking

As mentioned in the previous chapter, methods in ColdFusion Components can return types through the use of the returntype attribute of cffunction. Consider this example:

```
<cffunction name="listFilms" returnType="query" output="false">
```

Here, the method must return a variable with a data type of query. Any other return type would cause an error. For example, it might make sense to return a value of the Boolean false because no valid query could be returned, but that would throw an error. Instead, you'd want to return an empty query or throw a custom error.

You can also specify data types as arguments for methods. In any cfargument, you can specify the type that your method must return (just as with cfparam). This specification can prevent you from having to create a lot of custom error-handling code in your application to check the data types of arguments passed in, and it also helps in introspection (covered in more depth later in this chapter and also in Chapter 26, "Building Reusable Components"). In addition, the cfproperty tag allows you to document for introspection local variables and define a type that the arguments will have for self-documentation.

The data type attributes of cffunction and cfargument are required when creating Web services (see Chapter 68, "Creating and Consuming Web Services," in *Adobe ColdFusion 8 Web Application Construction Kit, Volume 3: Advanced Application Development*, for more information).

Table 27.1 lists the allowed data types.

Table 27.1 Type Values Used for `returntype` (`cffunction`) and `type` (`cfargument`, `cfproperty`)

TYPE	DESCRIPTION
Any	Can be any type.
Array	ColdFusion Array complex data type.
Binary	String of 1s and 0s.
Boolean	Can be `1`, `0`, `true`, `false`, `yes`, or `no`.
Date	Any value that can be parsed into a date. Note that POP dates (see the `ParseDateTime` function) and time zones are not accepted, but simple timestamps and ODBC formatted dates and times are accepted.
GUID	The argument must be a UUID or GUID of the form xxxxxxxx-xxxx-xxxx-xxxx-xxxxxxxxxxxx where each x is a character representing a hexadecimal number (0-9A-F)
Numeric	Integer or float.
Query	ColdFusion Query Result Set.
String	ColdFusion String simple data type.
Struct	ColdFusion Struct complex data type.
UUID	The argument must be a ColdFusion UUID of the form xxxxxxxx-xxxx-xxxx-xxxxxxxxxxxxxxxx where each x is a character representing a hexadecimal number (0-9A-F).
variableName	A string formatted according to ColdFusion variable naming conventions (a letter, followed by any number of alphanumeric characters or underscores).
Void	Does not return a value.

If anything else is specified as a return type, ColdFusion processes it as returning a component for which properties have been defined. This technique allows components to define complex types for Web services. Chapter 67, "Using Server-Side HTTP and FTP," in Vol. 3, *Advanced Application Development*, discusses this feature in depth. Typically, though, the standard data types will suffice.

Our Actors master-detail application has two data-access actions—currently each one a `cfquery` on each of the two CFML pages. Our Actors component, then, will have two methods, each defined with a `<cffunction>` tag. `<cffunction>` uses the same introspection attributes as `<cfcomponent>`: `displayname` and `hint`.

Another attribute, `output`, can be set to `"no"` if your function doesn't write anything out. This works like a virtual `<cfsilent>` tag, and causes all the whitespace in a pure code function to be discarded by ColdFusion. If you set it to `"yes"`, your function works as if the entire function is wrapped in a `<cfoutput>` tag, and anything in number signs (#) will be interpreted as ColdFusion variables. If you don't specify the `output` attribute, it works like any other ColdFusion code—you need to either wrap output in `<cfoutput>` or use the `WriteOutput()` function.

Finally, there are two additional arguments you can use when defining components in ColdFusion: roles, used to secure functionality by user; and access, used to hide implementation details. We'll come back to these later in this chapter.

Using the GetMetaData() Function

You can dump a component with cfdump. For example, you can dump FilmRotationCFC.cfc from the previous chapter as shown here:

```
<cfobject component="FilmRotationCFC" name="cfcFilmRotation">
<cfdump var="#cfcFilmRotation#">
```

The result is shown in Figure 27.1.

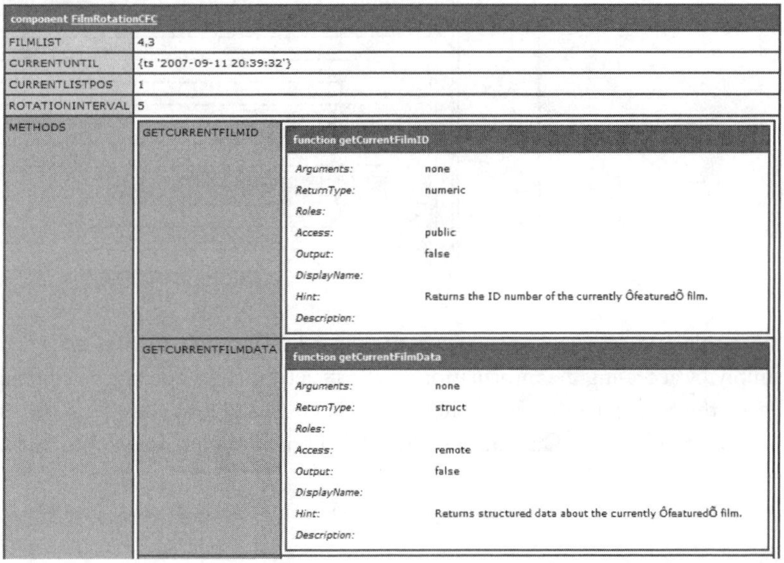

Figure 27.1

The cfdump output for a component.

As you can see, the dump shows the component's methods and instance data. This data can be useful to your code. ColdFusion provides a means to programmatically examine an instance of a component to get this data: the getMetaData() function. The getMetaData() function returns a structure containing the same information that you can see in the HTML view of a component that cfdump provides.

There are two syntaxes for using the getMetaData() function. From outside of a component, pass the function a reference to the component object. Within a component, pass the function the component's own scope keyword THIS. So, for example, the code

```
<cfobject component="FilmRotationCFC" name="cfcFilmRotation">
<cfdump var="#getMetaData(cfcFilmRotation)#">
```

will produce a structure similar to that shown in Figure 27.2.

Figure 27.2

The cfdump output for getMetaData().

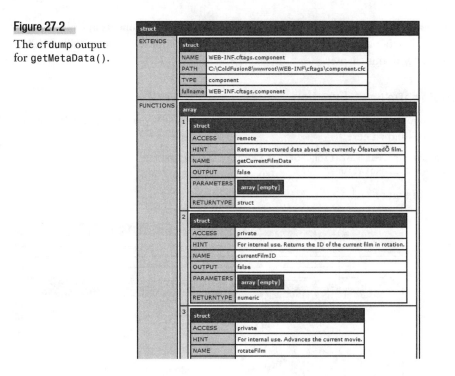

With this data, you could produce component HTML documentation in whatever form you wish, simply by accessing the information in the structure. This approach can be useful when you want to check the properties of a component that's been passed into a function or verify whether a method is implemented in it. This specification is demonstrated in Listing 27.1.

Listing 27.1 getMetaData.cfm—Display Data Using getMetaData()

```
<!---
  getMetaData.cfm
  Demonstrate use of getMetaData() function
--->
<!--- instantiate the FilmRotationCFC object into cfcfilmRotation --->
<cfobject component="FilmRotationCFC" name="cfcFilmRotation">
<!--- now get the metadata, into the ourMetaData function --->
<cfset ourMetaData = getMetaData(cfcFilmRotation)>

<cfoutput>
<!--- Show the displayName and size; we could also show the hint,
  path, etc. --->
<h3>Welcome to the #ourMetaData. Name#!</h3>
Enjoy our #arrayLen(ourMetaData.functions)# functions:
<ul>
<!--- loop through and show each function's name; could also show
    hint, parameters array, etc. but let's keep it simple. --->
<cfloop index="thisFunction" from="1" to="#arrayLen(ourMetaData.functions)#">
<li>#ourMetaData.functions[thisFunction]. Name#</li>
</cfloop>
</ul>
</cfoutput>
```

Managing Components

Now that we've made a component, learned how to use it, and documented its capabilities, we need to figure out how it best fits into the overall architecture of an application.

The first question to answer is where to put the physical component files. They will be accessible from any of the following:

- Web server directories—both physical and virtual
- ColdFusion mappings directories
- ColdFusion custom tag directories

In other words, just about anywhere! The location does, however, matter very much in the way that components interact. This is where component packages come into the architecture of your application. As components increase in complexity, the amount of code contained in a single component file can become unwieldy. It's very useful to be able to divide component code among multiple files, generally grouped by common functionality.

Packages really are nothing more than directories containing CFC files. They are best used for organizing the components that may be common to a particular application or task. For example, an intranet application may have our Actor Management system as one of many smaller applications. In that case, it would be wise to have a folder for the entire intranet application, under which would be a folder for each of the subapplications:

```
[Web root]\OWS\Components\ActorManager\Actors.cfc
[Web root]\OWS\Components\FilmManager\Actors.cfc
```

This arrangement would allow components to avoid naming conflicts as well—a component for one application can be named the same as that of another application as long as it is located in a different package—in other words, in a different directory.

Working with Inheritance

Frequently it is useful to have components that implement similar functionality in different ways. For example, you might have a *circle* component and a *square* component. Each has a *draw* method: The circle component draws a circle on the screen, and the square component draws a square. Each also has independent properties: for example, the circle has *circumference*, and the square has *length*. The two components also have a lot in common: They each have *perimeter* and *area*. The square and circle components are special cases of a shape; they have everything a shape has, plus more. Thus, it would make sense to create a single *parent* component called *shape* that has the information that is common to all types of shapes, and to have *child* components that inherit this information and also add their own. Thus, square, as a child of shape, would have all the things that shape has plus length, and it would implement its own variation of draw.

Just as we can use the word *my* to refer to a CFC's THIS scope ("*my* ID is 123 and *my* First Name is Fred…"), in *inheritance*, we can think of the words *is a*. A square *is a* shape. An actor *is a* person. A cat *is a* mammal. In these cases, *actor*, *square*, and *cat* are children of *person*, *shape*, and *mammal*. Some parents can exist by themselves; there can be a person who is not an actor. Some other parents, though, are abstract; *shape* can't draw itself without knowing what shape it is. Rather, the parent is intended as more of a handy template upon which more specific things can be based.

In a movie studio application, actors and directors are both types of people, with some properties that are common and some that are unique. So, for types of *people*, you could create a component to represent a *person* and have each of these variants inherit from it.

Listing 27.2 shows the basic person component. It has a first name and last name (stored in the THIS scope) and has one function that "shows" the person by outputting the first and last name.

Listing 27.2 `person.cfc`—The Basic person Component

```
<!---
  person.cfc
  Component that contains a "person", firstname and lastname only
  Modified by Ken Fricklas (kenf@fricklas.com)
  Modified: 8/1/2007
  Code from Listing 27.2
--->
<cfcomponent displayName="Person" hint="Parent Component - Person">

<cfparam name="THIS.firstName" default="John">
<cfparam name="THIS.lastName" default="Doe">

<cffunction name="showPerson" output="true" hint="showPerson in person.cfc" >
  <B>#THIS.firstName# #THIS.lastName#</B>
</cffunction>

</cfcomponent>
```

A component inherits from a parent component with the EXTENDS attribute of the `<cfcomponent>` tag. The value of the attribute is the name of the component upon which the new component should be based. Thus, a director component could consist of nothing more than this code:

```
<cfcomponent displayName="Movie Director" extends="person">
</cfcomponent>
```

Now, the director is an exact copy of the person component and has inherited all the properties and methods of its parent. A CFML page, then, could create an instance of the director and invoke the methods of the person component as though they were part of the director component:

```
<cfobject component="director" name="myDirector">
<cfoutput>#myDirector.showPerson()#</cfoutput>
```

NOTE

In fact, *every* component inherits from a root component: `WEB-INF.cftags.component`. This component is literally the mother of all components. In its default case, it is simply an empty file without any functions or properties, but you can implement custom logging, debugging, and other behavior by modifying this root component.

Overriding Properties and Methods

Just because the parent does something doesn't mean that the child is stuck with it. The component can override parts of the parent component. If we want the director component to set the first-Name and lastName properties to different values than those of the person component, we simply add code that redefines the values. The director, because it's the one being invoked, will take precedence. So the director component is now coded like this:

```
<cfcomponent displayName="Movie Director" extends="person">
  <cfset THIS.firstName = "Jim">
  <cfset THIS.lastName = "Jarofmush">
</cfcomponent>
```

When invoked from the CFML page, this component now will output "Jim Jarofmush" instead of "John Doe". The THIS scope assignments made in a child override those of its parent. Likewise, adding a showPerson function to the director component will override the showPerson function from the parent:

```
<cffunction name="showPerson" output="true" hint="showPerson in director.cfc">
  <B>A swell director named #THIS.firstName# #THIS.lastName#</B>
</cffunction>
```

Using the SUPER Scope

What if a child component needs to use the functionality in a method in its parent, but it has redefined that method already? In our director component, we could call the parent showPerson method, but we want to add our own information to it. We do this with the special scope SUPER. SUPER acts similarly to THIS, but instead of referring to a property or method in the current component, it refers to the property or method in the component's parent. We could redefine showPerson in the director component like this:

```
<cffunction name="showPerson" output="true" hint="showPerson in director.cfc">
  <B>A swell director</B> - #super.showPerson()#
</cffunction>
```

This code calls the showPerson method in the person component.

In addition to the child's being able to invoke functions that are really part of the parent component (and overriding them, if desired), the parent can call functions that are part of the child by referencing them in the instance's THIS scope. Say we added a function called showDetail to the director component:

```
<cfset THIS.credits = arrayNew(1)>
<cfset THIS.credits[1] = "The Phantom Dentist">
<cfset THIS.credits[2] = "Austin Showers">
<cfset THIS.credits[3] = "Men in Slacks II">

<cffunction name="showDetail" output="true">
  Credits include:
  <UL>
  <cfloop index="i" from="1" to="#arrayLen(THIS.credits)#">
```

```
      <LI>#THIS.credits[i]#</LI>
      </cfloop>
      </UL>
   </cffunction>
```

We could then modify the showPerson function in the person component to optionally call showDetail:

```
<cffunction name="showPerson" output="true" hint="showPerson in person.cfc">
  <cfargument name="showDetail" required="false" type="boolean"
    default="false">
  <B>#THIS.firstName# #THIS.lastName#</B>
  <cfif arguments.showDetail>
    <BR>#THIS.showDetail()#
  </cfif>
  </cffunction>
```

Since the director component wants the showPerson method to call its showDetail method, we change its showPerson method to pass in this argument, like this:

```
<cffunction name="showPerson" output="true" hint="showPerson in director.cfc">
  <B>A swell director</B> - #super.showPerson(true)#
</cffunction>
```

In the calling template now, we can call the showPerson function in the director component:

```
<cfobject component="director" name="myDirector">
<cfoutput>#myDirector.showPerson()#</cfoutput>
```

The result of our showPerson function now will be a combination of showPerson from the person component and showDetail from the director component:

```
A swell director - Jim Jarofmush
Credits include:
· The Phantom Dentist
· Austin Showers
· Men in Slacks II
```

This technique can be useful when multiple components are descendents of the same parent but require slightly different methods. Say we based an actor component on the same "person" parent using this code:

```
<cfcomponent displayName="Movie Actor" extends="person">
  <cfset THIS.firstName = "Judi">
  <cfset THIS.lastName = "Dents">

  <cffunction name="showDetail" output="true">
    Star of the hit <EM>The Importance of Being Sternest</EM>.
  </cffunction>

</cfcomponent>
```

When the showPerson function is invoked, the appropriate showDetail function is used, depending on whether the component is an actor or director (see Listing 27.3).

Listing 27.3 `index.cfm`—Calling Components to Show Inheritance

```
<!--- instantiate an actor and a director --->
<cfobject component="director" NAME="myDirector">
<cfobject component="actor" NAME="myActor">
<!--- demonstrate that showPerson calls different showDetail functions for each --->
<cfoutput>
  Directed by:<br>
    #myDirector.showPerson()# <!--- overridden in the director component --->
  <br>
  Starring:<br>
    #myActor.showPerson(true)# <!--- must pass argument true to have the showPerson
call showDetail, since it's not overridden --->
</cfoutput>
```

This code results in this output:

```
Directed by:
A swell director - Jim Jarofmush
Credits include:
· The Phantom Dentist
· Austin Showers
· Men in Slacks II
Starring:
Judi Dents
Star of the hit The Importance of Being Sternest.
```

Must you use inheritance in your ColdFusion applications? Certainly not. But it can be very useful in ways similar to other code-reuse techniques. Components can be built-in "branches," as in a family tree with chains of ancestral parent components, each providing base functionality to their children.

Component packages can help with this type of organization, too, to make applications more easily maintainable. In that case, the `extends="..."` attribute uses the same package path syntax as a `<cfinvoke>` tag. For example, to inherit from a component called `"person"` in the package `myApp.components`, the `<cfcomponent>` tag would be coded like this:

```
<cfcomponent extends="myApp.components.person">
```

Defining Interfaces

When designing components, it's frequently useful to define a template for anyone passing components to general functions. For example, you might create a function that takes as an argument an instance of a cast or crew member of a movie and calls a method named `getResume` to get a copy of the crew member's resume as a query, and another method named `showPersonHTML` that shows the crew member's name and information in an HTML display.

When requesting several implementations of this function to implement different types of cast members, actors, directors, producers, and so on, you might want these components to each do everything differently—you don't want them to inherit from a common parent, but they all have to implement a minimum set of functionality to meet the requirements of the system.

The definition of functions without actual implementation is a special type of component definition called an *interface*. An interface is basically a contract between a component and a system. You define an interface in a file with an extension of .cfc, but instead of enclosing the component with cfcomponent tags, you use a new–for–ColdFusion 8 tag called cfinterface. Any component that implements the interface must contain all the methods defined in it, or the system will display an error.

Listing 27.4 contains an interface for the component just described.

Listing 27.4 `iCastCrew.cfc`—An Interface

```
<cfinterface hint="cast or crewmember interface">
    <cffunction name="getResume" access="public" returntype="query" hint="return
resume as query">
    </cffunction>
    <cffunction name="showPersonHTML" access="public" returntype="string" hint="show
person information as HTML">
        <cfargument name="detail" type="boolean" required="no" default="true"
hint="show detailed information">
    </cffunction>
</cfinterface>
```

Introspection and inheritance (via the extends attribute of cfinterface) can be used with interfaces the same way as with components. Figure 27.3 shows the introspection when you open iCastCrew.cfc in a browser.

Figure 27.3

Component introspection.

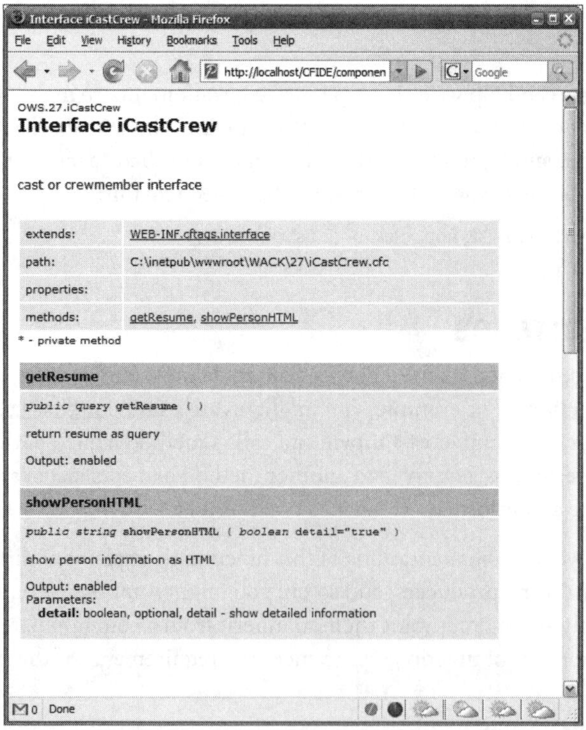

NOTE

Interfaces are typically given names that start with a lowercase *i*–for example, `iComponent.cfc`–to distinguish them from other components.

To make sure that a component implements an interface, you use the `implements` keyword in the `cfcomponent` tag; for example, to make the director an implementation of `iCastCrew`, you would change the first line to:

```
<cfcomponent displayName="Movie Director" extends="person" implements="iCastCrew">
```

If you ran this code, you would get the error shown in Figure 27.4, since the director component is missing some of the functions defined in the interface.

Figure 27.4

Interface error.

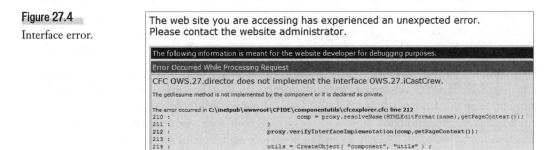

The web site you are accessing has experienced an unexpected error.
Please contact the website administrator.

The following information is meant for the website developer for debugging purposes.

Error Occurred While Processing Request

CFC OWS.27.director does not implement the interface OWS.27.iCastCrew.

The getResume method is not implemented by the component or it is declared as private.

The error occurred in **C:\inetpub\wwwroot\CFIDE\componentutils\cfcexplorer.cfc: line 212**

```
210 :                        comp = proxy.resolveName(HTMLEditFormat(name),getPageContext());
211 :                    }
212 :                    proxy.verifyInterfaceImplementation(comp,getPageContext());
213 :
214 :                    utils = CreateObject( "component", "utils" ) ;
```

Implementing Security

ColdFusion provides two ways to secure the functionality that you encapsulate in a ColdFusion component: roles-based authorization, and access control. Chapter 61, "Understanding Security," in Vol. 3, *Advanced Application Development*, discusses application user authentication and authorization, which allows the assignment of roles to your application's users. This roles-based security can also be applied to the functions in a CFC. The second technique, access control, was used in the preceding chapter in every `cffunction` tag as the attribute `access="..."`.

Implementing Access Control

The `access` attribute of the `<cffunction>` tag basically answers the question, "Who can use this function?" The attribute has four options: `private`, `package`, `public` (the default), and `remote`. These four options represent, in that order, the degree of openness of the function.

The `access` options range from a narrow group of potential consumers to a very broad audience. The consumers allowed by each option are as follows:

- **Private**. Only other functions within the same CFC can invoke the function.
- **Package**. Only components in the same package can invoke the function.

- **Public**. Any CFML template or CFC on the same server can invoke the function.

- **Remote**. Any CFML template or CFC on the same server can invoke the function, as can Adobe Flash applications (using Flash Remoting) and Web Services clients.

Within any given CFC, you can have functions of any type mixed together. Remember, it's the function and not the component itself to which you grant or deny access.

Let's take a look at each `access` option to see how they can be used.

Private

I was at a hotel one weekend and passed by a room from which drifted some terrific music and the sound of laughing, happy people. Naturally I wanted to see what the occasion was and join in the festivities. At the door, though, I was met by a gruff and rather large gentleman who blocked my way and shook his head. He pointed to a small sign on a brass post that read "Private Function."

Silly story, but you see the connection. Private functions are the most "exclusive." Any consumer (that is, a CFML page, Web service client, Flash application, and so on) outside of a CFC cannot use a function that has been designated as `access="private"`. Private functions are for use only in the CFC where they are coded. How can they be used at all, then, you ask? They are used by other functions in the same CFC. Generally, private functions are functions whose only purpose is to help other functions. In Chapter 26, `FilmRotationCFC` had a number of private functions: for example, `randomizedFilmList` and `currentFilmID`. Neither of these functions would ever be accessed directly from outside of the component. Rather, they are called from other functions, as we saw with the `getCurrentFilmID` method. We should mark them private, because they are only used internally to the CFC, and by exposing them to the outside world we risk letting people in on our implementation.

Why bother? You should always hide as much information about implementation as you can. Hiding information gives you the flexibility to change the component's implementation at a later time, due to changed requirements or developing a better algorithm. It also protects the user from changes in your implementation, because code can become dependent on functionality that was never intended to be exposed, and break when it changes. Marking the code private forces your CFC's users to play by your rules when using it.

TIP

Within a component, methods can call each other using function syntax instead of `<cfinvoke>` (see the earlier section "Inheritance"). Since private methods are only available for use by other methods within the same component, you'll probably find yourself always invoking them as functions.

Now, here's something to watch out for: If you try to invoke a private function from anywhere but inside the component itself, you'll get an error that says "The method `'myPrivateFunction'` could not be found in component (*whatever*)." You'll then think that you typed the name wrong, and go back and check and reenter your code, and still get the same error. "But I can see the function *right there*! How can it not be found?!?" you'll cry to the heavens. You've not lost your mind—it's just a private function. To be certain, look at the self-documenting view of the CFC in a browser. You'll see an asterisk next to the function's name: `"aPrivateFunction*"`. Then, under the methods list at the top of the page, you'll see a teeny explanation: `*private method`.

Package

Earlier in this chapter, you saw how component packages could help you organize the components in an application. Likewise, `access="package"` can help you control the access to your component's functionality within applications. A primary use of package access can be to prevent applications that happen to have functions with the same name from accidentally calling each other.

For example, Orange Whip Studios uses an application that lets the catering department order sandwiches for the movie shoots. A component in this application has a method that adjusts the number of sandwiches needed for a given day. The studio also uses a casting department application that can hire and fire actors. In that application, there is a component that helps calculate staff levels and make the firing decisions. Both of these methods have the apt but far-from-original name of `updateQuantity`. Without access control at the package level, someone developing an application could inadvertently end up firing 300 actors and leaving the remaining ones very hungry.

Public

The default option for a function's access setting is `public`. It's a somewhat confusing term, in that it doesn't mean "Anyone in the public can use this function." People who mistake the meaning of `public` usually find themselves coming to the assumption, "I don't want this function to be available as a Web service, so I shouldn't make it publicly accessible. It's just for my application, so I guess that would make it a private function." They then code a page somewhere that tries to invoke that function, and they get the less-than-intuitive error type that was mentioned earlier for `private` access: "The method (*whatever*) could not be found."

Public really means "accessible by the ColdFusion server in which the component is running." So any other component can invoke the function, as can any CFML page.

NOTE

Public (the default access level) makes CFCs behave just like custom tags and are as equally secure.

Here again, those people who *cannot* use a public function are precisely those you would ordinarily consider to be the "public"—other people on the Internet somewhere trying to use a Web service, for example.

Watch out for HTTP and form posts and public functions. Because the page that you post to happens to be on the same machine as the component that it invokes, many people think that posting a form to a public function should work. But a form post, just like a URL invocation, uses HTTP—it does not access the function from *within* the server. An HTTP request is just like any other remote request and thus necessitates the most open access option, `remote`.

Remote

A remote function is what you might have thought a public function is. It's open to anyone who wants it—the whole "public." The function can be used by the same component, another component (regardless of the package in which it's placed), any CFML page (on the server), HTTP requests, Web Services clients, and Adobe Flash applications.

To sum up, you can see how a lack of attention to the access attribute of a function can cause lots of trouble. A function that performs some sensitive business function could be inadvertently made available to the whole world if it were set as remote instead of private. Likewise, a business partner who tries to consume a Web service from your application may not find it in the WSDL ColdFusion creates for your component if you forgot to set the function's access to remote. (Refer to Chapter 68 in Vol. 3, *Advanced Application Development*, for more information on creating Web services and WSDL with ColdFusion.)

Implementing Role-Based Security in CFCs

In some applications, you'll want to control access to a component's functions based on who is using your application. This will be most common in traditional, HTML-based user interface applications, but it may also be true of Adobe Flash applications. Role-based security is not, however, a common approach to securing access to Web services, since a Web service client is a *program* and not an *individual*.

To see this technique in action, let's go back to the actors component that was created earlier in this chapter—the one that retrieves information about all actors. Part of the Orange Whip Studios Web application allows studio executives to review the salaries of the stars—how much should the studio expect to fork over for their next box-office smash? Of course, this information is not exactly something that they want just anybody seeing.

First we need to create the basic security framework for this part of the application, with the security tags in ColdFusion: <cflogin>, <cfloginuser>, and <cflogout>. (We discuss this process in detail in Chapter 23, "Securing Your Applications," online.)

For the purposes of this exercise, we'll just test by running the cfloginuser tag with the role we want to test with:

```
<cfloginuser name="Test" password="dummy" roles="Producers">
```

Any roles for the logged-in user will be the roles that correspond to those listed in our component function—more on this after we create the function (Listing 27.5).

The function will be simple: It takes an Actor ID as an argument, queries that actor's salary history, and returns a recordset. Notice, though, that the roles attribute in the <cffunction> tag has a comma-delimited list of values. Only users who have authenticated and been assigned one or more of those roles will be allowed to invoke the method.

Listing 27.5 `actor.cfc`—The Salary Method

```
<!--- Demonstrate roles --->
<cffunction name="getActorSalary" returnType="query" roles="Producers, Executives">
  <cfargument name="actorID" type="numeric" required="true"
    displayName="Actor ID" hint="The ID of the Actor">
  <cfquery name="salaries" dataSource="ows">
    SELECT Actors.ActorID, Actors.NameFirst, Actors.NameLast,
      FilmsActors.Salary, Films.MovieTitle
    FROM Films
    INNER JOIN (Actors INNER JOIN FilmsActors
     ON Actors.ActorID = FilmsActors.ActorID)
       ON Films.FilmID = FilmsActors.FilmID
    WHERE Actors.ActorID = #Arguments.actorID#
  </cfquery>
  <cfreturn salaries>
</cffunction>
```

The roles assigned to this function are Producers and Executives—they don't want any prying eyes finding this sensitive data. All we need now, then, is a page to invoke the component—something simple, as in Listing 27.6.

Listing 27.6 `showSalary.cfm`—Show Salary Page

```
<!---
  showSalary.cfm
  Demonstrate CFC roles
  Modified by Ken Fricklas (kenf@fricklas.com)
  Modified: 8/17/2007
--->
<HTML>
<HEAD>
<TITLE>What were they paid?</TITLE>
</HEAD>

<BODY>
<!--- Make sure they are logged in. Change roles to "User" to see what happens if
they don't have sufficient access. --->
<cfloginuser name="Test" password="dummy" roles="Producers">
<!--- Invoke actors component.  getActorSalary method will fail unless
  they have sufficient access. --->
<cfinvoke
 component="actor"
 method="getActorSalary"
 returnVariable="salaryHistory">
  <cfinvokeargument name="actorID" value="17"/>
</cfinvoke>
<h1>Salaries of our stars...</h1>
<cfoutput>
<H2>
#salaryHistory.NameFirst# #salaryHistory.NameLast#</H2>
<cfloop query="salaryHistory">
  #MovieTitle# - #dollarFormat(Salary)#<BR>
</cfloop>
</cfoutput>
</BODY>
</HTML>
```

ColdFusion now has all it needs to control the access to the component. The process will work in this order:

1. The Show Salary page is requested by a browser.

2. The `<cfinvoke>` tag is encountered, specifying the `Actor` component and the `getActorSalary` method.

3. An instance of the component is created, and the function is found.

4. Since the function has values specified in the `roles` attribute, a comparison is automatically made between the values in the `roles` attribute of the `<cffunction>` tag and those in the `roles` attributes that were set in the `<cfloginuser>` tag. If the user is not logged in, this function will fail.

5. A match will allow the function to be executed as usual; a failure will cause the following error: "Error Occurred While Processing Request—The current user is not authorized to invoke this method."

Notice that an unauthorized attempt to execute a secured function causes ColdFusion to throw an error. Consequently, you should put a `cftry` around any code that invokes secured functions (Listing 27.7).

Listing 27.7 `showSalary_final.cfm`—Catching a Secure Function Invocation

```
<!---
   showSalary_final.cfm
   Demonstrate CFC roles
   Modified by Ken Fricklas (kenf@fricklas.com)
   Modified: 8/17/2007
--->
<HTML>
<HEAD>
<TITLE>What were they paid?</TITLE>
</HEAD>

<BODY>
<!--- Make sure they are logged in. Change roles to "User" to see what happens if
they don't have sufficient access. --->
<cfloginuser name="Test" password="dummy" roles="Producers">
<!--- Invoke actors component.  getActorSalary method will fail unless
  they have sufficient access. --->
<cftry>
  <cfinvoke
    component="actor"
    method="getActorSalary"
    returnVariable="salaryHistory">
    <cfinvokeargument name="actorID" value="17"/>
  </cfinvoke>
  <cfcatch>
    What? Trying to steal company secrets? Get lost!
    <cfabort>
  </cfcatch>

  <h1>Salaries of our stars...</h1>
  <cfoutput>
```

Listing 27.7 (CONTINUED)

```
<H2>
#salaryHistory.NameFirst# #salaryHistory.NameLast#</H2>
<cfloop query="salaryHistory">
  #MovieTitle# - #dollarFormat(Salary)#<BR>
</cfloop>
</cfoutput>
</BODY>
</HTML>
```

This is not the only way to secure component functionality, of course. You could use the isUserIn-Role() function to check a user's group permissions before even invoking the function, or you could use Web server security for securing the CFML files themselves. The role-based security in CFCs is, however, a good option particularly if you are already using the ColdFusion authentication/authorization framework in an application.

Using the OnMissingMethod **Method**

It would be nice if all the CFCs that we write could handle their own errors. Starting in ColdFusion 8, any component can have a special method named OnMissingMethod that will run whenever code attempts to run a method that hasn't been defined in it. We can use this method to serve several purposes:

- Implement custom error handling. The OnMissingMethod method can be especially useful when methods in different child classes might be called, even though they are not implemented in a particular component. For example, we could use OnMissingMethod to handle a call to getActorSalary made to a director component.

- Run different code for several methods in a common place. If the same code can take the place of several methods, OnMissingMethod can provide a way to run the common code from a single point. This approach is not recommended, however; it's more straightforward to define all the methods separately and call the common code from each.

- Act as a proxy that calls another object or component that will actually implement the function. For example, you could create a component that is empty except for onMissingMethod that takes any method passed to it and calls a Web service on another machine that consumes the method name and its arguments and returns a value. This approach is a good way to implement a flexible, distributed system.

The onMissingMethod function takes exactly two arguments, which contain the name of the method that was being called and a structure with the arguments that were passed to it. For example, here is a simple onMissingMethod method:

```
<cffunction name="onMissingMethod">
  <cfargument name="missingMethodName" type="string">
  <cfargument name="missingMethodNameArguments" type="struct">
    Hey! You called <cfoutput>#arguments.missingMethodName#</cfoutput> and I haven't
got one!
</cffunction>
```

NOTE

Since onMissingMethod always returns successfully, if you can't handle an error in this method, you should throw a new error.

Distributed CFCs, Serialization, and ColdFusion 8

The previous chapter discussed storage of CFCs in the session scope. One problem with storing CFCs in this way is that when more than one server is in use, each server has its own session variables; if a user moves to another server during the course of a visit to your site, the session data can be lost. One way to solve this problem is to create "sticky" sessions, which requires special software or hardware—but what if the Web server goes down?

Many Java application servers that ColdFusion runs on can support distributed sessions. Basically, what the servers do is "serialize" the data in the session scope, which means that a server writes the data in a flat form (turns it into a string, in the same way that CFWDDX does) and passes it to all other servers in the cluster that might process the new request. No matter which server is used, it has a copy of the session data.

Before ColdFusion 8, components could not be serialized, so they would not be passed between machines as part of the session. In ColdFusion 8, however, components can be serialized and distributed.

NOTE

In Java parlance, this means that ColdFusion 8 CFCs now support the Java serializable interface. You can read more about this at `http://java.sun.com/developer/technicalArticles/Programming/serialization/`.

In addition, you can directly call the Java's `java.io.ObjectOutputStream` API to write objects to a file.

Listing 27.8 shows some sample code that checks to see whether a CFC exists in the session scope. If the CFC isn't found in the session, the code checks to see if a serialized copy of the component exists in a file and loads that. Finally, if the CFC is neither in the session nor on the disk, the CFC is instantiated and written out as a new serialized copy.

Listing 27.8 `serialize.cfm`—Serializing a CFC

```
<!---
   serialize.cfm
   Demonstrate CFC serialization
   Created by Ken Fricklas (kenf@fricklas.com)
   Modified: 9/10/2007
--->
<!DOCTYPE html PUBLIC "-//W3C//DTD XHTML 1.0 Transitional//EN"
"http://www.w3.org/TR/xhtml1/DTD/xhtml1-transitional.dtd">
<html xmlns="http://www.w3.org/1999/xhtml">
<head>
<meta http-equiv="Content-Type" content="text/html; charset=utf-8" />
<title>Serialize CFC</title>
</head>

<body>
<cfapplication sessionmanagement="yes" name="serialdemo">
<cfif not isdefined("session.cfcDirector")>
   <!--- check to see if we've got a copy --->
    <cftry>
       <cfset fileIn = CreateObject("java", "java.io.FileInputStream")>
         <cfset fileIn.init(expandpath("./serialized_director.txt"))>
```

Listing 27.8 (CONTINUED)

```
            <cfset objIn = CreateObject("java", "java.io.ObjectInputStream")>
            <cfset objIn.init(fileIn)>
            <cfset session.cfcDirector = objIn.readObject()>
            Read!
            <cfcatch>
                <!--- no copy to load, create it --->
                <cfset session.cfcDirector = createObject("component", "director")>
                <!--- save it --->
                <cfset fileOut = CreateObject("java", "java.io.FileOutputStream")>
                <cfset fileOut.init(expandpath("./serialized_director.txt"))>
                <cfset objOut = CreateObject("java", "java.io.ObjectOutputStream")>
                <cfset objOut.init(fileOut)>
                <cfset objOut.writeObject(session.cfcDirector)>
                Written!
            </cfcatch>
        </cftry>
    </cfif>
    <cfoutput>
        #session.cfcDirector.showPerson()#
    </cfoutput>
    </body>
    </html>
```

CFC Good Practices

Now that you have some understanding of ColdFusion Components—how to create and use them, how to extend them with OO concepts, and how to secure them—let's close with a few things that are always good to remember when using CFCs in your applications. Notice the heading for this section doesn't say "Best Practices"—CFCs are going to be used differently by everyone. They are not a strict framework. You may use them as a sort of "next generation" custom tag, or as the foundation of an implementation of an extremely formal OO pattern, or anything in between. Whatever your intent, here are some things that should become habit whenever you use components.

Use Hints

It may seem obvious to you what a particular function does or what the general use is for a component, but it may not be obvious to anyone else! This may be an incorrect attribution, and the quotation marks are mine—but a story goes that T.S. Eliot once gave a lecture toward the end of his life; he opened up the floor to questions. An eager young student began speaking about line four-hundred-something in *The Waste Land*, where Eliot had written some cryptic phrase; the student asked, "What, exactly, did you mean by that?" Eliot paused and, finally answered, "Young man, when I wrote that line only two people knew what it meant; myself and God. Now…God only knows!"

So use the hint attribute in every <cffunction> and <cfcomponent> tag. Use <cfproperty> to let your users know what properties your component makes available and what they contain. Anyone who reviews the work, including you, will use the CFC's self-documenting feature to much more advantage when brief, concise hints are included.

Avoid ACCESS="REMOTE"

CFC functions should only have their accesses set as remote if you *really* intend them to be used remotely. If you are not using SOAP Web Services or Flash Remoting in your application, and you don't intend to call the component directly from a URL, don't use this attribute. If a major point of CFCs is to encapsulate your business logic, then that is precisely the code you don't want to leave open to the "outside world."

Don't Expose Yourself Unless You Need To

Only use the THIS scope inside a component when you intend for your component's properties to be used directly. If you want to hide the details of your component's operation, create a function called getMyName() instead of allowing your components' users to use THIS.name. In this way you avoid allowing code that invokes your component to change its values without your component's being aware of it.

Use Data Types

<cffunction> has the attribute returntype="...", and <cfargument> has the attribute type="..." for setting data types of incoming arguments and outgoing return values. Use them! If you are using the component for SOAP Web Services, you have no choice. Without these attributes set properly, ColdFusion cannot make the WSDL to describe the service, and the Web service consumer will not know how to use it. When ColdFusion is using the component, these data type specifications are not required but are desirable. They will also make the self-documenting view of the component more useful.

For example, this line tells us without confusion that the method requires a numeric argument and returns a query recordset:

```
query getActorDetail ( required numeric actorID )
```

Design for Your Project

Don't feel bullied into using one specific design pattern when developing with ColdFusion Components. Each methodology has its own strengths and weaknesses, so feel free to select the methodology that best fits your specific project—or don't choose any! CFCs are flexible for a reason.

Use CFCs!

The best "good practice" on which to end this chapter is simply to use CFCs in all of your applications. There is no application so simple that it would not benefit from the inclusion of components. That one-page, single-access database query, tabular-output application needs a clean separation of logic and presentation as much as the most complex e-commerce site. An application built with CFCs is just as easy to build and will pay you back many times over in maintainability, code reuse, openness, and development team benefits. And all of these benefits come at no additional performance cost over ordinary methods of code reuse/encapsulation. Adobe has published performance numbers that show CFCs, custom tags, and user-defined functions all perform nearly the same.

PART VI

ColdFusion Configuration and Performance

CHAPTER 28

ColdFusion Server Configuration

The ColdFusion Administrator

The ColdFusion Administrator is a Web-based console that gives you an easy way to adjust the way ColdFusion behaves. Adobe provides this simple, straightforward Administrator so that we developers don't have to fiddle around with configuration files to get ColdFusion to behave the way we need it to.

Because the Administrator is Web-based, you can use it to monitor and configure your ColdFusion server from nearly anywhere, armed with nothing more than a browser and a password.

The primary functions of the ColdFusion Administrator are:

- Tweaking and monitoring the server's performance

- Telling ColdFusion where to find various external resources, such as databases, Verity full-text search collections, and mail servers

- Installing extensions to the CFML language, in the form of CFX tags, event gateways, and more

- Administrative tasks, such as backing up applications, reviewing log files, and securing portions of the server

This chapter will walk you through each part of the ColdFusion Administrator, explaining important settings and making recommendations along the way. Let's begin.

The Administrator Home Page

Log in to the Administrator as was explained back in Chapter 3, "Accessing the ColdFusion Administrator," in *Adobe ColdFusion 8 Web Application Construction Kit, Volume 1: Getting Started*.

Once you log in, the Administrator's home page appears. The Administrator is designed much like many other Web application interfaces, with a toolbar along the top and a navigation column along the left-hand side. This contains links to various online resources related to ColdFusion and the CFML developer community.

One really important—and often overlooked—screen is the System Information screen (there is a link at the top right of the page; look for a blue circle containing a white letter *i*). This screen has two primary uses:

- **Serial Number Change.** This screen is used to enter a new serial number, perhaps to upgrade the Developer Edition to a commercial edition, or upgrade ColdFusion Standard to ColdFusion Enterprise. This can be performed without a reinstallation and without restarting the server.

- **System Information.** Displays a detailed list of system settings, including ColdFusion information (version, edition, serial number, and more), and Java settings (JVM details, class path, and more).

TIP

If you get confused at any time during your visit to the ColdFusion Administrator, the Help link at the top-right corner of the screen will provide you with context-sensitive help about whatever Administrator page you happen to be on.

Server Settings

Let's begin our page-by-page tour of the ColdFusion Administrator with the Server Settings section, which makes up the first part of the left-hand navigation column. The pages in this section pertain mostly to tweaking the server's performance. Aside from the Data Sources page in the next section, this is the most important portion of the ColdFusion Administrator, and the part you will probably become most familiar with.

The Settings Page

The Settings page contains various options related to tweaking the server's performance and responsiveness to page requests from your users. It also contains options for controlling what happens when errors occur.

Timeout Requests After (Seconds)

To understand this setting, let's consider a metaphor. Let's say that your ColdFusion Server is a short-order cook in a busy downtown diner. This cook, who goes by the name of Gus, is new to the job and can handle five orders (page requests) at a time efficiently. However, at lunch hour, when office workers crowd the diner, Gus is suddenly flooded with 20 orders at a time. Bewildered by the avalanche of orders, Gus tries to fill all the orders at once. Unfortunately, because of his lack of experience, Gus's efficiency plunges, all the orders take longer, and the diner patrons become impatient.

We'll revisit Gus shortly, but for now, let's say that Gus is doing his usual thing, working on five orders at once. But, for whatever reason, one of the orders is taking much longer than usual (maybe he burned a burger, or dropped an order of fries on the ground, or ran out of egg salad and so has started making more). That order is taking up all of Gus's resources, keeping him from being able to start on the next person's order.

Gus always wants to be more efficient, so he puts a new policy into place. If any order takes him longer than three minutes to complete, he'll simply throw it away and forget about it! This will irritate the person who was waiting for that order, but it will allow him to complete more orders overall.

The analogy is pretty clear here. If you want to make sure that ColdFusion spends no more than 20 or 30 seconds working on a particular page request, go ahead and check the Timeout Requests After checkbox, and provide the appropriate value for the number of seconds. If a page takes longer than the number of seconds you specify, the page will simply halt and display an error message.

I strongly suggest that you enable this option, and set it to a relatively low number to start off with, perhaps 20 or 30. The idea is that any page that takes longer than 20 or 30 seconds has probably encountered some kind of serious problem (perhaps an unresponsive database) and thus won't be able to produce the desired output anyway, so it might as well be cut off so the server can move on to other page requests which should be easier for it to generate quickly.

You can override the request timeout you provide for this setting on a page-by-page basis. Just use the <cfsetting> tag, specifying the maximum number of seconds that you would like the page to be allowed to execute as the requesttimeout attribute. This use of <cfsetting> lets you provide a reasonably short timeout value in the Administrator, while still allowing certain pages (which you know really should take a while) to run for as long as they need to. For instance, if you wanted a particular page to run for up to five minutes (perhaps it performs a large file transfer operation with <cfftp>), you would use the following code, near the top of the page:

```
<!--- Allow this page to execute for up to five minutes --->
<cfsetting
 requesttimeout="300">
```

Keep in mind, however, that a long-running page could block other pages from executing. If you have set the maximum number of simultaneous requests to ten (as discussed in the previous section), and ten different page requests for the page with the <cfsetting> shown above were received around the same time, the server would essentially be unable to respond to any other page requests for up to five whole minutes. You might, therefore, want to use the <cflock> tag to make sure that only one instance of the long-running page is able to execute at the same time. You would use the <cflock> attribute with a name attribute that was unique to that particular ColdFusion file, like this:

```
<cftry>
<cflock
name="MyLongRunningFTPTransferPage"
type="EXCLUSIVE"
timeout="30">

<!--- Allow this page to execute for up to five minutes --->
<cfsetting
```

```
requesttimeout="300">

<!---
...long running code would go here...
--->
</cflock>

<!--- If the lock can't be obtained, display a message and stop --->
<cfcatch type="Lock">
Sorry, but another user is currently using this page.
Because this page is hard on the server, only one person is
allowed to execute it at once. Please try again in a few minutes.
<cfabort>
</cfcatch>
</cftry>
```

Alternatively, you could use a `name` value that was the same for all long-running pages; this would ensure that only one of the long-running pages was allowed to execute at one time.

➡ For more information about `<cflock>`, see Chapter 19, "Introducing the Web Application Framework," in Vol. 1, *Getting Started*.

NOTE

Of course, you can customize the look of the error message that appears if a page takes longer than the number of seconds you specify. See the Site-Wide Error Handler setting, later in this section, and the discussion of the `<CFERROR>` tag in Chapter 19.

Enable per App Settings

Settings defined in the ColdFusion Administrator apply to all applications running on the server. ColdFusion allows specific settings to be overridden at the application level. For example, the Custom Tags folder is shared by all applications. If two applications create custom tags with the same name, there is a real risk that the wrong tag will be invoked inadvertently. The capability to define a different Custom Tag folder for each application (overriding the default location that is specified) solves this problem.

Per-application settings are not defined in the ColdFusion Administrator. Rather, they are defined programmatically in the application's `Application.cfc` file.

➡ `Application.cfc` was introduced in Chapter 19.

To enable support for per-application settings, check the Enable per App Settings box.

Use UUID for `cftoken`

As you learned in Chapter 20, "Working with Sessions," in Vol. 1, *Getting Started*, ColdFusion uses values called `CFID` and `CFTOKEN` to identify each browser machine. The `CFTOKEN` value is used as a kind of password that allows users to be connected to their client variables on the server. In addition, this value is also used (in concert with the notion of a session timeout) to connect users with their session variables on the server.

Historically, ColdFusion used a random number for the `CFTOKEN` value. You can use this option to have ColdFusion use a universally unique identifier (UUID) instead, which will guarantee that the `CFTOKEN` is unique, even across multiple servers in a cluster.

It's pretty unlikely that this value will have a real-world impact on your application, but it's safer to enable this setting if possible. I recommend that you go ahead and enable this option unless you have an existing application that uses the CFTOKEN internally in some manner and depends on it being a number.

TIP

If you need to be able to generate unique identifiers for your own use within your application, you can use the `CreateUUID()` function.

Enable HTTP Status Codes

This setting allows ColdFusion to return true HTTP status codes in the header of its response if an unexpected error occurs. For instance, if a user requests a ColdFusion page that doesn't exist on the server, ColdFusion will be able to return a true error message (HTTP status code number 404) that other machines can understand to mean "not found." If this option is unchecked, ColdFusion would simply display a page that contained a message saying the page could not be found (in English, which is fine for humans but not so helpful for proxy servers, search engines, or machines trying to access Web Services on your server).

Similarly, if ColdFusion needs to report an error message, the HTTP status code of the server's response will be set to 500 if this option is checked. If left unchecked, the error message is displayed, but the status code remains set to the normal HTTP status code, 200, which means that other automated systems on the network can't really tell that anything has gone wrong.

As a general rule, never keep this option checked on development servers. If desired, keep it checked on production servers only.

Enable Whitespace Management

When enabled, this option makes sure that extraneous white space (such as the various hard returns, spaces, and tabs that you use to indent your ColdFusion code) is removed from any generated HTML code before it's sent back to browsers. The idea is that since white space isn't significant to HTML, then white space in your ColdFusion templates should usually be ignored as well.

I recommend that this option be enabled in nearly all cases. There are a few special situations in which you would not want white space to be removed (for instance, if you are using <pre> blocks in your pages), but you can always turn off the white-space management on a case-by-case basis with the <cfprocessingdirective> tag.

➔ For more information about white-space management, see Chapter 31, "Improving Performance."

Disable CFC Type Check

ColdFusion Components methods (and user-defined functions) arguments are validated by ColdFusion: that is, if the argument expects a specific data type to be passed to it, ColdFusion checks that the correct type was indeed passed.

Arguments can accept lots of types, including ColdFusion Components. By default, when an argument accepts a ColdFusion Component, ColdFusion checks that the component passed is of the right type. This check can be time consuming (milliseconds, but still slower than other argument type checks). To improve performance, you can disable CFC type checking.

NOTE

> This option is meant for production servers only. On development (and testing) servers, you'll want to know if you are passing the wrong type of CFC as an argument.

➜ See Chapter 24, "Building User-Defined Functions," and Chapter 26, "Building Reusable Components," for more information on UDFs and CFCs.

Disable Access to Internal ColdFusion Java Components

ColdFusion features internal Java objects that can be used to perform all sorts of server administration. Indeed, the ColdFusion Administrator itself (and the Administrator APIs) use these Java objects extensively.

Because ColdFusion code can invoke Java objects, these internal objects can also be invoked and used. On shared servers, this can be a potential security problem, so you can block access to ColdFusion's internal Java components if needed.

➜ See Chapter 78, "Extending ColdFusion with Java," in *Adobe ColdFusion 8 Web Application Construction Kit, Volume 3: Advanced Application Development,* for more information on ColdFusion Java integration.

TIP

> As a rule, check this box on servers where you do not control all code and applications, and leave it unchecked if the server is all yours.

Prefix Serialized JSON With

JSON is an XML data format used in Ajax applications and by ColdFusion's Ajax controls. Web Services that return data in JSON format could contain JavaScript code and could therefore be compromised to allow JavaScript cross-site scripting attacks. Check this box to prefix potentially harmful strings to prevent them from executing.

➜ See Chapter 15, "Beyond HTML Forms: ColdFusion-Powered Ajax," in Vol. 1, *Getting Started,* and Chapter 34, "Advanced ColdFusion-Powered Ajax," to learn about ColdFusion and Ajax integration.

Watch Configuration Files for Changes

ColdFusion configuration settings are stored in external XML files. These files are typically never modified directly; they are updated as needed by ColdFusion itself (when changes are made using the ColdFusion Administrator or the Administrator API). If changes are made to the files directly, these changes will not be seen by ColdFusion until the server has been restarted.

However, if needed, ColdFusion can watch its own configuration files and reload their contents (the settings) if file changes have occurred. If this capability is needed, check this option.

TIP

If you are using ColdFusion on IBM WebSphere using network deployment, this option should be enabled (checked).

Enable Global Script Protection

Check this box to have ColdFusion check `URL`, `FORM`, `CGI`, and `COOKIE` variables for potential cross-site scripting attacks.

➔ This option is explained in Chapter 23, "Securing Your Applications," online.

Default `ScriptSrc` Directory

`<cfform>` tags (introduced in Chapters 12, "ColdFusion Forms," and 14, "Using Forms to Add or Change Data," in Vol. 1, *Getting Started*) use JavaScript files that are installed in a folder named `/CFIDE/scripts` under the ColdFusion root. If this location must be changed (for example, to lock down the entire `CFIDE` directory structure), you should provide the new path in this field.

Missing Template Handler

You can create a ColdFusion page that will be executed and displayed whenever a user requests a ColdFusion page that doesn't actually exist on the server. This page will take the place of the standard Not Found message that would ordinarily appear. The missing template handler can contain whatever ColdFusion code you like. Just specify its location here, in the ColdFusion Administrator. Be sure to include the complete file path to the file (including the `c:\` or whatever is appropriate), not just its name.

NOTE

Some Web servers provide options that will make sure that the requested file actually exists before passing the page request to Cold-Fusion. For instance, Microsoft IIS provides a Check That File Exists option for each file extension mapping (choose Configuration from the Home Directory tab of your site's Properties dialog in the Internet Information Services Manager). If you enable this option for `.cfm` files, ColdFusion will never request nonexistent files, and thus the Missing Template Handler you specify in the ColdFusion Administrator will never be used. For details, consult the documentation for your Web server software.

Sitewide Error Handler

You can also create a ColdFusion page that will be executed and displayed whenever an uncaught error (exception) is displayed. This page will take the place of the standard error message that would ordinarily appear. Again, just specify its location here, in the ColdFusion Administrator. Be sure to include the complete file path to the file (including the `c:\` or whatever is appropriate), not just its name.

➔ You can still specify customized error handling pages on a page-by-page or application-by-application basis with the `<cferror>` tag, as explained in Chapter 51, "Error Handling," online.

Maximum Size of Post Data

One type of server attack overloads the server by making it process requests with massive amounts of data attached. This type of attack uses POST submission, and so ColdFusion can be instructed to ignore (and terminate) any requests with POST data greater than a specified size. To implement this option, specify a size.

TIP

Enable this option only if you are absolutely sure that you will never need to accept data (including form submissions and HTTP file uploads) greater than the specified size.

Request Throttle Threshold

ColdFusion can throttle (forcefully slow down) incoming requests if needed. However, really small requests (those with a small *payload*) can be allowed through regardless of the throttle state. To allow small requests to be processed, specify the maximum allowed size (the default is a maximum of 4 MB).

Request Throttle Memory

To throttle requests, specify the maximum amount of memory allocated for the throttle. If not enough total memory is available, ColdFusion queues requests until enough memory is free.

The Request Tuning Page

The Request Tuning page is used to manage and control how ColdFusion handles the processing of concurrent requests.

Maximum Number of Simultaneous Template Requests

ColdFusion is fast and efficient, but it obviously can't handle an unlimited amount of page requests at once. At some point, any server will become overwhelmed if it tries to serve too many users at once. This setting allows you to tweak your server's performance by adjusting the maximum number of page requests that it can process at the same time.

NOTE

If you change this setting, you need to restart the ColdFusion Application Server to make the changes take effect.

To explain this option, we'll visit Gus again. Gus knows that if he had more experience, or if the kitchen were better organized, he could handle more orders at one time. Oh well. Gus can think on his feet, though, and has a clever idea. He instructs the waitresses to herd the hungry patrons into one line and take five orders at a time. That way, Gus stays at peak efficiency and can cook the maximum number of orders.

You can see where this metaphor is going. Of course, Gus is analogous to the ColdFusion server, the lunch orders are like requests for ColdFusion pages, and Gus's customers are like your application's users. Gus is able to improve the efficiency of his kitchen because he knows the maximum number of lunch orders that he can handle at once.

That's really important. Gus somehow knows the maximum number of orders he can work on at once without slowing way down. When it comes to this setting in the ColdFusion Administrator, the trick is to figure out the number of page requests that your server can process at once before it slows way down.

Because this setting can have a big impact on an application's performance, it would be nice if there were a hard-and-fast rule that you could use to determine the best value to provide. Unfortunately, there is no such rule. To understand why, let's think some more about Gus's situation.

Gus can limit the number of simultaneous orders to five, but unfortunately he can't tell ahead of time what the customers are actually going to order. If three or four out of five particular orders are really complicated, his efficiency will still go down; he really ought to take fewer orders at once for a while. On the other hand, if the next five orders are really simple, his efficiency will go back up. Also, if Gus gets a new stove (which might be like getting a new processor for your server), or more counter space installed (which might be like getting more RAM), or moves the refrigerator closer to the stove (which might be like getting a faster connection to your databases), his efficiency will go up, and he could start taking more orders at once. If the kitchen deteriorates or gets cluttered (like an aging hard drive or poor network connection), his efficiency will go down.

So Gus's efficiency, and thus the maximum number of orders he should process, depends on two main factors:

- The nature of the lunch orders
- The nature of his working environment

When talking about the ColdFusion server's efficiency, the maximum number of pages it should process simultaneously depends on two main analogous factors:

- The complexity of the pages being requested
- The physical capacity of the server

Gus's level of experience directly translates into your server's hardware specifications. The more powerful your hardware—a greater amount of RAM, faster processors, quicker hard drives, and faster network connections to your databases—the more requests it can handle at one time.

Therefore, depending on your hardware specifications, reducing the number of requests allows ColdFusion to devote its resources to a small number of tasks, thus executing all tasks more quickly. If you think your server can handle more requests, try your ColdFusion applications with the increased setting under load in a staging environment.

Here are some rules of thumb:

- Start with a value of 10, which is a pretty reasonable starting point.

- If your server has more than one processor, it's reasonable to assume that it will be able to handle more requests at once. Add more requests (perhaps 5 to 10) for each processor.

- If your server is extremely powerful in other ways, such as in its amount or type of RAM, type or number of disk controllers, network connections, or other physical characteristics, increase the number of simultaneous requests per processor. If the server is starting to show its age, decrease the number.

- If all your pages execute very quickly during development, you can probably increase the number a bit more per processor. On the other hand, if they take more than a second or two to complete their work even when the server isn't under load, then you should decrease the number.

- If most of your pages are very fast, but there are a few pages that you know will take a long time to execute because of their nature, you should probably increase the number of simultaneous requests (so that the fast pages aren't blocked by the slow pages at runtime). In addition, you could use the <cflock> tag to make sure that a large number of the slow pages aren't allowed to execute all at once. For instance, you could place a <cflock> tag with name="VerySlowProcess" and type="Exclusive" attributes around code that you know will be time consuming or generally hard on the server. See Chapter 19 for more information about locking.

- If your application uses shared variables, especially APPLICATION variables, in such a way that you often need to request an exclusive lock to protect against race conditions, you will probably want to decrease the number of simultaneous requests (so that fewer locks actually block one another at runtime). See Chapter 19 for more information about race conditions.

NOTE

This setting isn't available in the ColdFusion for J2EE Application Servers version of ColdFusion, which means that it won't be available if you are running ColdFusion under IBM WebSphere, BEA WebLogic, or Sun ONE Application Server. It's available only for ColdFusion installations that use Adobe JRun as the underlying engine (that includes the Standard and Enterprise editions). It modifies an underlying setting in the jrun.xml configuration file, which tells JRun how many concurrent threads to use.

TIP

There is another important approach that you can use to manage different applications and requests with differing loads and response times. ColdFusion Enterprise allows you to install multiple copies (instances) of ColdFusion on a single machine, and each instance can have its own settings optimized for its own use.

Maximum Number of Simultaneous Flash Remoting Requests

Most inbound requests to ColdFusion originate from Web browsers, but ColdFusion also accepts requests from Flash (and Flex) applications via Flash Remoting. Thus, it is possible (if your site has lots of Flash applications) that Web browser requests may be queued waiting for Flash Remoting requests to complete.

ColdFusion allows you to specify how many requests to allow for Flash Remoting.

Maximum Number of Simultaneous Web Service Requests

ColdFusion requests can also be Web Services (SOAP) requests. As with Flash Remoting requests, ColdFusion allows Web Services requests to be restricted.

TIP

If your site exposes many public-facing Web Services, you may want to increase this number to match the Maximum Number of Simultaneous Template Requests value.

➔ See Chapter 68, "Creating and Consuming Web Services," in Vol. 3, *Advanced Application Development,* to learn how to create and publish Web Services.

Maximum Number of Simultaneous CFC Function Requests

ColdFusion Components are usually invoked directly (from within other ColdFusion files and templates). CFCs can also be invoked via Flash Remoting and Web Services, and as already seen, this type of access can be capped if needed. ColdFusion Components can also be invoked via direct HTTP request. To cap this type of access, set the maximum here.

NOTE

This setting does not affect CFC invocations from within local CFML code.

Maximum Number of Running JRun Threads

When ColdFusion runs using the integrated JRun server, it must share the total available threads with JRun. In addition to the threads that ColdFusion needs for processing, the underlying JRun requires threads itself. Thus, this value should always be greater than the sum of the previous four values (20 higher is a good starting point).

NOTE

This option is available only if ColdFusion is deployed as a stand-alone server (Standard Edition, or the first installation option in Enterprise Edition).

Maximum Number of Queued JRun Threads

The underlying JRun server can accept Java and J2EE requests in addition to ColdFusion requests (which are processed by ColdFusion running within JRun). JRun queues requests until they can be processed (by their destination, wherever it is), and that queue size is specified here.

NOTE

This option is available only if ColdFusion is deployed as a stand-alone server (Standard Edition, or the first installation option in Enterprise Edition).

Maximum Number of Simultaneous Report Threads

ColdFusion has an integrated reporting engine (used by `<CFREPORT>`). As report processing can be very resource intensive (especially the concurrent processing of very large reports), there is a risk that ColdFusion will be so busy creating reports that all other requests suffer from poor performance.

Thus, ColdFusion allows you to specify the maximum number of threads that can be allocated to report generation. Any requests greater than the specified maximum will be queued until they can be processed.

TIP

Unless your application generates reports continuously, set this value to a value far lower than the total number of available requests.

→ See Chapter 16, "Graphing, Printing, and Reporting," in Vol. 1, *Getting Started,* to learn about ColdFusion reporting.

Maximum Number of Threads Available for CFTHREAD

ColdFusion requests are single threaded, but, using <cfthread>, ColdFusion applications can spawn additional threads to perform asynchronous processing. Although this feature can boost performance tremendously, it also introduces a risk that so many threads will be spawned that total system performance suffers.

Thus, ColdFusion allows you to specify the maximum number of threads that can be allocated for spawned thread processing. Any requests greater than the specified maximum will be queued until they can be processed.

→ See Chapter 30, "Managing Threads," to learn how to use threading and the <cfthread> tag.

Timeout Requests Waiting in Queue After *n* Seconds

If ColdFusion is busy processing as many requests as have been specified, any additional inbound requests will be queued until there is a free thread to process them. In theory, requests can be queued indefinitely, but in practice, you'll probably want to timeout the requests and display a custom error message.

The maximum request queue time can be specified in this option.

NOTE

This value should never be less than the Request Timeout value (the first option on the Settings Page, discussed previously in this chapter).

Request Queue Timeout Page

If queued requests time out, users will see a generic 500 message in their browser. To provide a custom error page, specify the path to a static HTML file (relative to the Web root) here.

CAUTION

Do not use a .cfm page as the custom error page. If pages are timing out in the queue, you don't want to queue another page to display an error message!

The Caching Page

The word *cache* is a general term that refers to the use of a temporary area of a computer's memory or disk drive to store information that can be time-consuming to retrieve or calculate normally. The idea is to perform the action or calculation once, store it in the cache, and then use the information in the cache (the *cached version*) for subsequent requests, rather than performing the action or calculation over and over again. There always needs to be some limit placed on the amount of information in the cache; otherwise the size of the cache would become unwieldy and inefficient.

The Caching page of the ColdFusion Administrator is used to control the cache that ColdFusion uses to cache your ColdFusion code files, and the database cache that ColdFusion uses whenever you use the `cachedwithin` or `cachedafter` attributes in a `<cfquery>` tag.

NOTE

> Don't confuse the caching options on this page of the Administrator with the `<cfcache>` tag, which is for caching individual pages. For details about `<cfcache>`, see Chapter 31," Improving Performance."

Maximum Number of Cached Templates

ColdFusion converts your ColdFusion templates to compiled Java classes in the background. Whenever someone visits one of your ColdFusion pages, ColdFusion checks to see if the page has been converted to a Java class, and whether the Java class is up to date (that is, whether the `.cfm` file has been changed since the Java class was compiled). The same goes for any included pages, custom tags, and components. Certain aspects of this decision-making process, as well as the compiled Java classes themselves, are cached in memory to improve performance.

This setting lets you tweak the size of this template cache to improve performance. Ideally, you would want the cache to be big enough to hold all your templates.

NOTE

> Remember, a template is just another name for a ColdFusion page. Any `.cfm` or `.cfc` file is a template.

Trusted Cache

Normally, when a user requests one of your ColdFusion pages, the server needs to check to see if the `.cfm` file has been changed since the last time the page was executed. If so, it recompiles the `.cfm` file into an updated version of the corresponding Java class; if not, the existing version of the Java class can be used. The same goes for any included files, custom tags, or ColdFusion components. It doesn't take much time for the server to check whether each file has changed, but even that little bit of time is for naught if you know that your ColdFusion files won't be changing over time.

Checking this option tells ColdFusion not to bother checking whether each ColdFusion file has changed. This can improve performance quite a bit, especially if the server is receiving a lot of page requests.

In general, you should enable this option on your production servers, since the files would not normally be changing often. Leave it unchecked on your development servers.

Save Class Files

The class files generated by ColdFusion .cfm source code may be cached in server memory or written to disk. To save class files to disk, check this option. This can improve performance on high-volume sites.

Don't enable this option on your development servers.

Cache Web Server Paths

ColdFusion can cache the paths to files and how these paths map to URLs to improve performance. Check this option to cache paths, but never check this option if you host multiple Web sites on the same server (as this could cause paths to get mixed up resulting in the wrong pages being served).

Maximum Number of Cached Queries

As you learned in Chapter 31, you can use the cachedwithin or cachedafter attributes of the <cfquery> tag to reuse query results so they don't have to be retrieved from the database with each and every page request. Of course, it's not possible for the server to cache an unlimited number of query result sets in memory; there's only so much memory to go around.

By default, ColdFusion will allow up to 100 cached result sets to reside in its memory; when the 101st query needs to be cached, the query that was cached first will be removed from the cache. Increasing the number will allow more cached result sets to remain in memory at once; decreasing the number will reduce the amount of RAM that the cached queries will use up.

Like some of the options discussed earlier (particularly the number of simultaneous requests), this setting is a matter of balance, and there is no hard and fast rule about what the best value is. Setting the value too high could cause ColdFusion to use too much memory, which might negatively impact the overall performance of your applications. Setting the value too low will reduce the likelihood of a page request being able to take advantage of a previously cached query, which would also negatively impact performance.

In general, if you use cached queries extensively in your code, and you find that your server still has plenty of available RAM after your applications have been running for a while, you can increase the value. On the other hand, if you find that your server tends to run out of available RAM, you should try decreasing this value.

The ColdFusion System Monitor can be used to determine which queries are being cached and whether the cache is being used effectively.

➜ Chapter 56, "Monitoring System Performance," in Vol. 3, *Advanced Application Development*, explains how to use the System Monitor.

The Client Variables Page

In Chapter 20, you learned about the CLIENT variable scope, which allows you to create variables that become associated with a particular Web browser. You can use CLIENT variables to create pages that show personalized information or that otherwise maintain state between each user's visits and page requests.

Choosing a Client Variable Storage Mechanism

In general, the idea behind CLIENT variables is to store the actual variables on the server, so that the burden (and responsibility) for remembering the values isn't placed on each browser machine. There are two methods for storing values on the server: in a database, or in the registry. (For Windows servers, *registry* refers to the Windows Registry, which is a special information store that is built into the operating system; for other servers, *registry* refers to a special text file that Adobe ships with ColdFusion.) Because the values are stored on the server side, the total size of all the accumulated client variables can become quite large over time. Either the database or the registry will have to become large enough to store the total size of all client variables for all users.

You can also choose to have your client variables stored as a cookie on the browser machine. This takes care of the problem of your servers having to store every client variable for every user, but has some significant trade-offs. Conceptually, you are trusting the browser to store the values for you. Savvy users know how to delete cookies to save disk space, and they may do so at any time—which means that you have no way to prevent your application's client variables from being deleted. Some users will disable cookies altogether, which means that your client variables won't work at all. Perhaps most importantly, browsers aren't required to store an unlimited amount of information in cookies, which means that the combined length of all client variables for each user can't be very large.

Adobe recommends that you only use the default registry option for development, and that you create a database storage mechanism for your staging or production machines (even if it's just a lowly Access database). You can set the database to be the default storage mechanism (as discussed in the next section) so that your code doesn't have to change as you move your applications out of development.

That said, the registry option is generally fine as long as your ColdFusion applications (at least, the ones that use client variables) won't be visited by too many unique visitors. So for intranet applications that are only used by a limited number of people, it's probably fine to just use the default registry option. On the other hand, if your client-variable-aware applications are going to be used by lots and lots of people, you should consider using a database. You can also use the cookie option, if the information in the client variables isn't critical and isn't particularly verbose.

NOTE

> The primary reason to use CLIENT variables is to share this information across multiple servers. As this can also be accomplished using SESSION variables, there is rarely a need to use CLIENT variables anymore.

Choosing the Default Storage Mechanism

To choose the default storage mechanism used for client variables, make the appropriate selection under the heading Select Default Storage Mechanism for Client Sessions; then click Apply.

> You can override this setting on an application-by-application basis by specifying a clientstorage attribute in your <cfapplication> tag. For details, see Chapter 19.

Purge Interval

CLIENT variables persist over time, and are purged (deleted) at a predetermined interval. The default interval is 1 hour 7 minutes, and this can be changed if needed.

The Memory Variables Page

In Chapter 19, you learned about APPLICATION variables, which allow you to maintain counters, flags, and other variables on an application-wide basis. In Chapter 20, you learned about SESSION variables, which provide a way to track variables for your users on a per-session basis.

This page of the Administrator allows you to change how these variables are tracked, and for how long. Either type of variable can be disabled by unchecking the Enable Application Variables or Enable Session Variables checkbox.

Use J2EE Session Variables

ColdFusion can manage SESSION variables, or it can rely on the underlying J2EE server to perform this task. To have the J2EE server manage the session, check this box.

TIP

> There are significant advantages to using J2EE session variables; ideally, this checkbox should be checked.

NOTE

> If you have existing applications that explicitly use CFID and CFTOKEN values, don't check this box without updating that code.

Enable Application Variables

To enable the use of APPLICATION variables, check this box.

NOTE

> As a rule, this box should always be checked.

Enable Session Variables

If any applications on your server will need to use SESSION variables, check this box.

NOTE

> As a rule, this box should always be checked.

Maximum Timeout

You can adjust the Maximum Timeout value for each type of variable, which gives you a way to make sure that no individual <cfapplication> tag is specifying a sessiontimeout or applicationtimeout value that is unreasonably long. If the <cfapplication> tag specifies a timeout value that exceeds the maximum value you supply here, the maximum value is used instead.

Default Timeout

You can also edit the Default Timeout value for each type of variable by typing in the desired number of days, minutes, hours, and seconds. This default value will be used whenever you don't specify a sessiontimeout or applicationtimeout attribute in your <cfapplication> tags. For instance, you can set a longer timeout session timeout if users are complaining that their session variables disappear while they're filling out long forms or making complex decisions. You can use a shorter timeout if you suspect that too much memory is being used to store your session variables.

The Mappings Page

The Mappings Page is used to define path mappings, aliases that are used in CFML code to refer to specific folders.

By default two mappings are created (cfide and gateway) and these should not be removed. To add your own mappings, enter the alias and path in the form displayed, and click Add.

NOTE

> If Enable Per App Settings (on the Settings page) is checked, you can define mappings for specific applications in Application.cfc.

The Mail Page

In Chapter 21, "Interacting with Email," online, you learned to create ColdFusion pages that send dynamic, personalized email messages with the <cfmail> tag. ColdFusion can also send automatically generated reports to server administrators in case of problems, as you will learn in the System Probes Page section, later in this chapter. Use the Mail Server page to establish an SMTP email server connection for ColdFusion to use for these purposes.

NOTE

> If you are using the ColdFusion Developer Edition, some of the options listed for this page may not be available.

Mail Server

Enter either the Internet domain name or the IP address for your company's outgoing mail server (also known as an SMTP server) in the Mail Server text box.

Username

If your SMTP server requires that you log in, enter the username here.

Password

If your SMTP server requires that you log in, enter the password here.

Verify Mail Server Connection

When defining your mail server, check this box to have ColdFusion Administrator attempt to connect to the mail server to verify the connection.

Server Port

Enter your email server's port number. This is almost always 25, so you can usually leave the port number alone.

Backup Mail Servers

If you have access to backup SMTP servers (which can be used if the primary SMTP server is unavailable), list these here.

Connection Timeout

This setting lets you specify the number of seconds ColdFusion should wait for a response from the email server. In general, the default value of 60 seconds is sensible. If your mail server is far away or available only via a slow network connection, you may need to increase this value.

Enable SSL Socket Connections to Mail Server

Select this checkbox to enable SSL encryption on the connections to the mail server.

NOTE

For you to use this option, your mail server must support SSL encryption.

Enable TLS Connection to Mail Server

Select this checkbox to enable transport level security (TLS) on the connection to the mail server.

NOTE

For you to use this option, your mail server must support SSL encryption.

Spool Interval

This setting lets you specify the number of seconds ColdFusion waits before checking to see if new email messages are waiting to be sent out. You can decrease this value if it's critical that your messages be sent out very soon after they are created; you can increase the value to conserve server resources. Note this value is ignored whenever you use the `spoolenable="No"` attribute in your `<cfmail>` tags.

Mail Delivery Threads

You can specify the maximum number of threads that the ColdFusion mail spooler can use. The higher this number, the greater the number of messages that will be deliverable at any given time.

NOTE
Before raising this value, make sure that your mail server supports multiple concurrent connections from the same client.

Spool Mail Messages for Delivery To

Mail is spooled by ColdFusion and then delivered by the spooler. Messages can be spooled to disk or to memory.

As a general rule, messages should be spooled to disk. While spooling to memory can be faster, it does increase memory load and also prevents delivery of mail after a system failure.

Error Log Severity

Mail delivered by ColdFusion can be logged for future analysis. The logs are saved in the `/ColdFusion8/Log` folder and can be viewed using the log viewer pages within the ColdFusion Administrator (see the section "The Log Files Page" later in this chapter). You can specify the log level here.

Log All Messages Sent by ColdFusion

To aid in troubleshooting, ColdFusion can log all messages (including all contents) if needed.

CAUTION
Do not leave this option checked for extended periods of time, as saving all messages can consume vast amounts of disk space.

Mail Charset Setting

To change the default character set used in generated email messages, specify the value here.

NOTE
UTF-8 is generally the preferred option for this setting.

The Charting Page

In Chapter 16, you learned how to use the ColdFusion <cfchart> tag to create dynamic charts and graphs that create visual representations of your application's data. ColdFusion automatically caches charts for later use. Conceptually, the chart cache is the charting equivalent of the query caching feature you learned about in Chapter 31. Its purpose is to improve performance by automatically reusing the results of a <cfchart> tag if all of its data and attributes are the same, rather than having to re-render each chart for every page request.

The Charting page of the ColdFusion Administrator contains a number of options that you can use to tweak the way the chart cache behaves.

Cache Type

You can set this to Disk Cache (the default value) or Memory Cache. The Memory Cache setting will perform better under high load, but will require more of the server's memory to do so. The Disk Cache setting may not perform quite as quickly, but it won't have much of an impact on the server's RAM. We recommend leaving this value alone unless you are specifically experiencing performance problems with <cfchart> under heavy load.

Maximum Number of Cached Images

You can increase this number to allow ColdFusion to store more charts in its cache, thereby improving performance if your application is serving up lots of different charts. If you are using the Memory Cache option, keep in mind that this will cause even more of the server's memory to be used for chart caching.

Maximum Number of Charting Threads

The maximum number of <cfchart> tags that you want ColdFusion to be willing to process at the same moment in time. Under high load, a higher number here may improve responsiveness for individual chart requests, but it will put more overall strain on your server.

Disk Cache Location

If you are using the Disk Cache option, you may adjust this value, which is the location where ColdFusion stores charts for later reuse.

The Font Management Page

Fonts are used by the ColdFusion printing and reporting features. When generating printed output, ColdFusion must know what fonts are available, what output type they support, and whether to embed fonts in generated output.

The Font Management page lists available fonts and allows you to specify a folder containing additional fonts to be installed.

➜ See Chapter 16 to learn about ColdFusion printing and reporting.

The Java and JVM Page

ColdFusion runs on top of the Java platform. Your ColdFusion pages are translated into Java classes, and those classes are executed within the context of a Java Virtual Machine (JVM). The Java and JVM page of the Administrator allows you to adjust which JVM is used to execute your pages. You can also make other JVM-related adjustments, such as the amount of memory that the JVM is allowed to use while executing your pages.

NOTE

> This page is only available when using ColdFusion with the integrated J2EE server. If ColdFusion is installed on a J2EE server, use the server management tools to define these settings.

Java Virtual Machine Path

In theory, ColdFusion should be able to use any up-to-date JVM. To use an alternate JVM, install it, change the Java Virtual Machine Path setting in the ColdFusion Administrator, and then restart the ColdFusion Application Server.

NOTE

> Before using a different JVM on your production servers, you should definitely test your applications with that same JVM on some kind of development, staging, or beta-testing server. You should also see whether the JVM is officially supported by Adobe.

NOTE

> You can always find out what JVM ColdFusion is running under by clicking on the System Information link at the top of the ColdFusion Administrator.

Minimum JVM Heap Size

This setting allows you to provide an initial amount of your server's memory that the JVM should claim when ColdFusion is started. By default, this setting is left blank, which means that the JVM will make its own decisions about how much memory it should claim at startup. If your server encounters a lot of traffic, the JVM will generally need to claim more memory. You may be able to save the JVM some time by telling it to claim a larger amount of memory at start-up. In general, this could make the whole start-up process (which includes the initial processing of your pages) more efficient.

If you provide a value for this setting, it's strongly recommended that you specify a size of at least 32 MB.

Maximum Memory Size

In a default ColdFusion installation, the JVM is instructed to use no more than 512 MB of memory for the ColdFusion runtime and your ColdFusion pages. If your server has considerably more than 512 MB of RAM installed, you may want to allow the JVM to use more of it, which would generally improve performance. Simply specify the maximum amount of memory that you wish the JVM (and thus the ColdFusion server, and thus your ColdFusion pages) to be able to use, in megabytes.

NOTE

Don't set this value to anything lower than 32 MB, because ColdFusion probably won't be able to start with less than that amount of memory.

ColdFusion Class Path

If your applications use any external Java objects that in turn refer to other Java classes (that is, any Java classes that aren't provided by the JVM itself), you can tell ColdFusion where to find the class files by adjusting the Class Path setting in the ColdFusion Administrator. By *Java objects*, I mean any Java classes that you are accessing via <cfobject> or CreateObject(), any servlets or JSP tag libraries that you are using via <cfimport>, CFX tags that have been written in Java, and so on.

In general, you will either be specifying the path to a directory or the path to a Java Archive (.jar) file. If you need to specify multiple directories or archives, separate them with commas. Whatever Java objects you are using should include documentation that tells exactly which files need to be accessible via the class path.

NOTE

If you're familiar with invoking Java on the command line, this Administrator setting is equivalent to the -classpath or -cp option.

JVM Arguments

If you want any additional arguments to be passed to the JVM when the ColdFusion server is started, you can specify them here. Separate multiple arguments with spaces. Presumably, you would provide such arguments if they were required by an external Java object that you wanted to use, or if the argument was suggested by the JVM vendor to improve performance or stability. The exact purpose and effect of the arguments will depend on the JVM and classes you are using.

Settings Summary

The Settings Summary page provides a quick overview of all ColdFusion Administrator settings. Detailed information about all data sources, CFX tags, mappings, Verity full-text archives, and nearly all other settings discussed in this chapter are displayed. Most of the information from the Version Information page is included in the report as well. You can print this page to get a hard-copy record of all ColdFusion settings on the server.

Data and Services

The Data and Services section of the ColdFusion Administrator contains pages that let you create, edit, and delete data sources and Verity full-text search collections. You can also create aliases for Web Services.

The Data Sources Page

The Data Sources page provides tools to manage the list of data sources available to ColdFusion. Any data source listed here can be used as the `data source` attribute of a `<cfquery>` (or `<cfinsert>`, `<cfupdate>`, `<cfgridupdate>`, or `<cfstoredproc>`) tag. If you have been following along with the examples in this book, you have probably already used this page of the ColdFusion Administrator to set up the ows data source.

To define a new data source, specify the name, select the data source type from the drop-down list, click the Add button, and then specify the database specific options as requested.

The Data Sources page is also used to verify that data sources are working. Click the Verify All Connections button to verify all data sources, or click the green check button for a specific data source to validate it alone.

The Verity Collections Page

ColdFusion features an integrated Verity full-text search engine. CFML includes three tags related to Verity: `<cfsearh>`, `<cfindex>`, and `<cfcollection>`. All three tags have a `collection` attribute, which refers to what Verity calls a *collection*. A collection is to Verity as data sources are to databases: it's a name that you can use to refer to or search a particular set of data.

→ See Chapter 39, "Full-Text Searching," to learn about ColdFusion's integrated Verity full-text search engine.

Add New Verity Collections

To create a collection, simply provide a name for the new collection and click the Create Collection button. By default, the new collection will be created in the `/verity/collections` folder under the ColdFusion root; if you want the collection files to be kept somewhere else, you can specify the location in the Path field.

Verity Collections

To delete a collection, click the Delete Collection icon for the collection in the Connected Local Verity Connections list.

TIP

You can also create and delete collections programmatically with the `<cfcollection>` tag, rather than using the ColdFusion Administrator. For details, see Chapter 39.

Next to each listed collection are four buttons (from left to right)

- **Index Collection** re-indexes a Verity collection.

- **Optimize Collection** performs optimization on the Verity collection to improve performance (this is generally used for collections that are being constantly updated).

- **Purge Collection** empties a Verity collection.

- **Delete Collection** deletes a Verity collection completely.

The Verity K2 Server Page

Verity support is provided by the Verity K2 engine, which must be running in order to use any Verity functionality. By default ColdFusion uses a local K2 server, but an alternate server may be specified in this screen if required.

The Web Services Page

ColdFusion allows you to use (*consume*) Web Services via the <cfinvoke> or <cfobject> tag, or via the CreateObject() function. You can use the Web Services page to create aliases for the Web Services that you plan to use. You can then use the alias name instead of providing the full URL for the Web Service in every <cfinvoke> tag. If the Web Service requires a username and password, they can be associated with the alias as well, which means that the username and password don't have to appear in your ColdFusion code at all.

To create an alias for a Web Service, enter the alias in the Web Service Name field. Provide the URL for the service's WSDL description in the WDSL URL field (if the service requires a username and password, enter them as well), then click the Add Web Service button. The new alias will appear in the Active ColdFusion Services list at the bottom of the page. You can now use the alias name as the Webservice attribute for <cfinvoke>, <cfobject>, or CreateObject() where you would normally need to provide the complete WSDL URL.

The Flex Integration Page

ColdFusion can be used as a powerful backend for Flash and Flex applications, as well as for applications powered by LiveCycle Data Services.

➜ See Chapters 35, "Understanding ColdFusion-Powered Flex," and 36, "Building ColdFusion-Powered Flex Applications," to learn about ColdFusion and Flex integration.

Enable Flash Remoting support

To allow ColdFusion Components to be accessed via Flash Remoting, check this box.

Enable Remote Adobe LiveCycle Data Management Access

ColdFusion features an integrated Adobe LiveCycle Data Services server (if that option was selected during installation). Usually this integrated server will be sufficient for ColdFusion integration. However, if you need to connect ColdFusion to an external (or remote) LiveCycle Data Services server, check this box (and specify the server identity).

Enable RMI over SSL for Data Management

RMI is used for communication between ColdFusion and external LiveCycle Data Services servers. To secure this connection, check this box and provide the key information as required.

Select IP Addresses Where LiveCycle Data Services Are Running

To secure communication between ColdFusion and external LiveCycle Data Services servers, you can specify the IP addresses of those servers allowed to connect to ColdFusion. If any IP addresses are specified, any connections not listed will be refused.

Debugging and Logging

The Debugging and Logging section of the ColdFusion Administrator provides a set of tools that can help you understand what your applications are doing, where and when any performance bottlenecks are occurring, and whether any error messages are occurring without your knowledge. There is also a rich set of debugging options that make it easier to troubleshoot errors while coding. In short, this section is all about making it easier for you to identify and avoid problems, both during and after the development process.

The Debug Output Settings Page

The Debugging Settings page allows you to customize what exactly appears in the debugging output. This page also lets you monitor the ColdFusion server externally, via the command line or the System Monitor in Windows.

➜ See Chapter 17, "Debugging and Troubleshooting," in Vol. 1, *Getting Started*, to learn about ColdFusion debugging options.

Enable Robust Exception Information

ColdFusion error messages provide lots of useful information about your server and code so as to help you diagnose problems. Unfortunately, this information may also be useful to hackers trying to gain unauthorized access to your server. As such, this option should be enabled on development machines but not on production servers.

Enable AJAX Debug Log Window

To enable the pop-up Ajax debug window, check this box.

➜ See Chapter 34 to learn about Ajax debugging.

Enable Request Debugging Output

Check this option to enable debugging output. Information about variables, queries, execution times, and more will begin appearing at the bottom of each page processed by ColdFusion. You can customize what information is included in the debugging output.

NOTE
This option appends content to the generated page, so it should not be used when generating XML output.

TIP

Even when this option is enabled, you can make sure that only the appropriate people (presumably yourself and the other developers on your team) see the debugging output by restricting the output by IP address. This is discussed shortly, in the Debugging IP Addresses page.

Custom Debugging Output

You can customize exactly what is included in the debugging output and how it's displayed with the options in this section. Table 28.1 provides a summary of the options available in this section.

Table 28.1 Custom Debugging Output Options

OPTION	DESCRIPTION
Select Debugging Output Format	ColdFusion lets you switch between debugging output formats. As of this writing, the output formats that ship with the product are classic output, which displays the debugging output in the no-nonsense format familiar to veteran ColdFusion developers, and the dockable format, which displays the output in a less obtrusive, more interactive style. You can even create your own output formats by creating new ColdFusion templates in WEB-INF/debug folder (under the ColdFusion root). Check out the code in the existing templates to see how it's done.
Report Execution Times	It's usually helpful to see execution times in your debugging output, so you can understand how long each of your ColdFusion files takes to execute. Enable this option to include execution times in the debugging output.
Highlight Execution Time	By default, ColdFusion will highlight the execution time of any template that takes more than 250 milliseconds to execute. Increase the value to highlight fewer execution times, or decrease the value to highlight more of them.
Execution Time Output Mode	You can choose between summary and tree. Summary shows the amount of time that ColdFusion spends processing each ColdFusion file involved in the page request (such as <cfinclude> files, custom tags, and ColdFusion Components); if a file is used more than once, the execution times are totaled so that the actual display shows one execution time per ColdFusion file. Tree provides more detail, showing execution times for every single use of a file, and displaying the various included files in a tree-like format so you can easily see which pages are being included by which. In other words, the tree mode is better for applications that use lots of separate files to process each page request. That said, the tree mode can take a bit longer to display, so you might want to enable it only when you need the extra level of precision.

Table 28.1 (CONTINUED)

OPTION	DESCRIPTION
General Debug Information	Select this box to display server version, time stamp, browser information, IP address, and other basic debug information. This checkbox should generally be checked.
Database Activity	Check this option to include database-related information, such as query execution times, in the debugging output.
Exception Information	Check this option to include information about each exception raised while the template was executing.
Tracing Information	Check this option to allow messages included by the `<cftrace>` tag to be shown in the page output. Uncheck the option to turn off the messages included by `<cftrace>`. Note that even when this option is enabled, `<cftrace>` messages will only be visible to the IP addresses listed in the Debugging IP Addresses page, discussed shortly.
Timer Information	If checked, timer information (collected by using the `<cftimer>` tag) will be displayed with the debug data.
Flash Form Compile Errors and Messages	If checked, any Flex compiler errors (generated by Flash forms) will be displayed. This option should be used only on development servers.
Variables	These options allow you to include variables from the various built-in variable scopes, such as `CLIENT`, `SESSION`, `APPLICATION`, `URL`, `FORM`, and so on. You can uncheck the scopes you're not interested in at the moment to reduce the amount of debugging information displayed so you can concentrate on the task at hand.

Enable Performance Monitoring

If you're using ColdFusion with Windows, you can monitor the ColdFusion server with the standard Performance Monitor application that comes with Windows. This is the same application that you use to monitor internal Windows processes such as memory management and CPU use, or other Microsoft applications such as IIS or SQL Server.

Check this option to tell ColdFusion to make information available to the Performance Monitor. When enabled, the Performance Object called ColdFusion Server will be available for display and monitoring within the Performance Monitor.

To monitor performance with the Performance Monitor, follow these steps:

1. Make sure the Enable Debugging option is checked, since it affects all options on this page of the Administrator.

2. Make sure the Enable Performance Monitoring option is checked.

3. Launch the Windows Performance Monitor (choose Start > Run > Perfmon) and select ColdFusion from the Performance Object list as the process to monitor. Select All Counters or add individual counters from the list.

The Performance Monitor will show a live graph of the various counters available, such as the number of database interactions per second, the average page execution time, and the number of currently executing page requests. If you wish, you can also add counters from other Performance Objects, such as the IIS object (to monitor the IIS Web server) or the Processor object (to monitor the CPU itself). Use the Help icon on the Performance Monitor toolbar for more information.

Enable CFSTAT

For non-Windows servers, you can use the CFSTAT command-line utility to take the place of the Performance Monitor. It doesn't show up as a nice graph, but it displays the same information.

To use CFSTAT, follow these steps:

1. Make sure the Enable Debugging option is checked, since it affects all options on this page of the Administrator.

2. Make sure the Enable CFSTAT option is checked.

3. Do whatever is appropriate for the operating system you're using to execute the cfstat executable in the /bin folder (under the ColdFusion root). It's helpful to add a command-line switch of 1, so that the statistics will be updated once per second).

Table 28.2 shows the command-line arguments (also called switches) supported by CFSTAT.

Table 28.2   CFSTAT Command-Line Arguments

ARGUMENT	DESCRIPTION
1, 2, etc.	Refresh interval. You can provide any number as an argument to cfstat, which will cause it to display updated statistics on a separate line every few seconds. So, cfstat 2 updates the statistics every 2 seconds, and so on.
-s	Use the -s option with a refresh interval to cause CFSTAT to accumulate statistics for the desired number of seconds, and then display the aggregated statistics on a single line at the end of the period. So, cfstat -s 30 will collect statistics for 30 seconds; at the end of the 30 seconds, a single line of statistics will report on what happened during those 30 seconds.
-n	Use the -n option to omit the column headers that normally appear above the statistics.
/?	Use cfstat /? to get further help on using CFSTAT, including the meaning of each statistic it displays.

The Debugging IP Addresses Page

While ColdFusion's debugging output is certainly helpful to you as a developer, you probably don't want your users or beta testers to see it. You may also want to get rid of it from time to time while you work, to see what your pages will look like without it.

Rather than having to turn the debugging output on or off for the entire server at once, ColdFusion allows you to turn it on only for specific IP addresses. This way, you can turn on debugging but still make it show up for only the appropriate people. Also, you can remove your own IP address from the list to get rid of the display on your own computer, without affecting everyone else on your team.

To add an IP address, go to the Debugging IP Addresses page, type it in the IP Address field, and click Add. To remove an IP address, select it from the list and click Remove Selected.

TIP

To add your own IP address with one click, you can just click the Add Current button.

The Debugger Settings Page

ColdFusion provides an Eclipse-based interactive debugger. To use the debugger, you must enable support on this page.

Allow Line Debugging

To turn on Eclipse debugging support, check this box.

NOTE

Checking this setting requires restarting the ColdFusion Server.

Debugger Port

The ColdFusion debugger communicates with ColdFusion on a designated port. By default, this is port 5005, but any port value can be used if needed.

NOTE

Do not use the same port that is used by ColdFusion or your Web server.

TIP

If you are debugging against a remote server, make sure that your firewall allows communication via the specified port.

Maximum Simultaneous Debugging Sessions

ColdFusion allows multiple concurrent debugging sessions. Specify the maximum number of sessions needed here.

TIP

Don't set this number higher than necessary, and if you are the only developer using a local server, set it to 1.

The Logging Settings Page

ColdFusion keeps detailed log files that can be extremely helpful for monitoring or debugging an application. This page controls how ColdFusion maintains the log files, and allows you to turn on some additional log files that aren't kept by default.

Log Directory

By default, ColdFusion stores all log files in the /logs folder (beneath the ColdFusion root). You can use this option to change the location of the log files.

Maximum File Size

When log files get very large, they can become unwieldy and hard to read. Use this option to set the maximum amount of information to keep in each log file. The default value is 5000 KB. When a log file exceeds this size, its contents are copied into a *log archive* file. Log archives are the same as the original log files, except that they are given an extension of .1, .2, and so on, instead of .log.

Maximum Number of Archives

A new archive file will be created each time the log file reaches 5000 KB (or whatever you specify). If you don't want an indefinite number of these archive files hanging around forever, you can tell ColdFusion to only maintain a certain number of archives for each log file. By default, a limit of ten archives is used. If, when the actual log file reaches 5000 KB, there are already ten archives present (perhaps application.1 through application.10), the oldest archive file is deleted.

Log Slow Pages

If you enable this option, a special entry in the server.log file will be made for any ColdFusion pages that take longer than the specified number of seconds to execute. You can use this information to identify bottlenecks in your application.

Log All CORBA Calls

In you happen to be using CORBA objects in your application, enable this option to have ColdFusion log all CORBA interactions to the server.log file.

→ CORBA integration is covered in Chapter 77, "Extending ColdFusion with CORBA," in Vol. 3, *Advanced Application Development*.

Enable Logging for Scheduled Tasks

If you are using ColdFusion's built-in task scheduler (see "The Scheduled Tasks Page" section, later in this chapter), you can enable this option to have all scheduler-related actions logged to a special log file called scheduler.log.

The Log Files Page

The Log Files page allows you to view and manage all of the log files on your server. Each `.log` file in the `/log` folder (or whatever log file location you have specified) is listed. For each log, icons are provided for viewing, archiving, downloading, or deleting the log. When viewing a log, you can click on the Launch Filter button to launch the Log Viewer filter window.

The Scheduled Tasks Page

ColdFusion has a built-in task scheduler, which allows you to create ColdFusion pages that run every few minutes or hours, or that execute at a certain time of day. Such pages are usually used to do things like sending mail, indexing Verity collections, deleting temporary files that are no longer needed, and other administrative tasks.

➔ For more information about scheduling tasks, see Chapter 40, "Event Scheduling."

TIP

You can also schedule tasks programmatically with the `<cfschedule>` tag, instead of using the ColdFusion Administrator.

The System Probes Page

The System Probes page allows you to set up *probes* that check to see whether a particular page is executing normally. If not, ColdFusion can send you an email message so that you are among the very first to know when problems occur.

The System Probes page lists all currently defined probes. Icons are provided to edit or delete each probe. There is also a Disable/Enable icon for each probe, which you can use to temporarily turn a probe on or off. Finally, you can use the Run Probe icon to run a probe immediately, rather than waiting for it to run at its normally scheduled time or interval.

Define New Probe

To create a new probe, click the Define New Probe button. The Add/Edit System Probe page appears. Table 28.3 briefly explains each of the fields on this page. When you're finished, click the Submit button to create the probe.

Table 28.3 Options Available for Each System Probe

OPTION	DESCRIPTION
Probe Name	A name for the new probe.
Frequency	The frequency at which you want the probe to check your ColdFusion page. You can specify the frequency in terms of hours, minutes, and seconds. You must supply a start time; if you wish you may also provide an end time.
URL	The URL of the ColdFusion page (or other document) that you want the probe to check. Any URL that can be accessed via a browser is acceptable. The page doesn't have to be on the same server, or even on the same local network.
User Name	If the page requires authentication, supply a valid user name here.

Table 28.3 (CONTINUED)

OPTION	DESCRIPTION
Password	If the page requires authentication, supply the corresponding password.
Timeout	The number of seconds to wait for the page to respond. If the page doesn't respond within the specified timeout, ColdFusion will consider the probe to have failed and will notify people accordingly.
Proxy Server	If there is a proxy server between the ColdFusion server and the page being tested, enter the address and port number for the proxy server here.
Probe Failure	Check this option to have ColdFusion examine the actual text returned by the page being tested. You can use the Contains option to make sure that the page is generating the content that it's supposed to, by entering a string that should appear near the bottom of the page. Or you could use the Does Not Contain option to make sure that the page doesn't contain an error message or some other "canary in the coal mine."
Failure Actions	You can have ColdFusion send out an email message whenever the probe finds a problem. The message will be sent to and from the addresses discussed in the previous section.
Publish	Enable this option if you want ColdFusion to save the content returned by the page you are checking. If you enable this option, fill in the File field as well.
File	Relevant only when the Publish option is checked. The path and file name to save the tested page's content to. The content will be saved to the server's drive at the location you specify here.
Resolve URL	Relevant only when the Publish option is checked. Enable this option if you want ColdFusion to resolve any internal URLs (such as URLs for images and links) so that the saved version of the page can be viewed correctly in a browser.

System Probe Options

At the bottom of the System Probes page, you will find a number of options to control the way ColdFusion handles notification when a probe finds a problem:

- **Notification Email Recipients.** Provide a list of email addresses that ColdFusion should use when sending out a notification that a probe has found a problem. Everyone you specify here will receive a notification about every failed probe.

- **e-mail.** Specify a valid email address that ColdFusion's notification messages should use as their *from* field.

- **Probe.cfm URL.** Internally, the probe mechanism needs to be able to execute the Probe.cfm template in the CFIDE folder within your Web server root. If for some reason you need to move the template or place it on a different virtual server, edit the URL accordingly. The Probe.cfm template is encrypted; you aren't meant to be able to edit or customize it.

- **Probe.cfm Username and Password.** If you have used your Web server software to secure access to the Probe.cfm file with a username and password, enter that username and password here.

The Code Analyzer Page

While every effort is made to ensure backwards compatibility with prior versions of ColdFusion, it's always best to check your code before upgrading your server. The Code Analyzer page can help you identify most of the potential compatibility issues ahead of time, before you even try to run your application under ColdFusion.

To run the analyzer, specify the location of the application files you would like to test in the Directory to Analyze field, then click Run Analyzer. If you click the Advanced Options button, you will be able to tell ColdFusion which files to inspect (the default is all .cfm files), which incompatibilities to check for (the default is to check for all incompatibilities), which language elements to check, whether to display only serious problems (the Warn or the Info option), and more.

The License Scanner Page

Every non-Developer Edition of ColdFusion must be licensed. To help the system administrator, the License Scanner page can scan your local network and report the ColdFusion servers present and their license numbers.

NOTE

The License Scanner checks the local subnet only, and does not report information to any external locations. This is purely a local reporting option for system administrators.

Server Monitoring

The Server Monitoring section has a single page, which provides access to the ColdFusion Server Monitor.

➔ To learn about the ColdFusion Server Monitor, see Chapter 56, "Monitoring System Performance," in Vol. 3, *Advanced Application Development.*

The Server Monitor Page

The ColdFusion Server Monitor is a Flex application (requiring Flash Player 9 or higher).

Launch Server Monitor

This option launches the server monitor in a separate window. The Server Monitor is used to monitor a single server only, as well as to define system alerts.

Launch Multiserver Monitor

This option launches a dashboard page that can be used to monitor as many ColdFusion servers as needed, both local and remote. Each server must be registered, and a valid server login must be provided. The dashboard will then display the health of each server, and it will provide easy access to the Server Monitor for each of the listed servers.

Extensions

ColdFusion supports several extensibility options, including writing CFX tags with Java or C++, by using CORBA objects, and more. The Extensions section of the Administrator allows you to manage certain options related to extensibility.

The Java Applets Page

You can use the Java Applets page to create aliases for client-side Java applets that you use often throughout your applications. These aliases let you add the applets to individual pages with simpler, more manageable code. Once the alias has been created, you include the actual applet in your pages with the <cfapplet> tag.

The CFX Tags Page

It's possible to create new tags for ColdFusion that are written with Java or C++, rather than CFML; these are called CFX tags. CFX tags are usually created to add some kind of capability that is intrinsically easier or more sensible to implement with Java or C++ than with ColdFusion code. For instance, if you already have C++ code available that completes a particular task, why translate it into the corresponding ColdFusion code when you can just create a CFX tag that leverages the existing C++ code?

Before a CFX tag can be used in your ColdFusion pages, it must be registered using the ColdFusion Administrator. The first thing you will need to know is whether the CFX tag in question was written with Java or C++. If you have been given a .class file (or files), the CFX was written with Java. If it has a .dll extension, it was created with C++.

Registering a Java CFX

To register a Java CFX, follow these steps:

1. On the CFX Tags page, click Register Java CFX. The Add/Edit Java CFX Tag page appears.

2. Enter the name of the CFX tag in the Tag Name field. The name must start with CFX_ (but it's not case sensitive).

3. Enter the name of the class file that implements the CFX tag in the Class Name field. You should type the name of the .class file (but without the .class extension). The class name is case sensitive, so make sure to get the capitalization exactly right. The actual .class file (as well as any other classes or files that the .class file depends on) must be located somewhere within the Java class path (see the Java and JVM Page section, earlier in this chapter).

4. If you wish, provide a description for the CFX tag.

5. Click the Submit button to register the CFX tag. Assuming that there are no problems with the CFX tag internally, and assuming that the .class file can be found in the Java class path, you can now use the CFX tag in your ColdFusion pages.

Registering a C++ CFX

To register a CFX tag that was written in C++, follow these steps:

1. On the CFX Tags page, click Register C++ CFX. The Add/Edit C++ CFX Tag page appears.

2. Enter the name of the CFX tag in the Tag Name field. The name must start with `CFX_` (but it's not case sensitive).

3. Enter the name and location of the file that implements the CFX tag in the Class Name field. Most likely, this is a dynamic link library (`.dll`) file. You can use the Browse Server button to locate the file without typing.

4. Leave the Procedure field set to `ProcessTagRequest` unless you have been told otherwise by whoever created the CFX.

5. If you wish, provide a description for the CFX tag.

6. Click the Submit button to register the CFX tag. Assuming that there are no problems with the CFX tag internally, you can now use the CFX tag in your ColdFusion pages.

NOTE

Until you know how a CFX tag behaves on your system, and until you can be sure of its safety and reliability, it is best to uncheck the Keep Library Loaded option.

The Custom Tag Paths Page

The default location for custom tags is the `/CustomTags` folder directory beneath the ColdFusion root.

To add a new custom tag path, enter the location in the New Path field and click Add Path. Once the path has been created, you can now place custom tag files within the folder you specified, and they will be found automatically, as if they were placed in the default folder.

To edit or delete an existing tag path, use the icons provided for each entry in the Current Custom Tag Paths list.

NOTE

If Enable Per App Settings (on the Settings page) is checked, you can define custom tag locations for specific applications in `Application.cfc`.

The CORBA Connectors Page

If you plan to invoke CORBA objects or services within your ColdFusion pages, you need to set up a CORBA connector for the ORB you plan to use to broker your requests. ColdFusion ships with support for Borland's VisiBroker product. If you need support for a different ORB vendor's product, you will need to contact Adobe.

Assuming you intend to use the VisiBroker support rather than some other ORB, you need to add a connector for VisiBroker by following these steps:

1. Click the Register CORBA Connector button on the CORBA Connectors page of the Administrator. The Edit CORBA Connector page appears.

2. In the ORB Name field, enter a descriptive name for the connector, such as `visibroker`.

3. In the ORB Class Name field, enter `coldfusion.runtime.corba.VisibrokerConnector`

4. Leave the `Classpath` field blank.

5. In the ORB Property File field, enter the path to the `vbjorb.properties` file in ColdFusion's lib folder. For a default Windows installation, the correct path would be `C:\ColdFusion8\lib\vbjorb.properties`.

6. Click Submit to create the connector.

7. Edit the `SVCnameroot` property in the `vbjorb.properties` file appropriately so that ColdFusion is able to find the root.

In addition, you will need to provide the appropriate value to the `SVCnameroot` property in the `vbjorb.properties` file. You will also need to make sure that the `vbjorb.jar` file is present (this file is distributed with VisiBroker) and that the path to `vbjorb.jar` is part of ColdFusion's Java class path setting (see the Java and JVM Page section, earlier in this chapter).

➜ CORBA integration is covered in Chapter 77.

Event Gateways

Event gateways are the means by which ColdFusion connects to external systems (to generate message as well as to respond to inbound requests). This section is used to define and manage event gateways and their settings.

➜ Event gateways are covered in detail in Chapter 80, "Working with Gateways," in Vol. 3, *Advanced Application Development*.

The Settings Page

The Setting page is used to enable or disable event gateway processing, and to define gateway settings.

Enable ColdFusion Event Gateway Services

The gateway engine must be enabled to perform any gateway processing, and can be turned off to reduce overhead if gateways aren't being used.

Event Gateway Processing Threads

By default, 10 threads are allocated for gateway processing. If you have a large number of active gateways, or very heavy gateway load, you should increase this number. Higher numbers will improve gateway performance but will also increase server resource usage.

NOTE

The defaults and values are lower in the ColdFusion Developer Edition.

Maximum Number of Events to Queue

The maximum number of events to be queued is set to 25,000 by default. When this number is reached, no additional events will be placed in the processing queue.

SMS Test Server

ColdFusion includes an SMS test server that can be used to simulate the SMS world so as to build SMS applications. The SMS test server can be started and stopped as needed.

➜ The SMS Gateway is covered in detail in Chapter 81, "Integrating with SMS and IM," in Vol. 3, *Advanced Application Development*.

The Gateway Types Page

Gateways are written in Java, and must be registered on the server before they can be instantiated. Gateway Type management is performed in this page.

To add a gateway, provide a name, a description, and the location of the Java `.class` file. Then click the Add button.

To edit or delete defined gateways, use the icons to the left of the Configured Gateway Type list.

The Gateway Instances Page

Gateway instances are defined in this. One or more instances of any gateway type may be defined.

To add a gateway instance, provide a unique ID (name), select a type, provide the path to the CFC file that should process gateway requests, specify an optional configuration file, and select a startup mode. Then click the Add Gateway Instance button.

To edit or delete defined gateways, or to start and stop gateway instances, use the icons to the left of the Configured Gateway Instances list.

Security

ColdFusion provides a number of security-related features. Some of these features let you add login and role-based security mechanisms to your own applications. The options in the Security portion of the ColdFusion Administrator, in contrast, are about securing the server itself so that only the proper people have the ability to administer ColdFusion. You can also lock down various parts of the server (tags, files, data sources, and so on) so that each application only has the right to use its own files and data.

The Administrator Page

The ColdFusion Administrator enables the configuration and management of the ColdFusion server. Therefore, the ColdFusion Administrator should generally be password protected to prevent unauthorized access.

ColdFusion Administrator Authentication

To support a single administration login and password, select the first option. To support multiple administrators, each possibly with a different level of access, select the second option. To allow access without a password, select the third option.

CAUTION

Use of the third option is not recommended.

Root Administrator Password

Use this option to change the primary ColdFusion Administrator password.

The RDS Password Page

RDS is used to provide development time access to ColdFusion data sources, files, reporting building, and more. Because RDS can expose sensitive files and data, it should always be secured.

NOTE

RDS should never be installed on production servers.

RDS Authentication

To support a single RDS login and password, select the first option. To support multiple RDS logins, each possibly tied to a different sandbox, select the second option. To allow access without a password, select the third option.

CAUTION

Use of the third option is not recommended.

RDS Single Password

Use this option to change the primary RDS password.

The Sandbox Security Page

ColdFusion includes a feature called *sandbox security*. This feature is mostly aimed at Internet service providers or people running large enterprise-wide servers, where a server may have many different ColdFusion applications written by many different developers. In such a situation, there needs to be some way to keep one set of developers from accessing the data sources that are being used by another set of developers. Similarly, there needs to be some way to keep one application from being able to use <cffile> or <cfdirectory> to read or destroy files that are important to another application.

The idea behind sandbox security is to enable you to tell the server that the ColdFusion pages in certain directories either have more or fewer privileges than all other ColdFusion pages. For each of these special directories ("sandboxes"), you can tell ColdFusion to:

- Allow or forbid ColdFusion pages from accessing certain data sources via <cfquery>, <cfinsert>, <cfupdate> or similar tags.

- Allow or forbid ColdFusion pages from using accessing certain files or directories via <cfdirectory>, <cffile>, <cfexecute> and related tags and functions.

- Allow or forbid ColdFusion pages from using certain CFML tags and functions altogether.

- Allow or forbid ColdFusion pages from accessing other servers over the Internet with the <cfhttp>, <cfftp>, <cfmail> or similar tags.

There are basically two ways to go about managing sandboxes for your ColdFusion server:

- If there is a particular application (or developer) that you don't trust to behave nicely, you can create a sandbox for its root directory that denies it access to everything but what it actually needs. All other applications, including those created in the future, will be unaffected.

- If you would rather consider all applications to be untrustworthy (or if the applications shouldn't be considered to trust one another), you can create a larger sandbox for your entire document root that denies access to everything. You then create smaller sandboxes for each individual application, specifically granting access to only what that application needs.

In general, the second approach is the most flexible, and doesn't require very much extra effort.

Server sandbox security is managed in the Sandbox Security page.

Enable ColdFusion Security

By default sandbox security isn't enabled. To enable sandbox security, check this box. Changing this setting will require a ColdFusion server restart.

Add Security Sandbox

To create a new security sandbox, enter the path to the directory you want to make more or less omniscient in the Add Security Sandbox field (you can use the Browse Server button to specify the directory without typing). When you click the Add button, the new sandbox is added to the Defined Directory Permissions list.

TIP

If you want, you can select an existing sandbox from the drop-down list, which will cause all the access rights from the selected sandbox to be copied to the sandbox you're creating. This can be a real time-saver if you are creating multiple sandboxes with similar access rights.

Defined Directory Permissions

To edit a sandbox—including one you just added—click the Edit icon for the sandbox. To remove a sandbox, click the Delete icon.

When you click the Edit icon for a sandbox, the Security Permissions page appears. This page has five tabs across the top, the first of which is Data Sources.

Data Sources

ColdFusion pages in the sandbox directory you're editing will be able to access all the data sources in the Enabled Data Sources list (on the left). To disable access to a data source, select it and click the >> button to move it into the Disabled Data Sources list. Continue to move the data sources back and forth until only the appropriate data sources are enabled.

NOTE

The special `<<ALL DATA SOURCES>>` item behaves like a wild card. It represents all data sources that exist now as well as ones that are created in the future. If you move this item to the disabled side of the page, the sandbox won't have access to any data sources at all (unless access is specifically granted by some other nested sandbox).

CF Tags

You can restrict access to CFML functions as needed. To restrict the use of CFML tags, move them from the Enabled Tags list to the Disabled Tags list.

CF Functions

You can restrict access to CFML functions as needed. To restrict the use of CFML functions, move them from the Enabled Functions list to the Disabled Functions list.

Files/Dirs

Use the Files/Dirs tab to keep the `<cffile>`, `<cfdirectory>`, `<cfexecute>` and similar tags and functions from being able to freely access or change the files on the server's drive. When you create a sandbox, two paths are automatically added to the Secured Files and Directories list.

NOTE

Restricting the files and directories that can be accessed via the `<cffile>` and `<cfdirectory>` tags is separate from enabling or disabling the tags themselves. To disable the actual tags for a sandbox, use the CF Tags tab (discussed in the previous section).

Servers/Ports

For each sandbox, you can restrict the ability of ColdFusion pages to access other servers on the Internet via the `<cfhttp>`, `<cfmail>`, `<cfpop>`, `<cfldap>`, or `<cfftp>`. By default, any of these tags can access any machine on the Internet. For each sandbox, you can add entries for specific machines and IP ports. From that point forward, the tags can only access the machines and IP ports you added. Any attempt to access some other machine or port number will fail.

For instance, you might want to let most of your applications be able to use the `<cfhttp>` tag, but you want to make sure that the `<cfhttp>` tag can only be used to retrieve pages from certain sites, for instance Google and Yahoo! You don't want ColdFusion code to be able to retrieve pages from arbitrary URLs on the Internet. This is easily accomplished by specifically enabling IP port 80 for each of the desired sites.

Once sandbox security access has been defined, click the Finish button to save changes.

The User Manager Page

As seen previously, both the ColdFusion Administrator and RDS support single-password logins and multiple logins. To use the latter, you define users using this page.

Click the Add User button to add a user and then define the username, password, and permissions for this user.

Packaging and Deployment

ColdFusion applications are collections of files that can easily be copied and moved between servers. But moving individual files is a highly error-prone exercise, and so ColdFusion provides more manageable ways to distribute and deploy applications.

The ColdFusion Archives Page

At any point during your application's development, you can use the ColdFusion Administrator to create a *ColdFusion archive* of your application. ColdFusion archives are files that can contain all the files needed to run your application, such as your ColdFusion (`.cfm`) pages, image files, XML files, desktop database files, Flash movies, and any other files that your application depends on.

But ColdFusion archives can include more than just your application files; they can also include any Administrator settings that your application depends on. In other words, the idea behind the Cold-Fusion archive feature is to give you a way to create a single file that contains everything needed to make your application work. It's a great way to back up your work.

ColdFusion archives are also about deployment. Once you have created an archive for your application, you can copy the single archive file to another ColdFusion server. Your application can then be installed in one step. All of your application's files will be unpacked from the archive and placed in the appropriate places on the server, and all of the required configuration changes (such as setting up data sources and mappings) will be made automatically. In most cases, this means that you can move your applications from your development servers to your staging or production servers without having to manually copy individual files or make changes in each server's ColdFusion Administrator.

ColdFusion Archives are created and used from within the ColdFusion Archives page.

Deploy an Existing Archive

It's easy to restore all the files and settings stored in an archive, or to deploy an archive to a new ColdFusion server. Just follow these steps:

1. If necessary, copy the .car file to a folder on the server's drive (or place it at a location that is accessible to the ColdFusion service on your local network).

2. In the Deploy an Existing Archive field, provide the location and file name of the .car file. You can use the Browse Server button to browse for and select the archive file without typing.

3. Click the Deploy button. The Archive Wizard appears, displaying information about what files and settings are contained in the archive.

4. When you click Next, the Deploy Location step appears. You can use this page to provide a different location for each of the folders that were originally added to the archive. You might want to change the locations if you are deploying the archive to a ColdFusion server whose document root is on a different drive or folder location than the server you created the archive on. You might also want to change the locations if you don't want the files in the archive to overwrite the files that are currently on your server, or if you just want to test the archive functionality.

5. When you click Next again, the archive will be deployed. All the files in the archive will be unpacked and placed in the appropriate locations on your server, and the settings for any data sources, directory mappings, CFX tags, or other items that you selected while creating the archive definition will be added or changed in the ColdFusion Administrator for you.

CAUTION

When you deploy an archive, any existing files on the server will be overwritten with the version of the files in the archive. If you are using an archive file that contains an older version of your application, make sure you specify different folder locations before you deploy.

Creating a New Archive

There are two steps to creating a ColdFusion archive for your application. First, you use the Cold-Fusion Administrator to create a new *archive definition*. The archive definition is just a list of the files and settings that should be included in the archive. Once the archive definition has been created, you can use the definition to *build* an actual archive (.car) file at any time. The archive will include a snapshot of the current files and settings. When the files change and you want to create a new snapshot, you can build the archive again, using the same definition.

To create an archive definition, simply type a name in the Archive Name field in the Create New Archive section of the Archives and Deployment page, then click Create. The Archive Wizard appears, which walks you through the processes of selecting which files and which settings should be included in the archive each time it's built. The first step of the Archive Wizard simply asks you to provide an optional description to explain the purpose of the archive.

NOTE

In addition, there are Select All and Deselect All buttons on this screen. Clicking the Select All button is a shortcut for checking all the options on subsequent steps of the wizard; Deselect All unchecks them all.

NOTE

Selecting a data source in the Archive Wizard just means that the data source definition (that is, the Administrator settings) will be included in the archive. It doesn't mean that the database itself will be included in the archive. If you are using a file-based database such as Access, you could include the `.mdb` file in the archive using the previous step; assuming that you are using a server-based database system such as Oracle or SQL Server, you probably want your application to continue connecting to the same external database server.

The same basic process applies to the other portions of the Archive Wizard. When you are finished making your selections, click Close Window to return to the ColdFusion Administrator.

Current Archive Definition List

Now that you have created an archive definition, you can take a snapshot of your application at any time by building an archive (`.car`) file. Just click on the Build Archive icon for your archive definition at the bottom of the Archives and Deployment page. The Build CAR File Archive wizard appears with some summary information about what will be included in the archive.

When you click Next, the Archive File Location step appears, which allows you to choose a file location for the new archive file. The new archive file will be saved to this location on the server's drive. You can use the Browse Server button to browse for the directory location. You must specify a file name with a `.car` extension. If you choose a `.car` file that already exists, it will be overwritten without warning.

When you click Next again, the archive will be built. You will see status messages while ColdFusion adds items to the archive. When the build process is complete, a Build Successful message will be displayed.

Now look in the folder you specified for the archive location. You will see your new archive there. You can now burn the archive to a CD or tape to back up your work, or copy the archive to another ColdFusion server to deploy your application in one step.

CAUTION

ColdFusion may show the Build Successful message before the archive is actually complete. Make sure the archive has finished building (by watching the size of the archive until it stops increasing) before you copy the file to another location.

ColdFusion Archive (`.car`) files are similar conceptually and structurally to ZIP (`.zip`) archives or Java Archive (`.jar`) files. A program like WinZip will be able to make some sense of the file, but it will probably not be able to unpack the files correctly. The archive files are designed to only be unpacked by a ColdFusion server.

You can edit or delete an existing archive definition at any time by clicking the Edit Archive Definition or Delete Archive icons at the bottom of the Archives and Deployment page.

Deleting an archive definition just removes the definition from the Administrator, not any actual archive (`.car`) files that you may have built with the definition in the past. You need to delete the archive files yourself.

The J2EE Archives Page

Java applications deployed on J2EE servers are usually deployed as EAR or WAR files. As ColdFusion itself is a Java application, it can be installed as an EAR or a WAR, as can applications you create. J2EE archive packaging is managed from the J2EE Archives page.

Add New Archive

To create a new deployment archive, enter an archive name and click the Add button to display the Add/Edit J2EE Archive screen. You will be prompted for the location of your application, the location to store the created archive, the destination serial number, as well as the ColdFusion features to include in the deployment package. Once you have specified these values click Submit to create the deployment package.

Configured Archives

Packages may be modified and deleted as needed. Package deployment is performed using your J2EE server management tools.

CHAPTER 29

Improving the User Experience

Usability Considerations

This chapter concentrates on issues regarding the overall user experience and ways to improve it. The term *user experience* is vague and hard to measure, and different people define it differently. For our purposes, think of the quality of the user experience as being affected mainly by the combination of an application's performance, usability, and friendliness.

In other words, do people have a pleasant experience when they use your application?

Put Yourself in the User's Shoes

One of the best ways to ensure that your application is pleasant for your users is just to keep them in mind as you do your development work. When you are deep into a development project, perhaps rushing to meet a deadline, it's easy to produce code that works well enough for you to move on to the next task, without asking yourself whether it's really good enough for the user.

Even if you aren't responsible for the design or navigation, you still should keep the user in mind as you put together each data-entry screen, or code each query. If users are happy, your application will probably be successful. If they spend too much time waiting, or get confused, your application probably won't be successful. In most situations, especially applications aimed at the general public, it's as simple as that.

Think About Navigation

Entire books have been written on great ways to set up navigation elements for Web sites. Navigation elements should not only look good, but also be clear and easy to use. They shouldn't offer too many choices, especially on your application's first page. At the same time, most Web sites try to put the most important content no deeper than three levels (clicks) into the navigation structure. The most important or most commonly used items should appear before the less important ones, even if this makes the sequence less predictable.

Studying the navigation elements used by your favorite Web sites—the ones you use often—can help. What do these sites have in common? What's the theory behind the navigation on each page? For instance, does it adapt itself to context, or does it remain consistent from page to page? Why do some elements appear on the home page, but others on a second-level page? Try to come up with rules that explain which items appear on which pages, and where. For instance, some sites tend to put "verbs" (actions) in a toolbar at the top of each page and "nouns" (articles, accounts) in the left margin; other sites do the reverse. Try to come up with similar rules for what goes where within your own application.

TIP

Discussions on navigation and other design elements can be found on a number of developer-related Web sites. One good place to start is the Dimitry's Design Lab section at the WebReference Web site (`www.webreference.com/dlab`).

Why It's Good to Be Predictable

When describing a book or a movie, the word "predictable" isn't much of a compliment. But when describing a Web application, predictability is to be pursued and cherished. As users move from page to page, they will feel most comfortable if they can predict or guess what's going to appear next.

Anticipating the User's Next Move

As you put together a page, don't think only about what users are going to do on that page; try to imagine what they're likely to do next. If users are filling out a registration form, they might want to know your company's privacy policy. If they're reading a press release, they might appreciate links to the company's corporate information and facts about its management team.

In general, on any page, try to put yourself in the user's shoes and ask yourself whether it's clear how to get to the next step or the next piece of information.

Scripting, Rollovers, and Widgets

JavaScript and Dynamic HTML can help make your applications more exciting to your users, but they also can cause problems. For instance, image rollovers are great when used judiciously but can really slow a page down if you go overboard.

In particular, Dynamic HTML functionality is notorious for behaving differently from browser to browser, version to version, and platform to platform. If you use Dynamic HTML, try to find cross-browser scripts you can adapt until you understand the specific limitations. As a start, `www.webreference.com` and `www.builder.com` are good places to look for scripts that work reasonably well in a variety of browsers.

You may want to consider using Flash instead of Dynamic HTML, since a Flash movie almost always behaves the same way no matter what browser or platform it is viewed with.

Dealing with Problems Gracefully

Even the best-crafted application can encounter problems or error conditions, so make your error messages friendly and encouraging to users, so they don't lose trust in your Web site.

For instance, consider customizing all error messages so they match the site's look and feel. For instructions, see the section "Customizing the Look of Error Messages" in Chapter 19, "Introducing the Web Application Framework," in *Adobe ColdFusion 8 Web Application Construction Kit, Volume 1: Getting Started.* Also see Chapter 51, "Error Handling," online.

Easing the Browser's Burden

If an application isn't running as fast as you want, look for a source of trouble on the server side, such as a `<cfquery>` tag that is taking too long to execute. Also, think about how much work the browser is doing to display your pages.

If you're having performance troubles, turn on the debugging options in the ColdFusion Administrator so you can see the execution time for the page. This shows you how long the server is taking to complete your CFML template(s). If the server execution time is nice and short (under a couple of hundred milliseconds, say) but pages still seem to come up slowly for some users, the problem is probably something like image size, the overuse of tables, or some other topic discussed in this section. If, on the other hand, the server execution time is long, then you need to work on the code in your CFML templates themselves.

Dealing with Image Size

No matter how ardently you strive to make your application generate sensible HTML, and no matter how hard you work to ensure that all your queries and other server-side code runs quickly, a lot of large images can slow your pages. Not only can such images take a long time to download, they also take up room in the browser machine's memory. This can affect the user's computer, depending on how much RAM and virtual memory are available.

Here are some suggestions to keep image size in check:

- **Create or resave your images using a program that can compress or optimize images for use on the Web.** You give up a bit of image quality for a smaller file size, but the trade-off is generally worth it. Adobe's Fireworks product also does a great job of compressing image files and generally optimizing them for display on the Web. Adobe Photoshop CS includes a terrific Save for Web option on the File menu, which lets you preview how your images will look after they are optimized.

- **Create or resave JPEGs using a progressive JPEG option, so the images can be displayed in increasingly finer detail as they are downloaded.** This is more pleasant for users because they don't have to wait for the whole file to download before they can get a sense of the image. Most graphic-manipulation packages let you save progressive JPEGs.

- **The `width` and `height` attributes you supply to an `img` tag don't have to reflect the actual width and height of the image file.** You could, for instance, create an image file that is 50 by 50 pixels, yet provide `width` and `height` attributes of `100` each. The image's file size would be much smaller, but it would take up the same amount of space on the page. Of course, it would appear pixelated, but depending on the nature of the artwork, that might not matter.

- **Always try to provide a sensible `alt` or `title` attribute for each `<img>` tag to describe the image.** Most browsers display any text you provide in an `alt` or `title` attribute while the image is loading or as a tool tip when the mouse pointer hovers over the image. This lets the user anticipate what each image is before it is actually displayed.

- **Consider using the `lowsrc` attribute for your larger `<img>` tags.** With the `lowsrc` attribute, a small version of the image is displayed while the full-size one is being downloaded. Consult the HTML Reference section of the Dreamweaver or HomeSite+ online help for details.

Finally, ask yourself if big images are really necessary. Can they be eliminated, or at least be made a bit smaller? Look at the Web sites you use on a daily basis. How many images do you see? Most likely, not that many. Popular sites often use other techniques (especially type size and background colors) to give a page visual impact, and they use images sparingly.

NOTE

Always provide `width` and `height` attributes for each `<img>` tag. This lets the browser display the rest of the page correctly before it has loaded the images. Without `width` and `height`, the browser might have to wait until all the images have loaded to display anything, or it might have to reflow the document several times as each image loads. The exact behavior varies from browser to browser.

Use Tables Wisely

HTML tables are a great way to display information in any type of rows-and-columns format, such as the next-n examples shown later in this chapter. These tips will help you make the most of them without placing an undue burden on the browser:

- **Whenever possible, provide `width` attributes for each `<th>` or `<td>` cell in the table.** This usually speeds up the display of the table.

- **Specify the `width` attribute for an entire table as a percentage.** For instance, `width="100%"` tells the browser to make the table take up the entire available width of the page. You can also use percentages for the widths of each `<th>` and `<td>` cell. For instance, if three `<td>` cells were in a table row, you could use `width="50%"` for the first one and `width="25%"` for the second two. This is helpful when you want content to spread itself evenly across the page regardless of screen resolution. If the user resizes the page, the table automatically resizes as well.

- **Use tables instead of solid images to add color, style, and callout sections to a page.** If you want to fill a section of the screen with a light blue color, why send a light blue image to the browser when you can just include a light blue table cell instead, by seeing the cell's `bgcolor` to blue? The result will be smaller file size and faster speed.

- **Try not to use tables to control an entire page's layout.** Because tables usually can't be displayed incrementally, a table often won't be displayed until the closing `</table>` tag is encountered. If your whole page is laid out using a single, large table, the page might not be displayed at all until the whole page has been received (regardless of what you do with the `<cfflush>` tag discussed below). Sometimes, however, a table can be displayed incrementally. The exact behavior varies from browser to browser. See the `cols` attribute for the `<table>` tag in an HTML reference for details.

Using External Script and Style Files

We don't discuss the use of JavaScript and Cascading Style Sheets (CSS) in this book, but they often become important parts of ColdFusion applications. CSS and JavaScript code usually are included as part of the HTML document itself, generally in the `<head>` section. If you use the same JavaScript functions or CSS classes over and over again on a number of pages, consider moving the script or CSS code into separate files.

This way, the browser must download the file only once, at the beginning of each session (depending on how the user has set up the browser's caching preferences), rather than as a part of each page. This can make your pages display more quickly, especially for modem users—and especially if your script or CSS code is rather long.

To move frequently used JavaScript functions into a separate file, save the JavaScript code to a file with a `.js` extension. The file should not include opening and closing `<script>` tags; it should contain only the JavaScript code. Next, in place of the original `<script>` block, include a reference to the `.js` file using the `src` attribute of the `<script>` tag, like this (the closing `</script>` tag is required):

```
<script language="JavaScript" src="MyScripts.js"></script>
```

Similarly, to move frequently used CSS code into a separate file, save it to a file with a `.css` extension. The file shouldn't include any `<style>` tags, just the CSS code. Now, in place of the original `<style>` block, include a reference to the `.css` file using the `<link>` tag:

```
<link rel="stylesheet" type="text/css" href="MyStyles.css">
```

Browser Compatibility Issues

Not all browsers support all HTML tags. For instance, neither Internet Explorer nor Netscape 6 (or later) supports the `<layer>` tag that was introduced in Netscape Communicator 4.0. Netscape browsers don't support the `<marquee>` tag introduced by IE. Support for various tags also differs across browser versions—for instance, the `<iframe>` tag wasn't supported in Netscape browsers until version 6.0. Support for more advanced technologies, such as JavaScript and Dynamic HTML, varies even more widely.

You can use the automatic `CGI.http_user_agent` variable to determine which browser is being used to access the currently executing template. The `http_user_agent` value is a string provided by the browser for identification purposes. You can look at the string with ColdFusion's string functions to determine the browser and version number. For instance, the following line of code can be placed in `Application.cfc` to determine whether the Microsoft Internet Explorer browser is being used:

```
<cfset REQUEST.isIE = CGI.http_user_agent contains "MSIE">
```

You then could use the `REQUEST.isIE` variable in any of your application's pages (including custom tags or modules) to display Internet Explorer–specific content when appropriate:

```
<cfif REQUEST.isIE>
 <!--- Internet Explorer content goes here --->
<cfelse>
 <!--- Non-IE content goes here --->
</cfif>
```

Remembering Settings

One way to make your application more helpful is to have it remember certain settings or actions as users interact with it. For instance, in Chapter 20, "Working with Sessions," in Vol. 1, *Getting Started*, ColdFusion's Client Management feature was used to remember the words the user searched for last. When the user later returns to the search page, the user's most recent search phrase is already filled in. This improves the user experience by saving time and making users feel at home.

Remembering Usernames and Passwords

If your application requires visitors to log in by providing a username and password, consider adding some type of "remember me" option on the login form. This would cause the username to be pre-filled when the user next logs in. You can use the same basic technique used in the `SearchForm1.cfm` and `SearchForm2.cfm` templates in Chapter 20. Instead of using the `CLIENT` scope to remember the last search phrase, use it to remember and prefill the username.

Of course, this makes your application less secure, because anyone with physical access to the machine could see the person's user name. Do whatever makes sense for your application.

Other Helpful Settings to Remember

Many other things can be remembered between visits to save users time and make them feel more at home:

- If the users have indicated which country they live in, you could show them content relevant to their country each time they return to your site, perhaps even translated into the appropriate language.

- If the user has a favorite color, you could store the color in the `CLIENT` scope and use it to set the `bgcolor` for the `<body>` tags at the top of each page.

Avoid the "Big Brother" Effect

Once you start thinking about remembering settings for users, it becomes clear that you probably could retain information on just about everything they do, on which pages, and when. However, if your application begins to flaunt its knowledge of users' actions, you may start to lose their trust. People enjoy having sites personalized for them, but they don't like to feel as if their every move is being watched and recorded. Also, be sure you aren't violating your client or company's privacy policy.

Creating Next-n Records Interfaces

Sooner or later, you will run into a situation in which you need to build what we call a *next-n interface*. A next-n interface is used in any Web page that lets the user view a portion of a large number of records—say, 10 or 20 at a time. Such interfaces are common on search-engine Web sites, which might have 1,000 records to look through. Instead of showing you all 1,000 records at once, the page provides buttons or links labeled Next and Back that let you move through them in more reasonable chunks.

Advantages of Next-n Interfaces

This type of interface has a number of advantages:

- **Familiarity.** Because next-n interfaces are so common, many users expect them whenever they are presented with a large number of records. If they see a ton of records without such an interface, your application might appear unfinished.

- **Performance.** Next-n interfaces put an upper boundary on the size of the generated HTML, so pages that use them usually are easier on both the browser machine and the ColdFusion server.

- **Readability.** Most importantly, next-n interfaces usually enable users to more easily find the information they are looking for: reading a small page is faster than reading a large one.

When to Create a Next-n Interface

It will usually be obvious when you need to add a next-n interface to a particular display page. Other times, though, it becomes evident only over time, as the number of records in the database grows. A year after an application is deployed, what was once a nice, compact data-display page may have ballooned to the point of being slow and unmanageable. So, consider creating some variation on the next-n interface presented in this chapter whenever you think the user might sometime need to look at a large number of records.

TIP

You might come up with an internal policy stipulating that whenever a user will be presented with more than 50 records, a next-n interface should be implemented. You might pick a larger cutoff point if your users have fast connection speeds, or a smaller one if many users will connect via slow modems.

Creating the Basic Interface

Say you have been asked to create a simple expense report area for Orange Whip Studios' intranet. You have only been told to create a page in which employees can review all expenses, but folks in the accounting department say they usually want to see the most recent expenses. You decide to display the expense records in reverse order (the most recent expense first), with a next-10 interface. This way, users can see the new expenses right away, and page through the older records ten at a time.

This section presents four versions of a typical next-n interface, each version a bit more sophisticated than the one before it.

Limiting the Number of Records Shown

A number of approaches can be taken to create a next-n interface. Listing 29.1 demonstrates a simple, effective technique you can easily adapt to your needs.

The code relies on a URL parameter named `startRow`, which tells the template which records to display. The first time the page is displayed, `startRow` defaults to 1, which causes rows 1–10 to be displayed. When the user clicks the Next button, `startRow` is passed as 11, so rows 11–20 are displayed. The user can continue to click Next (or Back) to move through all the records.

NOTE

Before this listing will work, the `APPLICATION.dataSource` variable needs to be set in your `Application.cfc` file, as shown in Listing 29.2. Listing 29.3, later in this chapter, also must be in place.

Listing 29.1 `NextN1.cfm`—A Simple Next-n Interface

```
<!---
 Filename: NextN1.cfm
 Created by: Nate Weiss (NMW)
 Purpose: Displays Next N record-navigation interface
 Please Note Includes NextNIncludeBackNext.cfm template
--->

<!--- Retrieve expense records from database --->
<cfquery name="getExp" datasource="#APPLICATION.DataSource#">
 SELECT
 f.FilmID, f.MovieTitle,
 e.Description, e.ExpenseAmount, e.ExpenseDate
 FROM
 Expenses e INNER JOIN Films f
 ON e.FilmID = f.FilmID
 ORDER BY
 e.ExpenseDate DESC
</cfquery>


<!--- Number of rows to display per Next/Back page --->
<cfset rowsPerPage = 10>

<!--- What row to start at? Assume first by default --->
```

Listing 29.1 (CONTINUED)

```
<cfparam name="URL.startRow" default="1" type="numeric">

<!--- We know the total number of rows from query --->
<cfset totalRows = getExp.recordCount>

<!--- Last row is 10 rows past the starting row, or --->
<!--- total number of query rows, whichever is less --->
<cfset endRow = min(URL.startRow + rowsPerPage - 1, totalRows)>

<!--- Next button goes to 1 past current end row --->
<cfset startRowNext = endRow + 1>

<!--- Back button goes back N rows from start row --->
<cfset startRowBack = URL.startRow - rowsPerPage>

<html>
<head><title>Expense Browser</title></head>
<body>
<cfoutput><h2>#APPLICATION.companyName# Expense Report</h2></cfoutput>


<table width="600" border="0" cellSpacing="0" cellPadding="1" cols="3">
 <!--- Row at top of table, above column headers --->
 <tr>
 <td colSpan="2">
 <!--- Message about which rows are being displayed --->
 <cfoutput>
 Displaying <b>#URL.startRow#</b> to <b>#endRow#</b>
 of <b>#totalRows#</b> Records<br>
 </cfoutput>
 </td>
 <td></td>
 <td align="right">
 <!--- Provide Next/Back links --->
 <cfinclude template="NextNIncludeBackNext.cfm">
 </td>
 </tr>

 <!--- Row for column headers --->
 <tr>
 <th width="100">Date</th>
 <th width="250">Film</th>
 <th width="150">Expense</th>
 <th width="100">Amount</th>
 </tr>

 <!--- For each query row that should be shown now --->
 <cfloop query="getExp" startRow="#URL.startRow#" endRow="#endRow#">
 <cfoutput>
 <tr valign="baseline">
 <td width="100">#lsDateFormat(ExpenseDate)#</td>
 <td width="250">#MovieTitle#</td>
 <td width="150"><em>#Description#</em></td>
 <td width="100">#lsCurrencyFormat(ExpenseAmount)#</td>
 </tr>
```

Listing 29.1 (CONTINUED)

```
</cfoutput>
</cfloop>

<!--- Row at bottom of table, after rows of data --->
<tr>
<td colSpan="4" align="right">
<!--- Provide Next/Back links --->
<cfinclude template="NextNIncludeBackNext.cfm">
</td>
</tr>
</table>


</body>
</html>
```

NOTE

This listing relies on the `startRow` and `endRow` attributes for the `<cfloop>` tag. See Chapter 9, "Programming with CFML" in Vol. 1, *Getting Started*, for detailed information about `<cfloop>`.

First, a query named `getExp` is run, which retrieves all expense records from the `Expenses` table, along with the associated `MovieTitle` for each expense. The records are returned in reverse date order (most recent expenses first). Next, a variable called `rowsPerPage` is set to the number of rows that should be displayed to the user at one time. You can adjust this value to `20`, `50`, or whatever you feel is appropriate.

TIP

You could set the `rowsPerPage` variable in `Application.cfc` if you wanted to use the same value in a number of different next-n interfaces throughout your application.

The `URL.startRow` parameter is established via the `<cfparam>` tag and given a default value of `1` if it isn't supplied in the URL. Then, a `totalRows` variable is set to the number of rows returned by the `getExp` query.

TIP

Sometimes it's worth setting a variable just to keep your code clear. In this template, you could skip the `<cfset>` for the `totalRows` variable and use `getExp.recordCount` in its place throughout the rest of the code. But the name of the `totalRows` variable helps make the role of the value easier to understand, and the extra line of code entails virtually no performance penalty.

Next, a variable called `endRow` is calculated, which determines the row that should be the last to appear on a given page. In general, the `endRow` is simply `rowsPerPage` past the `startRow`. However, the `endRow` should never go past the total number of rows in the query, so the `min` function is used to ensure that the value is never greater than `totalRows`. This becomes important when the user reaches the last page of search results. The `URL.startRow` and `endRow` values are passed to the `startRow` and `endRow` attributes of the `<cfloop>` that displays the expense records, effectively throttling the display so it shows only the appropriate records for the current page.

startRowNext and startRowBack represent what the new startRow value should be if the user clicks the Next or Back link. If the user clicks Next, the page is reloaded at one row past the current endRow. If the user clicks Back, the display moves back by the value stored in rowsPerPage (which is 10 in this example).

After this small set of variables has been calculated, the rest of the template is simple. An HTML table is used to display the expense results. The first row of the table displays a message about which rows are currently being shown. It also displays Next and Back links, as appropriate, by including the NextNIncludeBackNext.cfm template (see Listing 29.3). The next row of the table displays some simple column headings. Then the <cfloop> tag is used to output a table row for each record returned by the getExp query, but only for the rows from URL.startRow through endRow. Finally, the last row of the HTML table repeats the same Next and Back links under the expense records, using an identical <cfinclude> tag.

For now, don't worry about the fact that the query must be rerun each time the user clicks the Next or Back link. ColdFusion's query-caching feature can be used to ensure that your database isn't queried unnecessarily. See Chapter 31, "Improving Performance," for details.

The Application.cfc file shown in Listing 29.2 establishes the APPLICATION.DataSource and APPLICATION.CompanyName variables used in Listing 29.1. Because they are set in the special APPLICATION scope, these variables are available for use within any of this folder's templates, including any custom tags (see Chapter 25, "Creating Custom Tags"). This is an excellent way to establish global settings for an application, such as data source names, and is used in most of the Application.cfc templates in the second half of this book. In addition, session management is turned on, which is needed by some of the later examples in this chapter. See Chapter 20 for more information about session management and session variables.

Listing 29.2 Application.cfc—Providing Application Settings

```
<!---
  Filename: Application.cfc
  Created by: Raymond Camden (ray@camdenfamily.com)
  Please Note Executes for every page request
--->

<cfcomponent output="false">

  <!--- Name the application. --->
  <cfset this.name="OrangeWhipSite">
  <!--- Turn on session management. --->
  <cfset this.sessionManagement=true>

  <cffunction name="onApplicationStart" output="false" returnType="void">

    <!--- Any variables set here can be used by all our pages --->
    <cfset APPLICATION.dataSource = "ows">
    <cfset APPLICATION.companyName = "Orange Whip Studios">

  </cffunction>

</cfcomponent>
```

Adding Next and Back Buttons

Listing 29.3 provides the code that includes the Back and Next links above and below the expense records. The idea is simply to show Back and Next links when appropriate. The Back link should be shown whenever the startRowBack value is greater than 0, which should always be the case unless the user is looking at the first page of records. The Next link should be shown as long as the startRowNext value is not after the last row of the query, which would be the case only when the user is at the last page of records.

Listing 29.3 NextNIncludeBackNext.cfm—Back and Next Buttons

```
<!---
Filename: NextNIncludeBackNext.cfm
Created by: Nate Weiss (NMW)
Purpose: Displays Back and Next links for record navigation
Please Note Included by the NextN.cfm templates in this folder
--->

<!--- Provide Next/Back links --->
<cfoutput>

  <!--- Show link for Back, if appropriate --->
  <cfif startRowBack gt 0>
  <a href="#CGI.script_name#?startRow=#startRowBack#">
  <img src="../images/BrowseBack.gif" width="40" height="16"
  alt="Back #rowsPerPage# Records" border="0"></a>
  </cfif>

  <!--- Show link for Next, if appropriate --->
  <cfif startRowNext lte totalRows>
  <a href="#CGI.script_name#?startRow=#startRowNext#">
  <img src="../images/BrowseNext.gif" width="40" height="16"
  alt="Next #rowsPerPage# Records" border="0"></a>
  </cfif>
</cfoutput>
```

As you can see, the Next and Back links always reload the current page, passing the appropriate startRow parameter in the URL. Now the user can navigate through all the query's records in digestible groups of 10. Figure 29.1 shows what the results look like in a browser.

NOTE

Because the CGI.script_name variable is used for the Back and Next links, this code continues to provide the correct links even if you change the file name for Listing 29.1. If you find this confusing, you could replace the CGI.script_name with the name of the template the user will be accessing (in this case, NextN1.cfm).

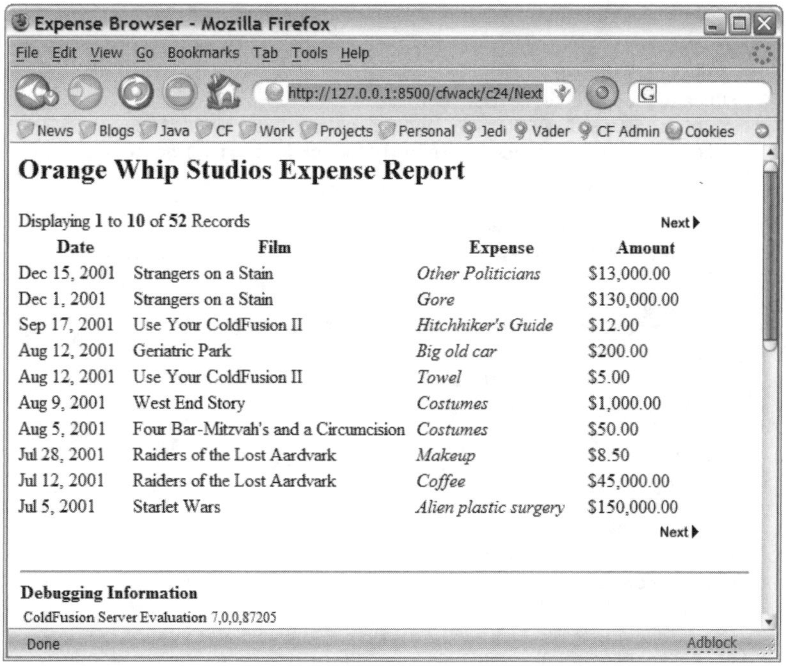

Figure 29.1

Creating a simple
Next 10 interface for
your users is easy.

Alternating Row Colors for Readability

Listing 29.4 is a revised version of Listing 29.1. This version adds some basic formatting via CSS syntax and presents the rows of data in alternating colors, as shown in Figure 29.2.

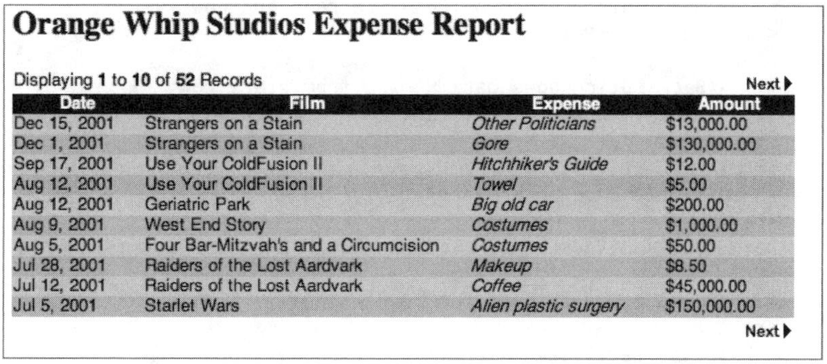

Figure 29.2

The background
colors of table cells
can be alternated to
make the display easier
to read.

Listing 29.4 `NextN2.cfm`—Adding CSS-Based Formatting

```
<!---
Filename: NextN2.cfm
Created by: Nate Weiss (NMW)
Purpose: Displays Next N record-navigation interface
Please Note Includes NextNIncludeBackNext.cfm template
--->

<!--- Retrieve expense records from database --->
<cfquery name="getExp" datasource="#APPLICATION.DataSource#">
 SELECT
 f.FilmID, f.MovieTitle,
 e.Description, e.ExpenseAmount, e.ExpenseDate
 FROM
 Expenses e INNER JOIN Films f
 ON e.FilmID = f.FilmID
 ORDER BY
 e.ExpenseDate DESC
</cfquery>


<!--- Number of rows to display per Next/Back page --->
<cfset rowsPerPage = 10>

<!--- What row to start at? Assume first by default --->
<cfparam name="URL.startRow" default="1" type="numeric">

<!--- We know the total number of rows from query --->
<cfset totalRows = getExp.recordCount>

<!--- Last row is 10 rows past the starting row, or --->
<!--- total number of query rows, whichever is less --->
<cfset endRow = min(URL.startRow + rowsPerPage - 1, totalRows)>

<!--- Next button goes to 1 past current end row --->
<cfset startRowNext = endRow + 1>

<!--- Back button goes back N rows from start row --->
<cfset startRowBack = URL.startRow - rowsPerPage>

<html>
<head><title>Expense Browser</title></head>
<body>
<cfoutput><h2>#APPLICATION.companyName# Expense Report</h2></cfoutput>

<!--- Simple Style Sheet for formatting --->
<style>
 th { font-family:sans-serif;font-size:smaller;
 background:navy;color:white}
 td { font-family:sans-serif;font-size:smaller}
 td.DataA { background:silver;color:black}
 td.DataB { background:lightgrey;color:black}
</style>

<table width="600" border="0" cellSpacing="0" cellPadding="1">
 <!--- Row at top of table, above column headers --->
```

Listing 29.4 (CONTINUED)

```
<tr>
<td width="500" colSpan="3">
<!--- Message about which rows are being displayed --->
<cfoutput>
Displaying <b>#URL.startRow#</b> to <b>#endRow#</b>
of <b>#totalRows#</b> Records<br>
</cfoutput>
</td>
<td align="right">
<!--- Provide Next/Back links --->
<cfinclude template="NextNIncludeBackNext.cfm">
</td>
</tr>

<!--- Row for column headers --->
<tr>
<th width="100">Date</th>
<th width="250">Film</th>
<th width="150">Expense</th>
<th width="100">Amount</th>
</tr>

<!--- For each query row that should be shown now --->
<cfloop query="getExp" startRow="#URL.startRow#" endRow="#endRow#">
<!--- Use class "DataA" or "DataB" for alternate rows --->
<cfset class = iif(getExp.currentRow mod 2 eq 0, "'DataA'", "'DataB'")>

<cfoutput>
<tr valign="baseline">
<td class="#class#" width="100">#lsDateFormat(ExpenseDate)#</td>
<td class="#class#" width="250">#MovieTitle#</td>
<td class="#class#" width="150"><i>#Description#</i></td>
<td class="#class#" width="100">#lsCurrencyFormat(ExpenseAmount)#</td>
</tr>
</cfoutput>
</cfloop>

<!--- Row at bottom of table, after rows of data --->
<tr>
<td align="right" colspan="4">
<!--- Provide Next/Back links --->
<cfinclude template="NextNIncludeBackNext.cfm">
</td>
</tr>
</table>

</body>
</html>
```

Defining Styles

The <style> block in Listing 29.4 specifies that all <th> cells should be displayed with white letter-ing on a navy background. Also, two style classes for <td> cells are defined, called DataA and DataB. By displaying alternate rows with these two classes, the expenses are displayed with alternating background colors, as shown in Figure 29.2.

Inside the <cfloop> tag, the code alternates between the DataA and DataB style classes by using ColdFusion's mod operator. The mod operator returns the modulus of two numbers, which is the remainder left over when the first number is divided by the second. When the currentRow is an even number, dividing it by 2 results in a remainder of 0, so the class variable is set to DataA. Otherwise, class is set to DataB. The class variable is then used as the class attribute for the <td> cells that display each row of expenses. The result is the pleasant-looking rendition of the next-n interface shown in Figure 29.2.

TIP

The DataA and DataB style classes could vary in more than just background color. They could use different typefaces, font colors, character formatting, and so on. See a CSS reference for details.

If you don't want to use CSS-based formatting, you could use the iif() test in Listing 29.4 to switch between two color names instead of class names. You would then feed the result to the bgcolor attribute of the <td> tags, instead of the class attribute. This would ensure that the rows displayed with alternating colors, even for browsers that don't support CSS (CSS support appeared in version 4.0 of Internet Explorer and Netscape Communicator). Of course, you could also choose to alternate both the class and bgcolor values.

A Note on the Use of iif()

The line that sets the class attribute uses the iif() function, which enables you to choose between two expressions depending on a condition. The iif() function is comparable to the ? and : operators used in JavaScript and some other languages. The first parameter is the condition; the second determines what the result should be when the condition is True; and the third is what the result should be when condition is False.

When iif() is used to switch between two strings, as shown previously in Listing 29.4, the second and third parameters must have two sets of quotes, because they each will be evaluated as expressions. If the second parameter were written as "DataA" instead of "'DataA'", an error would result because ColdFusion would try to return the value of a variable called DataA, which doesn't exist. The inner set of single quotation marks tells ColdFusion that the literal string DataA should be returned.

The iif() function is used here because it often improves code readability in cases such as this, due to its brevity. If you find it confusing, you can achieve the same result by replacing the single <cfset> line with this:

```
<cfif getExp.currentRow mod 2 eq 0>
 <cfset class = "DataA">
<cfelse>
 <cfset class = "DataB">
</cfif>
```

Letting the User Browse Page by Page

Many next-n interfaces that you see on the Web provide numbered page-by-page links in addition to the customary Back and Next links. If there are 50 records to display, and 10 records are shown per page, the user can use links labeled 1–5 to jump to a particular set of 10 records. This give the user a way to move through the records quickly, and the collection of clickable page numbers serves as a visual cue that provides a sense of how many records there are to look through.

For clarity, the page-by-page links are implemented in a separate file called NextNIncludePageLinks .cfm. Listing 29.5 shows the code for this new file.

Listing 29.5 NextNIncludePageLinks.cfm—Page-by-Page Links

```
<!---
 Filename: NextNIncludePageLinks.cfm
 Created by: Nate Weiss (NMW)
 Purpose: Displays Page 1, Page 2... links for record navigation
 Please Note Included by the NextN.cfm templates in this folder
--->

<!--- Simple "Page" counter, starting at first "Page" --->
<cfset thisPage = 1>

<!--- Loop thru row numbers, in increments of RowsPerPage --->
<cfloop from="1" to="#totalRows#" step="#rowsPerPage#" index="pageRow">

 <!--- Detect whether this "Page" currently being viewed --->
 <cfset isCurrentPage = (pageRow gte URL.startRow) and (pageRow lte endRow)>

 <!--- If this "Page" is current page, show without link --->
 <cfif isCurrentPage>
 <cfoutput><b>#thisPage#</b></cfoutput>
 <!--- Otherwise, show with link so user can go to page --->
 <cfelse>
 <cfoutput>
 <a href="#CGI.script_name#?startRow=#pageRow#">#thisPage#</a>
 </cfoutput>
 </cfif>

 <!--- Increment ThisPage variable --->
 <cfset thisPage = thisPage + 1>
</cfloop>
```

Like the Back and Next code shown in Listing 29.3, this template is responsible for generating a number of links that reload the current template, passing the appropriate startRow parameter in the URL.

First, a variable named thisPage is set to 1. This variable changes incrementally as each page-by-page link is displayed. Next, a <cfloop> tag is used to create each page-by-page link. Because the step attribute is set to the value of rowsPerPage, the pageRow variable rises in increments of 10 for each iteration of the loop, until it exceeds totalRows. So, the first time through the loop, thisPage and pageRow are both 1. The second time through the loop, thisPage is 2 and pageRow is 11, and so on.

The next <cfset> determines whether the user is already looking at the page of results currently being considered by the loop. If the current value of pageRow is between the startRow and endRow values (see Listing 29.4), isCurrentPage is True. Now the page number can be displayed by outputting the value of `thisPage`. If `thisPage` is the page currently being viewed, it is shown in boldface. If not, the page number is presented as a link to the appropriate page by passing the value of `pageRow` in the URL as the `startRow` parameter. Now users can see where they are in the records by looking for the boldface number, and can jump to other pages by clicking the other numbers, as shown in Figure 29.3.

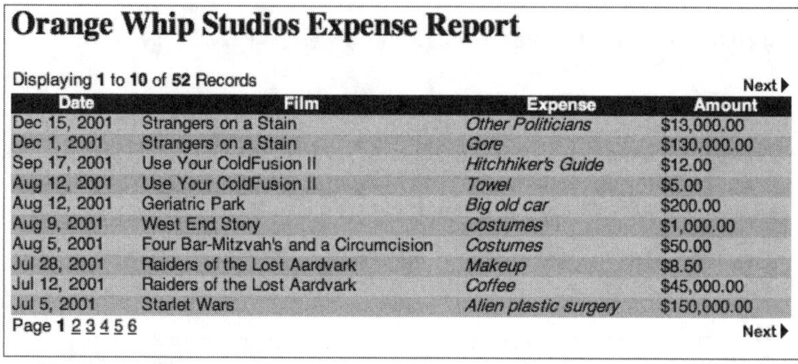

Orange Whip Studios Expense Report

Displaying **1** to **10** of **52** Records Next ▸

Date	Film	Expense	Amount
Dec 15, 2001	Strangers on a Stain	*Other Politicians*	$13,000.00
Dec 1, 2001	Strangers on a Stain	*Gore*	$130,000.00
Sep 17, 2001	Use Your ColdFusion II	*Hitchhiker's Guide*	$12.00
Aug 12, 2001	Use Your ColdFusion II	*Towel*	$5.00
Aug 12, 2001	Geriatric Park	*Big old car*	$200.00
Aug 9, 2001	West End Story	*Costumes*	$1,000.00
Aug 5, 2001	Four Bar-Mitzvah's and a Circumcision	*Costumes*	$50.00
Jul 28, 2001	Raiders of the Lost Aardvark	*Makeup*	$8.50
Jul 12, 2001	Raiders of the Lost Aardvark	*Coffee*	$45,000.00
Jul 5, 2001	Starlet Wars	*Alien plastic surgery*	$150,000.00

Page **1** 2 3 4 5 6 Next ▸

Figure 29.3
For easy navigation, the completed interface includes Back, Next, page-by-page, and Show All links.

Now that the code has been written, it can be included in the next-n interface with a simple `<cfinclude>` tag:

```
<!--- Shortcut links for Pages of search results --->
Page <cfinclude template="NextNIncludePageLinks.cfm">
```

The `NextN3.cfm` template (downloadable from the book Web site) builds on the previous version (see Listing 29.4) by adding this `<cfinclude>` tag in the appropriate place. The code is otherwise unchanged. You can also see this `<cfinclude>` tag in the next version of this template (see Listing 29.6).

Adding Show All and Filter Options

Although next-n interfaces are great for keeping your pages from getting too large to navigate comfortably, your users sometimes might need a way to see all the records at once (for instance, when they need to print a hard copy). Therefore, it's worth considering the addition of a Show All link, which essentially serves to override the next-n interface if the user so desires.

Listing 29.6 is the feature-complete version of the next-n interface, which now includes a Show All option as well as the page-by-page navigation included in the previous version. As you can see, only a few lines of new code were necessary to put the Show All option into place.

This version of the template also gives the user a way to filter the records being displayed in the next-n interface. The user is able to filter the records by movie name, the text of the expense description, or by expense date. In general, this is a simple matter of including a Filter form on the page, and then querying the database dynamically based on the user's entries. You saw all this in Chapter 12, "ColdFusion Forms," in Vol. 1, *Getting Started.*

The only trick is the fact that this next-n page will be reloaded over and over as the user navigates through the records. The user shouldn't have to keep reentering the filter criteria, so session variables will be used to remember the filter throughout the user's interaction with the interface. Luckily, Cold-Fusion's session variables make it easy to provide this basic usability feature. Three session variables are used to remember the filter: SESSION.expenseReport.userFilter, SESSION.expenseReport.dateFrom, and SESSION.expenseReport.dateThru.

At the top of the template, <cfparam> tags are used to initialize these variables to empty strings. Next, a simple <cfif> tests whether the user is currently submitting the Filter form. If so, the submission is saved in the three session variables. These session variables are then used in the page's <cfquery> to filter the records according to the user's wishes. The session variables are also used to prepopulate the three <cfinput> tags within the Filter form each time the page is reloaded, giving the user an easy way to experiment with various filters.

Listing 29.6 NextN4.cfm—Adding a Way to View All Records at Once

```
<!---
Filename: NextN4.cfm
Created by: Nate Weiss (NMW)
Purpose: Displays Next N record-navigation interface
Please Note Includes NextNIncludeBackNext.cfm and NextNIncludePageLinks.cfm
--->

<!--- Maintain ExpenseReport filtering variables at session level --->
<cfparam name="SESSION.expenseReport.userFilter" type="string" default="">
<cfparam name="SESSION.expenseReport.dateFrom" type="string" default="">
<cfparam name="SESSION.expenseReport.dateThru" type="string" default="">

<!--- If the user is submitting the "filter" form, --->
<!--- we'll make their submission be the filter for rest of session --->
<cfif isDefined("FORM.userFilter")>
 <cfset SESSION.expenseReport.userFilter = FORM.userFilter>
 <cfset SESSION.expenseReport.dateFrom = FORM.dateFrom>
 <cfset SESSION.expenseReport.dateThru = FORM.dateThru>
</cfif>

<!--- Retrieve expense records from database --->
<cfquery name="getExp" datasource="#APPLICATION.dataSource#">
 SELECT
 f.FilmID, f.MovieTitle,
 e.Description, e.ExpenseAmount, e.ExpenseDate
 FROM
 Expenses e INNER JOIN Films f
 ON e.FilmID = f.FilmID
 WHERE
 0=0
 <!--- If the user provided a filter string, --->
 <!--- show only matching films and/or expenses --->
 <cfif SESSION.expenseReport.userFilter is not "">
 AND (f.MovieTitle LIKE '%#SESSION.expenseReport.userFilter#%' OR
 e.Description LIKE '%#SESSION.expenseReport.userFilter#%')
 </cfif>
 <!--- Also filter on From date, if provided --->
 <cfif isDate(SESSION.expenseReport.dateFrom)>
 AND e.ExpenseDate >= #CreateODBCDate(SESSION.expenseReport.dateFrom)#
 </cfif>
```

Listing 29.6 (CONTINUED)

```
<!--- Also filter on Through date, if provided --->
<cfif isDate(SESSION.expenseReport.dateThru)>
AND e.ExpenseDate <= #CreateODBCDate(SESSION.expenseReport.dateThru)#
</cfif>
ORDER BY
e.ExpenseDate DESC
</cfquery>


<!--- Number of rows to display per Next/Back page --->
<cfset rowsPerPage = 10>
<!--- What row to start at? Assume first by default --->
<cfparam name="URL.startRow" default="1" type="numeric">
<!--- Allow for Show All parameter in the URL --->
<cfparam name="URL.showAll" type="boolean" default="No">

<!--- We know the total number of rows from query --->
<cfset totalRows = getExp.recordCount>

<!--- Show all on page if ShowAll passed in URL --->
<cfif URL.showAll>
 <cfset rowsPerPage = totalRows>
</cfif>

<!--- Last row is 10 rows past the starting row, or --->
<!--- total number of query rows, whichever is less --->
<cfset endRow = min(URL.startRow + rowsPerPage - 1, totalRows)>

<!--- Next button goes to 1 past current end row --->
<cfset startRowNext = endRow + 1>

<!--- Back button goes back N rows from start row --->
<cfset startRowBack = URL.startRow - rowsPerPage>


<!--- Page Title --->
<html>
<head><title>Expense Browser</title></head>
<body>
<cfoutput><h2>#APPLICATION.companyName# Expense Report</h2></cfoutput>

<!--- Simple style sheet for formatting --->
<style>
 form { font-family:sans-serif;font-size:smaller;}
 th { font-family:sans-serif;font-size:smaller;
 background:navy;color:white}
 td { font-family:sans-serif;font-size:smaller}
 td.DataA { background:silver;color:black}
 td.DataB { background:lightgrey;color:black}
</style>

<!--- Simple form to allow user to filter results --->
<cfform action="#CGI.script_name#" method="post">
 <!--- Filter string --->
 <b>Filter:</b>
```

Listing 29.6 (CONTINUED)

```
<cfinput
type="text"
name="userFilter"
value="#SESSION.expenseReport.userFilter#"
size="15">

<!--- From date --->
 
<b>Dates:</b> from
<cfinput
type="text"
name="dateFrom"
value="#SESSION.expenseReport.dateFrom#"
size="9"
validate="date"
message="Please enter a valid date, or leave it blank.">

<!--- Through date --->
through
<cfinput
type="text"
name="dateThru"
value="#SESSION.expenseReport.dateThru#"
size="9"
validate="date"
message="Please enter a valid date, or leave it blank.">

<!--- Submit button to activate/change/clear filter --->
<input
type="submit"
value="Apply">
</cfform>


<table width="600" border="0" cellSpacing="0" cellPadding="1">
<!--- Row at top of table, above column headers --->
<tr>
<td width="500" colspan="3">
<!--- Message about which rows are being displayed --->
<cfoutput>
Displaying <b>#URL.startRow#</b> to <b>#endRow#</b>
of <b>#totalRows#</b> Records<br>
</cfoutput>
</td>
<td width="100" align="right">
<cfif not URL.showAll>
<!--- Provide Next/Back links --->
<cfinclude template="NextNIncludeBackNext.cfm">
</cfif>
</td>
</tr>
<!--- Row for column headers --->
<tr>
<th width="100">Date</th>
<th width="250">Film</th>
```

Listing 29.6 (CONTINUED)

```
<th width="150">Expense</th>
<th width="100">Amount</th>
</tr>

<!--- For each query row that should be shown now --->
<cfloop query="getExp" startRow="#URL.startRow#" endrow="#endRow#">
<!--- Use class "DataA" or "DataB" for alternate rows --->
<cfset class = iif(getExp.currentRow mod 2 eq 0, "'DataA'", "'DataB'")>

<cfoutput>
<tr valign="baseline">
<td class="#class#" width="100">#lsDateFormat(ExpenseDate)#</td>
<td class="#class#" width="250">#MovieTitle#</td>
<td class="#class#" width="150"><i>#Description#</i></td>
<td class="#class#" width="100">#lsCurrencyFormat(ExpenseAmount)#</td>
</tr>
</cfoutput>
</cfloop>

<!--- Row at bottom of table, after rows of data --->
<tr>
<td width="500" colSpan="3">
<cfif not URL.showAll and totalRows gt rowsPerPage>
<!--- Shortcut links for "Pages" of search results --->
Page <cfinclude template="NextNIncludePageLinks.cfm">
<!--- Show All link --->
<cfoutput>
<a href="#CGI.script_name#?&showAll=Yes">Show All</a>
</cfoutput>
</cfif>
</td>
<td width="100" align="right">
<cfif not URL.showAll>
<!--- Provide Next/Back links --->
<cfinclude template="NextNIncludeBackNext.cfm">
</cfif>
</td>
</tr>
</table>

</body>
</html>
```

Aside from adding the filter form and accompanying session variables, not too much has changed in this version of the template. Near the top, a new URL parameter called showAll is introduced and given a default value of No. Two lines later, a simple <cfif> test is used to set the rowsPerPage variable to the value of totalRows if URL.showAll is True. If the page is accessed with showAll=Yes in the URL, it displays all the records in one large group.

The only other difference is the addition of a few <cfif> tests throughout, so the Back, Next, and page-by-page links aren't shown when in Show All mode. The final results are shown in Figure 29.4.

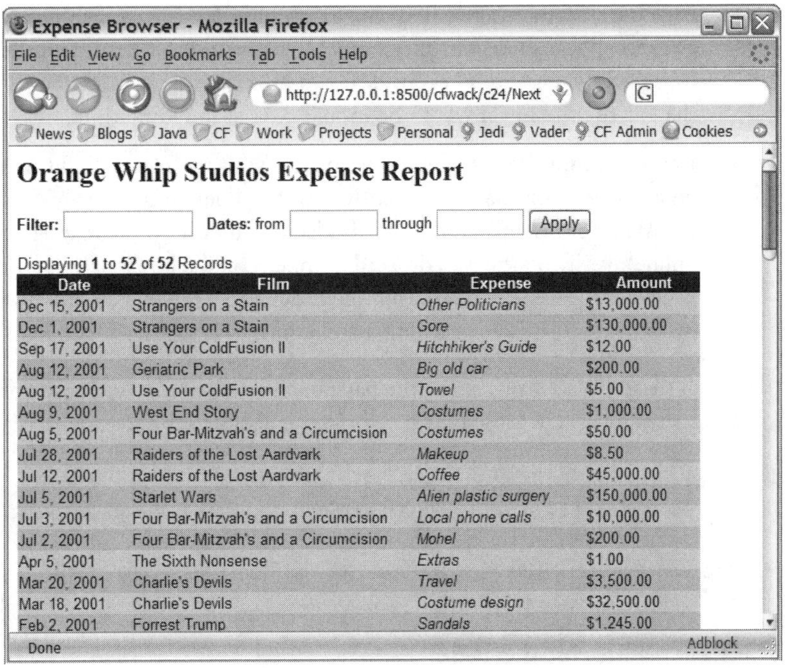

Figure 29.4

Users can apply filters and move back and next within the filtered results.

For now, don't worry about the fact that the query must be rerun each time the user clicks Next, Back, Show All, or one of the numbered page links. ColdFusion's query-caching feature can be used to ensure that your database is not hit too hard. See Chapter 31 for details.

Returning Page Output Right Away with `<cflush>`

By default, the output of all ColdFusion templates is automatically buffered by the server, which means the HTML for the entire page is sent to the browser at once, after all processing has been completed. In general, this isn't a problem. In fact, it helps ColdFusion pull off a number of cool tricks internally. See the section "When You Can't Flush the Buffer," later in this chapter.

That said, you will sometimes want ColdFusion to return the HTML it generates right away, while the template is executing. The browser can receive and display the HTML as it is generated, and meanwhile, ColdFusion can be finishing the rest of the template. The act of telling ColdFusion to send back the generated output right away is called *clearing the page buffer*.

When to Clear the Buffer

You might want to clear the page buffer in two basic situations:

- **Large Pages.** If the template you are working on will output a lot of information, such as a long article all on one page or a report with many records, you might want to flush the page buffer after every 1,000 characters of HTML have been generated. This causes the page to appear to display more quickly because the user can start reading the page before it has been completely received. It can also be easier on the ColdFusion server because the entire page never has to be in its RAM at the same time.

- **Long-running Pages.** Sometimes one of your templates might need to perform some type of operation that is inherently slow but doesn't necessarily output a large amount of HTML. For instance, if the user is placing an order (see Chapter 22, "Online Commerce," online), verifying their credit card number could take 10 or 15 seconds. By clearing the page buffer several times during the order process, you can display a series of "please wait" messages so the user can see that something is actually happening.

In both of these situations, clearing the page buffer judiciously can make your applications appear to be more responsive because they give more feedback to the user sooner.

NOTE

Don't start clearing the page buffer regularly in all your ColdFusion templates, however. Instead, use it when you think there would be a problem for ColdFusion to send back a particular page all at once. In particular, don't place a `<cfflush>` tag in your `Application.cfc` file. See the section "When You Can't Flush the Buffer," later in this chapter.

The Exception, Not the Rule

Most ColdFusion pages don't fall into either of the categories we've discussed. That is, most of your application's templates won't generate tons and tons of HTML code, and most will execute normally in well under a second.

So clearing the page buffer usually doesn't have much impact on the average ColdFusion template. And after the page buffer has been cleared, a number of features can no longer be used and will generate error messages (see the section "When You Can't Flush the Buffer," later in this chapter).

In short, the capability to flush the page buffer is helpful for dealing with certain special situations, as outlined previously. Unless the template you are working on will produce a large amount of output or will take a long time to process, let ColdFusion buffer the page normally.

Introducing the `<cfflush>` Tag

ColdFusion provides a tag called `<cfflush>` that lets you clear the server's page buffer programmatically. As soon as ColdFusion encounters a `<cfflush>` tag, it sends anything the template has generated so far to the browser. If the browser is able to, it displays that content to the user while ColdFusion continues working on the template.

The `<cfflush>` tag takes just one attribute—`interval`—which is optional. You can use `<cfflush>` without `interval`; that simply causes the page buffer to be flushed at the moment the tag is encountered. If you provide a number to `interval`, ColdFusion continues to flush the page cache whenever that many bytes have been generated by your template. So, `interval="1000"` causes the page buffer to be cleared after every 1,000 bytes, which would usually mean after every 1,000th character.

Flushing the Output Buffer for Large Pages

Look at the Show All option in Listing 29.7, earlier in this chapter. Over time, hundreds or thousands of records could exist in the Expenses table, causing the Show All display to become extremely large. Therefore, it becomes a good candidate for the <cfflush> tag.

For instance, near the top of Listing 29.7, you could change this code:

```
<!--- Show all on page if ShowAll is passed in URL --->
<cfif URL.showAll>
 <cfset rowsPerPage = totalRows>
</cfif>
```

to this:

```
<!--- Show all on page if ShowAll is passed in URL --->
<cfif URL.showAll>
 <cfset rowsPerPage = totalRows>

 <!--- Flush the page buffer after every 5,000 characters --->
 <cfflush interval="5000">
</cfif>
```

Now the page begins to be sent to the user's browser in 5,000-character chunks, instead of all at once. The result is that the page should display more quickly when the Show All option is used. Note, however, that the difference might not be particularly noticeable until the Expenses table gets quite large. Even then, the difference will likely be more noticeable for modem users.

Flushing the Output Buffer for Long-Running Processes

You have seen how <cfflush> can help with templates that return large pages to the browser. You also can use <cfflush> to deal with situations in which a lengthy process needs to take place (such as verifying and charging a user's credit card or executing a particularly complex record-updating process).

Simulating a Long-Running Process

To keep the examples in this chapter simple, the following code snippet is used to simulate some type of time-consuming process. Because this code should never be used in an actual, real-world application, it isn't explained in detail here. ColdFusion 8 adds a new function, sleep(), that can be used to make a page intentionally pause for a certain number of milliseconds.

For instance, this code will force ColdFusion to spin its wheels for five seconds:

```
<cfset sleep(5000)>
```

Displaying a Please-Wait Type of Message

The FlushTest.cfm template shown in Listing 29.7 demonstrates how you can use the <cfflush> tag to output page content before and after a lengthy process. Here, the user is asked to wait while an order is processed.

Listing 29.7   `FlushTest.cfm`—Displaying Messages

```
<!---
Filename: FlushTest.cfm
Created by: Nate Weiss (NMW)
Purpose: Demonstrates use of <cfflush> for incremental page output
--->

<html>
<head><title>&lt;cfflush&gt; Example</title></head>
<body>

  <!--- Initial Message --->
  <p><strong>Please Wait</strong><br>
  We are processing your order.<br>
  This process may take up to several minutes.<br>
  Please do not Reload or leave this page until the process is complete.<br>

  <!--- Flush the page output buffer --->
  <!--- The above code is sent to the browser right now --->
  <cfflush>

  <!--- Time-consuming process goes here --->
  <!--- Here, ColdFusion is forced to wait for 5 seconds --->
<cfset sleep(5000)>
  <!--- Display "Success" message --->
  <p><strong>Thank You.</strong><br>
  Your order has been processed.<br>

</body>
</html>
```

As you can see, the code is very simple. First, a "please wait" message is displayed, using ordinary HTML tags. Then, the `<cfflush>` tag is used to flush the page buffer, which lets the user see the message immediately. Next, the time-consuming process is performed (you would replace the `sleep()` snippet with whatever is appropriate for your situation). The rest of the page can then be completed normally.

If you visit this template with your browser, you should see the "please wait" message alone on the page at first. After about 5 seconds, the thank-you message will appear. This gives your application a more responsive feel.

Displaying a Graphical Progress Meter

With the help of some simple JavaScript code, you can create a graphical progress meter while a particularly long process executes. The code in Listing 29.8 is similar to the previous listing, except that it assumes there are several steps in the time-consuming process that the template needs to accomplish. When the page first appears, it shows an image of a progress indicator that reads `0%`. As each step of the lengthy process is completed, the image is updated so the indicator reads `25%`, `50%`, `75%`, and finally `100%`.

Listing 29.8   `FlushMeter.cfm`—Displaying a Progress Meter

```
<!---
Filename: FlushMeter.cfm
Created by: Nate Weiss (NMW)
Purpose: Diplays a progress meter as a lengthy task is completed
--->


<html>
<head><title>&lt;cfflush&gt; Example</title></head>
<body>

<!--- Initial Message --->
<p><strong>Please Wait</strong><br>
We are processing your order.<br>

<!--- Create the "Meter" image object --->
<!--- Initially, it displays a blank GIF --->
<img name="Meter" src="../images/PercentBlank.gif"
width="200" height="16" alt="" border="0">

<!--- Flush the page buffer --->
<cfflush>

<!--- Loop from 0 to 25 to 50 to 75 to 100 --->
<cfloop from="0" to="100" step="25" index="i">
<!--- Time-consuming process goes here --->
<!--- Here, ColdFusion waits for 5 seconds as an example --->
<!--- Do not use this technique in actual code! --->
<cfset sleep(5000)>
<!--- Change the SRC attribute of the Meter image --->
<cfoutput>
<script language="JavaScript">
document.images["Meter"].src = '../images/Percent#i#.gif';
</script>
</cfoutput>
<cfflush>
</cfloop>

<!--- Display "Success" message --->
<p><strong>Thank You.</strong><br>
Your order has been processed.<br>
</body>
</html>
```

First, an ordinary `<img>` tag is used to put the progress indicator on the page. The image's `src` attribute is set to the `PercentBlank.gif` image, which is an empty, transparent (spacer) image that won't show up (except as empty space) on the page. The `<cfflush>` tag is used to ensure that the browser receives the `<img>` tag code and displays the placeholder image right away.

Next, the `sleep` function is used to simulate some type of time-consuming, five-step process. Because of the `step` attribute, the value of `i` is 0 the first time through the loop, then 25, then 50, then 75, and then 100. Each time through the loop, a `<script>` tag is output that contains JavaScript code to change the `src` property of the meter `<img>`, which causes the meter effect. The buffer is flushed with <cfflush> after each <script> tag, so the browser can receive and execute the script right away. The first time through the loop, the <img> is set to display the Percent0.gif file, then Percent25.gif, and so on. The end result is a simple progress meter that helps users feel they are still connected during whatever time-consuming processes they initiated. Figure 29.5 shows what the meter looks like in a browser.

Figure 29.5

The <CFFLUSH> tag enables you to display progress indicators during lengthy processes.

NOTE

There isn't room here to fully cover the use of an image's src property to swap the images it displays. For more information, consult a JavaScript reference book, or the scripting reference section under HTML Reference in ColdFusion Studio's online help.

If the user's browser doesn't support JavaScript, the <img> tag will simply continue to display the PercentBlank.gif image (which the user won't notice because it is invisible).

Flushing the Output Buffer Between Table Rows

In Listing 29.7, a Show All link was added to the next-n interface for browsing Orange Whip Studios' expenses. Depending on the number of rows in the Expenses table, that page could produce a lot of output. You might want to consider flushing the page output buffer after every few rows of data, so the user will start to see the rows while the page is being generated.

Listing 29.9 shows how you can add a <cfflush> tag in the middle of an output loop, so that groups of rows are sent back to the browser right away. In this example, the rows are sent back in groups of five; in practice, you might want to choose a higher number of rows, such as 20 or 30.

Listing 29.9 NextN5.cfm—Sending Content to the Browser

```
<!---
 Filename: NextN5.cfm
 Created by: Nate Weiss (NMW)
 Purpose: Displays Next N record-navigation interface
 Please Note Includes NextNIncludeBackNext.cfm and NextNIncludePageLinks
--->

<!--- Retrieve expense records from database --->
<cfquery name="getExp" datasource="#APPLICATION.dataSource#">
 SELECT
 f.FilmID, f.MovieTitle,
 e.Description, e.ExpenseAmount, e.ExpenseDate
 FROM
 Expenses e INNER JOIN Films f
 ON e.FilmID = f.FilmID
 ORDER BY
 e.ExpenseDate DESC
</cfquery>


<!--- Number of rows to display per Next/Back page --->
<cfset rowsPerPage = 10>

<!--- What row to start at? Assume first by default --->
<cfparam name="URL.startRow" default="1" type="numeric">

<!--- Allow for Show All parameter in the URL --->
<cfparam name="URL.showAll" type="boolean" default="no">

<!--- We know the total number of rows from query --->
<cfset totalRows = getExp.recordCount>
<!--- Show all on page if ShowAll passed in URL --->
<cfif URL.showAll>
 <cfset rowsPerPage = totalRows>
</cfif>

<!--- Last row is 10 rows past the starting row, or --->
<!--- total number of query rows, whichever is less --->
<cfset endRow = min(URL.startRow + rowsPerPage - 1, totalRows)>

<!--- Next button goes to 1 past current end row --->
<cfset startRowNext = endRow + 1>

<!--- Back button goes back N rows from start row --->
<cfset startRowBack = URL.startRow - rowsPerPage>


<!--- Page Title --->
<html>
<head><title>Expense Browser</title></head>
<body>
<cfoutput><h2>#APPLICATION.companyName# Expense Report</h2></cfoutput>

<!--- simple style sheet for formatting --->
<style>
```

Listing 29.9 (CONTINUED)

```
  th { font-family:sans-serif;font-size:smaller;
  background:navy;color:white}
  td { font-family:sans-serif;font-size:smaller}
  td.DataA { background:silver;color:black}
  td.DataB { background:lightgrey;color:black}
</style>

<table width="600" border="0" cellSpacing="0" cellPadding="1">
<!--- Row at top of table, above column headers --->
<tr>
<td width="500" colSpan="3">
<!--- Message about which rows are being displayed --->
<cfoutput>
Displaying <b>#URL.startRow#</b> to <b>#endRow#</b>
of <b>#TotalRows#</b> Records<br>
</cfoutput>
</td>
<td width="100" align="right">
<cfif not URL.showAll>
<!--- Provide Next/Back links --->
<cfinclude template="NextNIncludeBackNext.cfm">
</cfif>
</td>
</tr>

<!--- Row for column headers --->
<TR>
<TH WIDTH="100">Date</TH>
<TH WIDTH="250">Film</TH>
<TH WIDTH="150">Expense</TH>
<TH WIDTH="100">Amount</TH>
</TR>

<!--- For each query row that should be shown now --->
<cfloop query="getExp" startRow="#URL.startRow#" endRow="#endRow#">
<!--- Use class "DataA" or "DataB" for alternate rows --->
<cfset class = iif(getExp.currentRow mod 2 eq 0, "'DataA'", "'DataB'")>

<!--- Actual data display --->
<cfoutput>
<tr valign="baseline">
<td class="#class#" width="100">#lsDateFormat(ExpenseDate)#</td>
<td class="#class#" width="250">#MovieTitle#</td>
<td class="#class#" width="150"><i>#Description#</i></td>
<td class="#class#" width="100">#lsCurrencyFormat(ExpenseAmount)#</td>
</tr>
</cfoutput>

<!--- If showing all records, flush the page buffer after every 5th row --->
<cfif URL.showAll>
<cfif getExp.currentRow mod 5 eq 0>
<!--- End the current table --->
</table>
<!--- Flush the page buffer --->
<cfflush>
```

Listing 29.9 (CONTINUED)

```
     <!--- Start a new table --->
     <table width="600" border="0" cellSpacing="0" cellPadding="1">
     <!--- Simulate a time-intensive process --->
<cfset sleep(1000)> </cfif>
     </cfif>

     </cfloop>

     <!--- Row at bottom of table, after rows of data --->
     <tr>
     <td width="500" colSpan="3">
     <cfif not URL.showAll and totalRows gt rowsPerPage>
     <!--- Shortcut links for "Pages" of search results --->
     Page <cfinclude template="NextNIncludePageLinks.cfm">
     <!--- Show All Link --->
     <cfoutput>
     <a href="#CGI.script_name#?showAll=Yes">Show All</a>
     </cfoutput>
     </cfif>
     </td>
     <td width="100" align="right">
     <cfif not URL.showAll>
     <!--- Provide Next/Back links --->
     <cfinclude template="NextNIncludeBackNext.cfm">
     </cfif>
     </td>
     </tr>
     </table>


     </body>
     </html>
```

This code listing is mostly unchanged from an earlier version (see Listing 29.4). The only significant change is the addition of the <cfif> block at the end of the <cfloop> block. The code in this
block executes only if the user has clicked the Show All link, and only if the current row number is
evenly divisible by 5 (that is, every fifth row).

If both of these conditions apply, the current <table> tag (the one opened near the top of the list-
ing) is ended with a closing </table> tag. The page buffer is then flushed using <cfflush>, and a
new table is started with an opening <table> tag that matches the one from the top of the listing. In
other words, the expense records are shown as a series of five-row tables that are each sent to the
browser individually, rather than as one long table that gets sent to the browser at once. Because
each of these mini-tables is complete, with beginning and ending <table> tags, the browser can dis-
play them as it receives them (most browsers can't properly render a table until the closing </table>
tag has been encountered).

After the page buffer is cleared, this template waits for one second, using the same time-delay
technique that was used in the progress meter example (see Listing 29.9). Again, never use
this technique in your actual code templates. It is used here only as a simple way of causing
ColdFusion to pause for a moment, so you can see the effect of the page flushes.

If you visit Listing 29.9 with your Web browser and click the Show All link, you will see that the rows of data are presented to you in small groups, with a one-second pause between each group. This shows that the buffer is being cleared, and that a user accessing a very long page over a slow connection would at least be able to begin viewing records before the entire page had been received.

NOTE

Of course, in practice, you wouldn't have the time-delay loop at all. It's included here only to make the effect easier to see while developing.

When You Can't Flush the Buffer

This section has introduced the <cfflush> tag and pointed out several situations in which it can be helpful. However, because it causes the content your templates generate to be sent to the browser in pieces, rather than the whole page at once, certain ColdFusion tags and features that depend on being capable of manipulating the page as a whole can't be used after a <cfflush> tag.

Restrictions on Cookie Use

After the <cfflush> tag has been used on a page, you can no longer tell ColdFusion to set a cookie in the browser. This is because cookies are set by sending special HTTP headers to the browser, and all HTTP headers must be sent to the browser before any actual HTML content. So, after a <cfflush> tag has been used, you can't send additional headers, so it's too late for ColdFusion to set any cookies.

If you really need to set a cookie after a <cfflush>, you can use JavaScript to do it. For your convenience, a custom tag called <cf_setCookieViaJS> has been included in this chapter's folder at the book Web site). The custom tag supports three attributes—cookieName, cookieValue, and expires—which correspond to the name, value, and expires attributes for the regular <cfcookie> tag. The expires attribute is optional.

So, instead of

```
<cfcookie
  name="MyCookie"
  value="My Value">
```

you would use

```
<cf_setCookieViaJS
  cookieName="MyCookie"
  cookieValue="My Value">
```

Note that the cookie will be set only if the user's browser supports JavaScript and if JavaScript has not been disabled.

NOTE

This example custom tag is not supported. We are merely presenting it as a work-around for situations in which you must set a cookie after a `<cfflush>` tag. Whenever possible, set cookies using the usual `<cfcookie>` and `<cfset>` methods explained in Chapter 20.

If you are familiar with JavaScript, you could study the `SetCookieViaJS.cfm` custom tag (mentioned previously) as an example of how custom tags can be used to generate JavaScript code.

The `PATH`, `SECURE`, and `DOMAIN` attributes from `<cfcookie>` aren't supported by this custom tag, but they could easily be added by editing the custom tag template.

Restrictions on `<cflocation>`

After a `<cfflush>` tag has been encountered, you can no longer use the `<cflocation>` tag to redirect the user to another page. This is because `<cflocation>` works by sending a redirect header back to the browser. When the first `<cfflush>` tag is encountered on a page, the page's headers have already been sent to the browser, so it's too late to redirect the browser to another page using the usual methods provided by HTTP alone.

There are two work-arounds to this problem. Both rely on the browser to interpret your document in a certain way, and they aren't part of the standard HTTP protocol. That said, these methods should work fine with most browsers.

The first work-around is to include a `<meta>` tag in the document, with an `HTTP-EQUIV` attribute set to `Refresh`. Then, provide the URL for the next page in the `CONTENT` attribute, as shown below. Most browsers interpret this as an instruction to go to the specified page as soon as the tag is encountered.

So, instead of this:

```
<cflocation url="MyNextPage.cfm">
```

you would use this:

```
<meta http-equiv="Refresh" content="0; URL=MyNextPage.cfm">
```

TIP

If you want the redirect to occur after 5 seconds rather than right away, you could change the **0** in the previous snippet to **5**. Consult an HTML reference for more information about this use of the `<meta>` tag.

Another work-around is to use JavaScript. The following snippet could also be used in place of the `<cflocation>` shown previously. However, if JavaScript is disabled or not supported by the client, nothing will happen. See the scripting reference in Dreamweaver or HomeSite+ for more information about this use of the `document.location` object:

```
<script language="JavaScript">
<!--
 document.location.href ="MyNextPage.cfm";
//-->
</script>
```

Other Restrictions

Several other tags (and one function) can't be used after a `<cfflush>` tag has been encountered, for the same basic reasons the `<cfcookie>` and `<cflocation>` tags can't be used— they all need to send special HTTP headers to the browser before your HTML code begins.

These tags and functions can't be used after a `<cfflush>`:

- `<cfcontent>`
- `<cfcookie>`
- `<cfform>`
- `<cfheader>`
- `<cfhtmlhead>`
- `<cflocation>`
- `setLocale()`

CHAPTER **30**

Managing Threads

ColdFusion MX 7 event gateways introduced asynchronous programming in CFML. Asynchronous coding allows requests to run concurrently yet independently of each other. The asynchronous CFML gateway allows developers to run code parallel to the user request. The template requested in the browser can issue multiple calls to the gateway. The code running in the gateway is completely autonomous, meaning that it runs in its own thread, consumes its own resources, and does not depend on the parent request thread. The parent thread continues execution without waiting for CFML gateway requests to be complete. This approach allows multiple tasks to finish simultaneously in contrast to the sequential execution of traditional procedural programming.

TIP

> The terms *parent thread*, *parent request*, and *page-level thread* are all synonyms for the ColdFusion template or page requested in the client browser.

The problem with the CFML gateway is that it provides limited feedback and interaction with the page-level thread. The CFML gateway sends messages to CFC methods and provides a status message only to the page-level thread. Although it can access shared scoped variables (such as Server, Application, and Session), CFML gateway requests run in a thread pool separate from the page-level thread, so they cannot share the Request scope or provide output to the user. ColdFusion 8 offers a better solution, with ColdFusion threads.

ColdFusion threads are also autonomous and allow asynchronous, simultaneous code execution. They are created with the `<cfthread>` tag. Like the CFML gateway, the `<cfthread>` tag is called in the request or page thread, and it creates additional threads that run independent of the page thread. However, ColdFusion threads can provide output to and interact with the page thread. ColdFusion threads can also process synchronously, by suspending execution of the page thread until the thread execution finishes. Table 30.1 summarizes the differences between the CFML gateway and Cold-Fusion threads.

Table 30.1 CFML Gateway Compared to ColdFusion Threads

CFML GATEWAY	COLDFUSION THREADS
Initialized by `sendGatewayMessage()` call to a gateway CFC.	Initialized with `cfthread`.
`SendGatewayMessage()` returns status value to page thread.	Thread scope containing metadata variables accessible by page thread.
Data passed by `CFEvent` scope.	Data passed by `Attributes` scope.
Can access shared scopes but not `Request` scope.	Can access all scopes.
Strict autonomous execution; page thread continues processing without waiting for gateway thread completion.	Flexible autonomous execution; can suspend page thread until thread completion.
Provides asynchronous processing.	Provides synchronous or asynchronous processing.
Thread runs in event gateway thread pool.	Thread runs in separate thread request pool.
Limited interaction with other gateway requests.	Threads can interact with and join each other.
Nesting allowed.	Nesting allowed, but child thread generation is unsupported.
Cannot set priority.	Can set thread priority.
Cannot suspend execution.	Can suspend thread execution.
Does not provide user feedback.	Can provide output to page-level thread.
Difficult to debug.	Provides `Error` metadata variable containing error information.

Using the `<cfthread>` Tag

The `<cfthread>` tag manages ColdFusion threads. Developers use `<cfthread>` to:

- Start thread execution
- Suspend thread execution
- Stop thread execution
- Join threads to each other or the page-level request

Only a page-level request can generate threads with `<cfthread>`—child threads are not supported. You can pass thread-specific attributes to the `<cfthread>` tag. Code inside the `<cfthread>` body executes in a separate thread pool. The thread pool limit is set in the ColdFusion Administrator; any threads created beyond this limit are queued. Table 30.2 lists the `<cfthread>` attributes and descriptions.

Only <cfthread> calls with action="run" can have a tag body. All other actions must not have tag bodies and must use a slash (/) to end the tag.

ColdFusion supports nested <cfthread> calls, but only the outermost <cfthread> can specify action="run". Generation of child threads is currently not supported.

Table 30.2 <cfthread> Attributes

ATTRIBUTE	DESCRIPTION	APPLIES TO	REQUIRED
action	Action to perform; options are join, run (default), sleep, and terminate.	All	No
duration	Number of milliseconds to suspend processing.	sleep	Yes
name	Name of the thread receiving the action	join, run, terminate	Yes if action is join or terminate
priority	Run-level priority for the thread. Options are HIGH, LOW, and NORMAL (default).	run	No
timeout	Number of milliseconds (default = 0) that the page-level thread waits for running threads or threads being joined to complete before continuing processing.	join	No

Starting Threads

Call <cfthread> with the action attribute set to run to start a new thread. Name the thread with the name attribute to provide a control handle for interaction with the page-level thread or other threads. Use the priority attribute to specify a runtime processing priority level for individual threads. Valid values are NORMAL, HIGH, and LOW. The page-level thread continues processing while the thread is running, unless it is suspended with the sleep function or by the joining of threads.

You may want to suspend the page thread to allow <cfthread>-generated threads to finish and return output for the page thread. Since threads process nonsequentially in a separate queue from the parent request, they typically do not affect the total page execution time. However, suspending the page-level thread to allow spawned threads to finish increases the total page execution time by the value of the sleep function, thus increasing the risk of eclipsing the configured request timeout. To prevent this, use the cfsetting tag and set the requestTimeout attribute equal to or greater than the total value of all the coded sleep functions, including any inside the cfthread body.

Here is the syntax:

```
<cfthread name="thread name" [action="run" [, priority="NORMAL|HIGH|LOW" [,
attributes]]]>
    Code to execute
</cfthread>
```

TIP

Page-level code always has a priority of NORMAL.

Suspending Threads

Occasionally you may want one or more threads to pause or suspend execution while another thread begins and then continue execution simultaneous to that thread. For example, you may start ThreadA, but it may depend on data generated in ThreadB, so you need to suspend ThreadA until ThreadB provides the necessary data. To suspend a thread, either call the sleep function within the <cfthread> body or provide the sleep value to the <cfthread> action attribute.

TIP

The cfthread sleep action and the sleep function are equivalent. Essentially, they both call java.lang.Thread.sleep(n).

Here is the syntax:

```
<cfthread action="sleep" duration= "milliseconds" />
```

Ending Threads

Specify terminate for the <cfthread> action attribute to end running or suspended threads. Remember that threads run in their own execution pools; there is no request timeout value applicable to threads, so they can potentially run forever. For example, the following code creates an infinite loop:

```
<cfloop condition="1">
  <cfset sleep(10000) />
</cfloop>
```

This code performs a continuous loop over a 10-second sleep call. If you run this code in a regular template with a timeout request enabled, ColdFusion will kill the page after it reaches the timeout limit. However, if you call this code inside <cfthread>, the page-level request will end, but the loop will continue in the thread. Use <cfthread> with action="terminate" and the name attribute set to the thread name to kill this runaway thread.

Here is the syntax:

```
<cfthread name="thread name" action="terminate" />
```

Joining Threads

Normally threads run independently of each other and the page-level thread. Sometimes, though, you may need co-dependent threads, where one thread depends on the completion of one or more threads before it can continue processing. Other times you may need synchronization with the page-level thread, to display thread-generated output for example.

Specify join for the <cfthread> action attribute to join threads. Joining threads effectively suspends the execution of the thread creating the join as it waits for the join operation to finish. Provide the name of the threads to be joined in the name attribute. You can join multiple threads using a comma-separated list. Use the `timeout` attribute to specify the amount of time a request waits for the thread join operation to finish.

NOTE

The default `timeout` value is 0, which tells the request to wait indefinitely for thread join to complete. If the current thread is the page-level thread, then the page request continues to wait for the thread join to complete. If you have hung or long-running threads, this will cause the page-level thread to execute beyond the configured request timeout in the ColdFusion Administrator.

Here is the syntax:

```
<cfthread action="join name="thread name [, thread name]… " [,
timeout="milliseconds" />
```

Accessing Thread Data

ColdFusion threads have access to all ColdFusion scopes. Threads perform processing simultaneously, but they share access to data, so it is paramount that shared data access be protected to ensure integrity. ColdFusion threads also have their own scopes for managing data internally. They provide metadata variables containing thread-specific data for processing at the page level.

Thread Scopes

ColdFusion threads have three scopes:

- THREAD-LOCAL scope

- ATTRIBUTES scope

- THREAD scope

In addition, a special CFTHREAD scope is available to the page-level request.

THREAD-LOCAL Scope

THREAD-LOCAL scope is a private scope containing variables available only to the current thread. Variables in this scope exist only for the life of the thread. They cannot be accessed by other threads or the page-level thread. Create variables in the thread-local scope by defining them in the `<cfthread>` body without a prefix:

```
<cfset counter = 1 />
```

TIP

You can also define thread-local variables using the `var` keyword: for example, `<cfset var counter = 1 />`. However, such variable definitions must occur immediately after the `<cfthread>` tag.

ATTRIBUTES Scope

The ATTRIBUTES scope contains any user-defined attributes specified for the `<cfthread>` tag individually or with the `attributesCollection` attribute. Variables in this scope exist only for the life of the thread and are available only to the current thread. This restriction provides thread safety because other threads cannot access attribute data. Because the attributes are thread safe, threads can have the same attribute names, which is useful when you are dynamically defining threads in a loop:

```
<cfparam name="URL.numOfThreads" default="5" type="integer" />
<cfloop index="i" from="1" to="#URL.numOfThreads#">
  <cfthread name="thread#i#" action="run" loopCtr="#i#">
    <cfset counter = ATTRIBUTES.loopCtr />
  </cfthread>
</cfloop>
```

This code block shows the `loopCtr` passed as an attribute to `<cfthread>` and accessed in the thread body with the ATTRIBUTES keyword prefix. ColdFusion makes a deep copy of variables before passing data to the `<cfthread>` attribute, which ensures that the values manipulated inside the `<cfthread>` body are independent of the original values. For example, this approach protects CFC instances passed to the thread; any manipulation of the CFC instance inside the thread does not affect the external CFC instances, and vice versa.

TIP

In general, use proper locking with `<cflock>` to prevent race conditions and deadlocks in all your CFML. Here is a good rule of thumb: If you are not sure it's thread-safe, lock it.

THREAD Scope

The THREAD scope contains thread-specific variables and metadata about the thread. Variables in the THREAD scope are available to the current thread and external threads. Only the current thread can write to this scope. All external threads in the page request (including the page-level thread) have read-only access. THREAD scope variables exist while the page and any threads in that page are still running. You create variables in the THREAD scope by prefixing them with either the thread name or the THREAD keyword:

```
<cfset THREAD.message = THREAD.name & " is initialized..." />
```

Use the thread's name to access THREAD scope data in external threads:

```
<cfset dataFromThreadA = THREADA.data />
```

NOTE

Be aware that variables in the THREAD scope can persist beyond the current page request if any threads generated in that request continue to run after the page request finishes.

TIP

THREAD scope data is available only to the current page request. If you need cross-request thread access, store the thread data in a shared scope (`Server`, `Application`, or `Session`), database, or file.

CFTHREAD Scope

The special CFTHREAD subscope of ColdFusion's Request scope contains the THREAD scope variables and metadata for all threads generated in the current page request. CFTHREAD exists for the entire page request or the life of the last running thread, whichever is longer. CFTHREAD is a ColdFusion structure whose keys are the thread names. Use the CFTHREAD keyword and the thread name to access data:

```
<cfoutput>#CFTHREAD.threadName.data#</cfoutput>
```

Since you can also use the thread name to access thread data, there are only a few instances where you might actually need to call CFTHREAD:

- When accessing dynamically named threads

- When threads have the same name as a Variables scoped variable

TIP

Remember that CFTHREAD belongs to the page request, so all threads in the current request can access it.

Thread Metadata

The THREAD scope contains several thread-specific variables. This metadata is available for every ColdFusion thread. Access the metadata as you would other THREAD scope variables by using either the thread name or CFTHREAD.threadName as a prefix. Thread metadata is also available for the duration of the page request or while a thread is running, whichever time is longer. This approach allows access to thread variables and metadata after the thread has finished processing. Table 30.3 lists the <cfthread> metadata variables.

Table 30.3   <cfthread> Metadata Variables

VARIABLE	DESCRIPTION
elapsedTime	Total processor time spent running the thread.
error	ColdFusion structure containing errors that occur during thread execution.
name	The name of the thread; corresponds to the <cfthread> name attribute.
output	Displays thread-generated output in page-level code.
priority	Thread processing priority as specified in the <cfthread> priority attribute; valid values are HIGH, LOW, and NORMAL.
starttime	The time thread processing began.
status	The current status of the thread.

TIP

If you dump the THREAD scope, the error metadata variable may be missing. It is present in the THREAD scope only if an error occurred during thread processing.

Other ColdFusion Scopes

ColdFusion threads have access to all ColdFusion scopes. All threads created in the same template (.cfm, .cfc, and so on) share the same variables and This scope. All the threads created in any templates within a single page request share the same Form, URL, Request, CGI, Cookie, Session, Application, Server, and Client scopes. Let's examine this point:

1. The user makes a request to index.cfm.

2. Index.cfm creates threads A, B, and C (ThreadA, ThreadB, and ThreadC) and then invokes the getFeeds method of component rss.cfc.

3. The getFeeds method creates threads D, E, and F.

    Threads A, B, and C share the same variables and This scope; threads D, E, and F share separate variables and This scope.

    Threads A through F share the same Form, URL, Request, CGI, Cookie, Session, Application, Server, and Client scopes.

Threads share ColdFusion scopes, so you need to protect simultaneous access to these variables with <cflock> and the appropriate scope attribute value. Threads have concurrent access to the variables and Request scope of the page-level request, so use the new Request scope lock to provide thread safety. Use name locks when accessing other shared resources such as FTP connections.

Good coding practices call for scoping of all variables. ColdFusion checks for unscoped variables inside the thread body in the following order:

1. FUNCTION-LOCAL

2. THREAD-LOCAL

3. ATTRIBUTES

4. VARIABLES

5. THREAD or CFTHREAD

Listing 30.1 shows the basic idea of <cfthread>. Threads.cfm uses a URL parameter (numOfThreads) to dynamically spawn threads inside <cfloop>. It creates variables in the THREAD-LOCAL and THREAD scopes. The loopCtr attribute determines which threads are suspended. The special CFTHREAD scope provides access to thread-specific and metadata variables (Figure 30.1).

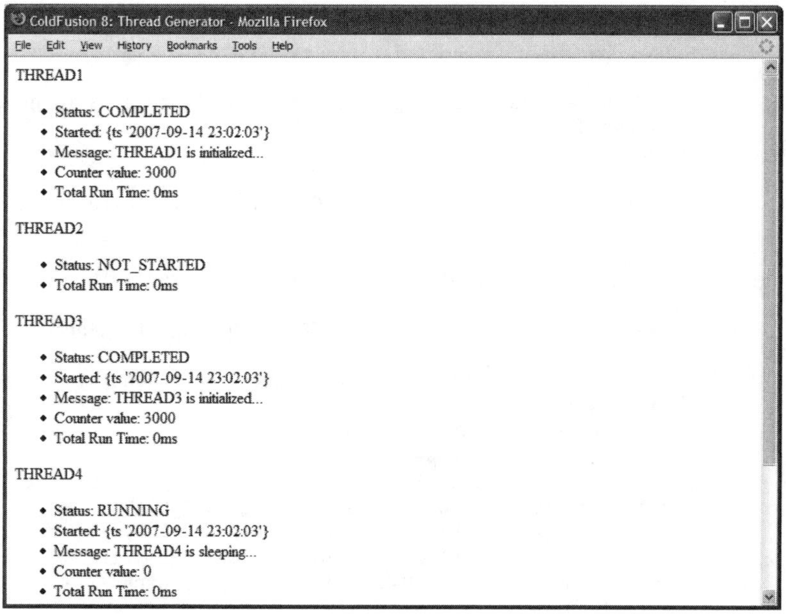

Figure 30.1

Dynamically generating threads and displaying their metadata.

Listing 30.1 `threads.cfm`—`<cfthread>` Example

```
<cfsilent>
<!---####
  File name: threads.cfm
  Description: Demonstrates <cfthread>.
  Assumptions: None
  Author name and e-mail: Sarge (sarge@sargeway.com) www.sargeway.com/blog/
  Date Created: September 11, 2007
####--->
<cfparam name="URL.numOfThreads" default="5" type="integer" />
<cfloop index="i" from="1" to="#URL.numOfThreads#">
  <cfthread name="thread#i#" action="run" loopCtr="#i#">
    <!---#### Initialize Thread-local scope variable. ####--->
    <cfset counter = 0 />

    <!---#### Initialize Thread scope variables.  --->
    <cfset THREAD.ctr = 0 />
    <cfset THREAD.message = THREAD.name & " is initialized..." />

    <!---#### Suspend all even numbered threads for 1/2 second. ####--->
    <cfif NOT ATTRIBUTES.loopCtr % 2>
       <cfset THREAD.message = THREAD.name & " is sleeping..." />
       <cfthread action="sleep" duration="500" />
    </cfif>
    <!---#### Update thread-level variable as loop counter. ####--->
    <cfloop index="j" from="1" to="3000">
      <cfset counter = j />
    </cfloop>
    <cfset THREAD.ctr = counter />
  </cfthread>
```

Listing 30.1 (CONTINUED)

```
    </cfloop>

    <!---#### Suspend page-level processing to allow threads to process. ####--->
    <cfset sleep(5) />
  </cfsilent>
  <html>
    <head><title>ColdFusion 8: Thread Generator</title></head>
    <body>
  <cfoutput>
    <cfloop index="k" from="1" to="#structCount(cfthread)#">
      <cfsilent>
  <!---#### Create a deep copy of the CFTHREAD scope to handle thread variables. ####-
  --->
        <cfset VARIABLES.demoThread = duplicate(cfthread["thread"&k]) />
      </cfsilent>
      <p>#VARIABLES.demoThread.name#
      <ul id="threadList" type="disc">
        <li>Status: #VARIABLES.demoThread.status#</li>
        <cfif VARIABLES.demoThread.status neq "NOT_STARTED">
          <li>Started: #VARIABLES.demoThread.starttime#</li>
          <li>Message: #VARIABLES.demoThread.message#</li>
          <li>Counter value: #VARIABLES.demoThread.ctr#</li>
        </cfif>
        <li>Total Run Time: #VARIABLES.demoThread.elapsedTime#ms</li>
      </ul><cfflush />
    </cfloop>
  </cfoutput>
  </body>
  </html>
```

Using the Thread Status

Every ColdFusion thread has a status. ColdFusion records the thread's status in the THREAD scope's
status metadata variable. The page-level and other threads can use the status to determine the processing state of a thread and take appropriate actions. For example, if the page-level thread requires
data from a spawned thread, it can check the thread's status to see if the thread has finished before
attempting to join the thread. Table 30.4 lists the status variable values.

Table 30.4 status Metadata Variable Values

VALUE	DESCRIPTION
NOT_STARTED	The thread has been queued.
RUNNING	The thread is being processed.
TERMINATED	Thread processing has stopped running because of one of the following actions: • A <cfthread> tag specifies action="terminate". • A <cfabort>, <cfrethrow>, or <cfthrow> is called in the thread body. • An exception occurred in the thread that caused the thread to terminate. • An administrator issued a kill instruction from the ColdFusion Server Monitor or Server Monitoring API.

Table 30.4 (CONTINUED)

VALUE	DESCRIPTION
COMPLETED	The thread ended normally.
WAITING	Thread execution is suspended by a `<cfthread>` tag with `action="join"`, and the thread is waiting for the joining thread or threads to finish processing.

Displaying Thread Output

ColdFusion threads can generate output, but they do not have access to the output buffer. Cold-Fusion restricts access to the output buffer to the page-level request to prevent conflicts. So how do you return thread-generated output to the page-level request?

ColdFusion stores thread-generated output in the THREAD scope's `output` metadata variable. The `output` variable contains all output including HTML and plaintext, generated text inside `<cfoutput>` tags, and `<cfdump>` content. The page-level request can access thread-generated output by calling `threadName.output`.

TIP

ColdFusion stores the generated text of `<cfdump>` in the `output` variable. Use `<cfoutput>` to display the color-coded `<cfdump>` contents—for example, `<cfoutput>#threadName.output#</cfoutput>`. `<cfdump>` simply displays the generated text.

Note the following important thread output considerations:

- ColdFusion populates the `output` metadata variable only when the thread process ends.

- All tags and tag attributes that create output inside the thread body must generate plaintext or HTML.

- You can use `<cfdocument>`, `<cfimage>`, `<cfpresentation>`, and `<cfreport>` only if you redirect their output to disk (a file or directory).

- You cannot use `<cfflush>` inside the thread body.

Monitoring and Administering Threads

ColdFusion thread management is ultimately the developer's job. Developers must responsibly spawn ColdFusion threads with thread safety and unresponsiveness in mind. Use proper locking techniques for shared scope access. Provide reasonable timeouts to prevent runaway threads. Use good error handling techniques to capture thread exceptions.

Handling Thread Exceptions

Errors in ColdFusion threads do not affect page-level requests. As with the CFML gateway, Cold-Fusion will not return an exception to the page request. Unhandled thread-level exceptions will terminate thread processing and populate the THREAD scope's error metadata variable with the exception object (Figure 30.2). External threads can access this variable and determine a resulting course of action.

Figure 30.2

Use <cfthrow>
to populate the
THREAD scope's Error
metadata variable.

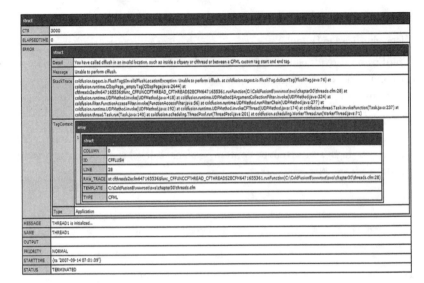

Threads cannot use page- or application-level error handling. Recall that threads do not have access to the output buffer, so you cannot use <cferror> or the onError application event handler for thread-level exceptions. Use the following techniques to handle thread-level exceptions:

- Trap errors within the thread body by using <cftry> or <cfcatch> or their CFScript equivalents. When catching thread errors with the try-catch paradigm, ColdFusion does not create the Thread.Error variable and sets Thread.Status to COMPLETED. The CFCATCH data is displayed in the Thread.Output variable (Figure 30.3).

Figure 30.3

Try-catch sends
exception data to the
THREAD scope's
Output metadata
variable.

struct	
CTR	0
ELAPSEDTIME	16
MESSAGE	THREAD1 is initialized...
NAME	THREAD1
OUTPUT	<p>Unable to perform cfflush.</p> <p>You have called cfflush in an invalid location, such as inside a cfquery or cfthread or between a CFML custom tag start and end tag.</p>
PRIORITY	NORMAL
STARTTIME	{ts '2007-09-14 23:21:18'}
STATUS	COMPLETED

- Use `<cfabort>`, `<cfrethrow>`, or `<cfthrow>` to terminate thread processing immediately, populate the `Thread.Error` variable, and set the `Thread.Status` variable to `TERMINATED`.

- Use the `threadName.Error` metadata variable to handle thread errors outside the thread. You can extend your application error logic by combining `threadName.Error` with `threadName.Status`.

The `watcher.cfm` template in Listing 30.2 provides an example of the handling of thread exceptions and other concepts discussed in this chapter. The code accepts a `URL.timeout` parameter to control page-level suspension: for example, `http://localhost:8500/ows/30/watcher.cfm?timeout=5000`. A browser request to `watcher.cfm` will create a dynamically named thread whose body includes the `runaway.cfm` template within a try-catch block. `Runaway.cfm` contains an infinite loop and increments a `Request` scope variable, shared by all the templates and threads in the request. The page-level thread pauses processing as it waits to joins the spawned thread. If the spawned thread exceeds the timeout value, the page-level thread terminates the child thread and displays the available `THREAD` scope metadata, including output and error values. If an error occurs anywhere during processing, the child thread terminates, and error messages are displayed (Figure 30.4).

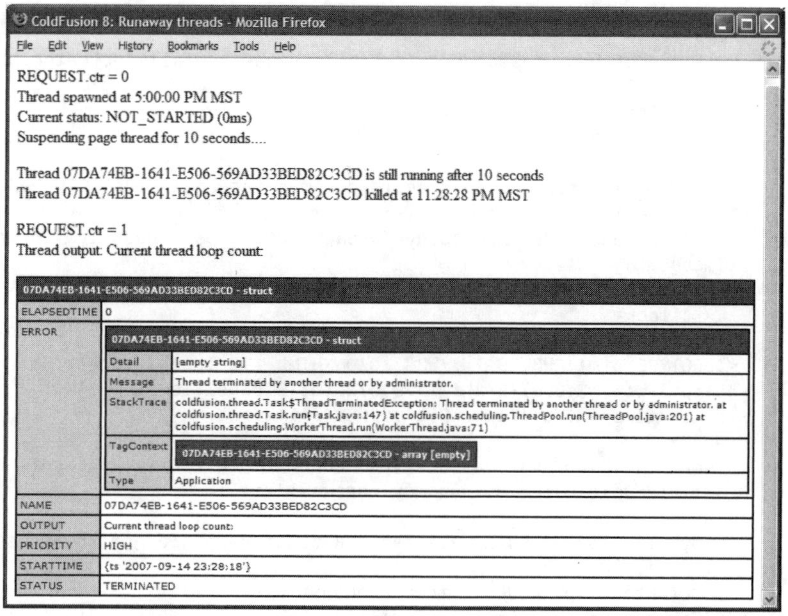

Figure 30.4

Terminating threads and handling thread-level exceptions in a page thread.

Listing 30.2 `watcher.cfm`—Error Handling Example

```
<cftry>
<cfsilent>
<!---####
   File name: watcher.cfm
   Description: Demonstrates joining and terminating threads, as well as exception
handling.
```

Listing 30.2 (CONTINUED)

```
    Assumptions: Timeout requests disabled or set higher than URL.timeout value.
    Author name and e-mail: Sarge (sarge@sargeway.com) www.sargeway.com/blog/
    Date Created: September 11, 2007
####--->
    <cfparam name="URL.timeout" default="10000" type="integer" />
    <cfparam name="REQUEST.ctr" default="0" type="integer" />

    <!---#### Dynamic name value ####--->
    <cfset variables.dynThreadName = createUUID() />

    <!---#### Create dynamically named threads to prevent deadlocks ####--->
    <cfthread name="#dynThreadName#" action="run" priority="high">
    <cftry>
        Current thread loop count:
        <cfinclude template="runaway.cfm" />

        <!---#### Demonstrate thread and included template share Request scope.
####--->
        <cfset Thread.ctr = Request.ctr>
        <cfoutput>#Thread.ctr#</cfoutput>
        <cfcatch type="any">
        <!---#### Throw thread-specific exception to page-thread for handling.
####--->
            <cfthrow message="#cfcatch.Message#" detail="#cfcatch.Detail#" />
        </cfcatch>
      </cftry>
    </cfthread>

    <!---#### Create a pointer to dynamic thread in the CFTHREAD scope to handle
thread variables. ####--->
    <cflock name="#variables.dynThreadName#" type="readonly" throwontimeout="yes"
timeout="5">
      <cfset Variables.demoThread = CFTHREAD[variables.dynThreadName] />
    </cflock>
</cfsilent>
<!DOCTYPE html PUBLIC "-//W3C//DTD XHTML 1.0 Transitional//EN"
"http://www.w3.org/TR/xhtml1/DTD/xhtml1-transitional.dtd">
<html xmlns="http://www.w3.org/1999/xhtml">
<head>
  <meta http-equiv="Content-Type" content="text/html; charset=utf-8" />
  <title>ColdFusion 8: Runaway threads</title>
</head>
<body><!---#### Display available Request variable and Thread scope
metadata. ####--->
    <cfoutput><p>REQUEST.ctr = #Request.ctr#<br />
    Thread  spawned at #timeFormat(Variables.demoThread.starttime, "full")#<br />
    Current status: #Variables.demoThread.status#
(#Variables.demoThread.elapsedTime#ms)<br />
    Suspending page thread for #URL.timeout/1000# seconds....</p></cfoutput><cfflush>

    <!---#### Suspend page-level thread until timeout is reached. ####--->
    <cfthread action="join" name="#Variables.demoThread.name#"
timeout="#URL.timeout#" />

    <!---#### Kill thread if it runs beyond the timeout. ####--->
    <cfif FindNoCase("RUNNING", Variables.demoThread.status)>
```

Listing 30.2 (CONTINUED)

```
        <cfoutput>Thread #Variables.demoThread.name# is still running after
#Variables.demoThread.elapsedTime/1000# seconds<br /></cfoutput><cfflush>
        <cflock name="runaway_killer" type="EXCLUSIVE" throwontimeout="yes" timeout="5">
            <cfthread action="terminate" name="#Variables.demoThread.name#" />
            <!---#### Log the killed thread. ####--->
            <cflog application="yes" date="yes" file="threads" time="yes" thread="yes"
text="#variables.dynThreadName# terminated!" />
        </cflock>
        <cfoutput>Thread #Variables.demoThread.name# killed at #timeFormat(now(),
"full")#<br /></cfoutput>
    </cfif>

    <!---#### Check value of Request variable. ####--->
    <p><cfoutput>REQUEST.ctr = #Request.ctr#</cfoutput><cfflush>

    <!---#### Display available Thread output. ####--->
    <cfif len(trim(Variables.demoThread.output))><cfoutput><br />Thread output:
#Variables.demoThread.output#</cfoutput></cfif></p>

    <!---#### Dump the Thread scope ####--->
    <cfdump label="#Variables.demoThread.name#" var="#Variables.demoThread#">
</body>
</html>
    <cfcatch type="any">
    <!---#### Determine if the CFTHREAD scope is populated. ####--->
     <cfif structCount(CFTHREAD)>
        <!---#### Kill spawned thread in event of any page-level exception. ####--->
        <cflock name="runaway_killer" type="EXCLUSIVE"  throwontimeout="yes"
timeout="5">
            <cfthread name="#dynThreadName#" action="terminate" />
            <!---#### Dump the Thread scope Error data. ####--->
            <cfdump var="#cfthread[variables.dynThreadName].Error#">
            <!---#### Log the killed thread. ####--->
            <cflog application="yes" date="yes" file="threads" time="yes" thread="yes"
text="#variables.dynThreadName# terminated!" />
        </cflock>
    </cfif>
    <cfdump var="#cfcatch#">
    </cfcatch>
</cftry>
```

Administrator Tools

The ColdFusion Administrator and Server Monitor provide tools for controlling and viewing information about threads. The Maximum Number of Threads Available for CFTHREAD setting in the Tag Limit Settings section of the ColdFusion Administrator Server Settings > Request Tuning page specifies a limit for the number of concurrently running <cfthread>-generated threads. Any threads created by <cfthread> beyond this limit are queued. The default value is 10.

TIP

Ten is also the default value for ColdFusion 8 Standard Edition. You may be able to increase this number in the ColdFusion Administrator, but the Standard Edition allows only two concurrent ColdFusion threads and will queue the remaining threads.

The ColdFusion 8 Server Monitor provides several views for monitoring ColdFusion threads. You will find details on the ColdFusion Server Monitor in Chapter 56, "Monitoring System Performance," in *Adobe ColdFusion 8 Web Application Construction Kit, Volume 3: Advanced Application Development*.

- Statistics > Request Statistics section

Active ColdFusion threads
Lists all currently active threads launched by `<cfthread>`.

Report view
Lists the thread name, the template path that spawned the thread, the execution time, and the Java thread name. It also provides the method to terminate individual threads manually.

Detail view
Displays the CFML and Java stack traces for the thread selected in the Report view.

TIP
You can also double-click a thread to invoke the Detail view.

Chart view
Displays the processing time for running and queued ColdFusion threads.

Slowest ColdFusion threads
Lists the slowest-running ColdFusion threads. Double-click a thread to view thread statistics including response times, request sizes, expanded template paths, and CFML stack traces.

- Statistics > Memory Usage section

ColdFusion threads by memory usage
Lists the ColdFusion threads that are consuming more memory than the configured number of kilobytes. Double-click a thread to see memory details including variable names, values, and sizes (in bytes).

TIP
Memory tracking must be started to be able to track `cfthread` memory usage.

NOTE
At the time of publication, the ColdFusion Server Monitor alerts do not monitor ColdFusion threads. If any `<cfthread>`-generated threads run beyond the page request that spawned them, the only way to kill them is to either manually use the Server Monitor Active ColdFusion Threads page or code your own ColdFusion thread monitor using the Server Monitoring component that is part of the Administrator API (see Chapter 66,"Using the Administration API," in Vol. 3, *Advanced Application Development*).

Best Practices

The following are best-practice techniques for generating and controlling ColdFusion threads. Add these to your coding methodology to ensure better performance and thread safeness.

- Do not overuse ColdFusion threads; performance gains may be realized by leveraging the ColdFusion CFML gateway for some tasks.

- Keep thread names unique.

- Always specify a timeout when joining threads. Specify a `timeout` value that is less than the ColdFusion Administrator Timeout Request setting when joining threads to the page-level request.

- Properly scope all variables inside the thread body. Remember that unscoped variables default to the THREAD-LOCAL scope and are not accessible outside the thread.

- Use the thread's name to access THREAD scope variables. Use CFTHREAD when accessing dynamically named threads.

- Use <cflock> to prevent potential deadlocks and race conditions between threads. Use the proper scope locks when threads access shared server resources: Server-, Application-, or Session-scoped variables. Use a Request scope lock when threads modify variables or Request-scoped variables. Use named locks when threads access shared resources such as Microsoft Exchange Server or FTP connections.

- Use the `cfthread output` metadata variable in page-level code to display thread-generated text.

- Use <cfabort>, <cfrethrow>, or <cfthrow> to send thread-level exceptions to the page-level code and properly set the `threadName.Error` and `threadName.Status` metadata variables.

- Use the `theadName.Error` metadata variable to handle thread-specific exceptions in external threads.

- Use <cflog> and <cftrace> to help track threads.

- Use the ColdFusion Administrator's Maximum Number of Threads Available for CFTHREAD setting to control the pool size for concurrently running ColdFusion threads.

- Use the ColdFusion Server Monitor or the Server Monitor API to monitor and terminate hung threads.

CHAPTER 31

Improving Performance

Options in the ColdFusion Administrator

This chapter discusses a number of ways to improve the performance of your ColdFusion templates, some of which are a bit involved. Before getting into the specific solutions, you should be aware of a number of server-wide options provided by the ColdFusion Administrator that can affect the overall performance of your applications.

The Administrator options most likely to directly affect performance are:

- **Maximum Number of Simultaneous Template Requests.** This option on the Server Settings > Request Tuning page of the Administrator should be set to a fairly low number (but not as low as 1) for best performance. The best value for your application will depend on how heavily it is used and how much processing is done per page request.

- **Maximum Number of Simultaneous Flash Remoting, Web Service, and CFC Function Requests.** Also found under Server Settings > Request Tuning, these three options allow you to control the number of remote requests to CFCs, whether they be Flash Remoting, Web Service, or direct CFC calls. As with the previous setting, the best values will vary.

- **Maximum Number of Cached Templates.** Ideally, this option on the Caching page should be set to a number greater than (or at least close to) the number of ColdFusion templates that get used on a regular basis.

- **Trusted Cache.** This option on the Caching page should be enabled for best performance, but only when your application has moved into a production mode (after you have completely finished writing your code).

- **Maintain Connections.** This option for each of your data sources should be enabled for best performance. When configuring or editing a data source, click the Show Advanced Settings button to configure this option.

- **Limit Connections.** In general, if you choose Maintain Connections (above), this option (found in the same location) should also be enabled for each of your data sources, and you should provide a sensible number for the Restrict Connections To field next to the Limit Connections checkbox. As a rough guide, consider starting with a value that is approximately the same as the number you provided for Maximum Number of Simultaneous Requests, above.

→ See Chapter 28, "ColdFusion Server Configuration," for details on each of these options.

Improving Query Performance with Caching

Nearly all ColdFusion applications have a database at their heart, and most ColdFusion templates contain at least one <cfquery> or other database interaction. In fact, depending on the type of application you are building, your ColdFusion templates might be solely about getting information in and out of a database. In such a situation, ColdFusion is basically behaving as database middleware, sitting between your database and your Web server.

Because database access is such an integral part of ColdFusion development, the server provides a number of features relevant to the performance of your database queries. This section helps you understand which options are available and how to make the most of them.

In particular, we will discuss the following:

- Query caching, which cuts down on the amount of interaction between your database and ColdFusion. This can improve performance dramatically.

- Helping ColdFusion deal with larger query results via the blockfactor attribute.

Understanding Query Caching

To improve performance, ColdFusion provides a wonderful feature called *query caching*. Basically, query caching allows ColdFusion to keep frequently used query results in its internal memory, rather than retrieving the results from the database over and over again.

You tell ColdFusion to cache a query by adding a cachedWithin or cachedAfter attribute to the <cfquery> tag. If one of your templates is visited often and contains a query that won't return different results each time it runs, you can usually give the page an instant performance boost by simply using one of these two special attributes. Table 31.1 explains what each of the attributes does.

Table 31.1 `<cfquery>` Attributes Relevant for Query Caching

ATTRIBUTE	PURPOSE
`cachedWithin`	Optional. Tells ColdFusion to cache the query results for a period of time, which you can specify in days, hours, minutes, or seconds. You specify the time period using the `createTimeSpan()` function.
`cachedAfter`	Optional. Tells ColdFusion to cache the query results based on a particular date and time. This attribute is generally less useful in real-world applications than `cachedWithin`. If you know that your database will be updated at a certain moment in time, perhaps after some type of external batch process, you can specify that date and time (as a ColdFusion date value) here.

Query caching is really easy to use. Say you use the following query in one of your ColdFusion templates:

```
<cfquery name="GetFilms" datasource="ows">
 SELECT FilmID, MovieTitle FROM Films
</cfquery>
```

Assuming that the data in the Films table doesn't change very often, it would probably be sufficient to only query the database occasionally, rather than with every page request. For instance, you might decide that the database really only needs to be checked for new or changed data every 15 minutes. Within each 15-minute period, the data from a previous query can just be reused. To get this effect, simply add a `cachedWithin` attribute that uses `createTimeSpan()` to specify a 15-minute interval, like this:

```
<cfquery name="getFilms" datasource="ows"
 cachedWithin="#createTimeSpan(0,0,15,0)#">
 SELECT FilmID, MovieTitle FROM Films
</CFQUERY>
```

That's all you have to do. The first time the query runs, ColdFusion interacts with the database normally and retrieves the film records. But instead of discarding the records when the page request is finished—as it would do normally—ColdFusion stores the query results in the server's RAM. The next time the template is visited, ColdFusion uses the records in its memory instead of contacting the database again. It continues to do so for 15 minutes after the first query ran (or until the Cold-Fusion server is restarted). The next time the template is visited, the original records are flushed from the server's RAM and replaced with new records, retrieved afresh from the database.

There's more. Queries aren't cached on a per-page basis. They are cached on a server-wide basis. If two `<cfquery>` tags on two different pages specify exactly the same SQL code, `datasource`, `name`, `dbtype`, `username`, and `password`, they will share the same cache. That is, the first time either page is accessed, the database is contacted and the records are retrieved. Then, for the next 15 minutes (or whatever interval you specify), a visit to either page will use the cached copy of the query results.

NOTE

The SQL statements in the two `<cfquery>` tags must be exactly the same, including any white space such as tabs, indenting, and spaces. If they aren't the same, the two queries will be cached independently.

Clearly, if a query is at all time-consuming, the performance benefits can be tremendous. Every template that uses the cached query will be sped up. Plus, if the database and ColdFusion are on different machines, using query caching will likely cut down dramatically on network traffic. This tends to improve performance as well, depending on how your local network is configured.

NOTE

A possible disadvantage to caching a query is that changes to the actual data in the database won't show up in the cached version of the query, because the database isn't actually being contacted. Any new records (or updates or deletes) will show up only after the cache interval has expired. For details and solutions, see "Refreshing Cached Queries Programmatically" later in this chapter.

Using Cached Queries

One obvious situation in which ColdFusion's query caching feature can be of great benefit is when you're building a next-n type of record-browsing interface, such as the one presented in Chapter 29, "Improving the User Experience."

Listing 31.1 takes the NextN4.cfm template from Listing 29.7 of Chapter 29 and adds a cached-Within attribute to the <cfquery> at the top of the template. Now ColdFusion doesn't need to keep rerunning the query as the user browses through the pages of records.

Listing 31.1 NextNCached.cfm—Adding the cachedWithin Attribute to Speed Up Record Browsing

```
<!---
 Filename: NextNCached.cfm
 Created by: Nate Weiss (NMW)
 Purpose: Displays Next N record-navigation interface
 Please Note Includes NextNIncludeBackNext.cfm and NextNIncludePageLinks.cfm
--->

<!--- Maintain ExpenseReport filtering variables at session level --->
<cfparam name="SESSION.expenseReport.userFilter" type="string" default="">
<cfparam name="SESSION.expenseReport.dateFrom" type="string" default="">
<cfparam name="SESSION.expenseReport.dateThru" type="string" default="">

<!--- If the user is submitting the "filter" form, --->
<!--- we'll make their submission be the filter for rest of session --->
<cfif isDefined("FORM.userFilter")>
 <cfset SESSION.expenseReport.userFilter = FORM.userFilter>
 <cfset SESSION.expenseReport.dateFrom = FORM.dateFrom>
 <cfset SESSION.expenseReport.dateThru = FORM.dateThru>
</cfif>

<!--- Retrieve expense records from database --->
<cfquery name="getExp" datasource="#application.dataSource#"
 cachedWithin="#createTimeSpan(0,0,15,0)#">
 SELECT
 f.FilmID, f.MovieTitle,
 e.Description, e.ExpenseAmount, e.ExpenseDate
 FROM
 Expenses e INNER JOIN Films f
 ON e.FilmID = f.FilmID
 WHERE
 0=0
```

Listing 31.1 (CONTINUED)

```
<!--- If the user provided a filter string, --->
<!--- show only matching films and/or expenses --->
<cfif SESSION.expenseReport.userFilter is not "">
AND (f.MovieTitle LIKE '%#SESSION.expenseReport.userFilter#%' OR
e.Description LIKE '%#SESSION.expenseReport.userFilter#%')
</cfif>
<!--- Also filter on From date, if provided --->
<cfif isDate(SESSION.expenseReport.dateFrom)>
AND e.ExpenseDate >= #createODBCDate(SESSION.expenseReport.dateFrom)#
</cfif>
<!--- Also filter on Through date, if provided --->
<cfif isDate(SESSION.expenseReport.dateThru)>
AND e.ExpenseDate <= #createODBCDate(SESSION.expenseReport.dateThru)#
</cfif>
ORDER BY
e.ExpenseDate DESC
</cfquery>


<!--- Number of rows to display per Next/Back page --->
<cfset rowsPerPage = 10>
<!--- What row to start at? Assume first by default --->
<cfparam name="URL.startRow" default="1" type="numeric">
<!--- Allow for Show All parameter in the URL --->
<cfparam name="URL.showAll" type="boolean" default="No">

<!--- We know the total number of rows from query --->
<cfset totalRows = getExp.recordCount>
<!--- Show all on page if ShowAll passed in URL --->
<cfif URL.showAll>
 <cfset rowsPerPage = totalRows>
</cfif>
<!--- Last row is 10 rows past the starting row, or --->
<!--- total number of query rows, whichever is less --->
<cfset endRow = min(URL.startRow + rowsPerPage - 1, totalRows)>
<!--- Next button goes to 1 past current end row --->
<cfset startRowNext = endRow + 1>
<!--- Back button goes back N rows from start row --->
<cfset startRowBack = URL.startRow - rowsPerPage>


<!--- Page Title --->
<html>
<head><title>Expense Browser</title></head>
<body>
<cfoutput><h2>#application.companyName# Expense Report</h2></cfoutput>

<!--- Simple style sheet for formatting --->
<style>
 FORM { font-family:sans-serif;font-size:smaller;}
 TH { font-family:sans-serif;font-size:smaller;
 background:navy;color:white}
 TD { font-family:sans-serif;font-size:smaller}
 TD.DataA { background:silver;color:black}
 TD.DataB { background:lightgrey;color:black}
```

Listing 31.1 (CONTINUED)

```
  </style>


  <!--- Simple form to allow user to filter results --->
  <cfform action="#CGI.script_name#" method="POST">
   <!--- Filter string --->
   <b>Filter:</b>
   <cfinput
   type="text"
   name="userFilter"
   value="#SESSION.expenseReport.userFilter#"
   size="15">

   <!--- From date --->
    
   <b>Dates:</b> from
   <cfinput
   type="text"
   name="dateFrom"
   value="#SESSION.expenseReport.dateFrom#"
   size="9"
   validate="date"
   message="Please enter a valid date, or leave it blank.">

   <!--- Through date --->
   through
   <cfinput
   type="text"
   name="dateThru"
   value="#SESSION.expenseReport.dateThru#"
   size="9"
   validate="date"
   message="Please enter a valid date, or leave it blank.">

   <!--- Submit button to activate/change/clear filter --->
   <input
   type="Submit"
   value="Apply">
  </cfform>


  <table width="600" border="0" cellspacing="0" cellpadding="1">
   <!--- Row at top of table, above column headers --->
   <tr>
   <td width="500" colspan="3">
   <!--- Message about which rows are being displayed --->
   <cfoutput>
   Displaying <b>#URL.startRow#</b> to <b>#endRow#</b>
   of <b>#totalRows#</b> Records<br>
   </cfoutput>
   </td>
   <td width="100" align="right">
   <cfif not URL.showAll>
   <!--- Provide Next/Back links --->
   <cfinclude template="NextNIncludeBackNext.cfm">
```

Listing 31.1 (CONTINUED)

```
</cfif>
</td>
</tr>

<!--- Row for column headers --->
<tr>
<th width="100">Date</th>
<th width="250">Film</th>
<th width="150">Expense</th>
<th width="100">Amount</th>
</tr>

<!--- For each query row that should be shown now --->
<cfloop query="getExp" startRow="#URL.startRow#" endrow="#endRow#">
<!--- Use class "DataA" or "DataB" for alternate rows --->
<cfset class = iif(getExp.currentRow mod 2 eq 0, "'DataA'", "'DataB'")>

<cfoutput>
<tr valign="baseline">
<td class="#class#" width="100">#lsDateFormat(expenseDate)#</td>
<td class="#class#" width="250">#movieTitle#</td>
<td class="#class#" width="150"><i>#description#</i></td>
<td class="#class#" width="100">#lsCurrencyFormat(expenseAmount)#</td>
</tr>
</cfoutput>
</cfloop>

<!--- Row at bottom of table, after rows of data --->
<tr>
<td width="500" colspan="3">
<cfif not URL.showAll and totalRows gt rowsPerPage>
<!--- Shortcut links for "Pages" of search results --->
Page <cfinclude template="NextNIncludePageLinks.cfm">
<!--- Show All link --->
<cfoutput>
<a href="#CGI.script_name#?&showAll=Yes">Show All</a>
</cfoutput>
</cfif>
</td>
<td width="100" align="right">
<cfif NOT URL.showAll>
<!--- Provide Next/Back links --->
<cfinclude template="NextNIncludeBackNext.cfm">
</cfif>
</td>
</tr>
</table>

</body>
</html>
```

If you want, you can watch which queries ColdFusion is actually caching by turning on the Database Activity option in the Debug Output Settings page of the ColdFusion Administrator. Whenever a query is returned from the cache, the execution time will be reported as 0ms, accompanied by the words `Cached Query`, as shown in Figure 31.1. When the cache timeout expires, you will see the execution time reappear, in milliseconds, as it does normally.

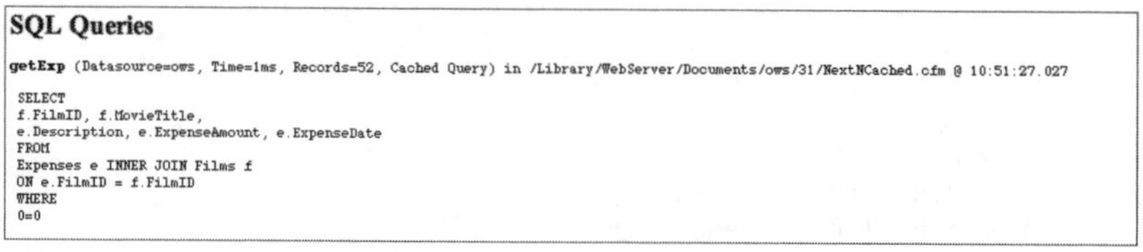

Figure 31.1

Cached queries are fetched directly from ColdFusion's internal memory, which can greatly improve performance.

```
SQL Queries

getExp (Datasource=ows, Time=1ms, Records=52, Cached Query) in /Library/WebServer/Documents/ows/31/NextNCached.cfm @ 10:51:27.027

SELECT
f.FilmID, f.MovieTitle,
e.Description, e.ExpenseAmount, e.ExpenseDate
FROM
Expenses e INNER JOIN Films f
ON e.FilmID = f.FilmID
WHERE
0=0
```

> **NOTE**
>
> Before you try this file in your browser, copy the `Application.cfc`, `NextNIncludeBackNext.cfm`, and `NextNIncludePageLinks.cfm` files from the book Web site.

Refreshing Cached Queries Programmatically

Query caching is most often used for queries that don't change often over time, or in situations where it is acceptable for your application to show information that might be slightly out of date. However, you might run into situations in which you want a query cached for several hours at a time (because the underlying data hardly ever changes), but where it is very important for any changes that *do* get made to the database to be reflected right away.

Flushing a Specific Cached Query After an Update

ColdFusion doesn't provide a specific attribute for flushing a particular cached query, but you can achieve the same effect by including a `<cfquery>` tag with a negative `cachedWithin` value right after a relevant change is made to the database. This will force ColdFusion to contact the database and fetch the updated records. From that point on, the updated version of the query results will be what is shared with other pages that use the same query.

> **NOTE**
>
> Of course, this technique is not effective if the database is being updated via some application other than ColdFusion. Your Cold-Fusion application needs to be aware of when to discard a cached version of a query.

For instance, let's say you are using the following cached query in your code:

```
<cfquery name="getFilms" datasource="ows"
 cachedWithin="#createTimeSpan(0,3,0,0)#">
 SELECT * FROM Films
</cfquery>
```

Left to its own devices, this query's cache will only be refreshed every three hours. Now say that some other page updates one of the film records, perhaps using a `<cfupdate>` tag, like so:

```
<cfupdate datasource="ows" tablename="Films">
```

Again, left to its own devices, the SELECT query will continue to show the cached records until the three-hour timeout expires. Only then will the changes that the <cfupdate> made be fetched from the database. However, you could force the updated records into the cache by placing the following query right after the <cfupdate>:

```
<cfquery name="getFilms" datasource="ows"
 cachedWithin="#CreateTimeSpan(0,0,0,-1)#">
 SELECT * FROM Films
</cfquery>
```

Now, when the first SELECT query is next executed, it will read the updated records from the cache. Your application will always show the most current version of the records, even though it is usually reading the records from the query cache.

NOTE

The SQL statements in the two <cfquery> tags (the one that uses the cachedWithin of three hours and the one that uses the negative cachedWithin value) must be exactly the same, including indenting and other white space. The name and datasource attributes must also be identical, as well as any dbtype, username, and password attributes you might be providing. If not, ColdFusion will consider the queries separate for caching purposes, which means that the second query won't have the desired effect of refreshing the first.

Flushing All Cached Queries

As you just saw, you can use a negative value for a specific query's cachedWithin attribute to make sure a particular query gets removed from the query cache. This method is simple and straightforward, but you may also find that there are situations in which you would like to discard *all* cached query records. One way to do this is to simply restart the ColdFusion application server.

You can also refresh all cached queries programmatically, using the <cfobjectcache> tag. At this time, <cfobjectcache> takes one attribute, action, which must always be set to Clear. When Cold-Fusion encounters this tag in your code, all cached queries are discarded. The next time a <cfquery> tag is encountered for the first time, it will re-contact the database and retrieve the current data from your tables.

Here is how the tag would look in your code:

```
<!--- Discard all cached queries --->
<cfobjectcache
 action="Clear">
```

NOTE

This tag was present but undocumented in previous versions of ColdFusion. As of ColdFusion MX, it is a documented and supported part of the product.

Limiting the Number of Cached Queries

To ensure that your cached queries don't take up crippling amounts of the server's RAM, Cold-Fusion imposes a server-wide limit on the number of queries that can be cached at any given time. By default, the limit is set to 100 cached queries. If a new <cfquery> tag that uses cachedWithin or `cachedAfter` is encountered after 100 queries are already in the cache, the oldest query is dropped from the cache and replaced with the new query.

NOTE

You can increase this limit by editing the Maximum Number of Cached Queries field in the Caching page of the ColdFusion Administrator. Keep in mind that the final SQL code determines how a query is cached. If you use a ColdFusion variable in the SQL portion of a `<cfquery>` tag, and the query is run with 10 different variable values during a given period, that will count as 10 queries toward the limit of 100. See Chapter 28 for details about using the ColdFusion Administrator.

Controlling the Number of Records Fetched at Once

Normally, ColdFusion retrieves each record from your database individually. That said, if you know a query will return more than a few records, you can speed up ColdFusion a bit by giving it a hint about how many records are likely to be returned. To do so, provide a `blockFactor` attribute in your `<cfquery>` tags. In using `blockFactor`, make a reasonable guess as to how many records the query might return.

Don't provide a `blockFactor` value that is more than the number of records the query returns. If you do, your database driver will tell ColdFusion that the specified `blockFactor` is invalid, and ColdFusion will try again—this time repeatedly subtracting 1 from the value you supplied until `blockFactor` no longer exceeds the total number of records. This could slow down your query. Unfortunately, ColdFusion can't determine the appropriate `blockFactor` automatically.

For instance, if you know that the `Films` table will contain 25 or more records for the foreseeable future, you should provide a `blockFactor` value of 25, like this:

```
<cfquery name="getFilms" datasource="ows" blockFactor="25">
 SELECT * FROM Films
</cfquery>
```

The larger the number of records involved, the more effect `blockFactor` is likely to have on overall query performance. Don't obsess about getting `blockFactor` exactly right. Just think of it as a way to let ColdFusion know whether to expect a large number of records or just one or two. At the very least, consider providing a `blockFactor="100"` attribute for all queries that will return hundreds or thousands of records.

NOTE

If you are using stored procedures, it's worth noting that the `<cfstoredproc>` tag also supports the `blockFactor` attribute. See Chapter 42, "Working with Stored Procedures," online, for details.

NOTE

Currently, the maximum value that `blockFactor` allows is `100`. If a query might return hundreds or thousands of records, you should still go ahead and set `blockFactor="100"`. Because ColdFusion will be retrieving the records in 100-record chunks, this can often improve performance rather dramatically.

Caching Page Output

You already have learned that ColdFusion allows you to cache query results. It also provides a page-caching feature, which enables you to cache the complete HTML page that each of your templates generates. Similar to query caching, ColdFusion's page-caching feature is designed to improve your Web pages' overall performance.

The idea is simple. If you have certain ColdFusion templates that are time-consuming or get hit often, you can tell ColdFusion to cache them for a specified period of time. This can have a huge effect on overall application performance. The caching can take place on the browser machine, on the server machine, or on both.

Introducing the `<cfcache>` Tag

If you want ColdFusion to cache a page, place the `<cfcache>` tag at the top of the template, before any other CFML or HTML tags. The most important attribute for the `<cfcache>` tag is the `action` attribute, which tells ColdFusion whether you want the page cached on the client machine, on the ColdFusion server machine, or on both.

Client-Side Page Caching

The `<cfcache>` tag can provide two types of caching: client-side page caching and server-side page caching. Both are of great benefit. Let's look first at client-side page caching, which is of particular relevance when you're putting together personalized pages that might take some time to display. Then we will look at server-side page caching, which is most useful for putting together nonpersonalized pages that get hit very often.

Finally, we will see how to use client-side and server-side page caching together, usually the best option.

Background

All modern Web browsers provide some type of internal page-caching mechanism. As you use your Web browser to visit sites, it makes local copies of the HTML for each page, along with local copies of any images or other media files the pages contain. If you go back to that same page later, the browser will show you the local copies of the files, rather than refetching them from the Web server. Your browser also provides settings you can use to control where the cached files are kept and how large the collection of all cached files can get. If it weren't for your browser's cache, most casual Web browsing would be much slower than it is.

Normally, the browser just relies on these settings to determine whether to display a page from its local cache or to recontact the Web server. If you haven't adjusted any of these settings, your own browser is probably set to use the cached copy of a page until you close the browser. When you reopen the browser and visit that same page, the browser recontacts the Web server and fetches the page afresh.

NOTE

To view the current cache settings for a Firefox browser, choose Tools > Options > Privacy > Cache. For Internet Explorer, choose Internet Options from the Tools menu, then click the Settings button under Temporary Internet Files.

Gaining More Control

The `<cfcache>` tag gives you programmatic control over when the browser should use its local, cached copy to display a page to the user. You use the `timeSpan` attribute to tell ColdFusion how old the browser's cached version of the page can be before ColdFusion should refetch it from the server. If the browser fetched its local copy of the page after the date you specify, it uses the local copy to show the page to the user. If not, it visits the template normally. Table 31.2 summarizes the attributes relevant for this use of `<cfcache>`.

Table 31.2   `<cfcache>` Tag Attributes Relevant for Client-Side Caching

ATTRIBUTE	PURPOSE
action	Must be set to `ClientCache` to use client-side caching only. You can also set this attribute to several other values to enable server-side caching, which the next section describes. You can also set it to `CACHE`, which uses both client-side and server-side mechanisms (see "ColdFusion-Optimized Caching," later in this chapter).
timeSpan	The period of time you want the page to remain cached by the user's browser. You can specify this period using any combination of days, hours, minutes, or seconds, by providing a value returned by the `createTimeSpan()` function. If a simple number is passed, it is the number of days the cache is used. For example, 0.5 would result in a cache of one half day. A value of 1 would result in a cache lasting one day.

For instance, if you wanted the browser to use its local copy of a page for six hours at a time, you would include the following at the top of your ColdFusion template:

```
<!--- Let browser use a cached version of --->
<!--- this page, from up to six hours ago --->
<cfcache
 action="ClientCache"
 timeSpan="0.25">
```

TIP

If you wanted to cache all pages in an application, you could simply place the `<cfcache>` tag in your `Application.cfc` file. That would cause all page requests to be cached (except for form submissions, which never are).

The first time a user visits the page, ColdFusion processes the template normally and sends the generated page back to the browser. The browser then stores the page in its local cache. The next time the user visits the same page, the browser quickly contacts the server, providing the server with the exact date and time that the page was visited the first time (that is, the date and time the local copy was saved). If the browser tells the server that its local copy is not older than the date specified in `timeSpan`, the server then tells the browser to show the local copy to the user and immediately stops processing the rest of the template. Otherwise, ColdFusion tells the browser that the local copy is now out of date, processes the rest of your code normally, and returns the newly generated version to the browser, where it can be cached locally for the next six hours (or whatever interval you specify).

What It Means

By using `<cfcache>`, you can keep the amount of interaction between the browser and server to a minimum. Yes, the browser will contact the Web server, and ColdFusion will begin executing your template code. But as soon as ColdFusion encounters the `<cfcache>` tag—which should be at the top of your CFML code—ColdFusion will often be able to tell the browser to just use its local copy of the page. This is a fast operation because only the initial handshake between browser and server is necessary to determine whether the local copy can be used.

This improves performance in three important ways:

- The browser can display the template more quickly. This is because it can just use the local copy instead of waiting for your template code to generate the template and refetch it over the Net. The longer the page and the more time-consuming your CFML code is, the greater the benefit.

- It cuts the amount of work ColdFusion needs to do. As long as the browser's local copy is still valid, ColdFusion can stop processing your template as soon as it encounters the `<cfcache>` tag. This frees ColdFusion to complete its next task more quickly, which benefits all your users. The more often the same users revisit your pages, the greater the benefit.

- By reducing the number of times complete pages must be sent back to browsers, traffic on your local network is kept to a minimum. This makes better use of your network bandwidth. Again, the more often the same users revisit your pages, the greater the benefit.

Server-Side Page Caching

You can also use the `<cfcache>` tag to enable ColdFusion's server-side page caching mechanism. Like client-side caching, this method takes advantage of a previously generated version of your template code. However, server-side caching doesn't use the cached copy of the page that might be on the browser machine. Instead, it looks for a cached copy of the page that ColdFusion stores on the server's drive.

Enabling Server-Side Caching

To enable server-side caching for one of your templates, place a `<cfcache>` tag at the top of the template before your other CFML and HTML tags. As you can see in Table 31.3, a number of attributes are relevant for using `<cfcache>` to do server-side caching. They are all optional, however, and most of them are relevant only if your template is secured via SSL encryption or a username and password. Most of the time, you can just specify `action="ServerCache"` and whatever `timeSpan` you desire.

Table 31.3 `<cfcache>` Tag Attributes Relevant for Server-Side Caching

ATTRIBUTE	PURPOSE
action	Set this attribute to `ServerCache` to enable server-side caching for your template. You can also set it to `ClientCache` to enable client-side caching only, as discussed above. Finally, you can set it to `Cache` (the default), which uses both client-side and server-side mechanisms (see the section "ColdFusion-Optimized Caching," later in this chapter).
timeSpan	As with client-side caching, this is the period of time that you would like the user's browser to cache the page. You can specify this period using any combination of days, hours, minutes, or seconds by providing a value returned by the `createTimeSpan()` function. If a simple number is passed, it is the number of days the cached is used. For example, 0.5 would result in a cache of one half day. A value of 1 would result in a cache lasting one day.
directory	Optional. The directory in which you want ColdFusion to store cached versions of the page. If this is omitted, ColdFusion stores the cached versions in a `cache` directory within the `ColdFusion` directory (or wherever you installed ColdFusion).
username	Optional. If the template you want to cache normally requires the user to enter a username and password, you must provide the appropriate username here. Depending on the Web server software you are using, remember that the username might be case sensitive.
password	Optional. If the template you want to cache normally requires the user to enter a username and password, you must provide the appropriate password here. Again, depending on your Web server, the password might be case sensitive.
protocol	Optional. Specify either `http://` or `https://`, depending on whether the template you want to cache is being served using SSL encryption. Normally, you can omit this attribute. This value defaults to the protocol of the current request.
port	Optional. If the Web server is serving documents at a nonstandard HTTP port, specify that port number here. Otherwise, you can omit this attribute, in which case it defaults to the port of the current request.

For instance, you could place the following snippet at the top of any of your ColdFusion templates. It tells ColdFusion that your template code only needs to execute once every 30 minutes at most:

```
<!--- Let browser use a cached version of --->
<!--- this page, from up to six hours ago --->
<cfcache
 action="ServerCache"
 timeSpan="#createTimeSpan(0, 0, 30, 0)#">
```

The first time the template is accessed, ColdFusion processes your code as it would normally do. But before it sends the generated page back to the browser, it also saves the page as a separate, static file on the server's drive. The next time the page is accessed, ColdFusion simply sends back the static version of the file without executing any code that appears after the `<cfcache>` tag. ColdFusion will continue to send this static version back to all visitors until 30 minutes have passed. After the 30 minutes have elapsed, the next page request re-executes your template normally.

For most situations, that's all you have to do. Your visitors will immediately begin to see improved performance. The more often your pages are hit and the longer your template code takes to execute, the larger the benefit.

Listing 31.2 is a simple example that demonstrates this effect. The template uses the timeFormat() function to output the current time. At the top of the template, the <cfcache> tag allows the page to be cached for 30 seconds at a time. Try visiting this page repeatedly in your browser.

Listing 31.2 ServerSideCache.cfm—Testing the Server-Side Cache Mechanism

```
<!---
 Filename: ServerSideCache.cfm
 Author: Nate Weiss (NMW)
 Purpose: Demonstrates use of server-side caching
--->

<!--- Cache this template for 30 seconds at a time --->
<cfcache
 action="ServerCache"
 timespan="#createTimeSpan(0, 0, 0, 30)#">

<html>
<head><title>Caching Demonstration</title></head>
<body>

 <!--- Display the current time --->
 <p>This page was generated at:
 <cfoutput>#timeFormat(now(), "h:mm:ss tt")#</cfoutput>

</body>
</html>
```

The first time you visit this template, it displays the current time. For the next 30 seconds, subsequent page accesses will continue to show that same time, which proves that your template code is not re-executing. Regardless of whether you access the page using another browser or from another machine, click the browser's Reload or Refresh button, or close and reopen the browser, you will continue to see the original time message until the 30 seconds have elapsed. Then the next page request will once again reflect the current time, which will be used for the next 30 seconds.

NOTE

Remember, if you are using <cfcache> for server-side caching (that is, with an action of Cache or ServerCache), the page won't be regenerated for each user. In particular, you should make sure that the page doesn't depend on any variables kept in the CLIENT, COOKIE, or SESSION scopes because the generated page will be shared with other users, without checking that their CLIENT, COOKIE, or SESSION variables are the same. So in general, you shouldn't cache personalized pages using server-side caching. For personalized pages, enable client-side caching with action="ClientCache" instead.

ColdFusion-Optimized Caching

So far, you have learned about client-side page caching (that is, using <cfcache> with action= "ClientCache") and server-side page caching (action="ServerCache").

As noted earlier in Tables 31.2 and 31.3, you can use both types of caching together by specifying action="Cache" or by omitting the action attribute altogether. For each page request, ColdFusion will first determine whether the browser has an appropriate version of the page in its local cache. If not, ColdFusion determines whether it has an appropriate version of the page in its own server-side cache. Only if there isn't an appropriate version in either cache will your template code re-execute.

The result is greatly enhanced performance in most situations.

NOTE

In previous versions of ColdFusion, the default value for `action` resulted in server-side caching only. In ColdFusion, the default is for both types of caching to be enabled. So if you move an application to ColdFusion and the code doesn't provide an `action` attribute, the server-side cache and client-side caches will both be enabled. This shouldn't be a problem, since nearly any situation that would benefit from server-side caching will benefit from client-side caching as well.

Caching Pages That Use URL Parameters

ColdFusion maintains a separate cached version of your page for each combination of URL parameters with which it gets accessed. Each version expires on its own schedule, based on the `timeSpan` parameter you provide. In other words, you don't need to do anything special to employ server-side caching with pages that use URL parameters to pass ID numbers or any other information.

ColdFusion doesn't cache the result of a form submission, regardless of whether the target page contains a `<cfcache>` tag, so `<cfcache>` is disabled whenever the `CGI.request_method` variable is set to `POST`.

NOTE

Remember, if you are using `<cfcache>` for server-side caching, the page won't be regenerated for each user, so server-side caching shouldn't be used for pages that are personalized in any way. The only type of caching that is safe for personalized pages is client-side caching (`action="ClientCache"`). See the important caution in the previous section.

Specifying the Cache Directory

By default, ColdFusion stores the cached versions of your templates in a folder called `cache`, located within the ColdFusion installation directory. If after visiting Listing 31.2, you look in the Cold-Fusion cache folder you will notice that ColdFusion has placed a file there, with a `.tmp` extension. If you open this `.tmp` file in a text editor, you will see that it contains the final, evaluated code that the ColdFusion template generated. A new `.tmp` file will appear in the folder whenever you visit a different template that uses server-side caching. In addition, a different `.tmp` file will appear for each set of URL parameters supplied to the templates when they are visited.

If you want to store the `.tmp` files in some other location, you can use the `directory` attribute to tell ColdFusion where to store them. You must provide a fully qualified file path to a folder on your server's drive.

For instance, the following would tell ColdFusion to store its cache files in a folder called `cachefiles`:

```
<!--- Cache this template for 30 seconds at a time --->
<cfcache
 action="Cache"
 timeSpan="#createTimeSpan(0,0,0,30)#"
 directory="c:\cachefiles">
```

You would, of course, need to create the `cachefiles` directory on the server machine before this would work.

The `directory` value shouldn't be within the Web server's document root. You don't want people to be able to request the `.tmp` files directly via their browsers.

Flushing the Page Cache

Earlier in this chapter, you learned about query caching and how to make a cached query refresh when the data in the underlying database tables change. You have the same option for server-side page caching, via the `flush` action provided by the `<cfcache>` tag. You can also delete ColdFusion's cache files manually.

Using `action="flush"`

To flush a page from the cache before it would time out on its own, simply use the `<cfcache>` tag with `action="flush"`. Table 31.4 shows the attributes relevant for flushing the server-side page cache.

Table 31.4   `<cfcache>` Tag Attributes Relevant for Server-Side Cache Flushing

ATTRIBUTE	PURPOSE
`action`	Must be set to `Flush` to flush pages from the server-side cache.
`directory`	Optional. The directory that contains the cached versions of your pages. In other words, provide the same value here that you provide to the `directory` attribute in your other `<cfcache>` tags (the ones that enable caching).
`expireURL`	Optional. A URL reference that represents which cache files to delete. If you don't provide this attribute, ColdFusion will flush the cache for all files in the specified directory. You can use an asterisk (*) in this attribute as a simple wildcard.

If one of your templates makes some type of change that your application should reflect immediately, even in pages that would otherwise still be cached, you could use the following line to delete all cached pages in the current directory. You would place this code in the change template, right after the `<cfquery>` or whatever else is making the actual changes:

```
<!--- Flush the server-side page cache --->
<cfcache
 action="Flush">
```

If you don't need to expire all cached pages from the directory, you can provide an `expireURL` attribute. For instance, suppose you are using server-side caching to cache a template called ShowMovie.cfm, and that movie accepts a URL parameter called FilmID. After some kind of update to the Films table, you might want to flush the ShowMovie.cfm template from the cache, but only for the appropriate FilmID. To do so, you might use code like the following:

```
<!--- Flush the server-side page cache --->
<cfcache
 action="Flush"
 expireURL="ShowMovie.cfm?FilmID=#FORM.FilmID#">
```

Or to flush the cache for all versions of the ShowMovie.cfm template (regardless of URL parameters), leaving all other cached pages in the directory alone, you would use something like this:

```
<!--- Flush the server-side page cache --->
<cfcache
  action="Flush"
  expireURL="ShowMovie.cfm?*">
```

Controlling White Space

One of the side effects of CFML's tag-based nature is the fact that white-space characters (such as tabs, spaces, and return characters) that you use to indent your CFML code are usually passed on to the browser as part of the final generated page. In certain cases, this white space can considerably inflate the size of the generated HTML content, and this in turn can hurt performance. ColdFusion provides several options for dealing with these extraneous white-space characters.

NOTE

ColdFusion's ability to automatically control white space is better than ever in ColdFusion. You will find that in most cases, you can just enable the automatic Whitespace Management feature (discussed in a moment) and never think about white-space issues again. Nonetheless, it is worthwhile to discuss the other options available to you, just in case.

Understanding the Issue

In a ColdFusion template, you use CFML and HTML tags together. The processing instructions for the server are intermingled with what you actually want to generate. That is, there is no formal separation between the code and the content parts of your template. Most other Web scripting environments separate code from content, generally forcing you to put the HTML code you want to generate into some type of Write() function or special block delimited by characters such as <% and %> (depending on the language).

The fact that you get to use CFML tags right in the body of your document is a big part of what makes ColdFusion development so powerful, but it has a disadvantage. Often ColdFusion can't easily determine which white-space characters in a template just indent the code for clarity and which should actually be sent to the browser as part of the final, generated page. When ColdFusion can't make the distinction, it errs on the side of caution and includes the white space in the final content.

Automatic White-Space Control

The good news is that ColdFusion already does a lot to eliminate excess white space from your generated pages. ColdFusion includes an automatic white-space elimination feature, enabled by default. As long as you haven't disabled this feature, it's already pulling much white space out of your documents for you, before the generated page is sent to the browser.

Enabling White-Space Suppression

On the Settings page of ColdFusion Administrator, you'll see an option called Enable Whitespace Management. When this is enabled, portions of your template that contain only CFML tags will have the white space removed from them before the page is returned to the browser. Basically,

ColdFusion looks at the template, finds the areas that contain only CFML tags, removes any white space (extra spaces, tabs, indents, new lines, or hard returns) from those areas, and then processes the template.

It's easy to see this in action. To do so, follow these steps:

1. Visit the `NextNCached.cfm` template (refer to Listing 31.1) via your Web browser.

2. Use the browser's View Source option to see the final HTML code that the template generated. Leave the source code's window open.

3. On the Settings page of ColdFusion Administrator, uncheck (or check) the Enable Whitespace Management option and submit the changes.

4. Visit the `NextNCached.cfm` template and view the source code again.

If you compare the two versions of the page source, you will see that the second (or first) version has a lot more blank lines and other white space in it. In particular, it has a lot more space at the very top, consisting of all the white space that surrounds the comments and various `<cfquery>`, `<cfparam>`, and `<cfset>` tags at the top of Listing 31.1. The first version of the page source has eliminated that white space from the top of the document.

There are very few situations in which this automatic suppression of white space would be undesirable. In general, you should leave the Enable Whitespace Management option enabled in Cold-Fusion Administrator.

Controlling White-Space Suppression Programmatically

You can turn off ColdFusion's automatic white-space suppression feature for specific parts of your document. Such situations are rare because HTML usually ignores white space, so there is generally no need to preserve it.

However, in a few situations you wouldn't want ColdFusion to remove white space for you. For instance, a few rarely used HTML tags like `<pre>` and `<xmp>` do consider white space significant. If you are using either of these tags in a Web document, ColdFusion's white-space suppression might eliminate the very space you are trying to display between the `<pre>` or `<xmp>` tags. You might run into the same problem when composing an email message programmatically using the `<cfmail>` tag (see Chapter 21, "Interacting with Email," online).

In such a situation, you can use the `suppressWhitespace="No"` attribute of the `<cfcfprocessing-Directive>` tag to disable the automatic suppression of white space. Place the tag around the block of code that is sensitive to white-space characters, like so:

```
<cfprocessingDirective suppressWhitespace="No">
 <pre>
 ...code that is sensitive to white space here...
 </pre>
</cfprocessingDirective>
```

Suppressing White-Space Output with `<cfsilent>`

Unfortunately, ColdFusion can't always correctly identify which parts of your code consist only of CFML tags and should therefore have white space automatically removed. This is most often the case with code loops created by `<cfloop>` and `<cfoutput>`.

If you find that a particular portion of code generates a lot of unexpected white space, you can add the `<cfsilent>` tag, which suppresses all output (even actual text and HTML tags). The `<cfsilent>` tag takes no attributes. Simply wrap it around any code blocks that might generate extraneous white space when executed, such as `<cfloop>` or `<cfoutput>` loops that perform calculations but don't generate any output that the browser needs to receive.

NOTE

The `<cfsilent>` tag doesn't just suppress white-space output. It suppresses all output, even output you would generally want to send to the browser (such as HTML code and text).

Suppressing Specific White Space with `<cfsetting>`

For situations in which ColdFusion's automatic suppression isn't suppressing all the white space in your generated pages (for instance, the first `<cfloop>` snippet in the previous section), but where `<cfsilent>` is too drastic, you can use the `<cfsetting>` tag to suppress output in a more selective manner.

The `<cfsetting>` tag takes a few optional attributes, but the only one relevant to this discussion is the `enableCFOutputOnly` attribute. When this attribute is set to `Yes`, it suppresses all output (similar to how the `<cfsilent>` tag works), except for `<cfoutput>` blocks. Any HTML code or text that should be sent to the browser must be between `<cfoutput>` tags, even if the code doesn't include any ColdFusion variables or expressions. This is different from ColdFusion's normal behavior, where it assumes that it can send any non-CFML text or code to the browser.

So if you find that a section of code is generating a lot of white space, but you can't easily use `<cfsilent>` because your code must be able to generate *some* output, then you should place a `<cfsetting>` tag with `enableCFOutputOnly="Yes"` just above the section of code, and a `<cfsetting>` tag with `enableCFOutputOnly="No"` just below the section. Within the section of code, make sure `<cfoutput>` tags surround any item (even plain text) that you want to include in the final, generated version of the page. This gives you complete control over all generated white space and other characters.

NOTE

Note that when you use `<cfsetting>` to control white space, it acts like a "stack." What do we mean by that? If you have two or more `<cfsetting>` tags, both of which turn on `enableCFOutputOnly`, you can imagine that ColdFusion has an internal value of 2 for suppressing white space. This means you would need to turn off the setting twice in order to return to the default behavior. The upshot? Be sure to always switch this setting off after turning it on, even if it is at the end of the page.

PART VII

Integrating with ColdFusion

Working with PDF Files

Since the introduction of `<cfdocument type="pdf">`, a longing to do more with PDF documents has existed. Well, wait no more—now that it is part of the Adobe product line, ColdFusion 8 brings so much PDF support that we're going to spend a whole chapter talking PDF sweetness and still not cover everything that ColdFusion brings to the table.

With ColdFusion 8, you have the capability to add watermarks, headers, footers, tables of contents, metadata (author, creator, keywords, and so on), bookmarks, and much more to PDF files. You can also populate PDF forms and receive PDF form submissions.

NOTE
Visit Adobe.com for more information about Portable Document Format (PDF):
`http://www.adobe.com/products/acrobat/adobepdf.html`.

Working with `cfpdf`

Most of the functionality found in Adobe Acrobat is now available in ColdFusion 8. One thing you cannot do is convert other document types to PDF format using `<cfpdf>`. This section discusses the procedures for manipulating, creating, and reading PDF documents using the `<cfpdf>` tag.

NOTE
`<cfdocument>` allows you to create PDF files using HTML and CFML and also allows you to save the output as a PDF file.

Creating PDF Files

ColdFusion lets you easily create PDF files. Listing 32.1 shows a simple example of `<cfdocument>` wrapped around HTML and passing the name variable to `cfpdf` as the source parameter.

Listing 32.1 CreatingPDFs1.cfm—Creating a PDF File

```
<!--- Create simple html content --->
<cfdocument name="cover" format="PDF">
<html>
    <body>
        <h1>Sample Content</h1>
        <h3>Created: <cfoutput>#DateFormat(now(),
                                 "mm/dd/yyyy")#</cfoutput></h3>
    </body>
</html>
</cfdocument>

<!--- Write the PDF to disk --->
<cfpdf action="write"
       source="cover"
       destination="pdfs/CreatingPDFs1a.pdf" overwrite="yes" />
```

Running this page does not yield any browser output, but the file is created in the /pdfs folder. There is nothing special here, but don't leave just yet.

Listing 32.2 builds on Listing 32.1, adding a few extra steps.

Listing 32.2 CreatingPDFs1a.cfm—Creating a PDF File with Metadata

```
<!--- Create simple html content --->
<cfdocument name="cover" format="PDF">
<html>
    <body>
        <h1>Sample Content</h1>
        <h3>Created: <cfoutput>#DateFormat(now(),
                                 "mm/dd/yyyy")#</cfoutput></h3>
    </body>
</html>
</cfdocument>

<!--- Write the PDF to disk --->
<cfpdf action="write" source="cover"
       destination="pdfs/CreatingPDFs1a.pdf" overwrite="yes" />

<!--- Set the PDF info --->
<cfset meta = StructNew() />
<cfset meta.Author = "John C. Bland II" />
<cfset meta.Title = "Adobe Derby" />
<cfset meta.Subject = "Adobe Derby Official Rules" />
<cfset meta.Keywords = "Adobe, Adobe Derby, Rules" />
<cfpdf action="setinfo" source="pdfs/CreatingPDFs1a.pdf" info="#meta#" />

<!--- Read the PDF info --->
<cfpdf name="info" action="read" source="pdfs/CreatingPDFs1a.pdf" />

<!--- Dump PDF info to the screen --->
<cfdump var="#info#" />
```

Notice first that the meta struct contains values for Author, Title, Subject, and Keywords followed by another cfpdf tag using the setinfo action. This code successfully sets the metadata of a PDF file, as evident in Figure 32.1, which shows a cfdump of the info variable.

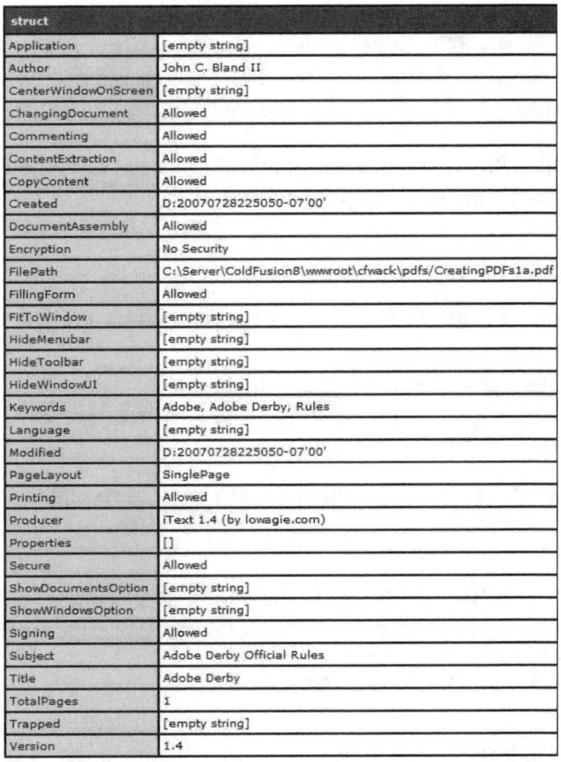

Figure 32.1

Dump of data obtained from `action="getinfo"`.

struct	
Application	[empty string]
Author	John C. Bland II
CenterWindowOnScreen	[empty string]
ChangingDocument	Allowed
Commenting	Allowed
ContentExtraction	Allowed
CopyContent	Allowed
Created	D:20070728225050-07'00'
DocumentAssembly	Allowed
Encryption	No Security
FilePath	C:\Server\ColdFusion8\wwwroot\cfwack\pdfs/CreatingPDFs1a.pdf
FillingForm	Allowed
FitToWindow	[empty string]
HideMenubar	[empty string]
HideToolbar	[empty string]
HideWindowUI	[empty string]
Keywords	Adobe, Adobe Derby, Rules
Language	[empty string]
Modified	D:20070728225050-07'00'
PageLayout	SinglePage
Printing	Allowed
Producer	iText 1.4 (by lowagie.com)
Properties	[]
Secure	Allowed
ShowDocumentsOption	[empty string]
ShowWindowsOption	[empty string]
Signing	Allowed
Subject	Adobe Derby Official Rules
Title	Adobe Derby
TotalPages	1
Trapped	[empty string]
Version	1.4

We'll return to the creation of PDF files later in this chapter; we'll use this capability when we apply PDF-file creation to our application.

Reading PDF Files

You've seen how to grab PDF meta information and dump it to the screen. Now look at Listing 32.3, which shows how to read the body of a PDF file.

Listing 32.3   ReadingPDFs1.cfm—Reading a PDF File

```
<!--- Read the PDF file --->
<cfpdf name="pdf" action="read" source="pdfs/CreatingPDFs1a.pdf" />

<!--- Dump PDF contents --->
<cfdump var="#pdf#" />
```

This code is almost the same as that used in Listing 32.2 with one slight change: `action="read"`. We now have an in-memory PDF file that we can manipulate in different ways by referencing the variable name. We'll use this capability later in the chapter.

NOTE

When the variable of an in-memory PDF file is used in `cfdump`, the resulting struct is very similar to the `cfdump` from `action="getinfo"` except that you cannot access the values in the struct from an in-memory PDF file like you can from a `getinfo` call. Calling `cfdump` on the in-memory PDF file produces an internal call to `getinfo`.

Now let's put this functionality to use in some practical scenarios: merging PDF files, creating thumbnails and watermarks, and deleting pages.

Merging PDF Files

Merging PDF files is easy. Listing 32.4 shows how we can merge two PDF files into one.

Listing 32.4 MergingPDFs.cfm—Merging PDFs with <cfpdf>

```
<cfpdf action="merge" overwrite="yes" source="pdfs/Sample Title.pdf, pdfs/Sample
Page.pdf" destination="pdfs/MergingPDFs.pdf" />
```

Alternatively we can use `cfpdfparam` tags within the `cfpdf` tag to specify the source files, as shown in Listing 32.5.

Listing 32.5 MergingPDFs-pdfparam.cfm—<cfpdf> with <cfpdfparam>

```
<cfpdf action="merge" overwrite="yes" destination="pdfs/MergingPDFs-pdfparam.pdf">
    <cfpdfparam source="pdfs/Sample Title.pdf" />
    <cfpdfparam source="pdfs/Sample Page.pdf" />
</cfpdf>
```

Both approaches achieve the same result; be sure to note that the order of the source files defines the actual order of text in the destination PDF file.

There is also another way to merge PDF files:

```
<cfpdf action="merge" overwrite="yes"
        directory="pdfs/pdfsToMerge"
        destination="pdfs/MergingPDFs-directory.pdf" />
```

The `directory` attribute tells ColdFusion to take all the PDF files from the specified directory and merge them into the `destination` PDF file. Obviously, being able to specify an order would be of great help, right? I'm glad you asked:

```
<cfpdf action="merge" overwrite="yes"
        directory="pdfs/pdfsToMerge"
        destination="pdfs/MergingPDFs-directory.pdf"
        order="name" ascending="yes" />
```

Notice the two additional parameters in this example: `order` and `ascending`. The `order` parameter can be assigned the value `name` or `time`, and `ascending` can be assigned the value `yes` or `no`. You can change the options to achieve your desired order of input for the destination PDF file.

When you use the `directory` attribute, ColdFusion throws an error if the directory contains a non-PDF file (for instance, an image file or CFM file) and the `stopOnError` attribute is set to `yes`. The default value for `stopOnError` is no. The `stopOnError` attribute is valid only when the `directory` attribute is used.

Listing 32.6 includes the additional `<cfpdf>` parameters discussed above.

Listing 32.6 `MergingPDFs-directory.cfm`—`<cfpdf>` with the directory Attribute

```
<!--- If you put a non-pdf file (image, cfm, etc),
      the following line will throw an error --->
<cfpdf action="merge" overwrite="yes"
       directory="pdfs/pdfsToMerge"
       destination="pdfs/MergingPDFs-directory.pdf"
       order="name" ascending="yes" stoponerror="yes" />
```

Later in the chapter, we will revisit merging using Document Description XML (DDX).

Creating Thumbnails

Here is the bare minimum code needed to create thumbnails:

```
<cfpdf action="thumbnail" source="pdfs/Comps.pdf" />
```

By default, ColdFusion creates a folder named `thumbnails` in the same directory as the CFM template running the code. You can control the target folder by using the `destination` attribute.

```
<cfpdf action="thumbnail" source="pdfs/Comps.pdf" destination="images/compThumbs"
overwrite="yes" />
```

NOTE

Unless you use the `overwrite` attribute, running this code with the thumbnails already in the destination folder will result in an error.

The images are created as JPEG files unless otherwise noted. You can also create PNG and TIFF images by using the `format` attribute. The default naming convention is `{pdf name or imageprefix attribute}_page_{page number}.{image extension}`. For example, the PDF file we used was named `Comps.pdf`, and it has three pages. Generating PDF thumbnails created the following images: `Comps_page_1.jpg`, `Comps_page_2.jpg`, and `Comps_page_3.jpg`. As noted, a prefix can be supplied to replace the PDF name. In this example, the resulting file names are `v1_page_1.jpg`, `v1_page_2.jpg`, and `v1_page_3.jpg`.

```
<cfpdf action="thumbnail" source="pdfs/Comps.pdf" destination="images/compThumbs"
overwrite="yes" imageprefix="v1" />
```

Figure 32.2 shows the original PDF file.

Figure 32.2

The original
Comps.pdf file.

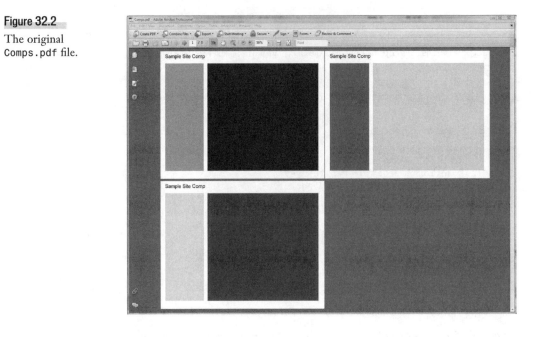

The images are created, so we can now look at them in the browser using a little more ColdFusion as shown in Listing 32.7.

Listing 32.7 Thumbnails.cfm—Displaying Thumbnail Images

```
<!--- Create the thumbnails --->
<cfpdf action="thumbnail" source="pdfs/Comps.pdf"
       destination="images/compThumbs"
       overwrite="yes" imageprefix="v1" />

<!--- Read the thumbnails directory --->
<cfdirectory directory="#ExpandPath('images/compThumbs')#"
             name="thumbs" filter="*.jpg"/>

<!--- Output the images to the browser --->
<cfoutput query="thumbs">
#currentRow#) <img src="images/compThumbs/#name#" align="top" />
<br />
      #name#
<br />
<hr />
</cfoutput>
```

Figure 32.3 shows the final output. The cfpdf code is the same code as before. The only change is the use of cfdirectory to read the images and generic HTML in a query output using cfoutput.

Figure 32.3

The final thumbnail output.

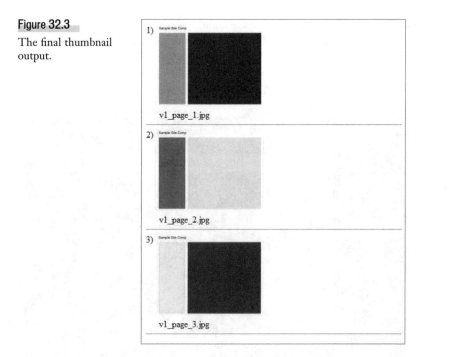

There are a few other attributes worth mentioning. The scale attribute is available to control the resulting size of the created thumbnails. All thumbnails are created at 25 percent of the original size by default. Figure 32.3 shows thumbnails at 200 x 150 pixels (25 percent of 800 x 600, the original size). Thumbnails are created with high quality by default, but you can create a low-quality thumbnail by using the resolution attribute, which accepts high or low as its value. When using the PNG image format, you can make the generated thumbnails respect transparency by using the transparent attribute, which takes a value of yes or no (no is the default value). Transparency is not available in the JPEG and TIFF formats.

Creating Watermarks

Watermarks are useful in any document type and are great for versioning. With the watermark action (see Listing 32.8), you now can easily add and remove watermarks (Figure 32.4).

Listing 32.8 Watermark.cfm—Adding a Watermark

```
<cfpdf action="addwatermark"
        source="pdfs/Comps-ImageWatermark.pdf"
        image="images/MyWatermark.png"
        foreground="yes" overwrite="yes" />
```

NOTE

The source file is a duplicate of Comps.pdf renamed for versioning purposes.

Here we used an actual image path, but the `image` attribute could be an in-memory image created with `cfimage`. We will look at a basic example of such an image later (see Chapter 33, "ColdFusion Image Processing," for more details).

Figure 32.4

The images/
MyWatermark.png
image as a watermark.

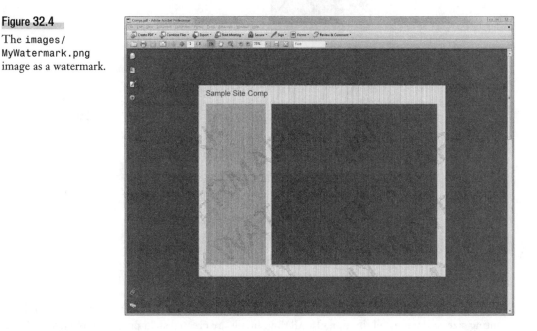

Instead of using an image as a watermark, you can use the first page of another PDF file. To do this, you use the `copyFrom` attribute instead of the `image` attribute:

```
<cfpdf action="addwatermark" source="pdfs/Comps.pdf"
       destination="pdfs/Comps-PDFWatermark.pdf"
       copyFrom="pdfs/PDF WATERMARK.pdf"
       foreground="yes" overwrite="yes" />
```

The watermark source PDF file (`pdfs/PDF WATERMARK.pdf`) is a PDF file created from Microsoft Word (Figure 32.5).

Figure 32.6 shows the initial results of the use of this PDF file as a watermark.

The watermark is at the top of the page, but it doesn't have to stay there; you can control the positioning and rotation with code, as shown in Listing 32.9.

Listing 32.9 Watermark-copyFrom.cfm—Adding a Watermark from PDF File

```
<cfpdf action="addwatermark" source="pdfs/Comps.pdf"
       destination="pdfs/Comps-PDFWatermark.pdf"
       copyFrom="pdfs/PDF WATERMARK.pdf"
       foreground="yes" rotation="45" position="375,-275"
       overwrite="yes"
       opacity="10" />
```

Figure 32.5

The original source for pdfs/PDF WATERMARK.pdf.

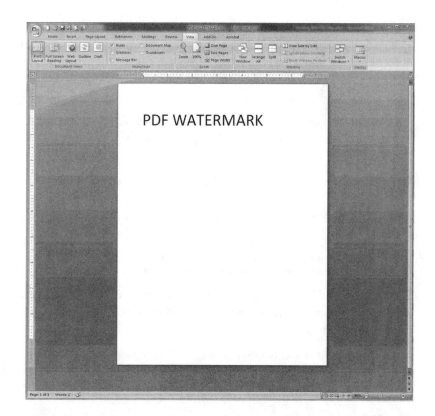

Figure 32.6

The initial results from the copyFrom attribute.

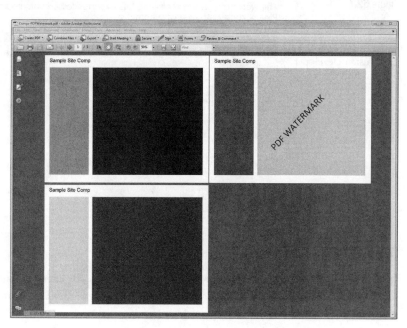

Here, the position, rotation, and opacity are set. For clarity, this example uses an opacity of 10, which is full opacity; available values are 0 to 10. The rotation is 45 degrees, but you have access to all 360 degrees. Positioning is based on x and y positioning of the fourth dimension (lower right) in the Cartesian coordinate system (`http://en.wikipedia.org/wiki/Cartesian_coordinate_system`).

TIP

Positioning a watermark can be tricky if you are not familiar with the Cartesian coordinate system. To counteract the need to learn it, you can position the text in your Word document before exporting to a PDF file. Later in the chapter we will cover another way to set a text-based watermark.

Removing a watermark is as easy as adding one, as you can see in Listing 32.10.

Listing 32.10 `Watermark-Remove.cfm`—Removing a Watermark

```
<cfpdf action="removewatermark"
       source="pdfs/Comps-ImageWatermark.pdf"
       destination="pdfs/Comps-ImageWatermark-Removed.pdf" />
```

This syntax should look familiar. We're taking the initial PDF file created earlier (`source="pdfs/Comps-ImageWatermark.pdf"`) and creating a new one (`destination="pdfs/Comps-ImageWatermark-Removed.pdf"`).

Not all watermarks can be removed, though. All PDF files created using the ColdFusion Developer and Trial Editions have a permanent watermark that cannot be removed (by ColdFusion or Acrobat). Figure 32.7 shows the error you will receive if you try to remove the watermark.

Figure 32.7

ColdFusion error after trying to remove a watermark from a ColdFusion Developer or Trial Edition PDF file.

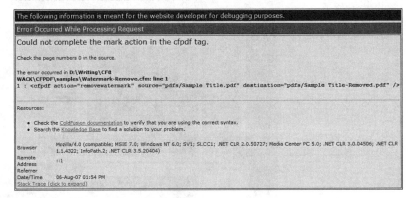

Deleting Pages

If you have ever used Adobe Acrobat to print or delete pages, the `page` attribute in ColdFusion will feel familiar. The `pdfs/Comps.pdf` file was duplicated for this example. It contains three pages; we're going to delete the last two:

```
<cfpdf action="deletepages" source="pdfs/Comps-DeletedPages.pdf" pages="2-3" />
```

The pages attribute, which is required, marks pages 2 to 3 for deletion. There are a lot of options for deleting pages. You can specify specific pages and ranges of pages. For example, the specification pages="1, 9-20, 23, 25" deletes pages 1, 9 through 20, 23, and 25.

TIP

If the pages attribute includes invalid page numbers (pages that don't exist in the PDF file), ColdFusion throws an error. It would be best to surround the deletepages call in a cftry block; then ColdFusion will catch the error, and no error will appear on the screen. See Chapter 51, "Error Handling," online, for more information about cftry and cfcatch.

NOTE

In addition to the deletepages action, the pages attribute can be used with the following cfpdf actions: thumbnail, merge, removeWatermark, and addWatermark.

Encryption, Permissions, and Passwords

Protecting PDF files is important, and ColdFusion answers the call with 4 levels of encryption, 10 levels of permissions, and user and owner password support.

Setting Passwords

To set a password, you specify action="protect" and then set a password type, a requirement for protect. There are two password types: newownerpassword and newuserpassword. Setting newuser-password requires a user to enter the password upon opening the PDF file. After the PDF file is opened, the user can edit the PDF file (Listing 32.11).

Listing 32.11 UserPasswordPDF.cfm—Setting a User Password

```
<cfpdf action="protect"
       source="pdfs/Comps.pdf"
       destination="pdfs/Comps-userpassword.pdf"
       newuserpassword="test" overwrite="yes" />
```

When this PDF file is opened, a password prompt appears.

This level of password protection is the easiest to implement. When newownerpassword is set, a world of options are available. The permissions attribute, which is required when setting newowner-password, allows the options, or combinations of them, listed in Table 32.1. The best part of these options is their clarity. For instance, you know if AllowPrinting is set, printing is allowed. If you do not explicitly set a permission for an option, the option is not allowed.

Table 32.1 Permissions Options

PERMISSIONS	DESCRIPTION
All	There are no restrictions on the PDF document.
AllowAssembly	Users can add the PDF document to a merged document.
AllowCopy	Users can copy text, images, and other file content. This setting is required to generate thumbnail images with the thumbnail action.

Table 32.1 (CONTINUED)

PERMISSIONS	DESCRIPTION
`AllowDegradedPrinting`	Users can print the document at low resolution (150 dpi).
`AllowFillIn`	Users can enter data into PDF form fields. Users can sign PDF forms electronically.
`AllowModifyAnnotations`	Users can add or change comments in the PDF document.
`AllowModifyContents`	Users can change the file content. Users can add the PDF document to a merged document.
`AllowPrinting`	Users can print the document at high resolution (print-production quality). This setting is required for use with the `cfprint` tag.
`AllowScreenReaders`	Users can extract content from the PDF document.
`AllowSecure`	Users can sign the PDF document (with an electronic signature).
`None`	Users can only view the document.

Source: `http://livedocs.adobe.com/coldfusion/8/`.

Let's explore some examples.

The goal in Listing 32.12 is to protect a PDF file with an owner password of `test` and to allow no permissions.

Listing 32.12 `OwnerPasswordPDF-none.cfm`—Setting an Owner Password with No Permissions

```
<cfpdf action="protect"
      source="pdfs/Comps.pdf"
      destination="pdfs/Comps-ownerpassword-none.pdf"
      newownerpassword="test"
      permissions="none" overwrite="yes" />
```

Figure 32.8 shows Adobe Acrobat 8's Security Properties window.

Changing the `permissions` attribute to `all` will remove all restrictions.

Listing 32.13 uses the same code as in the previous example but with different permissions.

Listing 32.13 `OwnerPasswordPDF-multiple.cfm`—Setting an Owner Password with Permissions

```
<cfpdf action="protect"
      source="pdfs/Comps.pdf"
      destination="pdfs/Comps-ownerpassword-multiple.pdf"
      newownerpassword="test"
      permissions="allowdegradedprinting, allowmodifycontents,
                   allowscreenreaders" overwrite="yes" />
```

The `allowdegradedprinting` and `allowprinting` options set Printing to Allowed. To see the differences, click Advanced in the File > Print window.

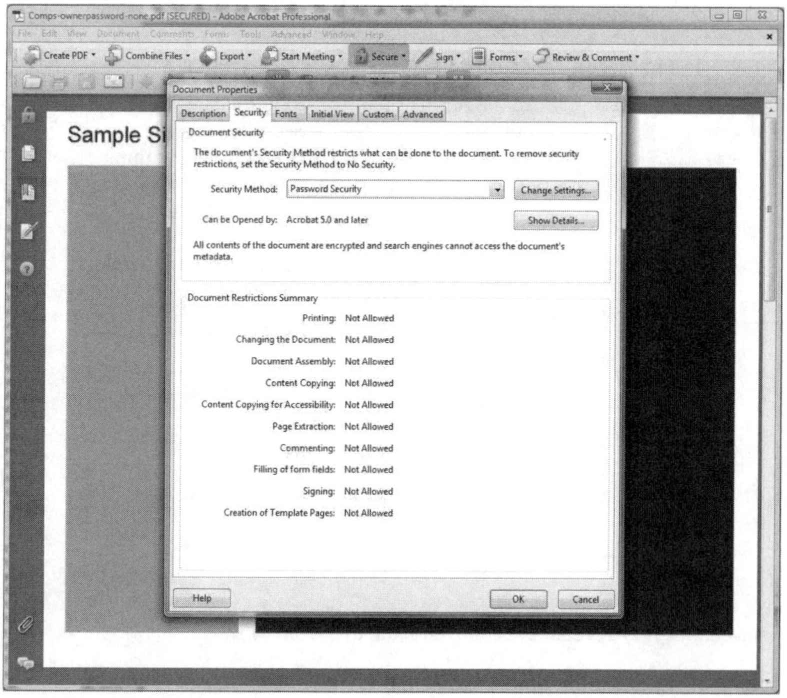

Figure 32.8

Adobe Acrobat 8's
Security Properties
window with "none"
permissions.

After permissions are set, they apply not only in Acrobat but also in ColdFusion. For PDF files with user passwords, the user must supply the password in the `password` attribute to read or manipulate the PDF file:

```
<cfpdf action="read" source="pdf source path" password=" mypassword" name="mypdf">
```

Adding Encryption

The available encryption algorithms are based on version compatibility (see Table 32.2).

Table 32.2   Encryption Algorithms

ENCRYPTION	ALGORITHM	COMPATIBILITY	DESCRIPTION
AES_128	Adobe Acrobat 7.0 and later	Advanced Encryption Standard (AES) specifies the Rijndael algorithm, a symmetric block cipher that can process data blocks of 128 bits. This is the highest encryption level.	This encryption algorithm lets users do the following: Encrypt all document contents. Encrypt all document contents except for the metadata. Encrypt only the file attachments.

Table 32.2 (CONTINUED)

ENCRYPTION	ALGORITHM	COMPATIBILITY	DESCRIPTION
RC4_128M	Adobe Acrobat 6.0 and later	RC4 specifies the RSA Security software stream cipher for algorithms such as Secure Sockets Layer (SSL), to protect Internet traffic, and WEP, to secure wireless networks.	This encryption algorithm lets users do the following: Encrypt all document contents. Encrypt all document contents except for the metadata.
RC4_128	Adobe Acrobat 5.0 and later	RC4 128-bit encryption.	This encryption algorithm lets users encrypt the document contents, but not the document metadata.
RC4_40	Adobe Acrobat 3.0 and later	RC4 40-bit encryption.	This is the lowest encryption level.
None			The document is not encrypted.

Source: `http://livedocs.adobe.com/coldfusion/8/`.

Encrypting a PDF file goes hand in hand with setting passwords; `newuserpassword` or `newowner-password` is required, along with `action="protect"` and source attributes:

```
<cfpdf action="protect" encrypt="aes_128"
       source="pdfs/Comps.pdf"
       destination="pdfs/Comps-userpassword-encrypted.pdf"
       overwrite="yes" newuserpassword="test" />
```

This code uses the same `Comps.pdf` file, sets the user password to `test`, and encrypts the PDF file with AES_128. In Acrobat, go to the Document Properties, Security tab and click Show Details (see Figure 32.9) to see the encryption information.

You can use the same code with different encryption as needed. Refer to Table 32.2 to ensure you're targeting the proper version of Adobe Acrobat.

NOTE

The metadata in a PDF file is used in Internet searches. When the document is encrypted, the metadata is no longer available to search engines. You also have to make sure that the encryption you choose works in the targeted Acrobat version.

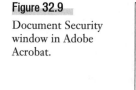

Figure 32.9

Document Security
window in Adobe
Acrobat.

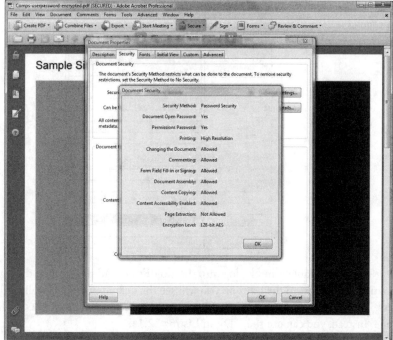

Working with <cfprint>

The cfprint tag prints only PDF files.

Using GetPrinterInfo and GetPrinters

Before actually printing something, let's look at a dump of printer information (Figure 32.10). Here the Adobe PDF printer is used, but any connected or networked printer could be used.

```
<cfdump var="#GetPrinterInfo('Adobe PDF')#">
```

NOTE

A printer name is not required. Call GetPrinterInfo() for the default printer.

NOTE

Printers are managed outside ColdFusion. Configure printer settings, security, and so on via your operating system.

The paper struct was closed for space reasons. This struct shows the available page sizes available for this printer; each printer may vary.

Figure 32.10

A cfdump of
GetPrinterInfo.

struct		
collate	no,yes	
color	no,yes	
copies	1	
defaults	**struct**	
	collate	yes
	color	yes
	copies	1
	fidelity	no
	jobname	ColdFusion Print Job
	orientation	portrait
	pages	1-2147483647
	paper	na-letter
	requestingusername	JCBII-9400$
fidelity	no,yes	
jobname	ColdFusion Print Job	
orientation	portrait,landscape,reverse-landscape	
pages	1-2147483647	
paper		
printer	Adobe PDF	
requestingusername	JCBII-9400$	

For a list of available printers, log into the ColdFusion Administrator; then go to the System Infor-mation page. Toward the bottom, you will see the default printer as well as all other available print-ers. This information would be useful in a `GetPrinters()` function, but ColdFusion doesn't provide one. Instead, you can use the UDF in Listing 32.14.

Listing 32.14 `GetPrinters.cfm`—Get Installed Printers

```
<!--- Author: Ben Forta --->
<!--- Get installed printers --->
<cffunction name="GetPrinters" returntype="array" output="no">
   <!--- Define local vars --->
   <cfset var piObj="">

   <!--- Get PrinterInfo object --->
   <cfobject type="java"
        action="create"
        name="piObj"
        class="coldfusion.print.PrinterInfo">

   <!--- Return printer list --->
   <cfreturn piObj.getPrinters()>
</cffunction>

<!--- dump printer list --->
<cfdump var="#GetPrinters()#" />
```

Figure 32.11 shows the resulting dump.

Figure 32.11

`<Cfdump>` for
GetPrinters().

array	
1	Send To OneNote 2007
2	QuickBooks PDF Converter
3	Microsoft XPS Document Writer
4	Microsoft Office Live Meeting Document Writer
5	Microsoft Office Document Image Writer
6	Macromedia FlashPaper
7	Fax
8	Adobe PDF

Printing PDF Files

Now that we have our printers and printer information, we can print a PDF file:

```
<cfprint source="pdfs/Comps.pdf" />
```

The preceding code is the bare minimum needed to print, if you have a default printer specified.

If you want to specify a printer, use the `printer` attribute or specify `attributestruct` with a `printer` attribute:

```
<!--- specify attributes directly --->
<cfprint source="pdfs/Comps.pdf" printer="\\myserver\myprinter" />

<!--- use an attribute collection --->
<cfset attributes = StructNew() />
<cfset attributes.printer = "\\myserver\myprinter" />

<cfprint source="pdfs/Comps.pdf" attributestruct="#attributes#" />
```

NOTE

Because PDF is the only print type, the `type` attribute is optional.

The following attributes are available: `autoRotateAndCenter`, `collate` or `sheetCollate`, `color` or `chromaticity`, `copies`, `coverPage` or `jobSheets`, `fidelity`, `finishings`, `jobHoldUntil`, `jobName`, `jobPriority`, `numberUp`, `orientation` or `orientationRequested`, `pages`, `pageScaling`, `pageSubset`, `paper`, `presentationDirection`, `printer`, `quality`, `requestingUserName`, `reversePages`, `sides`, and `usePdfPageSize`. (More on each attribute can be found on LiveDocs: `http://livedocs.adobe.com/coldfusion/8/htmldocs/Tags_p-q_02.html#2922772`).

When using attributes, you don't need to worry about whether the printer will accept the attributes. Attributes not available for the specified printer are ignored or replaced with reasonable alternates unless the `fidelity` attribute is set to `yes`. In this case, the print job will fail if the supplied attributes are not available for the specified printer.

ColdFusion keeps a log of all print jobs in the print log. Log into the ColdFusion Administrator, open Debugging and Logging, if needed, click Log Files, and click print.log. Figure 32.12 shows an example of the print log.

NOTE

If the print log does not exist, ColdFusion will create it when needed.

Figure 32.12

The print log from the ColdFusion Administrator.

Searching file : *print.log*			☐ Compact View		1 - 5 of 5
Date	Time	Severity	ThreadID	Application Name	
Aug 20, 2007	11:29 AM	Information	jrpp-8		
Print job 'Comps.pdf' was sent to printer. Printer: 'Send To OneNote 2007'. Total pages: 3.					
Aug 20, 2007	11:29 AM	Information	jrpp-8		
Print job 'Comps.pdf' started. Printer 'Send To OneNote 2007'.					
Aug 20, 2007	11:22 AM	Information	cfthread-0		
Print job 'Comps.pdf' started. Printer 'Adobe PDF'.					
Aug 20, 2007	11:15 AM	Information	jrpp-7		
C:\Servers\JRun4\servers\cfusion\cfusion-ear\cfusion-war\WEB-INF\cfusion\logs\print.log initialized					
Aug 20, 2007	11:15 AM	Information	jrpp-7		
Print job 'Comps.pdf' started. Printer 'Adobe PDF'.					

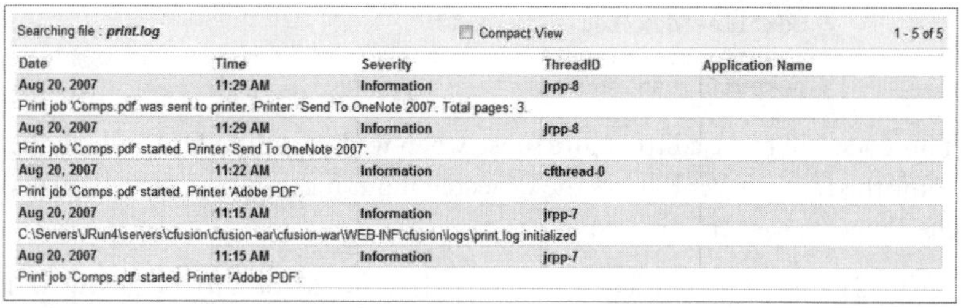

The printing of protected PDF files comes under the same scrutiny as the reading or writing of protected PDF files. The PDF document must have printing allowed, and where passwords are used, the `password` attribute must provide the PDF file's password.

```
<cfprint source="pdfs/Comps-userpassword.pdf" password="test" />
```

Even when a protected PDF file's password is supplied, the PDF file must have printing permissions, as must ColdFusion. ColdFusion, by default, runs as the Local System Account. If the Local System Account does not have printer privileges, ColdFusion can use a specific user account (see the tech note at `http://kb.adobe.com/selfservice/viewContent.do?externalId=tn_17279&sliceId=2` for more information).

Using DDX

Document Description XML, or DDX, is an XML-based syntax for constructing PDF files. You can create actual DDX files or use `cfsavecontent` to construct DDX on the fly. ColdFusion 8 does not provide support for the entire DDX language, but the available subset is still very useful and impressive. There are many DDX combinations and potential applications. Here we cover only the basics and some of the more popular PDF applications; we also don't cover every tag in full; for more information, read the LiveCycle DDX Reference (`http://livedocs.adobe.com/livecycle/es/sdkHelp/programmer/sdkHelp/wwhelp/wwhimpl/js/html/wwhelp.htm?href=ddxRefMain.150.1.html&accessible=true`).

Creating a Simple DDX Processing Application

To test the various DDX options, we'll be using a simple form created to show the available DDX files. All examples use the same PDF files, so all we'll need to do is switch DDX files and look at the results. Before we cover DDX syntax, let's explore the code for processing DDX and a simple application built for testing DDX files.

```
<cfset input = StructNew() />
<cfset input.TitlePage = "pdfs/Sample Title.pdf" />
<cfset input.SamplePage = "pdfs/Sample Page.pdf"/>
<cfset input.Comps = "pdfs/Comps.pdf" />

<cfset output = StructNew() />
<cfset output.Output1 = "output.pdf" />

<cfpdf name="myBook"
       action="processddx"
       ddxfile="ddx/toc-simple.ddx"
       inputfiles="#input#"
       outputfiles="#output#" />
```

This code will make a little more sense when we look at the DDX file in the next section. For now, know the `input` struct follows the expected input files, and the `output` struct follows the top-level PDF elements `result` attribute.

We'll take this same code as a base and apply a simple form to it (Listing 32.15). The finished code reads the `/ddx` directory and places those values in a `cfselect` element. When the form is submitted, a PDF file will be written with the same name as the selected DDX file, minus the `.ddx` extension.

Listing 32.15 `ProcessDDXSimple.cfm`—DDX Processing Application

```
<!--- Check for the form field "ddxfile" --->
<cfif structKeyExists(form, "ddxfile")>
    <!--- verify the file is valid DDX --->
    <cfif isDDX(ExpandPath("ddx/#form.ddxfile#"))>
        <!--- Construct input files struct --->
        <cfset input = StructNew() />
        <cfset input.TitlePage = "pdfs/Sample Title.pdf" />
        <cfset input.SamplePage = "pdfs/Sample Page.pdf"/>
        <cfset input.Comps = "pdfs/Comps.pdf" />

        <!--- Construct output files struct --->
        <cfset output = StructNew() />
        <cfset output.Output1 = "pdfs/"&Replace(form.ddxfile,
                                    ".ddx", "")&".pdf" />

        <!--- Process DDX --->
        <cfpdf name="myBook"
               action="processddx"
               ddxfile="ddx/#form.ddxfile#"
               inputfiles="#input#"
               outputfiles="#output#" />

        <!--- Output result --->
        <cfoutput>
            <h1>DDX instruction processing: #myBook.Output1#</h1>
        </cfoutput>
    <cfelse>
        <!--- Invalid DDX --->
        <cfoutput>
        <h1>ddx/#form.ddxfile# is not a valid DDX file</h1>
        </cfoutput>
    </cfif>
</cfif>

<!--- Filter the /ddx directory for all ddx files --->
<cfdirectory action="list"
             directory="#ExpandPath('ddx')#"
             name="ddxDirector"
             filter="*.ddx" />

<!--- Create a form for processing DDX;
      preservedata for ease of testing --->
<cfform name="DDXSelector"
        preservedata="yes">
    DDX File: <cfselect name="ddxfile"
                        query="ddxDirector"
                        required="yes"
                        display="name"
                        value="name" /><br />

    <cfinput name="submitButton" type="submit" value="Submit" />
</cfform>
```

Now that we have our testing application, we can look at some DDX examples.

Adding a Table of Contents

You add a table of contents (`toc`) with the `TableOfContents` element inside a PDF, PDFGroup, or StyleProfile element. Listing 32.16 uses the PDF element.

Listing 32.16 `ddx/toc-simple.ddx`—Simple DDX with Table of Contents

```
<?xml version="1.0" encoding="UTF-8"?>
<DDX xmlns="http://ns.adobe.com/DDX/1.0/"
    xmlns:xsi="http://www.w3.org/2001/XMLSchema-instance"
    xsi:schemaLocation="http://ns.adobe.com/DDX/1.0/ coldfusion_ddx.xsd">
    <PDF result="Output1">
      <PDF source="TitlePage"/>
      <TableOfContents/>
      <PDF source="SamplePage"/>
      <PDF source="Comps" />
    </PDF>
</DDX>
```

The PDF element has the `result` attribute set to Output1. If you look at our application's source, you'll see Output1 used in two places: in the output struct used in the `cfpdf` tag, and in the `result` output. Also notice the `source` attributes used in the internal PDF elements are used in the input struct. The names of both of these attributes are completely up to you. Instead of using TitlePage, SamplePage, and Comps, you could name them Doc1, Doc2, and Doc3, for instance. Running this DDX file through our application creates a table of contents for all PDF pages with bookmarks (Figure 32.13).

Figure 32.13

Generic table of contents.

NOTE

The file extension .ddx is not required. Initially the files were named with an .xml extension. The files can be edited in any text editor.

The Bookmarks view is expanded in Figure 32.13, and it shows all the bookmarked pages with the exception of the table of contents. The bookmark name is the same as that of the original PDF file. The Comp PDF file has three pages (Comp1, Comp2, and Comp3), and they flow one after another rather than being grouped. We can group the included PDF files into a single bookmark folder by using the bookmarkTitle attribute, as shown in Listing 32.17 (Figure 32.14).

NOTE

The includeInTOC attribute defaults to true, but it applies only when the bookmarkTitle attribute is used.

Listing 32.17 ddx/toc-simple-titles.ddx—DDX with bookmarkTitle Attribute

```xml
<?xml version="1.0" encoding="UTF-8"?>
<DDX xmlns="http://ns.adobe.com/DDX/1.0/"
    xmlns:xsi="http://www.w3.org/2001/XMLSchema-instance"
    xsi:schemaLocation="http://ns.adobe.com/DDX/1.0/ coldfusion_ddx.xsd">
    <PDF result="Output1">
        <PDF source="TitlePage" bookmarkTitle="Cover Page"/>
        <TableOfContents bookmarkTitle="Table of Contents" />
        <PDF source="SamplePage" bookmarkTitle="Sample Page" />
        <PDF source="Comps" bookmarkTitle="Site Designs" />
    </PDF>
</DDX>
```

Figure 32.14

Generic table of contents with bookmark labels.

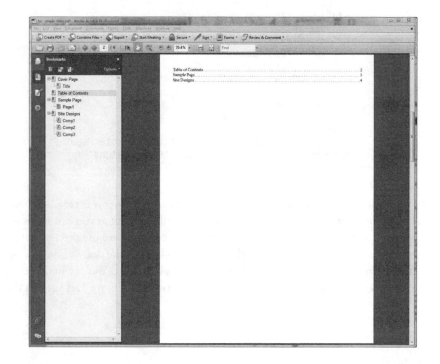

These PDF files are only one level deep, but you can embed multiple levels of bookmarks in a PDF file, and you can control the number of levels by using the `maxBookmarkLevel` attribute on the `TableOfContents` element.

A great feature of the generated table of contents is the live links applied to the page names. The `createLiveLinks` attribute, from the `TableOfContents` element, defaults to `true`. Set it to `false`, and the table of contents will be pure text, with no links.

We can also customize the look of the table of contents page by adding a few elements to the DDX, as shown in Listing 32.18.

Listing 32.18 `ddx/toc-simple-title-custom.ddx`—DDX with Table of Contents Customization

```
<?xml version="1.0" encoding="UTF-8"?>
<DDX xmlns="http://ns.adobe.com/DDX/1.0/"
    xmlns:xsi="http://www.w3.org/2001/XMLSchema-instance"
    xsi:schemaLocation="http://ns.adobe.com/DDX/1.0/ coldfusion_ddx.xsd">
    <PDF result="Output1">
        <PageLabel format="Decimal"/>
        <PDF source="TitlePage" bookmarkTitle="Cover Page"/>
        <TableOfContents bookmarkTitle="Table of Contents">
            <Header>
                <Center>
                    <StyledText>
                        <p font="Arial,18pt">Table of Contents</p>
                    </StyledText>
                </Center>
            </Header>
            <TableOfContentsEntryPattern>
                <StyledText>
                    <p font="Arial,10pt">
                        <_BookmarkTitle/>
                        <leader leader-pattern="solid" />
                        Page <_BookmarkPageCitation/>
                    </p>
                </StyledText>
            </TableOfContentsEntryPattern>
        </TableOfContents>
        <PDF source="SamplePage" bookmarkTitle="Sample Page" />
        <PDF source="Comps" bookmarkTitle="Site Designs" />
    </PDF>
</DDX>
```

We introduce a few new elements here: `TableOfContentsEntryPattern`, `StyledText`, and `Header`. The `Header` element will be covered in more detail later, but as you can see, it is very straightforward. To style each individual line of the table of contents, we use the `TableOfContentsEntryPattern` element with `StyledText`. In this DDX, we changed the dotted line to solid with the `leader` element and added the word `Page` before each page number. You can build on these few DDX examples to generate your own style of table of contents. Figure 32.15 shows the output.

Figure 32.15

Solid lines now replace the dotted lines, and a header has been added to the table of contents.

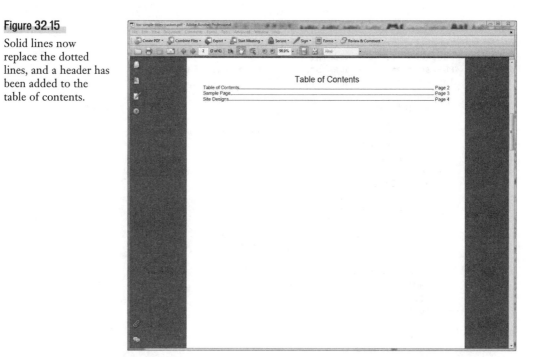

Adding Headers and Footers

The Footer element is similar to the Header element used in the preceding example. Both follow the same structure, as follows:

```
<Header or Footer …>
   <Left or Center or Right>
      <StyledText or PDF source>
         ...
      </StyledText or PDF source>
      <TargetLocale … />
   </Left or Center or Right>
</Header or Footer>
```

In Listing 32.19, we're going to throw in PDFGroup as well so the header and footer will be applied only to the grouped PDF files because the first PDF group comprises our title page and the second comprises the table of contents.

Listing 32.19 ddx/toc-simple-titles-custom-styled-header-footer.ddx—DDX with PDF Group

```
<?xml version="1.0" encoding="UTF-8"?>
<DDX xmlns="http://ns.adobe.com/DDX/1.0/"
    xmlns:xsi="http://www.w3.org/2001/XMLSchema-instance"
    xsi:schemaLocation="http://ns.adobe.com/DDX/1.0/ coldfusion_ddx.xsd">
```

Listing 32.19 (CONTINUED)

```
        <PDF result="Output1">
           <PageLabel format="Decimal"/>
           <PDF source="TitlePage" bookmarkTitle="Cover Page"/>
           <TableOfContents bookmarkTitle="Table of Contents">
              <Header>
                 <Center>
                    <StyledText>
                       <p font="Arial,18pt">Table of Contents</p>
                    </StyledText>
                 </Center>
              </Header>
              <TableOfContentsEntryPattern>
                 <StyledText>
                    <p font="Arial,10pt">
                       <_BookmarkTitle/>
                       <leader leader-pattern="solid" />
                       Page <_BookmarkPageCitation/>
                    </p>
                 </StyledText>
              </TableOfContentsEntryPattern>
           </TableOfContents>
           <PDFGroup>
              <Header>
                 <Center>
                    <StyledText>
                       <p font="Arial,18pt">My Header</p>
                    </StyledText>
                 </Center>
              </Header>
              <Footer>
                 <Center>
                    <StyledText>
                       <p font="Arial,18pt">My Footer</p>
                    </StyledText>
                 </Center>
              </Footer>
              <PDF source="SamplePage" bookmarkTitle="Sample Page" />
              <PDF source="Comps" bookmarkTitle="Site Designs" />
           </PDFGroup>
        </PDF>
     </DDX>
```

The Header and Footer elements used in the TableOfContents element have no effect on the PDF elements in the PDFGroup element. The Header and Footer elements have a direct relationship to the sibling elements—for example, putting the Header element in the initial <PDF result="Output1"> element would cause all pages to have the specified header (see Figure 32.16).

Figure 32.16

The PDFGroup header and footer; pages 1 and 2 do not have the same header and footer.

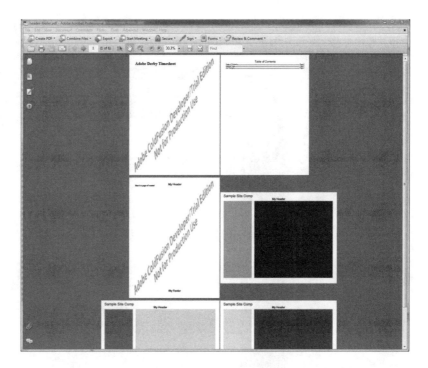

Adding Watermarks

You saw how to add a watermark earlier in the chapter, but you can also use DDX. The Watermark element allows you to set scale, horizontal and vertical offsets, opacity, and so on, and maybe best of all, you can type normal text without the need to use cfimage or another PDF. The use of a PDF file as a watermark is still an option as well. To save space, the example in Listing 32.20, based on the previous DDX example, shows only the Watermark element and the parent element (see the source file for the full script).

Listing 32.20 ddx/ toc-simple-titles-custom-styled-header-footer-watermark.ddx—
DDX with Watermark

```
<?xml version="1.0" encoding="UTF-8"?>
<DDX xmlns="http://ns.adobe.com/DDX/1.0/"
    xmlns:xsi="http://www.w3.org/2001/XMLSchema-instance"
    xsi:schemaLocation="http://ns.adobe.com/DDX/1.0/ coldfusion_ddx.xsd">
  <PDF result="Output1">
    <Watermark opacity="25%" rotation="30" fitToPage="true">
      <StyledText>
        <p>My Watermark</p>
      </StyledText>
    </Watermark>
    ... the remaining source ...
  </PDF>
</DDX>
```

This simple example added the text "My Watermark" to all pages at 25 percent opacity, rotated 30 degrees, and sized to properly fit the page—how easy is that! Figure 32.17 shows the results.

Figure 32.17

Custom DDX watermark.

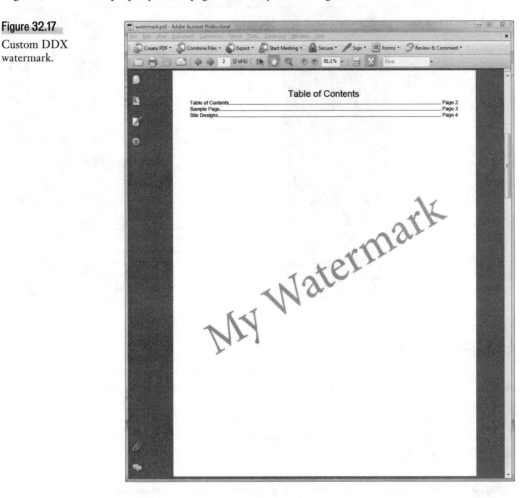

Using Style Profiles

You can use StyleProfile elements to create a named profile for referencing using the style-Reference attribute on the following elements: Background, Footer, Header, Watermark, and Table-OfContents. You can think of this profile as an internal CSS declaration: You create the style and then reference it by name.

Building on our current PDF example, suppose that you need to watermark the image pages and page 1 of the PDF file but not the rest of the document. You also want a specific footer on those pages. With page 1 and the rest of the PDF elements separated by the TableOfContents element, a StyleProfile will work perfectly.

Listing 32.21 follows previous examples but is changed quite a bit. We no longer use PDFGroup, and the main Watermark element has been removed.

Listing 32.21   ddx/ toc-simple-titles-custom-styled-header-footer-watermark-
styleprofiles.ddx—DDX with styleReference

```xml
<?xml version="1.0" encoding="UTF-8"?>
<DDX xmlns="http://ns.adobe.com/DDX/1.0/"
    xmlns:xsi="http://www.w3.org/2001/XMLSchema-instance"
    xsi:schemaLocation="http://ns.adobe.com/DDX/1.0/ coldfusion_ddx.xsd">
    <PDF result="Output1">
        <PageLabel format="Decimal"/>
        <PDF source="TitlePage" bookmarkTitle="Cover Page">
            <Watermark styleReference="MyWatermark" />
        </PDF>
        <TableOfContents bookmarkTitle="Table of Contents">
            <Header>
                <Center>
                    <StyledText>
                        <p font="Arial,18pt">Table of Contents</p>
                    </StyledText>
                </Center>
            </Header>
            <TableOfContentsEntryPattern>
                <StyledText>
                    <p font="Arial,10pt">
                        <_BookmarkTitle/>
                        <leader leader-pattern="solid" />
                        Page <_BookmarkPageCitation/>
                    </p>
                </StyledText>
            </TableOfContentsEntryPattern>
        </TableOfContents>
        <PDF source="SamplePage" bookmarkTitle="Sample Page" />
        <PDF source="Comps" bookmarkTitle="Site Designs">
            <Footer styleReference="CompsFooter" />
            <Watermark styleReference="MyWatermark" />
        </PDF>
    </PDF>
    <StyleProfile name="CompsFooter">
        <Footer>
            <Left>
                <StyledText>
                    <p font="Arial,10pt">
                        Page <_PageNumber/> / <_LastPageNumber/>
                    </p>
                </StyledText>
            </Left>
            <Right>
                <StyledText>
                    <p font="Arial,10pt">Last Modified: <_Modified/></p>
                </StyledText>
            </Right>
        </Footer>
    </StyleProfile>
    <StyleProfile name="MyWatermark">
```

Listing 32.21 (CONTINUED)

```
        <Watermark opacity="25%" rotation="30" fitToPage="true">
            <StyledText>
                <p>Copyright My Company</p>
            </StyledText>
        </Watermark>
    </StyleProfile>
</DDX>
```

For the PDF element with source="Comps", we have two subelements, and both use styleReference. One style sets up a footer, and the other controls the watermark. The initial PDF element, TitlePage, also uses the same watermark.

What we have done is watermarked our cover page and every page included from the Comps source PDF file. The table of contents and SamplePage source do not use the either StyleProfile, so the source pages are not affected.

StyleProfile elements allow you to create custom styles for the PDF document. They help you begin to develop a much more dynamic and cleaner DDX document, by separating the design from the layout.

Extracting PDF Text

DDX also provides a quick and easy way to index PDF text. Instead of using the PDF element as the main Output1 result, we use another element: DocumentText. This element requests information about the words that appear in the specified source documents. The DDX, in Listing 32.22, is quite simple. We'll strip away all previous DDX examples and just use the same source documents.

Listing 32.22 ddx/extractingtext.ddx—DDX Using DocumentText

```
<?xml version="1.0" encoding="UTF-8"?>
<DDX xmlns="http://ns.adobe.com/DDX/1.0/"
     xmlns:xsi="http://www.w3.org/2001/XMLSchema-instance"
     xsi:schemaLocation="http://ns.adobe.com/DDX/1.0/ coldfusion_ddx.xsd">
    <DocumentText result="Output1">
        <PDF source="TitlePage" />
        <PDF source="SamplePage"/>
        <PDF source="Comps" bookmarkTitle="Site Designs" />
    </DocumentText>
</DDX>
```

A change had to be made to the sample application in order to output an XML file instead of a PDF file. Listing 32.23 shows the final source with the changes highlighted.

Listing 32.23 ProcessDDX.cfm—DDX Test Application

```
<!--- Check for the form field "ddxfile" --->
<cfif structKeyExists(form, "ddxfile")>
    <!--- verify the file is valid DDX --->
    <cfif isDDX(ExpandPath("ddx/#form.ddxfile#"))>
        <!--- Construct input files struct --->
        <cfset input = StructNew() />
        <cfset input.TitlePage = "pdfs/Sample Title.pdf" />
```

Listing 32.23   (CONTINUED)

```
             <cfset input.SamplePage = "pdfs/Sample Page.pdf"/>
             <cfset input.Comps = "pdfs/Comps.pdf" />

             <!--- Construct output files struct --->
             <cfset output = StructNew() />
             <cfset output.Output1 = form.outputtype & "/"
                             & Replace(form.ddxfile, ".ddx",
                                          "")&"."&form.outputtype />

             <!--- Process DDX --->
             <cfpdf name="myBook"
                    action="processddx"
                    ddxfile="ddx/#form.ddxfile#"
                    inputfiles="#input#"
                    outputfiles="#output#" />

             <!--- Output result --->
             <cfoutput>
                 <h1>DDX instruction processing: #myBook.Output1#</h1>
             </cfoutput>
             <cfif form.outputtype EQ "xml" AND myBook.Output1 EQ "successful">
                 <cffile variable="xmloutput"
                         file="#ExpandPath(output.Output1)#"
                         action="read" charset="utf-8" />
                 <cfoutput>#XMLFormat(xmloutput)#</cfoutput>
             </cfif>
        <cfelse>
             <!--- Invalid DDX --->
             <cfoutput>
                 <h1>ddx/#form.ddxfile# is not a valid DDX file</h1>
             </cfoutput>
        </cfif>
    </cfif>

    <!--- Filter the /ddx directory for all ddx files --->
    <cfdirectory action="list"
                 directory="#ExpandPath('ddx')#"
                 name="ddxDirector" filter="*.ddx" />

    <!--- Create a form for processing DDX;
    preservedata for ease of testing --->
    <cfform name="DDXSelector" preservedata="yes">
       DDX File: <cfselect name="ddxfile"
                           query="ddxDirector"
                           required="yes"
                           display="name"
                           value="name" /><br />
       Output type:
       <cfselect name="outputtype">
          <option value="pdf">pdf</option>
          <option value="xml">xml</option>
       </cfselect><br />
       <cfinput name="submitButton" type="submit" value="Submit" />
    </cfform>
```

Processing DDX with `DocumentText` does not output a PDF file—it outputs XML—so the changes here basically check the selected `outputtype` and either read the generated XML file and then display it or operate as our previous examples did.

The following XML shows the result of running the `DocumentText` DDX:

```xml
<?xml version="1.0" encoding="UTF-8"?>
<DocText xmlns="http://ns.adobe.com/DDX/DocText/1.0/">
<TextPerPage>
<Page pageNumber="1">Adobe Derby Timesheet</Page>
<Page pageNumber="2">Here is a page of content</Page>
</TextPerPage>
</DocText>
```

This XML can be parsed, searched, stored, and so on to fit your needs.

Working with PDF Forms

PDF forms are not all the same, beyond the internal form elements. A PDF form created with Adobe Acrobat is different from one created with Adobe LiveCycle Designer. There are also two types of form submissions: HTTP and PDF.

Populating PDF Forms

You can populate PDF forms in several ways. To start, we will look at `<cfpdfsubform …. />`. The PDF form we are using (Listing 32.24) is a sample timesheet PDF form from Adobe LiveCycle Designer CS3 (Figure 32.18), which uses a more hierarchical PDF structure than Adobe Acrobat, which uses a flat structure.

Figure 32.18

Timesheet PDF.

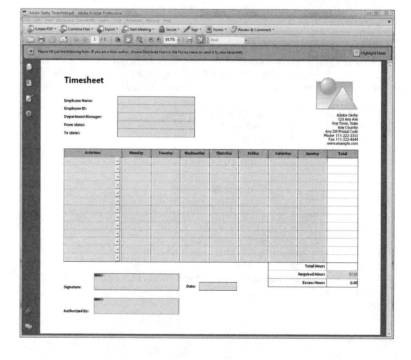

To populate the form, you need to know the names of the form fields you're populating. If you're using Acrobat, you can export the form data to XML by choosing Forms > Manage Form Data > Export Data, or you can choose Forms > Edit in Designer to open the PDF form in Adobe LiveCycle Designer. You can also read the PDF form and dump the result to the browser (see Listing 32.24).

Listing 32.24 `PopulatingPDFForms-Structure.cfm`—Sample Timesheet PDF Form

```
<cfpdfform source="pdfs/Adobe Derby Timesheet.pdf"
           result="result"
           action="read"/>
<cfdump var="#result#" />
```

To populate the form, we'll use `cfpdfsubform`, which specifies our PDF form's structure in CFML (Listing 32.25).

Listing 32.25 `PopulatingPDFForms.cfm`—Populating a PDF Form

```
<!--- Populate form data --->
<cfpdfform action="populate" source="pdfs/Adobe Derby Timesheet.pdf">
   <cfpdfsubform name="form1">
      <cfpdfformparam name="employeename" value="John C. Bland II" />
      <cfpdfformparam name="employeeid" value="32" />
      <cfpdfformparam name="departmentmanager" value="Ben Forta" />
      <cfpdfformparam name="date"
                      value="#DateFormat(now(), 'mm/dd/yyyy')#" />
      <cfpdfformparam index="1" name="monday" value="5" />
      <cfpdfformparam index="2" name="monday" value="10" />
      <cfpdfformparam index="1" name="tuesday" value="7" />
      <cfpdfformparam index="2" name="tuesday" value="18" />
      <cfpdfformparam index="1" name="activity" value='Project "A"' />
   </cfpdfsubform>
</cfpdfform>
```

Here we specify a few regular form fields (`employeename`, `employeeid`, `departmentmanager`, and `date`) and a few index-based fields (`Monday`, `Tuesday`, and `activity`). The index-based fields are merely fields with the same name, like an array of fields, and they are accessed like an array:

```
<cfpdfformparam index="1" name="monday" value="5" />
```

This code sets the `monday` box of index 1 to the value 5. The `index` attribute is required only if you want to set a specific `index` value. Otherwise, for an index-based field, the default `index` value, 1, is used.

```
<!--- index defaults to 1 --->
<cfpdfformparam name="monday" value="5" />
```

NOTE

Specification of an `index` value is not based on position in the code. You can specify index 2 before index 1, for instance.

NOTE

The `monday` field expects a number. If anything else is passed in, the field defaults to `0.0`.

cfpdfsubform has an index property and serves the same purpose. For PDF forms with multiple subforms, you can use the index attribute to access a specific subform. In our example, we specified the exact name of the subform since only one subform is available. Running the code loads the same timesheet in the browser but with our fields populated.

You can also populate this form using XML. The structure of a PDF form populated with XML is quite different from that of a form populated with cfpdfsubform. A PDF form created in Adobe LiveCycle Designer uses XML Forms Architecture (XFA), whereas one created in Adobe Acrobat uses XML Forms Data Format (XFDF). Our sample PDF form was created with LiveCycle. The XML in Listing 32.26 populates the PDF form with the same information as in our previous cfpdf-subform example.

Listing 32.26 PopulatingPDFs-LiveCycle.xml—XML PDF Form Data

```
<?xml version="1.0" encoding="UTF-8"?>
<form1>
    <EmployeeName>John C. Bland II</EmployeeName>
    <EmployeeID>32</EmployeeID>
    <DepartmentManager>Ben Forta</DepartmentManager>
    <Date>08/27/2007</Date>
    <Monday>5</Monday>
    <Monday>10</Monday>
    <Tuesday>7</Tuesday>
    <Tuesday>18</Tuesday>
    <Activity>Project "A"</Activity>
</form1>
```

TIP

Instead of writing the entire structure and worrying about which format to use, export the form data in Adobe Acrobat (choose Forms > Manage Form Data > Export Data). You can also use Ray Camden's toXML component (see http://www.coldfusionjedi.com/projects/toxml/) to convert the result struct from a PDF file to XML.

To populate a PDF form via XML, you can use the following code:

```
<!--- Populate form data from XML --->
<cfpdfform action="populate"
           source="pdfs/Adobe Derby Timesheet.pdf"
           xmldata="xml/PopulatingPDFs-LiveCycle.xml" />
```

In addition to an external XML file, you can use inline XML, shown in Listing 32.27.

Listing 32.27 PopulatingPDFForms-XML-inline.cfm—Populating a PDF Form with Inline XML

```
<!--- Save XML info to a variable --->
<cfsavecontent variable="pdfxml">
<form1>
    <EmployeeName>John C. Bland II</EmployeeName>
    <EmployeeID>32</EmployeeID>
    <DepartmentManager>Ben Forta</DepartmentManager>
    <Date>08/27/2007</Date>
    <Monday>5</Monday>
    <Monday>10</Monday>
    <Tuesday>7</Tuesday>
```

Listing 32.27 (CONTINUED)

```
    <Tuesday>18</Tuesday>
    <Activity>Project "A"</Activity>
</form1>
</cfsavecontent>

<!--- Populate form data from XML --->
<cfpdfform action="populate" source="pdfs/Adobe Derby Timesheet.pdf"
xmldata="#pdfxml#" />
```

TIP

Use `overwriteData="yes"` to overwrite prefilled form values.

TIP

Use the `destination` attribute to save the populated PDF form to a new PDF file instead of displaying the PDF file in the browser.

Submitting PDF Forms

There are two types of form submissions: HTTP and PDF. ColdFusion allows you to manage both submission types, but they are slightly different. For the examples here, the sample timesheet PDF form has been copied and saved as two separate PDF forms: one for each submission type.

Handling HTTP Submissions

A PDF form with an HTTP Submit button points to a specific location. To access the submitted information, you treat it almost like a regular HTML form submission. The big difference is that the submitted values are in the hierarchy of the PDF form. To demonstrate, Listing 32.28 uses the previous code for populating the PDF form with XML.

Listing 32.28 `SubmittingPDFForms-http.cfm`—Submitting a PDF Form via HTTP

```
<!---
Expects a PDF with the following submit type:
    - HTTP Post
--->
<cfif isDefined("form.form1")>
   <!--- Dump the contents of the form submission --->
   <cfdump var="#form#" />
<cfelse>
   <!--- Prepopulate form data --->
   <cfpdfform action="populate"
              source="pdfs/Adobe Derby Timesheet - HTTP Post.pdf"
              xmldata="xml/PopulatingPDFs-LiveCycle.xml" />
</cfif>
```

If the variable `form.form1` exists, we dump the contents of `form`; otherwise, we load the PDF file in the browser. After the PDF file is loaded in the browser, the page is done processing and merely waits for the PDF form to be submitted. The dumped form values are shown in Figure 32.19.

Figure 32.19

A cfdump of an HTTP post submission.

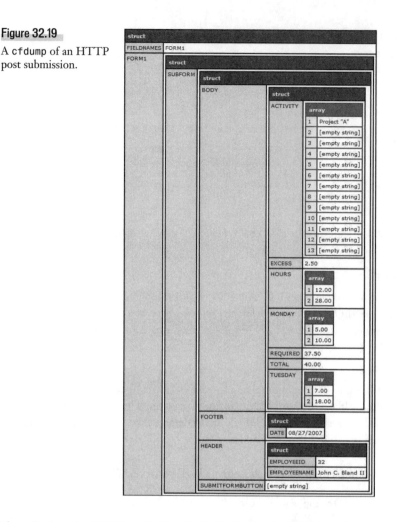

If you look at the PDF form in LiveCycle Designer, the PDF form is set up with Header, Footer, and Body elements within the Subform element, which is in the main form1 element (see Figure 32.20).

Handling PDF Submissions

A PDF form post does not fill the form scope. Instead, the PDF scope is filled with a binary content variable. You cannot access the data inside of PDF.content until you read it. This requirement does add one more step, but it is painless. Listing 32.29 shows the code.

Figure 32.20

Hierarchy tab.

Listing 32.29 SubmittingPDFForms-pdf.cfm—Submitting a PDF Form via PDF

```
<!---
Expects a PDF with the following submit type:
   - PDF
--->
<cfif isDefined("PDF")>
   <!--- Read the PDF contents into a variable --->
   <cfpdfform action="read" source="#PDF.content#" result="timesheet" />
   <!--- Dump the contents of the PDF variable --->
   <cfdump var="#timesheet#" />
<cfelse>
   <!--- Prepopulate form data --->
   <cfpdfform action="populate"
              source="pdfs/Adobe Derby Timesheet - PDF Post.pdf"
              xmldata="xml/PopulatingPDFs-LiveCycle.xml" />
</cfif>
```

We follow the same steps as for the HTTP post, but we check for the PDF variable, read the PDF.content variable, and then dump the result of the read (Figure 32.21).

As you can see, this dump doesn't follow the exact PDF form structure but is more of a flat hierarchy. For both submission types, multiple form fields with the same name are submitted as an array (see the Activity array in Figure 32.21).

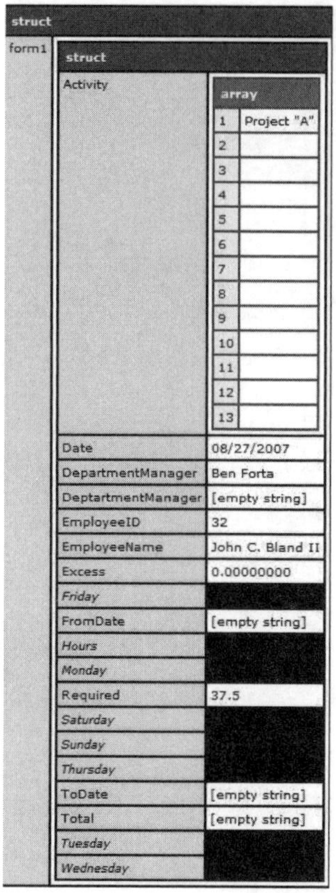

Figure 32.21

A `cfdump` of
an HTTP post
submission; several
nodes are closed to
save space.

Embedding PDF Forms

Using `cfdocument` (see Chapter 16, "Graphing, Printing, and Reporting," in *Adobe ColdFusion 8 Web Application Construction Kit, Volume 1: Getting Started*), you can embed a PDF form into a static PDF file. Only one `cfpdfform` tag can be included in a `cfdocument` tag, and the `cfpdfform` tag should be a child of `cfdocument`, not of `cfdocumentsection` or any other `cfdocument` child node. Also, in case you're thinking of changing `format="flashpaper"` to see if the PDF form can be converted, I'll save you the time: It can't. The `cfdocument` format value must be PDF.

```
<cfdocument format="pdf">
   <cfdocumentsection>
      PDF Form examples...
   </cfdocumentsection>

   <cfpdfform action="populate"
              source="pdfs/Adobe Derby Timesheet - PDF Post.pdf"
              xmldata="xml/PopulatingPDFs-LiveCycle.xml" />
</cfdocument>
```

TIP

To remove the interactivity of a PDF form, you use the `flatten="yes"` attribute in a `cfpdf write` action.

CHAPTER 33

ColdFusion Image Processing

One often repeated request of ColdFusion developers prior to version 8 was the capability to manipulate images directly in ColdFusion. Adobe has listened to ColdFusion's developer community and has given developers, with just a few lines of code, the ability to dynamically resize images, inspect image metadata, and much more. ColdFusion 8 now lets developers remove much of the drudgery of working with images in applications and even allows developers to create new types of graphically rich applications. So without further ado, let us jump into ColdFusion's new image processing capabilities.

Introducing <CFIMAGE>

Probably at some point, every ColdFusion developer has had to create an application or Web site that uses multiple sizes of the same image, such as in a thumbnail gallery that links to larger, high-resolution images. This scenario often requires tedious editing of images to make smaller, thumbnail sizes of the full-scale image.

ColdFusion 8 now lets you create such multiple versions simply by using the new <CFIMAGE> tag. Instead of walking through the incredible number of new image functions and attributes, let's first look at a few examples. For this exercise, you can use any image you want, but we will use the image of a scorpion found at Wikipedia under the GNU free license. You can find that image at `http://upload.wikimedia.org/wikipedia/commons/9/93/Black_scorpion.jpg` and also with the code samples for this book.

NOTE

Image processing and <CFIMAGE> is a huge topic. With more than 18 attributes for <CFIMAGE> and 50 image manipulation functions, there is just not enough space to cover every possible function and use of <CFIMAGE> here. So for this chapter, we will focus on the most common and important points and suggest that you review the full power of <CFIMAGE> and image processing functions at Adobe's LiveDocs site: `http://livedocs.adobe.com/coldfusion/8/htmldocs/`.

Now create a directory under your Web root called 33. Make sure that the scorpion image is in this directory. Then create a file called resizeimage.cfm in this directory as shown in Listing 33.1. Remember to edit the source and destination fields to reflect your file paths.

Listing 33.1 resizeimage.cfm—Image Resizing Example

```
<cfimage
    action = "resize"
    height = "25%"
    source = "#ExpandPath( './Black_scorpion.jpg' )#"
    width = "25%"
    destination = "#ExpandPath( './NewBlack_scorpion.jpg' )#"
    overwrite = "true"
    >

<table width="200" border="1">
  <tr>
    <td><img src="Black_scorpion.jpg"></td>
    <td><img src="NewBlack_scorpion.jpg"></td>
  </tr>
  <tr>
    <td><div align="center">Old Image</div></td>
    <td><div align="center">New Image</div></td>
  </tr>
</table>
```

If you run this code and look in the same directory in which you put Black_scoprion.jpg, you should see a new file called NewBlack_scorpion.jpg, and if you look at it you will see that it is 25 percent smaller than the original. You should see something like Figure 33.1 if you compare the images side by side.

NOTE

Why a scorpion you ask? Well, ColdFusion 8's code name during development was Scorpio.

Figure 33.1

Black scorpion image resized to 25 percent of its previous size.

So with one simple tag, we are able to consume an image, resize it to 25 percent of its height, and then write out the new image to the file system. If we look at the code syntax for <CFIMAGE> more closely for resizing it has this general form:

```
<cfimage
    action = "resize"
    height = "number of pixels|percent%"
    source = "absolute pathname|pathname relative to the web root|URL|#cfimage
variable#"
    width = "number of pixels|percent%"
    destination = "absolute pathname|pathname relative to the web root"
    isBase64 = "yes|no"
    name = "cfimage variable"
    overwrite = "yes|no">
```

As you can see, the attributes for the tag are pretty self-explanatory, with the four attributes desti-nation, isBase64, name, and overwrite being optional. Several of the <CFIMAGE> tag's attributes have multiple options, allowing a wide variety of uses. For example, you can get the scorpion image directly from the URL by changing the source in Listing 33.1 from:

```
source = "#ExpandPath( './Black_scorpion.jpg' )#"
```

to:

```
source = "http://upload.wikimedia.org/wikipedia/commons/9/93/Black_scorpion.jpg"
```

If you run the code, you will see that <CFIMAGE> has retrieved the image from the Web, resized the image, and written it to the file system again. Adobe's development team has added an incredible amount of functionality, which shows in the <CFIMAGE> tag's 18 attributes. Table 33.1 lists these attributes and describes how they can be used.

Table 33.1 <CFIMAGE> Attributes

ATTRIBUTE	ACTION	REQUIRED	DEFAULT	DESCRIPTION
action	N/A	Optional read		Action to take. Must be one of the following: border, captcha, convert, info, read, resize, rotate, write, writeToBrowser.
angle	rotate	Required		The angle in degrees. Must be an integer.
color	border	Optional	black	Border color. This needs to be a hexadecimal value or supported named color; see the name list of valid HTML named colors. For a hexadecimal value, use the form ##xxxxxx or xxxxxx, where x = 0–9 or A–F; use two number signs or none.

Table 33.1 (CONTINUED)

ATTRIBUTE	ACTION	REQUIRED	DEFAULT	DESCRIPTION
destination	border, captcha, convert, resize, rotate, write	Optional (see description)		Absolute or relative pathname where the image output is written. The image format is determined by the file extension.
difficulty	captcha	Optional	low	Level of complexity of the CAPTCHA text. Specify one of the following levels of text distortion: low, medium, high.
fonts	captcha	Optional		Valid fonts for CAPTCHA text. Fonts supported are those the JDK can recognize. Multiple fonts can be used and should be separated by commas.
fontSize	captcha	Optional	24	Font size of the text in the CAPTCHA image. The value must be an integer.
format	writeToBrowser	Optional	PNG	Format of the image displayed in the browser. If you do not specify a format, the image is displayed in PNG format. You cannot display a GIF image in a browser. GIF images are displayed in PNG format.
height	captcha, resize	Required		Height in pixels of the image. For the resize attribute, you also can specify the height as a percentage (an integer followed by the percent (%) symbol). When you resize an image, if you specify a value for the width, you can let ColdFusion calculate the aspect ratio by specifying " " as the height. If specified, the value must be an integer.
isBase64	border, convert, info, read, resize, rotate, write, writeToBrowser	Optional	No	Defines whether image is Base64: Yes = Base64; No = not Base64.

Table 33.1 (CONTINUED)

ATTRIBUTE	ACTION	REQUIRED	DEFAULT	DESCRIPTION
name	border, convert, read, resize, rotate	Optional (see description)		ColdFusion image variable name. The read action requires a name attribute. The border, resize, and rotate actions require a name attribute or a destination attribute.
overwrite	border, captcha, convert, read, resize, rotate, write	Optional	No	Valid only if the destination attribute is specified. The overwrite values are Yes = overwrites the destination file and No = does not overwrite the destination file. If the destination file already exists, ColdFusion generates an error if the overwrite action is not set to Yes.
quality	write	Optional	0.75	Controls the quality of JPEG only. Valid values are fractions that range from 0 through 1 with 1 being maximum quality.
source	border, convert, info, read, resize, rotate, write, writeToBrowser	Required		Can be: • URL of the source image • Absolute pathname or a pathname relative to the Web root, such as c:\images\logo.jpg • ColdFusion image variable containing another image, BLOB, or byte array, such as #myImage# • Base64 string, such as data:image/jpg;base64,/9j/4AAQSkZJRgABAQA
structName	info	Required		Name of the ColdFusion structure to be created.
text	captcha	Required		Text string displayed in the CAPTCHA image.
thickness	border	Optional	1	Creates a border on the outside edge of the image. Border thickness is an integer and measured in pixels.

As you can see, <CFIMAGE> has a lot of attributes—so many that it is almost impossible to show examples of every possible use of <CFIMAGE> let alone, as we will see later, all the ColdFusion image manipulation functions.

TIP

<CFIMAGE> and ColdFusion image manipulation functions are mostly extensions or wrappers around Java classes and methods found in java.awt, java.image, and the Java Advanced Image API, which can be accessed directly from ColdFusion. If you run into a situation where ColdFusion cannot do something you need, you should explore ColdFusion's tight integration with Java, which is covered in Chapter 78, "Extending ColdFusion with Java," in *Adobe ColdFusion 8 Web Application Construction Kit, Volume 3: Advanced Application Development.*

Manipulating Images with <CFIMAGE>

Now that you have seen those attributes, let's put them to use by creating a more involved series of examples. We'll create a simple application that will let us upload or retrieve an image from a URL, display information about that image, resize the image, and more.

Resizing an Image

We will start by making a simple Web page that will allow us to view everyone in the contacts table of the OWS database, upload images for each person, and automatically create a thumbnails. First create a directory called cfimage, and under that directory create one called upload. Under upload, create an image called user_photos. You can also simply just download the examples from this book's Web site and unzip them, which will create the correct folder structure. After your directory structure is set up, create a file called image_upload_example.cfm as in Listing 33.2. This file will be used for most of the examples in this chapter.

Listing 33.2 image_upload_example.cfm—Image Upload Example

```
<cfset imageDirPath = ExpandPath("user_photos")>

<cfquery name="get_users" datasource="ows">
   SELECT *
   FROM Contacts
   ORDER BY lastname, firstname
</cfquery>


<cfif isDefined("form.fileToUpload") and form.fileToUpload neq "">
   <cfset userPhotoPath = "#imageDirPath#/user_#form.contactid#.jpg">
   <cfset userThumbPath = "#imageDirPath#/user_#form.contactid#_thumb.jpg">

   <!--- Accept the file upload --->
   <cffile
      action="upload"
      destination="#getTempDirectory()#"
      fileField="fileToUpload"
      nameConflict="overwrite">

      <!--- Get info about the photo --->
   <cfimage
      action="info"
      source="#cffile.serverDirectory#\#cffile.serverFile#"
      structName="uploadedFileInfo">

   <cfif uploadedFileInfo.width lt 200
      or uploadedFileInfo.height lt 200
      or uploadedFileInfo.width gt 1000
```

Listing 33.2 (CONTINUED)

```
        or uploadedFileInfo.height gt 1000>
        <cfthrow message="Please provide an image between 100 and 1000 pixels tall and
wide.">
    </cfif>

        <!--- Convert the photo --->
        <cfimage
            action="convert"
            source="#cffile.serverDirectory#\#cffile.serverFile#"
            destination="#userPhotoPath#"
            overwrite="true">

        <!--- Resize the photo to create a thumbnail --->
        <cfimage
            action="resize"
            width="100"
            height="100"
            source="#userPhotoPath#"
            destination="#userThumbPath#"
            overwrite="true">

</cfif>

<cfinclude template="upload_form.cfm">
<cfinclude template="user_list.cfm">
```

Note the two templates included with <cfinclude>. The first is the form for uploading files and goes in the same place as Listing 33.2. To create the upload form, make a new file called upload_form.cfm as shown in Listing 33.3 and save it in the upload directory.

Listing 33.3 Upload_form.cfm—Upload Form

```
<hr>
<form action="" method="post" enctype="multipart/form-data">
    Provide new image for:

    <!--- DROPDOWN LIST OF USERS --->
    <select name="contactid">
    <cfoutput query="get_users">
        <option value="#contactid#">#firstname# #lastname#</option>
    </cfoutput>
    </select>

    <!--- FILE UPLOAD UI --->
    <input type="file" name="fileToUpload">

    <!--- SUBMIT BUTTON --->
    <button type="submit">Upload</button>
</form>
<hr>
```

Now create a new file called user_list.cfm as in Listing 33.4 and save it to the upload directory. This file will display a list of users and their associated images.

Listing 33.4 User_list.cfm—User List UI

```
<cfoutput>
    <table>
```

Listing 33.4 (CONTINUED)

```
        <cfloop query="get_users">
        <tr>
            <td>
    <cfif FileExists(ExpandPath("user_photos") & '/user_#contactid#_thumb.jpg')>
        <a href="user_photos/user_#contactid#.jpg"><img
src="user_photos/user_#contactid#_thumb.jpg" border="0"></a>
        <cfelse>
        <a href="user_photos/user_#contactid#.jpg"><img src="user_photos/default.jpg"
border="0"></a>
    </cfif>
            </td>

            <td><h3>#firstname# #lastname#</h3></td>
        </tr>
        </cfloop>
    </table>
</cfoutput>
```

Assuming that you have placed these files in your webroot/chapter33/upload directory, you should be able to see the application by going to http://localhost/chapter33/upload/upload_image_example.cfm, and you should see something like Figure 33.2. By selecting a name from the resulting drop-down list, you can select a person, such as Ben Forta, and assign an image to that person (the URL to Ben's image here).

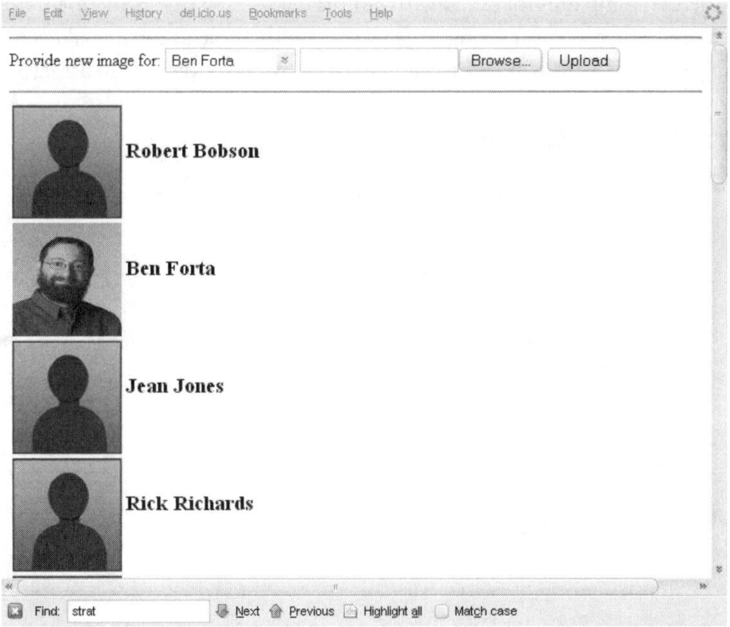

Figure 33.2

Sample output showing what you should see what you view the image management application in your browser.

When you assign an image to a person who does not yet have an image, the template first uploads the image to a specific directory and then uses the <CFIMAGE> tag to get information about the image, such as its size. To get information from for an image using <CFIMAGE>, use this format:

```
<cfimage
    action = "info"
    source = "absolute pathname|pathname relative to the web root|URL|#cfimage
variable#"
    structname="">
```

The info action lets you retrieve valuable information about an image, including the color model, height, width, and source, all written to a structure. Here, all we are interested in is the width and height, but depending on the scenario you may be interested in other information about the image.

Once you have the image information you need, you can have all images saved to your system in one format, such as the JPEG format. So the next thing you do in the code is use <CFIMAGE> to convert files from other formats to JPEG by using the syntax:

```
<cfimage
    action = "convert"
    source = "absolute pathname|pathname relative to the web root|URL|#cfimage
variable#"
    destination = "absolute pathname|pathname relative to the web root"
    overwrite="true|false">
```

NOTE

There are a number of practical reasons for standardizing on one image format, from ease of support to security.

Here, you simply write:

```
<cfimage
    action="convert"
    source="#cffile.serverDirectory#\#cffile.serverFile#"
    destination="#userPhotoPath#"
    overwrite="true">
```

<CFIMAGE> will now convert supported file formats from one format to the destination format (JPEG, GIF, TIFF, PNG, or BMP). Simply setting the destination without the action="convert" but being explicit improves code readability as well because some image conversions (such as conversion to a ColdFusion image variable) require that the action be set to "convert". You can test your code by adding a .gif or other image extension to one of names in the list. When you upload the image and check the user_photos directory, you should see that the image has been converted to JPEG.

NOTE

Image processing in ColdFusion is usually very fast but, depending on what actions you perform and how often, image processing can impose significant overhead on your server. Some ways around this are to work with small or lower-quality images or use asynchronous processes and ColdFusion gateways to perform batch operations on your images. For more about gateways and asynchronous processes, see Chapter 80, "Working with Gateways," in Vol. 3, *Advanced Application Development*.

Adding Borders

Now that we have made sure that all our images are a certain size and are of the same type, we can finally generate the thumbnail. You have to create a simple template that allows you to add images for people in a database, validate the uploaded image information, convert the images to other image file formats, and autogenerate thumbnails of a specific size—all with only about 50 lines of code. But let's do some more. Suppose that you are now asked to add more features to the photos in the gallery, including a border for the images, the person's name on the image, and a simple watermark.

We'll start with the border. To do this, use this syntax:

```
<cfimage
    action="border"
    source="absolute pathname|pathname relative to the web root|URL|#cfimage
variable#"
    destination="absolute pathname|pathname relative to the web    root|URL|#cfimage
variable#"
    thickness="in pixels"
    color ="supported colors"
    overwrite="true">
```

To change the code to add a border, change the lines:

```
<!--- Convert the photo --->
<cfimage
    action="convert"
    source="#cffile.serverDirectory#\#cffile.serverFile#"
    destination="#userPhotoPath#"
    overwrite="true">
```

to:

```
<!--- Convert the photo and write it to a variable--->

<cfimage
    action="convert"
    source="#cffile.serverDirectory#\#cffile.serverFile#"
    destination="user_#form.contactid#.jpg"
    name="tempImage"
    overwrite="true">

<!--- add a black border with a thickness of 5 pixels around the image --->
<cfimage
    source="#tempImage#"
    action="border"
    thickness="5"
    color="black"
    destination="#userPhotoPath#"
    overwrite="true">
```

Now if you try uploading a new image or even the same image for Ben Forta, you should see a border generated around the image. If you look at the code, you also see that we are doing something a little different in the <CFIMAGE> tag used to convert the images: We are using the tag name attribute, which allows us to create or store the image not as a file on the file system but as an object that is stored as a ColdFusion variable, allowing us to pass it to the next <CFIMAGE> tag as the source to which the tag applies a border. The name attribute allows you to save most <CFIMAGE> operations output to a ColdFusion variable, which is useful for many purposes, such as performing operations on an image before you write the file system.

Controlling JPEG Quality and Drawing Text

The next thing we need to do is add the person's full name to each image. To do this, you will use the image manipulation function ImageDrawText(). This function is one of the 50 image functions now in ColdFusion. The ImageDrawText() function simply draws a text string on an image with X-Y coordinates, starting in the upper-right corner of the image (the Y axis is inverted from a normal Cartesian coordinate system). The ImageDrawText() function uses this format:

```
ImageDrawText(name, str, x, y [, attributeCollection])
```

Tables 33.2 and 33.3 list the attributes and elements of this function.

Table 33.2 ImageDrawText Attributes

ATTRIBUTE	DESCRIPTION
name	The name of the ColdFusion image that you will draw on; it is required.
str	The text string you wish to draw on the image; it is required.
x	Starting point for the string on the horizontal axis in pixels; required. The origin is the upper-left corner of the image.
y	Starting point for the string on the vertical axis in pixels; required. The origin is the upper-left-corner of the image.
attributeCollection	A structure of text attributes; optional.

Table 33.3 ImageDrawText **Elements**

ELEMENT	DESCRIPTION
font	Font for your text. This is an optional element, and if it is left out, ColdFusion will switch to the system default.
size	Font point size; optional.
style	Style supports bold, italic, bold italic, and plain.
strikeThrough	Optional element. If set to Yes, a line will be drawn through each character.
underline	Optional parameter. If set to Yes, will underline the drawn text.

To use ImageDrawText() in our code, you will need to rewrite the code as in Listing 33.5.

Listing 33.5   `image_upload_example_text.cfm.cfm`—Image Upload with Text

```
<cfset imageDirPath = ExpandPath("user_photos")>

<cfquery name="get_users" datasource="ows">
   SELECT *
   FROM Contacts
   ORDER BY lastname, firstname
</cfquery>

<cfif isDefined("form.fileToUpload") and form.fileToUpload neq "">
   <cfset userPhotoPath = "#imageDirPath#/user_#form.contactid#.jpg">
   <cfset userThumbPath = "#imageDirPath#/user_#form.contactid#_thumb.jpg">

   <!--- Accept the file upload --->
   <cffile
      action="upload"
      destination="#getTempDirectory()#"
      fileField="fileToUpload"
      nameConflict="overwrite">

      <!--- Get info about the photo --->
   <cfimage
      action="info"
      source="#cffile.serverDirectory#\#cffile.serverFile#"
      structName="uploadedFileInfo">

   <cfif uploadedFileInfo.width lt 100
      or uploadedFileInfo.height lt 100
      or uploadedFileInfo.width gt 1000
      or uploadedFileInfo.height gt 1000>
   <cfthrow message="Please provide an image between 100 and 1000 pixels tall and
wide.">
   </cfif>

   <!--- Convert the photo and write it to a variable--->

   <cfimage
      action="convert"
      source="#cffile.serverDirectory#\#cffile.serverFile#"
      destination="user_#form.contactid#.jpg"
      name="tempImage"
      overwrite="true">
   <!--- add a black border with a thickness of 5 pixels --->
   <cfimage
      source="#tempImage#"
      action="border"
      thickness="5"
      color="black"
      destination="#userPhotoPath#"
      overwrite="true">

   <cfquery name="get_user" datasource="ows">
      SELECT *
      FROM Contacts
      Where  CONTACTID = #form.contactid#
   </cfquery>

   <!--- Resize the photo to create a thumbnail --->
```

Listing 33.5 (CONTINUED)

```
        <cfimage
            action="resize"
            width="100"
            height="100"
            source="#userPhotoPath#"
            destination="#form.contactid#_thumb.jpg"
            name="tempThumbImage"
            overwrite="true">

        <!--- Draw text --->
        <!--- Set the text attributes. --->
        <cfset attr = StructNew()>
        <cfset attr.underline = "yes">
        <cfset attr.size = 10>
        <cfset attr.style = "bold">
        <cfset ImageSetDrawingColor(tempThumbImage,"black")>

        <cfset ImageDrawText(tempThumbImage, "#trim(get_user.firstname)#
    #trim(get_user.lastname)#",5, 90, attr)>

        <!--- Write out image to the file system --->
        <cfimage
            source="#tempThumbImage#"
            action="write"
            destination="#userThumbPath#"
            overwrite="true">
    </cfif>

    <cfinclude template="upload_form.cfm">
    <cfinclude template="user_list.cfm">
```

As you can see in Listing 33.5, we have changed the code to add the individuals' first and last names to the thumbnail by using this code:

```
<!--- Draw text --->
<!--- Set the text attributes. --->
    <cfset attr = StructNew()>
    <cfset attr.underline = "yes">
    <cfset attr.size = 10>
    <cfset attr.style = "bold">
    <cfset ImageSetDrawingColor(tempThumbImage,"black")>

    <cfset ImageDrawText(tempThumbImage, "#trim(get_user.firstname)#
#trim(get_user.lastname)#",5, 90, attr)>
```

We first create a simple structure called attr to hold the attributes for the text we want to draw. We then use ImageDrawText to draw the text on the image, which is held in the tempThumbImage variable, and later in the code we use <CFIMAGE> once again to write the image to the file system. This is another good example showing why you may want to use ColdFusion variables to hold images as you apply multiple manipulations to them for writing them to their final destination.

Adding a Watermark

Now all we need to do is add a watermark to our images. For this example we are going to add a copyright image to the images. We are going to use the image copyright.gif, which can be found in the user_images directory in the sample code for this chapter.

ColdFusion allows you to add watermarks to existing images by essentially pasting one image on top of another using the image function `ImagePaste()`. The image that will be the watermark—in our case, `copyright.gif`—will be made transparent by using the image function `ImageSetDrawing-Transparency()`.

To generate the watermark, all you need to do is add this code right after line 41 in Listing 33.5, where we use the `<CFIMAGE>` tag to convert the images to JPEG format:

```
<!--- create a watermark from an existing image. --->
<!--- Create two ColdFusion images from existing JPEG files. --->

    <cfimage source="#imageDirPath#/copyright.gif" name="myImage2">

    <cfimage
        source="#myImage2#"
        action="convert"
        destination="copyright.jpg"
        name="tempCopyright"
        overwrite="true">

    <cfset ImageSetDrawingTransparency(tempImage,50)>
    <!--- Paste myImage2 on myImage at the coordinates (0,0). --->
    <cfset ImagePaste(tempImage,tempCopyright,0,0)>
```

As you can see, we first create a ColdFusion image from `copyright.gif`. We then use `ImageSet-DrawingTransparency()` to make the image 50 percent transparent. The function simply takes a ColdFusion image and then a percent value between 1 and 100 (decimal values are okay) to define the amount of transparency. Once we have made the image transparent, we can paste the copyright image on the main image in the upper-right corner. Your results should resemble Figure 33.3.

Figure 33.3

You can use the `ImageSetDrawing-Transparency()` function to add copyright information to an image.

Once again, with a few lines of ColdFusion code we have accomplished something that would be difficult and complex in another programming language.

Adding a CAPTCHA Test

Our simple template now supports a large number of image functions. Now let's add some security to our simple application to make sure that Web robots don't add images to our simple user gallery.

A common problem these days on the Internet is spammers who create bots, or programs that look for Web sites where users are allowed to post comments, links, suggestions, or photos and then these scripts to automatically post links to advertisements, distasteful Web sites, or images of items for sale. Often these scripts are smart enough to circumvent simple security solutions such as login names, email addresses, and other tests to confirm the user. One way to defeat these scripts is to create a Completely Automated Public Turing test to tell Computers and Humans Apart, or CAPTCHA test. One of the most common CAPTCHA tests on the Web requires the user to type the letters or characters in a distorted image. We'll add this simple CAPTCHA test to our code, so the user has to pass the test before uploading an image.

To create a CAPTCHA test, we once again use <CFIMAGE>, but this time we are going to use the action attribute and set it to CAPTCHA. Here is the basic syntax for <CFIMAGE> to create a CAPTCHA:

```
<cfimage
    action="captcha"
    fontsize="fontsize"
    text="#captchaText#"
    difficulty="difficut"
    fonts="fonts"
    width="width"
    height="height"/>
```

Table 33.4 lists the attributes for <CFIMAGE>, assuming the CAPTCHA action.

Table 33.4 <CFIMAGE> CAPTCHA Attributes

ATTRIBUTE	DESCRIPTION
fontsize	The font size in points.
text	A text string that will be used to generate the CAPTCHA characters.
difficulty	Set to low, medium, or high to govern how obfuscated the generated text in the image is.
fonts	Can be a list of JVM-supported fonts. You should define at least one font since the default is all supported fonts, which may result in human-unreadable CAPTCHAs.
width	Must be larger than the fontSize value times the number of characters in the text; otherwise, ColdFusion may throw an error.
height	Height of the CAPTCHA image.
size	Font point size; optional.

To use the CAPTCHA in our simple application, we need to change the UI a bit, so we are going to rewrite Listing 33.3. To get the form to look like Figure 33.4, we need to add some code to the upload form as shown in Listing 33.6, where we introduce some new UI elements as well as the CAPTCHA test.

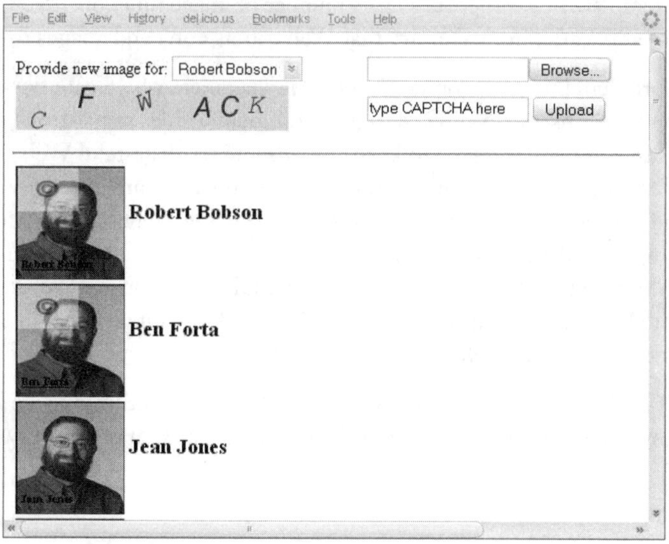

Figure 33.4

Example of the CAPTCHA output on the screen.

Listing 33.6 `upload_form2.cfm`—Upload Form

```
<hr>
<form action="" method="post" enctype="multipart/form-data">
    <table width="597" border="0">
    <tr>
    <td>Provide new image for:
    <!--- DROPDOWN LIST OF USERS --->
    <select name="contactid">
        <cfoutput query="get_users">
        <option value="#contactid#">#firstname# #lastname#</option>
        </cfoutput>
        </select></td>
        <td><input type="file" name="fileToUpload" /></td>
        </tr>
        <tr><!--- CFIMAGE being used to create a CAPTCHA image --->
        <td>
        <cfimage
            action="captcha"
            text="#captchaText#"
            difficulty="low"
            width="250"
            height="40"/></td>
        <td>
        <label>
        <input name="captchaTextField" value="type CAPTCHA here" type="text"
    id="captchaTextField" size="20" />
```

Listing 33.6 (continued)

```
            </label>
            <!--- SUBMIT BUTTON --->
            <button type="submit">Upload</button></td>
            </tr>
        </table>

    </form>
    <hr>
```

We need to make some changes to the main template to add logic for the simple CAPTCHA test. You can see these changes in Listing 33.7.

Listing 33.7 image_upload_example_captcha.cfm—Image Upload with CAPTCHA Test

```
<cfset imageDirPath = ExpandPath("user_photos")>
<!--- This is our default captcha text--->
<cfset captchaText = "CFWACK"/>
<!--- Form param for the captcha entered text --->
<cfparam name="FORM.captchaTextField" default=""/>
<!--- get the list of users from the DB --->
<cfquery name="get_users" datasource="ows">
    SELECT *
    FROM Contacts
    ORDER BY lastname, firstname
</cfquery>

<cfif isDefined("form.fileToUpload") and form.fileToUpload neq "">

    <!--- Check if the user is human --->
    <cfif captchaText eq TRIM(FORM.captchaTextField)>
        <cfset isHuman = true />
    <cfelse>
            <cfset isHuman = false/>
    </cfif>
    <!--- If the user passes as human then move on to handle the file upload --->
        <cfif isHuman eq true>

        <cfset userPhotoPath = "#imageDirPath#/user_#form.contactid#.jpg">
        <cfset userThumbPath = "#imageDirPath#/user_#form.contactid#_thumb.jpg">

        <!--- Accept the file upload --->
    <cffile
        action="upload"
        destination="#getTempDirectory()#"
        fileField="fileToUpload"
        nameConflict="overwrite">

        <!--- Get info about the photo --->
    <cfimage
        action="info"
        source="#cffile.serverDirectory#\#cffile.serverFile#"
        structName="uploadedFileInfo">

    <cfif uploadedFileInfo.width lt 100
        or uploadedFileInfo.height lt 100
```

Listing 33.7 (CONTINUED)

```
            or uploadedFileInfo.width gt 1000
            or uploadedFileInfo.height gt 1000>
        <cfthrow message="Please provide an image between 100 and 1000 pixels tall and
wide.">
    </cfif>
    <!--- Convert the photo and write it to a variable--->

    <cfimage
        action="convert"
        source="#cffile.serverDirectory#\#cffile.serverFile#"
        destination="user_#form.contactid#.jpg"
        name="tempImage"
        overwrite="true">
    <!--- create a watermark from an existing image. --->
    <!--- Create two ColdFusion images from existing JPEG files. --->
    <cfimage source="#imageDirPath#/copyright.gif" name="myImage2">

    <cfimage
        source="#myImage2#"
        action="convert"
        destination="logo.jpg"
        name="tempLogo"
        overwrite="true" />

    <cfset ImageSetDrawingTransparency(tempImage,50)>
    <!--- Paste myImage2 on myImage at the coordinates (0,0). --->
    <cfset ImagePaste(tempImage,tempLogo,0,0)>
    <!--- Write the result to a file. --->

    <!--- add a black border with a thickness of 5 pixels around the image --->
    <cfimage
        source="#tempImage#"
        action="border"
        thickness="5"
        color="black"
        destination="#userPhotoPath#"
        overwrite="true">

    <cfquery name="get_user" datasource="ows">
        SELECT *
        FROM Contacts
        Where  CONTACTID = #form.contactid#
    </cfquery>

    <!--- Resize the photo to create a thumbnail --->
    <cfimage
        action="resize"
        width="100"
        height="100"
        source="#userPhotoPath#"
        destination="#form.contactid#_thumb.jpg"
        name="tempThumbImage"
        overwrite="true">

    <!---  Draw text --->
```

Listing 33.7 (CONTINUED)

```
        <!--- Set the text attributes. --->
        <cfset attr = StructNew()>
        <cfset attr.underline = "yes">
        <cfset attr.size = 10>
        <cfset attr.style = "bold">
        <cfset ImageSetDrawingColor(tempThumbImage,"black")>
        <cfset ImageDrawText(tempThumbImage, "#trim(get_user.firstname)#
 #trim(get_user.lastname)#",5, 90, attr)>
        <!--- Write out image to the file system --->
        <cfimage
           source="#tempThumbImage#"
           action="write"
           destination="#userThumbPath#"
           overwrite="true">

        <cfelse>
        <cfabort>
        <!--- Refresh Page --->
           <cflocation url="#CGI.SCRIPT_NAME#"
                      addtoken="false"/>
        </cfif>
</cfif>

<cfinclude template="upload_form2.cfm">
<cfinclude template="user_list.cfm">
```

Now if you run the new code in your browser, you should have to pass the CAPTCHA test before you can upload your images.

Exploring Other ColdFusion Image Manipulation Techniques

We have explored some of the more common uses of <CFIMAGE>. Now let's look at some of the other powerful image manipulation options available in <CFIMAGE>. For all of these examples, we will be using our Ben Forta JPEG file.

We will start by seeing how to flip or invert an image, using the code in Listing 33.8.

Listing 33.8   `flip.cfm`—Image Flip

```
<cfset filename = ExpandPath("benfortalarge.jpg")>

<cfimage
   action="read"
   name="myimage"
  source="#filename#">

<cfset ImageFlip(myimage, "vertical")>

<cfimage
  action="writeToBrowser"
  source="#myimage#">
```

As you can see, we are introducing two new elements here. The first is the image manipulation function: `ImageFlip()`. This function uses this syntax:

> `ImageFlip(`*name* `[,` *transpose*`])`

It takes two parameters: the name of the ColdFusion image to be flipped and the transposition value, which can be vertical, horizontal, diagonal, antdiagonal, or degrees of rotation clockwise (90, 180, or 270 degrees only). If you do not select a transposition parameter, ColdFusion defaults to vertical.

The other new item you see here is the `<CFIMAGE>` action `writeToBrowser()`. The `writeToBrowser()` element for the `action` attribute tells ColdFusion to push the image directly to the Web browser without first writing it to a variable or the file system. There are many reasons why you may want to not save an image before you display it.

Now let's try rotating an image.

Rotating is just as simple as flipping an image. It makes use of another image manipulation function, called `ImageRotate()`, which has this syntax:

> `ImageRotate(`*name,*`[` *x, y,*`]` *angle*`[,` *interpolation*`])`

`ImageRotate()` has five attributes, listed in Table 33.5.

Table 33.5 `<CFIMAGE>` CAPTCHA Attributes

ATTRIBUTE	DESCRIPTION
name	The required ColdFusion image.
x	An optional parameter for the horizontal axis coordinate relative to the upper-left corner of the image. The default is the center of the image.
y	An optional parameter for the vertical axis coordinate relative to the upper-left corner of the image. The default is the center of the image.
angle	Required rotational angle in degrees.
interpolation	Optional interpolation type: • `nearest`: This is the default method. It uses the nearest-neighbor method. Image quality is lower than with other types, but it is the fastest setting. • `bilinear`: Uses the bilinear method, where image quality is less pixelated than nearest, but processing is slower. • `bicubic`: Applies the bicubic method of interpolation. Generally, the quality of the image is high, but processing is slow.

NOTE

Nearest-neighbor, bilinear, and bicubic interpolation are all mathematical methods for constructing new data points from a discrete set of known points. To learn more about the interpolation techniques, view the Wolfram Mathworld articles on each method at `http://mathworld.wolfram.com/`.

To rotate the Ben Forta image, we'll use the same code as before but replace `ImageFlip()` with `ImageRotate()`, like this:

```
<cfset ImageRotate(myimage, "90")>
```

You should see something like Figure 33.5.

Figure 33.5

An image rotated 90 degrees.

You can even turn the color JPEG into a grayscale image, with the `ImageGrayscale()` function:

```
<cfset ImageGrayscale(myimage)>
```

Or you can invert the pixel values on the image with the `ImageNegative()` function, like this:

```
<cfset ImageNegative(myimage)>
```

You can use some of the 50 other image manipulation functions to blur, transpose, and sharpen the image, and more. `<CFIMAGE>` and ColdFusion's associated image processing functions are too numerous and varied to cover in depth in this chapter, but by this time you should have a strong understanding of how `<CFIMAGE>` and image functions work. Almost any image manipulation or action you want to perform can be done in ColdFusion 8. All that is left now is for you to imagine and create.

Creating and Drawing Images with ColdFusion

So far, we have looked at methods and ways you can manipulate images in ColdFusion, but with ColdFusion 8 you can actually create images from scratch and even draw your own images. Among the image processing functions, ColdFusion has a number of basic drawing functions that allow you to draw basic lines, arcs, and shapes. For example, to create the drawing in Figure 33.6, you first draw a rectangle and then rotate it some number of times, as in Listing 33.9.

Figure 33.6

Geometric flower created by rotating the axis on which the square is drawn.

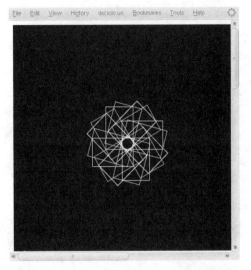

Listing 33.9 `flower.cfm`—Flower Image

```
<!--- Create a 400x400-pixel image. --->
<cfset myImage=ImageNew("",400,400)>
<!--- Turn on antialiasing to improve image quality. --->
<cfset ImageSetDrawingColor(myImage,"yellow")/>
<cfset ImageSetAntialiasing(myImage)>
<!--- Translate the origin to (200,200). --->
<cfset ImageTranslateDrawingAxis(myImage,200,200)>

<!--- draw a rectangle and keep rotating the axis to make flower --->
<cfset i = 15>
<cfloop condition="i LESS THAN OR EQUAL TO 360">
   <cfset ImageRotateDrawingAxis(myImage,i,10,10)>
   <cfset i = i + 15>
   <!--- Draw a rectangle at the offset location. --->
   <cfset ImageDrawRect(myImage,0,0,50,75)>
</cfloop>
<!--- Display the image in a browser. --->
<cfimage source="#myImage#" action="writeToBrowser">
```

In Listing 33.9, the first thing you will notice is the use of the function `ImageNew()`, which has this syntax:

ImageNew([*source*, *width*, *height*, *imageType*, *canvasColor*])

Table 33.6 explains its attributes.

Table 33.6 `ImageNew` **Attributes**

ATTRIBUTE	DESCRIPTION
source	Valid ColdFusion image source; optional.
width	Width of the image in pixels; valid only when source is not defined.
height	Height of image in pixels; valid only when source is not defined.
imageType	Type of ColdFusion image to create, which can be rgb, argb, or grayscale. You can use this attribute only when source is not specified.
canvasColor	Optional; color value of the image canvas: • Hexadecimal value of RGB color. • String value of color; default is "black". • List of three numbers for R, G, and B values. Each value must be in the range 0–255.

Next we will use the `ImageSetDrawingColor()` function, which has this syntax:

```
ImageSetDrawingColor(name, color)
```

The `name` attribute is simply a valid ColdFusion image, and `color` is a valid ColdFusion color, such as `yellow` or `##FFFFFF`. This function sets the color of our drawing.

We can then use the function `ImageSetAntialising()` to make the generated image look smoother and less blocky. It has this syntax:

```
ImageSetAntialiasing(name [, antialias])
```

Here, `name` is a ColdFusion image, and `antialias` is Yes or No.

The next function we will use is `ImageTranslateDrawingAxis()`, which has this syntax:

```
ImageTranslateDrawingAxis(name, x, y)
```

It takes three parameters: `name`, which identifies your ColdFusion image, and X and Y coordinates to reset the origin point. In Listing 33.9, we set the origin to `200,200`, which is the center of the new image on which we plan to draw.

Next we'll use a conditional loop, where we increment by 15 degrees until we have traveled 360 degrees, and for each increment we will rotate the axis also by 15 degrees, using `ImageRotate-DrawingAxis()`, which has this syntax:

```
ImageRotateDrawingAxis(name, angle [, x, y])
```

Here, `name` identifies a valid ColdFusion image, and `angle` is an angle in degrees; an optional set of X-Y coordinates allows you to further offset the drawing axis. For this example, we will offset the axis 10 pixels on both the X and Y axes, which will create the illusion of an open center in the drawing.

Finally, we will draw a rectangle using the function `ImageDrawRect()`, which has this syntax:

```
ImageDrawRect(name, x, y, width, height [, fill])
```

`ImageDrawRect()` has six parameters: `name` is a ColdFusion image, `x` and `y` are coordinates to start drawing from, `width` is the width in pixels, `height` is the height in pixels, and `fill` is a optional parameter that, if set to `Yes`, will fill the rectangle with the color we set earlier.

As you can see, it is pretty easy to programmatically create drawings using shapes. You can create similar programmatic drawings using `ImageDrawLine()`, which has this syntax:

```
ImageDrawLine(name, x1, y1, x2, y2)
```

The parameters are `name`, which identifies a valid ColdFusion image, and then two sets of X and Y coordinates, which the line will be drawn between. You can programmatically draw lines just as you can shapes. For an example, look at Listing 33.10.

Listing 33.10 `drawlines.cfm`—Draw Lines

```
<!--- Create the image variable --->
<cfset myImage = imageNew("",400,300) />
<!--- Set the drawing color to yellow. --->
<cfset ImageSetDrawingColor(myImage,"yellow") />
<!--- Turn on antialiasing to improve image quality. --->
<cfset ImageSetAntialiasing(myImage,"on") />
<cfset i=10>
<cfloop condition="i LESS THAN OR EQUAL TO 300">
   <cfset i = i+10>
   <cfset x1 = 300-i>
   <cfset x2 = 290>
   <cfset y1 = 290>
   <cfset y2 = i>
   <cfset ImageDrawLine(myImage, x1, y1, x2, y2)>

</cfloop>
<!--- Draw the text --->
<cfset stAtrCollection = structNew() />
<cfset stAtrCollection.font = "arial" />
<cfset stAtrCollection.size = 25 />
<cfset stAtrCollection.style = "bold" />
<cfset ImageDrawText(myImage,"Cool Line Drawing",20,20,stAtrCollection) />
<!--- Display the image in a browser. --->
<cfimage action="writeToBrowser" source="#myImage#" />
```

In this example, we again loop over some simple code, which draws a series of lines that creates an image as in Figure 33.7.

Figure 33.7

Using the ColdFusion `ImageDrawLine()` function to create a simple mesh surface.

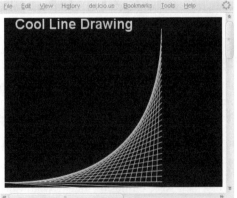

Drawing and creating images in ColdFusion is straightforward and simple, but we have hardly scratched the surface. ColdFusion functions also support various forms of arcs, curves, circles, and other drawing controls. Using these along with ColdFusion's other image processing functions, you should be able to fulfill your custom imagery needs.

Summary

Image processing in ColdFusion 8 is a deep topic. For almost any need you can think up, from drawing and creating images programmatically to rotating, resizing, copying, converting, and more, ColdFusion has a function. In this chapter, you saw how simple it is to create a photo gallery that automatically resizes and converts images while simultaneously adding borders, watermarks, and text to them. You also learned how to create your own images and draw shapes and lines programmatically.

By exposing and simplifying the underlying Java image processing classes and methods, the Cold-Fusion 8 team has allowed ColdFusion developers to perform, in a single line, operations that can be very difficult in plain Java.

34

Advanced ColdFusion-Powered Ajax

This chapter continues the discussion of Asynchronous JavaScript and XML—Ajax—begun in Chapter 15, "Beyond HTML Forms: ColdFusion-Powered Ajax," in *Adobe ColdFusion 8 Web Application Construction Kit, Volume 1: Getting Started.* In that earlier chapter, you learned the basics of working with Ajax and ColdFusion. In this chapter, you will delve deeper, learning about new Ajax-based layout controls, more binding options, JavaScript, and security options for your ColdFusion-based Ajax Web sites.

Ajax-Based Layout Controls

In the past, ColdFusion primarily focused on the back end of a Web site. There were few tabs that generated content. The `<cftable>` tag, for example, creates an HTML table, but this tag is rarely used by developers. ColdFusion 8 includes many new and improved layout controls that can greatly enhance the look of your applications. Some controls help you lay out your page, while others act as widgets or containers for other content. Let's start with the `<cflayout>` and `<cflayoutarea>` tags.

As you can probably guess, the `<cflayout>` tag is concerned with layout. It allows you to define a layout for a Web page. This layout can contain a left panel or a top panel or both, and it can contain a bottom panel and a right panel as well. It can also be used to create tabbed containers, providing a handy way to split complex forms into simpler sections. The type of layout used is based on the `type` attribute. The `<cflayout>` tag allows you to set up four types of layouts, summarized in Table 34.1.

Table 34.1   `<cflayout>` Layout Types

LAYOUT TYPE	FUNCTION
border	Creates an area with a simple border. This area can have five sections, placed at the top, left, right, bottom, and center.
hbox	Defines an area in which everything inside is laid out horizontally. This layout is not demonstrated in this chapter.

Table 34.1   (CONTINUED)

LAYOUT TYPE	FUNCTION
vbox	Defines an area in which everything inside is laid out vertically. This layout is not demonstrated in this chapter.
tab	Creates a tabbed panel in which all the sections are contained within a tab. A user can select which tab is visible by clicking the tab.

There are restrictions on what can be placed inside a `<cflayout>` tag. In general, you can use only non-output tags, including the `<cflayoutarea>` tag we will introduce shortly as well as tags such as `<cfloop>`. You put your HTML and other output inside `<cflayoutarea>` tags. Let's look at a simple example: Listing 34.1 demonstrates a border layout with a left panel.

Listing 34.1   `layout1.cfm`—Basic Layout

```
<!---
Name:        layout1.cfm
Author:      Raymond Camden (ray@camdenfamily.com)
Description: Basic layout
--->

<cflayout type="border">

    <cflayoutarea position="left" size="250">
    <p>
    Menu 1
    </p>
    <p>
    Menu 2
    </p>
    <p>
    Menu 3
    </p>
    </cflayoutarea>

    <cflayoutarea position="center">
    <p>
    This is the main body of the page.
    </p>
    </cflayoutarea>

</cflayout>
```

Listing 34.1 begins and ends with a `<cflayout>` tag that uses `type="border"`. Inside are two `<cflayoutarea>` tags. The `<cflayoutarea>` tag is used to define an area within `<cflayout>`. For border layouts, it defines a positioned panel. For the first tag, we set a position of left, setting the content at the left side of the page. A width of 250 is set for this area. The next area has a center position. Notice that no width is set. This lets the area expand as much as the browser allows. Figure 34.1 shows the result.

Figure 34.1

Simple `<cflayout>`
example.

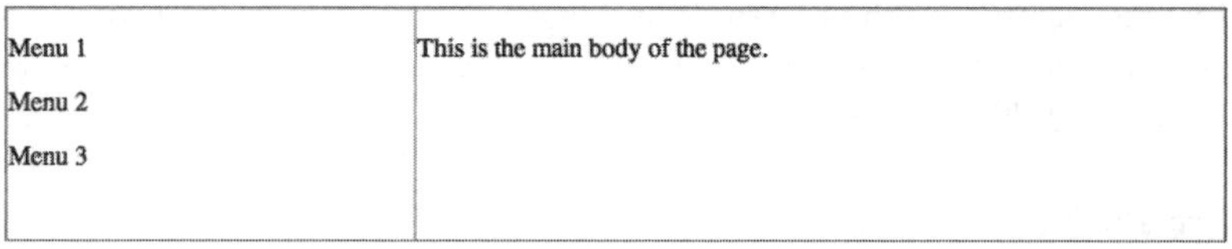

Menu 1	This is the main body of the page.
Menu 2	
Menu 3	

As mentioned in Table 34.1, the bordered `<cflayout>` can have five sections: left, right, top, bottom, and center. Which you use is up to you and your particular design needs. Listing 34.2 demonstrates a layout with all five sections in use.

Listing 34.2   `layout2.cfm`—All Layout Positions

```
<!---
Name:        layout2.cfm
Author:      Raymond Camden (ray@camdenfamily.com)
Description: Basic layout
--->

<cflayout type="border">

    <cflayoutarea position="left">
    <p>
    LEFT
    </p>
    </cflayoutarea>

    <cflayoutarea position="right">
    <p>
    RIGHT
    </p>
    </cflayoutarea>

    <cflayoutarea position="top">
    <p>
    TOP
    </p>
    </cflayoutarea>

    <cflayoutarea position="bottom">
    <p>
    BOTTOM
    </p>
    </cflayoutarea>

    <cflayoutarea position="center">
    <p>
    CENTER
    </p>
    </cflayoutarea>

</cflayout>
```

Listing 34.2 isn't much different from Listing 34.1. This time, however, all five positions of the `<cflayoutarea>` tag are used. Within each `<cflayoutarea>` tag, the name of the position is printed. Figure 34.2 shows the results in a browser.

Figure 34.2

Advanced `<cflayout>` example.

So far we've used the layout tags simply to position and partition areas of the page. You can also add interactivity to these partitions. Each area, except the center area, can be allowed to resize, collapse, or even go away. Table 34.2 summarizes the attributes of `<cflayoutarea>` that pertain to the border-based layout.

Table 34.2 `<cflayoutarea>` Attributes for Border-Based Layouts

ATTRIBUTE	FUNCTION
align	Sets the alignment for items inside `<cflayoutarea>`. Valid values are `left`, `right`, `justify`, and `center`.
closable	If set to true, `<cflayoutarea>` can be closed. If closed, `<cflayoutarea>` is removed from the page.
collapsible	If set to true, `<cflayoutarea>`, can be minimized. It can also be restored.
initcollapsed	Sets `<cflayoutarea>` as initially closed.
inithide	Sets `<cflayoutarea>` as initially hidden. Later in the chapter, you will learn about the JavaScript API that lets you work with ColdFusion's Ajax controls. One such API lets you show or hide an area.
maxsize	Sets the maximum size of an area; applicable only to resizable areas.
minsize	Sets the minimum size of an area; applicable only to resizable areas.

Table 34.2 (CONTINUED)

size	Sets the size of an area. Depending on the position of <cflayoutarea>, the size can apply to the width or height.
splitter	If true, a divider is placed between the areas. This divider lets you resize the <cflayoutarea> area.
title	Adds a title to <cflayoutarea>.

Listing 34.3 demonstrates some of these attributes in action.

Listing 34.3   layout3.cfm—<cflayoutarea> Options

```
<!---
Name:        layout3.cfm
Author:      Raymond Camden (ray@camdenfamily.com)
Description: Basic layout
--->

<cflayout type="border">

    <cflayoutarea position="left" align="center"
            size="400" collapsible="true" title="Menu">
    <p>
    Menu 1
    </p>
    <p>
    Menu 2
    </p>
    <p>
    Menu 3
    </p>
    </cflayoutarea>

    <cflayoutarea position="right" closable="true">
    <p>
    This area can be closed.
    </p>
    </cflayoutarea>

    <cflayoutarea position="top" size="100"
                splitter="true" minsize="50">
    <p>
    This area can be resized, but has a minsize of 50
    </p>
    </cflayoutarea>

    <cflayoutarea position="center">
    <p>
    CENTER
    </p>
    </cflayoutarea>

</cflayout>
```

This example has a lot going on, so let's look at it area by area. The left area is now collapsible and has a title of `"Menu"`. The right area is set to be `closable`. The top area can be resized with the splitter, but a `minsize` value was set to ensure that it doesn't get too small. Figure 34.3 shows the results.

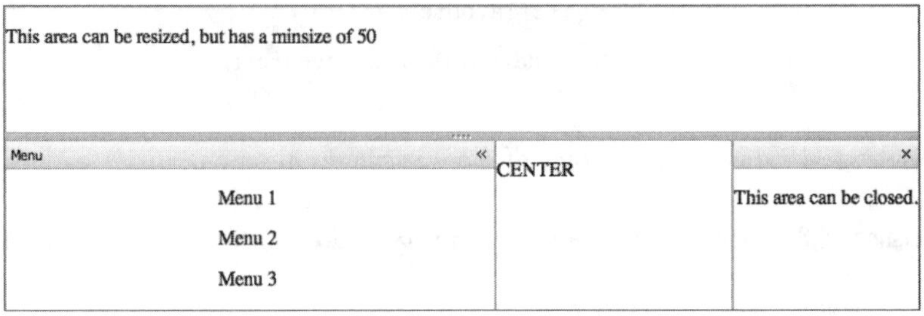

Figure 34.3

A `<cflayout>` example with different options.

Working with Tabs

One basic usability tip is not to overwhelm users with too much text. A page full of text or form controls is sure to cause users to either give up in frustration or leave your site. Tabs offer a way to exert some control over the amount of text on the screen. Consider the fairly standard checkout process. Normally this is a multipage process asking the user for shipping, billing, and credit card information. Instead of forcing the user to work through three pages of forms, you can employ tabs to provide the information in a nicely segmented, easy-to-work-with manner. Listing 34.4 creates a simple tabbed layout.

Listing 34.4 `tab1.cfm`—Tab Layout

```
<!---
Name:        tab1.cfm
Author:      Raymond Camden (ray@camdenfamily.com)
Description: Basic tabs
--->

<cflayout type="tab" tabheight="200">

    <cflayoutarea title="Tab One">
    <p>
    This is the first tab.
    </>
    <form>
    Name: <input type="text" name="name"><br />
    Email: <input type="text" name="email"><br />
    <input type="submit">
    </form>
    </cflayoutarea>

    <cflayoutarea title="Tab Two">
        <cfloop index="x" from="1" to="10">
        <p>
        This is the second tab.
        </p>
```

Listing 34.4 (CONTINUED)

```
      </cfloop>
    </cflayoutarea>

  </cflayout>
```

As with the earlier examples, we begin by wrapping our content with the `<cflayout>` tag. This time, however, the type is set to `tab`. When using this type, each `<cflayoutarea>` tag pair inside represents one tab. The `<cflayout>` tag allows a `tabheight` attribute when working with tabs. As you can guess, this sets the height for the total tabbed area. The first tab contains a simple paragraph of text and a basic form. The second tab contains 10 paragraphs of text generated by a simple `<cfloop>` tag. Figure 34.4 shows this layout, with the first tab selected and in another view with the second tab selected.

Figure 34.4

A tab-based layout.

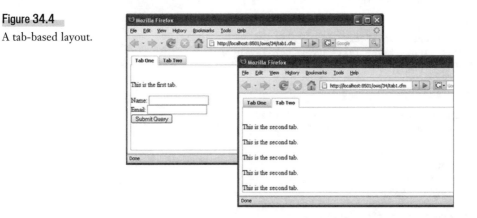

Pay particular attention to the content in the second tab. Note that because the content exceeded the space of the tab, ColdFusion automatically added a scroll bar. This behavior can be controlled with the `overflow` attribute. Valid values are `auto` (show scroll bars when needed), `hidden` (the additional content will not be visible), `scroll` (always show scroll bars), and `visible` (content will "leak" outside the layout area).

As with the border type, the tabs have options that let you add interactivity and other default behavior. Table 34.3 lists `<cflayoutarea>` attributes applicable to tabs.

Table 34.3 `<cflayoutarea>` Attributes for Tab-Based Layouts

ATTRIBUTE	FUNCTION
closable	If set to true, the tab can be closed. If closed, the tab is removed from the page.
disabled	If set to true, the tab is disabled and cannot be selected.
inithide	Sets a tab as initially hidden. Later in the chapter you will learn about the JavaScript API that lets you work with ColdFusion's Ajax controls. One such API lets you show or hide a tab.
selected	Sets the tab as selected. By default, the first tab is selected

Listing 34.5 creates tabs with various options applied to them.

Listing 34.5 `tabs2.cfm`—Tab Layout with Optional Settings

```
<!---
Name:       tab2.cfm
Author:     Raymond Camden (ray@camdenfamily.com)
Description: Basic tabs
--->

<cflayout type="tab" tabheight="200">

    <cflayoutarea title="Tab One">
    <p>
    This is the first tab.
    </p>
    <form>
    Name: <input type="text" name="name"><br />
    Email: <input type="text" name="email"><br />
    <input type="submit">
    </form>
    </cflayoutarea>

    <cflayoutarea title="Tab Two" selected="true">
        <cfloop index="x" from="1" to="10">
        <p>
        This is the second tab.
        </p>
        </cfloop>
    </cflayoutarea>

    <cflayoutarea title="Tab Three" disabled="true">
        <p>
        This tab content won't be shown.
        </p>
    </cflayoutarea>

</cflayout>
```

This listing is just slightly more advanced than the previous one. First we set the second tab as selected. The next change is the addition of a third tab. This tab is disabled, however, and cannot be selected by the user (although this behavior can be changed via the JavaScript API, as you will see later in the chapter). Figure 34.5 shows the new tabbed layout.

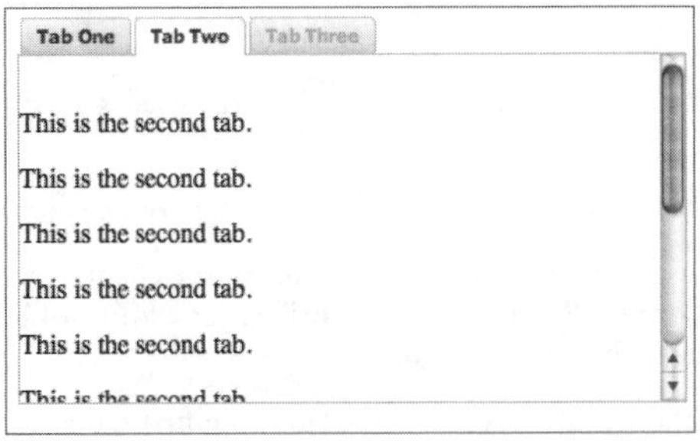

Figure 34.5

Tabs with additional options set.

Working with Pods

We've covered bordered and tabbed layouts; now we will look at basic containers, or widgets. The next set of controls are used to hold simple blocks of information. The simplest of these tags is `<cfpod>`. The `<cfpod>` tag creates a small block on a Web page. This block may have an optional title as well. Listing 34.6 creates a simple pod.

Listing 34.6 `pod1.cfm`—Simple Pod

```
<!---
Name:        pod1.cfm
Author:      Raymond Camden (ray@camdenfamily.com)
Description: Basic pod
--->

<cfpod title="Pods rule the world..." width="300"
       height="200">
<p>
This is the content of the pod. Groovy content
will go in here.
</p>
</cfpod>
```

As you can see, this code is fairly simple. The `<cfpod>` tag wraps the content, and a title, width, and height are provided to customize the pod. Figure 36.6 shows how a browser renders the pod.

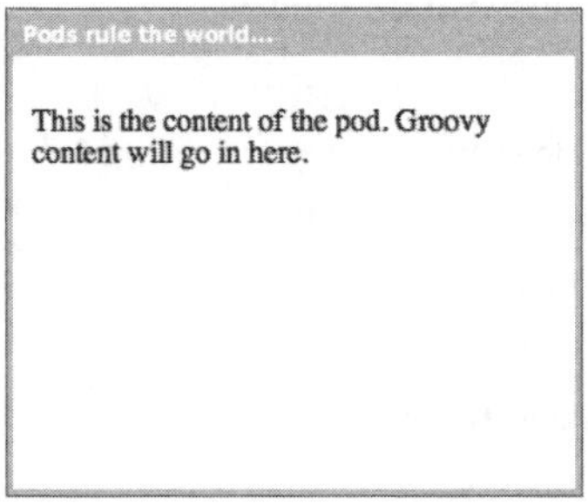

Figure 34.6

A simple pod.

Working with Windows

No, we don't mean the Windows operating system from Redmond, nor do we mean pop-up windows. The next control we will discuss is the `<cfwindow>` tag. This creates a UI element that looks like a new window, but is instead generated within the same main browser window. Like a real pop-up window, the window can be positioned, moved, resized, and even set as modal so that the user must interact with the window instead of the content beneath. Windows created by the `<cfwindow>` tag have many options, just as with the tab and border layouts. Table 34.4 lists the basic attributes of `<cfwindow>`.

Table 34.4   **Basic** `<cfwindow>` Attributes

ATTRIBUTE	FUNCTION
center	If set to true, the window is centered.
closable	If set to true, the window can be closed. If closed, the window is removed from the page.
draggable	If set to true, the window can be moved.
height	Height of the window.
initShow	By default, windows are *not* shown. That may seem a bit counterintuitive, but the idea is that windows are used for special operations and special circumstances; therefore, your window will not be visible. If you want the window to be displayed immediately, set this option to true.
minHeight	Sets the minimum height for a resizable window.
minWidth	Sets the minimum width for a resizable window.
modal	Sets the window so that it is the only item the user can interact with. Everything else on the page is dimmed.
resizable	If set to true, the window can be resized.
title	Sets the title of the window.
width	Sets the width of the window.
x, y	Sets the x and y positions of the window.

Now let's look at a simple example of `<cfwindow>` in action, in Listing 34.7.

Listing 34.7   `window1.cfm`—Simple Window

```
<!---
Name:        window1.cfm
Author:      Raymond Camden (ray@camdenfamily.com)
Description: Basic window
--->

<p>
This is content on the main page.
</p>

<cfwindow title="Logon Window" center="true" width="300"
          height="300" modal="true" initShow="true">
<p>
This is the content inside the window.
</p>
</cfwindow>
```

This listing creates a window using the `<cfwindow>` tag. The height and width are each set to 300, and the window is centered and set as modal. Remember that *modal* simply means that the window will be on top of any other content on the page. The last attribute, `initShow="true"`, forces the window to appear when the page is displayed. Figure 34.7 shows the browser with the window displayed.

Figure 34.7

A window created
by <cfwindow>.
Notice that the rest
of the page is dimmed
because of the modal
mode.

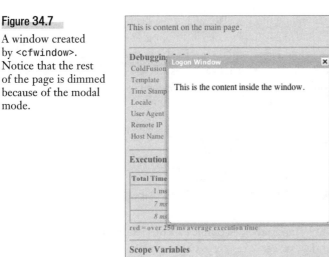

Normally you will not display a window immediately with the rest of the page. This is where the JavaScript API comes in. Commands to show, hide, and create windows are discussed later in the chapter.

Working with Menus

All of the previous tags have dealt with layouts or containers: items that contain other bits of HTML. Now we will discuss a few tags that simply generate a display of some sort. The first is the <cfmenu> tag. This tag creates dynamic, expandable menus, a common feature on most sites. The tag supports both vertical and horizontal menus and allows any level of nesting (but for your users' sake, you shouldn't go more than two or three levels deep). The <cfmenu> tag creates the menu as a whole, but the pieces of the menu (the labels and URLs) are made with the <cfmenuitem> tag. The <cfmenuitem> tag also allows dividers to help visually separate sections of a menu. Let's take a look at a simple example in Listing 34.8.

Listing 34.8 menu1.cfm—Horizontal Menu

```
<!---
Name:        menu1.cfm
Author:      Raymond Camden (ray@camdenfamily.com)
Description: Horizontal menu
--->

<cfmenu type="horizontal" bgcolor="##b6fa5d">
    <cfmenuitem display="Adobe"
            href="http://www.adobe.com" />
    <cfmenuitem display="Microsoft"
            href="http://www.microsoft.com" />
    <cfmenuitem display="CNN"
            href="http://www.cnn.com" />
    <cfmenuitem display="Raymond Camden's Blog"
            href="http://www.coldfusionjedi.com" />
</cfmenu>
```

Listing 34.8 begins by defining a horizontal menu. We also set a green background color for the menu. (Most of the Ajax controls discussed so far have numerous styling options that will be discussed later.) Inside the menu are four `<cfmenuitem>` child tags. Each tag defines a display (what you see in the browser) and an `href`. Note that each `<cfmenuitem>` tag is self-closed (that's the / at the end). This isn't done for stylistic reasons but for necessity: Every `<cfmenuitem>` tag must have a closing tag as well. Figure 34.8 shows the results.

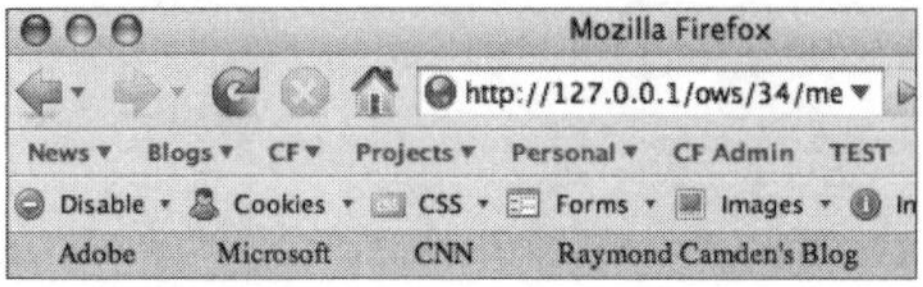

Figure 34.8

A menu with four items.

Most menus won't be a simple list of links but, rather, a complex set of sections and subsections. To create submenus, all you need to do is nest `<cfmenuitem>` tags under existing `<cfmenuitem>` tags. Listing 34.9 demonstrates a more realistic menu.

Listing 34.9   `menu2.cfm`—Advanced Horizontal Menu

```
<!---
Name:        menu2.cfm
Author:      Raymond Camden (ray@camdenfamily.com)
Description: Horizontal menu
--->

<cfmenu type="horizontal" bgcolor="##fffba0"
        selectedItemColor="##e7d844">

    <cfmenuitem display="Products">
        <cfmenuitem display="Books"
                href="products/books.cfm" />
        <cfmenuitem display="Music"
                href="products/music.cfm" />
        <cfmenuitem display="Movies"
                href="products/movies.cfm" />
        <cfmenuitem display="Video Games"
                href="products/vidgames.cfm" />
        <cfmenuitem display="Weapons of Mass Destruction"
                href="products/womd.cfm" />
    </cfmenuitem>

    <cfmenuitem display="Services">
        <cfmenuitem display="Car Washing"
                href="services/car.cfm" />
        <cfmenuitem display="Car Tuning"
                href="services/tuneup.cfm" />
        <cfmenuitem display="Starship Construction"
                href="services/starship.cfm" />
    </cfmenuitem>

    <cfmenuitem display="Our People">
        <cfmenuitem display="Entertainment">
```

Listing 34.9 (CONTINUED)

```
                <cfmenuitem display="Abba Jones"
                        href="people/aj.cfm" />
                <cfmenuitem display="Jacob Camden"
                        href="people/jc.cfm" />
            </cfmenuitem>

            <cfmenuitem divider />

            <cfmenuitem display="Finances">
                <cfmenuitem display="Jeanne Camden"
                        href="people/jc2.cfm" />
                <cfmenuitem display="Charlie Griefer"
                        href="people/sd.cfm" />
            </cfmenuitem>

            <cfmenuitem divider />

            <cfmenuitem display="Security">
                <cfmenuitem display="Alfonse Albertorinia"
                        href="people/aa.cfm" />
                <cfmenuitem display="Lynn Camden"
                        href="people/lc.cfm" />
                <cfmenuitem display="Noah Camden"
                        href="people/nc.cfm" />
            </cfmenuitem>
        </cfmenuitem>
    </cfmenu>
```

This menu is significantly bigger than the previous example, but it will help if you approach the code from an outside-in direction. Remember that menus must be wrapped in <cfmenu> tags, so the outer portion of the file contains beginning and end <cfmenu> tags. Inside are three sections of <cfmenuitem> tag pairs, named Products, Services, and Our People. Notice that these items do not have an href. They simply serve as section titles. Inside Products and Services are simple sets of <cfmenuitem> tags. Our People is more complex, however; it has sections of its own: Entertainment, Finances, and Security. To help differentiate these sections, the <cfmenuitem> divider tag is used; this tag places a divider between menu items. Note that none of the URLs in this listing actually work. Figure 34.9 shows this menu in action.

Figure 34.9

A menu with multiple sections and children.

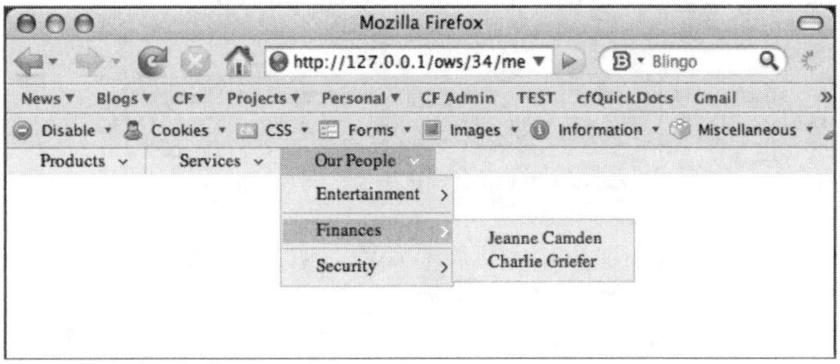

Adding Tooltips

Many applications use tooltips: text that appears when you pause your mouse over an item in the application. They are often used to explain graphical items: for instance, if you hover the mouse over a trash can icon, text may pop up that says "Contains the files and folders that you have deleted." ColdFusion allows you to add tooltips with the `<cftooltip>` tag. You can create a simple tooltip by wrapping a piece of content (text, graphic, form element, anything) and supplying the text attribute, as shown in Listing 34.10.

Listing 34.10 `tooltip1.cfm`—Tooltips in Action

```
<!---
Name:        tooltip1.cfm
Author:      Raymond Camden (ray@camdenfamily.com)
Description: Basic tooltip
--->

<form>

<cftooltip tooltip="This will delete the record forever!">
<input type="button" value="delete">
</cftooltip>

<cfsavecontent variable="archivetext">
This will archive the data so that it can be<br />
restored later. This will <b>not</b> delete<br />
the record.
</cfsavecontent>

<cftooltip tooltip="#archivetext#">
<input type="button" value="archive">
</cftooltip>

</form>
```

Listing 34.10 creates tooltips for two buttons in a simple form. The first tooltip is provided in line with the tag. The second tooltip's text is created within a pair of `<cfsavecontent>` tags. Either method is fine, but the second tooltip, with its additional text and HTML, is easier to read if you create it outside the `<cftooltip>` tag. Also notice that HTML is fine and dandy in a tooltip. You can even include images. Figure 34.10 shows the tooltips in action.

Figure 34.10

The `<cftooltip>` tag lets you easily add helpful text to your Web applications.

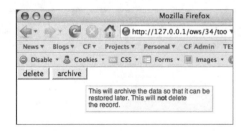

The <cftooltip> tag gives you control over how quickly the tooltip appears and disappears and when it goes away on its own. You can also specify an external URL for the tooltip, using the sourceForToolTip attribute.

Working with Trees

Yet another widget ColdFusion provides out of the box is the tree. Trees are UI interfaces based on nodes (branches) that can be opened to reveal more nodes (leaves) underneath. Previous versions of ColdFusion had a Java applet and Flash form of the tree, but ColdFusion 8 adds a completely HTML form of the control. The tree itself can be populated directly or via Ajax-style calls to the server. This section discusses static trees; later in the chapter, you'll learn how to dynamically load data for all of ColdFusion's Ajax-based controls.

To build a ColdFusion HTML tree, you work with the <cftree> and <cftreeitem> tags. Listing 34.11 demonstrates a simple, hard-coded, static HTML tree.

Listing 34.11 tree1.cfm—HTML-Based Tree

```
<!---
Name:        tree1.cfm
Author:      Raymond Camden (ray@camdenfamily.com)
Description: Basic tree
--->

<cfform name="main">
<cftree format="html" name="mytree">
   <cftreeitem display="Products" value="products"
           expand="false">
      <cftreeitem display="ColdFusion" value="cf"
              parent="products" >
      <cftreeitem display="Dreamweaver" value="dw"
              parent="products" >
      <cftreeitem display="Flash" value="flash"
              parent="products" >
   <cftreeitem display="Other" value="other"
           expand="false">
      <cftreeitem display="Alpha" value="alpha"
              parent="other" >
</cftree>

</cfform>
```

First and foremost, note that the <cftree> tag is a part of the overall <cfform> framework. Therefore, the listing begins and ends with <cfform> tags. The <cftree> tag uses a format value of html and the name mytree. Six <cftreeitem> tags are stored inside the <cftree> pair. Each item has a label (display) and a value. Some of the tags specify parents, which places the items under parent nodes (think branches) so that they can be expanded and collapsed. Figure 34.11 shows how this tree appears in a browser.

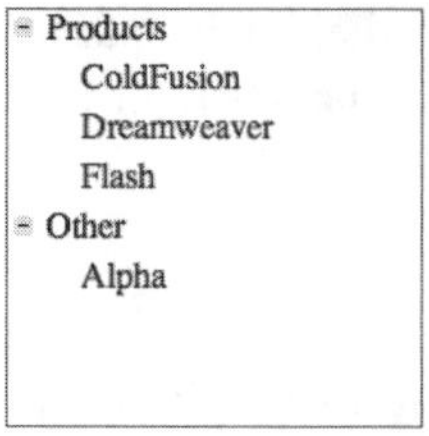

Figure 34.11

A simple `<cftree>` tag adds a dynamic tree control to a form.

```
─ Products
     ColdFusion
     Dreamweaver
     Flash
─ Other
     Alpha
```

Later in the chapter we will discuss how to tie the values of the tree to CFCs and other server-side data.

Dynamically Populating Ajax Controls

So far all the controls covered in this chapter have had static (or predefined) values. For example, the `<cfpod>` listing (Listing 34.6) showed the content of the pod stored directly inside the tag. Each control can instead be populated via an Ajax request, with the initial page loading in the browser first, followed by the content of the control. Let's look at the pod example to see how to move to Ajax data population. To populate the pod like this, you simply supply the source attribute. Consider Listing 34.12.

Listing 34.12 `pod2.cfm`—Ajax-Loaded Pod

```
<!---
Name:        pod2.cfm
Author:      Raymond Camden (ray@camdenfamily.com)
Description: Ajax populated pod
--->

<cfpod title="Pods with Ajax content" width="300"
     height="200" source="content1.cfm" />
```

The major change here compared to Listing 34.6 is the removal of all text from inside the `<cfpod>` tag pair. Next, a source attribute was added to the tag. When loaded in the browser, ColdFusion's Ajax code will load the contents of `content1.cfm` into the pod. The contents of `content1.cfm` are shown in Listing 34.13.

Listing 34.13 `content1.cfm`—Content for Pod

```
<!---
Name:        content1.cfm
Author:      Raymond Camden (ray@camdenfamily.com)
Description: Pod content
--->

<cfoutput>
<p>
This is the content.<br />
Here is a random number: #randRange(1,100)#
</p>
</cfoutput>
```

Listing 34.13 provides the content for the pod in Listing 34.12. A bit of randomness is used so that on multiple reloads, the content is slightly different every time. As you can see, no JavaScript code was needed. While JavaScript code was certainly generated by ColdFusion, as a developer you don't have to know a line of JavaScript to generate this Ajax-based code.

One final note about the `source` attribute and any remote source you use with ColdFusion's controls: The source must point to a local URL. This is not a ColdFusion limitation; the browser will not load data from a remote source as a security precaution.

Let's look at another example, this time using `<cfwindow>`. Listing 34.14 demonstrates how the source attribute can be added there as well.

Listing 34.14 `window2.cfm`—Ajax-Loaded Window

```
<!---
Name:        window2.cfm
Author:      Raymond Camden (ray@camdenfamily.com)
Description: Ajax-loaded window
--->

<p>
This is content on the main page.
</p>

<cfwindow title="Logon Window" center="true" width="300"
          height="300" modal="true" initShow="true"
          source="content1.cfm" />
```

As before, the main change here is the removal of the text inside the opening and closing `<cfwindow>` tags and the addition of a `source` attribute. We used the same content as in the pod example.

Let's look at yet another example. Listing 34.15 takes the earlier tab example in Listing 34.5 and mixes Ajax-loaded content with static content.

Listing 34.15 `tab3.cfm`—Ajax-Loaded Tabs

```
<!---
Name:        tab3.cfm
Author:      Raymond Camden (ray@camdenfamily.com)
Description: Tabs with ajax magic
--->

<cflayout type="tab" tabheight="200">

    <cflayoutarea title="Tab One">
    <p>
    This is the first tab.
    </>
    <form>
    Name: <input type="text" name="name"><br />
    Email: <input type="text" name="email"><br />
    <input type="submit">
    </form>
    </cflayoutarea>
```

Listing 34.15 (CONTINUED)

```
      <cflayoutarea title="Tab Two" selected="true"
              source="content1.cfm" />

      <cflayoutarea title="Tab Three"
              source="content1.cfm"
              refreshOnActivate="true" />

</cflayout>
```

Listing 34.15 is a modified version of Listing 34.5. The second and third tabs no longer have content inside. Instead, both point to content1.cfm for their source. Notice, though, that the third tab uses refreshOnActivate. By default, ColdFusion loads remote content only once, but with the use of refreshOnActive="true", the tab is reloaded each time it is activated. With the random content used in content1.cfm, you see a different number each time the tab is loaded.

Listing 34.16 presents yet another example, this time working with <cftooltip>.

Listing 34.16 tooltip2.cfm—Ajax-Loaded Tooltips

```
<!---
Name:        tooltip2.cfm
Author:      Raymond Camden (ray@camdenfamily.com)
Description: tooltip ajax example
--->

<cfloop index="x" from="1" to="5">

<cftooltip sourceForTooltip="tooltipcontent.cfm?id=#x#">
<cfoutput>
<p>
This is paragraph #x#. Mouse over the paragraph to get
interesting information about it.
</p>
</cfoutput>
</cftooltip>

</cfloop>
```

Listing 34.16 uses a simple loop to create five paragraphs of text. Each paragraph is wrapped by <cftooltip> tags. Unlike in the previous examples, instead of using a source attribute, this example uses a sourceForTooltip attribute. Although it has a different name, it acts the same as the source attribute. Listing 34.17 shows the content of the file loaded by the tooltip.

Listing 34.17 tooltipcontent.cfm—Content for Tooltip

```
<cfparam name="url.id" default="1">

<cfoutput>
<h2>Help for #url.id#</h2>
<p>
This is the dynamic help for paragraph #url.id#.
</p>
</cfoutput>
```

The tooltip content in Listing 34.17 isn't very complex. The tooltip in Listing 34.16 passed an ID, and this value is used in Listing 34.17. Although this value is simply displayed, you could load content from the database instead. Figure 34.12 shows the display of the tooltip in the browser.

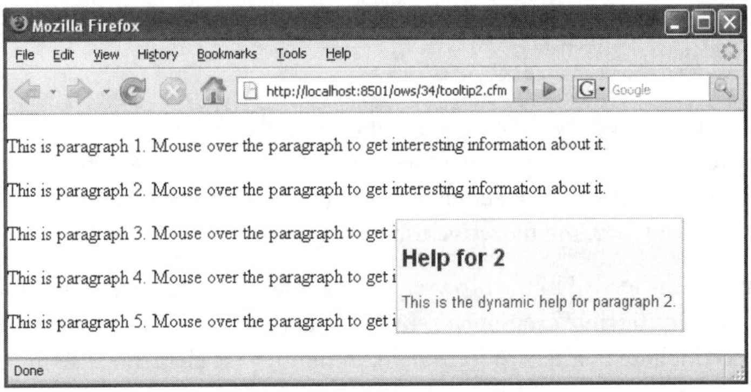

Figure 34.12

Dynamic tooltips that change with the content.

Using Bindings to Load Content

The previous examples all used the source (or a similar) attribute to load content for the controls. But as you learned in Chapter 15, ColdFusion controls can also be bound to remote data sources. In general, you can create bindings to these entities:

- ColdFusion Components
- JavaScript functions
- URLs (for example, content1.cfm)
- Other controls on the page

Bindings that point to external resources are typically specified with their type and location within one attribute. So, for example, to bind a control to a URL such as content1.cfm, you would use

```
bind="url:content1.cfm"
```

To link to a ColdFusion Component, the format would be

```
bind="cfc:someCFC.someMethod()"
```

To connect a control directly to a JavaScript function, the syntax would be

```
bind="javaScript:javascriptFunction()"
```

To introduce this concept, we will look at a new ColdFusion UI control: the <cfdiv> tag. The <cfdiv> tag creates a simple div, or block, on a page. This div is typically loaded with other content. Listing 34.18 demonstrates a simple example of <cfdiv>.

Listing 34.18   `div1.cfm`—`<cfdiv>` Example

```
<!---
Name:        div1.cfm
Author:      Raymond Camden (ray@camdenfamily.com)
Description: cfdiv example
--->

<cfdiv bind="url:content1.cfm" />
```

This template is extremely short, but if you haven't figured it out yet, most of the examples are relatively simple, and that speaks to the power of ColdFusion 8. The `<cfdiv>` tag in Listing 34.18 has one attribute: `bind`. Again, this should be familiar to you from Chapter 15. The `bind` attribute points to `content1.cfm`, the file we've used for a few sources now.

When this code is loaded in the browser, you see the same content you've seen before—nice and powerful, but not terribly exciting yet. But we can modify it to make it more dynamic. ColdFusion bindings can include pointers to form fields and other UI elements. Listing 34.19 demonstrates an Ajax-based search form.

Listing 34.19   `search1.cfm`—Ajax-Based Search

```
<!---
Name:        search1.cfm
Author:      Raymond Camden (ray@camdenfamily.com)
Description: Dynamic search example
--->

<form>
Search: <input type="text" name="search">
<input type="button" value="Search">
</form>

<cfdiv bind="url:movieresults.cfm?search={search}" />
```

Listing 34.19 uses a very simple form. Notice that there is no action or method for the `<form>` tag. Also note there is no Submit button—just a simple button. The last line is a `<cfdiv>` tag using a `bind` attribute that points to a URL: `movieresults.cfm`. Notice that it passes a value in the query string: `search`. The token `{search}` refers to the text input field named `search`. This is all it takes to bind the div to the form field. When the field changes, ColdFusion will automatically load the URL, with the value of the form field, into the div. Listing 34.20 shows the contents of `movieresults.cfm`.

Listing 34.20   `movieresults.cfm`—Search Results

```
<!---
Name:        movieresults.cfm
Author:      Raymond Camden (ray@camdenfamily.com)
Description: Dynamic search example
--->
<cfparam name="url.search" default="">

<cfinvoke component="movies" method="searchMovies"
        search="#url.search#" returnVariable="results">
```

Listing 34.20 (CONTINUED)

```
<table border="1">
   <tr>
      <td>Title</td><td>Summary</td>
   </tr>
   <cfoutput query="results">
   <tr>
      <td>#movietitle#</td>
      <td>#summary#</td>
   </tr>
   </cfoutput>
</table>
```

This template is rather simple. It takes a `url` parameter and passes it to a CFC, which performs a search against the Orange Whip Studios movie database. The results are then output in a simple table.

NOTE

For this code sample to work, you must copy `Application.cfc` and `movies.cfc` from the book Web site into the current folder.

Although this listing is slick, you may notice that the results don't change until you click somewhere on the page or on the button. By default, bindings to form fields look for a change event. If you are familiar with JavaScript, you'll recognize this as the `onChange` event. You can change the event that ColdFusion listens to by using the @ symbol and the event name, minus the `on` portion. You could change the bind in Listing 34.19 to this:

```
<cfdiv bind="url:movieresults.cfm?search={search@keypress}" />
```

This will fire off the Ajax request as soon as you start typing, providing a "filter as you type" interface to the search engine. You can find the listing for this version as `search2.cfm` at the book Web site.

Loading Content with `AjaxLink`

If you play with the loading of content within one of ColdFusion's UI elements such as the window or pod, you may notice something odd. A link will not load inside the element. Instead, it will completely overwrite the current document. If you want a link inside a pod, for example, to load inside the pod, you must use the `AjaxLink` function. Listing 34.21 demonstrates this function.

Listing 34.21 `ajaxlink1.cfm`—`AjaxLink()` Example

```
<!---
Name:        ajaxlink1.cfm
Author:      Raymond Camden (ray@camdenfamily.com)
Description: Ajax link example
--->

<cfpod title="Links">

<a href="content1.cfm">Without AjaxLink</a><br />

<cfoutput>
```

Listing 34.21 (CONTINUED)

```
<a href="#ajaxLink('content1.cfm')#">With AjaxLink</a>
</cfoutput>

</cfpod>
```

This template contains a pod with two links. The first link is a simple link. The second link uses the `AjaxLink` function to wrap the URL. If the first URL is clicked, the entire page is reloaded with the contents of `content1.cfm`. If the second link is clicked, however, the pod's content will reload with `content1.cfm`.

Working with the JavaScript API

Most of the Ajax controls discussed so far have both server-side options and an API that lets you work with them on the client side. So, for example, you can set a default selected tab using the `<cflayoutarea>` tag. But what if you want to change the selected tab with JavaScript? ColdFusion provides a set of APIs that allow you to perform many operations like this, including manipulating windows, updating tabs, and accessing the lower-level objects that make up the UI elements. A complete list of the available JavaScript APIs is available in the CFML Reference (online at `http://livedocs.adobe.com/coldfusion/8/htmldocs/help.html?content=Part_3_CFML_Ref_1.html`), but here are some of the actions possible with JavaScript APIs:

- Create windows (like those made with `<cfwindow>`)
- Load a URL into a UI element
- Disable, enable, and select tabs
- Submit forms
- Sort and refresh grids
- Reduce or expand layout areas
- Send debug messages (this action is discussed later in the chapter)

Listing 34.22 presents an example of a JavaScript API.

Listing 34.22 `jstabs.cfm`—JavaScript API Example

```
<!---
Name:        jstabs.cfm
Author:      Raymond Camden (ray@camdenfamily.com)
Description: JS Api Example
--->

<cflayout type="tab" tabheight="200" name="tabs">

    <cflayoutarea title="Tab One" name="tab1">
    <p>
    This is the first tab.
    </p>
    </cflayoutarea>
```

Listing 34.22 (CONTINUED)

```
      <cflayoutarea title="Tab Two" name="tab2">
      <p>
      This is the second tab.
      </p>
      </cflayoutarea>

   </cflayout>

   <p>
   <a href = ""
   onClick="ColdFusion.Layout.selectTab('tabs','tab1');
   return false;">select tab 1</a> /
   <a href = ""
   onClick="ColdFusion.Layout.selectTab('tabs','tab2');
   return false;">select tab 2</a>
   </p>

   <p>
   <a href = ""
   onClick="ColdFusion.Layout.enableTab('tabs','tab2');
   return false;">enable tab2</a> /
   <a href = ""
   onClick="ColdFusion.Layout.disableTab('tabs','tab2');
   return false;">disable tab2</a>
```

Listing 34.22 begins with a simple tab layout. Unlike the earlier tab examples, in this one we specifically named both the main layout and each tab. This wasn't required earlier, but it is necessary for the JavaScript API to work with the tabs. After the tabs, the first paragraph of links uses the JavaScript API function `ColdFusion.Layout.selectTab`. As you can guess, this function selects a tab. The function's first parameter is the name of the layout area, and the second parameter is the name of the tab. The next paragraph demonstrates two API functions: `ColdFusion.Layout.enableTab` and `ColdFusion.Layout.disableTab`. Again, the result is pretty obvious. If you click the disable tab link, the second tab will become dimmed and unselectable. This function even blocks the `selectTab` function.

Now let's look at a second example. You learned earlier about the `AjaxLink` function, which helps ensure that content is loaded in a UI element such as a pod or window. The API has a similar feature, shown in Listing 34.23.

Listing 34.23 `navigate.cfm`—Navigate Example

```
<!---
Name:        navigate.cfm
Author:      Raymond Camden (ray@camdenfamily.com)
Description: Navigate example
--->

<cfpod title="Load Stuff" name="mypod" />

<a href="" onClick=
"ColdFusion.navigate('content1.cfm','mypod');
return false">Load Content1</a>
```

Listing 34.23 (CONTINUED)

```
<a href="" onClick=
"ColdFusion.navigate('content2.cfm','mypod');
return false">Load Content2</a>
```

The listing begins with a simple pod. Notice that no content is defined inside the pod. Below the pod are two links. Both make use of `ColdFusion.navigate`. This function will load the contents of a URL into a UI element. In this example, the first link loads `content1.cfm` into the pod, and the second example loads `content2.cfm`. (This file is available as an electronic download at the book Web site.)

Working with `<cfajaxproxy>`

Ajax is all about connecting the front end (your browser) to the back end (ColdFusion). The closer the connection, the greater the integration possible between the two. ColdFusion 8 introduces a new tag that makes the connection between your JavaScript and ColdFusion code as close as possible. The `<cfajaxproxy>` tag has two main abilities. The first is to create a JavaScript proxy to a ColdFusion Component. The second is to easily bind a CFC, JavaScript function, or URL to a form element. Let's focus on the first feature. Table 34.5 lists the attributes we will use to create a proxy to a CFC.

Table 34.5 `<cfajaxproxy>` Attributes for Creating a CFC Proxy

ATTRIBUTE	FUNCTION
cfc	Specifies the CFC for which a proxy will be created. This CFC must be under the Web root.
jsclassname	Specifies the class name to use for the proxy.

For ColdFusion to create a proxy to a CFC, you must first ensure that the CFC is under the Web root, and you must use remote methods. Listing 34.24 creates a simple CFC that will be used for our examples.

Listing 34.24 `proxytest.cfm`—AjaxProxy Component

```
<cfcomponent>

<cffunction name="sayHello" access="remote"
        returnType="string" output="false">
  <cfargument name="name" type="string" required="true"
          default="Nameless">

  <cfreturn "Hello, #arguments.name#">
</cffunction>


</cfcomponent>
```

This code creates a simple component with just one method: `sayHello`. Note that it is marked `remote`; this is important for the JavaScript code coming in the next example, in Listing 34.25.

Listing 34.25   `ajaxproxy1.cfm—AjaxProxy Example`

```
<!---
Name:        ajaxproxy1.cfm
Author:      Raymond Camden (ray@camdenfamily.com)
Description: AjaxProxy example
--->

<cfajaxproxy cfc="proxytest" jsclassname="proxytest">

<script>
var myProxy = new proxytest();

function runProxy() {
    var name = document.getElementById("name").value;
    var result = myProxy.sayHello(name);
    alert(result);
}
</script>

<form>
<input type="text" id="name">
<input type="button" onclick="runProxy()"
       value="Run Proxy">
</form>
```

Listing 34.25 begins with the `<cfajaxproxy>` tag. The `cfc` attribute points to the CFC created in Listing 34.24, and `jsclassname` uses the same name, for simplicity. At this point, we have a JavaScript class that we can instantiate and use. The script block shows an example of this. The first line creates an instance of the class. The variable is named `myProxy`, and it can be considered a proxy to the CFC. Any remote method can be called by invoking the function within the JavaScript variable. The form at the bottom of the page contains a simple text field and a button that invokes the `runProxy` function. This function gets the `name` value from the field and then passes it to the `sayHello` method. This is the same method defined in Listing 34.24. The result is then reported. Figure 34.13 shows an example.

Figure 34.13

`<cfajaxproxy>` in action.

By default, calls to the CFC are synchronous. Thus, JavaScript makes the call to the CFC and waits for it to respond. This behavior isn't always desirable, however, especially if the call to the CFC is slow. The browser would then essentially be locked waiting for the response. Luckily, this is a behavior you can tweak. Table 34.6 lists this and other useful functions.

Table 34.6 `<cfajaxproxy>` **JavaScript Utility Functions**

FUNCTION	DESCRIPTION
setAsynchMode	Sets all calls within the proxy to be asynchronous, so that the browser will not be locked while the call is made.
setCallbackHandler	Sets the callback handler for the proxy. This is the function called whenever a remote operation is completed. If used, it sets the proxy to asynchronous.
setErrorHandler	Sets the error handler for the proxy. This is the function called whenever a remote operation throws an error. If used, it sets the proxy to asynchronous.
setForm	Tells the proxy to include the form identified in this function in all calls to the CFC.
setHTTPMethod	Sets the HTTP method for calls. The default is GET. Valid values are GET and POST.
setQueryFormat	Specifies how query data is returned. The default value (row) returns a query as an object with column names and an array of row arrays. The other value (column) tells ColdFusion to return a query in WDDX format: as an object containing the number of rows, an array of column names, and an object in which the column names are keys of the object and the values represent the rows.
setReturnFormat	Overrides the normal setting that returns data in JSON format. The default value is JSON. You can also specify plain (a simple, nonencoded string) or WDDX.
setSynchMode	Sets the proxy to work in synchronous mode. All calls made to CFCs will result in the browser's waiting for the response.

Let's look at an example that uses a few of these functions. Listing 34.26 is a new version of the CFC used in Listing 34.24.

Listing 34.26 `proxytest2.cfm`—Second `ProxyTest` CFC

```
<cfcomponent>

<cffunction name="sayHello" access="remote"
        returnType="string" output="false">
  <cfargument name="name" type="string" required="true"
         default="">
  <cfif arguments.name is "paris">
    <cfthrow message="Paris is NOT a valid name!">
  </cfif>
  <cfset sleep(1000)>
  <cfreturn "Hello, #arguments.name#">
</cffunction>
</cfcomponent>
```

This CFC is exactly like the earlier version except for two important changes. If the name value is paris, an exception will be thrown. Otherwise, the CFC will pause for 1000 milliseconds using the sleep function and then return a string.

Now consider Listing 34.27, a modified version of Listing 34.25.

Listing 34.27   ajaxproxy2.cfm—Second AjaxProxy CFC

```
<!---
Name:        ajaxproxy2.cfm
Author:      Raymond Camden (ray@camdenfamily.com)
Description: AjaxProxy example
--->

<cfajaxproxy cfc="proxytest2" jsclassname="proxytest">

<script>
var myProxy = new proxytest();
myProxy.setErrorHandler(handleError);
myProxy.setCallbackHandler(handleResult);


function handleResult(result) {
    alert(result);
}

function handleError(code,msg) {
    alert('Status Code: '+code+'\n'+'Message: '+msg);
}

function runProxy() {
    var name = document.getElementById("name").value;
    var result = myProxy.sayHello(name);
}
</script>

<form>
<input type="text" id="name">
<input type="button" onclick="runProxy()"
       value="Run Proxy">
</form>
```

Again let's focus on how this listing differs from the earlier version. The first change is that <cfajaxproxy> points to proxytest2 instead of proxytest. Next notice that within the script block, both an errorHandler and a callbackhandler are set. These will both set the proxy to asynchronous. The error handler is a function named handlerError. By default, a status code and message are passed to the method, so all the listing does is report these values.

The callback handler, handleResult, simply reports the result. Because this is a string, we should see what we saw in the earlier version. Open ajaxproxy2.cfm in your browser and enter a name. Notice that it takes a second for the result to return, but the page doesn't lock up. Then enter the name Paris. The error handler function will display the message that was used in Listing 34.26.

Using `AjaxProxy` as a Binding

As mentioned in the beginning of this section, `<cfajaxproxy>` can also be used as a binding. In this form, the tag creates a connection between a form or UI element (such as `<cftree>`) and a binding. The binding can be to a CFC, URL, or JavaScript function. You can use this approach as a simpler way to communicate with the server. Listing 34.28 demonstrates the use of the `<cfajaxproxy>` tag in this fashion.

Listing 34.28   `ajaxproxy3.cfm`—AjaxProxy as a Binding

```
<!---
Name:        ajaxproxy3.cfm
Author:      Raymond Camden (ray@camdenfamily.com)
Description: AjaxProxy example
--->
<cfajaxproxy
     bind="cfc:proxytest2.sayHello({name@keypress})"
     onError="handleError"
     onSuccess="handleResult">

<script>
function handleResult(result) {
    document.getElementById("result").innerHTML = result;
}

function handleError(code,msg) {
    alert('Status Code: '+code+'\n'+'Message: '+msg);
}
</script>

<form>
<input type="text" id="name">
</form>

<div id="result" />
```

This example begins with the `<cfajaxproxy>` tag. Instead of defining a JavaScript class name and CFC, a binding is used. The binding is to `proxytest2.cfc`, from Listing 34.26. The value from the form field is used in the binding as well the as key press event. The `onError` and `onSuccess` attributes are used to define which functions to run when an error occurs or when the binding is successful. Inside the script block, the error function, `handleError`, is the same as in the previous listing. The `handleResult` function is slightly different. Instead of using alerts, the `innerHTML` value of a `div` is updated with the result. This approach is quite a bit less annoying than the use of JavaScript alerts.

Working with JSON

JavaScript Object Notation, or JSON, provides a way to represent data in string format. In this, it is a lot like XML or WDDX, but JSON has a few advantages over XML. First, it can be quite a bit slimmer than XML; smaller data equals quicker data transfers between the server and the browser, and that's definitely a good thing. JSON also acts as a literal representation of JavaScript data. Thus, to convert JSON into "real" data, the browser just needs to evaluate it. ColdFusion 8 uses JSON for its communication between the various bits of Ajax plumbing, and for the most part, you don't have to worry about it. But if you want to get under the hood and play with JSON yourself, there are a few functions you should be aware of. The isJSON function checks whether a string represents valid JSON data, the SerializeJSON function converts ColdFusion data into JSON, and the DeserializeJSON function translates JSON back into ColdFusion data. Listing 34.29 shows a simple example.

Listing 34.29   json1.cfm—JSON Example

```
<!---
Name:        json1.cfm
Author:      Raymond Camden (ray@camdenfamily.com)
Description: JSON example
--->

<cfset string = "Jeanne,Jacob,Lynn,Noah">
<cfset array = ["Darth","Fetch","Nick","HDTV","Dharma"]>
<cfset struct = {name="Raymond",cool=true,age=34}>

<cfquery name="query"
   datasource="#application.datasource#" maxrows="4">
   select   filmid, movietitle, summary
   from    films
   order by movietitle asc
</cfquery>

<cfset json_string = serializeJSON(string)>
<cfset json_array = serializeJSON(array)>
<cfset json_struct = serializeJSON(struct)>
<cfset json_query = serializeJSON(query)>

<cfif isJSON(json_string)>
   <p>
   Yes, json_string is a JSON string.
   </p>
</cfif>

<cfoutput>
<p>
json_string=#json_string#
</p>
<p>
json_array=#json_array#
</p>
<p>
json_struct=#json_struct#
</p>
<p>
json_query=#json_query#
</p>
</cfoutput>

<cfset rString = deserializeJSON(json_string)>
<cfset rArray = deserializeJSON(json_array)>
<cfset rStruct = deserializeJSON(json_struct)>
<cfset rQuery = deserializeJSON(json_query)>
```

Listing 34.29 (CONTINUED)

```
<cfdump var="#rString#">
<cfdump var="#rArray#">
<cfdump var="#rStruct#">
<cfdump var="#rQuery#">
```

This is a rather large template, but all in all, not much is happening. First, the template creates a set of variables, including a string, an array, a structure, and a query. These are all then serialized to JSON using the serializeJSON function. Next, we test one of them, json_string, to see whether it is a valid JSON string. All the variables could have been checked, but only one is necessary here to get the point across. Next, all the variables are deserialized using deserializeJSON. Finally, the variables are all dumped to the browser. If you run this template, you will notice something odd. The query, when serialized and deserialized, becomes a structure, not a query. You can see this in Figure 34.14.

Figure 34.14

The query has become a structure.

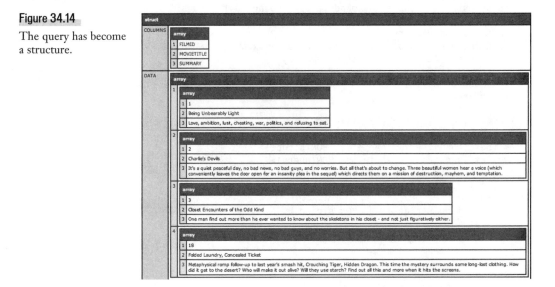

Why did this happen? A ColdFusion query doesn't translate to a native JavaScript variable. When the query was turned into JSON, it becomes an object with properties that represent the columns and rows of data. When translated back into ColdFusion, the closest representation of an object is a structure. The deserializeJSON function allows a second argument: strictMapping. It is true by default and enforces a strict conversion of data: hence, the structure. If set to false, though, the function will check whether the JSON string represents a query. If it does, then a query is created. Therefore, you can change the line

```
<cfset rQuery = deserializeJSON(json_query)>
```

to

```
<cfset rQuery = deserializeJSON(json_query,false)>
```

to get back a valid ColdFusion query.

Special Considerations for ColdFusion Ajax Applications

Although ColdFusion 8 goes out of its way to make working with Ajax applications as easy as possible, some things do require a bit of extra work. This section discusses a few special details you should be aware of.

Importing JavaScript Ajax Libraries

When you use one of the new ColdFusion 8 Ajax-related tags, the server will automatically import any JavaScript libraries needed for the code to work. But what if ColdFusion doesn't know that you are using a particular tag? Consider Listing 34.30.

Listing 34.30 ajaximport1.cfm—Ajax Import Example

```
<!---
Name:        ajaximport1.cfm
Author:      Raymond Camden (ray@camdenfamily.com)
Description: AjaxImport Test
--->

<cfpod source="tooltip2.cfm" title="cfajax import demo" />
```

This template has one line: a `<cfpod>` tag that points to one of the earlier `<cftooltip>` examples. If you run this code in your browser, though, you will get a lot of JavaScript errors.

Luckily, the error message is clear. It tells you that the imports for `<cftooltip>` are missing. It even tells you what to use: `<cfajaximport>`. As mentioned earlier, ColdFusion looks at the code to determine what JavaScript to load, but in Listing 34.30, the only tag *directly* on the page is `<cfpod>`. The pod ends up loading a page that uses `<cftooltip>`, but ColdFusion didn't know this. Luckily, the `<cfajaximport>` tag makes this problem easy to fix, as demonstrated in Listing 34.31.

Listing 34.31 ajaximport2.cfm—Ajax Import Example

```
<!---
Name:        ajaximport2.cfm
Author:      Raymond Camden (ray@camdenfamily.com)
Description: AjaxImport Test
--->
<cfajaximport tags="cftooltip">

<cfpod source="tooltip2.cfm" title="cfajax import demo" />
```

The only difference between Listings 34.31 and 34.30 is the addition of the `<cfajaximport>` tag. Because we know that `tooltip2.cfm` will need the tooltip JavaScript code, we specify `tags="cftooltip"`. If `<cfwindow>` was used as well, this could be used: `tags="cftooltip,cfwindow"`. The `<cfajaximport>` tag also allows you to specify alternative JavaScript and CSS locations.

Running Functions on Page Load

Another common task is running a set of JavaScript code when the page loads. Although this is normally a simple task, when a page is made up of a multiple Ajax-loaded items, it is more difficult to know when a page is really done. Thus, ColdFusion provides the `AjaxOnLoad` function. With this function, you simply specify the name of the function to be run, and ColdFusion will run it when the page is done: for example, `<cfset ajaxOnLoad("setup")>`.

Defining JavaScript Functions in Loaded Pages

If you are writing code for a page that will be included by another page (for example, the source for a pod or window), you must define JavaScript in a particular format. You can't use the normal "function name" format:

```
function doIt() { alert('Hi'); }
```

You must instead use this format:

```
doIt = function() { alert('Hi'); }
```

This format ensures that the functions can run properly when used inside containers such as a pod or window.

Integration with Adobe Spry

Adobe is currently working on an Ajax framework named Spry. Spry aims to make using Ajax as simple as possible, much like the Ajax tags do in ColdFusion 8. Spry focuses on working with XML, JSON, and other forms of data. It also includes widgets and effects (fade-in and fade-out, for example). The framework is free and doesn't require any server-side technology; it is completely written in JavaScript and CSS. Details on Spry can be found at `http://labs.adobe.com/technologies/spry/`. For users who want to integrate ColdFusion 8 Ajax work with Spry, ColdFusion provides the `<cfsprydataset>` tag. This tag makes it easier to bind with elements such as trees and grids. If you need to bind Spry data to one of ColdFusion's UI elements, then you should use this tag. Information about the tag can be found in the CFML Reference (online at `http://livedocs.adobe.com/coldfusion/8/htmldocs/`).

Debugging Ajax

Debugging with ColdFusion can be relatively simple, especially with the addition of a new Eclipse-based debugger in ColdFusion 8. Debugging Ajax applications can be tricky, however, especially when you have to worry about both server-side and client-side code. Luckily ColdFusion ships with an Ajax debugger to aid your development work. To begin, you must enable debug support for Ajax applications. In your ColdFusion Administrator, select Enable AJAX Debug Log Window on the Debug Output Settings page.

Ajax debugging follows the same IP restrictions as normal debugging, so ensure that your IP is listed on the Debugging IP Addresses page. Next, you have to enable debugging for the request. Visit any page that uses Ajax tags and add `?cfdebug` to the URL. Figure 34.15 shows the tab example with `?cfdebug` added to the URL. Notice the window in the upper right of the page.

Figure 34.15

The Ajax debugging window.

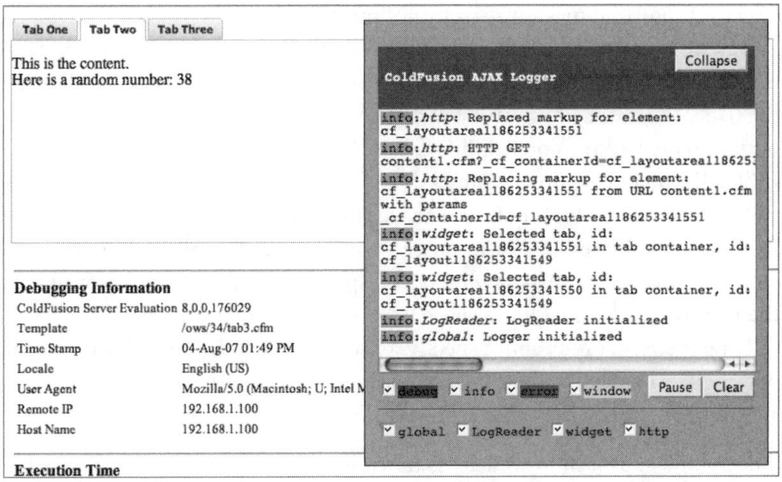

The window right away reveals a lot of information. You can see HTTP requests and other messages as the page is displayed. If you click the tabs multiple times, you will see additional messages. Along with messages that are automatically added to the window, you can use JavaScript to add your own messages. Table 34.7 lists the debugging functions available.

Table 34.7 Ajax Debugging JavaScript Utility Functions

FUNCTION	DESCRIPTION
ColdFusion.Log.debug	Logs a simple message to the debugging window. The message can include JavaScript variables. The second argument is a category value that can be any value you choose.
ColdFusion.Log.dump	Acts like the ColdFusion <cfdump> tag and dumps (converts into readable format) any JavaScript variable. This function also takes an arbitrary category attribute.
ColdFusion.Log.fin	Displays a message flagged as an information-level message in the debugging window. This function also takes an arbitrary category attribute.
ColdFusion.Log.error	Displays a message flagged as an error in the debugging window. This function also takes an arbitrary category attribute.

Implementing Security Options

Ajax applications are not any more secure or insecure simply because they are Ajax. In fact, because Ajax is the "Hot New Thing" for Web 2.0, it is safe to assume that hackers will turn quite a bit of attention to Ajax applications as a new way to attack Web sites. ColdFusion 8 has two main approaches to potential Ajax security risks.

The first approach makes use of JSON prefixes. A JSON prefix is a string that is placed in front of a JSON string. Because JSON is evaluated by the browser, this prefix essentially breaks the application. But if the client-side code is aware of the prefix, it can remove the prefix before working with the data. There are a few ways you can add a JSON prefix to your code. One way is to use a global option in the ColdFusion Administrator: Choose Server Settings > Settings > Prefix Serialized JSON With. This option creates a default prefix of //, but that can be changed. A second way to add a prefix is with `Application.cfc` variables. Two new variables can be added to the `This` scope in an `Application.cfc` file. For instance, `THIS.secureJSON` tells ColdFusion to add a prefix to JSON strings; `THIS.secureJSONPrefix` lets you specify a prefix. One more way to add a prefix is to add it at the method level. By adding `secureJSON="true"` to a CFC method, its JSON results will automatically be prefixed. (You cannot specify a prefix this way, however.) The best part of this feature is that once you've enabled it, ColdFusion automatically updates all client-side code. You don't have to do anything to remove the prefix from the code.

The second approach to security is more subtle. Imagine that you have a CFC method that is meant to be called only via Ajax, or a CFM page meant only to be used from Ajax. How can you ensure that someone doesn't open that page or call that CFC in a non-Ajax request? You have two options. For the CFC method, simple add `verifyClient="true"`. For the CFM file, add a call to the new `verifyClient` function: `<cfset verifyClient()>`. When these options are used, ColdFusion passes a special token when it makes the Ajax request. If the token is not passed, then the CFC method or CFM file will not respond. For this approach to work, you must enable session or client management. This approach should be used for any sensitive request.

CHAPTER 35

Understanding ColdFusion-Powered Flex

Traditionally, Web application development has been a matter of generating HTML from a server application language, giving you the powerful yet dangerous capability to intermix your server logic with the generated HTML. In the beginning, this is what made ColdFusion such a powerful option—-execute a query, generate a table, execute another query, generate some more HTML, and so on. This made sense in the limited world of HTML; however, with new technologies like Flex, presentation and business logic now have a clear division, with very specific bridges between the two.

The clear division of a Flex application allows you to design and build your application along the more traditional client-server model. This means clear lines between the presentation layer and the business logic. It also allows you to pass a lot of the work back to the client, so everything does not need to be done on the server—for instance, sorting and filtering are both great examples of work left on the client.

As you develop and build your ColdFusion applications with Flex, you will find that most of the ColdFusion code you write is accessed through a few specific CFC files (services) that are exposed to the Flex application and the rest of the world as a well-defined set of Web Services to power your application.

The addition of the LiveCycle Data Services (LCDS) to ColdFusion has increased your options dramatically. When Flex was created, the ColdFusion team made it a goal to make ColdFusion the easiest language you can use to build Flex applications. The LCDS Server provides three main types of interaction with the ColdFusion server:

- RPC
- REST
- Web Services

- Flash Remoting

- Data Messaging

- Publish and subscribe

The most common of these are the RPC services, specifically Flash Remoting. Flash Remoting uses a binary protocol (such as HTTP or FTP) called AMF that both the Flash Player and ColdFusion understand. Flash Remoting allows you to send data back and forth between the client and the server without needing to translate the data into some intermediate format, such as XML. This in turn removes the overhead of creating and parsing the XML and reduces the bandwidth requirements.

NOTE

Technically, you can invoke ColdFusion through REST requests and Web Services. But with Flash Remoting being a option, why? Flash Remoting is faster and easier to use. Leave REST and Web Services to the other languages that can't use Flash Remoting.

Truth be told, 80 percent of all applications need to use only Flash Remoting. Data management and the publish and subscribe functionality are very powerful, and when you need them they will be the greatest things in the world. So when should you use what?

Flash Remoting:

- All users have their own data sets, so you don't need to worry about conflicts between users.

- Your application works along the lines of the request/response model: for instance, the user clicks a button, so go to the server, get new data, and return.

Data Management:

- You have multiple users sharing and editing the same data.

- You are working with very large result sets and want to return only a subset of data at a time with the paging feature.

Publish and Subscribe:

- You need to send real-time notification of changes to many clients.

- You want to be able to push system messages to clients at any time.

All three of these features are installed and available to you in ColdFusion 8, so the decision of which to use should be based on the requirements of your application, not on the installation or software requirements.

In the next chapter, we will start by building an application with Flash Remoting and then change it to use data management and then add system notifications to the application using publish and subscribe. You will see that the differences between a Flash Remoting application and a data management application are very small, and that both are easy to use with ColdFusion.

What Is the LCDS Server?

When building Flex applications that access ColdFusion, you are actually using the Adobe Live-Cycle Data Services Server (LCDS Server) Express Edition.

NOTE
Adobe LiveCycle Data Services was previously known as Flex Data Server. It was renamed in version 2.5.1.

You can think of the role of LCDS Server as providing the plumbing layer for data between your client application (Flash) and the server-side code (ColdFusion). For instance, the LCDS Server does not have the ability to talk directly to a database. You still write the code to talk to the database in your language of choice, be it a CFC or even a Java class, but CFCs are easier to use. The LCDS Server just provides the ability for your client application to talk to your server code by going through the LCDS Server layer.

In ColdFusion 7, the integration between ColdFusion and the LCDS Server was performed by configuring two separate J2EE servers and configuring your client application to talk to one or the other. You pointed it at ColdFusion to talk to ColdFusion CFCs with Flash Remoting, or you pointed it at the LCDS Server to talk to ColdFusion with the data messaging feature or to listen for push events. However, in ColdFusion 8 the two servers have been integrated into one server, with one simple installer. This doesn't mean that the two-server option is no longer available; instead, you now have more options. The two-server configuration is still the preferred method if you are using a multi-instance configuration and want to isolate the Flex traffic to its own server, configure the JVM settings differently, or cluster the LCDS Servers differently than your ColdFusion servers. If you think about it, you can see that ColdFusion is doing the heavy lifting—querying the database, building the object, and manipulating the data. Flex is only providing the data layer between the client and the server—receiving the requests and forwarding them along. It's perfectly reasonable to assume then that your ColdFusion cluster will need to be larger than your LCDS Server cluster for the same traffic. By configuring ColdFusion and Flex as two separate server instances, you have this option.

RPC (Rest, Web Services, and Flash Remoting)

If you are familiar with the capability of the Flash application to talk to the server—a capability available since ColdFusion 6 and Flash 5—then you have heard of the product or feature called Flash Remoting. Until the LCDS Server came out, this was the only way to talk directly to a server with AMF.

Since Flash Remoting works with the request/response model—I ask for something, I get a response, I ask for something else, I get a response, and so on—it is considered an RPC type of data access.

NOTE
Wikipedia describes RPC as follows:

Remote procedure call (RPC) is a technology that allows a computer program to cause a subroutine or procedure to execute in another address space (commonly on another computer on a shared network) without the programmer explicitly coding the details for this remote interaction. That is, the programmer would write essentially the same code whether the subroutine is local to the executing program, or remote. When the software in question is written using object-oriented principles, RPC may be referred to as remote invocation or remote method invocation.

The other three types of RPC requests supported by the LCDS Server are HTTP, Web Services, and Flash Remoting. Technically, they are all HTTP requests and work over port 80; however, unlike the plain text of an HTTP request, Web Services use XML, and Flash Remoting uses a binary language called AMF (ActionScript Message Format). A key advantage of the AMF protocol is that because it's binary, the request size is smaller than for a plain text request, and you can send actual objects in the request and response data packets. You don't need to convert the objects to some simple string format, such as XML or JSON, and then back to an object on the server. This approach results in some interesting application architecture decisions and a noticeable performance advantage since you don't have the serialization and deserialization layers on the client side and again on the server side.

If you are familiar with Flash development, you may have noticed an overlap with the RPC features. Flash supports HTTP directly from the client without going through the server. While this is true sometimes, the problem is that the Flash Player has a built-in security sandbox restriction. Any Flash movie can call back to the domain that the movie was downloaded from; however, to prevent Flash from being used in any malicious way, a Flash movie cannot talk to any other server unless that server is configured specifically to allow Flash clients from other domains access. This is achieved with the `crossdomain.xml` file, which must be present in the Web root of the other servers. In the world of Web 2.0 applications and APIs, if your Flash client wants to call some of these other services being made available (Flickr, Google search, Amazon shopping, and so on), these other clients need to define their `crossdomain.xml` files for you. Some do, but many do not.

Flash support for HTTP is also limited to only GET and POST requests; however, the HTTP spec supports more methods than just GET and POST. There are PUT, DELETE, HEAD, OPTIONS, and TRACE as well. Many of the HTTP APIs available require the use of these methods, too. This is where the LCDS Server provides the plumbing. The HTTP support in the LCDS Server allows it to work as a proxy for your client applications and provides the capability to use the additional HTTP methods such as PUT and DELETE. Using the LCDS Server as a proxy also allows your Flash clients to go through the server and bypass the Flash sandbox restrictions because a Java server can call any HTTP URL. The LCDS Server provides your Flash application with support for the additional HTTP methods that may be needed.

Data Messaging

The LCDS Server data messaging functionality provides your application with true push. Unlike RPC where you need to request data to get data, data messaging allows you to send a message from a client to other clients through the LCDS Server or directly from the server to the client without the client's needing to periodically check for data.

For example, if you have a dashboard application used by the executives of your company to see the company sales figures in real time, you might use RPC and a timer to have all the dashboards check for new data every 30 seconds. As you can imagine, this is a lot of overhead and excess network traffic for nothing. However, if you use the data messaging feature, your application can send a single message to all of the connected clients when a new sale is recorded in the database, thus using network bandwidth only when something happens. With the cool Flex Charting components, the dashboard charts could be animating and changing in real time automatically. Imagine showing that application to your boss (make sure you ask for a raise when you do it).

The Flex data messaging functionality is modeled on other messaging frameworks, such as JMS in Java, using much of the same terminology and architecture. If you are familiar with these other languages, you will find Flex data messaging similar. Since Flex is a plumbing layer written on Java, you can even connect Flex to other messaging frameworks, JMS, or ColdFusion event gateways.

Like Flash Remoting, data messaging uses the AMF binary protocol to talk to the server. However, it doesn't use, by default, the HTTP protocol that Flash Remoting uses. Instead, the data messaging functionality uses a new protocol: Real-Time Messaging Protocol (RTMP). RTMP was originally developed for the Flash Media Server (originally called the Flash Communications Server) to provide audio, video, and data streaming. Unlike TCP/IP, which was designed for short bursts of traffic, RTMP was designed and optimized for thousands and thousands of concurrent connections.

Data Management

The third part of the LCDS Server data layer is the Flex data management functionality. Data management provides your application with two key pieces of functionality: data synchronization and conflict resolution. Data management is built as a layer on top of the push functionality provided by the Flex data messaging—which is how the data messaging keeps the data set in sync between clients.

Data synchronization allows you to link many clients to the same set of data (query result set, array, and so on), and when one person changes the data, all of the other clients will see the change immediately—well, as immediately as their bandwidth allows. This functionality can be clustered and scaled for a large number of connected clients.

Conflict resolution works in conjunction with the data synchronization and provides you with a client-side answer to the problem of what happens when two people try to edit and save the same data.

Imagine this: One user opens a record and changes the phone number but then gets distracted and doesn't save the record (but it's still open in the application). At the same time, another user opens the same record and edits the same phone number and saves it. Now the second user has his or her changes saved to the database, but the first client is out of sync. Flex data management comes to the rescue as the first user will get an alert saying that data—the phone number—is out of sync and allowing the user to either override this data with the new data from the second user or override the second user's changes with his or her own modifications. As you can imagine, this is a lot better experience for the user than having a form submitted back to the server, having a version ID or time stamp checked in the database, and giving the user an error message, making the user start over.

The LCDS Server does have the ability to fall back to HTTP for data messaging, but under the covers, all it is doing is adding a timer and periodically checking for new messages. This is not especially efficient, but it is guaranteed to work on all networks. RTMP requires two new ports to be open on the client's firewall. Luckily, the LCDS Server allows you to configure both protocols at the same time, so users who can use RTMP will, and users who have it blocked can default down to HTTP. This is not as great an experience but still good, and the application still works for all users.

How Does a Flex Application Communicate with ColdFusion?

Traditionally, ColdFusion and HTML were intermixed; there are even a number of tags in ColdFusion that generate HTML directly. When you want to change the HTML, you go through ColdFusion and reexecute the CFML page. However, when you are building a Flex application, the two are completely separate, with a small direct connection between the two.

Inside the Flex application, you will do everything client-side until you need to get or save new data, and then you call the ColdFusion server and execute a remote CFC method. On the server, you only create a set of services—basically one or more CFC files with all of the individual methods that your application will need to execute. This is the services layer of a service-oriented architecture. The nice side effect of building your application this way is that now you have a clean, well-defined services layer to the business side of your application. You can expose the same service to other developers in your company or in the world, and you know that the core of the application has already been built and tested, or you can use these same services next time you want to rewrite the front end of the application. You don't need to start over and rewrite the application from scratch (the database doesn't change, so why should the code that accesses the database?).

When comparing a Flex application to HTML, think of an HTML page with lots of DHTML layers, with different sections being visible or hidden at any one time, and instead of reloading the page, everything is done with Ajax calls back to the ColdFusion server. Flex works the same way, except you don't have to build your whole application in one HTML page and you have a lot more data access options than with an Ajax application (AMF, Messaging, data management, and so on).

Asynchronous Requests and Callbacks

At the core of data access in Flex is the concept of asynchronous requests, meaning that when you do call the server, Flex doesn't wait for a response. It doesn't matter if that call comes back 10 milliseconds later or 10 minutes later—Flex doesn't wait. Instead, when the server finally does return data, an ActionScript function that you wrote is called, and inside this function you can do what you need to with the result.

In a way, this is great because the Flash client doesn't wait for the response. This is why the Flex application does not stop and spin while some long-running query is being executed. The user can still move the mouse around, see a progress bar spinning, click other links, and so on—kind of like when you run batch jobs and then go to lunch. However, programming with asynchronous requests can be a little tricky when you need to execute things in sequence and you can't execute one item until the previous item is done.

No More Request/Response

The hardest part of learning how to build Flex applications for traditional Web developers—and I mean all Web developers: ColdFusion, ASP, PHP, and so on—is getting the idea of request/response out of their heads and starting to think of applications in an event-driven way. Typical Web applications work like this: I click a link (request), and the page reloads (response); I click another link (request), and a new page is loaded (response). Get this out of your head and forget about this concept of clicking a link and reloading a page. Now you're working on only the exact part of the application that you are interested in. It sounds simple, but by far this is the hardest thing for people to give up.

The interesting part of this is that events are in HTML, too, but only on form controls. So although you are probably familiar with programming a little JavaScript call when a `<select>` list changes, making this the core of the way that the application functions and changes is where things get tricky. But really, you can just think of Flex events in the same way as HTML events, except that everything in Flex has events that you can use, not just the form controls.

Session Scope

Where is the session scope? This is a common question for new Flex developers. You've just spent the last 10 years figuring out different ways to pass variables from page to page so you can remember a user: cookies, a server-side variable tied to a cookie, URL variables. However, with Flex, the application is the session. In Flex, you load one application, and as long as it is running, it maintains state. You don't need to pass variables when you switch screens.

But this doesn't mean that your server-side code can't share a session with the client. A cool side effect of how Flash works is that Flash actually uses the browser's HTTP engine when a call is made back to the server. This means that all of the cookies and browser information gets passed back and forth whenever you call the server. So if you set a cookie with `<CFCOOKIE>` every time you make a Flash Remoting request from Flex to the ColdFusion server, that same cookie is sent back each time. The CFC doesn't know if it's a CFM page or a Flash movie, and it can maintain state exactly the same way.

ColdFusion and Flex Configurations

When setting up ColdFusion and Flex, there are a number of different options, and no way to say that one is better than another. You can merge everything into one server or break up the servers and configure them separately.

What makes this possible is the remote structure of a Flex application. With standard CFM pages, the server did all the work, and it needed access to everything. However, with Flex, a lot of the application is running on the client's computer, and all the interaction with the server is done as individual HTTP requests. Just as with a request to get the HTML, in a Flex application you will have an individual request for every query, so there are lots of little requests instead of one big request.

ColdFusion Admin Settings

The ColdFusion Administrator has a new page dedicated to the integration of ColdFusion and Flex (Figure 35.1). However, most of these settings matter only if you have ColdFusion and Flex installed separately. If you have ColdFusion and Flex installed together, with the ColdFusion installer, only the first setting affects you.

- Enable Flash Remoting Support: This setting will turn on or off the ability to invoke ColdFusion CFCs with Flash Remoting. This is a security setting. If you are using CFCs with Flash Remoting and being careful about how you build your CFCs and which CFCs you put in your Web root, then you need this capability turned on. However, with this setting, you can just shut down this access so no one can build a Flash movie to call code on your server.

- Enable Remote Adobe LiveCycle Data Management Access: This is another on/off switch; however, you would disable this for performance and resource reasons instead of for security. Turning this setting off tells ColdFusion not to load the libraries it needs into memory and not to listen for RMI requests.

- Enable RMI over SSL for Data Management: This setting allows you to configure the keystore for the SSL connection between servers. This setting is useful if you have ColdFusion and Flex installed on different servers and are working with sensitive data.

- Select IP Addressesn Where LiveCycle Data Services Are Running: If you have enabled the remote data management access, this setting will let you lock this access down to a specific IP as an extra security precaution.

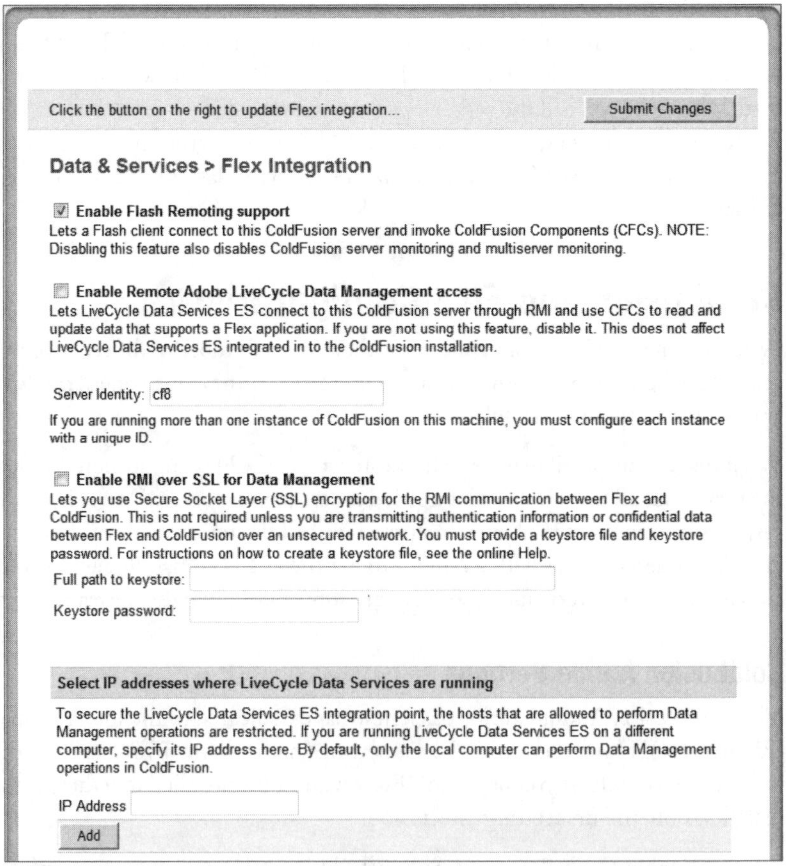

Figure 35.1

Flash Remoting and Data Services options are configured in the ColdFusion Administrator.

Click the button on the right to update Flex integration...   Submit Changes

Data & Services > Flex Integration

☑ **Enable Flash Remoting support**
Lets a Flash client connect to this ColdFusion server and invoke ColdFusion Components (CFCs). NOTE: Disabling this feature also disables ColdFusion server monitoring and multiserver monitoring.

☐ **Enable Remote Adobe LiveCycle Data Management access**
Lets LiveCycle Data Services ES connect to this ColdFusion server through RMI and use CFCs to read and update data that supports a Flex application. If you are not using this feature, disable it. This does not affect LiveCycle Data Services ES integrated in to the ColdFusion installation.

Server Identity: cf8

If you are running more than one instance of ColdFusion on this machine, you must configure each instance with a unique ID.

☐ **Enable RMI over SSL for Data Management**
Lets you use Secure Socket Layer (SSL) encryption for the RMI communication between Flex and ColdFusion. This is not required unless you are transmitting authentication information or confidential data between Flex and ColdFusion over an unsecured network. You must provide a keystore file and keystore password. For instructions on how to create a keystore file, see the online Help.

Full path to keystore:

Keystore password:

Select IP addresses where LiveCycle Data Services are running

To secure the LiveCycle Data Services ES integration point, the hosts that are allowed to perform Data Management operations are restricted. If you are running LiveCycle Data Services ES on a different computer, specify its IP address here. By default, only the local computer can perform Data Management operations in ColdFusion.

IP Address

Add

ColdFusion and Flex Together as One Server Instance

New to ColdFusion 8 is the merging of these two Adobe servers—ColdFusion and LCDS Server—in the same installer. The ColdFusion installer will install all of the files required for Flex and ColdFusion as well as modify all of the necessary Java configuration files to combine them all into one server.

If you are familiar with J2EE deployment, you should note that the installer combines the two servers under the same class loader with the same `Context-Root` and merges the `Web.xml` files instead of just deploying two J2EE applications next to each other in the same server instance.

In general, this installation is just the easier option, especially if you are installing the stand-alone version of ColdFusion. However, this approach also provides some interesting development options. Since all of the Java classes are loaded at the same level of the server (and not isolated from each other in different class loaders), you can call the Flex libraries from your ColdFusion pages, or you can call CFCs from your Java code, with CFCProxy. For instance, perhaps you want to use Hibernate for your database persistence layer, but you also want to use ColdFusion to generate PDF reports, send emails, and basically do everything else, and (here's the catch) they need to share the session scope. This is the installation you want to use to achieve this.

ColdFusion and Flex as Two Separate Server Instances

This option can mean a few things. Two J2EE applications can be deployed side by side in the same server instance with different context roots, or each server can be deployed on its own server instance. It doesn't matter if they are on the same server or a different server; the idea is that different servers are configured differently. This approach has advantages if your site requires it. You can define different resource requirements for the different servers, different security permissions, and even different hardware clusters.

It's the isolation between the two servers that makes this installation option worth looking at. By keeping the two servers independent, you have more options for configuration and updating. However, you'll need to install ColdFusion with the full version of JRun.

Note that the ColdFusion server still has Flex Express embedded in it, and all requests to Cold-Fusion CFCs with Flash Remoting go through the embedded LCDS Server in ColdFusion. ColdFusion data management and ColdFusion data push requests or Java Flash Remoting requests still need to go through the standard LCDS Server with this setup.

CHAPTER 36

Building ColdFusion-Powered Flex Applications

In Chapter 35, "Understanding ColdFusion-Powered Flex," we talked about how ColdFusion and Flex work together. Now we can start building our applications. In this chapter, we are going to build a simple master-detail application. We'll start using Flash Remoting to build a typical client application; we'll modify the application to use LiveCycle Data Services and Data Management instead.

Configuring Flex

Before we begin, there are a few configuration details you need to know about.

The `services-config.xml` File

Every application has a special configuration file you need to know about: the `\WEB-INF\flex\services-config.xml` file. This little file is the key to the whole system. This file tells the Flex server which Java classes to load for the different types of requests, the URL to use to access everything, security settings, level of logging, and so on.

NOTE

This file is used by both the Flex Builder IDE and the Flex server. Flex Builder uses the files to get the URL of the Flex server for the services you want to call. The Flex server uses it for everything else.

Channels and Destinations

The Flex server works with the concept of destinations: your CFC services that are accessed through specific channels. The protocol you use is AMF over HTTP or AMF over HTTPS. Every time you create a new CFC that you want to expose to a Flex application, you need to create a destination in the `services-config.xml` file. If you don't, Flex can't find the CFC.

However, before you start worrying about the maintenance nightmare this could become for your team, note that there is a special destination created for ColdFusion developers. The `ColdFusion` destination lets you define the path to your CFC in the code so that all your applications and all your developers can send their requests through one common destination, and no one needs to ever edit the `services-config.xml` file. Java developers can't use a common destination, so this is one more way in which ColdFusion makes building Flex applications easier than Java.

Configuring the Flash Remoting Destination

Here is a sample `<destination>` element in the `services-config.xml`. The ColdFusion destinations are made up of four sections: `channels`, `source`, `access`, and `property-case`. Only `channels` and `source` are required.

```
<destination id="ColdFusion">
    <channels>
        <channel ref="my-cfamf"/>
    </channels>
    <properties>
        <source>*</source>
        <!-- define the resolution rules and access
             level of the cfc being invoked -->
        <access>
            <!-- Use the ColdFusion mappings to find CFCs,
                 by default only CFC files under your
                 webroot can be found. -->
            <use-mappings>false</use-mappings>
            <!-- allow "public and remote" or just
                 "remote" methods to be invoked -->
            <method-access-level>remote</method-access-level>
        </access>

        <property-case>
            <!-- cfc property names -->
            <force-cfc-lowercase>false</force-cfc-lowercase>
            <!-- Query column names -->
            <force-query-lowercase>false</force-query-lowercase>
            <!-- struct keys -->
            <force-struct-lowercase>false</force-struct-lowercase>
        </property-case>
    </properties>
</destination>
```

channels

As mentioned earlier, channels are the protocols used to access a destination. Because requests to these destinations come directly from the client's computer, you don't have control over their configuration. For instance, perhaps they are behind a firewall that supports only HTTPS traffic. This is no problem; Flex supports multiple channels per destination, and the client can automatically fail over and try each one until it finds one that works. For Flash Remoting, this lack of control isn't usually a problem, since all the traffic is over HTTP. However, the data management and data push features can use the RTMP protocol, which is not on port 80, and it's very common for its port to be blocked. The `channels` feature allows Flex to use the RTMP protocol for users who can use it and to fall back to an HTTP polling protocol for the rest.

source

The `source` element specifies the path to your CFC service. In the preceding sample, the source is `*`, which is a wildcard character that tells the ColdFusion server to look in a property defined in the MXML or ActionScript code. However, if you replace `*` with a regular CFC path such as `com.services.Search`, ColdFusion ignores the ActionScript and MXML code and forces the request to this CFC. This behavior is a security precaution, so that if someone manages to upload their own Flash movie, they can't start calling any CFC they want—only the CFC exposed in the `services-config.xml` file.

access

ColdFusion considers a Flash Remoting request a remote request, meaning that it comes from outside a CFM page. Again, for security, the Flash Remoting request can access only CFC methods specifically exposed for outside use with the `access="remote"` attribute and placed under the Web root. If you can browse to it in a browser, then you can call it from a remote location. However, any other service can also call the same CFC (URL, Web Services, and so on), so to allow you to open CFCs for Flash Remoting but not as Web Services, you can change the `method-access-level` property to something other than `remote`: for example, `public`. Once you do this, Flash Remoting has the same access as a `.cfm` page, but the CFC is still not exposed as a Web Service for others to access. Should you lower this setting to `public`? There are appropriate situations in which to do so, but you also open up more CFC methods—ones that you many not want to expose. A better option might be to change the `use-mappings` setting instead and remove the CFC from your Web root. This way, the methods still have to be marked for remote access, but only Flash Remoting can find them.

property-case

ColdFusion is a case-insensitive language, and Flex is a case-sensitive language. As you might imagine, these two don't play together well. To make your life easier, you can use `property-case` settings to force all your ColdFusion variables to lowercase, giving you an absolute way to reference variables in Flash. If you are passing CFC value objects back and forth, these settings may not matter. If you pass a lot of queries, structs, and arrays back to Flash, however, these settings will be very useful.

Configuring the ColdFusion Data Messaging Destination

To set up a data messaging destination, you need to specify the channels, the component path to the assembler, the assembler scope, and the metadata identity field.

```
<destination id="ColdFusion_Example3">
    <adapter ref="coldfusion-dao"/>
    <channels>
        <channel ref="cf-dataservice-rtmp"/>
        <channel ref="cf-polling-amf"/>
```

```
        </channels>
        <properties>
            <component>ows.36.example2.components.ActorsAssembler</component>
            <scope>application</scope>
            <metadata>
                <identity property="ACTORID"/>
            </metadata>
        </properties>
    </destination>
```

channels

The `channels` property specifies the channels that the Flex client uses to access the server. The Flex client will automatically try each channel if any are blocked, for instance, by a firewall.

component

The `component` property specifies the ColdFusion dot notation path to the assembler that is required to work with the data messaging server.

scope

The `scope` property defines the caching method for the assembler CFC. If the value is `application`, the CFC will be created once, and all users will reuse the same CFC. Your other options are `session` and `request`. The `session` option creates a new instance of the assembler for each user, and `request` creates a new CFC every time. If you use `application` or `session`, be sure to test your code for any race conditions.

metadata

Data messaging handles all server calls from the client to the assembler. However, it can't do that unless it has a way to determine the status of an object and the action that is required; create or update. For Flex to do this, it needs to know which property of the CFC object maps to the primary key in the database, which is defined by the `metadata` property's `identity property` value.

Configuring the ColdFusion Data Push Destination

A data push destination is made of two elements: the ID of the ColdFusion Flex event gateway and the protocols for talking to ColdFusion. In this example, we define two channels. This tells Flex to first try the real-time RTMP protocol and, if that fails, to fall back to a built-in HTTP polling code.

```
    <destination id="ColdFusion_example4">
        <adapter ref="cfgateway" />
        <properties>
            <gatewayid>ows35_example4</gatewayid>
        </properties>

        <!-- You should use the ColdFusion specific channels -->
        <channels>
            <channel ref="cf-polling-amf"/>
```

```
        <channel ref="cf-rtmp"/>
    </channels>
</destination>
```

channels

To configure a new channel or protocol that can access a Flex server, use the `<channel-definition>` XML element. Here is the default ColdFusion channel:

```
<channel-definition id="my-cfamf"
                    class="mx.messaging.channels.AMFChannel">
<endpoint uri=http://{server.name}:{server.port}
              {context.root}/flex2gateway/"
          class="flex.messaging.endpoints.AMFEndpoint"/>
<properties>
   <polling-enabled>false</polling-enabled>
   <serialization>
      <instantiate-types>false</instantiate-types>
   </serialization>
</properties>
</channel-definition>
```

The important part of this XML is the `<endpoint>` tag. This defines the URL that the client uses to connect to Flex on the ColdFusion server. The sample includes three variables in the URL; however, you can easily hard-code the URL, too:

```
<endpoint uri="http://www.myserver.com:8500/flex2gateway/"
          class="flex.messaging.endpoints.AMFEndpoint"/>
```

These different endpoint URLs in the channel are what let a Flex application talk to a ColdFusion server for CFCs and a Flex server for Java classes in the same application.

TIP

If your application is having difficulty connecting to a ColdFusion server, make sure that the `endpoint` path and the port are correct.

Configuring Logging

In the Flex `services-config.xml` file, you can also configure the logging level for all traffic to and from ColdFusion. To do this, find the line shown here and set the level to `Error`, `Warning`, `Info`, or `Debug`.

```
<target class="flex.messaging.log.ConsoleTarget" level="Debug">
```

The default output destination of the log data is the console or the command window, but if you have ColdFusion running as a service, which is the default installation option, there is no console window for you to see. If you are familiar with the Java Log4J project, you can create your own custom output location, such as a file. An easier approach is to run ColdFusion from a command window during development.

For information about debugging, see the "Advanced Topics" section at the end of this chapter.

Configuring the Flex Builder `-services` Compiler Argument

The `services-config.xml` file contains the URLs that the client needs to use to call Flex, and the Flex server loads this file for its configuration settings, but how does the `.swf` file on the client's machine know this information? This information is provided automatically when the Flash movie is compiled. Using the `-services` compiler argument, Flex Builder loads and parses the `services-config.xml` file and pulls that `<endpoint>` value out of the XML file for the destinations you are using. Then when the Flex application needs to call the server, the movie already knows the URL to use.

To specify this setting in Flex Builder, right-click your open Flex project, choose Properties from the menu, and go to the Flex Compiler screen. This screen has a text input field labeled Additional Compiler Arguments. There, add this line:

```
-services "<path to your services-config.xml>"
```

NOTE

If you do development on a remote server, you can point Flex Builder to a local copy of `services-config.xml`. You don't have to use the exact same file; it just needs to have the same XML elements.

Configuring Your Flex Builder Project

Every new Flex project you create requires you to use the New Flex Project wizard. When you run the wizard, you will be presented with a ColdFusion-specific project type: ColdFusion Flash Remoting Service (Figure 36.1). Choose this project type, and all of the compiler arguments will be set up for you automatically. Then click Next to move on.

NOTE

If you use the Basic wizard type, you'll need to define the `-services` compiler argument yourself or use the runtime configuration described at the end of this chapter. Many people prefer to use the Basic option so that they have full control.

Figure 36.1

The Flex Builder New Flex Project wizard features explicit support for ColdFusion-powered Flex applications.

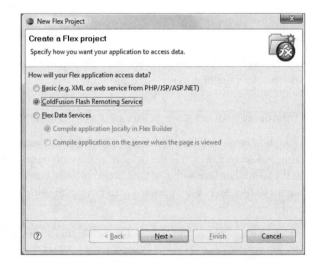

Next, you need to provide three pieces of information: the root folder, root URL, and context root (Figure 36.2). These fields allow Flex Builder to find `services-config.xml` and know how to launch the application when you run it from Flex Builder. This is the only step that is unique to the ColdFusion project wizard. The other screens are the same for all three types of new projects.

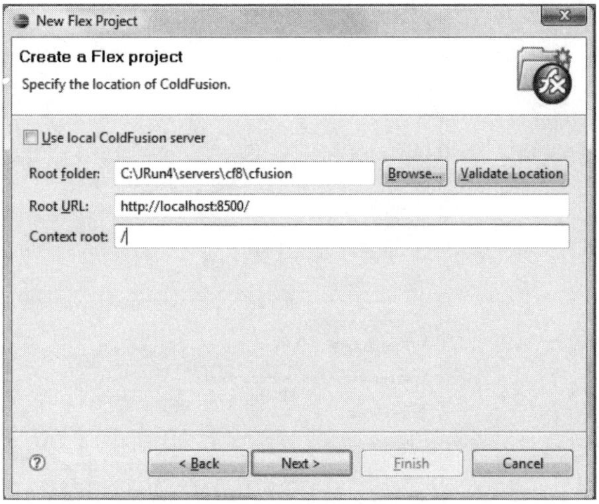

Figure 36.2

Flex Builder needs to know the location of the ColdFusion installation.

* Root Folder: This is Web root folder in your ColdFusion installation, the same folder that contains the `WEB-INF` folder.

* Root URL: This is the URL you use to browse the folder where Flex outputs the compiled movie. Usually this is a folder called `\bin` under your project root, but if you moved the default `\bin` folder or your project is in a subfolder or virtual directory, make sure that this path reflects this.

* Context Root: The stand-alone installation and the default J2EE installation use / as the context root. If you are running ColdFusion in a J2EE configuration, the root may be different.

On the next screen of the wizard, you define the name of the project and the location of your development folder: where you want the files to be created. The default location is a folder under the Eclipse workspace folder, but rarely will this be the same folder in which you do your development. Instead, it will usually be a folder under your Web root; for instance, with IIS it might be a folder under `/INETPUB/wwwroot/`.

On the final wizard screen (Figure 36.3), you can leave the defaults; however, it's considered a best practice to create a `/src` folder for your Flex files. This way, the system folders (`.settings` and `html-templates`), the compiled files, and the source files for the project are cleanly separated.

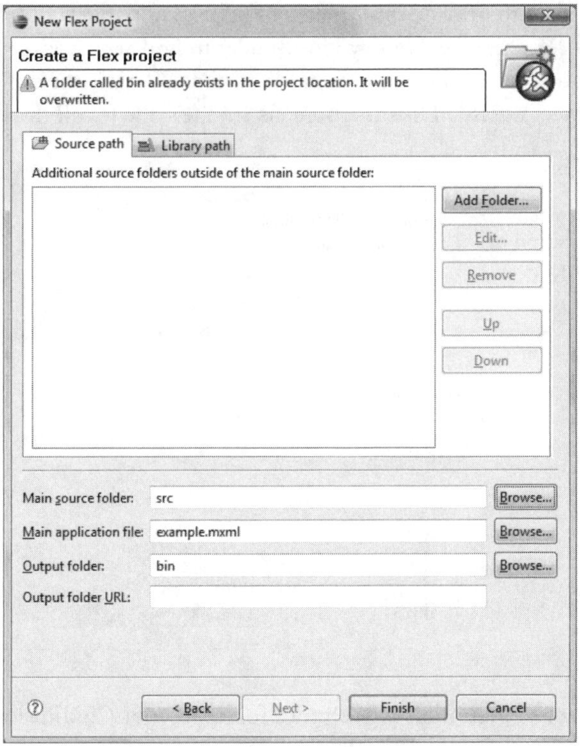

Figure 36.3

You can specify a folder to store the application source.

RPC Applications for Flash Remoting

We will now look at some RPC applications for Flash Remoting.

Populating a Data Grid

Our first application simply calls ColdFusion and displays the results of a query. You can think of this as the Flex version of the use of CFQuery and CFOUTPUT in an HTML page.

After creating our new Flex Builder project, we will create a new folder for ColdFusion components, \components, so your folder structure should look like this:

```
\project
    \bin
    \components
    \html-templates
    \src
```

NOTE

You'll notice when you compile this project that it will also copy the \components folder into the \bin folder, even though the code is not technically Flex code. This is a good thing, since you will be able to deploy just the \bin folder when you are done with development.

When starting a new Flex project, you first should define the services that the UI will access, so the first piece of code we will write is the ColdFusion component that our Flex project will access.

In the new `\components` folder, create a new file named `Example1Service.cfc` containing the code in Listing 36.1.

Listing 36.1 `Example1Service.cfc`

```
<cfcomponent alias="ows.35.example1.components.example1Service">
    <cffunction name="getData" access="remote" returnType="query">
        <cfset var qData="">

        <cfquery name="qData" datasource="ows">
        select ACTORID, NAMEFIRST, NAMELAST, AGE
        from APP.ACTORS
        </cfquery>

        <cfreturn qData/>
    </cffunction>
</cfcomponent>
```

As you can see, this CFC has one remote method with a simple query that returns the ID, age, and name of each of the actors in the database. There is nothing special about this method, nothing Flex specific; this CFC method could be called from any CFM page.

The next step in writing our application is to modify the MXML application that was created when the Flex project was created. To get our Flex application to talk to ColdFusion and to display the results of our query, we need three pieces: the remote object definition, the button to load the data, and the data grid to display the data.

First, we'll define the link between Flex and ColdFusion. To do this, we use the `<mx:RemoteObject>` tag, which defines a link between Flex and your CFC and allows Flex to call CFC methods via methods on the `RemoteObject` tag.

The source attribute of the `RemoteObject` tag is the path to CFC, just like when you call a CFC with `CFOBJECT`. However, don't forget that this source value must point to a ColdFusion component under the Web root.

```
<mx:RemoteObject id="ro"
                 destination="ColdFusion"
                 source="ows.35.example1.components.example1Service" />
```

TIP

To test your CFC mapping, take this source value and replace the period (`.`) with a slash (`/`) in your browser and make sure that you can browse the CFC. For example, in the browser the source value would be `http://localhost:8500/ows/35/example1/components/example1Service.cfc`.

Next, define a button that will call the CFC and load the data. This button has a click event, just like the HTML `onClick` event. When the button is clicked, this event calls the CFC method `.getData()` by going through the `RemoteObject` tag.

```
<mx:Button label="Load Actors"
           click="ro.getData()"/>
```

TIP

If you want this feature loaded automatically when the application starts, you can use the Flex `creationComplete` event on the application instead of the button:

```
<mx:Application xmlns:mx="http://www.adobe.com/2006/mxml"
                creationComplete="ro.getData()">
```

This is the Flex equivalent of the HTML `<body onLoad="">` event.

Next, we'll define `<mx:DataGrid>` to output our results.

When we create the grid, Flex can automatically define the columns based on the columns in the query, but this method does not allow any control of formatting or header text, so we will add child tags for each of the columns.

The `<mx:DataGrid>` grid is populated by passing in an array of objects that maps from ColdFusion as an array of structs: one struct for each row in our query.

NOTE

ColdFusion automatically performs this conversion from a query to an array of structs for you.

For the data grid to display the query returned from a ColdFusion CFC, we need to set the value of the `dataProvider` property on the Flex data grid to equal the results of our CFC method.

The `RemoteObject` tag has a special property we can use to create this binding: `lastResult`. Since Flex requests are asynchronous and multiple requests could be returned at different times in a different order, this `lastResult` property will always be the returned value from the last request sent, not the last response received. The format is remote object ID > CFC method name > `lastResult`.

```
<mx:DataGrid width="100%"
             height="100%"
             dataProvider="{ro.getData.lastResult}">
    <mx:columns>
        <mx:DataGridColumn dataField="ACTORID" headerText="id" width="50"/>
        <mx:DataGridColumn dataField="AGE" headerText="age" width="50"/>
        <mx:DataGridColumn dataField="NAMEFIRST" headerText="First Name"/>
        <mx:DataGridColumn dataField="NAMELAST" headerText="Last Name"/>
    </mx:columns>
</mx:DataGrid>
```

When you are done, the final MXML file should look like this:

```
<?xml version="1.0" encoding="utf-8"?>
<mx:Application xmlns:mx="http://www.adobe.com/2006/mxml" >

    <!-- define a connection to our CFC -->
    <mx:RemoteObject id="ro"
                     destination="ColdFusion"
                     source="ows.35.example1.components.example1Service"/>
    <mx:VBox width="100%" height="100%">
        <!--using the RemoteObject we defined we'll call our CFC method-->
        <mx:Button label="Load Actors" click="ro.getData()"/>

        <!-- Display the query that is returned from our CFC -->
```

```
            <mx:DataGrid width="100%"
                         height="100%"
                         dataProvider="{ro.getData.lastResult}">
            <mx:columns>
                <mx:DataGridColumn dataField="ACTORID"
                                   headerText="id" width="50"/>
                <mx:DataGridColumn dataField="AGE"
                                   headerText="age" width="50"/>
                <mx:DataGridColumn dataField="NAMEFIRST"
                                   headerText="First Name"/>
                <mx:DataGridColumn dataField="NAMELAST"
                                   headerText="Last Name"/>
            </mx:columns>
        </mx:DataGrid>
    </mx:VBox>
</mx:Application>
```

Adding Best-Practice Improvements to the Data Grid

The preceding application was very simple. There are a few modifications we can make to our application that don't directly change the functionality but are considered best practices.

To see these modifications, look at the \example1\src\example1a.mxml file.

The first change will be the way we define the RemoteObject tag. The RemoteObject tag allows you to specifically define each CFC method and the result and fault methods that should be called when a value is returned.

By default, Flex calls any method that you define in your code; however, the results and errors of all of the methods will share the same result and fault errors. This approach isn't desirable when you are trying to do different things with the different results—trying to put all of this logic into one method can very quickly become problematic.

To solve this problem, we can use a child tag of the <mx:RemoteObject> tag: <mx:method>. The <mx:method> tag allows you to define a different result and fault method for each ColdFusion method.

```
<mx:RemoteObject id="ro"
                 destination="ColdFusion"
                 source="ows.35.example1.components.project1Service">
    <mx:method name="getData"
               result="doGetDataResult(event)"
               fault="doErrorHandler(event)"/>
</mx:RemoteObject>
```

Instead of binding our grid to lastResult, we will bind DataGrid to a local property, which is set in the result handler of our method.

In RemoteObject, we define a result handler, with the result event as an argument:

```
result="doGetDataResult(event)"
```

Then in the doGetaDataResult(event) method, we set a local property:

```
private var qResults:ArrayCollection;
```

```
private function doGetDataResult(event:ResultEvent):void
{
    this.qResults = event.result as ArrayCollection;
}
```

Then we update the binding in `DataGrid` to this new local property:

```
<mx:DataGrid width="100%"
             height="100%"
             dataProvider="{this.qResults}">
    <mx:columns>
        <mx:DataGridColumn dataField="ACTORID" headerText="id" width="50"/>
        <mx:DataGridColumn dataField="AGE" headerText="age" width="50"/>
        <mx:DataGridColumn dataField="NAMEFIRST" headerText="First Name"/>
        <mx:DataGridColumn dataField="NAMELAST" headerText="Last Name"/>
    </mx:columns>
</mx:DataGrid>
```

Adding an Edit Form to the Data Grid

Displaying data is not enough. You need to be able to modify it, too. In this next example, we will add a pop-up edit form to the preceding application, allowing you to view and edit all the rows in your database.

To see this example, look at the \example2\src\example2.mxml file.

We will also add logic to the data grid that will call our method to launch a pop-up window with our edit form when a user double-clicks a row in the data grid.

NOTE

In Flex, a pop-up window is not another browser instance; it's just another box floating over the movie that looks like a pop-up window.

TIP

The `doubleClick` event is the only event for `DataGrid` that requires a second property, `doubleClickEnabled`, to turn on the `doubleClick` event.

```
<mx:DataGrid width="100%"
             height="100%"
             dataProvider="{this.qResults}"
             doubleClickEnabled="true"
             doubleClick="doEditActor(event)">
    <mx:columns>
        <mx:DataGridColumn dataField="ACTORID" headerText="id" width="50"/>
        <mx:DataGridColumn dataField="AGE" headerText="age" width="50"/>
        <mx:DataGridColumn dataField="NAMEFIRST" headerText="First Name"/>
        <mx:DataGridColumn dataField="NAMELAST" headerText="Last Name"/>
    </mx:columns>
</mx:DataGrid>
```

Next, we will add a new function, `doEditHandler(event)`, to handle the `DoubleClick` event. This function will use the Flex `PopUpManger` class to open a new component over the application.

```
private function doEditActor(event:Event):void
{
    // Create a new UI component.
    var popup:EditActor = new EditActor();
    popup.width = 300;
    popup.height = 400;

    // Set the actor property so the new form
    // knows which actor to edit.
    popup.actor = event.currentTarget.selectedItem;

    PopUpManager.addPopUp( popup, this, true );
    PopUpManager.centerPopUp(popup);
}
```

Finally, we'll create a new component, which will be our edit form.

TIP

A component can be more than a single MXML file, so in more complex components you may have multiple MXML files, ActionScript files, item renderers, events, commands, and so on. Thus, for good code maintainability, I recommend creating a new folder within a common /`components` folder–one for each component of your application–and then building your application with these components, like blocks stacked together.

Data Management Applications

We will now modify the preceding example to use the data management functionality to create a result set synchronized between clients. When this application is working, you will be able to open it in multiple browsers or on other servers, and when one client changes the code, all the other clients will see that change instantly.

The key difference between this example and the Flash Remoting example is that things happen automatically with data management. With Flash Remoting, you needed to code both the request and response handlers. You don't have to choose one approach or the other, however. In a large application, you likely will access some data through a synchronized result set and other data with simple one-off calls with Flash Remoting or with Web Services. One warning: You can't use data messaging and Flash Remoting on the same object; if you use data messaging to get the object, all changes have to go through data messaging, or the object will get out of sync between clients.

One server-side piece that is required to build a data management application is the assembler CFC. This CFC works like a gateway service for the Flex client and has four key functions:

- `fill`: This function returns an array populated with an array of CFC instances.

- `get`: This function returns a single CFC instance, based on the primary key ID.

- `sync`: This function is a smart method that can determine whether an object needs to be created or updated, usually by checking the primary key property of the object to see whether it has a value.

- `count`: This function is similar to the `fill()` method except that it returns a count instead of the full result set or array of CFC objects.

With these four functions, Flex can load objects, create new objects, and update existing objects. Flex decides when to invoke these methods for you based on actions and events in Flex application.

You can build the assembler CFC in either of two ways. The first, and easiest, way is to run the Create CFC wizard from the RDS plug-in in Flex Builder. We will discuss this approach later.

The second way is to write your own code, since every assembler is going to be custom to your application, database, and CFC. Let's go through the logic of what you need to write in your assembler CFC instead of looking at the actual code:

```
<cfcomponent output="false">

    <cffunction name="count" output="no"
                returntype="Numeric" access="remote">
        // These are the same param attributes that you would pass to the fill()
           method.
      <cfargument name="param" type="string" required="no">

        // 1. Run a query to get all of the items that match the parameters that are
           passed in.

        // 2. Return the #query.recordCount# variable.
    </cffunction>

    <cffunction name="fill" output="no"
                returntype="ACTORS[]" access="remote">
        // The parameters passed to the param attribute are defined by the client
           application.
        // These are usually the search parameters needed for a result set.
        <cfargument name="param" type="string" required="no">

        // 1. Run a query to get all of the items that match the parameters that are
           passed in.

        // 2. Loop over the results and create a CFC for each item in the result set.

        // 3. Add each new CFC to an array.

        // Return the new array full of CFC.
    </cffunction>

    <cffunction name="get" output="no"
                returnType="ACTORS" access="remote">
        <cfargument name="obj" type="struct" required="yes">
        // 1. Pull the primary key out of the obj argument.

        // 2. Query the database for the item matching the ID.

        // 3. Create a CFC instance for it.

        // 4. Return the CFC.
    </cffunction>

    <cffunction name="sync" output="no"
                returnType="array" access="remote">
        <cfargument name="changes" type="array" required="yes">
        // 1. Loop over the array of CFC instances.
```

```
        // 2. Check the primary key property of each CFC. If it's empty insert a new
        //    row in the database
        // and update the item with the new ID from the database insert.
        // If it's not empty, update the database instead.

        // 3. Return the array with the updated objects.
    </cffunction>
</cfcomponent>
```

Synchronizing the Data Grid

Currently, the Flash Remoting application we've built works fine for one user. However, if more than one user is looking at the same data, the users won't be able to see each other's changes without reloading the data. We can change that.

This example takes the Flash Remoting application we've already built and uses data management to create a synchronized `<mx:DataGrid>`, grid, so that when the application makes changes in one client, all the other clients will automatically see the changes immediately after.

NOTE

For this example, we are going to use the wizard to build our Assembler CFC.

First, open the ColdFusion RDS Data View Flex Builder plug-in from the Window > Views > ColdFusion menu. Then expand the list of data sources and select the ows data source. With the tables expanded, right-click the table and choose ColdFusion Wizards > Create CFC. You will see a window like the one in Figure 36.4.

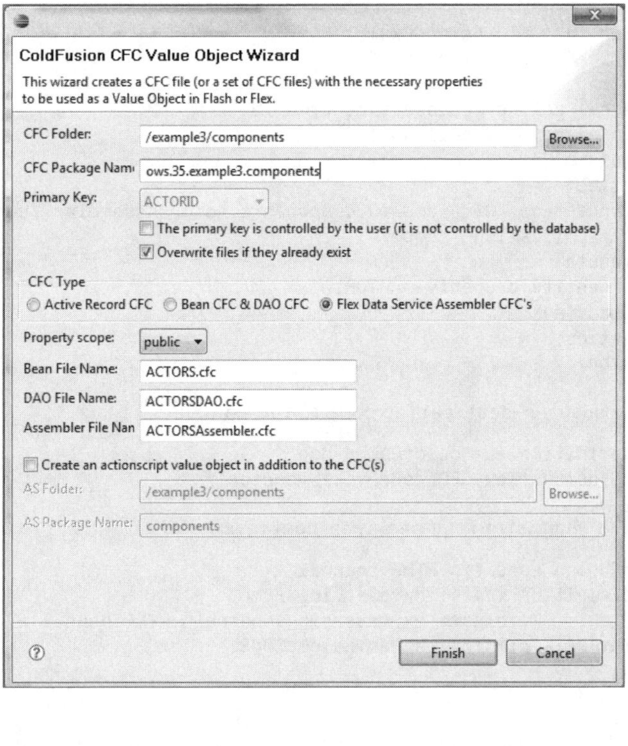

Figure 36.4

Flex Builder wizards can autogenerate CFC based on database tables.

Since we are building a data messaging application, we have to select the third CFC type: Flex Data Service Assembler CFC's. However, note that this wizard is a great tool for creating Flash Remoting applications and standard ColdFusion HTML applications, too. Because it creates two of the most common types of CFC, Active Record and Bean and DAO, you can use it with almost all of the ColdFusion frameworks that are out there.

You will need to define a path for ColdFusion CFC to be generated. A good place is in the same Flex project, but not in the \src folder where your Flex files are located. This is only reason I always use a separate \src folder for my Flex files.

You next need to change the CFC Package Name attribute. The wizard assumes that the application will be at the Web root of your Web server; however, it's common for that path to be incorrect. For instance, all of the examples in this book live three folders down, in \ows\35\example folder name, so we need to modify this setting.

Make sure that you have the Flex Data Service Assembler CFC's option selected for CFC Type. The rest of these settings you can leave as they are, but if you want to change them to follow your own naming convention, that's okay, too, and it won't change how our application works.

The next step is to configure the Flex server for our new assembler CFC. With a Flash Remoting application, we can define a reference to our CFC in the code directly. However, with a data messaging application, we need to configure a reference to our assembler CFC in the Flex services-config.xml file.

All of these files are located in the \%flex server%\WEB-INF\flex folder.

1. Add this destination to the data-management-config.xml file:

```
<destination id="ColdFusion_Example3">
    <adapter ref="coldfusion-dao"/>
    <channels>
        <channel ref="cf-dataservice-rtmp"/>
        <channel ref="cf-polling-amf"/>
    </channels>
    <properties>
        <component>ows.35.example2.components.ActorsAssembler</component>
      <scope>application</scope>
        <metadata>
            <identity property="ACTORID"/>
        </metadata>
    </properties>
</destination>
```

2. Add this adapter-destination code to the same file:

```
<adapter-definition id="coldfusion-dao"
class="coldfusion.flex.CFDataServicesAdapter"/>
```

3. Add these channels to the services-config.xml:

```
<!-- ColdFusion specific RTMP channel -->
<channel-definition id="cf-dataservice-rtmp"
                    class="mx.messaging.channels.RTMPChannel">
    <endpoint uri="rtmp://{server.name}:2048"
```

```
                    class="flex.messaging.endpoints.RTMPEndpoint"/>
    <properties>
        <idle-timeout-minutes>20</idle-timeout-minutes>
        <serialization>
            <!-- This must be turned off for any CF channel -->
            <instantiate-types>false</instantiate-types>
        </serialization>
    </properties>
</channel-definition>

<!-- ColdFusion specific HTTP channel -->
<channel-definition id="cf-polling-amf"
                    class="mx.messaging.channels.AMFChannel">
    <endpoint uri=http://{server.name}:{server.port}/
            {context.root}/messagebroker/cfamfpolling
            class="flex.messaging.endpoints.AMFEndpoint"/>
    <properties>
        <serialization>
            <!-- This must be turned off for any CF channel -->
            <instantiate-types>false</instantiate-types>
        </serialization>
        <polling-enabled>true</polling-enabled>
        <polling-interval-seconds>8</polling-interval-seconds>
    </properties>
</channel-definition>
```

4. Restart your Flex server.

In our Flex code, we need to remove the `<mx:RemoteObject>` tag that we added in the previous examples in this chapter and replace it with the `<mx:DataService>` tag. In the `<mx:DataService>` tag, you will need to set the destination to the same destination you defined in the `data-management-config.xml` file. This destination has the path to the CFC relative from the Web root.

```
<mx:DataService id="ds"
                autoCommit="false"
                autoMerge="true"
                destination="ColdFusion_Example3"/>
```

NOTE

To use FDS data messaging and the `<mx:DataService>` tag, you need to add the `fds.swc` and `rds.swc` files to your Flex project build path. You will find this project in `%FDS install folder%\frameworks\libs\fds.swc`.

The next change is a call to the CFC. In the earlier example, we called the `ro.getData()` method in our button click event. However, for data services you don't execute methods directly. Instead, you can call one of the predefined methods of the `<mx:DataService>` tag. Flex knows how to map these components to the assembler CFC methods. The first call to ColdFusion needs to be to the `fill()` method with an empty `arrayCollection` object. Flex will take this empty object and fill it with the array of CFCs returned from the CFC `fill()` method. This behavior allows you to bind to the `arrayCollection` variable before the results are returned, but note that Flex's binding mechanism will handle the results correctly when they are returned.

```
<mx:Button label="Load Actors"
           click="ds.fill(results)"/>
```

Next, we'll add a binding to the `results` variable:

```
<mx:DataGrid width="100%"
             height="100%"
             dataProvider="{this.results}">
```

At this point, if you run the application you should see `<mx:DataGrid>` populate with the results of your `fill()` method: all of the actors in the database.

The next step in our application development it to add the capability to edit these objects and see them synchronize across clients. Since our application is based on our earlier example, we already have the double-click code to open a pop-up edit form; however, we do need to change it a little. In our earlier example, we needed to call a save method to do the work. With data messaging, we don't call the server. Instead, we tell the data source to commit the changes, and the data messaging tag takes over.

First remove the `<mx:RemoteObject>` tag in the `/editActor/EditActor/EditActor.mxml` file:

```
<!--define a connection to our CFC-->
<mx:RemoteObject id="ro"
                 destination="ColdFusion"
                 source="ows.35.example1.components.project1Service">
    <mx:method name="save" result="doSaveResultHandler(event)"
               fault="doSaveFaultHandler(event)"/>
</mx:RemoteObject>
```

Now add a new property that is a reference to our `<mx:DataService>` tag instance:

```
public var dataService:DataService;
```

Next, in the `example3.mxml` file, set the `dataService` property for when we open the pop-up window:

```
private function doEditActor(event:Event):void
{
    var popup:EditActor = new EditActor();
    popup.actor = Actors(event.currentTarget.selectedItem);
    popup.dataService = this.ds;
    popup.width = 350;
    popup.height = 300;

    PopUpManager.addPopUp( popup, this, true );
    PopUpManager.centerPopUp(popup);
}
```

Now that the pop-up window has a reference to the `dataService` tag, it's easy to save the changes. We already have a `doSave()` function in this component: where we used to call the server in the earlier example. Now we just need to call the `commit()` function on the `dataService` property:

```
private function doSave():void
{
    dataService.commit();
    PopUpManager.removePopUp(this);
}
```

To see the data synchronization in action, open two or more browsers and try editing the information for an actor. When you save your changes, you will immediately see the same changes in all the open browsers.

NOTE

Flex also gives you another way to achieve this synchronization. Currently, we are explicitly deciding when to save data. However, Flex supports a function called `autoCommit`. With `autoCommit` enabled, any change you make to the data will automatically be implemented in real time. To see this function in action, remove the `dataServices` property and the `dataService.commit()` code in `EditActor.mxml`. In the file `example3.mxml`, change the `autoCommit` property of the `<mx:DataService>` tag to true.

```
<mx:DataService id="ds"
               autoCommit="true"
               autoMerge="true"
               destination="ColdFusion_Example3"/>
```

TIP

One other change you can try is to make the data grid in `example3.mxml` editable too. As you edit the data in the grid, the changes will also be saved and synchronized among all of the clients.

Adding Conflict Resolution to the Form

Now we have a synchronized data set, which is great. But what if two people edit the same item at the same time? In previous applications, there was really only one way to handle this: Before you inserted or updated the data in the database table, you needed to compare a date stamp or a version number on the server to make sure that the file hadn't changed since you pulled the record for editing. If it had, you threw an exception back to the client—not the best user experience. Luckily, Flex is smarter than this.

Flex data messaging can detect a conflict between one or more users' versions of the data and tell the users before they try to save the data.

Flex alerts the client applications with a special conflict event. In this event, you have access to the old data and the new data, allowing you to decide how to handle the event. You might not even tell the user there is a conflict and just overwrite the change with the new modifications automatically. For instance, maybe the user is a manager and always overwrites other users' changes.

You can also build a nice UI alert to show the user that the data has changed and let the user decide whether to overwrite his or her changes with the new changes or overwrite the other changes.

In `example3a.mxml`, we add a conflict handler with a UI that prompts the user for the right action.

To add a conflict handler, the first step is to add an event listener to the `<mx:DataService>` tag for the conflict event. When this `DataConflictEvent` event is triggered, it has a special `conflict` property. With this `conflict` object, Flex returns four elements: an array of the property names that were changed, the original object, your version of the object, and the modified object from the server.

```
<mx:DataService id="ds"
               autoCommit="false"
               autoMerge="true"
```

```
        destination="ColdFusion_Example3"
        conflict="dsConflictHandler(event)"  />
```

After you catch and handle this event, you can either decide which version to keep—the original or the server version—or you can make this decision automatically or by prompting the user for a decision. After the decision has been made, you will need to call one of two methods on the `DataService` object:

- `.acceptServer()`: Updates your version to match the server version.

- `.acceptClient()`: Replaces the server version with your version.

Data Messaging Applications

The third type of communication between Flex and ColdFusion is the publish and subscribe functionality, which allows Flex clients to receive messages (as strings) from the ColdFusion server or from other Flex clients, such as a chat application. You can also use this functionality to make ColdFusion and other Flex clients listen to messages being broadcast from the client. However, Flash Remoting and data messaging are usually the preferred ways to send messages back to just ColdFusion.

You might notice that data push and data messaging seem very similar to each other. They both automatically send messages between the server and the clients and from client to client. In fact, data messaging is built on top of the data messaging functionality.

A message can also be a trigger for your application to get more data. Consider the example of an executive dashboard that displays sales data in real time. Traditionally, your application would set up a timer and every 10 seconds or so ask the server if there is anything new. However, this approach can eat up a lot of bandwidth unnecessarily if nothing has changed. With the capability to subscribe to messages, every time you insert a new sale into the database, you can also send an event to all connected clients telling them to reload the data for the dashboard (charts) or send the updated data with the message and have the listener add it to the data provider directly.

In this next example, we are going to create a regular ColdFusion CFML page with a form to allow a system administrator to send a message, such as an emergency reboot of the server, to all users who are currently connected.

Creating an Event Gateway

First we need create and register a new ColdFusion event gateway. Since this example is only listening for events, this will be the easiest CFC you've ever written, shown in Listing 36.2.

Listing 36.2 empty.cfc

```
<cfcomponent>
</cfcomponent>
```

Yes, this is an empty CFC. To use an event gateway, we need to create an instance that is linked to a CFC. Since the CFC is going to process only outgoing messages, we don't need to write any functions to process the incoming events from the Flex clients.

To register our event gateway, we also need to link the gateway instance to a configuration text file. Create a new file (this is usually in the same directory as the CFC) as shown in Listing 36.3.

Listing 36.3 `example4.cfg`

```
#
# Flex event gateway configuration
#

# This is the destination of the messages.
#destination=ColdFusion_example4

# Hostname or IP address of the Flex Enterprise Server
#host=127.0.0.1
```

You'll notice that everything in this code is commented out. This is done because we are running ColdFusion and Flex together. If your Flex server is installed separately, uncomment the `host=` line and make sure that the IP address points to the location of your Flex server.

To register the new gateway instance, go to the ColdFusion Administrator, choose Event Gateways > Gateway Instances, and create a new gateway instance with the following settings:

- Gateway ID: `ows35_example4`

- Gateway type: `DataServicesMessaging`

- CFC path: The absolute path to the CFC you created

- Configuration file: The absolute path to the configuration text file you created

- Startup mode: `auto`

➜ For more information on creating, configuring and using the event gateways, see Chapter 80, "Working with Gateways," in *Adobe Cold-Fusion 8 Web Application Construction Kit, Volume 3: Advanced Application Development*.

The next step is to create our ColdFusion page and form to send the message. This CFML page has a `CFFORM` tag with a simple form handler. In the form handler, we will create a data struct to send through our event gateway. The two key items to include in this message struct are the body (the data to send) and the name of the destination defined in the `services-config.xml` file.

Notice that in the `body` variable, we are creating another struct to send to Flex instead of a string. You can send any ColdFusion data type in the body (strings, dates, structs, arrays, CFC instances, and so on). In this example, shown in Listing 36.4, we are sending the two form fields: `msgType` and `message`.

Listing 36.4 `gatewaytest.cfm`

```
<CFIF isDefined("form.submit")>
   <cfset flexMesssage = StructNew()>

   <cfset messageObject = structNew()>
   <cfset messageObject.message = form.message>
   <cfset messageObject.type = form.msgType>
```

Listing 36.4 (CONTINUED)

```
    <cfset flexMesssage.body = messageObject>

    <cfset flexMesssage.Destination = "ColdFusion_example4">
    <cfset ret = SendGatewayMessage("ows35_example4", flexMesssage)>
    <p>Message has been sent!</p>
</CFIF>

<CFFORM>
    <b>Type:</b>
    <CFINPUT type="radio" name="msgType" value="Information" selected="true">
    <CFINPUT type="radio" name="msgType" value="Warning">
    <CFINPUT type="radio" name="msgType" value="Error">
    <b>Message</b><br/>
    <CFTEXTAREA  id="message" name="message" rows="6" cols="50"/><br/>
    <CFINPUT type="submit" name="submit" value="Send Message">
</CFFORM>
```

Now we need to modify our Flex application. We'll build on the example in the preceding section; however, you can add this modification to any of the other examples in this chapter.

First we'll add the `<mx:Consumer>` tag to our application and link it to our `ColdFusion_example4` destination, defined in `services-config.xml`. We also need to give the tag an ID to reference later and register a function that will be called whenever a message is received.

```
<!--
Create a listener for ColdFusion messages
-->
<mx:Consumer id="consumer"
             destination="ColdFusion_example4"
             message="doMessageReceivedHandler(event)"/>
```

Next we need to create the `doMessageReceivedHandler` function. To keep this example simple, our new function will just display an alert with the message.

```
private function doMessageReceivedHandler(event:MessageEvent):void
{
    Alert.show(event.message.body.message, event.message.body.type);
}
```

Finally, we need to start the consumer. To do this, we will use the `creationComplete` event of the application to have the consumer subscribe itself to the server. When it does, the Flex application starts listening for events.

```
<mx:Application xmlns:mx="http://www.adobe.com/2006/mxml"
                creationComplete="consumer.subscribe()"
                layout="vertical" >
```

Advanced Topics

We've covered the basics. We'll now take a quick look at some advanced topics.

Debugging

As with any programming language, you can't do much if you don't have a way to debug your code. There are at least four ways to debug your Flex application, two of which require a separate application. You can use console output, ColdFusion debugging, a packet sniffer, and the new ColdFusion Debugging plug-in in Flex Builder.

Console Output

When developing your Flex application, run ColdFusion from a command prompt in a console window instead of running ColdFusion as a service. Watching the traffic going in and out can be very useful—so much so that you may want to always start your ColdFusion and Flex servers from a command prompt during development.

To see the Flex, traffic you need to change the Flex logging level to Debug. This setting is configured in \WEB-INF\flex\services-config.xml.

```
<logging>
    <target class="flex.messaging.log.ConsoleTarget" level="Debug">
        <properties>
            <prefix>[Flex] </prefix>
            <includeDate>false</includeDate>
            <includeTime>false</includeTime>
            <includeLevel>false</includeLevel>
            <includeCategory>false</includeCategory>
        </properties>
        <filters>
            <pattern>Endpoint.*</pattern>
            <pattern>Service.*</pattern>
            <pattern>Configuration</pattern>
            <pattern>Message.*</pattern>
        </filters>
    </target>
</logging>
```

There are a number of tweaks you can make to the logging settings. If you are curious, check the Flex documentation for descriptions of these settings. However, the default settings in most situations work great.

ColdFusion has startup scripts located in the \%install location%\bin folder. These are the exact same scripts that ColdFusion uses when it starts ColdFusion as a service. In the command window, this script is named cfstart.bat.

Open a command window (choose Start > Run and type cmd). Browse to your ColdFusion installation directory and run the ColdFusion start script.

When you run ColdFusion and Flex from a command window, you will see a lot of output from Flex, but most of the time, you should look for messages that start with one of these two strings (request = incoming and response = outgoing):

```
[Flex] Deserializing AMF/HTTP request
[Flex] Serializing AMF/HTTP response
```

Here is a sample request going into Flex. Most of the properties listed here are internal Flex properties; however, there are three that will matter to you: source will tell you what CFC is being invoked, operation will tell you the method name, and body will tell you the method arguments, if any, being passed in.

```
[Flex] Deserializing AMF/HTTP request
Version: 3
  (Message #0 targetURI=null, responseURI=/6)
    (Array #0)
      [0] = (Typed Object #0 'flex.messaging.messages.RemotingMessage')
        source = "ows.35.example2.components.exampleService"
        operation = "getData"
        messageId = "17D2C76D-C1A8-98E1-58EB-0EEF673F54ED"
        body = (Array #1)
        timeToLive = 0
        clientId = "F87123ED-040A-3CF2-321C-FA19C732C6AE"
        headers = (Object #2)
          DSEndpoint = "my-cfamf"
        destination = "ColdFusion"
        timestamp = 0
```

Here is a sample response coming out of ColdFusion and back to Flex. This example returns a query of two rows. As you can see, a query is returned as a flex.messaging.io.ArrayCollection data type, which is an array of objects.

```
[Flex] Serializing AMF/HTTP response
Version: 3
  (Message #0 targetURI=/6/onResult, responseURI=)
    (Typed Object #0 'flex.messaging.messages.AcknowledgeMessage')
      timestamp = 1.185661549358E12
      headers = (Object #1)
      body = (Externalizable Object #2 'flex.messaging.io.ArrayCollection')
        (Array #3)
          [0] = (Object #4)
            AGE = 56
            NAMEFIRST = "Sean"
            NAMELAST = "Conway"
            ACTORID = 1
          [1] = (Object #5)
            AGE = 45
            NAMEFIRST = "Harry5"
            NAMELAST = "Floyd4"
            ACTORID = 2
      correlationId = "17D2C76D-C1A8-98E1-58EB-0EEF673F54ED"
      messageId = "F876ABBB-4E08-C3CA-1E34-0198DBB06D47"
      timeToLive = 0.0
      clientId = "F87123ED-040A-3CF2-321C-FA19C732C6AE"
      destination = null
```

By using the console output for debugging, you can easily home in on a problem while debugging. If you see data going in and out of ColdFusion, then you know the problem is on the Flex side. If you see data going in but nothing coming out, or error messages in the console, then you know the problem is on the ColdFusion side. Also, the use of the console will help you handle simple case sensitivity issues. For instance, if you created your bindings with lowercase column names and nothing is showing up but you do see data coming in and out of ColdFusion, then you can use this console output to confirm the case of the column name binding variables in your Flex application. You should always be mindful of case sensitivity because it's very easy to flip the case of a property in memory without affecting your ColdFusion code.

TIP

> For Windows users, make sure that you increase the command window screen buffer size so you can scroll back up and see the debugging data.

ColdFusion Debugging

One of the biggest advantages of ColdFusion over other languages is the richness of the debugging data you get with every request to a CFML page. You know it well: it's all of the data at the bottom of every CFML page you run—if you have debugging enabled. With Flex 2.0 and ColdFusion 7.0.2, this same data is also available with every Flash Remoting request you make to ColdFusion. Remember, as far as ColdFusion is concerned, there is no difference between a CFML page being processed and a CFC method being called from a Flex application.

To see this debugging data, all you need to do is turn on debugging in the ColdFusion Administrator, just as with any other page. Nothing will change on the client, but all the data will be returned to the client, for you to look at if you want.

CAUTION

> If you turn on debugging, so much data will be returned to the Flex application that you will not be able to use the console for debugging.

To get access to this debugging data, you need to look in the `ResultEvent` object that is returned to your Flash Remoting result method. ColdFusion puts all of the debugging data in the header of the returned event. For instance, the following code dumps all of that data into an alert box. Dumping all the debugging data into an alert box isn't practical because there will be a lot more data that an alert can handle, but this simple example will get you started; later, you can build a custom control to format this data.

```
private function doResult(event:ResultEvent):void
{
var results = event.result;
   if( event.message.headers.debug != null )
   {
      var debugData = event.message.headers.debug
      Alert.show(ObjectUtil.toString(debugData));
   }
}
```

TIP

> If you don't want to write your own control, you can download, for free, a `DebugPanel` component from `http://www.mikenimer.com`. This component has custom formatters specifically for the ColdFusion debugging data, though it can handle any type of data. You can think of it as a `CFDump` tag for Flex.

Packet Sniffer

If you are working in an environment where you can't run ColdFusion from a command line—for instance, on a shared development server instead of on your own, local machine—you can use one of the many third-party sniffer applications available on the Web. ColdFusion ships with an IP sniffer called `sniffer.exe`. Depending on how you install ColdFusion, this program is in either the ColdFusion \bin folder or the JRun \bin folder. The `sniffer.exe` program can be a pain to use, however. It uses port forwarding, so that you need to modify your code to send all Flash Remoting requests to a new port and then let `sniffer.exe` forward the requests to the right port.

There is an easier solution: You can use a sniffer that works as a proxy for your browser. With such a sniffer, any requests from Internet Explorer or Firefox will be logged. A good sniffer to try is Service Capture. A simple Google search will find the latest version. Service Capture is smart enough to understand many formats—SOAP, JSON, XML, and the Flash AMF protocol—so you can see the data you are passing in and the data being returned with Flash Remoting. The `sniffer.exe` program will show you only the binary data that is passed back and forth between the client and the server.

Another sniffer frequently used by members of the Flex community is called Charles.

TIP
Any packet sniffer will help, but using one that understands AMF will make a big difference in your debugging work.

Flex Builder and ColdFusion Line Debuggers

Another option for debugging is a line-by-line debugger. For the client side, you can use Flex Builder to start your application in debugging mode and insert a breakpoint in your result method to see what is being sent back from ColdFusion.

For the server side, there is a new feature in ColdFusion 8: the Eclipse Debug plug-in. By running the plug-in inside Flex Builder, you can connect to a running instance of ColdFusion and insert a breakpoint in the CFC that is invoked with Flash Remoting to see what is being passed to ColdFusion.

If you have enough RAM, you can run both of these options together.

Value Objects

One of the main advantages to using Flash Remoting instead of a simple Web Service or XML REST service is support for value objects. A value object, also called data transfer objects (DTOs), is a pattern for passing class and CFC instances between languages. For instance, suppose that you have a Product CFC on the server side and all of the logic needed to create new instances, update existing instances, or return an instance of Product. It makes sense that if you are working with a Product object on the server, you will want to work with the same Product objects in your Flex application and not deal with the XML needed to transfer the objects back and forth and the logic needed to re-create the Product object.

The data messaging examples use this technique, and it works just as well with Flash Remoting. Instead of returning a query, they can just as easily return an array of CFC instances. Just change the first example in this chapter, in the section "Populating a Data Grid," so that it uses CFC instances instead of a query.

Adobe Flash Player and the Flex server work together to make this translation between server and client transparent to you for ColdFusion CFC and Java classes only. For all other languages, a translation layer needs to be written—another reason why ColdFusion provides the easiest way to build the back end of Flex applications.

After the proper linking is in place, when a ColdFusion CFC is returned, it will arrive in the result method as a Product AS class. The same is true the other way: If your CFC requires a Product CFC instance as an argument, you can create a new AS Product class and pass it as an argument to your CFC method (when you invoke the CFC with the `<mx:RemoteObject>` tag); it will automatically be converted to a Product CFC when it gets to ColdFusion.

You need to do a few things to set up this linking correctly. Once they are done, you won't need to worry about this again.

First, you must make sure that the property names—spelling, including case—and data types match exactly. The tricky part is that ColdFusion is typeless (everything is a string) and case insensitive, and AS3 in Flex is the strongly typed and case sensitive—not conducive to one-to-one mapping. To ensure a strong linkage without any chance that ColdFusion will guess wrong while it tries to perform the translation, use the `cfproperty` tag in your ColdFusion CFC. Until now, `cfproperty` was used only for documentation, but with Flash Remoting, the `cfproperty` tag is also your contract with Flash. ColdFusion will use the case of the `name` attribute and will convert the data, if possible, to the type of data defined by the `type` attribute.

```
<cfproperty name="ACTORID" type="numeric" default="0">
<cfproperty name="NAMEFIRST" type="string" default="">
```

The second task you need to do is define the path and name of the CFC with the `alias` attribute of the `cfcomponent` tag. ColdFusion provides a number of options for finding a CFC: in the same directory, under the Web root, under a `CFMAPPING` folder, or in your custom tags folder. The problem is that ColdFusion will use the path to the location of the CFC to define the alias of your CFC.

You might get lucky and link Flash and ColdFusion with the right paths; however, it's easy to break this link—all it takes is the addition of a new virtual directory or a new `CFMAPPING` definition, and ColdFusion suddenly finds the same CFC from a new direction and changes the metadata alias for the CFC.

To lock the path so the link can never suddenly change on you, define an alias for your ColdFusion Component and set this `alias` attribute to the exact same path you use in a `CFOBJECT` or `CREATE-OBJECT()` call when you invoke the CFC.

Using the application in "Creating an Event Gateway" as a basis, Listing 36.5 shows a sample CFC with the `alias` and the `cfproperty` tags defined.

Listing 36.5 `actors.cfc`

```
<cfcomponent output="false"
             alias="ows.35.example4.components.ACTORS">
  <cfproperty name="ACTORID" type="numeric" default="0">
  <cfproperty name="NAMEFIRST" type="string" default="">
  <cfproperty name="NAMELAST" type="string" default="">
  <cfproperty name="AGE" type="numeric" default="0">
  <cfproperty name="NAMEFIRSTREAL" type="string" default="">
  <cfproperty name="NAMELASTREAL" type="string" default="">
  <cfproperty name="AGEREAL" type="numeric" default="0">
  <cfproperty name="ISEGOMANIAC" type="numeric" default="0">
  <cfproperty name="ISTOTALBABE" type="numeric" default="0">
  <cfproperty name="GENDER" type="string" default="">

  <cfscript>
  // set the default values,
  // notice that the case of the property doesn't matter
  this.actorid = 0;
  this.nameFirst = "";
  this.nameLast = "";
  this.age = 0;
  this.nameFirstRead = "";
  this.nameLastReal = "";
  this.ageReal = 0;
  this.isEgoManiac = 0;
  this.isTotalBase = 0;
  this.gender = "";
  </cfscript>

</cfcomponent>
```

Now to link from the Flex side, you need to perform the same two tasks, but a little differently. First, define the properties with the matching data type and case of the CFPROPERTY tags:

```
public var ACTORID:Number = 0;
public var NAMEFIRST:String = "";
```

Next, remote the same `alias` attribute in the AS class, using the AS3 metadata tag `RemoteClass`. Note that the string in the `alias` attribute must be exactly the same as the alias in the CFC (including the case), and the alias must be a valid path that the CFC can use to invoke the CFC.

```
[RemoteClass(alias="ows.35.example3.components.ACTORS")]
```

Listing 36.6 shows the complete AS class that matches Listing 36.5.

Listing 36.6 `Actors.as`

```
package model.beans
{
    [RemoteClass(alias="ows.35.example3.components.ACTORS")]
    [Managed]
    public class Actors
    {
        public var ACTORID:Number = 0;
        public var NAMEFIRST:String = "";
        public var NAMELAST:String = "";
```

Listing 36.6 (CONTINUED)

```
        public var AGE:Number = 0;
        public var NAMEFIRSTREAL:String = "";
        public var NAMELASTREAL:String = "";
        public var AGEREAL:Number = 0;
        public var ISEGOMANIAC:Number = 0;
        public var ISTOTALBABE:Number = 0;
        public var GENDER:String = "";
    }
}
```

With this link set up, you can now work in straight OOP and pass objects back and forth instead of first creating generic structs and queries of the data.

TIP

Flash will link only if AS code that it knows is used, and it won't know about the AS class unless you reference it in your code as a data type for a variable or use it in a cast. So if you set up everything but your CFC isn't converted to the right AS class, add a `temp` variable so the compiler will make sure to include your AS class. This approach guarantees that the class is available at runtime. It doesn't matter where you put this variable as long as it's in the source code somewhere:

```
var  _t1:Actors;
```

Flex Builder Wizards

Along with building a server, the ColdFusion team has built a number of Eclipse plug-ins that can work with Flex Builder to help ColdFusion developers build applications even faster with Flex. If you're keeping a list, this is another reason that ColdFusion provides the easiest way to build Flex applications.

A number of plug-ins are available: an RDS database viewer, a CFC generator based on a database table, a CFC-to-AS generator, an AS-to-CFC generator, a services browser, and a line-by-line debugger. All of these plug-ins can be opened from the Window > Show Views > ColdFusion menu in Flex Builder.

- RDS Data View: If you're a former HomeSite user, this plug-in will be familiar to you. It's as close as possible to the database browser in HomeSite. This plug-in lets you view the data sources registered in ColdFusion along with the tables and columns.

- Create CFC Wizard: You invoke this wizard by right-clicking a table in the RDS Data View plug-in. This wizard automatically generates the CFC files and SQL queries needed to work with data in a specific table, and it can create the CFCs in three ways following two different patterns.

NOTE

The Create CFC Wizard plug-in can generate CFCs against only one table. If you need to run a more complex query, such as a join to get the data for a CFC, you can run this wizard against the main table and then modify the SQL and properties as needed.

- CFC-to-AS Wizard: If you create your CFCs first, you can use this simple wizard to create matching AS class value objects.

- AS-to-CFC Wizard: If you create your AS classes first, you can use this wizard to create matching CFC value objects.

- Services Browser: This plug-in lets you browse all of the CFCs and the methods on a server (using your RDS connection), to see what's available. You can also use it to parse a WSDL file and see all of the methods available for your to use. If you don't know what services you can call or how can you build an application, the Services Browser plug-in can help.

- Line-by-Line Debugger: This plug-in, new in ColdFusion 8, allows you to connect your Eclipse IDE to a running server instance of ColdFusion. Once this link is made, you can insert breakpoints in your ColdFusion and pause the processing of your ColdFusion code while you figure out what is happening: what arguments are coming in or out, the results of a query, the value of a variable, and so on.

Creating Presentations

Presentations are a part of our lives. If you've sat through one Microsoft PowerPoint presentation, you've sat through a hundred. While these presentations may not always be exciting, they can be an effective way to present information for educational, commercial, or even entertainment purposes. ColdFusion 8 adds a great new way to create presentations. These presentations need not be static, boring affairs but can be fully dynamic. Want to include sales figures? You can add the latest, up-to-the-minute figures when the presentation is requested. Want to include current stock prices? Use the new tags introduced in ColdFusion 8.

Presenting <cfpresentation>

ColdFusion 8 introduces three new tags to work with presentations. The first and most important tag is the <cfpresentation> tag. All presentations begin and end with <cfpresentation>. Table 37.1 lists the main attributes of the tag.

Table 37.1   Main <cfpresentation> Attributes

ATTRIBUTE	FUNCTION
title	Specifies the title of the presentation.
autoplay	Determines whether the presentation starts automatically. The default value is true.
control	Specifies the type of control to use in the presentation. Valid values are normal and brief. The default is normal.
controlLocation	Indicates the location of the controls. Valid values are left and right. The default is right.
directory	Specifies the directory in which to store the presentation. This attribute is optional; if it is not specified, the presentation will play in the browser.

Table 37.1 (CONTINUED)

ATTRIBUTE	FUNCTION
initialTab	Indicates the selected tab in the control area. The valid values are outline, search, and notes. The default is outline.
loop	Specifies whether the presentation should loop. The default value is false.
overwrite	If the directory option is used, specifies whether the files should be overwritten. The default value is yes.
showNotes, showOutline, showSearch	Determine whether the Notes, Outline, and Search tabs are visible.

By itself, the <cfpresentation> tag can't do much. To complete the presentation, you need to add slides. As you can probably guess, this is done with <cfpresentationslide>. Slides can be made with HTML or ColdFusion or using an external source such as an Adobe Flash SWF file or even a remote URL. You can also bind MP3 audio tracks to slides to provide narration or background music to the slide. Table 37.2 lists the main attributes for <cfpresentationslide>.

Table 37.2 Main <cfpresentationslide> Attributes

ATTRIBUTE	FUNCTION
advance	Allows you to override the autoPlay setting of <cfpresentation>. Valid values are auto, never, and click. If set to auto, the slide will automatically advance to the next slide. This will be the default if autoPlay is set to true. If set to never, the slide will not advance unless the user clicks the Advance button. If set to click, the entire slide becomes clickable, and clicking will advance the slide.
audio	Specifies the path to an MP3 file; cannot be used with video.
duration	Specifies the duration of the slide. If an MP3 file is used, the duration of the slide will default to the length of the MP3 file.
notes	Specifies notes to include with a slide.
presenter	Specifies the presenter associated with a slide; relates to the <cfpresenter> tag that will be discussed later.
scale	If HTML content is used for the slide, determines how much the content is scaled to fit into the presentation. Valid values are 0 to 1.
src	Specifies the source of the slide; used only if content is not provided in the <cfpresentationslide> slide. This attribute can point to content at either an absolute or relative path. A remote URL can also be used. If a SWF file is used, it must be served by a ColdFusion system.
title	Specifies the title of the slide.
video	Specifies a video to use for the presenter for the slide; cannot be used with audio. The video must be a SWF or FLV file and must be local to the file system.

Now that we've covered the basic attributes of the <cfpresentation> and <cfpresentationslide> tags, let's look at a simple example in Listing 37.1.

Listing 37.1   example1.cfm—Basic Presentation

```
<!---
Name:        example1.cfm
Author:      Raymond Camden (ray@camdenfamily.com)
Description: First presentation
--->

<cfpresentation title="First Presentation"
             autoPlay="false">

    <cfpresentationslide title="Welcome to CFPRESENTATION"
                   notes="These are some notes.">
<h1>Welcome to CFPRESENTATION</h1>

<p>
This is content for the first slide. I can include HTML
and it will be rendered by the presentation.
</p>
    </cfpresentationslide>

    <cfpresentationslide title="Sales Figures"
           notes="These are some notes for slide two.">
<h1>Sales Figures</h1>

<p>
Some fake data.
</p>

<p>
<table width="100%" border="1">
<tr>
    <th>Product</th>
    <th>Price</th>
</tr>
<tr>
    <td>Apples</td><td>$0.99</td>
</tr>
<tr>
    <td>Bananas</td><td>$1.99</td>
</tr>
<tr>
    <td>Nukes</td><td>$2.99</td>
</tr>
</table>
</p>
    </cfpresentationslide>
</cfpresentation>
```

Listing 37.1 is a simple presentation. It contains two slides, both of which contain simple, static text. You can see the result in Figure 37.1.

Figure 37.1

Simple presentation.

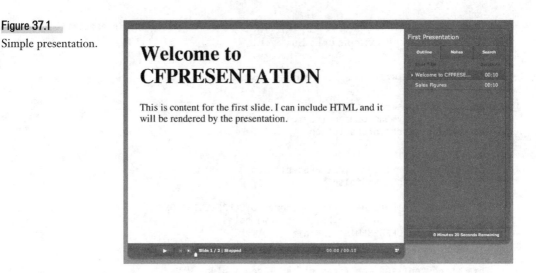

Now let's take a look at a truly dynamic presentation. Orange Whip Studios produces quite a few films. What if the company wants to create a presentation that shows its body of work? Listing 37.2 creates a simple portfolio. What's nice is that whenever a film is added to the database, the portfolio is automatically updated.

Listing 37.2 example2.cfm—Dynamic Presentation

```
<!---
Name:        example2.cfm
Author:      Raymond Camden (ray@camdenfamily.com)
Description: Dynamic presentation
--->

<cfquery name="getMovies" datasource="ows">
select   f.movietitle, f.pitchtext, f.amountbudgeted,
     f.summary, f.imagename, f.dateintheaters,
     r.rating
from  films f, filmsratings r
where f.ratingid = r.ratingid
</cfquery>

<cfpresentation title="Orange Whip Studios - Films"
            autoPlay="false">
   <cfpresentationslide
      title="Welcome to Orange Whip Studios"
            >
<h1>Welcome to Orange Whip Studios</h1>

<p>
Here is the latest gallery of our films.
</p>
   </cfpresentationslide>

   <cfloop query="getMovies">
      <cfpresentationslide title="#movietitle#">
```

Listing 37.2 (CONTINUED)

```
<cfoutput>
<h2>#movietitle#</h2>

<p>
<cfif len(trim(imagename))>
<img src="../images/#imagename#" align="right">
</cfif>
<b>Rating:</b> #rating#<br />
<b>Budget:</b> #dollarFormat(amountbudgeted)#<br />
<b>Date:</b>
#dateFormat(dateintheaters,"mmmm d, yyyy")#<br />
<b>Pitch:</b> #pitchtext#
</p>

<p>
<b>Summary:</b> #summary#
</p>
</cfoutput>

        </cfpresentationslide>

    </cfloop>

</cfpresentation>
```

Listing 37.2 begins with a query that gets information about the films from the Orange Whip Studios database. Normally this query should be in a ColdFusion Component, but it is included here for simplicity. The presentation begins with an introduction slide. After that, the query is used to generate dynamic slides. Each slide contains information about the movie, including an optional image. The code could be expanded even further to show directors, actors, and the budget, but the code as it is now gives a nice overview of the films. Figure 37.2 shows the presentation.

Figure 37.2

Dynamic presentation.

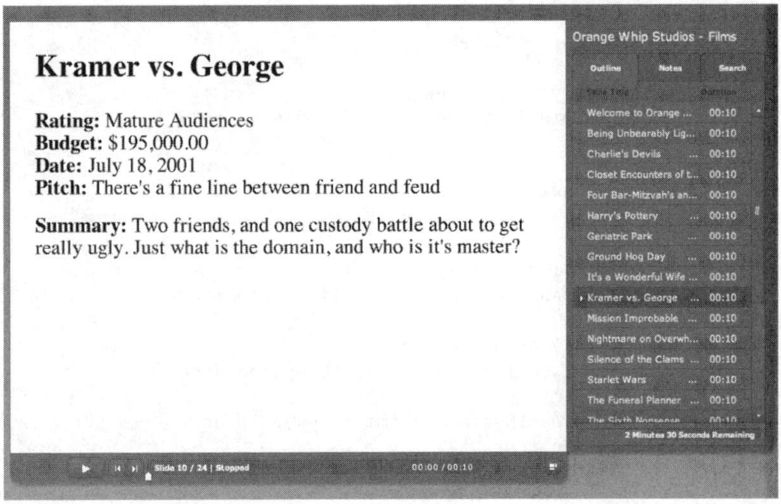

Setting Play and Control Options

Now that you've created a few presentations, let's discuss how to manipulate the way that the presentation plays and is controlled. Table 37.1 listed the attributes of `<cfpresentation>` that allow this sort of customization. Listing 37.3 is a modified version of Listing 37.2. This time the presentation is being built for a kiosk where no one will be there to click the Next button. The presentation needs to run by itself, without human intervention. Let's see how this can be done.

Listing 37.3 `example3.cfm`—Dynamic Presentation (Autoplay)

```
<!---
Name:           example3.cfm
Author:         Raymond Camden (ray@camdenfamily.com)
Description: Dynamic presentation, self run
--->

<cfquery name="getMovies" datasource="ows">
select   f.movietitle, f.pitchtext, f.amountbudgeted,
      f.summary, f.imagename, f.dateintheaters,
      r.rating
from  films f, filmsratings r
where f.ratingid = r.ratingid
</cfquery>

<cfpresentation title="Orange Whip Studios - Films"
            autoPlay="true" loop="true"
            control="brief">
   <cfpresentationslide
            title="Welcome to Orange Whip Studios"
            >
<h1>Welcome to Orange Whip Studios</h1>

<p>
Here is the latest gallery of our films.
</p>
   </cfpresentationslide>

   <cfloop query="getMovies">
      <cfpresentationslide title="#movietitle#">

<cfoutput>
<h2>#movietitle#</h2>

<p>
<cfif len(trim(imagename))>
<img src="../images/#imagename#" align="right">
</cfif>
<b>Rating:</b> #rating#<br />
<b>Budget:</b> #dollarFormat(amountbudgeted)#<br />
<b>Date:</b>
#dateFormat(dateintheaters,"mmmm d, yyyy")#<br />
<b>Pitch:</b> #pitchtext#
</p>

<p>
```

Listing 37.3 (CONTINUED)

```
<b>Summary:</b> #summary#
</p>
</cfoutput>

    </cfpresentationslide>

  </cfloop>

</cfpresentation>
```

This listing is pretty much the same as Listing 37.2. The critical change is in the `<cfpresentation>` tag:

```
<cfpresentation title="Orange Whip Studios - Films"
            autoPlay="true" loop="true"
            control="brief">
```

The first change was to set `autoPlay="true"`. This starts the presentation and makes it move through the slides by itself. Next, `loop="true"` ensures that the presentation will play forever. Last, `control="brief"` minimizes the controls. We can't remove the controls completely, but this setting makes them take up less space. Figure 37.3 shows the slimmer control scheme, at the bottom right.

Figure 37.3

A presentation that plays automatically.

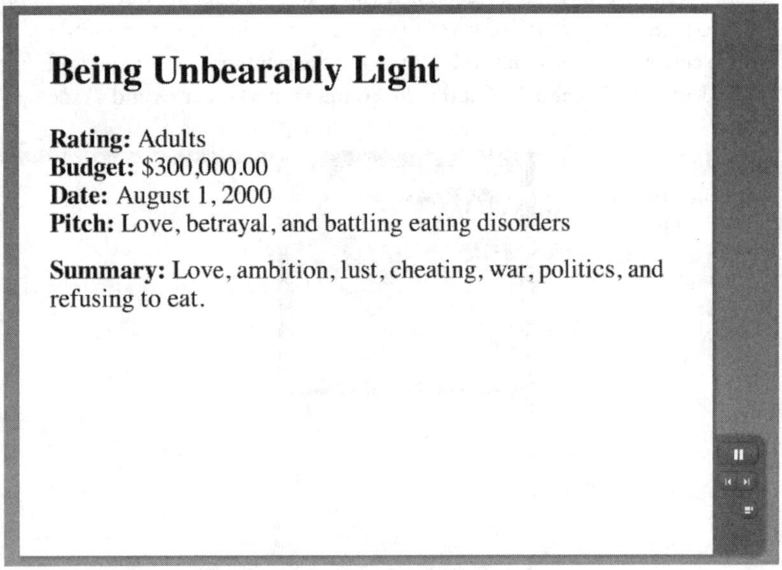

Being Unbearably Light

Rating: Adults
Budget: $300,000.00
Date: August 1, 2000
Pitch: Love, betrayal, and battling eating disorders

Summary: Love, ambition, lust, cheating, war, politics, and refusing to eat.

Embedding Content

Not all content for a presentation must be embedded directly in the presentation. Multiple options exist for providing content from outside the ColdFusion page. The `<cfpresentationslide>` tag supports a `src` attribute. This can point to a local ColdFusion file, a remote URL, or a local SWF file. Listing 37.4 shows a simple example of how to embed resources in presentations.

Listing 37.4 `example4.cfm`—Embedding Content in Slides

```
<!---
Name:        example4.cfm
Author:      Raymond Camden (ray@camdenfamily.com)
Description: Presentation with external content
--->

<cfpresentation title="Embedding Stuff!" showNotes="false"
        showSearch="false">

    <cfpresentationslide title="A Flash Slide"
        src="SimpleSearchMovie.swf" />

    <cfpresentationslide title="A CFM Slide"
        src="slide.cfm" />

    <cfpresentationslide title="An external URL"
        src="http://127.0.0.1/ows/37/slide2.cfm" />

</cfpresentation>
```

The presentation in Listing 37.4 contains three slides. The first slide points to a SWF file in the same directory. The second slide points to a CFM file. The third slide uses a full URL, but points to another file in the same directory. If you run this code on your own server, be sure to modify the URL to match the location for your machine, including the port number. As another example of how to customize the layout, the Notes and Search tabs were turned off. Figure 37.4 shows the result. Listings 37.5 and 37.6 show the contents of `slide.cfm` and `slide2.cfm`.

Figure 37.4

A presentation with external output.

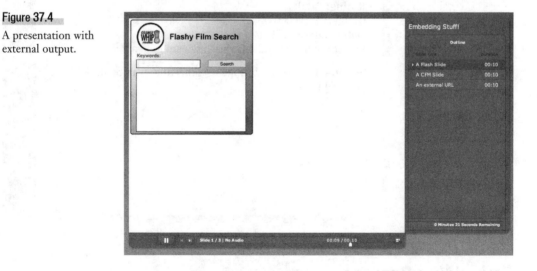

Listing 37.5 `slide.cfm`—Embedded Content

```
<!---
Name:        slide.cfm
Author:      Raymond Camden (ray@camdenfamily.com)
```

Listing 37.5 (CONTINUED)

```
Description: Content for a slide
--->

<cfoutput>
This will show up inside the slide.<br />
The date is #dateFormat(now(), "long")# and the time is
#timeFormat(now(), "long")#.
</cfoutput>
```

Listing 37.6 slide2.cfm – Embedded Content

```
<!---
Name:       slide2.cfm
Author:     Raymond Camden (ray@camdenfamily.com)
Description: Content for a slide
--->

<cfoutput>
This is a random number: #randRange(1,1000)#
</cfoutput>
```

NOTE

Both <cfpresentation> and <cfpresentationslide> provide attributes to support the requesting of information via a proxy server or HTTP authorization. See the ColdFusion documentation language reference for more information.

Styling Your Presentation

Although the default presentation display looks pretty nice, you may want to tweak the layout and add your own style. Table 37.3 lists the attributes related to styling presentations.

Table 37.3 <cfpresentation> and <cfpresentationslide> Design Attributes

ATTRIBUTE	FUNCTION
backgroundColor	Sets the background color for the presentation. The setting can be a hex color or named color. The default is #727971. Used in <cfpresentation>.
glowColor	Sets the color used for the "glow" around buttons. The setting can be a hex color or named color. Used in <cfpresentation>.
lightColor	Sets the color used for light and shadow effects. The setting can be a hex color or named color. Used in <cfpresentation>.
primaryColor	Sets the main color for the presentation. The setting can be a hex color or named color. Used in <cfpresentation>.
shadowColor	Sets the color used for shadow effects. The setting can be a hex color or named color. Used in <cfpresentation>.
textColor	Sets the color used for text. The setting can be a hex color or named color. Used in <cfpresentation>.
marginTop, marginLeft, marginRight, marginBottom	Sets the margin in pixels for a slide. The default is 0. Used in <cfpresentationslide>.

Listing 37.7 shows a rather ugly example of style customization.

Listing 37.7 `example5.cfm`—A "Stylish" Presentation

```
<!---
Name:        example5.cfm
Author:      Raymond Camden (ray@camdenfamily.com)
Description: Presentation with style
--->

<cfpresentation title="Designed Presentation"
            autoPlay="false" backGroundColor="green"
            glowColor="red" lightColor="pink"
            primaryColor="black" shadowColor="gray"
            textColor="blue">

    <cfpresentationslide title="Small Margins"
            marginleft="50" marginRight="50"
            marginTop="200" marginBottom="200"
    >
<h1>This is why I don't design</h1>

<p>
See how bad these colors go together? This is why I
don't do design work.
</p>
    </cfpresentationslide>

</cfpresentation>
```

As you can see, this presentation makes use of every design option listed in Table 37.3. The design choices aren't great, but this is something any decent designer can correct. Figure 37.5 shows why the author of this chapter isn't allowed to design.

Figure 37.5

A presentation with(out) flair.

Adding Presenters

What would a presentation be without a presenter? ColdFusion presentations can have one or more presenters associated with them, with any presenter assigned to any particular slide (but no more than one presenter per slide). To add a presenter to a presentation, simply use the `<cfpresenter>` tag. Table 37.4 lists the attributes of `<cfpresenter>`.

Table 37.4   `<cfpresenter>` Attributes

ATTRIBUTE	FUNCTION
biography	Specifies an optional biography of the presenter.
email	Specifies the email address of the presenter. If used, a Contact button is added to the control panel of the presentation.
image	Specifies a picture of the presenter. The image must be a JPEG file and set relative to the CFM page creating the presentation. If a video is used with the slide, the video takes the place of the picture.
name	Specifies the name of the presenter. This name will also be used to identify the presenter to slides.
logo	Specifies the logo for the presenter's company or organization. The logo must be a JPEG file and set relative to the CFM page creating the presentation.
title	Specifies the presenter's title, such as "Director of Marketing."

Listing 37.8 creates a presentation that makes use of the presenter feature.

Listing 37.8   `example6.cfm`—Adding Presenters

```
<!---
Name:        example6.cfm
Author:      Raymond Camden (ray@camdenfamily.com)
Description: Presentation with presentors
--->

<cfpresentation title="Presenting Presentors!">

  <cfpresenter name="Raymond Camden"
            email="ray@camdenfamily.com"
            title="ColdFusion Jedi Master"
            image="ray.jpg" logo="logo.jpg"
            biography="Raymond likes ColdFusion">

  <cfpresenter name="Boring Guy" title="Nothing Important"
            biography="This guy hasn't done anything.">

  <cfpresentationslide title="Slide 1"
        presenter="Raymond Camden">
<p>
This is the slide one. It is associated with
Ray.
</p>
</cfpresentationslide>
```

Listing 37.8 (CONTINUED)

```
<cfpresentationslide title="Slide 2"
      presenter="Boring Guy">
<p>
This is the slide two. It is associated with
Boring Guy.
</p>
</cfpresentationslide>

<cfpresentationslide title="Slide 3"
        presenter="Raymond Camden">
<p>
This is the slide three. It is associated with
Ray again.
</p>
</cfpresentationslide>

</cfpresentation>
```

The presentation in Listing 37.8 has two presenters. The first uses all the available options and is named Raymond Camden. The second is a presenter named Boring Guy. Then three slides are created. The first and third slides use Raymond Camden as the presenter. Be careful to ensure that the name exactly matches that in the <cfpresenter> tag. The second slide uses the Boring Guy presenter. The result is shown in Figure 37.6.

Figure 37.6

A presentation with a presenter.

Saving Your Presentation

So far, all presentations created in the listings were immediately displayed in the browser when requested. Although this process happens pretty quickly, you may want to store and save the presentation for use later. The <cfpresentation> tag supports an attribute named directory. If you use this attribute, the result of the presentation will be stored in the folder you specify. Listing 37.9 is a modified version of Listing 37.1. This time a `directory` attribute is provided.

Listing 37.9 example7.cfm—Saving Presentations

```
<!---
Name:        example7.cfm
Author:      Raymond Camden (ray@camdenfamily.com)
Description: First presentation
--->

<cfset directory = expandPath("./stored")>
<cfif not directoryExists(directory)>
   <cfdirectory action="create" directory="#directory#">
</cfif>

<cfpresentation title="First Presentation"
            autoPlay="false" directory="./stored">

   <cfpresentationslide title="Welcome to CFPRESENTATION"
              notes="These are some notes.">
<h1>Welcome to CFPRESENTATION</h1>

<p>
This is content for the first slide. I can include HTML
and it will be rendered by the presentation.
</p>
   </cfpresentationslide>

   <cfpresentationslide title="Sales Figures"
         notes="These are some notes for slide two.">
<h1>Sales Figures</h1>

<p>
Some fake data.
</p>

<p>
<table width="100%" border="1">
<tr>
   <th>Product</th>
   <th>Price</th>
</tr>
<tr>
   <td>Apples</td><td>$0.99</td>
</tr>
<tr>
   <td>Bananas</td><td>$1.99</td>
</tr>
<tr>
   <td>Nukes</td><td>$2.99</td>
</tr>
</table>
</p>
   </cfpresentationslide>
</cfpresentation>
```

The code begins by checking for the existence of a relative directory named "stored". If this directory doesn't exist, it is created. Next the <cfpresentation> tag is passed the directory attribute. If you run Listing 37.9 in the browser, you won't see anything, but a set of files is written to the "stored" folder. The index.htm file can now be opened directly in your browser either via HTTP (e.g., http://localhost:8500/ows/37/stored/), or via File > Open. The folder could be shipped on a CD or even emailed (if zipped, of course) to someone.

CHAPTER 38

Generating Non-HTML Content

About ColdFusion and Non-HTML Content

Normally, ColdFusion is used to generate Web pages and Web pages only. Its main purpose in life is to wait for requests from Web browsers and send back chunks of HTML in response. The Web browsers then render the HTML visually for your users. With the exception of the Flex listings in Chapter 35, "Understanding ColdFusion-Powered Flex," HTML generation is what every code example in this book has been about so far.

However, there's no law that says your ColdFusion templates have to send HTML back to the Web browser. If you think about it, the only reason HTML tags such as `<body>` and `<title>` are in the pages ColdFusion serves up is because you put them there. Take away the HTML tags, and your ColdFusion templates are really sending back plain old text files, of the kind you would create in Notepad or any other text editor.

So if you remove the HTML tags from a page, could you format or mark up the text in some other way? Sure you could. If the user's browser knows how to display text formatted in that particular way, it will do so. If not, it will try to invoke some other application to display the content to the user.

In this chapter, you learn about doing just that: getting ColdFusion to create other types of content on the fly.

About MIME Content Types

If you've been working with Web pages for long, you will have heard of MIME types and content types. But you may not have found much of an explanation regarding what exactly they are or what they are good for.

Basically, a MIME type is a short label that determines what type of content a particular document or URL contains. The idea is that every file format—word processing files, spreadsheets, HTML files, image files, multimedia files, and so on—has (or could have) its own MIME type. Any Web browser, e-mail client, or other device can use the MIME type to determine what do to with a file (or stream of content from a server), such as showing it as a picture, interpreting it as a document, or opening up the file in some other program (such as the appropriate word processing or spreadsheet application).

NOTE

In a way, the concept of a MIME type is similar to the notion of a file extension in Windows. The file extension tells Windows which icon to display in Windows Explorer and which program should be launched when a user double-clicks a file. MIME types are more flexible and appropriate for the Internet because they aren't Windows specific. But both are simple schemes for describing what exactly a computer should expect to find in a particular file or chunk of data.

Purists don't like it, but the terms MIME type, MIME content type, and content type are often used interchangeably. For purposes of this discussion, please consider them to be synonyms.

A MIME content type is always made up of two parts, separated by a forward slash:

- The first part describes the broad category that the content can be thought to belong to. The common ones are text (generally something that could sensibly be opened in Notepad or some other text editor), image, audio, video, and application. The application type is somewhat of a catchall, generally meaning that the content is meant for a specific application, such as Word or Photoshop.

- The second part, or subtype, is a more specific description of what exactly the content's format is. For instance, JPEG images, GIF images, and TIFF images been given MIME types of image/jpeg, image/gif, and image/tiff, respectively.

Some common content types are listed in Table 38.1.

Table 38.1 Examples of Common MIME Content Types

MIME TYPE	DESCRIPTION
text/html	Content that should be interpreted as HTML markup and thus rendered by a Web browser natively. By far the most common in use on the Web. Anything you would normally call a Web page has this content type.
text/plain	Normal text content, such as you would create if you were typing a note in Notepad or some other text editor.
text/vnd.wap.wml	Markup content intended for WAP-enabled wireless devices, such as cellular phones.
image/gif, image/jpeg	Common types of image content. Unlike the various text types listed above, images are binary files that mostly contain information about individual pixels and can't be opened in a text editor such as Notepad.
application/msword, application/msexcel	Content tailored specifically for (and probably generated or saved by) a specific application, such as Microsoft Word or Excel.

Table 38.1 (CONTINUED)

MIME TYPE	DESCRIPTION
`application/ x-shockwave-flash`	Multimedia presentations or movies to be displayed by the Adobe Flash Player.
`video/x-msvideo, video/vnd.rn-realvideo`	Multimedia presentations or movies to be displayed by the Windows Media Player or Real Player, respectively.
`application/unknown` or `application/octet-stream`	In general, a file or content that isn't really meant to be opened or viewed in any particular way. When you download an executable program (an `.exe` file, perhaps) from a Web site, the content type typically is set to this value. Web browsers usually respond to this content type by prompting the user for a download location with a Save As dialog box.

How Your Browser Handles MIME Types

A good way to get a list of MIME content types—and learn which program your particular browser will launch if it can't display the content itself—is to examine how the browser has been configured.

If you're using Netscape, select Content from the Preferences menu. In Firefox, choose Tools > Options > Manage, and then select the File Types option (depending on the version). You will be able to scroll through the list of applications and see the types of content the browser has been configured to launch for each application. For instance, URLs that return a content type of `application/msexcel` are passed off to Microsoft Excel for processing and viewing (Figure 38.1). This is how the dialog box looks with Firefox 2.0; other versions will look different but provide the same basic information.

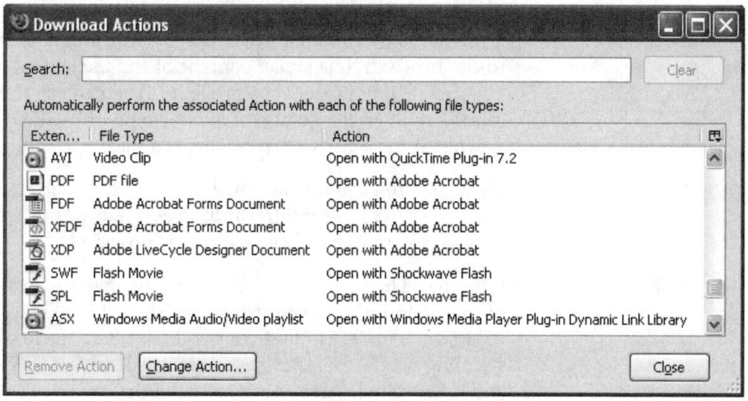

Figure 38.1

You can see how Firefox associates content types with applications in its Download Actions dialog.

If you're using Internet Explorer on a Windows machine, the equivalent place to look is in the File Types tab of the Folder Options dialog box, which you can get to by selecting Folder Options from the Tools menu in Windows Explorer (not Internet Explorer).

NOTE

If no content type is provided by the Web server for a given file or stream of content, the browser won't know what to do with the content. It will usually ask you what you want to do with the file, often by presenting a dialog in which you select the appropriate viewer or helper application. The exact behavior varies from browser to browser; it's generally the same behavior as when a content type of `application/unknown` or `application/octet-stream` is specified (refer to Table 38.1).

Although it's not exactly bedtime reading, you can read the formal specification for the MIME type scheme by visiting the WC3's Web site at `http://www.w3.org`.

Introducing the `<cfcontent>` Tag

The HTTP specification requires that every response from a Web server include the appropriate content type information. By default, ColdFusion always sends back a MIME type of `text/html`, which is why Web browsers assume that the text returned by your templates should be rendered as Web pages.

The `<cfcontent>` tag is provided for situations in which you want to send a different content type back to the browser along with the content your template generates. Table 38.2 lists the various attributes the `<cfcontent>` tag can take. The most important of these, as you might guess, is the `type` attribute.

Table 38.2 `<cfcontent>` Tag Syntax

ATTRIBUTE	PURPOSE
type	Optional. The MIME content type you want to send back to the browser along with the content your template is generating. This could be one of the types listed in Table 38.1 or some other type. For instance, if your template is written to generate plain text rather than HTML, you would set this value to `text/plain`. The MIME type can be followed by a semicolon and a character encoding value. If a value is not passed, ColdFusion will attempt to guess the proper MIME type for the file.
file	Optional. The complete path of a file on the server that you want to send back to the browser. The actual content of the file should match the content type you specified with the `type` attribute. You can use this to respond to a page request with an image or some other type of file that you want the user to download (perhaps a `.zip` or an `.exe` file).
deleteFile	Optional. You can set this attribute to `Yes`, which causes a file to be deleted from the server's drive after it has been sent to the browser. The default is `No`. Relevant only if the `file` attribute is provided.
reset	Optional. Defaults to `Yes`, which means that any text that might have been output before the `<cfcontent>` tag should be discarded (not sent to the browser). This is handy if your code needs to make some decisions before deciding which content type to specify. If it's set to `No`, all content—even spaces and other white space—that precedes the `<cfcontent>` tag will be sent back to the browser. This attribute is discussed later in this chapter, in the section "Generating Comma-Separated Text."

Experimenting with Plain Text

I said earlier that ColdFusion always sends back a content type of text/html unless you specify a different one using the <cfcontent> tag. As an experiment, you can try setting the content type to text/plain, which means the browser isn't obligated to parse the content as HTML. Instead, the browser can display the content literally, the way a simple text editor such as TextMate would.

Here's a simple exercise to illustrate this point. See Listings 38.1 and 38.2 at the book's Web site and compare the results. You can probably guess what Listing 38.1 will look like: the words The time is now will be in italics, and the current time will appear in bold on the next line. Listing 38.2, on the other hand, tells the browser that the content type is plain text rather than HTML, so it shows the text literally, without attempting to apply any tag-based formatting (Figure 38.2).

Listing 38.1 TestMessage1.cfm—A Simple Message, Without a Content Type

```
<!---
 Filename: TestMessage1.cfm
 Author:   Nate Weiss (NMW)
 Purpose: Outputting an HTML message normally
--->

<!-- Display the current time -->
<p><i>The time is now:</i><br>
<cfoutput><b>#timeFormat(now())#</b></cfoutput>
```

Figure 38.2

If the MIME type is set to text/plain, the browser won't know to interpret any HTML tags in your documents.

Listing 38.2 TestMessage2.cfm—Specifying text/plain as the Content Type

```
<!---
 Filename: TestMessage2.cfm
 Author:   Nate Weiss (NMW)
 Purpose: Outputting an HTML message normally
--->

<cfcontent type="text/plain">
<!-- Display the current time -->
<p><i>The time is now:</i><br>
<cfoutput><b>#timeFormat(now())#</b></cfoutput>
```

Comma-Separated Text

Now that you know how to use ColdFusion to serve plain text rather than HTML, let's try to put that knowledge to use. One thing people do with plain-text files is to use them to hold comma-separated text. Comma-separated text is a simple data format that gets used for many purposes. Because it's simple and easy to parse through, it's often used for various types of logging and simple integration projects. In fact, ColdFusion's own log files are kept in a comma-separated format. (Look at the files in the LOGS folder, within ColdFusion's program directory.) Many types of Web server software packages keep their logs in comma-separated format as well.

There are slightly different flavors of comma-separated text in common use, but they usually follow these rules:

- Each row of information sits in its own line in the text.

- Within each line, each column or field of information has a comma separating it from the next column or field.

- If the data in a particular column contains commas, it's traditional to put double-quote characters around the data so the "real" commas can be distinguished from the commas that separate the fields. If the data contains actual double-quote characters, they are usually escaped by using two double-quote characters together.

- It's common to put the names of each column on the first line, with each name surrounded by quotation marks and separated from one another with commas.

Generating Comma-Separated Text

To generate comma-separated text with a ColdFusion template, you'll usually create a .cfm file that does the following:

1. Retrieves the information that should be presented in column-separated format, using a database query or some other means.

2. Sets the content type for the request to text/plain using the <cfcontent> tag, so the generated content isn't mistaken for HTML.

3. Outputs the names of the columns as the first line of the generated content.

4. Outputs the actual rows of data, each on its own line.

The code in Listing 38.3 retrieves some data from a database table and sends the data back to the browser in a comma-separated text format (Figure 38.3).

Listing 38.3 FilmsCommaSep.cfm—Presenting Queried Data As Comma-Separated Text

```
<!---
 Filename: FilmsCommaSep.cfm
 Author: Nate Weiss (NMW)
 Purpose: Outputs film information as comma-separated text
--->
```

Listing 38.3 (CONTINUED)

```
Retrieving information about films...
<cfquery datasource="ows" name="getFilms">
 SELECT FilmID, MovieTitle
 FROM Films
 ORDER BY MovieTitle
</cfquery>

<!--- Now output as simple comma-separated text --->
<!--- Put the column names on first line, then --->
<!--- the actual data rows on their own lines --->
<cfcontent type="text/plain">"FilmID","MovieTitle"
<cfoutput query="getFilms">#FilmID#,"#MovieTitle#"
</cfoutput>
```

Figure 38.3

The <cfcontent>
tag makes generating
comma-separated text
on the fly easy.

```
"FilmID","MovieTitle"
1,"Being Unbearably Light"
2,"Charlie's Devils"
3,"Closet Encounters of the Odd Kind"
18,"Folded Laundry, Concealed Ticket"
21,"Forrest Trump"
4,"Four Bar-Mitzvah's and a Circumcision"
6,"Geriatric Park"
23,"Gladly Ate Her"
7,"Ground Hog Day"
20,"Hannah and Her Blisters"
5,"Harry's Pottery"
8,"It's a Wonderful Wife"
9,"Kramer vs. George"
10,"Mission Improbable"
11,"Nightmare on Overwhelmed Street"
17,"Raiders of the Lost Aardvark"
27,"Ray's Movie"
26,"Ray's Movie"
12,"Silence of the Clams"
13,"Starlet Wars"
```

NOTE

In HTML, white space (such as multiple spaces together or new lines) is ignored. Not so with comma-separated text. That's why there is a new line after the list of column names but not before; it's important that the names show up as the first line of text. That's also why there is a new line before the closing `</cfoutput>` tag but not after the opening `<cfoutput>` tag. You want Cold-Fusion to output a new line only after each row of data. This means you can't freely indent and skip lines the way you can when you're outputting normal HTML content.

You'll notice that the `Retrieving information about films` message isn't displayed by the browser. Because you haven't explicitly set the `reset` attribute of the <cfcontent> tag to No, it defaults to its Yes behavior, which is for all content that was generated before the tag to be discarded. If you were to remove the <cfcontent> tag, not only would the data no longer be displayed as plain text by the browser, but the retrieving message would be displayed, as you would expect it to normally (Figure 38.4). The same results would appear if you added `reset="No"` to the <cfcontent> tag.

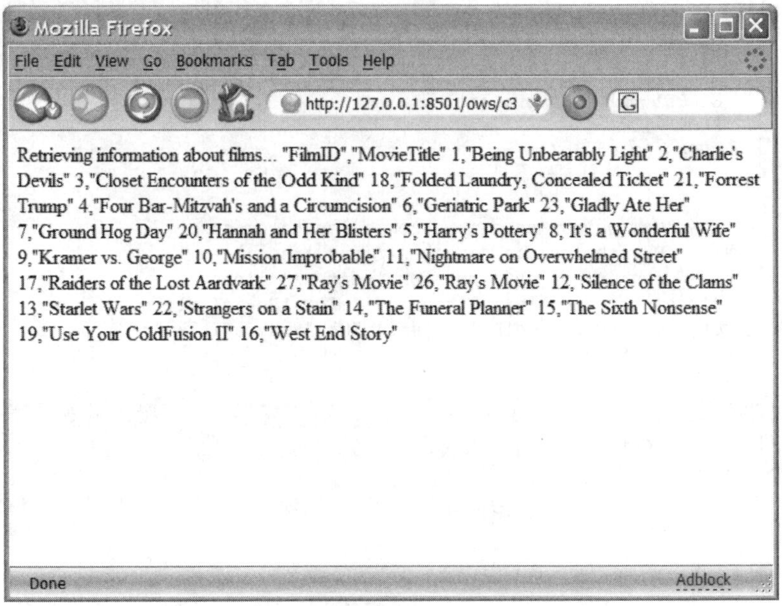

Figure 38.4

Without <cfcontent>, the new lines in the text are no longer displayed. Also, the message from earlier in the template is included in the output.

Adding a Content-Disposition Header for Internet Explorer

If you test Listing 38.3 with a Firefox browser, it should look like Figure 38.3. If you visit the listing with Internet Explorer 6, you might see much different behavior. For instance, you might find that the comma-separated text automatically opens in Adobe Dreamweaver as a file named FilmsCommaSep[1].cfm or similar. Internet Explorer takes the .cfm extension in the URL as an indication that the returned content is a ColdFusion template, which it clearly is not.

This illustrates one of Internet Explorer 6's policies. Unlike most other browsers, it thinks the file extension—and the format of the actual content itself—is more important than the specified content type. The content type is considered only if the file extension doesn't have an associated program, or when there is no file extension.

To get consistent behavior with IE, add a content-disposition header to the page request, using a <cfheader> tag, such as the following. The <cfheader> tag is the way ColdFusion enables you to send custom HTTP headers back to the browser, along with the content your template generates. You would add this line right before the <cfcontent> line in Listing 38.3:

```
<cfheader
  name="Content-Disposition"
  value="filename=films">
```

The content-disposition header suggests a file name for the file, if the user were to save it. When Internet Explorer sees this header, it thinks of the content as having an implied file name of films, rather than of FilmsCommaSep.cfm. Because films has no extension, Internet Explorer will then use the content type to decide how to display the content. The content therefore will be shown as plain text, as in Figure 38.3.

You could also provide a file name with an extension, like so:

```
<cfheader
 name="Content-Disposition"
 value="filename=films.txt">
```

If you now visit the listing with Internet Explorer and select Save As from the File menu, the Save Web Page dialog box will appear with `films.txt` prefilled as the file name. Firefox-based browsers will behave in the same way.

You can also add the word `Attachment` to the header, as shown here:

```
<cfheader
 name="Content-Disposition"
 value="Attachment; filename=films.txt">
```

This will cause Internet Explorer to prompt the user to save the content as an attachment right away when Listing 38.3 is visited, rather than displaying the content in the browser window. Firefox browsers don't do anything special with the `Attachment` keyword, so the added line of code shouldn't cause any harm. The `FilmsCommaSepIE.cfm` template (on this book's Web page) includes this `content-disposition` line.

NOTE

To read more about the `content-disposition` header and the `Attachment` and `filename` keywords (there is an `Inline` keyword, too), see RFC 1806 at `http://www.ietf.org`.

NOTE

If you want to know more about the way IE decides how to display incoming content, read article Q293336 in the Microsoft Knowledge Base at `http://support.microsoft.com`.

Retrieving the Comma-Separated Text with `<cfhttp>`

Listing 38.4 is a bit of a digression, but it demonstrates a way you can actually use comma-separated text in your applications. You can use ColdFusion's `<cfhttp>` tag to visit the URL for Listing 38.3, as if ColdFusion itself were a Web browser. The `<cfhttp>` tag grabs the comma-separated text generated by `FilmsCommaSep.cfm` and parses through it, effectively re-creating the query result set. You can then use the result set, as if it were returned by the original `<cfquery>` tag. This enables you to share data between two different ColdFusion servers over the Internet.

NOTE

We're a bit ahead of ourselves in using the `<cfhttp>` tag. It's discussed in full in Chapter 67, "Using Server-Side HTTP and FTP," in *Adobe ColdFusion 8 Web Application Construction Kit, Volume 3: Advanced Application Development*.

NOTE

ColdFusion's `<cfwddx>` tag gives you an even easier and more powerful way to share content between servers over the Internet, using a clever XML format instead of comma-separated text. To learn more about WDDX, see Chapter 47, "Using WDDX," online, or visit `http://www.openwddx.org`.

Listing 38.4 `FetchCommaSep.cfm`—The `<cfhttp>` Tag and Comma-Separated Text

```
<!---
 Filename: FetchCommaSep.cfm
 Author: Nate Weiss (NMW)
 Purpose: Retrieves comma-separated film information over the Web
--->

<!--- Visit our new "comma-separated" page, --->
<!--- and parse content into a query object --->
<cfhttp method="Get" url="http://localhost:8500/ows/38/FilmsCommaSep.cfm"
 name="getFilmsViaHTTP" delimiter=",">

<html>
<head><title>Fetching Comma-Separated Content</title></head>
<body>
<h3>Comma-Separated text has been fetched via CFHTTP</h3>

<!--- Now the "fetched" query may be used normally --->
<cfoutput query="getFilmsViaHTTP">
 Film <b>#FilmID#</b> is: <i>#MovieTitle#</i><br>
</cfoutput>
</body>
</html>
```

Generating Excel Files

You might have seen Web sites that enable users to access or view some type of information—like stock quotes— in spreadsheet or Excel format. Microsoft Excel has become the de facto standard for spreadsheet applications, and many PCs come with it preinstalled, so this type of feature can be very useful.

In this section, you will learn how to add this type of functionality to your own ColdFusion applications. This will enable you to provide your users with a way to open customized data in Excel (such as kind of personalized purchase history or a list of other employees if you're building an intranet application). If you do not have Excel, consider downloading OpenOffice, a free office suite application available for multiple operating systems. See `http://www.openoffice.org`.

Creating Spreadsheets with Tab-Separated Text

One of the file formats Excel knows how to import is tab-separated text. Tab-separated text is basically the same as comma-separated text, except it uses tab characters instead of commas to separate the columns on each line.

If you create a ColdFusion template that generates tab-separated text and specify a content type of `application/msexcel`, the user's browser will display the content to the user by launching Excel. Excel should then seamlessly import the tab-separated text and display it in the same way it would display a native `.xls` worksheet file. As far as the end user is concerned, your Web site presented them with a personalized spreadsheet file; only you know that it was simply some tab-separated text.

Listing 38.5 shows how easy it is to get this effect. This code is essentially the same as the code from Listing 38.3, with just a few minor changes. Most importantly, the type attribute of the <cfcontent> tag has been changed to application/msexcel.

Listing 38.5 FilmsToExcel.cfm—Generating Tab-Separated Text for Use with Excel

```
<!---
 Filename: FilmsToExcel.cfm
 Author: Nate Weiss (NMW)
 Purpose: Outputs film information for Microsoft Excel
--->

<!--- Don't output anything *not* in CFOUTPUT tags --->
<!--- This makes it easier to deal with whitespace --->
<cfsetting enableCFOutputOnly="Yes">

<!--- Retrieve information about films --->
<cfquery datasource="ows" name="getFilms">
 SELECT MovieTitle, AmountBudgeted
 FROM Films
 ORDER BY MovieTitle
</cfquery>

<!--- Set variables for special characters --->
<cfset tabChar = chr(9)>
<cfset newLine = chr(13) & chr(10)>

<!--- Suggest default filename for spreadsheet --->
<cfheader name="Content-Disposition" value="filename=FilmBudgets.xls">
<!--- Set the content-type so Excel is invoked --->
<cfcontent type="application/msexcel">

<!--- Output the header row, with column names --->
<!--- Put tab between columns, and newline at end --->
<cfoutput>MOVIE TITLE#tabChar#BUDGET#newLine#</cfoutput>
<!--- Output actual data rows, each on own line --->
<!--- Put tab between columns, and newline at end --->
<cfloop query="getFilms">
 <cfoutput>#MovieTitle##tabChar##AmountBudgeted##newLine#</cfoutput>
</cfloop>
```

NOTE

When the spreadsheet is displayed in Excel, you may see hash marks (a series of # signs) where the budget numbers belong. Just make the budget column a bit wider to see the full numbers..

Another difference is that this code uses the <cfheader> tag mentioned earlier to send a custom Content-Disposition header to the browser, along with the content type. The Content-Disposition header is used to suggest a default file name for the content going back to the browser (see the following notes and the section, "Adding a Content-Disposition Header for Internet Explorer," earlier in this chapter).

NOTE

A complete discussion of all HTTP headers is beyond the scope of this book and is something you don't need to know about because ColdFusion takes care of this kind of thing for you. In short, custom headers can be used to provide the browser with various pieces of information, or metadata, about the server's response.

NOTE

The `Content-Disposition` header really should be optional, but because of the way Internet Explorer determines how to handle incoming content, this particular `<cfheader>` tag is required for the code to work properly with IE. To decide which application to launch, IE doesn't look only at the MIME content type the code provides; it also relies on other factors, such as the suggested file name. Additionally, the extension of the suggested file name must be associated with Excel (that is, `.xls`), but the first part of the file name is up to you. To learn how IE decides how to display incoming content, read article Q293336 in the Microsoft Knowledge Base at `http://support.microsoft.com`.

Listing 38.5 also sets a couple of variables for the two special characters needed to produce the correct text, by using the `chr()` function. This can be a more manageable way to get special characters into your page output. Instead of actually pressing the Tab key to insert a tab character into your code (which would work but might be hard to notice or understand when you edit the code later), you can use the `chr()` function, which returns the character specified by the ASCII code you supply.

NOTE

`chr(9)` always returns a tab character, and a `chr(13)` followed by a `chr(10)` always returns a linefeed character followed by a carriage return. A linefeed followed by a carriage return is known as a newline, which is the standard way to indicate the end of a line in a text file.

Another difference is that this listing turns on the `enableCFOutputOnly` mode of the `<cfsetting>` tag, which causes ColdFusion not to output anything that isn't between `cfoutput` tags. Together with the `tabChar` and `newLine` variables, this code explicitly tells ColdFusion about every single character that needs to be output to the browser, rather than having to be overly careful about positioning the tags within the code (refer to Listing 38.3).

In any case, if you visit the URL for Listing 38.5 with your browser, it should launch Excel with the film data loaded as a spreadsheet. Depending on the browser and platform being used, Excel might be launched as a separate application, or it might appear within the browser window (Figure 38.5). Internet Explorer 7 will display a File Download dialog instead of automatically launching Excel. However, if you then click the Open button in the File Download dialog, Excel will be launched and will display the data in spreadsheet format.

NOTE

Of course, you could create a template based on Listing 38.5 that uses a URL parameter to dynamically return spreadsheet data based on some type of film ID, actor, and so on.

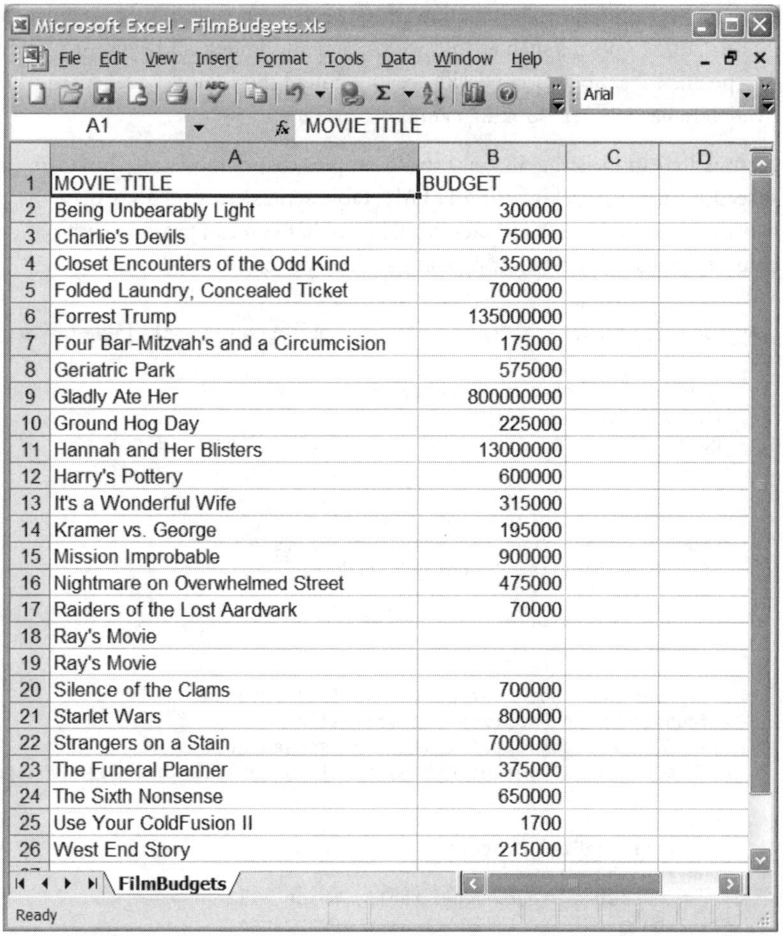
Microsoft Excel - FilmBudgets.xls
File Edit View Insert Format Tools Data Window Help
Arial
A1
MOVIE TITLE
A B C D
1 MOVIE TITLE BUDGET
2 Being Unbearably Light 300000
3 Charlie's Devils 750000
4 Closet Encounters of the Odd Kind 350000
5 Folded Laundry, Concealed Ticket 7000000
6 Forrest Trump 135000000
7 Four Bar-Mitzvah's and a Circumcision 175000
8 Geriatric Park 575000
9 Gladly Ate Her 800000000
10 Ground Hog Day 225000
11 Hannah and Her Blisters 13000000
12 Harry's Pottery 600000
13 It's a Wonderful Wife 315000
14 Kramer vs. George 195000
15 Mission Improbable 900000
16 Nightmare on Overwhelmed Street 475000
17 Raiders of the Lost Aardvark 70000
18 Ray's Movie
19 Ray's Movie
20 Silence of the Clams 700000
21 Starlet Wars 800000
22 Strangers on a Stain 7000000
23 The Funeral Planner 375000
24 The Sixth Nonsense 650000
25 Use Your ColdFusion II 1700
26 West End Story 215000
FilmBudgets
Ready

Figure 38.5

If you send tab-separated text back to the browser with the correct content type, it should be opened in Excel.

Creating Spreadsheets with HTML

For Excel 2000, Microsoft created a special flavor of HTML, which Excel can import as if it were a normal `.xls` file. If you have Excel 2000, Excel XP, or later, create a spreadsheet with a few columns and rows. Select Save As from the File menu, and save the spreadsheet as an HTML file. Now open that HTML file in a text editor such as Notepad or Dreamweaver. You will find a fair amount of what seems like extraneous code in there, but after a moment you'll realize that the spreadsheet has basically been converted into an ordinary HTML table, using the `<table>`, `<tr>`, and `<td>` tags you're already familiar with.

If you were to create a ColdFusion template that created a similar HTML file, Excel could render it as a spreadsheet, just as it could render the tab-separated text from Listing 38.5 as a spreadsheet. The advantage to using the special HTML format over the tab-separated format is that Microsoft designed the special HTML format to be more than just a data-export format; it actually holds all the Excel-specific information about the spreadsheet as well. This means you can dynamically specify formatting options such as font, color, and alignment, and even provide autocalculating formulas for specific cells. So you can easily create a fully functioning Excel spreadsheet on the fly, using relatively familiar HTML-looking syntax.

Listing 38.6 and Listing 38.7 are two examples that demonstrate how you can create formatted spreadsheets for Excel by using HTML table syntax. Listing 38.6 again creates a spreadsheet that lists the title and budget for each film. Note that you can provide width and alignment for the columns and specify formatting using ordinary <font> and <b> tags.

Listing 38.6 `FilmsToExcelPretty.cfm`—Outputting an HTML Table in Excel

```
<!---
 Filename: FilmsToExcelPretty.cfm
 Author: Nate Weiss (NMW)
 Purpose: Outputs film information for Microsoft Excel
--->

<!--- Retrieve information about films --->
<cfquery datasource="ows" name="getFilms">
 SELECT MovieTitle, AmountBudgeted
 FROM Films
 ORDER BY MovieTitle
</cfquery>

<!--- Set the content-type so Excel is invoked --->
<cfcontent type="application/msexcel">
<!--- Suggest default filename for spreadsheet --->
<cfheader name="Content-Disposition" value="filename=FilmBudgets.xls">

<html>
<head><title>Film Budgets</title></head>
<body>
<!--- Output ordinary HTML table, which will --->
<!--- be displayed by Excel as a spreadsheet --->
<table>
 <tr><th>Film</th><th>Budget</th></tr>
 <cfoutput query="getFilms">
  <tr>
   <td width="400">
    <font face="verdana">#MovieTitle#</font>
   </td>
   <td align="center">
    <font color="red"><b>#AmountBudgeted#</b></font>
   </td>
  </tr>
 </cfoutput>
</table>
</body>
</html>
```

Listing 38.7 is similar to Listing 38.6, except that it includes some additional color and formatting instructions, so the resulting spreadsheet looks quite nice. It also adds another row of cells to the bottom of the spreadsheet, which shows the total of the second column (the budgets of all films combined). This is a live, formula-based total; if the user changes any of the prices, Excel updates the total accordingly (Figure 38.6).

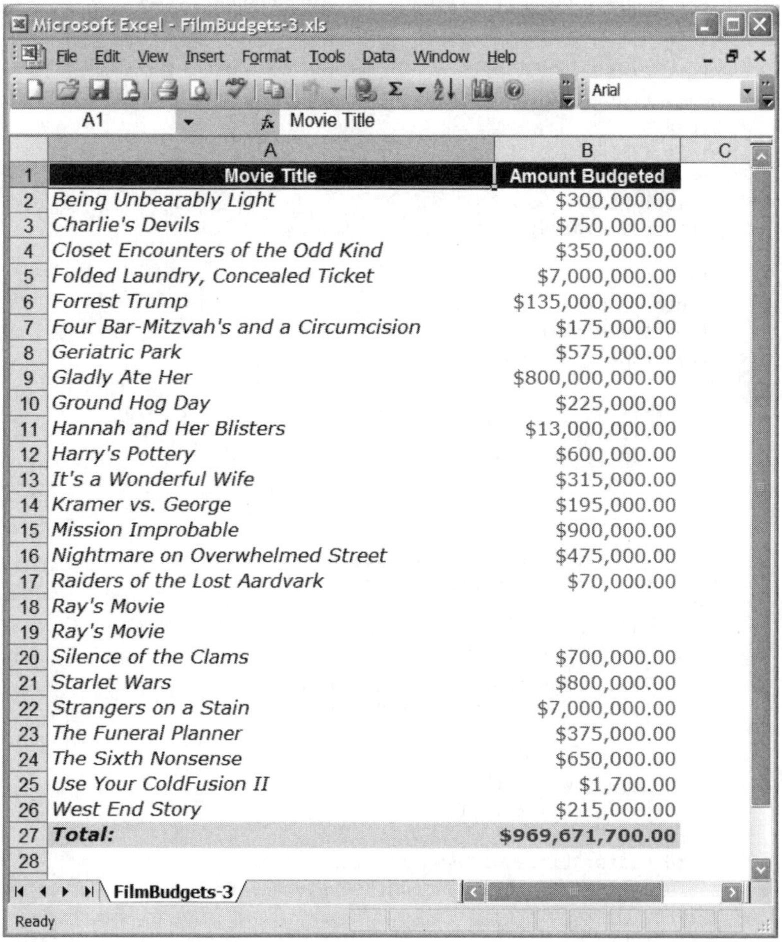

	A	B
1	Movie Title	Amount Budgeted
2	Being Unbearably Light	$300,000.00
3	Charlie's Devils	$750,000.00
4	Closet Encounters of the Odd Kind	$350,000.00
5	Folded Laundry, Concealed Ticket	$7,000,000.00
6	Forrest Trump	$135,000,000.00
7	Four Bar-Mitzvah's and a Circumcision	$175,000.00
8	Geriatric Park	$575,000.00
9	Gladly Ate Her	$800,000,000.00
10	Ground Hog Day	$225,000.00
11	Hannah and Her Blisters	$13,000,000.00
12	Harry's Pottery	$600,000.00
13	It's a Wonderful Wife	$315,000.00
14	Kramer vs. George	$195,000.00
15	Mission Improbable	$900,000.00
16	Nightmare on Overwhelmed Street	$475,000.00
17	Raiders of the Lost Aardvark	$70,000.00
18	Ray's Movie	
19	Ray's Movie	
20	Silence of the Clams	$700,000.00
21	Starlet Wars	$800,000.00
22	Strangers on a Stain	$7,000,000.00
23	The Funeral Planner	$375,000.00
24	The Sixth Nonsense	$650,000.00
25	Use Your ColdFusion II	$1,700.00
26	West End Story	$215,000.00
27	**Total:**	**$969,671,700.00**
28		

Figure 38.6

You can create dynamic spreadsheets that include live cell formulas.

Listing 38.7 `FilmsToExcelPrettier.cfm`—Adding CSS Formatting and Cell Formulas

```
<!---
 Filename: FilmsToExcelPrettier.cfm
 Author: Nate Weiss (NMW)
 Purpose: Outputs film information for Microsoft Excel
--->

<!--- Retrieve information about films --->
<cfquery datasource="ows" name="getFilms">
 SELECT MovieTitle, AmountBudgeted
 FROM Films
 ORDER BY MovieTitle
</cfquery>
```

Listing 38.7 (CONTINUED)

```
<!--- Set the content-type so Excel is invoked --->
<cfcontent type="application/msexcel">
<!--- Suggest default filename for spreadsheet --->
<cfheader name="Content-Disposition" value="filename=FilmBudgets.xls">

<html>
<head><title>Film Budgets</title></head>
<body>
<style TYPE="text/css">
 .rowHeads {
  color:white;
  background:blue;
 }
 .titleCol {
  width:400px;
  font-style:italic;
  font-family:verdana;
 }
 .priceCol {
  width:170px;
  font-family:verdana;
  color:red;
} ;
</style>
<!--- Output ordinary HTML table, which will --->
<!--- be displayed by Excel as a spreadsheet --->
<table>
 <!--- Top row --->
 <tr>
  <th class="rowHeads">Movie Title</th>
  <th class="rowHeads">Amount Budgeted</th>
 </tr>

 <!--- Data rows --->
 <cfoutput query="getFilms">
  <tr>
   <td class="titleCol">#MovieTitle#</td>
   <td class="priceCol">#AmountBudgeted#</td>
  </tr>
 </cfoutput>

 <!--- Last row, with "total" formula --->
 <cfset firstPriceCell = "B2">
 <cfset lastPriceCell = "B" & getFilms.RecordCount + 1>
 <cfset totalFormula = "SUM(#FirstPriceCell#:#LastPriceCell#)">
 <cfoutput>
  <tr>
   <td
    class="titleCol"
    style="font-weight:bold;background:yellow">Total:</td>
   <td
    class="priceCol"
    style="font-weight:bold;background:yellow"
  >=#TotalFormula#</td>
  </tr>
```

Listing 38.7 (CONTINUED)

```
  </cfoutput>
 </table>
 </body>
 </html>
```

Near the end of Listing 38.7, a ColdFusion variable called `totalFormula` is created, which will end up having a value of `SUM(B2:B24)` if 23 rows of film information exist.

TIP

Remember that the HTML approach used in Listing 38.7 is a solution only for Excel 2000 (sometimes called Excel 9) and later. This technique won't work for earlier versions of the product.

Generating Word Files

You can also use ColdFusion to create Microsoft Word files on the fly, using techniques similar to the ones for creating Excel files. This opens up the possibility of creating personalized or customized sales documents, pricing sheets, product documentation, and other documents you might want to deliver in the common Word file format.

Although the idea of using a proprietary document format to deliver such documents—rather than something more open, such as HTML—might rub some people the wrong way, there are some clear benefits. Most obviously, you can produce documents that end users can edit further, using their own, familiar copy of Word. Also, in a Word document you generally have much greater control over the way the document will look when printed (margins, headers, footers, leading, kerning, widow and orphan paragraphs, and so on) than you do with HTML.

Creating Documents with RTF

If you have exchanged documents between word-processing programs, you have probably encountered Rich Text Format. RTF is a somewhat older file format designed to store formatted information, especially documents such as those you create with a word processor. Word lets you work with RTF (`.rtf`) files in almost all the same ways you can work with real Word (`.doc`) files.

Most importantly to you, RTF is a plain-text format, so it's made up of normal ASCII characters, which ColdFusion is good at generating. So, just as you were able to create a tab-separated text to be sent to Excel via `<cfcontent>`, you can create RTF files to be sent to Word.

Creating an RTF Template Document

There are several approaches you could take to creating RTF files with ColdFusion. This section discusses a relatively simple one, which is similar to performing a mail-merge operation within a word processor. First, you will create a template document and save it as an RTF file on your ColdFusion server. Then you will customize the document using simple string-manipulation functions and send the customized version of the document back to the browser using the `<cfcontent>` tag.

To create your template document, do the following:

1. Open Word. Create some type of document, such as a form letter.

2. In the document, insert six placeholders by inserting the following terms somewhere in the text, including the percent signs: %CurrentDate%, %NameFirst%, %NameLast%, %NameFirstReal%, %NameLastReal%, and %FreePrize%.

3. Feel free to add some formatting to the document, using whatever features you want (styles, margins, font colors, tables, and so on). Do not include large pictures for the moment.

4. Select Save As from Word's File menu, select Rich Text Format from the drop-down list of file types, and save the document as DocTemplate.rtf in the same folder you're using to save code for this chapter.

5. Be sure you close the document in Word (otherwise, Word might keep it locked).

Now you can create a ColdFusion template that creates a personalized copy of the template, based on information you retrieve with a database query. Listing 38.8 shows one way to do this. As you can see, this template has two sections. When you visit the template normally (with no URL parameters), the top portion of the code executes and displays a list of actors. The user can then click an actor's name to cause the template to be executed again, this time with the appropriate ActorID passed as a URL parameter.

Listing 38.8 RetireActor.cfm—A Personalized Word Document from an RTF Template

```
<!---
 Filename: RetireActor.cfm
 Author: Nate Weiss (NMW)
 Purpose: Generates a retirement memo as an RTF document for Microsoft Word
--->

<!--- If no Actor ID passed, diplay list of links --->
<cfif not isDefined("URL.actorID")>

 <!--- Get a list of actors from database --->
 <cfquery name="getActors" datasource="ows">
  SELECT ActorID, NameFirst, NameLast
  FROM Actors
  ORDER BY NameLast, NameFirst
 </cfquery>

 <!--- Page Title, etc --->
 <html>
 <head><title>Actor Retirement System</title></head>
 <body>
```

Listing 38.8 (CONTINUED)

```
  <h3>Which Actor Would You Like To Retire?</h3>

  <!--- For each Actor, include simple link to --->
  <!--- this page, passing the Actor ID in URL --->
  <cfoutput query="getActors">
   <cfset linkURL = "#CGI.script_name#?actorID=#ActorID#">
   <a href="#linkURL#">#NameFirst# <b>#NameLast#</b></a><br>
  </cfoutput>
  </body>
  </html>

 <!--- If Actor ID passed, generate Word doc --->
 <cfelse>

  <!--- Make sure Actor ID in URL is a number --->
  <cfparam name="URL.actorID" type="numeric">

  <!--- Get this Actor's name from database --->
  <cfquery name="getActor" datasource="ows">
   SELECT NameFirst, NameLast,
    NameFirstReal, NameLastReal,
    (SELECT Min(DateInTheaters)
     FROM Films f, FilmsActors fa
     WHERE fa.FilmID = f.FilmID
     AND fa.ActorID = a.ActorID) AS DateFirstFilm
   FROM Actors a
   WHERE ActorID = #URL.actorID#
  </cfquery>

  <!--- How long has Actor been with company? --->
  <cfset monthsEmployed = dateDiff("m", getActor.DateFirstFilm, now())>

  <!--- Determine severance package --->
  <cfif monthsEmployed gte 36>
   <cfset sevPackage = "Gold Watch (Digital)">
  <cfelseif monthsEmployed gte 18>
   <cfset sevPackage = "$100 Starbucks Gift Certificate">
  <cfelse>
   <cfset sevPackage = "ColdFusion Web Application Construction Kit">
  </cfif>

  <!--- Location of our RTF "template" document --->
  <cfset thisFolder = getDirectoryFromPath(getCurrentTemplatePath())>
  <cfset templatePath = thisFolder & "DocTemplate.rtf">
  <!--- Read RTF template into variable called "RTF" --->
  <cffile action="read" file="#templatePath#" variable="rtf">

  <!--- Replace "placeholders" with specific information --->
  <cfset todaysDate = dateFormat(Now(), "dddd, mmmm d, yyyy")>
  <cfset rtf = replace(rtf, "%CurrentDate%", todaysDate,"ALL")>
  <cfset rtf = replace(rtf, "%FreePrize%", sevPackage,"ALL")>
  <cfset rtf = replace(rtf, "%NameFirst%", trim(getActor.NameFirst),"ALL")>
  <cfset rtf = replace(rtf, "%NameLast%", trim(getActor.NameLast),"ALL")>
  <cfset rtf = replace(rtf, "%NameFirstReal%", trim(getActor.NameFirstReal),"ALL")>
```

Listing 38.8 (CONTINUED)

```
<cfset rtf = replace(rtf, "%NameLastReal%", trim(getActor.NameLastReal),"ALL")>

<!--- Suggest default filename for document --->
<cfheader name="Content-Disposition" value="filename=RetireMemo.doc">
<!--- Set the content-type so Word is invoked --->
<cfcontent type="application/msword"><cfoutput>#rtf#</cfoutput>
</cfif>
```

When an actor ID is provided, the second part of the template executes, which is where the dynamic Word generation occurs. First, some basic information about the employee is retrieved from the database, using an ordinary <cfquery> tag. Then, a severance package is determined, depending on how long ago the actor's first film was released (if he was hired more than 12 months ago, he gets a gold watch).

Next, the <cffile> tag is used to read the DocTemplate.rtf file (which is just a text file) into an ordinary ColdFusion string variable called rtf. Now, you can use ColdFusion's Replace() function to replace the simple placeholders in the RTF file with the actor's actual first and last names and replace the %FreePrize% placeholder with the value of the SevPackage variable (which contains the determined severance package).

→ See Chapter 70, "Interacting with the Operating System," in Vol. 3, *Advanced Application Development,* for more information about using <cffile> to read in the contents of text files.

NOTE

In this example, ColdFusion looks for the DocTemplate.rtf file in the same folder the RetireActor.cfm file is in. The getCurrentTemplatePath() function makes this possible. In practice, you might want to keep the RTF template somewhere outside the Web server's document root, so it can't be downloaded directly.

Now the customized RTF text is sitting in the rtf variable. All that's left is to stream the RTF text to the browser. As with the Excel examples earlier in this chapter, this is done by including a <cfcontent> tag, this time with the type attribute set to application/msword. This causes the browser to launch the user's copy of Microsoft Word on the local machine. Note that you also must include the <cfheader> tag, which suggests a sensible default file name for the document (see the discussion of Listing 38.5).

If you use the DocTemplate.rtf file that was included with the chapter files (at the book Web site) the resulting Word document will be a personalized retirement memo (Figure 38.7).

Serving Media Files

You have seen how you can create various types of document-type files with a little help from the <cfcontent> tag. You also can use <cfcontent> to serve up images or other types of multimedia files, such as audio or video.

Figure 38.7

You can create Word files on the fly that the user can print or modify.

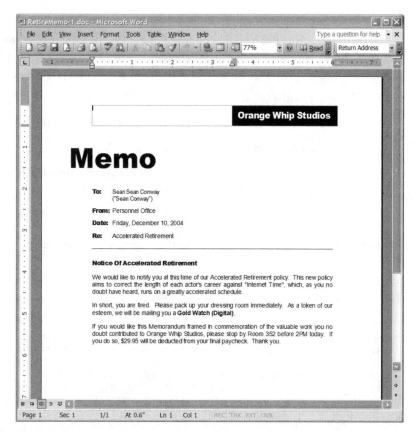

Turning ColdFusion into an Image Server

Let's say you've been asked to create a banner ad server application with ColdFusion. One requirement is that your ad server must be able to work with sites built with static HTML files. You need to be able to provide a simple <img> tag that people can cut and paste into their pages. But if the src of the <img> tag doesn't change each time a user views a page, how will the banner ad rotate? Like the other solutions discussed in this chapter, the answer to this head-scratcher involves the <cfcontent> tag.

Although it's certainly the norm, no law says the src for an image has to have a .gif or .jpg extension. The src can be the URL for a ColdFusion template, perhaps called AdServer.cfm. Rather than returning some type of text, such as HTML code, the template should return an image. In addition, it should specify a MIME content type of image/gif instead of the usual text/html content type. Because of the content type, the browser will understand that it's receiving what it expects to receive (an image) and should have no problems displaying it.

Serving Up Images

Listing 38.9 shows what this ad server template might look like. It assumes that a number of banner images are located in a subfolder called Ads. It selects one of the ads at random and then uses <cfcontent> to send the image back to the browser with the appropriate content type.

Before this example will work, however, you must do the following:

1. Save the code shown in Listing 38.9 to a ColdFusion template named AdServer.cfm.

2. Create a subdirectory called Ads in the same folder where you just saved AdServer.cfm.

3. Place several banner ads or other GIF files in the Ads subfolder. If you want, you can simply copy the images from the Ads subfolder from this chapter's folder at the book Web site.

Listing 38.9 AdServer.cfm—Using <cfcontent> to Respond with an Image

```
<!---
 Filename:  AdServer.cfm
 Created by: Nate Weiss (NMW)
 Purpose:  Responds with the binary content of a randomly selected image
--->

<!--- Ad Images are in "Ads" subfolder, within current folder --->
<cfset adDir = getDirectoryFromPath(getCurrentTemplatePath()) & "Ads\ ">

<!--- Get a listing of GIF image files in the Ads folder --->
<!--- Result is a query object with a row for each image --->
<cfdirectory directory="#adDir#" action="LIST" filter="*.gif" name="getAds">

<!--- Pick random number between one and number of images --->
<cfset adNum = randRange(1, getAds.recordCount)>

<!--- Grab the filename in chosen row of the GetAds query --->
<cfset adFileName = getAds.Name[adNum]>

<!--- Prepend directory to get full filesystem path to ad image --->
<cfset adFilePath = adDir & adFileName>

<!--- Send the chosen image back to the client --->
<cfcontent type="image/gif" file="#adFilePath#">
```

NOTE

Because it isn't returning HTML content, Listing 38.9 doesn't contain the <html>, <body>, and other standard tags you're used to seeing.

As you can see, you don't need a lot of code to serve up an image with ColdFusion. You simply select the file you want to serve, and supply its complete file name to the file attribute of the <cfcontent> tag, which is being used for the first time in this chapter (see Table 38.2). Any streaming and network communication issues are handled for you.

First, the adDir variable is set to the full file-system path of the Ads folder. This is a nice use of the getDirectoryFromPath() and getCurrentTemplatePath() functions. When you use the two together, as shown in Listing 38.9, they return the full path to the folder in which the currently executing template is located.

Next, the `<cfdirectgory>` tag is used to get a listing of all GIF files within the `Ads` folder. You can find out more about `<cfdirectory>` in Chapter 70. Here, it's used in a very basic way. It returns a query object, such as the results of a `<cfquery>`, where each row of the query represents a file that matches the `filter` attribute. The query object contains a column called `NAME`, which contains the file name (with the extension, but not the path) of each file.

Now, the `randRange()` function is used to pick a number between 1 and the number of rows in the query, which in turn is the number of GIF files in the `Ads` folder. So, if eight images are in the folder, the `adNum` variable will be set to a random number between 1 and 8. Next, the `adFileName` variable is set to the value of the `name` column of the appropriate row of the `getAds` query object. If `adNum` turns out to be 5, `adFileName` is set to the file name in the fifth row of the query.

TIP

You can gain more control over how random numbers are generated by using the `rand()` and `randomize()` functions together.

Finally, another variable called `adFilePath` is created, which concatenates the `adDir` and `adFileName` variables together, resulting in the complete file system path to the randomly selected image file. All that's left is to feed the path to the `file` attribute of the `<cfcontent>` tag.

You should be able to test the template at this point by visiting the `AdServer.cfm` template with your browser. All you should see is the randomly selected banner ad. If you reload the template's URL a few times, you should see that the ads rotate on a fairly even, random basis.

NOTE

If you visit the `AdServer.cfm` template and try to View Source with your browser, you will find that your browser either prevents it or shows garbage characters. This is because there is no HTML source to show. The template is returning the binary image information itself, not an `<img>` tag, which is a pointer to an image on the Net.

Displaying the Images in Other Web Pages

The goal of this exercise was to use a simple `<img>` tag to create a rotating banner ad system that could be used by static HTML files, and that's exactly what you have. You can include the following line of code in a static HTML file:

```
<img src="http://localhost:8500/ows/38/AdServer.cfm">
```

When the browser encounters the `<img>` tag, it communicates with the `AdServer.cfm` template and displays whatever image content is returned. As long as you use a fully qualified URL (including the `http://`), you're free to save the HTML file on any server in the world. It doesn't have to be on the same machine as the ad server.

Handling Click-Throughs

Listing 38.9 now correctly serves up banner ads, but it can't be really considered a fully featured ad-management system at this point. For instance, what about tracking the number of ads served? What happens when the user clicks an ad?

We don't have room here to develop a world-class ad server that would meet everyone's needs. But we can add a few lines of code to the `AdServer.cfm` template to make the example more complete.

NOTE

The main purpose of these examples is to demonstrate how `<cfcontent>` can be combined with client or session variables to build a useful application based on serving media files, such as images. If you were building a real-world ad-server utility, you would probably do some things differently (for instance, use a database).

Listing 38.10 shows an `Application.cfc` file that turns on ColdFusion's Session Management feature and then creates a structure called `SESSION.adsOnPages` if it doesn't exist already. Because the structure is kept in the `SESSION` scope, it's maintained separately for each user who is shown an ad. You'll see how this structure is used in a moment.

Listing 38.10 `Application.cfc`—Getting Ready to Track Ad Views

```
<!---
Filename: Application.cfc
Created by: Raymond Camden (ray@camdenfamily.com)
Please Note Executes for every page request!
--->

<cfcomponent output="false">

  <!--- Name the application. --->
  <cfset this.name = "AdServer">
  <!--- Turn on session management. --->
  <cfset this.sessionManagement = true>

  <cffunction name="onSessionStart" returnType="void" output="false">
    <cfset SESSION.AdsOnPages = structNew()>
  </cffunction>

</cfcomponent>
```

The version of `AdServer.cfm` in Listing 38.11 is almost the same as Listing 38.9. Only one line of code has been added, before the `<cfcontent>` tag at the end:

```
<!--- Record fact that this ad is now placed on this page --->
<!--- You could record the ad-showing in database instead --->
<cfset SESSION.adsOnPages[CGI.http_referer] = adFileName>
```

Listing 38.11 `AdServer2.cfm`—Recording Each Ad Hit in a Session Variable

```
<!---
Filename: AdServer2.cfm
Created by: Nate Weiss (NMW)
Purpose: Responds with the binary content of a randomly selected image
--->

<!--- Ad Images are in "Ads" subfolder, within current folder --->
<cfset adDir = getDirectoryFromPath(getCurrentTemplatePath()) & "Ads\ ">

<!--- Get a listing of GIF image files in the Ads folder --->
<!--- Result is a query object with a row for each image --->
<cfdirectory directory="#adDir#" action="LIST" filter="*.gif" name="getAds">
```

Listing 38.11 (CONTINUED)

```
<!--- Pick random number between one and number of images --->
<cfset adNum = randRange(1, getAds.recordCount)>

<!--- Grab the filename in chosen row of the GetAds query --->
<cfset adFileName = getAds.Name[adNum]>

<!--- Prepend directory to get full filesystem path to ad image --->
<cfset adFilePath = adDir & adFileName>

<!--- Record fact that this ad is now placed on this page --->
<!--- You could record the ad-showing in database instead --->
<cfset SESSION.adsOnPages[CGI.http_referer] = adFileName>

<!--- Send the chosen image back to the client --->
<cfcontent type="image/gif" file="#adFilePath#">
```

Here we exploit the fact that the browser will provide the referring page when it requests the image from the `AdServer.cfm` page. That is, the URL of the page in which the image is to appear will be available in the `CGI.http_referer` variable. Therefore, the `<cfset>` line shown previously places a new name/value pair in the `AdsOnPages` structure, where the referring URL is used as the name portion of the structure entry, and the file name of the ad being shown is the value portion.

Later, you can easily look up the ad's file name using the page's URL as the structure's key. In other words, the template is now tracking which users have seen which ads, on which pages. (See Chapter 8, "The Basics of CFML," in *Adobe ColdFusion 8 Web Application Construction Kit, Volume 1: Getting Started*, for a discussion about ColdFusion structures.)

NOTE

In addition to (or instead of) maintaining the `adsOnPages` structure, you could record each banner ad view in a database table called, for example, `adViews`. The table might have columns such as `AdID`, `PageURL`, and `ViewDate`. This would let you easily create reports based on usage.

Now that each ad view is being recorded in the `adsOnPages` structure, you can create a template to respond when an ad is clicked. You can use the code in Listing 38.12, assuming that this is the template that will be called when a user clicks an ad. It again uses the `CGI.http_referer` variable to determine the URL of the referring document, which should be the URL that the ad is on. The idea is to use the referrer URL to look up the last ad shown to this user on that page.

Listing 38.12 `AdClick.cfm`—Responding to a Banner Ad Click

```
<!---
 Filename:  AdClick.cfm
 Created by: Nate Weiss (NMW)
 Please Note This template executes when a user clicks on an ad
--->

<!--- Assuming we have shown an ad on the referring page --->
<cfif structKeyExists(SESSION.adsOnPages, CGI.http_referer)>

 <!--- What ad was last shown to this user on referring page? --->
 <cfset adFileName = SESSION.adsOnPages[CGI.http_referer]>
```

Listing 38.12   (CONTINUED)

```
<!---
At this point, you might record the "click" in database
  and then redirect the user to the appropriate site via
  the <cflocation> tag. Here, we will simply output the
  ad that the user clicked on, just to prove the concept.
--->
<cfoutput>
  You just came from: #CGI.http_referer#<br>
  You got here by clicking on the <b>#AdFileName#</b> ad.
</cfoutput>

<!--- If "KeyExists" fails, we don't know what ad was shown --->
<cfelse>

  We don't have any ad on record for you. Perhaps you didn't
  come here after seeing an ad, or your session timed out.

</cfif>
```

First, the structKeyExists() function is used to see whether a record exists for the URL. If so, the <cfset> line retrieves the value from the structure, assigning the ad's file name to the adFileName variable. This code then outputs the original file name of the ad, without redirecting the user somewhere else. As an exercise, you could take things further by using the file name to determine where to send the user in response to the ad click, log the click-through in a database, and then use <cflocation> to redirect the user to the advertiser's Web site.

The code in Listing 38.13 can be used to test the new ad server templates. The <img> tag displays the banner ad served up by AdServer.cfm (Figure 38.8), and the <a> tag causes the AdClick.cfm page to be called when the ad is clicked. This is an ordinary, static HTML file that doesn't need to be processed by ColdFusion.

Figure 38.8

ColdFusion templates can serve images, such as this banner ad, instead of documents.

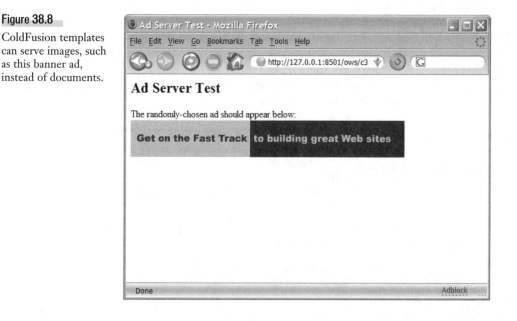

Listing 38.13 `AdServerTest.htm`—Displaying an Image Served by ColdFusion

```
<!---
 Filename:  AdServerTest.htm
 Created by: Nate Weiss (NMW)
 Please Note This is a static HTML file, not a CF template
--->

<html>
<head><title>Ad Server Test</title></head>
<body>

<h2>Ad Server Test</h2>
The randomly-chosen ad should appear below:<br>
<!--- Include banner ad supplied by "Ad Server" --->
<a href="AdClick.cfm">
<img src="AdServer2.cfm" width="468" height="60" alt="" border="0"></a>
</body>
</html>
```

Other Uses

You could apply this same idea—using ColdFusion to serve up media files—to many other situations. Here are a few ideas.

Other Types of Media Content

You also could adapt this ad server idea to serve up other kinds of multimedia content, such as Adobe Flash movies, or audio or video files. As long as you provide the correct MIME content type to the `type` attribute of the `<cfcontent>` tag, you can serve up just about any type of content.

Secure Downloads

If you look back at Listing 38.9, you will notice that `<cfcontent>`'s `file` attribute requires a full file system path (including the `c:\`, for instance, if you're using ColdFusion on a Windows machine). This means the banner images could be stored anywhere on the server's drives or local network. You're free to store the images in a folder that isn't within the Web server's document root, and thus not accessible via the Internet using an ordinary URL (a URL ending with `.gif`). The only way to get to the files would be via the `AdServer.cfm` template. If you think about it, there's no way for the outside world to know what the name of each image file is.

This means you easily can set up a secure download system for documents or other files your company wants to be accessible to only certain people. Or you could set up a software download page that requires people to register (or pay) before they can obtain your software. Because ColdFusion is in charge, you can use whatever queries or other special processing you need to determine whether the user has the right to get a particular image or file.

NOTE

If you want to give the downloaded file a name, or if you find that you don't get the Save As behavior you want, try using a `Content-Disposition` header, such as the Word and Excel examples earlier in this chapter.

CHAPTER 39

Full-Text Searching

Getting to Know Verity

By now you're convinced that ColdFusion is the greatest package on the planet for publishing database data to the Web—but you haven't yet learned how to create that most popular of Web-based applications, the search engine. The success of Yahoo!, Google, and other search engines has made the concept of a Web-based search tool nearly as ubiquitous on the Internet as the word "ubiquitous" itself. An intelligent search tool is a must-have for an increasing number of sites. This chapter shows how to integrate the Verity search technology into your ColdFusion applications.

ColdFusion includes a version of Verity search technology that can be leveraged within ColdFusion applications. This technology includes:

- An engine for indexing and searching large amounts of textual data

- A programming interface for searching the indexes

- A number of index optimization utilities

You can think of the combination of these tools as "the Verity search engine." The Verity search engine excels at finding words in large chunks of unstructured text, such as the documents human beings tend to write. As a developer, you tell it what to search—and what to search for—and it will faithfully try to find it.

Verity can search a variety of files in a variety of languages, and it does all the fancy stuff you'd expect from a sophisticated search engine, such as handling ANDs, ORs, wildcards, and so on. If you've ever used the search interface provided by Lexis/Nexis, you can expect the same type of functionality from your own applications that use Verity.

Conceptually, the Verity layer you will learn about in this chapter is similar to the data source/SQL layer we covered earlier in the book. The main difference is that while data sources and SQL excel at accessing neat rows and columns of information in structured database tables, Verity excels at accessing messy chunks of text strewn about in various folders on your hard drives.

Much of Verity's inner workings are thoughtfully hidden from ColdFusion developers. In a nut-shell, here's how you integrate text searching into your ColdFusion applications. First you index your textual data with the ColdFusion administrator or the `<cfindex>` tag. Then you build a search form for users. Then you build an *action* template that employs the `<cfsearch>` tag and formats the search results.

Searching for Different Types of Files with Verity

ColdFusion's Verity functionality supports most popular file types, including native files such as documents produced with many of the Microsoft Office applications. This feature provides great flexibility when it comes to making files searchable via a Web browser.

For instance, in an intranet situation, employees can continue to use the word-processing and spreadsheet applications they use every day. All they have to do is save the documents in a folder tree that is indexed in a Verity collection. With just a few lines of code, you can turn those documents into a fully searchable company library. Verity can index Office documents, MP3s, PDFs, and other binary formats. For a complete list, see the official documentation.

NOTE

Different file types can be freely mixed and matched in a Verity collection. Don't worry about keeping the HTML and Word files in separate folders or collections. Store them wherever you want.

Integrating ColdFusion with Other Search Engines

Including Verity functionality is a terrific way to add search capability to your application, making it behave somewhat like a mini-Google. However, it has nothing to do with actually integrating with Google, AltaVista, Yahoo!, or any other commercial search engines. If you want to integrate with one of these search engines, you certainly can include standard `href` links from your application to a commercial search engine—but doing so has nothing to do with the Verity functionality explained in this chapter.

You also could place on one of your pages a search form that has an appropriate URL (within the commercial search engine's domain) as its `action` parameter. Many of the commercial search engines have instructions about how to set this up—such as what to name the form `<input>` tags, for instance. See their sites for details.

Finally, you could use the `<cfhttp>` tag to place a search request to a commercial search engine and display the results on your page with the `#cfhttp.FileContent#` variable.

Creating a Search Tool for Your Documents

Let's say that Orange Whip Studios' Human Resources Department wants to make the company's personnel policies available online so employees can see what they are allowed to do (and not do) at any time. These policies are published internally and are not accessible to a large number of employees.

The documents are saved as various Word, plain-text, and Excel files. Collect all the documents into one folder on your Web server's local drive; explore what is necessary to make these documents searchable and retrievable from a Web browser using ColdFusion's Verity functionality as the back end. It's really pretty simple.

Understanding Collections

Verity's search functionality centers around a concept of a collection. A Verity *collection* is a mass of documents you want Verity to keep track of and make searchable. (Note that a collection also can consist of a query result set, which is explored later in this chapter.)

After Verity has been told which documents belong to a collection, it can index the documents and compile metadata about them for its own use. This index enables it to search through your documents quickly, without actually parsing through them line by line at run time. Conceptually, the key to Verity's strength is its capability to invest a certain amount of time up front in indexing and compiling information about your documents. You get the payoff on that investment when your users run their searches. Verity has already studied the documents and can therefore return information about them very quickly.

Again, you might find it useful to think of Verity collections as being the full-text search equivalent of data sources. Just as you need to set up a data source before you can use `<cfquery>` to retrieve data with SQL, you need to set up a collection before you can get started with Verity. As with setting up a new data source, you go to the ColdFusion Administrator to set up a new collection.

Creating a New Collection

Here are the steps needed to create the Verity collection for the Human Resources documents:

1. Go to the ColdFusion Administrator and click the Verity Collections link in the Data & Services section, as shown in Figure 39.1. This screen lists all collections and contains a form used to create new collections.

2. Name the new collection `owshr` (as in "Orange Whip Studios HR").

3. You can change the path if you want the collection to be stored in a location other than the default (`/verity/collections` under the ColdFusion root), but you should generally not do so unless you have a specific reason not to (such as drive space or file-permissions issues).

NOTE

The path you fill in when creating a new collection is simply where Verity's internal data about your documents will be kept. This is not the path to where the actual documents are.

4. Verity can perform intelligent searching if it knows the language that content is in. Select the primary language from the drop-down list.

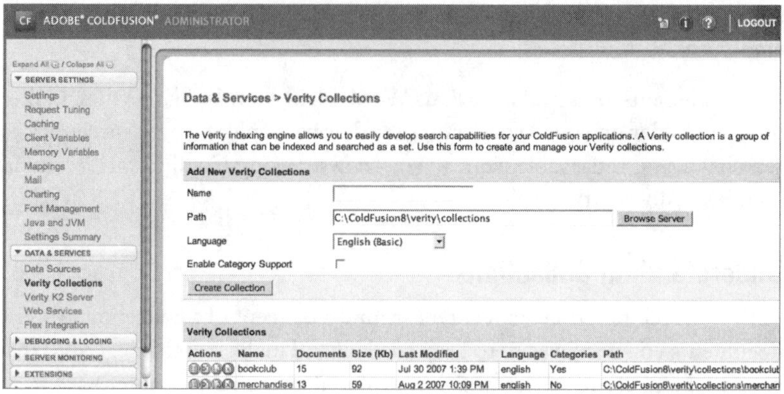

Figure 39.1

Verity Collections must be created in order to use ColdFusion full-text searching functionality.

NOTE

If only English is shown and you need non-English support, install the add-on Verity language pack.

5. Categories can be used within collections to group related documents (making locating data within very large collections much easier). To use categories be sure to check the Enable Category Support checkbox.
6. Click the Create Collection button. After a moment, your new collection will appear in the list of Verity Collections (along with any other existing collections).

Indexing the Collection

Creating the collection simply results in the creation of the basic Verity infrastructure that will be used for the collection. You must *index* the collection in order to make the collection searchable.

Indexing is simple and can be done via the ColdFusion Administrator or through the `<cfindex>` tag. Let's start by indexing a collection through the ColdFusion Administrator.

Indexing Your Files with the ColdFusion Administrator

Locate the newly created collection in the Verity Collections list, and click the Index icon (the left-most icon) for the collection to be indexed (or just click on the collection name). This displays the Index Collection page (seen in Figure 39.2). The form is used to specify the text content that is to be made searchable.

You must now tell ColdFusion what to index:

1. Enter the file extensions (comma delimited) as follows: `.html, .htm, .doc, .txt, .xls`
2. The `directory path` specifies the location on the server's disk where the data to be made searchable is located. Enter: `C:\ColdFusion8\wwwroot\ows\39\HR\DOCS` or the appropriate path for your server.

3. Check the Recursively Index Sub Directories (so that content in child folders is indexed too).

4. The `return URL` specifies the URL that will be used to return any content if the user searches for it. It is the path the Web server uses to find the content. Enter: `http://localhost:8500/ows/39/hr/docs/`or the appropriate URL for your server.

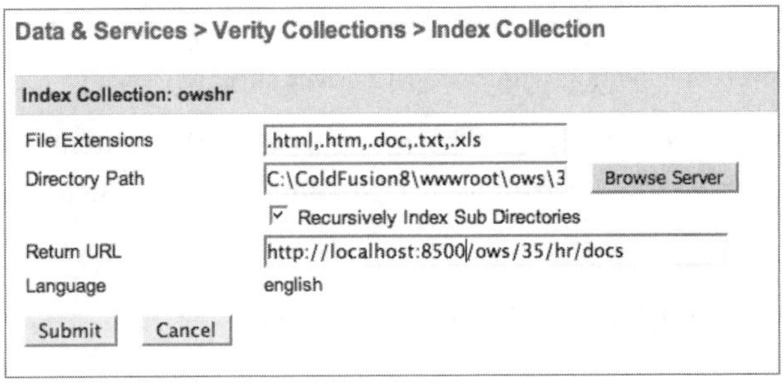

Figure 39.2

The Index Collection page is used to add items to a Verity collection, indexing them for searching.

Data & Services > Verity Collections > Index Collection

Index Collection: owshr

File Extensions	.html,.htm,.doc,.txt,.xls
Directory Path	C:\ColdFusion8\wwwroot\ows\3 [Browse Server]
	☑ Recursively Index Sub Directories
Return URL	http://localhost:8500/ows/35/hr/docs
Language	english

[Submit]   [Cancel]

NOTE

Again, it's assumed that you're using the stand-alone Web server. If you aren't, the directory path may be different.

At this point, click the Submit button to index the content. When indexing is complete (it will take a second or two), you'll be returned to the Verity Collection list page and the message "Collection owshr Indexed" will be displayed at the top.

You now know one way to index your documents. This method is handy for the following situations:

- When the documents change infrequently, or not on a fixed or predictable schedule

- When the documents live outside your ColdFusion application, such as in a folder full of Word files that employees might save and edit without your application knowing about it

- For testing and development

- With less complicated in-house applications

But other situations are likely to require the programmatic approach:

- When the documents are always changing.

- When it's critical that new documents become searchable right away

- When it's important that your application be as self-tuning as possible—such as when you are working as an outside consultant

- With more complicated applications

Let's see how the programmatic approach is used.

Indexing Your Files with the `<cfindex>` Tag

You've learned how to index a collection using the ColdFusion Administrator, but that approach isn't always good enough. Sometimes you'll need a ColdFusion application to do the indexing itself, programmatically.

The `<cfindex>` tag cues Verity to wake up and index (or re-index) the files in the folder you specify. This is the second step in the overall process of making a Verity application come alive. (The first step is creating the collection in the ColdFusion Administrator; the third is actually searching the collection with the `<cfsearch>` tag, which we will cover shortly.)

The template in Listing 39.1 uses the `<cfindex>` tag to index the content of the HR\Docs subdirectory. This content consists of some Microsoft Word and Excel documents as well as some text and HTML files.

Listing 39.1 `indexing.CFM`—Indexing the owshr Collection

```
<!---
Module:         indexing.cfm
Author:         Leon Chalnick & Ben Forta
Function:       Indexes HTML, Text, Word and Excel
 content for owshr collection.
Date created:   01/05/2005
--->

Indexing documents ...<br>
<cfflush>

<!--- Index the owshr collection --->
<cfindex collection="owshr"
         action="refresh"
         type="path"
         key="c:\ coldfusion8\ wwwroot\ ows\ 39\ hr\ docs\ "
         extensions=".htm, .html, .txt, .doc, .xls"
         recurse="yes"
         urlpath="http://localhost:8501/ows/39/hr/docs">

Done!
```

The `<cfindex>` tag tells Verity to index your actual documents, and the `<cfindex>` tag's various parameters give Verity the particulars about what you want it to do. Take a look at each of the parameters:

- `collection` tells Verity which collection to use.

- `action` tells Verity you're interested in refreshing any data currently in the collection with new information. Other values are possible for `action` other than `refresh`, and are discussed in the section "Maintaining Collections," later in this chapter.

- `type` tells Verity you're interested in adding documents from a directory path on your Web server. You'll learn about another possible value for `type` later, when the topic of using Verity to index database data rather than document files is covered. Refer to the section "Indexing Your Table Data: Verity to the Rescue," later in this chapter.

- `key` tells Verity from which directory path to add documents. This parameter must evaluate to the complete file system path to the actual documents you want to index. Be sure to edit this line to match the location where you saved the files.

- `extensions` tells Verity which documents in the specified folder should be indexed. This parameter is useful if you want only certain types of documents to become searchable.

- `recurse` tells Verity whether you want it to index files in subfolders of the folder you specified with the `KEY` parameter. Possible values are `YES` and `NO`. You would usually specify `YES`.

- `urlpath` tells Verity to maintain URLs for each document as it indexes, by appending the file name to the value you supply with this parameter. If `recurse="YES"` and the file is in a subfolder, the folder name is appended as well. As long as the value you supply here is the URL version of the value you supplied for `KEY`, Verity automatically records the correct URL for each file as it indexes. You will see this in action later when you use the `#URL#` column returned by the `<cfsearch>` tag. This is discussed later in the "Search Results Page" section. Be sure to edit this line to match your Web server information.

That's about all there is to indexing document files. Now all you have to do is ensure that the code in Listing 39.1 runs whenever new documents are saved to the `\ows\39\HR\Docs` folder.

Creating a Search Interface

Now that you've created the `owshr` collection and you've learned both techniques for indexing it, you can start putting together the ColdFusion templates to make your documents searchable. You'll see that the code you use to do this is similar in concept to the examples in Chapter 12, "ColdFusion Forms," in *Adobe ColdFusion 8 Web Application Construction Kit, Volume 1: Getting Started.*

Building the search interface involves constructing two pages. You need a simple search form page for users to enter their search criteria. This form's action template will actually conduct the search using `<cfsearch>`, and it can also display the search results.

The Search Form Page

Roll up your sleeves because we're writing more code: it's time to build a search form. Refer to Listing 39.2.

Listing 39.2 `searchform.cfm`—The Search Form Page

```
<!---
Name:         searchform.cfm
Author:       Leon Chalnick & Ben Forta
Description:  Presents a simple form for specifying
search criteria and number of rows to display
Date created:  01/05/2005
--->
<html>
```

Listing 39.2 (CONTINUED)

```
<head>
 <title>search form</title>
</head>
<body>

<h2>Personnel Policy Documents</h2>
<p>
<strong>Search Form</strong>

<!--- Create search form --->
<form action="searchresults.cfm" method="post">

<table>
 <tr>
  <td>Keywords:</td>
  <td><input type="text" name="criteria" size="30"></td>
 </tr>
 <tr>
  <td colspan=2>
   <input type="submit" value="Search">
  </td>
 </tr>
</table>

</form>

</body>

</html>
```

The Search Results Page

This form submits these two pieces of information to the searchresults.cfm template, which contains the code that actually runs the Verity search and displays the results of the search to the user.

Take a look at that template now. As Listing 39.3 shows, it contains only one ColdFusion tag that you're not familiar with yet—the <cfsearch> tag.

Listing 39.3 searchresults.cfm—The Search Results Page

```
<!---
Name:          searchresults.cfm
Author:        Leon Chalnick & Ben Forta
Description:   Runs CFSEARCH and displays results.
               The only tricky part is determining
               how to provide link to resulting file.
               It's dependent on type of file and
               is documented below.
Date created:  01/05/2005
--->

<!--- Run the search against the HRDocs collection --->
<cfsearch name="GetResults"
          collection="owshr"
```

Listing 39.3 (CONTINUED)

```
                criteria="#FORM.criteria#">

<!--- Display results --->
<html>
<head>
 <title>Search Results</title>
</head>

<body>
<h2>Personnel Policy Documents</h2>

<cfoutput>
Search Results: <strong>#FORM.criteria#</strong>
</cfoutput>

<p>

<!--- no files found for specified criteria? --->
<cfif GetResults.RecordCount is 0>

   <strong>No files found for specified criteria</strong>

<cfelse>

 <!--- Found a match --->
 <table cellspacing=0 cellpadding=2>

  <!--- Display results --->
  <cfoutput query="GetResults">
   <!--- alternate line background color --->
   <cfset bgcolor=IIf(CurrentRow Mod 2,
                      DE('ffffff'),
                      DE('ffffcf'))>
   <tr bgcolor="#bgcolor#" valign="top">
    <!--- current row number --->
    <td>#CurrentRow#</td>
    <!--- score --->
    <!--- file name with the link returning the file --->
    <td>
     <!---
    HREF to file is produced using either FILE protocol
    or HTTP, depending on whether this is a web document.
    so, we'll look at the file ext to determine if it's
    a web doc or not --->
     <cfset FileName=GetFileFromPath(Key)>
     <cfset Ext=ListLast(FileName, ".")>
     <!--- Display title if there is one, else name --->
     <cfif Trim(Title) IS "">
      <cfset display=GetFileFromPath(Key)>
     <cfelse>
      <cfset display=title>
     </cfif>
     <!--- Now display it --->
     <a href="#url#">#display#</a> (#score#)
     <br>
```

Listing 39.3 (CONTINUED)

```
         <small>#Context#</small>
       </td>
     </tr>
   </cfoutput>
  </table>

</cfif>

</body>
</html>
```

Clearly, the focus of this template is the `<cfsearch>` tag near the top. The `<cfsearch>` tag tells Verity to actually run a search: take the search criteria that the user supplies and try to find documents that match.

Do you recall that Verity searches are similar to data source/SQL queries? With that similarity in mind, it's worth noting that the `<cfsearch>` tag acts a lot like the `<cfquery>` tag when you're dealing with database tables.

Take a look at the specific parameters you're supplying to the `<cfsearch>` tag in Listing 39.3. As you do so, keep in mind that most of these parameters look like the ones you'd supply to a `<cfquery>` tag.

Here are the parameters for `<CFSEARCH>`, as used in Listing 39.3:

- `name` gives the search a name. Whatever results are found by Verity are available (for your use as a developer) as a query that has the name you supply here. You can use the search results in `<cfoutput>` tags and in any of the other ways you normally use query results.

- `collection` tells Verity in which collection to search for documents. In this case, we are using the just-created `owshr` collection.

- `criteria` is probably the most important parameter here. This is what you're actually asking Verity to look for. You're simply passing to this parameter whatever the user types in the search form.

NOTE

`<cfsearch>` also takes a `type parameter`. You can use `type="simple"` or `type="explicit"` in your search templates. `type="simple"` places the `stem` and `many` operators into effect automatically. Unless you specify `explicit`, `simple` is used by default. I recommend that you don't use `explicit` unless you have a specific reason to do so.

After the `<cfsearch>` is executed, the rest of Listing 39.3 displays the results to the user (as seen in Figure 39.3 for keyword `basic`). Here is the main thing to keep in mind: Now that the `<cfsearch>` has found its results, you treat it just as if it were a `<cfquery>` named `GetResults`.

First, a `<cfif>` tag performs the now-familiar check to ensure that the built-in `RecordCount` variable is not `0` (which would mean Verity didn't find any results).

Provided there are results to display, your code moves into the large `<cfelse>` block that encompasses the remainder of the template. `<table>`, `<tr>`, and `<td>` tags are used to establish an HTML table in which to display the results, with headers.

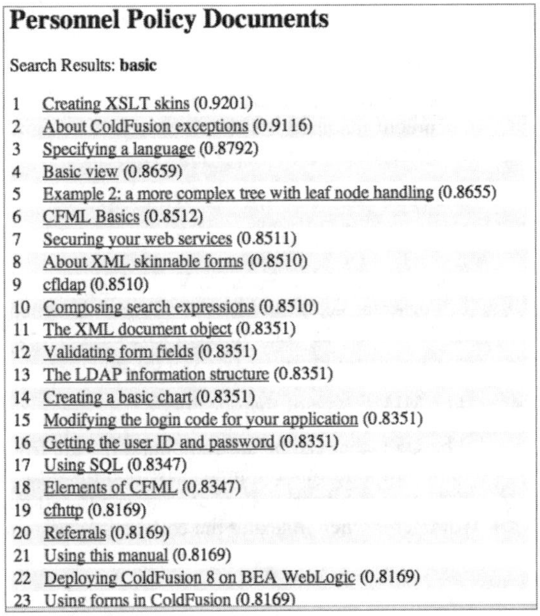

Figure 39.3

Results returned from a Verity search contain a score that can be used to determine how close a match each result is to the criteria. Note that your results may differ.

> **Personnel Policy Documents**
>
> Search Results: **basic**
>
> 1   Creating XSLT skins (0.9201)
> 2   About ColdFusion exceptions (0.9116)
> 3   Specifying a language (0.8792)
> 4   Basic view (0.8659)
> 5   Example 2: a more complex tree with leaf node handling (0.8655)
> 6   CFML Basics (0.8512)
> 7   Securing your web services (0.8511)
> 8   About XML skinnable forms (0.8510)
> 9   cfldap (0.8510)
> 10 Composing search expressions (0.8510)
> 11 The XML document object (0.8351)
> 12 Validating form fields (0.8351)
> 13 The LDAP information structure (0.8351)
> 14 Creating a basic chart (0.8351)
> 15 Modifying the login code for your application (0.8351)
> 16 Getting the user ID and password (0.8351)
> 17 Using SQL (0.8347)
> 18 Elements of CFML (0.8347)
> 19 cfhttp (0.8169)
> 20 Referrals (0.8169)
> 21 Using this manual (0.8169)
> 22 Deploying ColdFusion 8 on BEA WebLogic (0.8169)
> 23 Using forms in ColdFusion (0.8169)

Most of the important stuff happens in the large `<cfoutput>` block that follows. The `query="GetResults"` parameter in the `<cfoutput>` tag causes this code to be executed once for each row in the search results, where each row represents a document found. Within the `<cfoutput>` block, special columns named `key`, `title`, `score`, and `context` are being used. Unlike results returned by a `<cfquery>`—where you've specified which columns your results will contain by including them in the `SELECT` part of your SQL statement—results returned by Verity searches always contain the same, predefined column names, which are shown in Table 39.1.

Table 39.1   Columns Returned by Verity Searches

COLUMN	CONTAINS
AUTHOR	Author information (if it can be obtained from Microsoft Office and Adobe PDF files).
CATEGORY	A list of categories that this document is associated with.
CATEGORYTREE	A hierarchical category tree.
CONTEXT	An excerpt of the matched text with the match highlighted in bold.
CUSTOMn	The value of a custom field you specify when you populate the collection. See the section "Indexing Additional Columns with Custom Fields."
KEY	The document's file name.
RANK	The relative ranking in the search results.
RECORDSSEARCHED	The number of records Verity searched. In other words, the number of records in the collection(s).

COLUMN	CONTAINS
SCORE	The relevancy score for the document, which indicates how closely the document matched the search criteria. The score is always a value between 0 and 1, where a score of 1 indicates a perfect match.
SIZE	The number of bytes in the found document.
SUMMARY	Summary as generated when indexed.
TITLE	The title of the document, if Verity is capable of determining what the title is. For example, if the file is an HTML document, Verity obtains the title from the `<title>` tags in the document's `<head>` section. Verity might not provide a title for other types of documents.
TYPE	The MIME type of the document.
URL	The URL that can be used to obtain the file from your Web server. The information in this column is based on the information you supplied to the `<cfindex>` tag with its `urlpath` parameter. If you didn't specify a `URLPATH` parameter when indexing the collection, this column is blank.

Refining Your Search

Often, typing a few keywords isn't enough to find the documents you want. Verity provides a wealth of search operators to help you get the job done. By including special words such as AND, OR, and NOT in your search criteria, or by using various wildcards, users can tweak their searches so they find exactly what they're looking for.

As you read through this section, note how Verity search criteria end up looking like SQL statements. It's nice that some common ground exists between the two, but it's also important to keep in mind that Verity's search language is not the same thing as SQL.

Using AND, OR, and NOT

If you want to refine your search a little, you can use special search operators in your search criteria to get more specific. Only the most common search operators are discussed at this point. Many others are available for your use.

Table 39.2 briefly describes the effect of using AND, OR, and NOT in your search criteria. These operators are very similar to the AND, OR, and NOT Boolean operators discussed in Chapter 6, "Introducing SQL," in Vol. 1, *Getting Started*.

Table 39.2 Basic Search Operators

OPERATOR	EFFECT	EXAMPLE
AND	Searches for documents that have both words in them	`Verity AND Adobe`
OR	Searches for documents that have either word in them	`Verity OR Adobe`
NOT	Eliminates documents in which the word is found	`Verity NOT Adobe`

A comma can be used instead of **OR** in search criteria. A search for `Verity, Adobe` is therefore the same as a search for `Verity OR Adobe`.

Using Parentheses and Quotation Marks

Search criteria can look ambiguous after more than two search words are present. For instance, if you typed in `Verity AND Adobe OR ColdFusion`, what would that mean exactly? Documents that definitely contain Verity but that only need to contain Verity or ColdFusion? Documents that contain ColdFusion in addition to documents that contain both Verity and Adobe?

Use parentheses and quotation marks to indicate this type of criteria, in which the order of evaluation needs to be specified. They make your intentions clear to Verity and are fairly easy to explain to users. Table 39.3 summarizes the use of parentheses and quotation marks.

Table 39.3 Examples: Quotation Marks and Parentheses

CHARACTER	PURPOSE	EXAMPLES
(Parentheses)	Words within parentheses are considered a unit and are considered first.	
"Quotation Marks"	Quoted words or phrases are searched for literally. Useful when you want to search for the actual words "and" or "or."	`"Simple AND Explicit"` `Adobe AND "not installed"`

Using Wildcards

Verity provides a few wildcards you can use in your searches, so you can find documents based on incomplete search words or phrases. The wildcards should look familiar to you if you've used the `LIKE` operator with SQL queries, as discussed in Chapter 7, "SQL Data Manipulation," in Vol. 1, *Getting Started*. Table 39.4 summarizes the use of wildcard operators.

Table 39.4 Two Most Common Wildcards

WILDCARD	PURPOSE
*	Similar to the % wildcard in SQL, * stands in for any number of characters (including 0). A search for `Fu*` would find `Fusion`, `Fugazi`, and `Fuchsia`.
?	Just as in SQL, ? stands in for any single character. More precise—and thus generally less helpful—than the * wildcard. A search for `?ar?et` would find both `Carpet` and `Target`, but not `Learjet`.

Taking Case Sensitivity into Account

By default, a Verity search automatically becomes case sensitive whenever the characters provided as the `criteria` parameter are of mixed case. A search for `employee`—or for `EMPLOYEE`—finds `employee`, `Employee`, or `EMPLOYEE`, but a search for `Employee` finds only `Employee`, not `employee` or

EMPLOYEE. You might want to make this fact clear to your users by providing a message on your search forms, such as `"Type in all uppercase or all lowercase unless you want the search to be case sensitive."`

To have your application always ignore case regardless of what the user types, use ColdFusion's `LCase` function to convert the user's search words to lowercase when you supply them to `<cfsearch>`. For instance, by replacing the `<cfsearch>` in Listing 39.3 with the code below, you guarantee that the search criteria passed to Verity isn't of mixed case, so you know the search won't be case sensitive.

```
<!--- Run the search against the HRDocs collection --->
<cfsearch name="GetResults"
          collection="owshr"
          criteria="#LCase(FORM.criteria)#">
```

Indexing SQL Data

You've seen how easy it is to use ColdFusion's Verity functionality to index all sorts of files on your system. What if you want to index and search information in your database files? ColdFusion enables you to build a Verity index from data in your database as if the data were a bunch of document files.

In this section you will see how Verity lets you neatly get around the limitations that make SQL less than ideal for true text-based searching. By the time you're finished, you'll have a good understanding of when you should unleash Verity's rich search capabilities on your database data and when you're better off leaving things to SQL instead.

Searching Without Verity

You don't need to use Verity to make your database searchable, but it can make implementing a search interface much easier and help your users find what they want more easily. Look at what you'd need to do to search your data using the tools you already know: `<cfquery>` and SQL.

Say you want to set up a little search tool to enable your users to search the OWS database's `Merchandise` table. You want the user to be able to type a word or two into a form field and click Search to get the matching item.

The code in Listing 39.4 is a simple search form. The form is displayed in a browser.

Listing 39.4   MERCHANDISESEARCH_FORM1.CFM—Merchandise Search Form

```
<!---
Name:          merchandisesearch_form1.cfm
Author:        Leon Chalnick & Ben Forta
Description:   Presents simple search form for searching
               for merchandise
Date created:  01/05/2005
--->

<!--- Create a search form --->
```

Listing 39.4 (CONTINUED)

```html
<html>
<head>
   <title>Merchandise Search</title>
</head>

<body>

<h2>Please enter keywords to search for.</h2>

<form action="merchandisesearch_action1.cfm"
      method="post">
Keywords: <input type="text" name="criteria">
<br>
<input type="submit" value="Search">
</form>

</body>
</html>
```

The code in Listing 39.5 performs a simple search, then displays the results from the Merchandise table. Note that the LIKE keyword is used along with the % wildcard to search any part of the description.

Listing 39.5 MERCHANDISESEARCH_ACTION1.CFM—Searching the Inventory

```coldfusion
<!---
Name:          merchandisesearch_action1.cfm
Author:        Leon Chalnick & Ben Forta
Description:   Takes criteria from and
               searches against Merchandise
               Description field in db.
Date created:  01/05/2005
--->

<!--- Execute SQL query to do the searching --->
<cfquery name="GetResults" datasource="ows">
  SELECT MerchID, MerchDescription
  FROM Merchandise
  WHERE (MerchDescription LIKE '%#Form.Criteria#%')
</cfquery>

<!--- Display the query results --->
<html>
<head>
 <title>Search Results</title>
</head>

<body>
<cfoutput>
<h2>
#GetResults.RecordCount# Merchandise record(s) found for
"#FORM.Criteria#".
</h2>
</cfoutput>
```

Listing 39.5   (CONTINUED)

```
<!--- loop through each row outputting the description --->
<ul>
<cfoutput query="getresults">
  <li>#MerchDescription#</li>
</cfoutput>
</ul>

</body>
</html>
```

This would work fine as long as your application required only simple searching. If the user entered poster for the search criteria, SQL's LIKE operator would faithfully find all the merchandise that had the word poster somewhere in the description.

But what if the user entered something such as West End Tee? No records would be found because no records have those exact words in them (although one merchandise item does have the phrase West End Story Tee). That's a limitation your users probably won't find acceptable.

You could simply check for each word in the search string, so that if a user enters West End Story Tee you generate a SQL statement that would end up looking like this:

```
SELECT MerchID, MerchDescription
FROM Merchandise
WHERE MerchDescription LIKE '%West%'
 AND MerchDescription LIKE '%End%'
 AND MerchDescription LIKE '%Story%'
 AND MerchDescription LIKE '%Tee%'
```

That would work in this example, but you could end up with completely inappropriate results, too. And as the amount of data to search grows, so does the likelihood that you'll miss matches and return mismatches.

Indexing Your Table Data: Verity to the Rescue

ColdFusion's Verity functionality provides an easy-to-implement solution that addresses this problem. You create a custom Verity collection filled with documents that aren't really documents at all. Each document is actually just a record from your database tables.

It works like this: You write a <cfquery> that retrieves the data you want to make searchable. You pass this data to a <cfindex> tag, which indexes the data as if it were documents. Additionally, you tell Verity which column from the query should be considered a document "file name," which column should be considered a document "title," and which column(s) should be considered a document's "body."

To try this out, create a new collection named Merchandise (using the ColdFusion Administrator). But don't add anything to the index. Instead, you'll populate this new collection with data from the Merchandise database table.

Take a look at the code in Listing 39.6. Notice that the <cfindex> tag looks similar to Listing 39.1, in which you indexed your document files. The central differences here are the fact that you're setting type to custom instead of path and that you're referring to column names from a <cfquery>.

Listing 39.6 `INDEXDATA1.CFM`—Index a Collection with Database Data

```
<!---
Module:          indexdata1.cfm
Author:          Leon Chalnick & Ben Forta
Function:        Refreshes the Merchandise collection by
                 indexing a query result.
Date created:    01/05/2005
--->

<html>
<head>
 <title>Indexing Merchandise Data</title>
</head>
<body>


<!--- Feedback --->
Getting data ...<br>
<cfflush>

<!--- Retrieve all merchandise to be searched --->
<cfquery name="getresults" datasource="ows">
 select merchid, merchname, merchdescription
 from merchandise
</cfquery>

<!--- Feedback --->
Indexing data ...<br>
<cfflush>

<!--- Build 'custom' index on query result above --->
<cfindex action="refresh"
        collection="merchandise"
        key="merchid"
        type="custom"
        title="merchname"
        query="getresults"
        body="merchdescription">

<!--- Feedback --->
Done!

</body>
</html>
```

The `<cfquery>` part is very simple—just get the basic information about the books. (Obviously, if you only want certain books to be indexed, a WHERE clause could be added to the `<cfquery>`'s SQL statement.) Next comes a `<cfindex>` tag, which looks a lot like the `<cfindex>` tag you used earlier to index your normal document files.

This time around, though, you specify a few new parameters that are necessary when indexing a database table instead of normal documents:

- `action="refresh"` tells Verity that you're supplying new data.

- `type="custom"` says that you're dealing with table data, rather than document files.

- `query="GetResults"` specifies from which `<cfquery>` to get the data.

- `key, title, body` specify which query columns should be treated like which parts of a document.

That's really about all there is to it. After the `indexdata1.cfm` template is executed, you should be able to search the `Merchandise` collection in much the same way as you searched the `owshr` collection previously.

The code in Listing 39.7 searches through the newly indexed Merchandise collection, based on whatever criteria the user types in the search form. Except for the introduction of the `<cfsearch>` tag, this code is virtually unchanged from Listing 39.5; the results are displayed to the user.

Listing 39.7 MERCHANDISESEARCH_ACTION2.CFM—Searching and Displaying Records

```
<!---
Name:           merchandisesearch_action2.cfm
Author:         Leon Chalnick & Ben Forta
Description:    Takes criteria from and
                searches against Merchandise
                Description field in db.
Date created:   01/05/2005
--->

<!--- Perform a Verity search --->
<cfsearch collection="Merchandise"
          name="GetResults"
          criteria="#FORM.Criteria#">

<!--- Display the query results --->
<html>
<head>
 <title>Search Results</title>
</head>

<body>
<cfoutput>
<h2>
#GetResults.RecordCount# Merchandise record(s) found for
"#FORM.Criteria#".
</h2>
</cfoutput>

<!--- loop through each row outputting the description --->
<ul>
<cfoutput query="getresults">
  <li>#Title#</li>
</cfoutput>
</ul>

</body>
</html>
```

As you can see, exposing your database data to Verity was easy. You really didn't have to do much work at all. But the user will notice a tremendous difference: All of Verity's AND, OR, NOT, wildcarding, and other searching niceties are suddenly available.

Displaying a Summary for Each Record

In addition to the score and title, Verity also provides a summary for each record in the search results. The summary is the first three sentences—or the first 500 characters—of the information you specified for the body when you indexed the collection with the `<cfindex>` tag. The summary helps the user to eyeball which documents they are interested in.

To display the summary to the user, refer to it in your ColdFusion templates in the same way you refer to the key, score, or title. An example of this is shown in Listing 39.8. Figure 39.4 shows what the search results will look like to the user.

Figure 39.4

Returned summary data is useful for presenting a short snippet of matched content.

1 Merchandise record(s) found for "west end story tee".

80% **T-Shirt**
       T-Shirt Be the talk of the town with a West End Story Tee.

Listing 39.8 `MERCHANDISESEARCH_ACTION3.CFM`—Include a Summary for Each Document

```
<!---
Name:         merchandisesearch_action3.cfm
Author:       Leon Chalnick & Ben Forta
Description:  Takes criteria from and
              searches against Merchandise
              Description field in db.
Date created: 01/05/2005
--->

<!--- Perform a Verity search --->
<cfsearch collection="Merchandise"
          name="GetResults"
          criteria="#FORM.Criteria#">

<!--- Display the query results --->
<html>
<head>
 <title>Search Results</title>
</head>

<body>
<cfoutput>
<h2>
#GetResults.RecordCount# Merchandise record(s) found for
"#FORM.Criteria#".
</h2>
</cfoutput>
```

Listing 39.8 (CONTINUED)

```
<!--- Use definition list to display Verity output
 score, title and summary from each item found. --->
<dl>
<cfoutput query="GetResults">
 <dt><emp>#NumberFormat(Round(Score * 100))#%</emp>
 <strong>#Title#</strong>
 <dd><small>#Summary#</small></dd>
</cfoutput>
</dl>

</body>
</html>
```

Don't expect Verity summaries to always show the parts of the document that contain the search keywords; that's not how Verity summarization works. Verity selects each record's summary at the time the collection is indexed, and it's always the same for any given record, regardless of the search criteria that found it. The summary doesn't necessarily contain the keywords that were used as the search criteria.

Indexing Multiple Query Columns as the Body

In Listing 39.6 you indexed the Merchandise collection with the results from a query. In that listing, you declared that the MerchDescription column from the Merchandise table should be considered the body of each book record (by setting the body parameter of the <cfindex> tag to "MerchDescription").

By default, when your application runs a Verity search, only the Body part of each record is actually searched for matching words. The information in the Title part of the record isn't searched.

There are two ways to make the title searchable. One is to specify the title in the criteria parameter, using relational operators and the substring operator. See the section "Indexing Additional Columns with Custom Fields."

An easier way is to go back to your <cfindex> tag and supply the information you're giving to the title parameter to the body parameter as well. The body parameter can take a comma-separated list of column names ("MerchName,MerchDescription"), rather than only one column name ("MerchDescription"). The searchable part of each record in your database is composed of the MerchName of the item, followed by the MerchDescription of the item.

There's no need to stop there. You can put a bunch of column names in the body parameter, as shown in Listing 39.9. For each row returned by the query, ColdFusion concatenates the Merch-Description and MerchName columns and presents them to Verity as the body of each document. The result is that all textual information about the merchandise description and name is now part of your collection and instantly searchable. You don't have to change a thing about the code in any of your search templates.

Listing 39.9   `INDEXDATA2.CFM`—Supply Columns to the body Attribute

```
<!---
Module:         indexdata2.cfm
Author:         Leon Chalnick & Ben Forta
Function:       Uses multiple columns for the
                body param and refreshes the
                Merchandise collection by
                indexing a query result.
Date created:   01/05/2005
--->

<html>
<head>
 <title>Indexing Merchandise Data</title>
</head>
<body>


<!--- Feedback --->
Getting data ...<br>
<cfflush>

<!--- Retrieve all merchandise to be searched --->
<cfquery name="getresults" datasource="ows">
 select merchid, merchname, merchdescription
 from merchandise
</cfquery>

<!--- Feedback --->
Indexing data ...<br>
<cfflush>

<!--- Build 'custom' index on query result above --->
<cfindex action="refresh"
         collection="merchandise"
         key="merchid"
         type="custom"
         title="merchname"
         query="getresults"
         body="merchname,merchdescription">

<!--- Feedback --->
Done!

</body>
</html>
```

It's important to note that when you supply several columns to the `body` parameter, Verity doesn't maintain the information in separate columns, fields, or anything else. The underlying table's structure isn't preserved; all the information is pressed together into one big, searchable mass. Don't expect to be able to refer to a `#MerchName#` variable, for instance, in the same way you can refer to the `#Title#` and `#Score#` variables after a `<cfsearch>` is executed.

That might or might not feel like a limitation, depending on the nature of the applications you're building. In a way, it's just the flip side of Verity's concentrating on text in a natural-language kind of way, rather than being obsessed with columns the way SQL is.

However, ColdFusion and Verity do enable you to store a limited amount of information in a more database-like way, using something called *custom fields*.

Indexing Additional Columns with Custom Fields

ColdFusion lets you index up to four additional Verity fields when you're indexing database data. The fields—custom1, custom2, custom3, and custom4—are treated like the Title field you've already worked with. These custom fields come in handy when you have precise, code-style data that you want to keep associated with each record.

In Listing 39.10, you adjust the code from Listing 39.6 to fill the custom1 field with your FilmID. Conceptually, it's as if Verity were making a little note on each document that it makes from the rows of your query. The custom1 note is the FilmID. This example doesn't use the custom2 attribute, but it is used exactly the same way as custom1.

Listing 39.10 INDEXDATA3.CFM—Adding Custom Fields to a Collection

```
<!---
Module:         indexdata3.cfm
Author:         Leon Chalnick & Ben Forta
Function:       Uses multiple columns for the
                body param, and adds a custom
                field, and then refreshes the
                Merchandise collection by
                indexing a query result.
Date created:   01/05/2005
--->

<html>
<head>
 <title>Indexing Merchandise Data</title>
</head>
<body>


<!--- Feedback --->
Getting data ...<br>
<cfflush>

<!--- Retrieve all merchandise to be searched --->
<cfquery name="getresults" datasource="ows">
 select merchid, merchname,
        merchdescription, filmid
 from merchandise
</cfquery>

<!--- Feedback --->
Indexing data ...<br>
<cfflush>
```

Listing 39.10 (CONTINUED)

```
<!--- Build 'custom' index on query result above --->
<cfindex action="refresh"
         collection="merchandise"
         key="merchid"
         type="custom"
         title="merchname"
         query="getresults"
         body="merchname,merchdescription"
         custom1="filmid">

<!--- Feedback --->
Done!

</body>
</html>
```

Now that Verity knows the `FilmID` for each record in the collection, you can easily create a more sophisticated search tool that lets users select films along with their search words, similar to Listing 39.11.

Listing 39.11 `MERCHANDISESEARCH_FORM4.CFM`—Search Form with User Interface

```
<!---
Name:          merchandisesearch_form4.cfm
Author:        Leon Chalnick & Ben Forta
Description:   Presents simple search form for searching
               for merchandise
Date created:  01/05/2005
--->

<!--- Get the movie titles for drop down list --->
<cfquery NAME="GetFilms" datasource="ows">
 SELECT FilmID, MovieTitle
 FROM Films
</cfquery>

<!--- Create a search form --->
<html>
<head>
   <title>Merchandise Search</title>
</head>

<body>

<h2>Please enter keywords to search for.</h2>

<cfform action="merchandisesearch_action4.cfm">
Keywords: <cfinput type="text" name="criteria">
<br>
Movie: <cfselect name="FilmID"
                 query="GetFilms"
                 value="FilmID"
                 display="MovieTitle"
                 queryPosition="below">
       <option />
```

Listing 39.11 (CONTINUED)

```
            </cfselect>
    <br>
    <cfinput type="submit"
            name="sbmt"
            value="Search">
    </cfform>

    </body>
    </html>
```

Now you just need to teach the receiving template how to deal with the user's entries for the FilmID field. To specify the additional criteria, use Verity's MATCHES operator, which you use here for the first time.

The MATCHES operator searches specific document fields—rather than the body—and finds only exact matches. Document fields you can use MATCHES with include CF_CUSTOM1, CF_CUSTOM2, CF_CUSTOM3, CF_CUSTOM4, CF_TITLE, and CF_KEY, all of which correspond to the values you supply to the <cfindex> tag when you index the data.

TIP

Depending on the situation, you could use the Verity operators CONTAINS, STARTS, ENDS, and SUBSTRING in place of MATCHES in the this code. You also could use numeric operators, such as =, <, and >, with the CF_CUSTOM2 field.

Listing 39.12 demonstrates the use of the MATCHES search operator. At the top of the template, you use some <CFIF>, <CFELSE>, and <CFELSEIF> tags to decide what you're going to ask Verity to look for. If the user specifies a specific film (using the <SELECT> list, FilmID), you will ignore the keywords. If the FilmID is blank, search for the keywords that the user entered—but be sure the user specified either keywords or a film.

Depending on which field the user might have left blank, the TheCriteria variable will have slightly different values. The TheCriteria variable is then supplied to the <cfsearch> tag in its criteria parameter.

Listing 39.12 MERCHANDISESEARCH_ACTION4.CFM—MATCHES Search Operator

```
<!---
Name:          merchandisesearch_action4.cfm
Author:        Leon Chalnick & Ben Forta
Description:   Takes criteria from and
               searches against Merchandise
               Description field in db.
Date created:  01/05/2005
--->

<cfparam name="FORM.FilmID" default="">
<cfif FORM.FilmID NEQ "">
 <!--- FilmID is specified --->
 <cfset TheCriteria = "CF_CUSTOM1 <MATCHES> #Form.FilmID#">
<cfelse>
 <!--- Use text --->
 <cfset TheCriteria = "#Form.Criteria#">
```

Listing 39.12 (CONTINUED)

```
</cfif>

<!--- Perform a Verity search --->
<cfsearch collection="Merchandise"
          name="GetResults"
          criteria="#TheCriteria#">

<!--- Display the query results --->
<html>
<head>
 <title>Search Results</title>
</head>

<body>
<cfoutput>
<h2>
#GetResults.RecordCount# Merchandise record(s) found for:
#HTMLEditFormat(TheCriteria)#.
</h2>
</cfoutput>

<!--- Use definition list to disply Verity output
 score, title and summary from each item found. --->
<dl>
<cfoutput query="GetResults">
 <dt><emp>#NumberFormat(Round(Score * 100))#%</emp>
 <strong>#Title#</strong>
 <dd><small>#Summary#</small></dd>
</cfoutput>
</dl>

</body>
</html>
```

As you can see in Listing 39.12, variable TheCriteria refers to the field containing FilmID by using the Custom1 variable.

Combining Verity Searches with SQL Queries on the Fly

The custom fields you just learned about give you a lot of flexibility. In most cases, you'll be able to search and display records straight from your Verity collection(s), without bothering with the underlying database tables.

You might encounter situations in which you want to get information from Verity and from your database tables, presenting the information together to the user. This is quite easy to pull off: Use ColdFusion's ValueList function along with SQL's IN operator.

Say you want to run a Verity search on the Merchandise collection, but you want to be able to show the current, up-to-the minute price on each item. You consider the idea of feeding the MerchPrice column to CUSTOM1 or CUSTOM2, but you know that Orange Whip Studios changes the prices…well, hourly! So you decide you must get the live value directly from the database table.

You run a `<cfsearch>` just as you already have, but you won't display anything from it. Instead, you just use Verity's results as criteria for a normal SQL query. Verity supplies you with the key value for each document it finds, which you know happens to be the `MerchID` from your `Merchandise` table. You'll supply those MerchIDs to a normal `<cfquery>`.

Listing 39.13 shows how to use `<cfsearch>` results to drive a `<cfquery>` in this manner.

Listing 39.13 MERCHANDISESEARCH_ACTION5—Normal SQL Query

```
<!---
Name:           merchandisesearch_action5.cfm
Author:         Leon Chalnick & Ben Forta
Description:    Takes criteria from and
                searches against Merchandise
                Description field in db, and
                then queries a table using those
                results
Date created:   01/05/2005
--->

<cfparam name="FORM.FilmID" default="">
<cfif FORM.FilmID NEQ "">
 <!--- FilmID is specified --->
 <cfset TheCriteria = "CF_CUSTOM1 <MATCHES> #Form.FilmID#">
<cfelse>
 <!--- Use text --->
 <cfset TheCriteria = "#Form.Criteria#">
</cfif>

<!--- Perform a Verity search --->
<cfsearch collection="Merchandise"
          name="GetResults"
          criteria="#TheCriteria#">

<!--- Get --->
<cfquery name="GetPrices" datasource="ows">
 SELECT MerchID, MerchDescription, MerchPrice
 FROM Merchandise
 WHERE MerchID IN (#ValueList(GetResults.Key)#)
</cfquery>


<!--- Display the query results --->
<html>
<head>
 <title>Search Results</title>
</head>

<body>
<cfoutput>
<h2>
#GetPrices.RecordCount# Merchandise record(s) found.
</h2>
</cfoutput>

<ul>
```

Listing 39.13 (CONTINUED)

```
<cfoutput query="GetPrices">
 <li>#MerchDescription# - #DollarFormat(MerchPrice)#</li>
</cfoutput>
</ul>

</body>
</html>
```

NOTE

When you use this strategy, the search results are no longer sorted by relevance. Instead, they are sorted according to the ORDER BY part of your SQL statement. This can be a good or a bad thing, depending on your situation. Keep it in mind.

Understanding Verity and Your Table's Key Values

When you're indexing table data, it's important to understand that Verity doesn't think of the concept of a key in the same way your database tables do. Specifically, Verity doesn't assume or enforce any rules about uniqueness of values you feed it with <cfindex>'s key parameter. This means Verity can and will index two separate documents that have the same key value. This can lead to problems, especially if the data you're indexing is derived from two tables that have a master-detail relationship to one another.

For instance, say you want to include the names of the people who placed orders for each of the merchandise items into the Verity collection. As you will learn in Chapter 41, "More About SQL and Queries," online, creating a join query that retrieves this information from your database tables is fairly simple.

The problem is that any number of orders can be placed for each piece of merchandise. Therefore, if seven customers have ordered an item, seven rows will exist for that item in the result set. This poses a problem. Verity will dutifully index each of these rows as a separate document, without understanding that the seven rows all represent the same item. So a search that matches with the description of the item finds all seven records and displays them to the user. This can make your application look buggy.

ColdFusion provides no ready-made way out of this. <cfindex> doesn't have a group parameter like cfoutput does; you can't use group when you're displaying the records because the seven rows aren't guaranteed to be in consecutive rows when Verity finds them. You need to either avoid this kind of situation altogether or figure out some way of processing the data between <cfquery> and <cfindex>.

This may in fact not be a problem at all, depending on how the SQL is constructed (if you have the same WHERE clause repeated, it won't return extraneous rows). But, if this is indeed an issue, one solution to this problem is to query existing queries, as explained in Chapter 41.

Searching on More Than One Collection

To specify more than one Verity collection in a <cfsearch> tag, just specify all the collection names for the collection parameter and separate them with commas. All the collections are searched for matching documents.

If you want to allow your users to choose from several collections, you could add the code from Listing 39.14 to your search form.

Listing 39.14   MERCHANDISESEARCH_FORM6.CFM—Search More Than One Collection

```
<!---
Name:          merchandisesearch_form6.cfm
Author:        Leon Chalnick & Ben Forta
Description:   Presents simple search form for searching
               against multiple collections
Date created:  01/05/2005
--->

<!--- Create a search form --->
<html>
<head>
   <title>Merchandise Search</title>
</head>

<body>

<h2>Please enter keywords to search for.</h2>

<form action="merchandisesearch_action6.cfm"
      method="post">
Keywords: <input type="text" name="criteria">
<br>
Collections (select at least 1):
<INPUT TYPE="Checkbox"
       NAME="Collection"
       VALUE="Merchandise">Merchandise
<INPUT TYPE="Checkbox"
       NAME="Collection"
       VALUE="owshr">Personnel Policies
<br>
<input type="submit"
       value="Search">
</form>

</body>
</html>
```

Because of the convenient way check boxes are handled by ColdFusion, the value of the `Form.Collection` variable is set to `Merchandise,owshr` if the user checks both boxes. You would pass the variable directly to the `collection` parameter of the receiving template's `<cfsearch>` tag, like this:

```
<!--- Perform a Verity search --->
<cfsearch collection="#collection#"
          name="GetResults"
          criteria="#FORM.Criteria#">
```

NOTE

Note that you can freely mix normal document collections with database-table collections within a single `<cfsearch>` operation.

Maintaining Collections

In some situations, you might be able to simply create a Verity collection, index it, and forget about it. If the documents or data that make up the collection never change, you're in luck—you get to skip this whole section of the chapter.

It's likely, though, that you'll have to refresh that data at some point. Even when you don't have to refresh it, you might want to get it to run more quickly.

Repopulating Your Verity Collection

Whenever the original documents change from what they were when you indexed them, your collection will be a little bit out of sync with reality. The search results will be based on Verity's knowledge of the documents back when you did your indexing. If a document or database record has since been edited so that it no longer has certain words in it, it might be found in error if someone types in a search for those words. If the document is deleted altogether, Verity will still find it in its own records, which means your application might show a bad link that leads nowhere.

In a perfect world, Verity would dynamically watch your document folders and data tables and immediately reflect any changes, additions, or deletions in your collections. Unfortunately, the world isn't perfect, and this stuff doesn't happen automatically for you. The good news is that fixing it is no major chore.

If You Index Your Collections Interactively

As you recall, there are two ways of indexing a Verity collection: interactively with the ColdFusion Administrator or programmatically with the `<cfindex>` tag. If you did it interactively, there's not much I need to tell you; just go back to the Verity page in the Administrator and click the Purge button for your collection. Click the Index button, and do the same thing you did the first time. This should bring your collection up to date.

> **NOTE**
> You'd do the same basic thing if the location of the documents had changed.

If You Index Your Collections Programmatically

If you indexed the collection using `<cfindex>`—and you used `action="refresh"` in the `<cfindex>` tag, as seen previously—you should be able to bring your collection up to date simply by running the indexing template again.

> **TIP**
> You might consider scheduling this refresh template to be executed automatically at the end of each week, during off-peak hours. The indexing process can be resource intensive. It is therefore best to schedule this type of activity during off-peak hours.

➜ For more information on ColdFusion's built-in template scheduler, see Chapter 40, "Event Scheduling."

Instead of `action="refresh"`, you can use `action="update"` in your `<cfindex>` tag. This updates information on documents already indexed but without deleting information on documents that no longer exist. You also can use `action="purge"` to completely remove all data from the collection. The `action="refresh"` previously recommended is really the same thing as a `purge` followed by an `update`.

Deleting and Repopulating Specific Records

If your application is aware of the moment that a document or table record is deleted or edited, you might want to update the Verity collection right then, so your collection stays in sync with the actual information. Clearly, you don't have to repopulate the entire collection just because one record has changed. ColdFusion and Verity address this by enabling you to delete items from a collection via the key value.

The following code snippet deletes the Verity record for a specific key value:

```
<!--- Delete a record from the Verity collection --->
<cfindex action="delete"
         collection="Merchandise"
         KEY="#Form.MerchID#">
```

To update a single row use the data index techniques seen previously, but use `<cfquery>` to *only* retrieve the row to be updated. So long as `action="refresh"` is being used (instead of `action="update"`) only that row will be updated, and all other Verity data will be left as is.

Administering Collections with `<cfcollection>`

The `<cfcollection>` tag enables you to administer collections programmatically in your own templates, as an alternative to using the ColdFusion Administrator. If you want your application to be capable of creating, deleting, and maintaining a collection on its own, the `<cfcollection>` tag is here to help.

This section will be of special interest if you are developing prebuilt applications that other people will deploy on their servers without your help, or if you are presented with a project in which you want to completely remove any need for anyone to interact with the ColdFusion Administrator interface. For example, you could use `<cfcollection>` in a template that acted as a setup script, creating the various files, Registry entries, database tables, and Verity collections your application needs to operate.

Optimizing a Verity Collection

After a Verity collection gets hit many times, performance can start to degrade. Depending on your application, this might never become a problem. If you notice your Verity searches becoming slower over time, you might want to try optimizing your collection. Optimizing your collection is similar conceptually to running Disk Defragmenter on a Windows machine.

Two ways to optimize a collection are available: You can use the ColdFusion Administrator or create a ColdFusion template that uses the `<cfcollection>` tag to optimize the collection programmatically.

To optimize a collection with the ColdFusion Administrator, locate the collection in the Verity Collections page and click the Optimize button. Verity whirs around for a minute or two as the collection is optimized. Because optimization can take some time—especially with large collections—you should optimize a collection during off-peak hours if possible.

To optimize a collection with the <cfcollection> tag, just include the tag in a simple ColdFusion template. The tag must include an action="optimize" parameter, and the collection name must be provided in the collection parameter. For instance, the code in Listing 39.15 can be used to optimize the owshr collection created earlier in this chapter.

NOTE

You might find that you want to optimize your collections on a regular basis. You could schedule the template shown in Listing 39.15 to be automatically run once a week, for example, by using the ColdFusion scheduler (explained in Chapter 40).

Listing 39.15   OPTIMIZE.CFM—Optimizing a Collection

```
<!---
Module:          Optimize.cfm
Author:          Leon Chalnick & Ben Forta
Function:        Optimizes a collection.
Date created:    01/05/2005
--->

<html>
<head>
 <title>Optimizing Verity Collection</title>
</head>
<body>


<!--- feedback --->
Performing optimization ...<br>
<cfflush>

<!--- optimize the verity collection --->
<cfcollection action="optimize"
              collection="owshr">

<!--- feedback --->
Done!
<cfflush>

</body>
</html>
```

Repairing a Collection

If Verity's internal index files for a collection become damaged, ColdFusion provides repairing functionality that enables you to get the collection back up and running quickly in most cases. Most likely, you will never need to repair a Verity collection. But if you do, use the <cfcollection> tag with action="repair". For instance, you could use the code shown in Listing 39.15—just change the action parameter to repair.

NOTE

Searches can't be made against a collection while it is being repaired.

This procedure will generally never be needed. But if searches return inconsistent results and you can't re-create the collection from scratch, this may be an alternative.

Deleting a Collection

To delete a collection altogether, use the <cfcollection> tag with action="delete". Again, you could use the basic code shown in Listing 39.15 by simply changing the action to delete. After the collection has been deleted, ColdFusion displays an error message if a <cfsearch> tag that uses that collection name is encountered. The collection name will no longer appear in the ColdFusion Administrator, and Verity's index files will be removed from your server's hard drive. Note that only Verity's internal index files will be deleted, not the actual documents that had been made searchable by the collection.

TIP

Alternatively, you could use the Delete button on the Verity Collections page of the ColdFusion Administrator to delete the collection.

Creating a Collection Programmatically

The <cfcollection> tag can also be used to create a collection from scratch. Basically, you supply the same information to the tag as you would normally supply to the ColdFusion Administrator when creating a new collection there. Provide a name for the new collection in the tag's name parameter, and provide the path for the new collection's internal index files with the path parameter.

Listing 39.16 demonstrates how to use <CFCOLLECTION> to create a new collection called MoreHRDocs.

NOTE

If you have the ColdFusion Verity Language Pack installed on your ColdFusion server, you also can provide a **LANGUAGE** attribute to specify a language other than English. The languages you can supply with the **LANGUAGE** attribute include Danish, Dutch, English, Finnish, French, German, Italian, Norwegian, Portuguese, Spanish, and Swedish.

Listing 39.16 CREATE.CFM—Creating a Collection

```
<!---
Module:          create.cfm
Author:          Leon Chalnick & Ben Forta
Function:        Create a new collection.
Date created:    01/05/2005
--->

<html>
<head>
 <title>Creating Verity Collection</title>
</head>
<body>
```

Listing 39.16 (CONTINUED)

```
<!--- feedback --->
Creating collection ...<br>
<cfflush>

<!--- Create the new verity collection --->
<cfcollection action="create"
              collection="finance"
              path="c:\ cfusionmx7\ Verity\ Collections\ ">

<!--- feedback --->
Done!
<cfflush>

</body>
</html>
```

NOTE

Remember that the newly created collection can't be searched yet, because no information has been indexed. You still need to use the `<cfindex>` tag–after the `<cfcollection>` tag–to index documents or data from your database tables, as discussed earlier in this chapter.

You can't use the name of an existing local collection. However, if the collection already exists on another server in your local network, you can create a mapping to it simply by using the UNC directory name when you create the collection. ColdFusion will recognize the earlier Verity collection and will create the mapping to it (rather than creating a new collection in that location).

NOTE

You also can use these techniques to map to an existing collection that was produced by Verity outside of ColdFusion.

Depending on how your local network is configured, you might have permissions issues to deal with before ColdFusion can access the files on the other server. On Windows NT, you might need to go to the Services applet in the Control Panel; there you adjust the Windows NT username that the Adobe ColdFusion service logs in as.

If you delete a collection that is mapped to a Verity collection on another server, Verity's internal index files on the other ColdFusion server don't get deleted–only the mapping itself does. The same goes for collections created using the Map an Existing Collection option in the ColdFusion Administrator.

Understanding Verity's Search Syntax

You've explored a number of ways to index information and make it searchable on the Web. You've also discovered using AND, OR, and wildcards, which make your search criteria work more easily for you.

It doesn't stop at AND and OR. Verity provides a fairly rich set of operators that you can use in your search criteria. Your users probably won't use these operators along with their keywords when they're running a search—most people won't go beyond ANDs and ORs. However, you might, in certain circumstances, want to use some of these operators behind the scenes. Table 39.5 lists all the operators available by category.

Table 39.5   Verity Operator Quick Reference

OPERATOR	DESCRIPTION
AND	Find documents where all words/conditions are found.
OR	Find documents where any one word/condition is found.
STEM	Find documents matching words that are derived from the search words.
WORD	Match the search words.
WILDCARD	Match search words with *, ?, and so on.
NEAR	Find only if words are close together.
NEAR/N	Find only if words within n words of each other.
PARAGRAPH	Find only if words in the same paragraph.
PHRASE	Find only if words in the same phrase.
SENTENCE	Find only if words in the same sentence.
CONTAINS	Find words that are within a specific field.
MATCHES	The text of an entire field.
STARTS	At the start of a specific field.
ENDS	At the end of a specific field.
SUBSTRING	Within a specific field as (fragments).
=,<, >, <=, >=	For numeric and date values.
CASE	To change Verity's behavior so that the search is case-sensitive.
MANY	Documents are ranked by relevance.
NOT	Matching documents should not be found.
ORDER	Words must appear in documents in order.

The document fields you can specify with relational operators, such as CONTAINS, STARTS, ENDS, and so on, are:

- CF_TITLE

- CF_KEY

- CF_URL

- CF_CUSTOM1

- CF_CUSTOM2

- CF_CUSTOM3

- CF_CUSTOM4

These fields correspond to the values (TITLE, KEY, URL, and so on) you specify in the <cfindex> tag used to index a collection.

Finally, it's worth noting that ColdFusion uses a limited version of the Verity K2 Server. For example, you can't index more than 250,000 documents with the ColdFusion Enterprise implementation, and 125,000 documents with the ColdFusion Standard implementation. You can overcome these limitations by upgrading to the commercial versions of the Verity products from Verity.

CHAPTER 40

Event Scheduling

ColdFusion Event Scheduling Concepts

The automated scheduling of activities is a part of everyday life. We schedule automatic monthly mortgage payments from our bank accounts, the recording of various television shows with our DVRs, notifications from our handheld devices and many other activities. By scheduling these events to occur in an automated fashion, we free up other resources to focus on issues that require our explicit interaction. It simply makes our lives easier knowing that the scheduled activity is going to get done without requiring our attention or time.

Of course, when we develop computerized systems to replace or enhance manual processes, we often want to schedule events to occur on a regular basis with the very same goals in mind. ColdFusion provides its own event scheduling mechanism that enables us to invoke one-time or recurring events. Through ColdFusion's scheduling mechanisms, you are able to invoke a specific ColdFusion template at a specific time. Because that template can be used to do just about anything that ColdFusion can do, this becomes a very powerful tool for the ColdFusion developer.

Here are some ideas for scheduled events:

- **Content management.** You can schedule the generation of static HTML pages from content that is stored in a database. This technique is commonly used in content management systems to improve site performance.

- **Automated email applications.** You can schedule a process to check a POP3 server for email and respond to it automatically with various prescribed messages or actions. This frees up the site administrator from a tedious task.

- **Verity collection updates.** You can schedule the recurring update of the Verity collection that you've created for your site. This assures you that when visitors search your site, their results will reflect the site's current contents.

ColdFusion provides two mechanisms for executing automated events or *scheduled tasks*:

- The Scheduled Tasks page in the ColdFusion Administrator

- The <cfschedule> tag

The functionality provided by the Add/Edit Scheduled Task page and the <cfschedule> tag is essentially the same. Both enable you to create, update, run, and delete tasks. However, you should be aware of a few distinctions:

- If you want to see a list of all the scheduled tasks on your server, you must use the Scheduled Tasks page in the ColdFusion Administrator.

- The Add/Edit Scheduled Task page is simply an HTML form. You create or modify a task in the form, so it's a bit easier to work with than writing code.

- The <cfschedule> tag can be used without access to the ColdFusion Administrator.

It's important to recognize that when ColdFusion runs a scheduled task, it's run as if someone requested the URL (template) specified in the task. If you need a specific user to run that task (perhaps based on security concerns), you can specify the username and password. If output is to be generated by the task (perhaps for debugging purposes) you can specify that the output is to be published and then specify the file to which the output will be written.

➡ These concepts will be discussed in more detail in the section "Creating, Modifying, and Deleting Scheduled Events" later in this chapter.

Also note that ColdFusion logs the execution of scheduled tasks in the scheduler.log file.

ColdFusion Scheduling vs. Other Kinds of Scheduling

As you may already know, there are other ways to schedule automated tasks in computerized systems.

- Most advanced operating systems, such as Windows (NT, 2000, XP and Server 2003), Unix, and Linux, provide their own mechanism for scheduling tasks.

  In Windows you have the AT command (and there are some GUI utilities that work with AT as well).

- Many powerful database products, such as Microsoft SQL Server and Oracle, come with their own scheduling capabilities as well.

ColdFusion's scheduling capability is limited to requesting URLs through HTTP. With this in mind, there are situations in which one of the other approaches is more appropriate. For example, suppose you've built an index with the Verity Spider command-line utility (which is discussed in more detail in Chapter 39, "Full-Text Searching"). Because the Verity Spider runs from the command line prompt you could execute the command using <cfexecute>, but it would probably be more appropriate to run this through the operating system. If you needed your database to dump some of its data in some XML format to a file every night, you could use a ColdFusion template and a scheduled task to do this, but the database's native exporting tools and scheduling mechanism (assuming it had one) would probably be more appropriate.

Using ColdFusion's task scheduler has a couple of important benefits that are not necessarily provided by other scheduling approaches:

- The output from the specified URL can be saved to a file.

- The ColdFusion scheduler writes log entries each time a scheduled task is executed—and this log can be valuable in debugging.

- It can come in extremely handy if your application is hosted by an ISP that has limited your ability to run command-line programs or create scheduled tasks using their database server.

  In this situation, consider using ColdFusion's event scheduling capabilities. Even if the ISP doesn't provide you access to the ColdFusion Administrator, you can use the `<cfschedule>` tag to run your task.

Creating, Modifying, and Deleting Scheduled Tasks

You can use either the ColdFusion Administrator or the `<cfschedule>` tag to create, modify, run and delete scheduled tasks. Your server's administrator may have decided to prevent developers from accessing the ColdFusion Administrator. If you don't have access, you can still get the job done programmatically using the `<cfschedule>` tag. If you do have access to the ColdFusion Administrator, you'll find this method preferable under most circumstances.

→ See Chapter 28, "ColdFusion Server Configuration," for a description of the ColdFusion Administrator usage.

Administering Scheduled Tasks

The ColdFusion Administrator can be used to list, create, modify, delete, run, and log the execution of scheduled events or tasks. Newly scheduled events are immediately recognized and will run as soon as they are scheduled to do so.

Scheduled Task Logging

You have the option of configuring the ColdFusion Administrator to log the execution of scheduled tasks. This setting is made at the bottom of the Logging Settings page.

NOTE

Note that even if you don't enable logging of scheduled tasks, scheduled tasks that you manually execute will be logged.

Whenever a scheduled task is executed, an entry is written to the file `scheduler.log` in the Logs directory (below the directory in which ColdFusion is installed). (See Chapter 17, "Debugging and Troubleshooting," in *Adobe ColdFusion 8 Web Application Construction Kit, Volume 1: Getting Started,* for more information on ColdFusion's logging capabilities.) You can review the entries in this log through the Log Files pages in the ColdFusion Administrator. The log file itself is a simple quote and comma-delimited text file, as seen in Figure 40.1.

Figure 40.1

The scheduler.log file is a simple quote and comma-delimited text file.

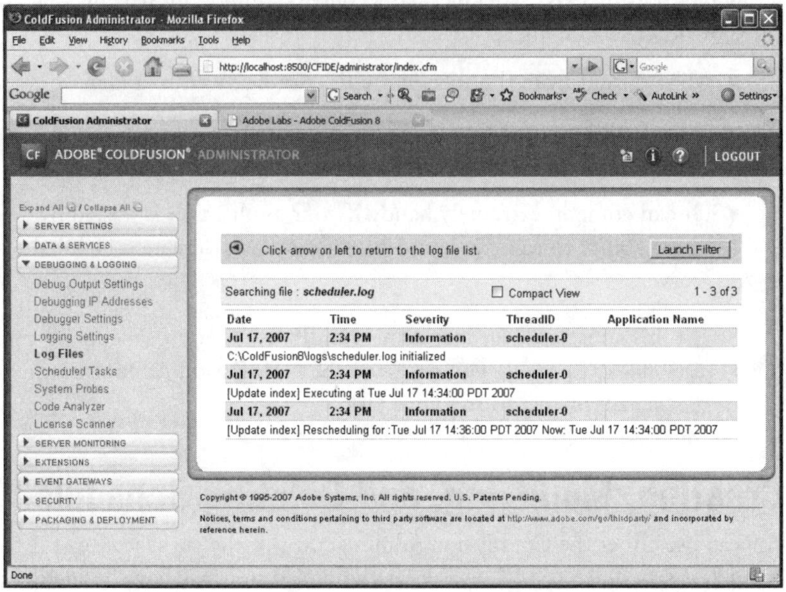

The data presented in the log file is discussed in Table 40.1.

Table 40.1 Interpreting the scheduler.log File

VALUE	DESCRIPTION
"Information"	Severity; in this case, simply informational
"scheduler-0"	Thread ID
"Jul 17, 2007"	Date of task execution
"2:34PM"	Time of task execution
null value	Application name. This is null in the scheduler log. It does not reflect the name of your ColdFusion application.
[Update Index] Executing at Tues…	This message indicates the name of the scheduled task that is being referenced in this log entry.

As you browse through the scheduler.log file, you'll note that ColdFusion makes one entry when the event is executed. If it's a recurring event, you'll see another to indicate the rescheduling of the event's execution.

NOTE

Note that the log does not provide information regarding the success or failure of whatever underlying function is being provided by the task that you're scheduling. Techniques for this kind of analysis are presented later in this chapter, in the section "Scheduling Application Examples."

Creating Scheduled Tasks with the ColdFusion Administrator

The ColdFusion Administrator's Scheduled Tasks page provides a listing of all scheduled tasks, as seen in Figure 40.2. This listing is where you start when you want to create, modify, delete, and run those tasks.

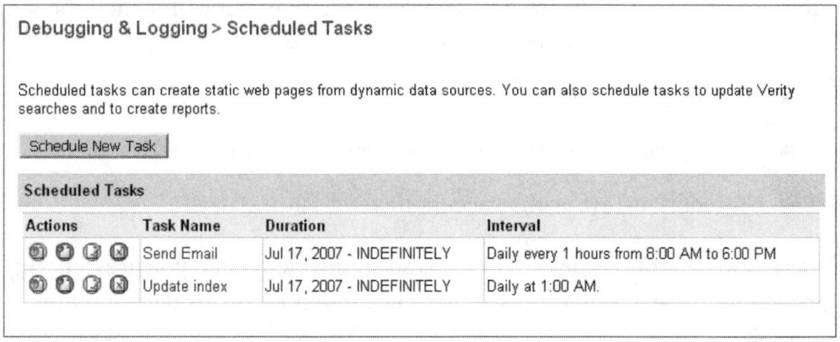

Figure 40.2

The Scheduled Tasks page in the ColdFusion Administrator is used to list, add, delete, modify, and run scheduled tasks.

Click the Schedule New Task button to create a new task. Doing so opens the Add/Edit Scheduled Task Form, as seen in Figure 40.3. Each field is explained in the following sections.

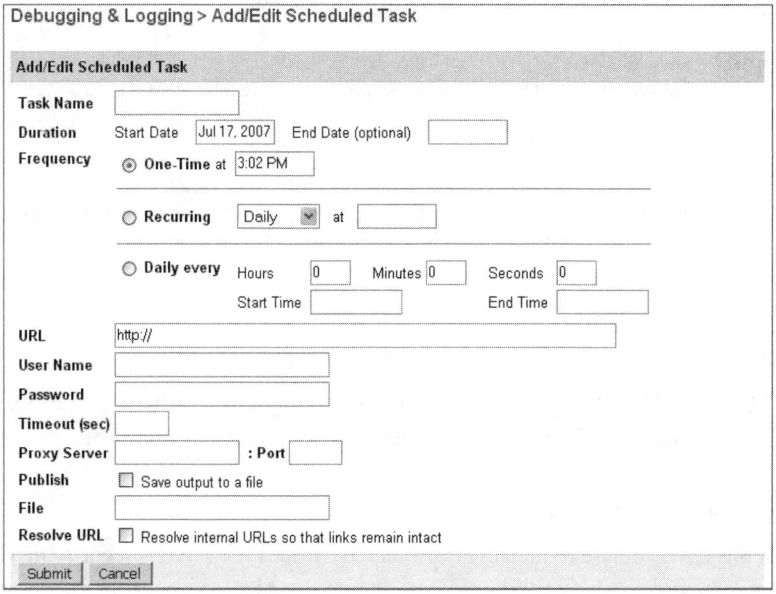

Figure 40.3

The Add/Edit Scheduled Task form.

Task Name

This is the name that you want to give this task. It will appear in the list on the Scheduled Tasks page.

Duration

These two fields are used to define a period of days over which the task will run. You must specify a Start Date. The End Date is optional and is only needed if you do not want a repeated task to run indefinitely.

Frequency

This part of the form enables you to specify the time frame in which the scheduled task operates. The time frame for execution can be:

- A one-time event

- A recurring event that occurs once a day, once a week or once a month

- A recurring event that occurs throughout the day

In any case you must at least enter a valid start time. When you are defining a task that must recur throughout the day, you must specify how often it recurs by entering hours, minutes or seconds (or a combination). You cannot run tasks more frequently than once per minute.

Select the appropriate radio button and enter the time at which the task should run (or start running, in the Daily every section). If you are scheduling a task that occurs more than once a day, also enter the appropriate interval and if you like, enter an end time (after which the task will not be run again, until you reach the start time the following day).

NOTE

Note that you can enter times in either 12- or 24-hour formats (i.e., 2:30:00 PM and 14:30:00 mean the same thing and either will work).

TIP

It's important to recognize that each scheduled task that requests a URL from your server adds to your server's overall workload and can affect performance. Think carefully about the frequency with which each scheduled task must occur because you don't want to make your server do a lot of unnecessary work.

URL

This is the URL that you want ColdFusion to request, i.e., the task to be executed. You can run URLs using only HTTP; you can't use HTTPS, FTP, or other protocols.

Username and Password

If the URL you are requesting is protected by the Web server's security mechanisms, you may need to authenticate with a valid username and password in order for the request to go through. Enter these values in these two fields.

NOTE

Note that the only authentication that can be passed is basic clear text. If the server administrator has employed something more secure or proprietary, ColdFusion may not be able to authenticate when it executes this task. You can verify whether this is the case by saving the output of the URL request to a file. This technique is described in the section "Publish and File" later in this chapter.

Timeout (Seconds)

If you are requesting a URL that is complex or may take a while to complete, you may need to tell ColdFusion to give this request a longer timeout.

NOTE

Note that ColdFusion's default request timeout duration is set on the Settings page in the ColdFusion Administrator.

➡ See Chapter 28 for a description of this setting.

In this situation, you can enter a longer time period, in seconds.

Proxy Server (and Port)

If your ColdFusion server goes through a proxy server to reach to the URL you're requesting, enter the proxy server and port information in these to fields.

Publish and File

If you want the output from the task to be saved to a file, select this check box and enter the pathname of the file in the File field (e.g., `c:\temp\output.htm`).

TIP

This feature is useful for debugging the execution of your task. If your task is something that doesn't really produce output for publishing (like HTML), you may still want to use this feature to write a date and time stamp or some other debugging information to a file to give you an indication of what happened with your process.

Resolve URL

If you are requesting a URL from an external site but you need to be able to use its internal references (perhaps you're requesting a URL from an external Web site that you plan on publishing on your server), you should check this box to resolve the URLs that are used within the page you're requesting.

TIP

When you're done creating a task, be sure to use the Submit button at the bottom of the form to save the new task.

Running, Modifying, and Deleting Scheduled Tasks

The Scheduled Tasks page in the ColdFusion Administrator lists all of the scheduled tasks in your ColdFusion server. There are four icons at the left of each entry. The first icon is for running the task, the second is for pausing the task, the third is for modifying the task, and the fourth is for deleting the task.

Running Scheduled Tasks

To run the task now, click the leftmost icon with the "!". This ad hoc method of executing a scheduled task is most helpful when you're getting your task set up and debugging the process.

TIP

If you configured the task to publish its output to a file, you can open that file after running the task to see what happened. If the URL you entered was incorrect or there was some other problem requesting it, you should have enough valuable information in the saved output to debug the situation.

Pausing a Scheduled Task

Starting with ColdFusion 8, you have the capability to easily, temporarily cease the execution of a scheduled task. Simply click the pause icon. Your request to pause the task is submitted to the Cold-Fusion Administrator, which will report back that the task has been paused. The task will not run again until you've resumed it, by clicking the second icon again. And when you do, the icon will change back to its earlier appearance.

Modifying Scheduled Tasks

The third icon at the left of the task list (in the Scheduled Tasks page in the ColdFusion Administrator) is used to modify the configuration of that task. You can also just click on the task's name in the list. Clicking either the icon or the task name loads the Add/Edit Scheduled Task page.

The fields all work just as they did when you created the task. Make whatever changes are required and save the task using the Submit button at the bottom of the form.

NOTE

Note that the act of saving a scheduled task like this creates its own entry in the `scheduler.log` file. This entry indicates that the task is being activated.

Deleting Scheduled Tasks

When you determine that you no longer need to keep a scheduled task, you can delete it by clicking the rightmost icon (of the four) in the Scheduled Tasks list. Having no-longer-scheduled tasks in the list doesn't hurt anything, but if there are a lot that are no longer running, it may make sense to delete some of them to make the list easier to read.

When you click the delete icon, you'll be prompted to confirm that you do indeed want to delete the task. Assuming you do, click the OK button; the task is removed from the list and the list is refreshed.

Creating, Modifying, and Deleting Tasks Using <CFSCHEDULE>

As explained in the section "ColdFusion Event Scheduling Concepts," you can use either the Cold-Fusion Administrator or the <cfschedule> tag to manage scheduled tasks. You've already learned how to employ this functionality using the ColdFusion Administrator. This section demonstrates the use of <cfschedule> to accomplish the same things.

The <cfschedule> tag is commonly used when your server administrator has configured the Cold-Fusion Administrator so that you don't have access to the Scheduled Tasks list. When you can't use the ColdFusion Administrator's form-based interface, the <cfschedule> tag comes in very handy.

NOTE

Note that you actually could build a form-based interface to the <cfschedule> tag. You could start by copying the HTML code from the ColdFusion Administrator and saving it somewhere that allows users access. You'd then have to build a template to validate the user's input. Assuming the input was good, you'd feed it to the <cfschedule> tag. Using this approach, the ColdFusion Administrator would remain protected and users would still have an easy-to-use, form-based interface for creating scheduled tasks.

Creating a Scheduled Task with <cfschedule>

Table 40.2 lists and describes the <cfschedule> tag attributes. Note that items marked with an asterisk (*) are required only under certain circumstances. The specific cases are noted in the description of the attribute.

Table 40.2 <CFSCHEDULE> Tag Attributes

ATTRIBUTE	REQUIRED	DESCRIPTION
Task	Yes	A descriptive name for the task.
Action	Yes	Delete, Update, Pause, Resume, or Run. Specifies which action is required of the task scheduler with respect to the named task. Note that Update produces a new task if the named task doesn't already exist. If the named task does exist, using Update will overwrite that task. Run executes the task now and Delete deletes it now.
Operation	Yes*	The type of operation to be performed but can be set only to Httprequest. Required only if the Action attribute is Update.
Startdate	Yes*	The date on which you want the scheduled event to begin. This attribute is required when the Action attribute is Update.
Starttime	Yes*	The time at which you want the scheduled event to begin executing. This attribute is required when the Action attribute is Update. Provide a complete time value in 12- or 24-hour format.
URL	Yes*	The URL to be requested when the task is executed. Required when the Action attribute is set to Update. It must start with http:// and indicate the complete URL; relative addresses won't work. You can include a port in the URL (if you're using one other than 80, the default) or you can use the PORT attribute to specify the port (but don't do both).
interval	Yes*	The interval at which the scheduled task is to be executed. Valid values are Once, Daily, Weekly, Monthly, or a time interval in seconds (an integer value). This is required only when the Action attribute is set to Update. Use seconds to specify intervals that recur throughout the day (e.g., every hour = 3600).

Table 40.2 (CONTINUED)

ATTRIBUTE	REQUIRED	DESCRIPTION
Publish	No	Indicates whether the results of the URL request are to be saved to a file. Valid values are Yes and No.
Path	Yes*	The path, ending with "\", where the file specified in the FILE attribute is to be created. This is required only if Publish is set to Yes.
File	Yes*	The file name for the results of the scheduled task. This is required only when the PUBLISH attribute is set to Yes.
Enddate	No	The date on which the scheduled task should stop being executed.
Endtime	No	The time at which the scheduled task should stop being executed. You can use either 12- or 24-hour time formats.
Requesttimeout	No	The request timeout period (in seconds) that should be used for this request.
Resolveurl	No	Indicates whether you want the internal URLs (in the content of the requested URL) to be resolved so that they work when this page is loaded from a server other than the original server. Defaults to No.
Username	No	The username to use to authenticate when requesting a protected URL.
Password	No	The password to use to authenticate when requesting a protected URL.
Proxyserver	No	The hostname or IP address of a proxy server. This is required only if your ColdFusion server needs to use a proxy server to reach the requested URL.
Proxyport	No	The port used by your proxy server. It is used only if your proxy server works on a port other than 80.
Port	No	The port to be used by your server when executing this task. Defaults to 80. If you include the port in your URL, don't include a Port attribute.

When you're using <cfschedule> to create scheduled events, you set the Action attribute to Update. Suppose you wanted to create a scheduled task that involves updating the Verity index of your site. First you'd write the ColdFusion template that would update the Verity index. In this simple example, let's assume that this template is called collection_update.cfm and is located in a directory off the Web server's root named "/ows/40/". The task it creates will be named "Update collection". You want to keep the Verity collection up to date so you want this task to run nightly. Because you don't want it to run when there's a lot of traffic on your server, you want it to run every day at 09:00 A.M. See the <cfschedule> tag that you could use for this task in Listing 40.1.

Listing 40.1 `Create_VerityUpdate.cfm`—Using `<cfschedule>` to Create a New Scheduled Task

```
<!---
Name:          Create_VerityUpdate.cfm
Author:        Leon Chalnick
Description:   Creates a scheduled task to
               run collection_update.cfm
        once per day at 9am
--->
<cfschedule
  action="UPDATE"
  task="Update collection"
  operation="HTTPRequest"
  url="http://localhost:8500/ows/40/collection_update.cfm"
  startdate="7/18/2007"
  starttime="09:00 am"
  interval="Daily"
>
```

After executing this code and opening the ColdFusion Administrator, you can see the resulting scheduled task displayed in the form.

As you can see in Listing 40.1, you do not have to write a lot of code to create a recurring task. Let's review what each attribute does.

- `Action="Update"`. Tells ColdFusion to update an existing task with the name specified in the TASK attribute. If that task does not exist, ColdFusion will create a new one.

- `Task="Update collection"`. Tells ColdFusion the name of the task to update (or create, as in our case).

- `Operation="HTTPRequest"`. Tells ColdFusion that this request is to be made through HTTP (this is the only way that requests currently can be made).

- `URL="http://localhost:8500/OWS/40/collection_update.cfm"`. Indicates the URL to be requested.

- `Startdate="7/18/2007"`. Indicates the date on which the task is to be first executed.

- `Starttime="09:00 am"`. Indicates the time at which the task is to begin running.

- `Interval="Daily"`. Indicates the time interval at which this event is to recur.

A more detailed example will be provided later in this chapter.

Modifying, Deleting, and Running Scheduled Tasks with the `<cfschedule>` Tag

Modifying scheduled tasks through use of `<cfschedule>` works virtually the same way as creating a scheduled task with `<cfschedule>`. The previous section provided a simple example of its usage for creating a scheduled task.

Suppose after updating the Verity collection nightly for a month, it became apparent that you don't need to update the collection more than once a week. The following code would make this modification (see Listing 40.2).

Listing 40.2 `Modify_VerityUpdate.cfm`—This Code Modifies an Existing Task

```
<!---
Name:            Modify_VerityUpdate.cfm
Author:          Leon Chalnick
Description:     Updates a scheduled task to
                 run Collection_Update.cfm
                 once per week at 11:30pm
--->
<cfschedule
  action="UPDATE"
  task="Update collection"
  operation="HTTPRequest"
  url="http://localhost:8500/ows/40/collection__update.cfm"
  startdate="9/18/2007"
  starttime="11:30:00 PM"
  interval="Weekly"
>
```

Deleting a scheduled task with `<cfschedule>` is simply a question of setting the `ACTION` to `Delete` and naming the task:

```
<cfschedule Action="Delete" Name="Update collection">
```

To execute a scheduled task immediately, use this code:

```
<cfschedule Action="Run" Name="Update collection">
```

You can programmatically pause execution of a task like this:

```
<cfschedule Action="Pause" Name="Update collection">
```

After pausing, you'll need to resume execution before you can do anything else with the task:

```
<cfschedule Action="Resume" Name="Update collection">
```

Scheduling Application Examples

You're now ready to put your new understanding of ColdFusion's scheduling capabilities to use. First, you'll create a scheduled task for a POP3 application (List Unsubscriber) presented in Chapter 21, "Interacting with Email," online. Then you'll build two simple scheduling applications. The first application sends email out on a regular basis. The second updates the Verity index that gets built in Chapter 39.

Creating a Scheduled Task for a POP3 Application

First, please quickly review the POP3 application developed in Chapter 21. This application checks a POP3 email account and looks for incoming messages to the `mailings@orangewhipstudios.com` account in which the subject includes the word "remove". When a message like this is found, the template identifies the sender in the Contacts table and sets the value of `MailingList` field to 0, flagging it as an account that should not have promotional email sent to it.

When you run this template, it will operate on the messages it finds in the `mailings@orangewhip-studios.com` account. But running this template only once is of limited usefulness. Moreover, you don't want to rely on a person to remember to execute this task from time to time. The ColdFusion task scheduler is ideally suited for this application.

Note that people may unsubscribe throughout the day. And yet, OWS staff may continue to send SPAM, ahem, make that "promotional email" throughout the day. So we want to find a schedule that minimizes the opportunity for someone to unsubscribe and then wind up with three new emails from OWS. At the same time, we don't want to bog down ColdFusion by running this script every minute. Once an hour seems like a good compromise.

Listing 40.3 creates a scheduled task to run the `ListUnsubscriber.cfm` template from Chapter 21.

Listing 40.3 `ListUnsubscribe_Task.cfm`—Create a Scheduled Task

```
<!---
Name:          ListUnsubscribe_Task.cfm
Author:        Leon Chalnick
Description:   Creates a scheduled task to
               Run ListUnsubscriber.cfm
               once per hour starting at
               2:00:00 AM on 7/18/2007.
--->
<cfschedule
  task="Mailing list unsubscriber"
  action="UPDATE"
  operation="HTTPRequest"
  url="http://localhost:8500/ows/21/ListUnsubscriber.cfm"
  interval="3600"
  startdate="7/18/2007"
  starttime="02:00:00 AM"
>
```

This task will begin running at 2:00 A.M. each night and will run on the hour. Please refer to Figure 40.4.

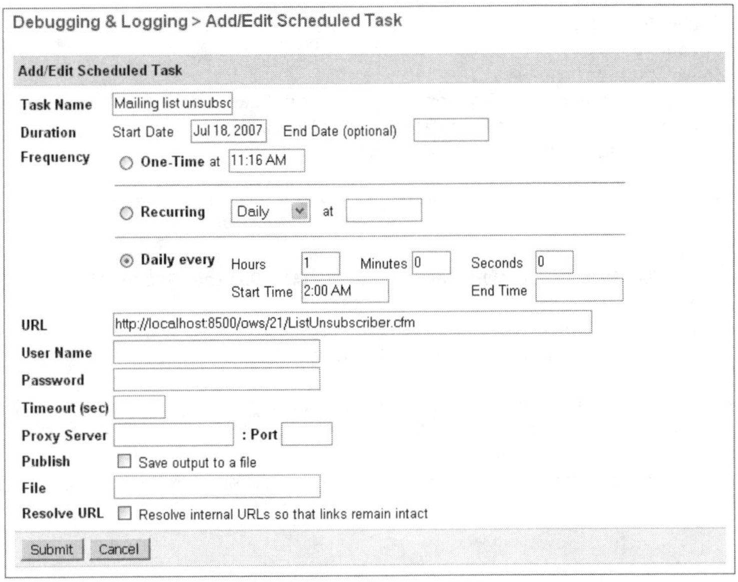

Figure 40.4

The Scheduled task created by Listing 40.3.

Building an Automatic Promotional Email Application

Let's assume that OWS's marketing department wants to capitalize on the large media blitz under way to support the new releases. It wants to send out promotional emails to local memorabilia dealers once a week that list the current merchandise available at the online store. To make matters tougher, the marketing department wants the email to be waiting in the dealers' in-boxes when they first check their email each Monday morning.

Therefore, you must build a ColdFusion scheduling application that has two parts:

- A page that queries the database for the current merchandise available, displays the results in an HTML table and sends the email page to the dealer group email alias.

- A scheduled task page that sends the promotional email once each week on Monday morning.

Building the Email Application

The email application consists of two parts: the query that collects the data and the `<cfmail>` tag that sends it. See Listing 40.4 for this part of the application.

Listing 40.4 `Promo_Email.cfm`—The Email Application

```
<!---
Name:          Promo_Email.cfm
Author:        David Golden, Leon Chalnick
Description:   Queries database and generates email
--->

<!--- Get all merchandise info from database --->
<cfquery name="GetMerchInfo" datasource="OWS">
    SELECT MerchName, MerchDescription, MerchPrice
    FROM Merchandise
    ORDER BY FilmID
</cfquery>
<!--- Produce the email --->
<cfmail to="dealers@ows.com" from="store@ows.com"
 subject="Merchandise Currently Available"
 server="mail.ows.com" type="HTML"
 groupcasesensitive="yes">
<!DOCTYPE HTML PUBLIC "-//W3C//DTD HTML 4.0 Transitional//EN">
<html>
<head>
    <title>Available Merchandise From OWS Online Store</title>
</head>
<body>
<p>Greetings from Orange Whip Studios!</p>

<p>Here is a list of merchandise currently
available from the online store at Orange Whip
Studios. To order any of these items, go to
<a href="http://www.ows.com/store/">http://www.ows.com/store/</a>.
</p>
```

Listing 40.4 (CONTINUED)

```
<!--- Display merchandise from query --->
<table border="1">
<tr>
   <th>Item name</th>
   <th>Description</th>
   <th>Price</th>
</tr>
<cfoutput query="GetMerchInfo">
   <tr>
      <td>#MerchName#</td>
      <td>#MerchDescription#</td>
      <td>#DollarFormat(MerchPrice)#</td>
   </tr>
</cfoutput>
</table>
</body>
</html>
</cfmail>
```

The `<cfquery>` tag selects all the merchandise in the database. The `<cfmail>` tag sends the mail to an email list of dealers. Notice the use of the TYPE attribute in the `<cfmail>` tag. By setting it to "HTML", you are able to send nicely formatted email.

NOTE

Another way you could send this listing would be as an attached PDF file. To do this, you would separate the production of the PDF merchandise listing from the sending of the email. You could create a separate scheduled task to run this new page and save its output to a PDF file using `<cfreport>`. Another scheduled task would then be executed to send the mail and you would use the `<cfmailparam>` tag to attach the new PDF listing output created by the first new scheduled task.

The `<cfoutput>` within the `<cfmail>` is used to output the query results in the body of the message.

Scheduling the Task

The second part of this application requires scheduling the task. In this sample application, you'll use your knowledge of the ColdFusion Administrator Scheduled Tasks page to accomplish this.

In the ColdFusion Administrator, click on Scheduled Tasks and view the Scheduled Tasks list, as seen in Figure 40.4 (note that the list may contain different scheduled tasks on your ColdFusion sever). Click the Schedule New Task Button and open the Add/Edit Scheduled Task form. Complete the form as seen in Figure 40.5.

Scheduling Updates to a Verity Collection

OWS wants Web site visitors to be able to do full-text searches of their Web site's content. A Verity collection was created to these ends (see Chapter 39 for more information about Verity collections). In a nutshell, a Verity collection is a searchable index of one or more documents that you build in ColdFusion (either through the ColdFusion Administrator or through the `<cfcollection>` tag). You can then search these documents for words or phrases using the `<cfsearch>` tag.

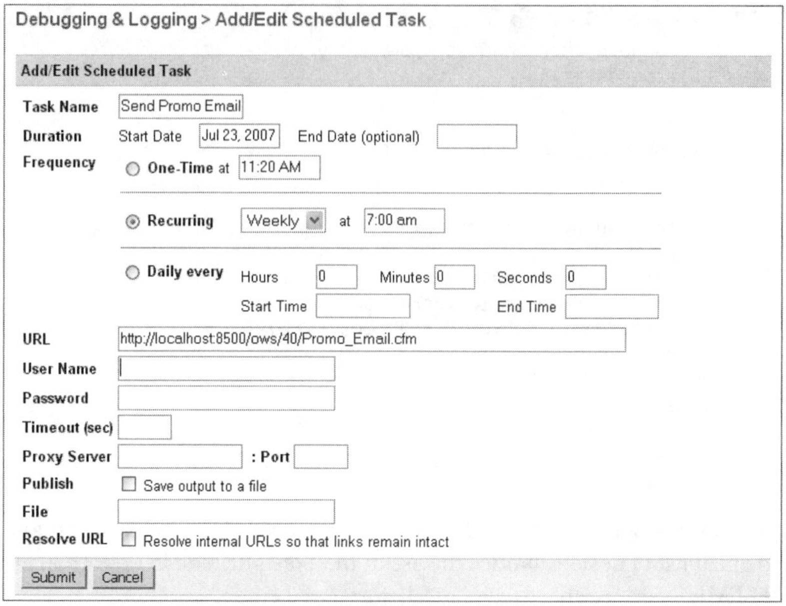

Figure 40.5

The newly scheduled task will run the Promo_Email.cfm template weekly, on Monday mornings (as July 23, 2007 is a Monday) at 7:00 A.M.

As the content of OWS's site changes from time to time, it is important to update the Verity collection to reflect these changes. It has been determined that this should take place nightly at 11:30 P.M.. As with most scheduled tasks, there are two parts to the solution. You must create the code to be run by the scheduled task and you must create the task itself.

Updating the Verity Collection

You can programmatically update a Verity collection through ColdFusion with the <cfindex> tag. The collection of the OWS site is created in Chapter 39. Here, we're simply going to produce a template to update it. See Listing 40.5 for the code that updates the Verity collection.

Listing 40.5   OWS_Verity_Update.cfm—Updating the OWS Verity Collection

```
<!---
Name:          Collection_Update.cfm
Author:        Leon Chalnick
Description:   Updates the OWS Verity collection
--->

<!--- Update the OWS collection --->
<cfindex collection="ows" action="update" type="path"
  key="C:\ColdFusion8\wwwroot\ows\39\HR\Docs">
<!--- Create debugging output to display last update of OWS
      collection --->
<cfoutput>
OWS collection last updated: #DateFormat(now())#
#TimeFormat(now(), "h:mm:ss tt")#
</cfoutput>
```

Note that a little bit of text is being output at the bottom of Listing 40.5. In the next section, you'll create a <cfschedule> tag to create the task. You'll configure this scheduled task so that the output is saved to a file. This debugging comment will be written to the specified file each time the task is executed.

Creating the Scheduled Task with <cfschedule>

Rather than create this task through the ColdFusion Administrator as you did in the previous example, this time you'll create it through code. See Listing 40.6. The task must be scheduled to run each night at 11:30 P.M. It must also save its output to a file named ows_verity_update_output.htm in a folder named c:\ temp\.

Listing 40.6 Sched_Verity_Update.cfm—Invoking OWS_Verity_Update.cfm

```
<!---
Name:          Sched_Verity_Update.cfm
Author:        Leon Chalnick
Description:   Creates a scheduled task to
               update the OWS Verity collection
               nightly and write output to file.
--->
<CFSCHEDULE
  TASK="OWS Verity Update"
  ACTION="UPDATE"
  OPERATION="HTTPRequest"
  URL="http://localhost/ows/40/OWS_Verity_Update.cfm"
  PORT="8500"
  INTERVAL="Daily"
  STARTDATE="7/18/2007"
  STARTTIME="11:30:00 PM"
  PUBLISH="Yes"
  PATH="c:\temp\"
  FILE="VerityUpdate_out.txt"
>
```

When you run this template through your browser, it instructs ColdFusion to create this scheduled task.

NOTE

Note that when the this task is run, it won't work unless you have already created the OWS Verity collection and have a directory named c:\temp\.

When this scheduled task does actually run, it will create the output file, VerityUpdate_out.txt, in the c:\temp\ folder.

INDEX